Churchill, Chamberlain and Appeasement

Was Churchill correct when he claimed the Second World War could easily have been prevented if Chamberlain had not appeased Hitler? How far did Churchill and Chamberlain differ on defence and foreign policy? To what extent was Chamberlain responsible for military defeats in 1940? In this new account of appeasement, G. C. Peden addresses these questions and provides a comparative analysis of Chamberlain's and Churchill's views on foreign policy and strategic priorities; explores what deterrence and appeasement meant in the military, economic and political contexts of the 1930s; and looks at where Chamberlain and Churchill agreed and disagreed on how best to deter Germany. Beginning in 1931 when Chamberlain became chancellor of the exchequer, this book explores the evolution of British policy towards Germany through to the Munich Agreement and its aftermath within the context of Britain's power to influence international affairs in the 1930s and of contemporary intelligence.

G. C. Peden is Emeritus Professor of Stirling University. His previous publications include *Arms, Economics and British Strategy: From Dreadnoughts to Hydrogen Bombs* (2007), *The Treasury and British Public Policy, 1906–1959* (2000) and *British Rearmament and the Treasury, 1932–1939* (1979). He is a fellow of the Royal Society of Edinburgh, Scotland's national academy.

Churchill, Chamberlain and Appeasement

G. C. Peden

University of Stirling

CAMBRIDGE
UNIVERSITY PRESS

CAMBRIDGE
UNIVERSITY PRESS

Shaftesbury Road, Cambridge CB2 8EA, United Kingdom

One Liberty Plaza, 20th Floor, New York, NY 10006, USA

477 Williamstown Road, Port Melbourne, VIC 3207, Australia

314–321, 3rd Floor, Plot 3, Splendor Forum, Jasola District Centre,
New Delhi – 110025, India

103 Penang Road, #05–06/07, Visioncrest Commercial, Singapore 238467

Cambridge University Press is part of Cambridge University Press & Assessment,
a department of the University of Cambridge.

We share the University's mission to contribute to society through the pursuit of
education, learning and research at the highest international levels of excellence.

www.cambridge.org
Information on this title: www.cambridge.org/9781009201988

DOI: 10.1017/9781009201995

First published 2023

A catalogue record for this publication is available from the British Library.

Library of Congress Cataloging-in-Publication Data
Names: Peden, G. C., author.
Title: Churchill, Chamberlain and appeasement / G. C. Peden, University
of Stirling.
Description: Cambridge ; New York, NY : Cambridge University Press, 2023. |
Includes bibliographical references and index.
Identifiers: LCCN 2022011036 (print) | LCCN 2022011037 (ebook) | ISBN
9781009201988 (hardback) | ISBN 9781009201964 (paperback) | ISBN
9781009201995 (epub)
Subjects: LCSH: Churchill, Winston, 1874-1965. | Chamberlain, Neville, 1869-
1940. | Munich Four-Power Agreement (1938) | World War, 1939-1945–
Causes. | Great Britain–Foreign relations–1936-1945. | Great Britain–Politics
and government–1936-1945.
Classification: LCC DA587 .P38 2023 (print) | LCC DA587 (ebook) | DDC
940.53/112–dc23/eng/20220427
LC record available at https://lccn.loc.gov/2022011036
LC ebook record available at https://lccn.loc.gov/2022011037

ISBN 978-1-009-20198-8 Hardback

Contents

Figures

Tables

Acknowledgements

I am particularly grateful to Gill Bennett and Alison Peden who read and commented on the whole of the draft manuscript. Iain Johnston-White and Steven Morewood also read chapters, and Steven shared the extensive reading list for his special subject on British defence and foreign policies in the 1930s. Jonathan Slater checked references at The National Archives of the United Kingdom when pandemic-related restrictions made it impracticable for me to go there. The responsibility for remaining errors and omissions is mine alone.

I thank the Bodleian Libraries, Oxford; the British Library of Political and Economic Science, the London School of Economics; the Cadbury Research Library, University of Birmingham; Cambridge University Library; the Churchill Archives Centre, Churchill College, Cambridge; Glasgow University Archives; the Liddell Hart Centre for Military Archives, King's College London; The National Archives of the United Kingdom, Kew; the National Maritime Museum, Greenwich; and Trinity College Library, Cambridge, for access to documents and permission to publish passages based on copyright material. I also record my appreciation of the helpful staff in these places and at the National Library of Scotland and Stirling University Library.

I gratefully acknowledge financial assistance from the Carnegie Trust for the Universities of Scotland.

Abbreviations

ADM	Admiralty records
ADR	Air Defence Research
AIR	Air Ministry records
ATB	Advisory Committee on Trade Questions in Time of War
BEF	British Expeditionary Force
c./cc.	column/columns
CAB	Cabinet Office records
CC	Cabinet conclusions
CD	*Diaries of Sir Alexander Cadogan*
CHT	Chatfield papers
CID	Committee of Imperial Defence
CIGS	chief of the imperial general staff
Cmd	Command paper
COS	Chiefs of Staff Committee paper
CP	Cabinet paper
CWP	*Churchill War Papers*
DBFP	*Documents on British Foreign Policy*
DC(M)	Defence Committee (Ministerial)
DGFP	*Documents on German Foreign Policy*
DP(P)	Defence Plans (Policy) Sub-Committee
DPRC	Defence Policy and Requirements Sub-Committee
DPR (DR)	Defence Policy and Requirements (Defence Requirements)
DRC	Defence Requirements Sub-Committee
FCI	Industrial Intelligence in Foreign Countries Sub-Committee
FO	Foreign Office records
fol./fos.	folio/folios
FP	Foreign Policy (Sub-Committee of Cabinet)
FRUS	Foreign Relations of the United States
GC&CS	Government Code and Cypher School
GDP	gross domestic product

HC Deb.	House of Commons Debates
HMSO	Her Majesty's Stationary Office
HNKY	Sir Maurice Hankey papers
IIC	Industrial Intelligence Centre
JMK	*Collected Writings of John Maynard Keynes*
LSE	London School of Economics
NC	Neville Chamberlain papers
NCDL	*Neville Chamberlain Diary Letters*
NCM	Naval Conference Ministerial
n.d.	no date
NDC	National Defence Contribution
OECD	Organisation for Economic Co-operation and Development
PREM	Prime Minister's Office paper
RAF	Royal Air Force
SAC	Strategic Appreciation Sub-Committee
SIS	Secret Intelligence Service
T	Treasury records
TA	Territorial Army
TNA	The National Archives of the United Kingdom
WM	War Cabinet conclusions
WO	War Office records
WSCC	*Winston S. Churchill Companion*

Introduction

There are few more contrasting historical reputations than those of Winston Churchill and Neville Chamberlain. On the one hand, there is the hero who led Britain in its finest hour when it stood alone against Nazi Germany in 1940. On the other, there is the man of Munich who attempted to appease Hitler by agreeing to his territorial demands on Czechoslovakia in 1938. Appeasement subsequently became a byword for weakness and shameful failure to stand up to dictators. Even today diplomatic compromise with an authoritarian regime is frequently criticised as another Munich.

Churchill is dominant in history partly because of what he achieved as prime minister, but also because of what he wrote in his best-selling history of the Second World War. Volume one, which appeared in 1948, established an enduring narrative of government failure to heed his warnings and of missed opportunities to halt Hitler before Germany became too powerful. Churchill's account still influences popular perceptions of Chamberlain. In contrast, academic historians have debated the pros and cons of appeasement for six decades without reaching a consensus. Surprisingly, this book is the first to compare Churchill and Chamberlain systematically in relation to both foreign and defence policy. It places their ideas in the context of Britain's power to influence international affairs through armed force or diplomacy, and of advice from the Foreign Office, the Treasury, the armed forces and the intelligence services as to what should be done. By doing so it demonstrates not only the uncertainty facing statesmen in the 1930s but also why historians find it difficult to agree what would have happened if statesmen had taken different decisions.

Chamberlain was accused by Churchill and by many historians since of failing to stand up to Hitler and of not preparing the country to face the danger it was in. Yet it was Chamberlain, the self-styled man of peace, who declared war on Germany in 1939 and who supported Churchill's decision to fight on in 1940. The Battle of Britain was won with aircraft ordered by Chamberlain's government. These apparent contradictions can only be understood in the context of what happened between the Great Depression of the early 1930s and the first stages of the Second World War.

This book is an attempt to clarify issues that continue to divide historians. Could war have been prevented as Churchill claimed? In what respects did Churchill and Chamberlain differ on defence and foreign policy? Did appeasement end in 1939? To what extent was Chamberlain responsible for military defeats suffered by Britain in the early phases of the war? The book is distinctive in three respects. First, it pays equal attention to defence and diplomacy. Second, it considers the practicality of Churchill's alternatives to Chamberlain's policies. Third, it poses moral questions for readers to consider before coming to their own conclusions about Churchill, Chamberlain and appeasement.

1 Churchill, Chamberlain and Historians

1.1 Chamberlain: Guilty Man?

One of the most cited works in the literature on appeasement is *Guilty Men*, a best-selling polemic written by three journalists – one of them, Michael Foot, a future leader of the Labour Party – in a few days in the summer of 1940, when Britain faced the threat of invasion. Under the pseudonym 'Cato', the authors condemned Chamberlain for trusting Hitler and failing to rearm adequately.[1] They echoed the Labour Party's criticisms that the Conservative-dominated National Government formed in 1931 had undermined the rule of international law and collective security through the League of Nations by acquiescing in the Japanese seizure of Manchuria and the Italian conquest of Ethiopia, and failed to prevent Germany and Italy intervening against the democratically elected Republican government in the Spanish Civil War.[2] The original 'guilty man' thesis thus came from the left. After Chamberlain's death in November 1940, his family sought to defend his reputation by commissioning Keith Feiling, an Oxford historian with Conservative leanings, to write a biography. Feiling used Chamberlain's private papers, particularly his diary and his weekly letters to his sisters Ida and Hilda, to put the former prime minister's case in his own words. He drew attention to Chamberlain's hatred of war and his belief that it was impossible to ask Britons to die in order to stop the German-speaking minority in Czechoslovakia seceding. He also set out Chamberlain's conception of defence policy as a balance between producing arms and maintaining economic resources with which to wage war.[3]

Feiling's biography was published in 1946, but its impact was overshadowed by the appearance two years later of the first volume of Churchill's *The Second World War* covering the years 1919–40. Although Churchill gave an impression of objectivity, his purpose was to reassert the case he had made in the 1930s that appeasement only encouraged aggression. The 'fatal course' taken at Munich would have been avoided, he said, if British and French statesmen had been guided by a sense of honour. Churchill claimed Hitler could 'easily' have been stopped in 1938 by a combination of Britain, France and the Soviet Union, and that Chamberlain's unwillingness to fight earlier than 1939 led to a decision to go to war over Poland in the worst possible circumstances, without a Soviet alliance and with Germany strengthened by absorbing the resources of Czechoslovakia. The focus of the book was very much on the threat from Germany, with comparatively little said about the threats from Japan and Italy.[4]

Churchill's arguments remained largely unchallenged by historians until 1961, when A. J. P. Taylor raised a storm in academic circles with his book, *The Origins of the Second World War*. In Taylor's account, the Treaty of Versailles, and in particular its denial of self-determination to German minorities in Eastern Europe after the First World War, lacked legitimacy in the eyes of informed British opinion. He claimed Chamberlain was motivated by the rights of German speakers in Czechoslovakia, not military weakness or fear of air attack. Munich was described as a triumph that had been praised by almost every British newspaper. Taylor admitted that some members of the Foreign Office disliked Chamberlain's policy, but believed they offered no alternative. To him it was inconceivable the Soviets would have committed themselves to the defence of the status quo and therefore it was pointless to speculate whether an Anglo-Franco-Soviet alliance such as Churchill advocated could have prevented war.[5]

Taylor was widely regarded as a maverick. Nevertheless, by 1965 Donald Watt could accurately forecast the rise of a revisionist school against the Churchillian orthodoxy.[6] The publication of volumes in the Foreign Office Historians' series of *Documents on British Foreign Policy* and a similar selection from the German archives enabled Keith Robbins to challenge prevailing beliefs about Munich in a well-received book in 1968. To him Chamberlain was not naïve about the potential threat from Nazi Germany, and his dual policy of appeasement and rearmament was described as an appropriate response. Robbins thought historians were bound to disagree about moral issues raised by the Munich settlement, such as the rival rights of ethnic groups, or the preservation of peace by surrender to the threat of force.[7] Robbins was a young historian, but revisionism was also embraced by the senior figure of W. Norton Medlicott, one of the editors of *Documents on British Foreign Policy*, who pointed to continuities in British foreign policy before and after Chamberlain became prime minister, and said that Chamberlain, like Sir Robert Vansittart, the permanent under-secretary of the Foreign Office, thought diplomacy should aim to gain time until Britain's defence preparations were complete in 1939.[8]

Revisionism thus preceded the flood of new evidence released under the Public Records Act of 1967, which reduced the normal period of closure of government archives from fifty years to thirty. Nevertheless, the sudden availability of Cabinet papers and the files of the Prime Minister's Office, the Foreign Office, the Treasury and the defence departments made it easier to understand how policy had been decided. Moreover, Chamberlain's own papers were made generally available to researchers in 1975. With the publication of Norman Gibbs's official history of grand strategy in 1976, followed by books on the Treasury's influence on rearmament, it became fully apparent how far ministers and their advisers had been influenced by economic constraints.[9] Grand strategy could be studied in its widest sense as the co-ordination and direction at the highest level of the nation's resources to achieve major military and political objectives. In the 1980s, revisionist historians like David Dilks and John Charmley portrayed Chamberlain as someone who pursued a rational policy of addressing legitimate German griev- ances through diplomacy, while rearming at an economically sustainable rate in the hope that Hitler would be deterred from going to war.[10]

To some historians, revisionism smacked of *tout comprendre, c'est tout pardoner* (to understand everything is to forgive everything). Drawing on much the same archival material as Dilks and Charmley, Keith Middlemas, Sidney Aster, Larry Fuscher and Williamson Murray produced a substan- tial body of anti-revisionist work along Churchillian or even more severely critical lines.[11] In 1993 Alastair Parker took an intermediate position with what he called a counter-revisionist interpretation. Parker accepted the revisionist case that Chamberlain's options had been restricted by economic and strategic circumstances. However, he argued that Chamberlain had chosen conciliation rather than resistance whenever he had to make a choice. Parker rejected Churchill's portrait of Chamberlain as narrow-minded and lacking experience in European affairs, and likewise the charge by the authors of *Guilty Men* that he had recklessly neglected rearmament. Nevertheless, he concluded that Chamberlain's obstinacy in pursuing appeasement, his caution regarding the effects of rearmament on the economy and his opposition to a Soviet alliance removed any chance of creating an effective deterrent. Parker believed Chamberlain should have followed Churchill's advice to form a close Anglo-French nucleus around which other states, including the Soviet Union, could have gathered in collective opposition to aggression.[12]

Parker's one caveat was that, despite the partial opening of Soviet arch- ives after 1989, he felt even in 2000 that evidence of Stalin's intentions was still lacking.[13] However, Michael Jabara Carley, on the basis of his research in the Moscow archives, had no doubt an Anglo-Franco-Soviet alliance could have been concluded in the summer of 1939 had it not been for Chamberlain's anti-Communist prejudice. Louise Grace Shaw, in an explicitly anti-revisionist study of British elite attitudes towards the Soviet Union, came to the same conclusion.[14] For Carley and Shaw, Chamberlain's failure to make an alliance with Stalin was no less reprehensible than the Munich agreement. Keith Neilson, however, found ideological antipathy an insufficient explanation of Chamberlain's position. The Soviet Union was, after all, a Communist state and therefore 'essentially hostile to British interests', and there was good reason to examine critically Soviet offers of co-operation.[15]

Differences between anti-revisionist and revisionist historians have tended to widen. Zara Steiner, in her magisterial international history of the 1930s, recognised the scale of the strategic problems Chamberlain faced. She accepted he was hoping for the best and preparing for the worst while conducting his dual policy of appeasement and rearmament. However, in her judgement, his 'hubristic' diplomatic ambitions, fear of risk, 'fatally flawed' reading of Hitler's character and 'obsession' with preserving peace led him to place more emphasis on appeasement than on rearmament.[16] Niall Ferguson was more Keynesian than Keynes in dismissing the economic case for limiting rearmament and contended that the most appropriate course of action would have been to conscript the unemployed into the army and to wage a preventative war. Keynes in fact thought in 1937 that the scale of borrowing to finance rearmament was potentially inflationary and would place a strain on the balance of payments.[17] Most anti-revisionist historians have focused on what they considered to be the immorality of appeasement rather than on economic constraints and grand strategy.[18] Revisionists, on the other hand, have linked diplomacy with the need to make strategic choices. For example, James Levy argued that appeasement and rearmament were logical and appropriate strategies: appeasement being aimed primarily at preventing, and only secondarily at delaying, war, and rearmament being primarily aimed at deterrence and only secondarily at creating the means to fight. Drawing on historians' research, Christopher Layne criticised his fellow international relations theorists for being too willing to accept Churchill's version of events, and emphasised the threat war posed to Britain's position as a world power; the lack of resources to meet multiple threats from Germany, Japan and Italy; and Chamberlain's use of deterrence as well as diplomacy.[19] However, Chamberlain's contribution to defence policy has not been universally admired. Greg Kennedy rated him as the worst of Britain's interwar strategic foreign policymakers on the grounds that, both as chancellor and as prime minister, he opted for defence on the cheap through air power that was severely limited in capability, held back the navy so that it was inadequate to defend the Empire, and failed to develop a co-operative relationship with the United States or an effective alliance system in Europe.[20] There have been similar divisions of opinion on Chamberlain's diplomacy. John Ruggiero condemned him for precipitating the war in 1939 by sabotaging an Anglo-Soviet alliance and by being so obsequious towards Hitler that the latter was convinced that Britain and France would not fight for Poland.[21] In contrast, Peter Neville believed it was Stalin's decision to make a pact with Hitler, rather than British foot-dragging in negotiations with Moscow, that made war inevitable and that Chamberlain made it plain to Hitler that an invasion of Poland would mean war.[22]

Many differences between historians arise from different assumptions of what would have happened if different policies had been adopted. As Robert Self, Chamberlain's by no means uncritical biographer, observed, the reality of the 1930s was neither as simple nor as clear as it may appear in hindsight to anti-revisionists, and that failure to preserve peace did not imply the existence of an alternative strategy that would have avoided war.[23] Andrew Stedman examined a range of alternatives to appeasement, including collective security through the League of Nations, formation of alliances and greater rearmament, and concluded that none would have deterred Hitler.[24]

Churchill himself long escaped historical criticism. In 1954, a short and little-noticed article by the American historian Richard Powers commented on how Churchill's parliamentary speeches had supported the appeasement of Italy when Mussolini attacked Ethiopia in 1935, had accepted the *fait accompli* of Hitler's occupation of the Rhineland in 1936 and as late as December 1937 had shown willingness to contemplate colonial concessions to Germany.[25] However, the first seriously researched challenge did not come until 1970 when Robert Rhodes James asked how, if war could have been easily avoided, Churchill failed to convince contemporaries to take appropriate action. One reason identified by Rhodes James was that Churchill focused on the German threat and did not share the passionate conviction of Labour and Liberal politicians that the League of Nations should halt Japanese aggression in China and Italian aggression in Ethiopia. Moreover, his anti-Communism led him to take a neutral stance over the Spanish Civil War. Churchill thus cut himself off from substantial potential public support. His position within the Conservative Party suffered from his opposition to the National Government's proposals for Indian self-government and his support for King Edward VIII in the Abdication Crisis. His reputation as someone who enjoyed war did not help at a time when the nation longed for peace. Rhodes James showed that, while

Churchill's warnings about the need for greater rearmament and firmer diplomacy were prescient, he failed to convince the House of Commons until the German occupation of the rump of Czechoslovakia in March 1939.[26]

Churchill's account of the 1930s in *The Second World War* was powerfully restated by Martin Gilbert in volume 5 of the official biography, which appeared in 1976. Gilbert incorporated substantial extracts from Churchill's papers in the text, and edited companion volumes of documents, most of them written by Churchill.[27] Churchill was thus his own historian for a second time. Nevertheless over the past thirty years a number of historians have revised Churchill's version of events. In 1993, John Charmley noted that the main difference between Churchill and the government over rearmament concerned how quickly the air force should be expanded. Charmley was critical of what he took to be Churchill's neglect of problems arising from rapid technical change in aircraft and from the scarcity of workers with the right skills to produce them, and argued that, had the government taken Churchill's advice, the result would have been higher output of obsolescent machines that would have been of no use in the summer of 1940. Charmley also doubted the practicality and efficacy of Churchill's concept of a grand alliance of Britain, France, the Soviet Union and smaller European powers, asking where was the evidence that other powers, particularly those that suspected the Soviets of hostile intentions, would have collaborated, and would not Germany have been tempted to strike against Britain while such an alliance was being negotiated? He saw no evidence to support Churchill's hopes of obtaining American support. In Charmley's view, Churchill grossly overestimated British strength, did not think in terms of strategic choices or long-term consequences of his actions and, consequently, while avoiding defeat in 1940, won a pyrrhic victory in 1945.[28] Brian McKercher also thought Churchill's criticisms of the National Government's defence and foreign policy lacked a rational strategic basis, and claimed they were motivated as much by his hopes of regaining office as by concern with national security.[29]

Donald Watt pointed out that Churchill's arguments in *The Second World War* depended upon counterfactuals that remain imponderable. In particular, Watt doubted whether Hitler would have been overthrown by a military coup even if Chamberlain had taken a firm stand in 1938. Watt also noted that Churchill's emphasis on air rearmament rather than on the army wrongly assumed the Germans feared strategic bombing as much as the British.[30] Likewise, David Reynolds, in a forensic study of how Churchill wrote *The Second World War*, showed that omissions and careful phrasing lent plausibility to counterfactuals such as Hitler could have been stopped in 1936 or 1938.[31] David Carlton demonstrated that Churchill had by no means been consistent earlier in seeing the Soviet Union as a counterbalance to Nazi Germany, being at least as anti-Communist as Chamberlain. He added that both men favoured friendship with Fascist Italy and it was only from 1938 that they diverged on the related issues of whether to fight Germany and whether to seek an Anglo-Soviet alliance.[32] Notwithstanding all these criticisms, Churchill's status as a great man whose virtues outweighed his faults has remained unimpaired.[33] Even Charmley acknowledged that. The question is, rather, whether Churchill's version of events should dominate historical analysis.

1.2   Why Historians Differ on Appeasement

Appeasement was long an uncontroversial term for the improvement of international relations by the peaceful settlement of grievances through rational negotiation and compromise.[34] In 1927 a Foreign Office memorandum referred to the Locarno Treaty of 1925 whereby Britain and Italy guaranteed the frontiers between Germany and France and Belgium (but not between Germany and Czechoslovakia and Poland) as part of a 'policy of appeasement'.[35] In 1936, in a speech praised by Churchill, Anthony Eden, the foreign secretary, said his objective was 'the appeasement of Europe'.[36] Churchill himself had used the term in 1921 when he spoke of the need for 'an appeasement of the fearful hatreds and antagonisms which exist in Europe', and in 1932 he said Germany's 'just grievances' ought to be removed before Britain and France agreed to disarm to the level set for Germany by the Treaty of Versailles in 1919. For Churchill, appeasement from strength was a wise policy.[37] Chamberlain had a similar understanding of appeasement as a policy of conciliation and he did not accept that the Munich settlement amounted to shameful surrender.[38] Some, but not all historians, attach a derogatory meaning to appeasement, and it is impossible for agreement to be reached when arguing from different premises. To avoid ambiguity, Medlicott proposed that the word should not be used by scholars.[39] That is impossible. In this book the word normally retains its original meaning – to pacify by making concessions, not necessarily from a position of weakness – and it is made clear when it is used in its pejorative sense by Chamberlain's critics.

Appeasement was only half of Chamberlain's policy, the other being deterrence. However, the precise meaning of the term is hard to pin down. In a speech in 1936 Chamberlain spoke of his 'enthusiasm' for an air force which, when fully developed, would have 'terrific striking power' and would be 'the most formidable deterrent to war that could be devised'.[40] Air warfare was widely expected to include the use of gas as well as high explosive and incendiary bombs against cities. For example, in 1937 the Air Staff estimated that 600,000 people would be killed and 1,200,000 injured in 60 days of air attacks on Britain. In the event, civilian casualties in 120 days from September to December 1940 were 23,767 killed and 84,529 injured.[41] It was the greatly exaggerated estimates that shaped policymakers' thinking in the 1930s. Harold Macmillan, who was prime minister during the Cuban missile crisis in 1962, was exaggerating only slightly when he said in 1966 that people in Britain in the 1930s thought of air warfare 'rather as people think of nuclear warfare today'.[42] Nevertheless, it would be anachronistic to equate Chamberlain's conception of deterrence with theories developed in the nuclear age. While the Air Ministry certainly hoped to create a bomber force that would deter Germany, such a force was not yet technically feasible.[43] Malcolm Smith believed Chamberlain's primary purpose in backing expansion of the Royal Air Force (RAF) from 1934 was to persuade the Germans to agree to an air arms limitation pact, thereby preventing bombers becoming a significant new factor in international relations. In Smith's view, Britain's air 'deterrent' was integral to appeasement and not an alternative to it.[44] In the event, an air pact proved to be a Will o' the Wisp. The British government was left pursuing a policy of 'parity' with Germany as a means of maintaining diplomatic credibility without any clear conception of how air power would be applied in war.

Once it was apparent British aircraft production was lagging behind Germany's, Chamberlain changed tack and gave priority to Britain's air defences, with the army's preparations to fight in Europe at the outbreak of war being delayed until these defences were complete. Brian McKercher argued that until then the army had been central to deterrence of Germany, by showing that Britain was committed to maintaining the continental balance of power, and claimed that by abandoning that commitment Chamberlain was taking the path to appeasement.[45] The decision on the army can be understood only in the context of another conception of deterrence: the Treasury doctrine that economic stability – the 'fourth arm of defence' – would give Britain the staying power to withstand a long war in which Germany would be worn down by blockade, as was believed to have been the case in the First World War. From this point of view, defence expenditure should not exceed a level that would destabilise the economy. By early 1939, as both the British and German economies showed signs of strain from the arms race, the Foreign Office advised that the issue of peace or war seemed likely to be decided within 12 months, and Chamberlain focused on short-term deterrence. [46] He agreed to the restoration of the army's continental role even as production of a new generation of heavy bombers for the RAF was being prepared. Deterrence in the 1930s thus involved air, land, sea and economic power, with varying emphases over time. What all these forms of deterrence had in common was an assumption that Britain's only major ally in a European war would be France. Churchill's conception of a grand alliance including the Soviet Union and smaller European powers won little support in Whitehall.

A feature of historians' debates on foreign and defence policy in the 1930s is the high level of conviction with which the contrasting arguments are put forward. Chamberlain's critics reminded David Dilks of the remark made by the nineteenth-century prime minister Lord Melbourne about the historian Thomas Macaulay: 'I wish I were as sure of anything in this world as [he] is of everything'.[47] Historians have to take account of two kinds of uncertainty: the uncertainty that historical characters felt about what was then the future, and the uncertainty historians ought to experience when they try to imagine what would have happened if historical characters had acted differently. Following John Maynard Keynes, I distinguish what is uncertain from what is more or less probable. Something is more or less probable if there are grounds for a rational expectation that it will occur, the degree of probability depending on the weight of the evidence. Uncertainty describes a situation in which there is no scientific basis on which to form any calculable probability. Writing in 1937, Keynes gave the prospect of a European war as an example of something that was uncertain.[48]

It is difficult for historians, informed by hindsight, to do justice to the uncertainty experienced by Chamberlain, Churchill and their contemporaries. It can be argued that Hitler's authorship of *Mein Kampf*, with its claim that Germans needed *Lebensraum* ('living space'), and brutal treatment of Jews left little reason to doubt the nature of the Nazi regime.[49] On the other hand, Churchill published an essay in 1937 in which he said 'we cannot tell whether Hitler will ... let loose upon the world another war in which civilization will irretrievably succumb', or whether he would bring 'the great Germanic nation ... serene, helpful and strong, to the forefront of the European family circle. It is on this mystery of the future that history will pronounce.'[50] Even after the event, historians have disagreed strongly about whether Hitler was an opportunist or had fixed aims from which he could not be deflected. For example, Taylor argued in *The Origins of the Second World War* that Hitler continued the foreign policy of his Wilhelmine and Weimar predecessors and that war resulted from faulty political calculation rather than from fulfilling a programme based on *Mein Kampf*. His Oxford colleague, Hugh Trevor-Roper, took the contrary view and said in a review that the book would do harm, perhaps irreparable harm, to Taylor's reputation as a serious historian. Taylor retorted that the review might have harmed Trevor-Roper's reputation as a serious historian, if he had one. It was fortunate for Taylor that Trevor-Roper did not know he had not read *Mein Kampf* before writing his book, apparently in the belief that statesmen do not plan but react to events. [51] Ian Kershaw convincingly portrayed Hitler as intent on a war of conquest, but flexible on timing according to the shifting balance of power, and prepared to gamble in 1939 that Britain would not go to war over Poland. [52] It was difficult for contemporaries to know whether such a man could be deterred or when war would occur.

Historians of the intelligence services have criticised Chamberlain for failing to heed warnings of Hitler's intentions. [53] However, the prime minister received a mass of information from various sources, not all of it pointing in the same direction. The hardest part of intelligence history is assessing the influence reports had, or should have had, on policy. British intelligence records from the 1930s began to be released in the 1990s, but historians are still grappling with the problem of putting them into their decision-making context. [54] Intelligence is only one component in the policymaking process. It is not surprising, therefore, that research on the work of the intelligence services has not as yet done much to reduce differences in historical interpretations of appeasement.

Although historians have the advantage of hindsight, hindsight does not extend to what did not happen. Much of Churchill's case against appeasement rests on an implication that alternatives would have produced better results. However, each of these alternatives would have had a range of possible outcomes, about which there is room for legitimate disagreement. That is particularly true of any counterfactual regarding recourse to war. As Clausewitz observed, war is characterised by interplay of possibilities that cannot be calculated and by chance. [55] Even factors that can be measured may easily be interpreted differently. Nations vary greatly in area, natural resources, population and capacity to produce armaments, and in the balance they maintain between air, land and naval forces. How does one compare the strength of a predominantly naval power like Britain with a predominantly land power like Germany? Which aspects of British power were most likely to deter or defeat Hitler? These are difficult questions, especially as the balance of power was changing from year to year as countries rearmed at different rates.

Some historical controversies reflect disputes within Whitehall in the 1930s and the nature of Cabinet records. Ministers argued from different departmental viewpoints. The Foreign Office was acutely aware of the difficulties of diplomacy without the backing of adequate armaments.

Three separate defence departments, the Admiralty, the Air Ministry and the War Office, competed for funds and industrial resources. In the absence of a ministry of defence, the Treasury tried not only to set some limit to defence expenditure but also to ensure that contracts were placed in an orderly way in accordance with priorities decided by the Cabinet. Each of these departments generated records that tend to support its own view, and historians have to read widely and critically to avoid simply replicating intra-Whitehall disputes.

Historians bring different perspectives to their work, reflecting the views of people who taught them or otherwise influenced their approach to the discipline. It was not by chance that the first revisionist history of Munich was written by one of A. J. P. Taylor's students, Keith Robbins. Perhaps I should let the reader know how my own perspective developed. Doing so gives an opportunity to acknowledge long-term intellectual debts. I was fortunate as an undergraduate at Dundee to have a professor, Donald Macdonald, who required all students of modern history also to study economics. My doctoral thesis at Oxford, which was published in 1979 as *British Rearmament and the Treasury*, was examined by Sir Alec Cairncross, an economist who had worked in the Ministry of Aircraft Production during the war, and who took an interest in my subsequent research, as did Thomas Wilson, an economist who had worked in Churchill's Prime Minister's Statistical Branch. They greatly deepened my understanding of the application of theory to the real world. William Ashworth was my mentor in economic history when I taught the subject at Bristol University and shared with me his experience of writing about aircraft and munitions contracts in the official history of the Second World War.[56]

Regarding military and international history, I was fortunate at Oxford to be supervised by Norman Gibbs, who was then completing the official history of grand strategy in the interwar period. I also attended lectures by Alistair Parker and both he and Donald Watt, who examined my thesis, took an interest in my work, as did David Dilks while I taught international history at Leeds University. I have thus long been accustomed to discuss revisionist and post-revisionist interpretations of appeasement amicably, in contrast to the tone of some of the literature. The best insights for writing this book, however, have come from many years of conversations with Gill Bennett, quondam chief historian at the Foreign and Commonwealth Office, an editor of *Documents on British Foreign Policy* and *Documents on British Policy Overseas*, and also an expert in intelligence history. I write, therefore, from the standpoint of someone who has taught both economic and international history. I use economics to analyse the constraints on policymakers. However, the choices they made were guided by politics and can be understood only through critical study of documentary evidence. That in turn requires an understanding of the personalities of the documents' authors and the positions they occupied in the policymaking process.

2   Personalities and Policymaking

2.1   Two Contrasting Personalities

'The key to Neville Chamberlain's Munich policy is to be found in his character and temperament', wrote Sir Horace Wilson, the prime minister's confidential adviser.[1] Churchill's opposition to appeasement likewise reflected his character and temperament. The two men differed markedly in upbringing, experience and ways of thinking. Both were born into political families. Chamberlain's father, Joseph, had been colonial secretary; Churchill's father, Lord Randolph, had been chancellor of the exchequer. However, there were social distinctions. Joseph Chamberlain, a wealthy Birmingham businessman, had been the first of his family to enter national politics. The Churchills were members of a landed class long accustomed to social and political dominance. Lord Randolph was a younger son of the seventh Duke of Marlborough, the dukedom having been bestowed by Queen Anne on John Churchill, the victor of Blenheim. By the years when Neville Chamberlain and Winston Churchill were born, 1869 and 1874, respectively, old and new wealth were beginning to combine, the marriage of Lord Randolph to Jennie Jerome, the daughter of a New York financier, in 1873 being a notable example. Nevertheless, there were still differences in lifestyles. Chamberlain was austere and tried to live within his means when his income from business interests fell in the 1920s and 1930s. Churchill consumed alcohol and cigars on a lavish scale, and the income from his prodigious output of books and newspaper articles was rarely sufficient to pay for his extravagant lifestyle. Chamberlain did not share Churchill's enjoyment of gambling at Monte Carlo. Chamberlain had a lifelong love of fishing and birdwatching, recreations best pursued alone. Churchill preferred the conviviality of fox hunting and polo.

Both men adored their fathers but had problematic relationships with them. When Neville Chamberlain was six years old, his mother died, and his distraught father became more remote as he repressed grief in public service. Moreover, whereas Neville's older half-brother, Austen, was groomed for national politics, Neville was trained for business. Lord Randolph was also a distant father, the more so after he and his wife became estranged when Winston was eleven. Both Neville and Winston were educated at public schools, Rugby and Harrow, respectively, but neither went to university. Chamberlain was sent to study science, metallurgy and engineering at Mason College, Birmingham, which had yet to be granted university status. Churchill went to Sandhurst, where he trained to be a cavalry officer. Both men had early, but very different, experiences of the British Empire. Chamberlain was entrusted by his father to manage a sisal plantation in the Bahamas (a venture that proved to be an expensive failure). Churchill served on India's north-west frontier with Afghanistan and took part in a cavalry charge at the Battle of Omdurman during the conquest of Sudan. After resigning his commission in order to enter politics, he became famous as a newspaper correspondent during the Boer War when he was captured and then escaped. Whereas Chamberlain was a man of peace, Churchill was happiest as a warrior.

Chamberlain was shy and reserved in public and avoided socialising with fellow MPs. Churchill was self-confident and gregarious. Chamberlain was sensitive to criticism. Churchill had the hide of a rhinoceros. People who worked for Chamberlain found he was considerate and had a quiet sense of humour, but these characteristics were known to few. Churchill was largely insensitive to other people's interests, requiring staff to work long and irregular hours, but won the affection of those who could stand the pace. Neither man was sustained by religious faith. Chamberlain had a Unitarian background, but his father had given up attending church when Neville's mother died. Churchill was nominally Anglican, as most Conservative politicians of his time were, and told his private secretary in the 1950s, 'I am not a pillar of the church but a buttress. I support it from the outside.'[2] Both Chamberlain and Churchill had supportive wives. Chamberlain married Anne Vere Cole, who came from an Irish 'county' family and had the social assurance he lacked. She suffered from 'nerves' after a difficult menopause, but Chamberlain told his sisters in 1939 she was 'wonderfully good in a crisis' and 'refrain[ed] from worrying suggestions'.[3] Indeed, she seems to have been unable to believe her husband could ever be wrong. In contrast, Churchill's wife, Clementine Ogilvy Hozier, a granddaughter of the Earl of Airlie, acted as a candid confidante, giving shrewd political advice, which was not always taken, and helped her husband through his fits of depression. Her influence moderated his egotism and sometimes smoothed his relations with colleagues.

The main source for Chamberlain's character is his correspondence with his spinster sisters, Ida and Hilda, to whom he confided his innermost thoughts. The letters betray conceit concerning his own ability and arrogance towards his critics, and some historians have taken a strong dislike to him as a result.[4] However, the tone of Neville's half-brother Austen's correspondence with Ida and Hilda suggests no less vanity. For example, when foreign secretary, Austen claimed all the credit for negotiating the Treaty of Locarno, and wrote in a self-congratulatory way about the king conferring the order of the garter on him as a reward.[5] Yet Austen is generally considered to have been a successful foreign secretary. Self-confidence is necessary, although not sufficient, for progress in a political career. Moreover, Neville's correspondence suggests his motive for entering politics was approbation within a family where public service was expected of its members, rather than egotism. For Churchill, hope of fame was the spur. He expected to die young, like his father, and aimed to achieve success early. He often struck people as a bumptious self-advertiser and was far from modest. In 1906, when discussing human mortality with Violet Asquith, he remarked: 'We are all worms. But I do believe I am a glow-worm.' When she told her father, H. H. Asquith, she had encountered genius for the first time, he replied: 'Well, Winston would certainly agree with you there – but I am not sure you will find many others of the same mind.'[6] Nevertheless, when Asquith became prime minister two years later, he appointed Churchill to his first Cabinet post, president of the Board of Trade, at the early age of 33.

Chamberlain and Churchill both made reputations as social reformers. Chamberlain gained experience at the municipal level as chairman of Birmingham General Hospital's management board and as a city councillor who chaired an investigation into housing conditions of the poor. Churchill was made aware of social conditions by reading Seebohm Rowntree's *Poverty: A Study of Town Life* (1901), a survey of York, and was responsible at the Board of Trade for minimum wage legislation, labour exchanges and unemployment insurance. He pressed an ambitious programme of social reform on Asquith, claiming that a minister who adopted it would leave 'a memorial which time will not deface'.[7] As chancellor of the exchequer from 1924 to 1929, he collaborated with Chamberlain in extending national insurance to widows, orphans and old-age pensions. However, Churchill was better known for financial orthodoxy: the defence of free trade, restoration of the gold standard in 1925 and the enunciation in 1929 of the Treasury view rejecting proposals by Lloyd George and Keynes for reducing unemployment by borrowing to pay for public investment.[8] Chamberlain dominated social policy in the interwar period. As minister of health in the 1920s, he was responsible for supervising local government, particularly housing and health services, and the poor law, in England and Wales. In the 1930s, as chancellor and prime minister, he promoted a scheme for what he called the regeneration of the national physique, involving physical training through voluntary organisations. He hated the idea that rearmament might be financed at the expense of measures to improve the condition of the people. As one Treasury official, casting around for possible cuts in public expenditure, observed in 1938: 'Physical training is a thing on which progress might be slowed down, but it is so dear to the prime minister's heart that it might be imprudent to raise it.'[9]

Chamberlain and Churchill had vastly different experiences of war in 1914–18. As lord mayor of Birmingham, Chamberlain busied himself on the home front with measures such as improved antenatal care and a pioneering blackout to foil air raids. However, his entry into national politics as director-general of national service in 1916–17 was not a success. The post was created by Lloyd George as an improvised response to complex problems without giving sufficient thought to how work would be divided between Chamberlain, the War Office, which retained responsibility for military recruitment, and a new Ministry of Labour, which handled labour exchanges and industrial relations. Chamberlain lacked experience of Whitehall politics and resigned when Lloyd George failed to support him. Subsequent relations between the two men were acerbic, and in the 1930s, Chamberlain blackballed Lloyd George from participation in the National Government, whereas Churchill and Lloyd George admired each other.

Churchill played prominent, although not invariably successful, roles in the war. As first lord of the Admiralty from 1911, he had worked tirelessly to expand the Royal Navy, but at heart he was a soldier. When in October 1914 the Cabinet decided everything possible should be done to prevent Antwerp from falling into German hands, Churchill volunteered to go there to encourage Belgian resistance and to report on the situation. He acted as if he were in charge of the defence of the city, bringing in the Royal Marine Brigade and half-trained men of the Royal Naval Division, a new unit he had created from seamen. He sent Asquith a telegram offering to resign as first lord and to take command of these men, plus an infantry division and a cavalry division that had been earmarked to be sent to Antwerp, provided he was given an appropriate military rank. Asquith told him to come home as his services could not be dispensed with at the Admiralty. When the prime minister read out Churchill's telegram to the Cabinet, his colleagues laughed.[10] Churchill's aspiration to be a soldier-statesman in the mould of his ancestor, the first Duke of Marlborough, was, after all, not matched by experience beyond a few years as a junior officer in the cavalry. Following the fall of Antwerp, Churchill continued to press Asquith for a command in the field, but to no avail.

It was as first lord of the Admiralty that Churchill became associated with military defeat in 1915. Field Marshal Kitchener, the secretary of state for war, asked for a naval demonstration at the Dardanelles, the straits leading to Constantinople, in order to relieve Turkish pressure on Russia. Churchill proposed a combined operation to force the straits, and when Kitchener said there were no troops to spare, decided to go ahead with warships alone. The naval attack in March failed, and the Turks, duly warned, reinforced their defences on the Gallipoli Peninsula, where a combined operation in April failed. Churchill was by no means solely responsible for the defeat, but, not for the last time, his audacious strategic vision had been influenced more by optimism than by attention to practical details. The Conservatives insisted on Churchill's removal from the Admiralty when Asquith formed a coalition with them in May 1915. Asquith kept him on in the Cabinet as chancellor of the Duchy of Lancaster, but in November, Churchill resigned and sought an army commission. He served on the Western Front as commander of a battalion for five months in 1916 before returning to the backbenches. In 1917 Lloyd George put him in charge of the Ministry of Munitions, where he carried out a much-needed reorganisation and applied his dynamism to industrial production and to investigating military requirements. After the armistice with Germany, he was appointed secretary of state for war and air and used his position to promote British intervention in the Russian Civil War – another military failure resulting from his fervour blinding him to reality. Nevertheless, he had the unique distinction of having been minister responsible at some time or another for all three armed services as well as munitions production, and could thus draw on exceptional experience when he urged faster rearmament in the 1930s.

Chamberlain and Churchill drew very different conclusions from their experiences. Chamberlain's revulsion against war was reinforced by the death in action in 1917 on the Western Front of his cousin Norman Chamberlain, to whom he had been close and whose pre-war social work he admired. Churchill deplored the heavy casualties, but retained his late-Victorian social Darwinism. To him, life was a struggle for survival; war brought out the best in men and accelerated improvements, whereas peace bred complacency and retarded progress.[11] In the 1930s Chamberlain could not conceive that Hitler or Mussolini could actually want war and believed they would work with him to prevent it. Churchill had a better insight into the dictators' minds.

Chamberlain and Churchill differed in their attitudes to party politics. Chamberlain was consistently loyal to the Conservatives, although he called himself a Liberal Unionist even after the party of that name, which his father had founded, had merged with the Conservatives. Churchill entered Parliament in 1900 as a Tory, but crossed the floor of the House in 1904 to become a Liberal because, as a free trader, he opposed tariffs advocated by Joseph Chamberlain. Churchill's return to the Conservatives in 1924, and to office as chancellor of the exchequer, left him open to the charge of being an unprincipled opportunist. However, in 1931 he challenged the Conservative Party leader Stanley Baldwin over the latter's support for a gradual move towards Indian self-government, and sustained opposition to what became the Government of India Act of 1935 ensured Churchill's exclusion from office. India linked Churchill with some of the most reactionary elements in the Conservative Party. Yet, when warning of the threat from Hitler and campaigning for greater air rearmament, he developed connections with the League of Nations Union and the Labour and Liberal parties. There is no reason to doubt the sincerity of Churchill's views on rearmament (or India), but he still hoped for office under Baldwin and offered to moderate his criticism of the government 'if there were any chance' of the latter appointing him minister to co-ordinate defence in 1936.[12]

Chamberlain and Churchill had contrasting parliamentary styles. Churchill loved the cut and thrust of the House of Commons debates. Chamberlain had a technocratic attitude to government and disliked the party-political point scoring and rowdy conduct of the adversarial style of British politics. Having worked out what he regarded as the best solution to a problem, Chamberlain was inclined to regard opposition as evidence of stupidity or hypocrisy. When Baldwin told him he always gave the impression he looked on the Labour Party as dirt, Chamberlain noted that intellectually, with few exceptions, Labour MPs were dirt.[13] Unsurprisingly, this attitude was resented. Churchill too was a hate figure for some on the left – he was blamed for the shooting of rioters in South Wales by troops he despatched to reinforce police when he was home secretary in 1910–11, and he took a prominent part in the defeat of the General Strike in 1926. He was a fierce critic of Labour in Parliament, but was always careful to maintain good personal relations. In particular, from 1924 he formed a friendship with Clement Attlee, who became leader of the Labour Party in 1935.

Chamberlain dominated the House of Commons and the Cabinet through his mastery of details. His analytical mind could break down problems into their constituent parts, identify which points mattered most and come to a conclusion unclouded by sentiment. David Margesson, the government chief whip, wrote that Chamberlain 'makes up his mind with extraordinary rapidity, and having made it up never alters it'. In fact,

Chamberlain did authorise major changes in defence and foreign policy in 1939, but Margesson's comment that, even for a man approaching his seventieth year, Chamberlain was 'more than usually tenacious of his views and unreceptive to the views of others' was fair.[14] This tenacity made Chamberlain slower than Churchill to respond to events. In contrast, Churchill relied on intuition rather than analysis. The War Cabinet minutes reveal how in discussion he would develop an idea that had apparently just struck him. He was prepared to change his mind when presented with a powerful argument. Attlee, who had five years' experience of Churchill as a War Cabinet colleague, said he had 'courage, imagination, a great knowledge of things, but he always wanted someone by him at a certain point to say, "Now don't be a bloody fool."'[15]

Chamberlain and Churchill both enriched their minds by extensive reading. Chamberlain's favourite was Shakespeare, and the Cambridge-educated undersecretary of state at the Foreign Office, R. A. Butler, said the prime minister had 'a great mastery of English such as I have never before experienced'.[16] Chamberlain was an effective communicator with the public, both on the radio and cinema newsreels. Churchill's prose was strongly influenced by Gibbon and Macaulay, and his speeches were marked by hyperbole and archaic language. It was only in wartime that his rhetorical style became popular with the general public.

Margesson noted how Chamberlain found all military and naval matters 'extremely distasteful'.[17] Churchill was fascinated by them. The contrast can be seen in the correspondence of Captain Basil Liddell Hart, the military correspondent of *The Times*. In 1937 Liddell Hart sent Chamberlain a copy of his book, *Europe in Arms*, which argued that Britain should limit its commitments in war to air and naval forces, apart from two high-quality armoured divisions. Chamberlain replied briefly that he found Liddell Hart's ideas extremely useful. The book fitted in with Chamberlain's ideas about giving priority to the air force, but he showed no interest in technical details. Churchill, on the other hand, while discussing with Liddell Hart the reorganisation required for mechanising the army, asked for information on the length of road an armoured division would occupy and how fast it could move.[18] Churchill was sometimes carried away with unwarranted enthusiasm for new weapons. For example, in March 1938 he advised Chamberlain that conventional aircraft with fixed, forward-firing guns, such as the Hurricane and Spitfire, were likely to be less successful as interceptors than an aircraft with a powered turret, such as the Defiant, which was capable of engaging with an enemy on a parallel course.[19] In the event the Defiant proved to be at such a disadvantage against conventional fighters, it had to be withdrawn from frontline service during the Battle of Britain.

Chamberlain had strong views about defence priorities regarding the relative importance of measures against Germany and Japan, or of air and land warfare, and he believed grand strategy should be related to Britain's economic resources. Nevertheless, within broad limits, he left strategic planning to the heads of the armed forces, the chiefs of staff. In contrast, Churchill applied his fertile imagination to conceiving all manner of plans to defeat an enemy, without, however, counting the cost. Moreover, his intuitive brilliance militated against the calm calculation required to weigh up alternative courses of action within a consistent grand strategy. He was also often over-optimistic about the capabilities of potential allies and their willingness to co-operate with Britain.

Chamberlain distrusted Churchill's warlike instincts. In March 1936, when Anglo-French conversations on how to react to the German occupation of the Rhineland were going on, Chamberlain explained to his sisters why he was thankful Churchill was not in the government: 'He is in the usual excited condition that comes on him when he smells war, and if he were in the Cabinet we should be spending all our time in holding him down instead of getting on with our business.' In March 1938, after a private conversation with Churchill about future policy towards Czechoslovakia, Chamberlain wrote: 'I can't help liking Winston although I think him nearly always wrong and impossible as a colleague.'[20] Chamberlain and Churchill had been rivals as potential successors to Baldwin as party leader, and Chamberlain was in no hurry to fulfil Churchill's hopes of being brought into his government.

Churchill described his relations with Chamberlain in the 1930s as 'cool, easy and polite'.[21] In 1937 he wrote a pen portrait of him as a loner who had had to fight every inch of his upward way in politics, and who might well be suspicious of the easy eminence which birth could give.[22] Churchill could recall only one intimate social conversation with Chamberlain, and that after confidence and goodwill had developed between them in the War Cabinet. On 13 November 1939, Churchill and his wife invited Mr and Mrs Chamberlain to dinner for four. Chamberlain relaxed and reminisced about his attempt to grow sisal in the Bahamas. Churchill thought to himself, 'What a pity Hitler did not know when he met this sober English politician with his umbrella at ... Munich that he was actually talking to a hard-bitten pioneer from the outer marches of the British Empire!'[23] This thought did not soften Churchill's judgement that Chamberlain, although business-like and efficient, was very opinionated and lacked the experience necessary to cope with European affairs. However, Churchill did credit Chamberlain with moral courage in his efforts for peace, and said he would have been willing to serve under him in the summer of 1939 when there was a press campaign for Churchill's return to government.[24]

Notwithstanding their differences, Chamberlain and Churchill had much in common. Both men had encyclopaedic knowledge, prodigious memories and remarkable capacity for hard work. Apart from gout, Chamberlain enjoyed good health until he was diagnosed with cancer in 1940. Churchill, notwithstanding his lifestyle, displayed formidable energy. Both had the physical and mental resilience required of a prime minister. Both were patriotic and upheld the British Empire. Both loathed Hitler's regime. Writing to his sisters in 1934, Chamberlain said he hated Nazism and all its works.[25] Attempts to link Chamberlain with pro-fascist sympathisers are unconvincing. Alvin Finkel and Clement Leibovitz contended in *The Chamberlain-Hitler Collusion* that Chamberlain's anti-Communism led him to make common cause with fascism, but they reached this conclusion by inference rather than evidence.[26]

2.2   Who Was Who in Whitehall

Churchill wrote of Chamberlain in April 1939 that 'no prime minister in modern times has had so much personal power to guide affairs' and never before had there been 'such a one-man government'.[27] However, Chamberlain exercised this power within the conventions of Cabinet government. Whereas members of an American president's cabinet advise him only on matters relating to their individual offices, members of the British Cabinet share collective responsibility. Ministers who cannot publicly support all of the government's policies are expected to resign. On the other hand, although the prime minister selects his Cabinet, he must retain their support and that of his party. Otherwise he must resign, as the Labour leader James Ramsay MacDonald did in 1931 when he was unable to persuade most of his colleagues to agree to cuts in unemployment benefit during the financial crisis of that year, and as Chamberlain did in 1940 when a vote of confidence in the House of Commons showed he no longer commanded sufficient support in the Conservative Party to continue in office.

MacDonald, who headed the National Government from 1931 to 1935, was in an unusually weak position for a prime minister. Few MPs followed him when he left the Labour Party to form a coalition, and he could act only with the support of Baldwin as leader of by far the largest number of MPs: 473 Conservatives after the general election of 1931 compared with 13 National Labour and 35 Liberal Nationals, plus 33 free-trade Liberals who resigned the following year. Nevertheless, National Labour and Liberal National politicians were given senior Cabinet positions at the expense of Conservatives, including Churchill. (In what follows, ministers in the National Government were Conservatives unless identified otherwise.) MacDonald took an active interest in foreign policy. He was quick to recognise the Nazi threat, but reluctant to abandon negotiations for disarmament. He was suspicious of France and hostile to a return to the pre-war system of alliances which, he believed, had caused the 1914–18 war (which he had opposed). By 1934 he was in failing health and had difficulty in reading papers and often rambled badly in discussion.[28] On 7 June 1935, he and Baldwin changed places with MacDonald taking the latter's title of lord president of the council, without, however, having any influence on policy.

Baldwin was 67 in 1935, and by the following summer he was suffering from nervous exhaustion. He stayed on to deal with the abdication of Edward VIII in December 1936 and to see George VI crowned six months later, but colleagues knew Neville Chamberlain would become prime minister after the coronation, and Baldwin's grip on policymaking relaxed. Even before then, Baldwin preferred to let colleagues get on with their responsibilities and to co-ordinate policy by chairing Cabinet committees. He sought consensus and could give an impression of being indecisive while he waited for one to emerge. His historical reputation suffered from the claim – originally made by Churchill in 1948 and endorsed by Baldwin's first biographer – that he had put party before country by not seeking a mandate for rearmament for fear of losing the 1935 general election, given the prevailing strength of pacifist feeling.[29] Churchill misrepresented Baldwin's position. Baldwin tried cautiously during the campaign to educate the public about the threat posed by Nazi Germany and the need to match German airpower.[30] On the other hand, although he affected to be a supporter of collective security, he told a delegation of Conservative peers and MPs in 1936 he would not get Britain into a war with anybody for the League of Nations. Nor would he support France if it attacked Germany as a consequence of the Franco-Soviet treaty of mutual assistance signed the previous year. He remarked that '[i]f there is any fighting in Europe to be done, I should like to see the Bolshies and the Nazis doing it'.[31] Baldwin had essentially a negative attitude towards European security.

Chamberlain, who became prime minister on 28 May 1937 at the age of 68, was very different both in his conduct of government business and his attitude to Europe. Whereas Baldwin tended to speak in generalities, Chamberlain gave close attention to detail. Baldwin's hands-off approach meant that down to 1937 foreign policy had been largely in the hands of the foreign secretary. In contrast, Chamberlain asserted his right to take the lead. He was not the first prime minister to do so: Benjamin Disraeli and David Lloyd George had conducted negotiations at the Congress of Berlin in 1878 and the Paris Peace Conference in

1919, respectively. Lord Salisbury had combined the offices of prime minister and foreign secretary in the 1880s, as had MacDonald in 1924. Chamberlain was irritated by what he saw as the Foreign Office's obstructiveness and was inclined to bypass it. In common with a large part of British public opinion, he thought an attempt to maintain the balance of power through military alliances, as before 1914, would lead to war. Rather than divide Europe into opposing blocs, he hoped through appeasement to enable democracies and totalitarian states to work together to settle differences and limit armaments.[32] His hostility to Churchill's concept of a grand alliance with France and the Soviet Union thus reflected more than anti-Communism. It was only in 1939 that he reluctantly accepted the need for alliances to deter Hitler, but until then his views were at odds with senior Foreign Office officials who had continued to believe in the utility of alliances to protect British interests.[33]

Despite his self-confidence, Chamberlain relied on two or three men to give him moral support. Down to 1937 the most important of these was Sir Warren Fisher, permanent secretary of the Treasury and head of the Civil Service from 1919 to 1939. As chancellor of the exchequer, Chamberlain consulted Fisher on more than financial matters, the two men having established a rapport during Chamberlain's first chancellorship in 1923–24. For example, in January 1935 Chamberlain had long talks with him about his (Chamberlain's) political future.[34] Fisher was a man of dynamic energy, given to quick enthusiasms. In the autumn of 1933, alarmed by the rise of Hitler, he urged a review of Britain's defence requirements. He had no faith in the League of Nations and was convinced of the vital necessity of rearmament. He believed Britain should improve relations with Japan, regardless of the effect on American opinion, in order to concentrate on the German menace. He was no appeaser. Indeed, he fell out with Chamberlain over the Munich agreement. By then, however, following Chamberlain's move from the Treasury to 10 Downing Street, the highly strung Fisher had been displaced as Chamberlain's principal adviser by the imperturbable Sir Horace Wilson.[35]

Chamberlain's biographer, Robert Self, described Wilson as the prime minister's *éminence grise*, serving as 'gatekeeper, fixer, and trusted sounding board', and one of his few personal friends.[36] It had been on Fisher's recommendation that Wilson had been seconded in 1935 from the Board of Trade, where he was chief industrial adviser, to the Prime Minister's Office to act as Baldwin's personal adviser. Until then the most senior members of the office had been middle-ranking civil servants acting as private secretaries and Baldwin felt he needed more support. Wilson was very unusual in the upper ranks of Whitehall in that he came from a modest social background – his father was a furniture dealer and his mother kept a boarding house – and he had entered the Civil Service as a boy clerk. Whereas most senior civil servants were Oxford or Cambridge graduates, his degree was a B.Sc. (Econ) taken by part-time study at the London School of Economics. He made his reputation at the Ministry of Labour through his skill in negotiating agreements between trade unionists and employers – hardly appropriate experience for dealing with fascist dictators. Nevertheless, so great was Wilson's confidence in his own ability, he could not conceive he could be wrong on any issue. He acted as Chamberlain's emissary to Hitler immediately prior to the Munich Conference and was an important channel for the prime minister's views reaching Germany. He often met the permanent under-secretary of the Foreign Office, Sir Alexander Cadogan, to discuss matters in 1938 and 1939, but they did not normally communicate in writing, which makes it difficult to know how far Wilson kept Cadogan informed, as he claimed he did, about initiatives from 10 Downing Street. There were occasions when Cadogan learned of them only from intelligence reports. Cadogan thought Wilson was out of his depth in foreign affairs, but believed he would have been removed from his post if he had refused to work with him. Wilson denied that he was as influential as Cadogan's diary indicated, and certainly Chamberlain did not always follow Wilson's briefs. Nevertheless there is no doubt Wilson strongly encouraged Chamberlain's conciliatory approach towards Germany and Italy, while his anti-Communism reinforced the prime minister's distrust of the Soviet Union. Chamberlain's confidence in him was such that he appointed him permanent secretary of the Treasury and head of the Civil Service when Fisher retired in 1939. Thereafter Wilson divided his time between advising the prime minister and the chancellor of the exchequer.[37]

Another man with a reputation as an *éminence grise* was Major (from 1936 Sir) Joseph Ball, the director of the Conservative Party's Research Department. Little is known about him, partly because he was careful to keep himself out of the public eye, and partly because he burned most of his papers. A former member of the Security Service who retained close associations with senior intelligence officials, he had been persuaded in 1927 to join the Conservative Central Office by J. C. C. Davidson, the party's chairman, to whom he had long supplied information. Ball was tough and slightly sinister. He was close to Chamberlain as a confidant and friend (the two men went fishing together). Ball's activities ranged from spying on Chamberlain's opponents, speech-writing, propaganda and management of the press, to informal diplomacy, most notably when Chamberlain used him in 1938 as an intermediary with the Italian ambassador, in order to bypass the foreign secretary, Anthony Eden. The weekly publication *Truth*, which Ball controlled, was pro-appeasement and hostile to Churchill.[38] Like Wilson, Ball was strongly anti-Communist. As with Wilson, it is difficult to know whether he was an independent influence on Chamberlain's thinking or was simply someone whom the prime minister could rely on to carry out his wishes.

The Foreign Office was the principal, but not the only, department responsible for external affairs. There were also a separate Dominions Office for independent members of the Commonwealth, the India Office for the most populous part of the Empire and the Colonial Office for the rest of the Empire. The Treasury kept a firm grip on negotiations relating to war loans and reparations. Foreign Office officials advised on political aspects of commercial policy, but that policy was formulated by the Board of Trade and negotiated by the Department of Overseas Trade, a joint charge of the Board and the Foreign Office. It was not until 1932 that the Foreign Office created its own Economic Relations Section in 1932, and it was small and rather ineffective.[39]

The influence of the Foreign Office varied according to who was foreign secretary. Sir John Simon (1931–35), leader of the small Liberal National group, was intellectually gifted: he was a fellow of All Souls College, Oxford; could make speeches in French, Italian and Spanish, and read German; and his legal talents had led to his appointment as attorney-general four years after entering Parliament in 1906. On the other hand, Chamberlain described him as someone able to summarise the pros and cons of a case but who was 'temperamentally unable to make up his mind to action when a difficult situation arose'.[40] Simon's failure in a speech to the League of Nations on 7 December 1932 to make an unqualified denunciation of Japan's invasion of Manchuria damaged his reputation with proponents of collective security. He seems not to have grasped that Hitler would regard any agreement as a temporary expedient and rejected the advice of his permanent under-secretary, Sir Robert Vansittart, that Germany would probably have to be contained by force.[41] In March 1935, Vansittart told MacDonald that Foreign Office officials had lost all confidence in Simon and were certain he would mishandle forthcoming negotiations in Berlin. Vansittart begged that Eden, the lord privy seal, should be sent to Berlin with Simon, and the prime minister agreed, noting in his diary that the foreign secretary was 'vain, weak, passionate for his own decoration and unreliable'.[42] When Baldwin reconstructed the National Government on 7 June 1935, Simon was replaced by Sir Samuel Hoare.

Chamberlain welcomed the change: in contrast to Simon, Hoare was decisive and happy to discuss foreign policy with Chamberlain.[43] Hoare had qualities that might have made him successful as a foreign secretary. A talented linguist, he had been head of the British intelligence mission in Russia and then Italy in the First World War. However, he was exhausted in 1935 after four years as secretary of state for India, having been responsible for the passage of the controversial Government of India Bill. Hoare found the Foreign Office over-excited compared to the India Office, and complained there seemed to be no generally accepted body of opinion on the main issues. Under Vansittart's influence, he believed the best policy was to gain time for rearmament and to avoid a permanent breach with Mussolini over his invasion of Ethiopia.[44] Hoare had to resign on 22 December 1935 after the press learned of an agreement he had signed with the French premier, Pierre Laval, to offer Mussolini territory and economic concessions in Ethiopia, in return for peace (see pages 125–6). As prime minister, Chamberlain regularly consulted Hoare and Simon on foreign policy, and the three men came to be regarded on the left of British politics as jointly responsible for appeasement. Hoare and Simon were unrepentant in their memoirs; indeed Hoare's contained a sustained defence of Chamberlain's policies.[45]

Hoare's successor, Eden, had had an unusually long apprenticeship at the Foreign Office. He was parliamentary private secretary to the foreign secretary, Austen Chamberlain, in 1926–29; under-secretary of state from September 1931 to the end of 1933; and lord privy seal without a seat in the Cabinet until 7 June 1935, when he became minister for League of Nations affairs. He was only 38 when he became foreign secretary six months later. Eden brought outstanding personal and intellectual qualifications to the post – he had won the Military Cross while serving on the Western Front, and had been awarded first class honours in oriental languages at Oxford – and he had film-star looks. He was an experienced diplomat, having handled disarmament negotiations at Geneva in 1933, and visited Hitler, Mussolini and Stalin in 1934–35. On the other hand, his health was uncertain – he suffered severe heart strain in April 1935 – and he had an emotional temperament. In particular, he was sensitive to criticism and easily lost his temper. After an initial period of amicable collaboration with Chamberlain, he took badly to the prime minister intervening in foreign policy. Chamberlain, for his part, came to feel that Eden was an obstacle to reaching agreements with Hitler and Mussolini. Eden resigned on 20 February 1938 following a row with the prime minister over the conduct of Anglo-Italian relations. He subsequently cultivated and defended an image of himself as an anti-appeaser.[46] He was certainly not an appeaser in the pejorative sense of the word, but his record in office suggests he believed the appeasement of Europe was possible. He had come away from his interview with Hitler in

1934 finding it hard to believe that someone who had fought on the Western Front wanted war.[47] On the other hand, Eden repeatedly expressed concern about the extent to which British rearmament lagged behind Germany's. In the House of Commons debate on the Munich agreement, he spoke against the exclusion of the Soviet Union from the councils of Europe.[48] However, he had not shown enthusiasm for co-operation with Moscow while in office, remarking in February 1936 that he had 'no intention of hugging the bear too closely for I am fully conscious of what happens to people who hug bears'.[49]

His successor, Lord Halifax, had been associated with the Foreign Office as lord privy seal in 1935–37 and lord president of the council in 1937–38 prior to becoming foreign secretary. He was intellectually distinguished, having graduated with first-class honours in modern history from Oxford and won an All Souls College fellowship in 1903. Halifax brought to the Foreign Office the faith in reason, conciliation and compromise allied with firmness that had served him well in India when dealing with Mahatma Gandhi, and it took some time for him to adapt to dealing with Hitler and Mussolini. Halifax aimed to preserve national unity and regularly saw Churchill, Eden and Labour Party leaders. Chamberlain, for his part, was glad to have a foreign secretary with a markedly calmer temperament than Eden's. The minutes of the Cabinet's Foreign Policy Committee show that the prime minister and the foreign secretary were close in their views on how to approach the Czechoslovakian problem for most of 1938, but in the September crisis Halifax, urged on by his permanent under-secretary, Cadogan, led the opposition in Cabinet to acceptance of Hitler's terms (see page 203). Subsequently, Halifax played an important role in the decision early in 1939 to prepare the army for war in Europe; he pushed a reluctant Chamberlain into guaranteeing Polish independence, and was quicker than the prime minister to accept that an alliance with the Soviet Union was necessary to make that guarantee effective. Chamberlain could not afford to lose a foreign secretary for a second time, and Halifax exercised greater influence on policy than Eden had been able to.

The Foreign Office also had a junior minister, the under-secretary of state, who acted as the foreign secretary's deputy in the House of Commons, but who normally had little or no input into the formulation of policy. R. A. Butler, who was under-secretary from February 1938 to May 1940, was more active than most since Halifax sat in the House of Lords. Chamberlain noted in June 1939 that Butler was the only minister to support his opposition to a Soviet alliance, but was 'not a very influential ally'.[50]

The foreign secretary was advised by the permanent under-secretary, who saw and commented on all papers before they reached him. The permanent under-secretary was also responsible for the running of the Office, giving instructions to the diplomatic corps and helping to choose ambassadors. In addition, he was responsible for liaison with the intelligence agencies, since the foreign secretary had ministerial responsibility for the Secret Intelligence Service and the Government Code and Cypher School, and the permanent under-secretary handled requests from all the intelligence agencies for money from the Secret Vote. Vansittart, who was permanent under-secretary from 1930 to the end of 1937, was a flamboyant character, whose minutes and memoranda were characteristically vehement and often unnecessarily lengthy. His experience as the head of the Foreign Office's American Department from 1924 to 1928 had made him conscious both of the need to maintain good Anglo-American relations and of the difficulty in doing so. He was one of the first men in Whitehall in 1933 to warn that the Nazi regime was likely to start another European war and pressed his views on ministers persistently. Hoare described Vansittart's fertile mind and knowledge of European politics as invaluable, but it was Vansittart's advice that led to the Hoare-Laval Pact and the foreign secretary's resignation.[51]

Vansittart's reputation in Whitehall was damaged by that event. Despite being a civil servant, he considered resignation, but decided against it because he felt no guilt. He had a difficult relationship with Eden, who was irritated by the didactic tone of his advice.[52] More important, Eden had greater misgivings than Vansittart about closer ties with the Soviet Union, was less sensitive to the risk of driving Italy closer to Germany and was prepared to consider limiting an agreement with Germany to Western Europe, whereas Vansittart insisted that Britain should seek a general European settlement which included guarantees for Eastern Europe.[53] Eden longed to be rid of his permanent under-secretary, but Vansittart declined the offer of the Paris embassy in September 1936, and again when Baldwin raised the subject with him in December 1936 and January 1937. Without the prime minister's support, Eden could not force Vansittart to go. In March 1937, Eden's private secretary, Oliver Harvey, recorded in his diary that the foreign secretary had openly expressed his lack of confidence in the permanent under-secretary's judgement.[54] However, it was not until the end of the year that Eden, with Chamberlain's support, had Vansittart side-lined to the newly created post of chief diplomatic adviser. Vansittart's minutes and memoranda seem thereafter to have been routinely ignored. However, he maintained a private intelligence network and contacts with the German opposition to Hitler, and his warnings about the latter's hostile intentions towards Britain had some influence on Halifax from the autumn of 1938 to the spring of 1939.

Vansittart is central to debates on appeasement because his conception of alliance diplomacy is seen by some of Chamberlain's critics as a better alternative to the prime minister's bilateral attempts to come to terms with Germany. Vansittart's advice was guided by the pre-1914 doctrine that Britain should prevent any state dominating Europe, although, like Churchill, he disguised balance-of-power strategy as collective security through the League of Nations in deference to the widely held opinion that pre-1914 alliance diplomacy had made conflict more likely. He sided with the War Office in its attempts to create an expeditionary force capable of supporting continental allies at the outbreak of war. Even when his hopes of a settlement with Germany dimmed to the point of extinction by 1935, he believed that continued negotiations served to gain time for rearmament. Initially he looked to Italy to supplement France as a counterweight to Germany, but when it became clear Italy would not be a reliable ally, he recommended a policy of closer relations with the Soviet Union. [55] Vansittart was prescient regarding the German threat, but Gladwyn Jebb, his private secretary, thought that he was disconcertingly vague when asked, 'what would you actually do about it, Van, declare war?'[56]

Cadogan, who became permanent under-secretary on 1 January 1938, was a complete contrast to Vansittart. Cadogan's minutes and memoranda were short and to the point. He gave the appearance of being imperturbable, although his diary shows that inwardly he felt deeply about the ethics of appeasement.[57] Jebb, whom he took over as private secretary, described him as 'cautious, reserved, conventional, clearly shy, clearly repressed emotionally', but a 'man of quiet charm and native intelligence'.[58] Cadogan's experience as head of the Foreign Office's League of Nations section from 1923 to 1933 had been ultimately disillusioning in view of the League's ineffectiveness over Manchuria. As Britain's representative in China in 1933–36, he had to recommend a policy of playing for time in the face of Japanese aggression. He was invited by Eden to return to become the senior deputy under-secretary at the Foreign Office, taking up the post in October 1936, correctly anticipating it would be a stepping stone to becoming permanent under-secretary. Indeed, during 1937 Eden came, increasingly, to rely on Cadogan rather than Vansittart for advice.

Cadogan thought Germany had real grievances arising from the Versailles Treaty and he was less pessimistic than Vansittart about the prospects of achieving peaceful change in Eastern Europe. He was also more suspicious than Vansittart of the Soviet Union. Cadogan found Vansittart's continued presence in the Foreign Office as chief diplomatic adviser tiresome, interpreting his minutes on Foreign Office papers as an attempt to become a super permanent under-secretary. He thought Vansittart's vehemence was 'all façade' and thought he had nothing constructive to offer.[59] Cadogan regarded the role of permanent under-secretary as being to give advice on the choices available to the foreign secretary rather than to declaim on the need for greater rearmament. He was for the most part able to steady the often impulsive Eden and to help Halifax to come to different conclusions from Chamberlain. He also penetrated the prime minister's notoriously reserved manner and developed great respect and affection for him, even when he disagreed with his policies.[60]

Most of the work of the Foreign Office was allocated geographically. Europe was divided between the Northern Department, which dealt with the Soviet Union, the Baltic States and Scandinavia; the Southern Department which dealt with Italy, Central Europe and the Balkans; and the Central Department which had general oversight of the continent and dealt with France, Germany and Poland. Groups of departments were supervised by an assistant under-secretary, who commented on minutes from heads of departments before forwarding them to the permanent under-secretary or his deputy. Assistant under-secretaries and heads of department were thus key figures in policymaking. Orme Sargent, the assistant under-secretary who supervised the Central and Southern departments, was universally known as 'Moley' and noted for his dry humour. Despite a reserved outward appearance, he was described by Jebb as 'a rather passionate character ... enormously respected for his intelligence and knowledge', and 'basically of the "Van" school of thought but with a sharper cutting-edge to his mind'.[61] Sargent accepted that civil servants existed to serve ministers, but came to hold the Chamberlain Cabinet in contempt.[62] However, it would be simplistic to label Sargent as an 'anti-appeaser'. Initially he was a proponent of coming to terms with Germany, although between 1934 and 1938 he gradually became disillusioned with the prospects of such a policy. Sargent's influence declined after Cadogan replaced Vansittart.[63]

The head of the Central Department until his death early in 1937 from lung cancer, aged only 46, was Ralph Wigram. His views on policy were similar to Vansittart's and Sargent's, and he and Sargent were often at odds with Laurence Collier, the head of the Northern Department. Collier had no illusions about Soviet sincerity, but believed the Nazi threat gave Britain, France and Russia common interests. He thought the Franco-Soviet treaty of mutual assistance in 1935 would help to check Germany, whereas Sargent feared it would encourage Germany and Japan to draw together, as indeed they did when they signed the Anti-Comintern Pact in 1936. Sargent's suspicions of the Soviet Union were shared by William Strang, Wigram's successor as the head of the Central Department. Strang had developed an aversion to the Soviet system while serving in Moscow from 1930 to 1933 and, although he found attendance at the Munich Conference a distressing experience, he doubted whether the Soviet Union would have intervened effectively in the crisis even if it had not been excluded from the negotiations. Strang was unusual among officials in having attended a grammar school and University College London, rather than public school and Oxford or Cambridge, but the ability that would lead to his appointment as permanent under-secretary in 1949 was already apparent. He carried more weight in official discussions than Collier, and in 1939 work on negotiations for an Anglo-Soviet alliance was allocated to the Central Department, not the Northern Department.[64]

Normally, communications from ambassadors would reach ministers via the permanent under-secretary, who would comment on them. However, Sir Nevile Henderson, who was ambassador to Germany from 28 May 1937 to the outbreak of war, corresponded directly with Chamberlain, Halifax and Sir Horace Wilson. Henderson was also present to give advice at Cabinet meetings in February and August 1938. In contrast to his predecessors in Berlin, Sir Horace Rumbold (1928–33) and Sir Eric Phipps (1933–37), who warned that the Nazi regime was a threat to peace, Henderson hoped Germany would revert to civilised ways and that there was a limit to Hitler's ambitions. He believed he was on a mission to secure peace through reason and negotiation instead of resorting to force, although he recognised that rearmament was essential for successful negotiation. Even after war broke out, he made no apology for appeasement.[65] The charge made by historians against Henderson is that he failed to understand the nature of German eastward expansion; was reluctant to provoke Hitler by giving blunt warnings about the consequences of invading Czechoslovakia; and misunderstood the German leadership, imagining there were Nazi moderates who could rein in Hitler, and failing to realise that Hitler was the greatest extremist of all. In Donald Watt's words, 'Henderson misrepresented Britain to Hitler and Hitler to Britain.'[66] Henderson's dispatches infuriated Vansittart and Cadogan – for example, the latter complained in February 1939 of the ambassador being 'completely bewitched by his German friends'[67]. However, they could not prevent Henderson encouraging Chamberlain's optimism regarding the possibility of appeasing Hitler.

Chamberlain's views on policy were strongly influenced by his experience as chancellor of the exchequer. The Treasury aspired to greater influence on grand strategy beyond its formal responsibilities for financial policy, control of government expenditure and the organisation of the Civil Service. Its permanent secretary, Fisher, aimed to make the Treasury a 'general staff', forming independent views on policy questions while controlling expenditure. The Treasury was well placed to influence defence policy as there was no ministry of defence. Ministers in charge of separate departments for the army, navy and RAF negotiated annually for funding with the chancellor, who could block expenditure pending a decision by the Cabinet. Fisher also thought the Treasury must concern itself with foreign affairs, which he characterised in 1936 as 'now-a-days largely economics, finance and rearmament'.[68] However, many foreign policy questions did not give rise to expenditure and therefore the Foreign Office had no need to consult the Treasury about them. In his memoirs, Eden complained about Fisher's attempts to influence Foreign Office appointments.[69] As head of the Civil Service, of which the Foreign Office was then a part, Fisher had the right to advise the prime minister on senior appointments, but his purpose in doing so was to integrate the Foreign Office more closely with the Home Civil Service, something the Foreign Office resisted.

Fisher devoted much of his time to improving the efficiency of and teamwork in the Civil Service, and the chancellor's chief adviser on all important aspects of financial policy and control of government expenditure was the next most senior official, the Second Secretary, Sir Richard Hopkins. In contrast to Fisher's dominating personality, Hopkins was mild in manner, possessed an impish sense of humour, and was held in great affection by his colleagues, to whom he was known as 'Hoppy'. He was not an economist, having studied classics and history at Cambridge, but he had been chairman of the Board of Inland Revenue before joining the Treasury in 1927 and had read books on economics. Hopkins was influential on account of his capacity for taking up, developing and expressing in simple but compelling terms ideas that other people had originated. He and Fisher worked in close partnership, but Fisher (who had studied Greats – classics, philosophy and ancient history – at Oxford) freely admitted to not understanding financial technicalities and deferred to Hopkins on purely financial issues. The principal draftsmen of the chancellor's budget were Hopkins and the under-secretary in charge of the Treasury's home and overseas finance divisions, Sir Frederick Phillips. Working with officials from the boards of Inland Revenue and Customs and Excise, and in consultation with the chancellor, they would draw up tax proposals in conditions of secrecy. Phillips, who had studied mathematics and natural sciences at Cambridge, had entered the Treasury after coming first in the Civil Service examinations in 1908. He was familiar with the writings of Keynes, but relied on the Treasury's sole professional economist, Ralph Hawtrey, to interpret economists' advice. The formal channel for economic advice was the Committee on Economic Information, which met infrequently, but whose members included Keynes, and which Phillips joined in 1935.[70] Phillips was reserved and taciturn in conversation, but lucid and even brilliant on paper. Keynes recorded that Phillips's grunts of assent or dispute were as well understood in Washington or Ottawa as in Whitehall; at the League of Nations in Geneva he could be silent in several languages and few men could say more in so few, clear words.[71]

Another key man in the Treasury, although ranking below Hopkins and Phillips, was Edward Bridges, the head of the division dealing with the defence departments and the Foreign Office from 1934 to 1938. Bridges' duties included briefing the chancellor on the annual estimates submitted by these departments for expenditure in the coming financial year, and on defence and foreign policy questions generally, making critical comments that could be used in discussion with other ministers. Chamberlain was so impressed by the quality of Bridges' work that he made a point of getting to know him and described him as a man of exceptional ability and brilliance. Bridges had studied Greats at Oxford and was a fellow of All Souls College, but had practical experience of war. He had been awarded the Military Cross as an infantry officer on the Western Front, and had first entered the Treasury as a temporary official in 1917 after being severely wounded. When he had sufficiently recovered, he returned to active service and only became a permanent official after the armistice. Once, when reviewing defence expenditure in 1937, he recalled the experience of the shell shortage in 1915, when the British artillery had been rationed to a couple of rounds per gun per day, and commented that he had nothing but the strongest sympathies for an army insufficiently supplied with munitions.[72] That experience did not lead him to recommend unlimited rearmament. On the contrary, in 1937, when the defence departments were adding new items to programmes agreed only the previous year, he commented that there was a danger that the industrial capacity required would exceed Britain's resources and that 'money and effort would be wasted in building isolated parts of a structure planned on so gigantic a scale that it could not be completed'.[73] Bridges played a key role in ensuring that grand strategy was considered in its wider economic context.

Defence policy was co-ordinated through the Committee of Imperial Defence (CID) and its sub-committees. Membership of the CID included the prime minister, the chancellor of the exchequer, the foreign secretary and the ministers in charge of departments responsible for defence (the Admiralty, the Air Ministry and the War Office) and the Dominions Office, the Colonial Office and the India Office, together with their official advisers. The chiefs of staff produced an annual review for the CID of the country's military position in the light of political information supplied by the Foreign, Colonial and India Offices. The CID made recommendations, but final decisions were made by the full Cabinet.

Most of the work was done in sub-committees. For example, a pro-gramme to deal with deficiencies in the armed forces in the light of the international situation was drafted in 1933–34 by the Defence Requirements Sub-Committee (DRC), comprising the chiefs of staff, the permanent secretary of the Treasury, the permanent under-secretary of the Foreign Office and the cabinet secretary. Subsequently, substantial changes to the recommended allocation of finance were made by minis-ters in another sub-committee, before a report was submitted to the Cabinet. The exercise was repeated in 1935. Gaines Post reckoned that the compromises involved in interdepartmental committees caused indecision, delays and disorder.[74] However, it is not clear that greater departmental independence would have created a more orderly govern-ment. The committee system facilitated the resolution of interdepart-mental disputes and, allied to Treasury control of expenditure, avoided the departmental competition for industrial capacity that had marked munitions production in the First World War.

The cabinet secretary, Sir Maurice Hankey, played a key role in servicing and co-ordinating the work of the Cabinet, the CID and their numerous sub-committees. A former royal marine and member of naval intelligence, he was respected by the chiefs of staff and ministers for his unrivalled experience – he had been the CID's secretary since 1912 and cabinet secretary since 1916. He was close to MacDonald and Baldwin, but much less so to Chamberlain. By 1937, Hankey was showing signs of exhaustion and, on his retirement in July 1938, his job was split between Bridges, whom Chamberlain selected to be cabinet secretary, and Colonel Hastings Ismay, Hankey's deputy since 1936, who became secretary to the CID (later renamed the Secretariat of the War Cabinet) and the Chiefs of Staff Committee. Ruggiero is mistaken in thinking that Chamberlain forced Hankey out of office.[75] Hankey had passed the normal age of retirement for a civil servant and the fact that Chamberlain appointed him as minister without portfolio in the War Cabinet in 1939 hardly suggests incompatibility.

There was strong pressure in the press in early 1936 for a minister of defence with his own staff to replace the CID, which was criticised as inadequate, lacking as it did executive power. Hankey was hostile to the idea because such a minister would come between him and the prime minister. Chamberlain, however, was by no means satisfied with the existing system. He believed the reports of the DRC in 1934 and 1935, which had been drafted by Hankey, simply put together the separate plans of the Admiralty, Air Ministry and War Office.[76] Hankey responded by preparing a scheme whereby a minister for the co-ordination of defence would chair the CID, when the prime minister was not present, and some CID sub-committees. Churchill would gladly have accepted the post and was not alone in being surprised when Sir Thomas Inskip, the attorney general, was appointed. Inskip had been in naval intelligence during the First World War, but had shown no interest in defence debates. However, he brought to his task a lawyer's ability to master a brief and was accepted as impartial by the defence departments. Like the CID, he had no executive authority and could only make recommendations. Having only a middle-ranking official as his secretary, Inskip relied heavily on Hankey for advice. At the end of 1938 a revolt of junior ministers against the government's record on rearmament led Chamberlain to transfer Inskip to the Dominions Office in January 1939. The new minister, Lord (until 1937 Sir Ernle) Chatfield, had ample experience of defence questions, having previously been first sea lord and chief of naval staff, chairman of the Chiefs of Staff Committee and chairman of a committee on Indian defence. However, as Chatfield admitted, his lack of political experience was a severe handicap and he was frustrated by his limited role as a co-ordinator.[77]

Until Churchill became prime minister in 1940 and took the additional title of minister of defence, executive authority for defence policy remained with the ministers in charge of the three defence departments. Churchill's cousin, the Marquess of Londonderry, who was in charge of the Air Ministry from November 1931 to June 1935, was a lightweight whose advancement had owed much to his wife, a noted political hostess who had formed an unlikely friendship with Ramsay MacDonald. As a peer, Londonderry could not defend the government in the House of Commons and he was not strong in debate in the Lords. When Hitler claimed in March 1935 to have achieved air parity with Britain, Londonderry's Cabinet colleagues wanted the RAF to be expanded more quickly than he or his professional advisers thought wise, and a small ministerial sub-committee was set up under the chairmanship of the colonial secretary, Philip Cunliffe-Lister, to produce a new air pro-gramme. On becoming prime minister on 7 June, Baldwin replaced Londonderry with Cunliffe-Lister.

The minutes of the secretary of state's progress meetings show Cunliffe-Lister was an effective head of the Air Ministry. He appointed Lord Weir, a Glasgow industrialist, as an adviser, drawing upon his experience as director-general of aircraft production in the First World

War and minister in charge of the RAF in 1918. Chamberlain, as chancellor, was willing to give the Air Ministry all the money it could spend, but aircraft production lagged behind Germany's. Cunliffe-Lister's decision in November 1935 to go to the House of Lords with the title of Viscount Swinton meant that, like Londonderry, he could not defend the government in the House of Commons, and Chamberlain felt forced to dismiss him on 6 May 1938 in the face of mounting criticism of the Air Ministry's performance from MPs, including Churchill, aircraft firms and the press. Weir was so angry at Swinton's treatment he resigned too.[78] Swinton's successor, Sir Kingsley Wood, was a capable minister who could defend the government effectively in the Commons and make the department's case in Cabinet. He established good personal relations with Sir Charles Bruce-Gardner, the chairman of the Society of British Aircraft Constructors, and won the confidence of the aircraft industry.

Successive secretaries of state for war had to defend the army against Chamberlain's belief that Britain could not afford both a powerful air force and an army capable of intervention in Europe at the outbreak of war. Viscount Hailsham, who was in charge of the War Office from 5 November 1931 to 7 June 1935, was also leader of the House of Lords and prominent in the Conservative Party. He was as effective in making his department's case as could be expected when the RAF enjoyed greater public support. His successor, Lord Halifax, was in post too briefly to defend even one year's annual estimates. From 22 November 1935 Duff Cooper was a doughty defender of the army's continental role. His career as a Foreign Office official from 1913 to 1924 had been interrupted by distinguished service on the Western Front with the Grenadier Guards, and on entering the House of Commons he quickly established a reputation as a formidable debater. He had experience of the War Office as a junior minister: as financial secretary in 1928–29 and under-secretary in 1931–34, and was the official biographer of Field Marshall Earl Haig. Chamberlain was favourably impressed by Duff Cooper when the latter was junior minister (financial secretary) at the Treasury in 1934, but repeated differences over the role of the army led him to regard Cooper as a failure at the War Office. 'D.C. has been lazy and until lately has shown no sign of getting down to work on any of the big problems', he wrote to his sisters in May 1937. However, Chamberlain recognised Cooper's 'undoubted ability' and, on becoming prime minister, gave him 'another chance' as first lord of the Admiralty.[79]

Chamberlain's choice as secretary of state for war in May 1937 was Leslie Hore-Belisha, a Liberal National whom he had come to know as financial secretary of the Treasury in 1932–34. Hore-Belisha had risen to the rank of major in the Army Service Corps in the First World War and had been a successful minister of transport, introducing such innovations as pedestrian crossings and driving tests at a time when increasing car ownership was associated with rising road casualties. Hore-Belisha embarked on what he called 'vitalisation of a stagnant atmosphere' at the War Office and the elimination of 'Buggins' Turn' in promotions. Influenced by Liddell Hart, who acted as his unofficial adviser in 1937–38, he believed the army had a '1914–18 mentality', preparing for a repetition of the Western Front, to the detriment of mechanisation or anti-aircraft defence, and an 'obsession' with India, where a third of British troops were based.[80] Hore-Belisha responded to the army's long-standing failure to attract enough recruits to fill its ranks by improving pay and conditions, and laying the foundations of what became a citizens' army during the war. For these achievements he has been rated a great secretary of state.[81] He was not, however, universally popular in the War Office, partly because of his penchant for self-publicity and lack of punctuality, but more importantly because he agreed with Chamberlain in 1937 that the army need not be made ready to fight in France at the outbreak of war.

The Admiralty enjoyed a much higher reputation than the Air Ministry or the War Office, and the minister, the first lord of the Admiralty, could count on popular support, mobilised by the Navy League, an effective lobby group. Sir Bolton Eyres-Monsell, the first lord from 5 November 1931 to 5 June 1936, had served in the Royal Navy from 1894 to 1906 before embarking on a political career, and had returned to active duty during the First World War. He thus enjoyed a rapport with his professional advisers. In particular, he and the first sea lord, Chatfield, worked effectively together to rebuild the fleet after years of Treasury-imposed retrenchment. Eyres-Monsell was successful in making the Navy's case in Cabinet when Chamberlain, as chancellor, tried to limit naval expenditure. Eyres-Monsell's successor, Samuel Hoare, the former foreign secretary, won Chatfield's approbation for diligently learning about the Admiralty and the fleet.[82] Hoare, however, had less than a year in which to make a mark, before being moved to the Home Office and was replaced by Duff Cooper. Cooper fought the Navy's corner with the same vigour as he had fought the army's, but was unable to persuade the Cabinet to adopt the standard of naval strength that the Admiralty believed was necessary to defend the Empire. In 1938 he was the leading dissident in Cabinet over Chamberlain's policy of appeasement and resigned in protest against the Munich agreement. In his place Chamberlain appointed Earl Stanhope, whose principal qualification was the prime minister's personal affection for him and his wife, who regularly acted as weekend hosts at their country house.[83] The Navy lacked a powerful presence in Cabinet thereafter until Churchill returned at the outbreak of war to the post of first lord that he had first occupied in 1911–15.

While ministers were responsible for defence policy, advice as to what it should be and its execution were in the hands of the chiefs of staff, who acted in two capacities. As first sea lord, chief of the air staff and the chief of the imperial general staff, each was, respectively, the principal adviser to his own minister. However, as members of the Chiefs of Staff Committee, they were supposed to offer collective advice to the CID. There was an inevitable tension between interdepartmental competition for scarce resources, both financial and industrial, and coming to a collective view on grand strategy. There was a tendency for the Admiralty to emphasize the threat from the Japanese navy to Britain's interests in the Far East, the Air Ministry the threat from the Luftwaffe to Great Britain, and the War Office the need to defend Belgium and Holland. Inskip thought in 1937 that any attempt to involve the chiefs of staff collectively in allocating finance between the three defence departments would lead to each fighting for his own service.[84] The period when Chatfield was first sea lord, January 1933 to November 1938, coincided with the Navy's turn to take the chair of the Chiefs of Staff Committee. He had wide experience, having fought at Jutland, played a prominent role in negotiating the Washington naval treaty with the United States, Japan, France and Italy in 1921–22, and resisted Treasury demands for retrenchment in the 1920s. As first sea lord, he saw his three principal tasks in 1933 as rebuilding the battle fleet, increasing cruiser construction, and reclaiming control of the Fleet Air Arm from the Air Ministry.[85] The last of these tasks involved a bitter interdepartmental dispute, which Inskip resolved in the Admiralty's favour. Chatfield's successor as first sea lord (but not chairman of the Chiefs of Staff Committee), Sir Roger Backhouse, had to retire in June 1939, dying shortly thereafter from a brain tumour. He was replaced by Sir Dudley Pound, who was very deaf and rarely spoke at chiefs of staff meetings except on naval matters.[86]

The historical reputations of the men who held the post of chief of the imperial general staff in the 1930s suffered from unfair criticism by Liddell Hart, who portrayed them as irresolute or reactionary regarding mechanisation of the army.[87] In fact Sir George Milne, who was chief of the imperial general staff from 1926 to 1933, sponsored experiments with tank formations at a time of severe financial constraint. His successor, Sir Archibald Montgomery-Massingberd (February 1933 to April 1936) established the 1st Tank Brigade as a permanent formation and took the decision in 1934 to create the first armoured division (then known as the mobile division). Sir Cyril Deverell (April 1936 to December 1937) was dismissed by Hore-Belisha on account of reluctance to implement policies that would have impaired the army's ability to fight in France at the outbreak of war. Deverell's successor, Lord Gort, was a fine fighting soldier, but lacked the qualities required to give advice to ministers and to discuss and defend it in committee. Matters were not improved by the mutual dislike that developed between him and Hore-Belisha.[88] On the outbreak of war, Gort went to France in command of the BEF and his place as chief of the imperial general staff was taken by Sir Edmund Ironside. Ironside had served in Russia, Central Europe and the Middle East, as well as on the Western front, but had no previous experience of the War Office and was not suited temperamentally to the job, his judgement during the Norwegian campaign in April 1940 being erratic.[89] By May he was exhausted and Churchill replaced him on the eve of Dunkirk with Sir John Dill, a much more able staff officer.

The chief of air staff at the outset of rearmament, Sir Edward Ellington (May 1933 to September 1937), had been unexpectedly appointed following the premature death of his predecessor, Sir Geoffrey Salmond, and failed to make a favourable impression in Whitehall. Warren Fisher thought Ellington was unable to hold his own against the other chiefs of staff on the DRC, and the secretary of that committee thought Ellington was 'extremely weak in discussion and his utterances most confused'.[90] Ellington's successor, Sir Cyril Newall (September 1937 to October 1940) had never attended Staff College and had a narrow conception of warfare. He succeeded Chatfield as chairman of the Chiefs of Staff Committee in November 1938 because it was the RAF's turn, but contented himself with reporting the views of its individual members rather than offering comprehensive strategic views. Neither Ellington nor Newall, at least before the war, questioned the offensive doctrine established by Sir Hugh Trenchard when he was chief of air staff between 1919 and 1929, and who continued to be an influential figure in his retirement.

With the exceptions of Chatfield and Backhouse, the pre-war chiefs of staff were not impressive strategists. Warren Fisher was typically hyperbolic when he wrote in 1939 that there had been no chief of the imperial general staff since Milne 'who could think' and 'since Hugh Trenchard, we have had no chief of the air staff (except in name)'. [91] However, even the more temperate Bridges thought Newall was the only good chief of staff in the opening months of the war (the not-good ones being Pound and Ironside).[92] Chamberlain had grounds for doubting whether the chiefs of staff could collectively rethink defence priorities.

2.3   The Intelligence Services

Intelligence work has three aspects: collection of information, analysis and interpretation, and distribution to people who can use it in making policy or conducting operations. The British intelligence services were not well placed to carry out these functions in the 1930s. The Secret Intelligence Service (SIS, also known from about 1938 as MI6), which was responsible for acquiring overseas intelligence through espionage, was understaffed, underfunded and could run few agents abroad. The Government Code and Cypher School (GC&CS) had very limited access to German coded radio traffic prior to breaking the Enigma key, with French and Polish help, in January 1940. The chief of SIS from 1923, Admiral Sir Hugh Sinclair, also controlled GC&CS. He saw ministers rarely, but the permanent under-secretary of the Foreign Office frequently, and he also developed good relations with Warren Fisher and Hankey. Chamberlain took a keen interest in the work of SIS, and by the time of Munich Sinclair was providing the prime minister and foreign secretary not only with intelligence appreciations but also with advice as to what policy should be.[93]

SIS and GC&CS provided intelligence for all Whitehall departments. However, responsibility for analysis and interpretation lay with the departments, not SIS or GC&CS. Departments also had their own sources of intelligence. The Foreign Office received a flow of information from diplomatic contacts and Vansittart had his own private intelligence networks. The Admiralty, Air Ministry and War Office each had its own intelligence branch. The Security Service, MI5, which operated in Britain, established contacts in the German embassy that provided the Foreign Office with important intelligence.[94] As regards the use of intelligence, the biggest weakness was lack of interdepartmental and inter-service co-operation. A Joint Intelligence Committee (JIC) was set up as a sub-committee of the Chiefs of Staff Committee in July 1936, but without representation from the Foreign Office until November 1938, or from SIS. The JIC advised the Joint Planning Sub-Committee and the Joint Planning Staff of the Chiefs of Staff Committee, but had yet to evolve into the powerful body that bears its name today. Interdepartmental barriers broke down only gradually. For example, in 1937 the Air Ministry representative on the JIC resisted the creation of an interdepartmental sub-committee to examine and correlate intelligence on air warfare in the Spanish Civil War, on the grounds that the necessary work was being done in the Air Ministry (although, on the insistence of the Admiralty, such a sub-committee was created).[95] The JIC was concerned mainly with long-term assessments of other countries' capabilities rather than intentions and had virtually no impact on policymaking before the war. Matters began to change only when the Foreign Office's Situation Report Centre, which had been created after the German occupation of the rump of Czechoslovakia in March 1939, was merged with the JIC on 3 August 1939, with the Foreign Office providing the chairman. Only then did the JIC's functions include preparation of daily reports and weekly commentaries on the international situation.

There were also weaknesses at the departmental level. The Foreign Office had no separate department devoted to the analysis of intelligence. The permanent under-secretary and the heads of departments received a flow of information, mainly from diplomatic sources, and took account of it while carrying out their daily advisory and executive functions. Jebb, who as private secretary to the permanent under-secretary was the point of liaison with the intelligence agencies, believed that many 'secret' reports he saw were really gossip.[96] There were no arrangements for collating or comparing Foreign Office appreciations with those of the defence departments. The Admiralty, Air Ministry and War Office had attachés at major embassies, but the Foreign Office normally forwarded their reports to the defence departments without commenting on them unless asked to do so. Indeed, the Foreign Office did not feel it necessary to consult the defence departments before forming its own views as to the significance of the reports, and Vansittart refused to share with the Air Ministry all information about the Luftwaffe reaching him from private sources. Within the defence departments, intelligence branches suffered from neglect after 1918 and were concerned more with collection of information than analysis and interpretation. They directed insufficient effort to following military technical progress and scientific innovation in foreign countries.

The growing importance of intelligence from 1935 was reflected in the appointment of more senior officers to deal with it. However, in the judgement of the official historian, the defence departments' intelligence branches were deficient in numbers and quality of staff until the influx of civilians after the outbreak of war.[97] From a Foreign Office perspective, Orme Sargent thought the defence departments lacked imagination when making forecasts of German rearmament: 'Our service departments seem to me to be not particularly good judges of pace. (Our Air Ministry is a hearse.)', he remarked.[98] Air Staff officers assumed wrongly their German counterparts would place a premium on efficiency rather than speed, and that the limiting factors in the expansion of the Luftwaffe were the training of personnel and the construction of air bases rather than aircraft manufacture.[99]

Economic intelligence was co-ordinated by two CID bodies: the Advisory Committee on Trade Questions in Time of War (the ATB

Committee), which dealt with plans for economic warfare and had a Foreign Office chairman and representatives of the Admiralty and the Board of Trade; and the Industrial Intelligence in Foreign Countries Sub-Committee (FCI), which studied industrial mobilisation abroad and had a chairman from the Department of Overseas Trade and representatives of the Board of Trade, Foreign Office, Treasury and the defence departments. In 1936 the FCI's remit was extended to include air targets. Serving both the ATB and FCI from 1934 was the Industrial Intelligence Centre (IIC), headed by the legendary Desmond Morton, best known to history as the man who provided information to Churchill on Germany's capacity to expand its air force. Morton had a military and SIS background, but had acquired a sufficient grasp of science and industry to know where to seek expert help, and he could interpret and analyse industrial intelligence, and present it in a suitable form for the ATB, FCI or CID. From 1934 he worked closely with the intelligence branch at the Air Ministry on estimates of German aircraft production that impressed readers in the CID secretariat and the Foreign Office, although ministers were slow to draw the conclusion that comparable industrial mobilisation was required in Britain. IIC reports on the German economy, particularly as regards shortages of raw materials, encouraged a belief in Whitehall that Germany would be vulnerable to economic warfare. Given the small size of the IIC and the variable quality of the intelligence it had to interpret and analyse, it is not surprising that its estimates and statistics were not always accurate, although they often were.[100] The main problem with economic intelligence, however, as with other forms of intelligence, was lack of systematic interdepartmental discussion of its significance. In the words of the official historian of intelligence, 'Whitehall was in no position to make a judgement on whether Hitler would be restrained by economic considerations'.[101]

One subject that seems to have escaped intelligence historians is financial intelligence. The Treasury maintained financial advisers at the embassies in Washington, Paris and Berlin. Their functions included making reports on the financial and economic position in the countries in which they were stationed. In Berlin, G. H. G. Pinsent's contacts included Hjalmar Schacht, the president of the Reichsbank (1933–39) and minister of economics (1934–37). Pinsent's reports tended to confirm the IIC picture of Germany being in growing economic difficulty, but with an additional financial dimension, including the effects of an armaments boom on the currency and external debt. Pinsent believed that the limits to Germany's rearmament were set not by its financial system, but by access to raw materials, the size of its labour force (which was fully employed by 1938) and by the willingness of its population to accept privation as the state diverted resources from civilian consumption.[102] Secret information reaching Fisher from German sources in January 1935 on the extent to which German rearmament was financed by debt led Chamberlain to abandon opposition to a defence loan, thereby facilitating planning rearmament on an enlarged scale (see pages 120–1). Intelligence could thus have a decisive effect on policy.

However, the pre-war intelligence services provided fragmented, incomplete and sometimes misleading information from which policymakers were able at best to form only a partial picture of the world around them. Chamberlain asked Lord Hankey, minister without portfolio, to investigate the working of the intelligence services as a whole in December 1939, and although Hankey produced an interim report in March 1940 no full report had been produced by the time Chamberlain's government fell. Churchill showed greater urgency. A week after becoming prime minister on 10 May 1940, he decided the JIC was to be the central body for producing intelligence appreciations. In the event, the JIC did not achieve real co-ordinating authority before May 1941, when the chiefs of staff gave it adequate assessment staff. Nevertheless, in the field of intelligence, Churchill, who had been fascinated by the subject, and particularly by signals intelligence, since the First World War, proved to be a better manager than Chamberlain.[103]

2.4   Churchill and Whitehall in the 1930s

Although Churchill was out of office for more than ten years before the Second World War, he was well connected to the policymaking process. He served as an outlet for Whitehall insiders who felt ministers were insufficiently responsive to warnings about the danger facing the country. For example, Wigram, the head of the Foreign Office's Central Department, leaked to him Vansittart's private intelligence on German aircraft production (with the latter's permission) for use in his campaign for greater air rearmament. Churchill also credited Wigram with fortifying his views on Hitler in frequent conversations.[104] Churchill's principal source of assessments of German air strength was Morton, who showed him both IIC and Air Ministry papers. Churchill reciprocated by forwarding reports he received from his own sources and asking for Morton's comments. For example, at least three French premiers passed French estimates of German air strength to Churchill, and in May 1938 Morton advised him that, whereas the French expected the Luftwaffe to expand to 300 squadrons by April 1939, the latest British forecast was 400.[105] The two men were neighbours and met frequently at Churchill's house, and much of what was communicated is undocumented. However, Gill

Bennett, Morton's biographer, doubts whether Churchill was told any-thing he was not entitled to know, given that he was sworn to secrecy as a privy councillor, and he was invited by the CID to comment on Air Ministry memoranda which were based on secret information.[106]

More questionable were the activities of RAF officers Charles (Torr) Anderson, director of the Training School, and Lachlan MacLean, a senior staff officer at Bomber Group headquarters, who informed Churchill of deficiencies in the RAF, supplying him with Air Ministry papers. On one occasion Churchill assuaged Anderson's conscience by telling him 'loyalty to the state *must* come before loyalty to the service'.[107] Churchill had contacts at the highest level in the Admiralty. The first sea lord, Chatfield, wrote to him about a number of issues, including the vulnerability of battleships to air attack, and took him to see a demon-stration of how the navy's new top-secret asdic (sonar) made it easier to detect submarines.[108] Churchill corresponded with Sir Henry Strakosch, a member of the League of Nations Financial Committee, and Morton on the economic aspects of German rearmament. For example, in November 1935 Morton consulted the Treasury about Strakosch's cal-culation of probable German expenditure on armaments and received what he called 'a long and interesting memorandum' to the effect that Sir Henry had overestimated. Morton did not show Churchill the Treasury memorandum, but gave him the Treasury's figures for his private information.[109]

The most striking evidence that Churchill was an insider in Whitehall was his membership of the CID's sub-committee on Air Defence Research (ADR). The sub-committee had been created in response to pressure from Churchill and Professor Frederick Lindemann, who held the chair in physics at Oxford and was a friend whom Churchill relied on to explain scientific matters. In June 1935 Churchill elicited by a parlia-mentary question the information that the ADR sub-committee had met only twice in the three months since it had been formed. He called for more urgency, and Baldwin responded by inviting him to become a member. The prime minister assured Churchill he would continue to be free to debate air policy and programmes in Parliament, and thus the leading critic of the government's failure to match German air rearma-ment was given access to technical secrets. Churchill later claimed this access 'imposed silence' and that he regretted having joined the sub-committee.[110] Certainly radar could not be mentioned in parliamentary debates, but Churchill's speeches betrayed little inhibition in his attacks on the government and, significantly, he did not resign.

Baldwin's invitation to join the ADR sub-committee did not extend to Lindemann, but Churchill insisted on him becoming a member of a committee of scientists who advised the Air Ministry on technical matters. Lindemann soon offended his colleagues by his harsh intolerance of alternative views to his own and the committee was reconstituted with the same chairman, Henry Tizard, but without Lindemann. Churchill's contributions in the ADR sub-committee were not always helpful. He took up a lot of time arguing for research on aerial mines, an impractical idea of Lindemann's for dropping explosives on bombers by parachute. In April 1938 Churchill proposed eliminating research that would not produce practical results within three years, prompting Hankey to point out that the progress of radar had been unexpectedly rapid and it was impossible to prophesy how quickly other projects would produce results.[111] Churchill's relationship with the ADR sub-committee was fractious, but he benefited from being kept up to date with developments in air warfare and arguably the sub-committee benefited from the energy he imparted to its proceedings and the high profile his participation gave it in Whitehall.

There was a limit to Whitehall's tolerance of Churchill's activities. In October 1937 Hankey received from Churchill a copy of a letter about the RAF's deficiencies sent to him by a senior staff officer. Although the cabinet secretary shared Churchill's concern about the lack of progress in rearmament, he replied he was shocked that RAF officers were in direct contact with a critic of the Air Ministry. He thought such communications must be subversive to discipline and urged Churchill (unsuccessfully) to discourage them. Churchill's service contacts included his son-in-law, Duncan Sandys, who, as a junior officer in the Territorial Army, was aware of grave deficiencies in London's anti-aircraft defences. Sandys was also an MP, and in June 1938 he sent the secretary of state for war, Hore-Belisha, a draft parliamentary question that was clearly based on secret information. Hore-Belisha referred Sandys to the attorney-general (the chief legal adviser to the Crown), who told him that he would be liable to prosecution under the Official Secrets Act unless he disclosed the name of his informant. Sandys demanded that a parliamentary select committee be set up to establish whether the Act applied to MPs discharging their responsibilities and the resulting Committee of Privileges decided it did not.[112]

3   Britain and the Balance of Power

3.1   Measuring Power

One reason why historians disagree about appeasement is they make different assumptions about Britain's ability to influence events. Power may be defined as the capability to compel other states to give way by the threat or use of military force or economic sanctions. The most comprehensive study of the balance of power in the 1930s by a historian is Paul Kennedy's *The Rise and Fall of the Great Powers*.[1] The book compares defence expenditure, aircraft production and shares of world manufacturing output, together with discussion of strategic choices and diplomatic developments. Kennedy argued that rising powers tend to take on commitments that they struggle to defend once other countries catch up. His prime example was the British Empire, which had expanded while Britain was a technological leader during the late eighteenth and early nineteenth centuries, but became increasingly vulnerable as other powers industrialised. Kennedy is not an economic determinist. Indeed, he emphasised that political leaders have a degree of choice in how to cope with long-term trends. Nevertheless, he has been criticized by some international historians for going too far in privileging measurable factors like national income, volume of trade and industrial capacity, and taking insufficient account of intangibles, such as leadership, will and imagination. Taking sea power and global reach into account, Kennedy's critics concluded that he had exaggerated the extent of British decline before 1939, but by how much they could not say, given their stress on intangibles.[2]

International relations theorists have attempted quantitative comparisons of great power capabilities. Paul MacDonald and Joseph Parent used estimates of gross domestic product (GDP) to identify relative great-power decline.[3] German GDP grew more rapidly than the United Kingdom's from 1933 (Figure 3.1). Although annual estimates of GDP were not available to policymakers in the 1930s, MacDonald and Parent regarded it as a proxy for trade statistics or tax receipts which were. However, GDP data, which record the value of goods and services

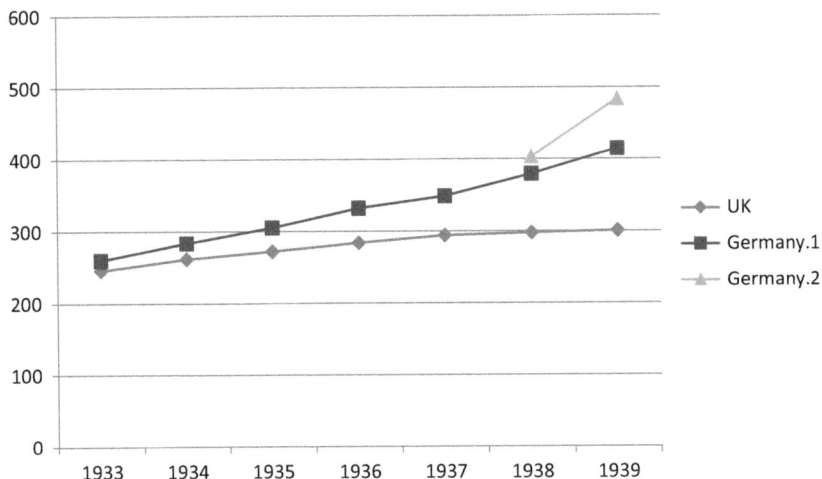

Figure 3.1 GDP of the German Reich and the UK at constant prices in
1990 international dollars (billions)
Note: Germany.1 excludes, and Germany.2 includes, Hitler's gains
from seizing Austria in 1938 and Czechoslovakia in 1939.
Source: Maddison Project http://www.ggdc.net/MADDISON/oriindex.htm[4]

produced within an economy in a year, say nothing about international
purchasing power represented by gold and foreign exchange reserves,
overseas assets that could be sold or used as security for borrowing
abroad, or control of colonial resources. In all these respects Germany
was at a disadvantage compared with Britain. GDP data are useful as
measures of the relative size of economies, but on their own are
inadequate as a measure of relative power or of how power was perceived
at the time.

Another international relations theorist, Randall Schweller, used an
index of power that gave equal weight to military, industrial and demo-
graphic factors. He drew on data on manpower in armed forces, defence
expenditure, steel production, energy consumption, and urban and total
population to give a single figure for each great power's capability. He
then compared the relative strengths of the great powers as a percentage
share of total great power capabilities. He concluded that the international system was bipolar in the early 1930s, with the United States
and the Soviet Union as the two poles, but by the later 1930s it had
become tripolar, with Germany overtaking the Soviet Union and almost
catching up on the United States in 1939. Britain, on his measure, was in
the second rank of great powers, although it was stronger than France,

Japan or Italy.[5] The picture given by Schweller's table for the relative strength of the powers is shown graphically in Figure 3.2a and b.

One problem with both Schweller's and MacDonald and Parent's work is that they equated British power with that of the United Kingdom. However, as Zara Steiner pointed out, measurement of British power has to take account of the dominions and colonies, with their natural resources and reserves of manpower.[6] The economic historian Mark Harrison compared data for area, population and GDP in 1938, and showed that, while the United Kingdom was inferior to Germany on all three measures, the British Commonwealth and Empire, including the United Kingdom, was superior to Germany on all three.[7] The population of Greater Germany, including Austria, was 75.4 million; the United Kingdom, 47.5 million. On the other hand, Britain could draw on the support of Canada, Australia, New Zealand and South Africa (combined population about 30 million) and India and the colonies (about 690 million). Much of the Empire was underdeveloped, but GDP data give a broad indication of the scale of the Commonwealth and Empire's economic resources compared with other major powers (compare Figure 3.3a and b). Once one takes account of the imperial dimension, it is not clear that Schweller was justified in consigning Britain to the second rank of great powers.

Once more, however, GDP data are only part of the story. The Commonwealth and Empire involved worldwide defence commitments: in the Far East against Japan, in the Middle East against Italy and in India against the Soviet Union, as well as imperial communications throughout the world.[8] Since the burden of imperial defence was borne in peacetime largely by the United Kingdom, the Commonwealth and Empire represented a liability as well as an asset. The dominions were constitutionally free to choose whether to support the United Kingdom in war. When the Commonwealth prime ministers met in May 1937 William Lyon Mackenzie King warned that Canadian participation would depend upon circumstances and public opinion. J. B. M. Hertzog said South Africa could not be expected to join in a conflict arising from unwillingness to redress German grievances in Central Europe, and South Africa came close to remaining neutral in 1939. Ireland, which was still constitutionally a dominion, although it had ceased to act like one, did opt for neutrality in 1939, thereby denying the Royal Navy the use of naval bases that Chamberlain had handed over in 1937 in an unsuccessful attempt to appease the Irish leader Eamon De Valera.[9] Given the uncertainty about what the dominions would do, their armed forces, existing and potential, had to be regarded in Whitehall as extra assets, not to be taken into account in pre-war planning. The dominions' armies were mainly made

(a)

(b)

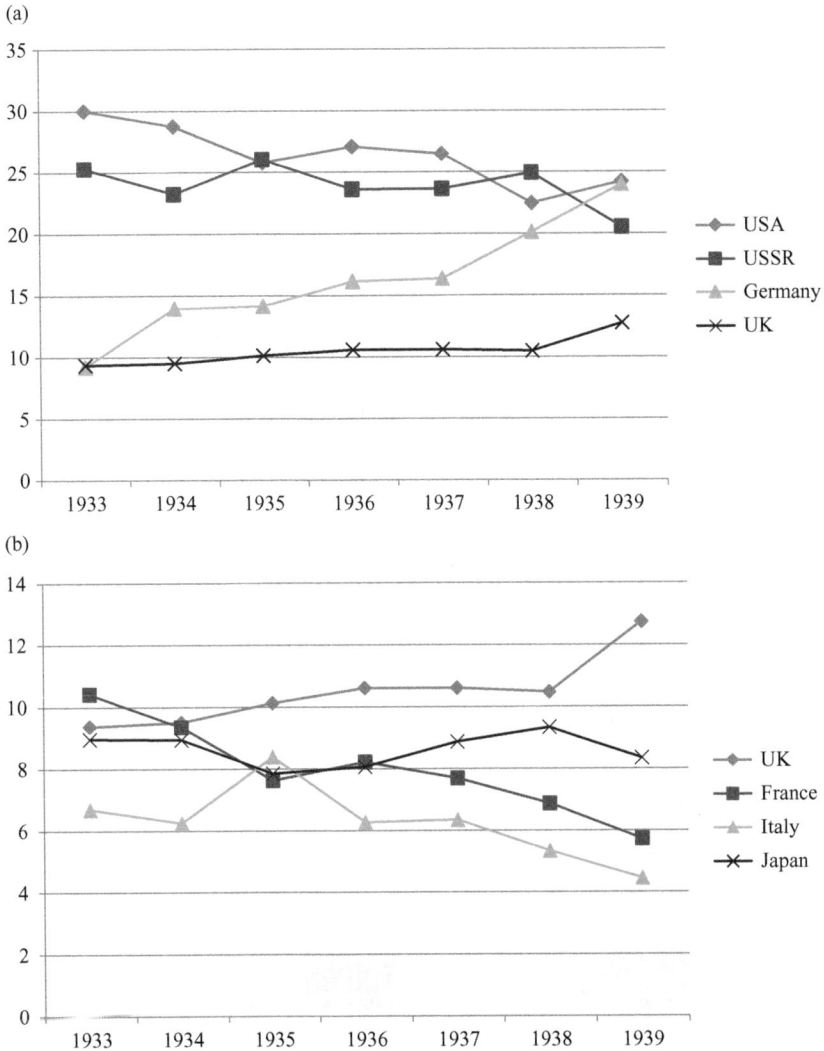

Figure 3.2 (a) Percentage shares of major power capabilities (USA, USSR, Germany and UK). (b) Percentage shares of major power capabilities (UK, France, Italy and Japan)

Note: The rise in Italy's share in 1935 reflects expenditure on the war in Ethiopia.

Source: Randall L. Schweller, *Deadly Imbalances: Tripolarity and Hitler's Strategy of World Conquest* (New York: Columbia University Press, 1998), p. 31.

(a)

(b)

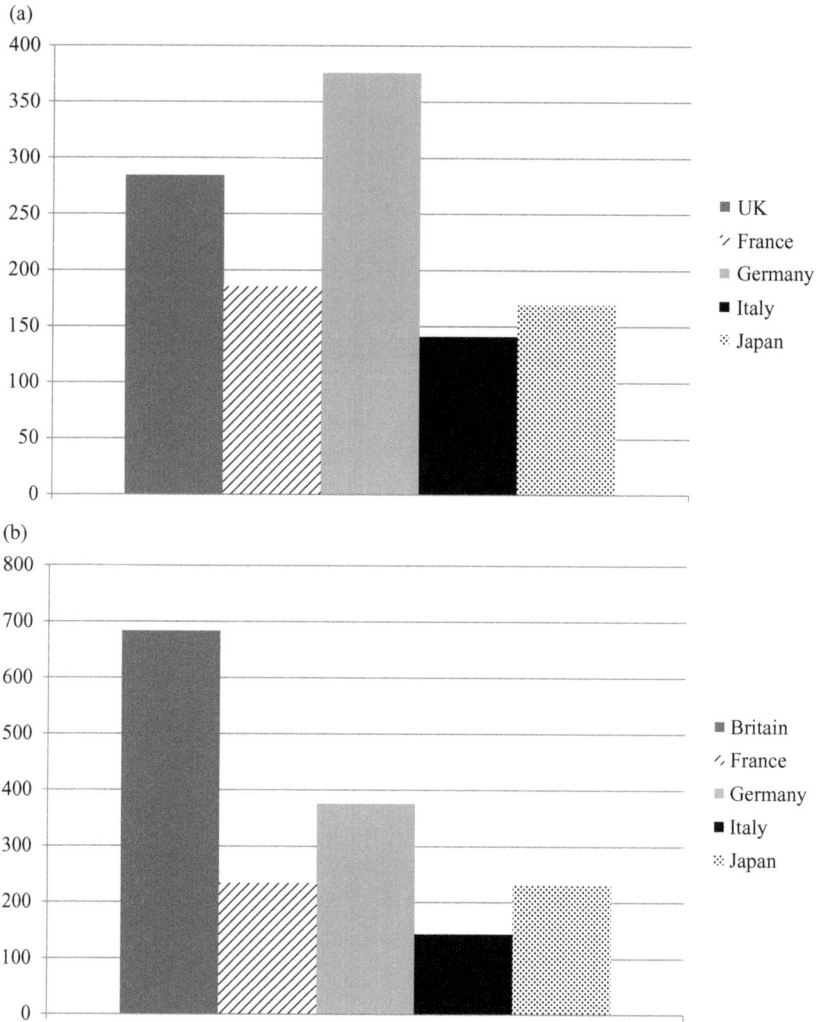

Figure 3.3 (a) GDP of major powers in 1938 (excluding colonies and dominions) in 1990 international dollars (billions). (b) GDP of major powers in 1938 (including colonies and dominions) in 1990 international dollars (billions)

Source: Mark Harrison (ed.), *The Economics of World War II: Six Great Powers in International Comparison* (Cambridge University Press, 1998), p. 3.

up of part-time soldiers who required further training before they would be ready to fight; their air forces were little more than training organisations with obsolescent equipment; only their navies were ready for war, but these were small.[10] The dominions had huge military potential: for example, by the middle of the war, Australia, New Zealand and South Africa were providing about 25 per cent of the 'British' army in North Africa; a greatly expanded Canadian navy was playing a key role in protecting North Atlantic convoys, and the dominions and Commonwealth air training schemes were supplying the RAF with a high proportion of its aircrews.[11] However, the only large dominion units committed in the first ten months of the war were a Canadian division sent to France, an Australian division and a (small) New Zealand division in the Middle East, and a South African brigade in East Africa. Consequently the United Kingdom had initially to rely mainly on its own resources.

British rearmament was slower than that of the leading totalitarian states, Germany and the Soviet Union; about the same as Japan's; but faster than that of the other great powers, including the United States (Figure 3.4a and b). Defence expenditure is an incomplete measure of power. German forces were concentrated in Europe; British forces were dispersed round the Empire (in 1938 more British troops were deployed maintaining order in Palestine than were available to send to France). As an island, the United Kingdom had long enjoyed greater security from invasion than continental European powers, but the advent of air power posed a new threat. On the other hand, the Royal Navy and bases round the Empire gave Britain global reach, which Germany lacked. Power depended not only on the scale of defence expenditure but also on grand strategy.

There is no single set of figures that can measure Britain's comparative strength in the European balance of power. The best one can do is to study Britain's relative capacity to wage war. That, the chiefs of staff observed in 1939, 'depend[ed] not only upon the strength and efficiency of the fighting forces, but also upon the organisation of the whole of the industrial and financial resources and of the available manpower of the nation and on the maintenance of civil morale'.[12] The next sections look at these different aspects of power.

3.2 Sea Power

Britain had ceded its position as the world's leading naval power at the Washington Conference in 1921–22, when it agreed to limit its tonnage in major warships to the same level as the United States. Thereafter the Admiralty was under pressure to reduce the annual naval estimates

(a)

(b)

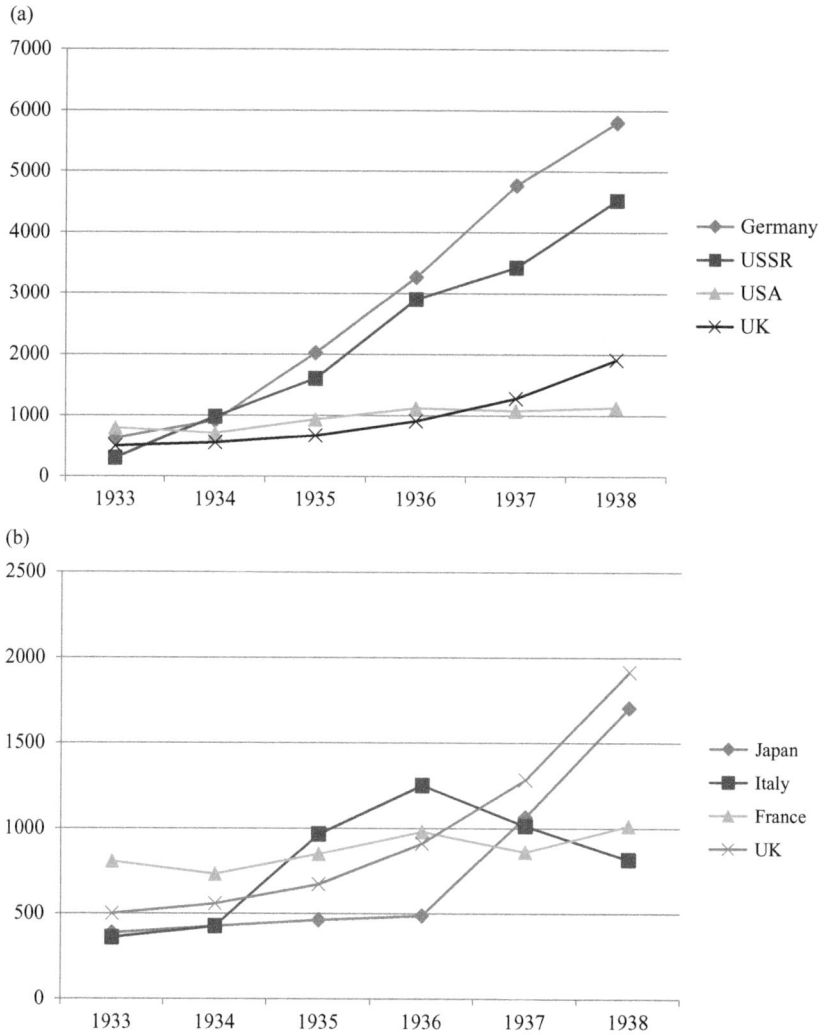

Figure 3.4 (a) Defence expenditures of Germany, the USSR, the USA
and the UK (millions of current dollars). (b) Defence expenditure of
Japan, Italy, France and the UK (millions of current dollars)
Note: Italian expenditure includes the cost of fighting in Ethiopia and
Spain, but the Japanese figures exclude the cost of fighting in China.
Source: Paul Kennedy, *The Rise and Fall of the Great Powers* (London: Unwyn
Hyman, 1988), p. 296.

Table 3.1. *Warships of great powers as at February 1939*

	British Commonwealth	USA	Japan	France	Italy	Germany
Capital ships	15	15	9	6	4	2
'Pocket Battleships'						3
Aircraft carriers	6	5	5	1		
8-in gun cruisers	15	17	12	7	7	
5.1/6.1-in gun cruisers	45	15	21	11	12	6
Destroyers	159	209	83	58	48	17
Submarines	54	87	58	76	104	43

Notes: The table excludes ships used primarily for training. The British Commonwealth figures include two Australian 8-in and four 6-in gun cruisers and one New Zealand 6-in gun cruiser. Source: Cmd. 5936, UK Parliamentary Papers 1938–39.

down to 1932, including while Churchill was chancellor from 1924 to 1929. As chancellor and prime minister, Chamberlain gave priority to the RAF rather than the navy. Nevertheless, the Royal Navy was still unsurpassed in size in 1939 (see Table 3.1). Fleets in the interwar period were compared principally in terms of capital ships, a category that included battleships, vessels with big guns and heavy armour, and battlecruisers, which also had big guns but had lighter armour and were faster than battleships. Britain and the United States had equal numbers of capital ships, and Britain had as many as Japan, Germany and Italy combined. During the Second World War, aircraft carriers became the principal warships; Britain had more than any other fleet in 1939, although American and Japanese carriers carried more aircraft. In other categories of surface warships, Britain exceeded all other navies except the United States'.

The Admiralty nevertheless thought a larger navy was required to defend the Empire and its trade routes. Since the Washington Conference naval planning had been based on a one-power standard, defined as sufficient strength to enable the main fleet to match any other fleet, wherever situated, and to have local forces capable of preventing vital damage pending the arrival of the main fleet. In practice, war against the United States was ruled out and the 'other fleet' was the Japanese navy. In the rearmament programme approved by the Cabinet in 1936 the one-power standard – by then referred to as the DRC Standard – was retained on the assumption there would be no abnormal German and Italian naval construction. The Admiralty argued, however,

Table 3.2. *Standards of strength for the Royal Navy*

	DRC Standard 1936	New Standard 1937
Capital ships	15	20
Aircraft carriers	10	15
Cruisers	70	100
Destroyers	16 flotillas	22 flotillas
Submarines	55	82

Source: DP(P) 3, CAB 16/182.

that a two-power standard was required and proposed what it called the New Standard, which was intended to make it possible to send to the Far East a fleet adequate to act on the defensive and be a strong deterrent to Japan, while maintaining in all circumstances in home waters a fleet able to meet the requirements of a war with Germany at the same time. Although, at Chamberlain's instigation, the Cabinet never formally approved the New Standard, the Admiralty used it when planning new construction.[13] A comparison of Tables 3.1 and 3.2 shows that in 1939 the Royal Navy was five capital ships and nine aircraft carriers short of a two-power standard.

Numbers of warships alone are an imperfect measure of sea power. Britain had an aging battle-fleet by the 1930s. At the Washington Conference Britain, the United States, Japan, France and Italy had agreed not to build new capital ships for ten years – with an exception being made for Britain, which was allowed two new ones – and at the London Naval Conference of 1930 Britain, the United States and Japan extended this building 'holiday' to the end of 1936. By the 1930s all the Washington signatories had aging battle fleets. However, other naval powers, particularly Japan, spent more than Britain on modernising older capital ships. Moreover, from 1929 Germany began building big-gun ships that nominally complied with the 10,000-ton limit imposed on it by the Treaty of Versailles – hence the nickname 'pocket battleships' – but which displaced considerably more. France and Italy refused to join in the post-1930 building holiday, and soon there was a European naval arms race. The Admiralty hoped to secure international agreement on limiting the size (and therefore the expense) of capital ships.[14] There was considerable uncertainty about the size of German, Italian and Japanese vessels under construction. The first British capital ships to be laid down in 1937 were designed within the 35,000-ton Washington limitation and proved to be smaller than their German, Italian and Japanese contemporaries. However, the quality of ships is not determined by size alone.

For example, the Royal Navy pioneered the use of ship-borne radar, which gave it a considerable advantage in night-fighting over the Italian navy, which had none.

Successful deployment of the main fleet to the Far East depended not only upon numbers of warships but also on the existence there of a fortified base with a dockyard, intermediate defended bases and fuelling stations, support vessels and adequate reserves of oil. All these require-ments had been neglected, partly because Churchill, while chancellor, had believed there was not the slightest chance of war with Japan, and partly because his Labour successor, Philip Snowdon, had imposed even greater restraint on expenditure than Churchill had done.[15] Work on the Singapore base was expedited from 1934, and by 1939 a new graving dock had been opened and the coastal defences were nearing comple-tion. Admiralty planning proceeded on the basis that Japan, with its dependence on imports of food, raw materials and oil, would be vulner-able to blockade by cruisers backed by a fleet based at Singapore.[16] The Singapore strategy remained in place despite German rearmament because the Admiralty believed that the Anglo-German Naval Agreement of 1935, whereby Hitler had offered to limit his surface fleet to 35 per cent of the size of the Royal Navy, gave Britain a margin with which to match the Japanese – provided the latter did not build beyond nine capital ships.[17] The Admiralty took the view that some numerical inferiority could be accepted, in the belief that the Japanese navy was only 80 per cent as efficient as the Royal Navy. The basis of this dubious estimate appears to have been a report from the naval attaché in Tokyo claiming that Japanese officers lacked independent judgement and Japanese technical personnel were deficient in training and skill.[18] Australia and New Zealand were assured at the Imperial Conference in 1937 that the main fleet would be sent to Singapore in the event of Japanese aggression. However, in May 1939, after Sir Roger Backhouse had replaced Sir Ernle Chatfield as first sea lord, Admiralty policy changed to one of sending only four capital ships against Japan's nine, unless Italy were neutral or had been defeated. Chatfield, as minister for co-ordination of defence, challenged this change, and an assessment by the chiefs of staff stated that seven capital ships could be sent to the Far East, if the Mediterranean were to be abandoned.[19]

These developments can be taken as evidence of a lack of power. On the other hand, in a strategic assessment in November 1937 the chiefs of staff noted that, against Germany and Italy, Britain and France would have such marked naval superiority they should be able to exercise decisive economic pressure in a prolonged war.[20] Moreover, the changes in Admiralty thinking in 1939 reflected confidence that Italy, with its dependence on seaborne imports, was vulnerable to blockade and could be eliminated by offensive action.[21] There was also some wishful thinking in London – fostered by secret and noncommittal Anglo-American naval staff talks in 1938 and 1939 – that assistance would be forthcoming from the US Navy in the event of a Japanese descent on South-East Asia. In fact, the balance of opinion in Washington was opposed to pulling Britain's imperial chestnuts out of the fire.[22] Even so, Churchill, as first lord of the Admiralty from the outbreak of war, and then as prime minister from May 1940, took the view that the United States might well become involved if Japan entered the war and he concentrated Britain's naval power in European waters.[23]

Naval rearmament took place in a period of rapid technical change. The Admiralty fended off an Air Ministry claim in 1934 that land-based bombers would give greater value than aircraft carriers, and launched as many aircraft carriers as capital ships in the 1930s. In contrast, Germany and Italy failed to complete a single aircraft carrier, giving the Royal Navy a considerable advantage. In 1936 the Admiralty and Air Staff debated the vulnerability of capital ships to aircraft, with the Admiralty denying that bombers were more cost-effective than capital ships and claiming that anti-aircraft guns offered adequate protection.[24] Churchill, briefed by his Admiralty contacts, strongly supported the resumption of capital ship construction in 1937.[25] Regarding anti-submarine warfare, he urged the construction of more destroyers in 1938 to take on escort duties but, after being given a demonstration of asdic, he declared submarines were obsolete. Indeed, in January 1939 he thought neither aircraft nor submarines posed a mortal threat to either warships or merchant ships.[26] In the event, wartime experience would show that both he and the Admiralty were much too optimistic in these respects.

Material weaknesses in British sea power were to some extent offset by intangible advantages. The Royal Navy had more long-service sailors than any other fleet and more could be recruited from what was still the world's largest merchant navy. Centuries of tradition imbued officers and men with confidence and an offensive spirit. Senior officers had experienced combat. Churchill, on becoming first lord in September 1939, felt he had at his disposal the 'finest-tempered instrument of naval war in the world', and thought it would be unjust to the Chamberlain government to suggest that the Royal Navy had not been adequately prepared for a war with Germany and Italy.[27]

Sea power gave Britain a means of putting pressure on Germany, but blockade would require time to take effect. As the chiefs of staff observed in March 1938, Germany would not be deterred from aggression if a war with Britain and France was expected to be short. In particular, the chiefs of staff thought the deterrent effect of sea power depended on whether the Germans believed Britain could be knocked out quickly by the ruthless use of air power.[28] It is to the question of relative air power that we now turn.

3.3   Air Power

In contrast to his views on the navy, Churchill described the loss of Britain's lead over Germany in the air in the 1930s as a 'disaster of first magnitude', leaving London exposed to 'immeasurable threats'.[29] Baldwin had stated as far back as 1923 that Britain must have a 'Home Defence Air Force of sufficient strength adequately to protect us against air attack by the strongest air force within striking distance of this country'.[30] However, as long as the air power in question was France, the RAF's Home Defence scheme was given little priority; indeed, it was still incomplete when Baldwin renewed his pledge in March 1934 in response to public alarm about covert German rearmament. Churchill kept up pressure on the government, but the RAF was slower to rearm than the Luftwaffe until 1939. In his account of the Second World War, Churchill stated that the outbreak of war found Britain with barely half the German numbers of aircraft.[31]

How great was Germany's advantage in air strength? Gibbs's volume in the official history of the Second World War gave comparative figures for September 1939 as Britain: 1,660 first-line aircraft (including 204 in the Fleet Air Arm) plus 2,200 reserves; Germany: 4,320 first-line plus 4,900 reserves.[32] However, Gibbs took his figures from a War Cabinet paper dated 29 September 1939, where, although the British figures were accurate, the German ones were based on overestimates, particularly of reserves, by the Air Ministry's intelligence branch.[33] M. M. Postan, in the official history of war production, derived a figure of 3,609 for German first-line strength at the outbreak of war from the records of the German Air Ministry – 16.5 per cent below the figure in Gibbs's book.[34] There is room for debate even about Postan's figure. As Richard Overy has pointed out, calculations of air strength are fraught with difficulty. He drew a distinction between first-line strength, that is the number of aircraft allocated to operational units, and serviceable first-line strength, which takes account of the proportion of these aircraft that were under repair or otherwise unavailable for operations. During the Luftwaffe's rapid expansion, serviceability was fairly low as technical support was still under development. Overy estimated German serviceable first-line strength in September 1939 at 2,893, or 20 per cent below Postan's figure. In Overy's view, estimates for Germany's air strength down to 1937 are meaningless, as many squadrons were below

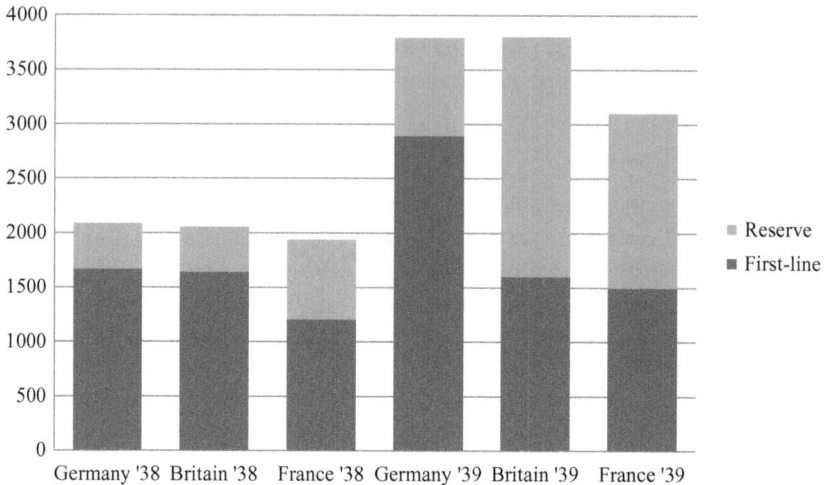

Figure 3.5 Serviceable first-line aircraft of Germany, Britain and France, September 1938 and September 1939
Source: R. J. Overy, *The Air War 1939–1945* (London: Europa Publications, 1980), p. 23.

establishment or were not ready for operations, and it was only from 1938 that the Luftwaffe became an effective fighting force.[35] Nevertheless, skilful German propaganda and misleading intelligence gave an impression of superior air power earlier.

Figure 3.5 shows that German serviceable first-line strength increased rapidly between Munich and the outbreak of war, from 1,669 to 2,893, whereas British serviceable first-line strength actually fell slightly, from 1,642 to 1,600. However, it does not follow that Germany was becoming relatively stronger. During their rapid expansion, both air forces were compelled to put most of their modern aircraft into the first line, and consequently lacked reserves to replace combat losses. Between September 1938 and September 1939, the British put a high proportion of new aircraft into reserve. In contrast, Hitler never grasped the necessity of reserves for sustained operations.[36] Figure 3.5 also shows that the combined air strength of the RAF and the French *l'Armée de l'Air* always exceeded the Luftwaffe's. However, the British took little comfort from this, being discouraged by reports to the CID on the capacity of the French aircraft industry and the inferior quality of its products.[37] Moreover, if the RAF and *l'Armée de l'Air* failed to co-ordinate their operations, each could be outnumbered by the Luftwaffe concentrating its power first against one and then against the other.

RAF doctrine did not encourage Anglo-French collaboration. Determined to maintain an independent service, the Air Ministry prioritised strategic bombing to the detriment of tactical operations in support of the army. The main purpose of Bomber Command was to weaken the German economy and morale, with the Ruhr the prime target, but, as with naval blockade, the strategy required time to take effect. In the short term, the French would benefit from strategic bombing only if British bombers forced the Germans to divert fighter aircraft or anti-aircraft guns to home defence. To the Air Staff, the effectiveness of strategic bombing was a matter of faith and was not rigorously tested. Similar ideas could be found in other countries, but the US Army Air Corps was the only other air force where strategic bombing theory prevailed over tactical support for ground forces. Geography allowed Britain and the United States to maintain smaller armies than other great powers, making it easier to devote resources to other purposes.[38] The Luftwaffe's first chief of air staff, Walther Wever, was a proponent of strategic bombing, but most of his staff thought that tactical support for the army was more important. Wever died in 1936 and his successor, Albert Kesselring, placed orders for medium bombers that were cheaper and more versatile than the large aircraft required for long-range operations. The prototypes built while Wever was alive were underpowered, and their successor, the Heinkel He 177, suffered from persistent technical problems. Like their British counterparts, the German air staff believed in an offensive strategy, but, for the purpose of limited continental wars, medium bombers were adequate and a strategic bomber force was a long-term project that was never fulfilled.[39] The predominant need to support a large army also prevailed against strategic bombing theory in the Soviet Union, where large numbers of heavy bombers were constructed in the early 1930s, but strategic bombing was abandoned in 1940 and priority given to ground attack aircraft and medium bombers.[40] Italy was home to the noted advocate of strategic bombing, Giulio Douhet, but the *Regia Aeronautica* failed to develop clear ideas of how to employ bombers, either strategically or in support of the army and navy.[41] The French air force had strategic aspirations, but had to defer to the army's demands for air superiority over the battlefield and support for army operations. Multi-purpose aircraft designed for bombing, reconnaissance and long-range escort tasks proved to be ill-suited to any of them.[42] France had only a handful of long-range aircraft, and Anglo-French collaboration in air warfare was confined to the provision of bases in France for RAF bombers with insufficient range to reach the Ruhr from England, and a small proportion of the RAF allocated to supporting the British Expeditionary Force.

Table 3.3. *RAF expansion schemes, 1934–9: planned numbers of front-line bombers and fighters*

Scheme	A	C	F	L	M
Date	July 1934	May 1935	Feb. 1936	Apr. 1938	Nov. 1938
Bombers	476	816	1,580	1,352	1,360
Fighters	336	300 + 120	280 + 140	448 + 160	640 + 160
Fighters as % of bombers	70.6	51.5	26.6	45.0	58.8

Note: The second number for fighters in Schemes C to M is for aircraft in the ten squadrons earmarked for work with the army and therefore not available for home defence except at the outbreak of war.
Source: Malcolm Smith, *British Air Strategy between the Wars* (Oxford University Press, 1984), pp. 328–335.

The best-known prophecy in Britain about air warfare was a speech in 1932 by Baldwin in which he said 'the bomber will always get through'.[43] However, the Air Staff never thought that *every* bomber would get through, and Britain invested heavily in its air defence system even before the development of radar shifted the balance between attack and defence.[44] Nor, although they greatly overestimated the casualties that would result from bombing, did the Air Staff believe that an air force could deliver a 'knock-out blow', if by that was meant defeating a nation in 24 hours. Rather, they thought an air force that seized the initiative and attacked with maximum intensity at the outbreak of war might strike a blow from which its victim would be unable to recover. Britain was more vulnerable than Germany to air attack because London was a more concentrated target than the Ruhr. The Air Staff argued that fighter squadrons must be able to conduct operations at whatever level of intensity was dictated by the enemy, and must therefore have 100 per cent reserves, even if bomber squadrons, for financial reasons, were to have a lower level during the period of expansion. The numbers of first-line fighters for home defence were determined by the anticipated scale of attack, and planned numbers were increased in 1938 as the numbers and range of Luftwaffe bombers increased (see Table 3.3). Nevertheless, the Air Staff held to the principle that the best form of defence was attack, including counter-bombing against air bases or other targets that would force the enemy on the defensive. RAF expansion programmes were designed to achieve parity with Germany in bomber strength. The proportion of bombers to fighters rose in the first three expansion schemes, and the reduction in planned numbers of bombers in 1938 was offset by the fact that the aircraft to be ordered were able to carry heavier loads of bombs over longer ranges than those in service. Despite decisions by the Cabinet in December 1937 and November 1938 that fighters were to have priority, the Air Ministry was able to secure additional industrial capacity for the new bombers.

The 1930s saw dramatic changes in the performance of aircraft. More powerful engines were developed, and streamlined monoplanes began to replace biplanes. The best RAF fighters in service down to 1937 could be outpaced by the bombers that began to enter service with the Luftwaffe in that year; hence the importance of the Hurricane and Spitfire monoplanes that were produced in large numbers from 1938. In general, the aircraft available for production when rearmament began in 1936 were of value only for training purposes by 1939. The range of bombers increased, making the RAF less dependent on continental air bases and therefore on Anglo-French co-operation. With technical improvement in aircraft came greater expense: the RAF's new heavy bomber in 1937 cost more than twice the design it replaced, or about four times as much as a contemporary fighter. Chamberlain, who feared the burden of rearmament would weaken the economy and yet was under political pressure to increase aircraft production, had financial reasons to challenge the Air Staff's emphasis on bombers.[45]

Moreover, when in October 1937 Chamberlain enquired what the position of air defence would be in January 1938, he was told that Bomber Command was in no way fit for war.[46] Deliveries of modern bombers capable of attacking targets in Germany from British bases had hardly begun. The need to maximise production for political reasons led the Air Ministry to order large numbers of aircraft with limited range and bomb load, and even at the outbreak of war half of Bomber Command was equipped with these pseudo-strategic bombers. Moreover, rapid expansion with inadequate training meant that, even with improved bomb sights, aircrews were unlikely to drop bombs closer than 150 yards from a target in daylight. As late as May 1939 the officer in charge of Bomber Command, Air Chief Marshal Sir Edgar Ludlow-Hewitt, warned the Air Council he could not predict when his force would be ready for war.[47]

In contrast, Britain was developing the best air defence system in the world. All information on enemy air movements were reported to the RAF's headquarters for the air defence of Great Britain, and command and control was improved by the development of radio communications between ground and air, and between aircraft. Radar greatly increased the chances of successful interception of bombers. The first successful tests did not occur until 1935, and in October 1937 the Air Staff advised that radar was still at an experimental stage. Nevertheless, progress was sufficient for ministers to feel confident Britain would be able to deflect an initial blow from the Luftwaffe once the air defence system was complete.[48]

Uri Bialer argued that fear of air attacks led to grand strategy prioritising the RAF, to the detriment on Britain's ability to intervene by land in a continental war.[49] However, apocalyptic visions of an aerial knock-out blow did not go unchallenged in Whitehall. For example, at a CID meeting in February 1935 the chief of the imperial general staff, Sir Archibald Montgomery-Massingberd, said he was unable to believe an air attack could be delivered on a scale that would paralyse the nation's ability to continue the war. On that occasion the prime minister, MacDonald, said that it was not the soldiers who might be knocked out, but the public who might become so demoralised as to get into unrestrained panic. In June 1937 the Admiralty's Director of Plans, Captain Tom Phillips, wrote there was 'no reason to suppose in theory and no evidence to prove in fact, that aircraft can play a decisive role save in support of the army and navy'.[50] In November 1937, a chiefs of staff report, no doubt reflecting Admiralty and War Office views, noted there was no proof that German military opinion as a whole believed victory could be achieved by air power alone, and that the relative strengths of Britain and France on the one hand and Germany and Italy on the other would not encourage the Germans to risk a war in which hope of success would depend almost entirely upon the Luftwaffe.[51] In contrast, the chiefs of staff collectively accepted that an air offensive was the most promising way for Germany to defeat Britain quickly, and on 16 March 1938 they reported that 'the outcome of unrestricted air attack on this country ... is impossible to forecast with any accuracy', given that Britain's defence preparations were incomplete.[52] Drawing on German records, Williamson Murray has shown the Luftwaffe was unprepared to launch bombing attacks against Great Britain at the time of the Munich crisis, or later.[53] However, ministers had to deal with uncertainty as to what German strategy would be or how the civilian population would react to bombing. Ministers were not helped by the failure of the Air Ministry to carry out a feasibility test on its gross overestimate of the weight of bombs that the Luftwaffe could deliver, given the amount of fuel required for flights from Germany.[54] It is not surprising that ministers were reluctant to risk war until Britain's air defences were closer to completion than they were in 1938.

3.4   Land Power

Germany could also hope to evade the effects of blockade if it could win an early, decisive victory over France, which would greatly increase the air and naval threats to Britain. The question of what support should be given to France on land was thus central to debates in Whitehall on grand strategy. Apart from the expansion of the British Army from six to 70 divisions during the First World War, it had always been accepted that the price of naval supremacy was the acceptance of inferiority on land compared with other European great powers. By the 1930s the army also came behind the RAF in the priorities of most politicians, including Churchill, who always participated in debates on the Air Ministry's annual estimates but did so rarely on the War Office's estimates. From 1934 Chamberlain challenged the need to have an army ready to fight in Europe at the outbreak of war, and sought to limit Britain's liability to send troops to the continent. He instigated a review by Sir Thomas Inskip, the minister for co-ordination of defence, which led to the Cabinet deciding in December 1937 that the army's primary roles were manning anti-aircraft guns in the United Kingdom and imperial defence. It was not until February 1939, when Britain's air defences had been strengthened and France had been weakened by the loss of its ally Czechoslovakia, that Chamberlain was persuaded the army's field units had a role to play in deterring Germany.

In the 1930s the Regular Army had about 195,000 men, of whom no fewer than 90,000 were deployed in the Empire, including 55,000 serving with the Indian Army. The Indian Army had about 150,000 native troops, commanded largely by British officers, and British and native regiments served together in brigades. Under the Cardwell system introduced in the 1870s, units based in Britain supplied drafts for, and periodically replaced, units serving in the Empire. As European warfare became increasingly mechanized, there was a divergence between the equipment and training required for colonial and continental service: in 1934 the chief of the imperial general staff, Montgomery-Massingberd, remarked that, even if foreign armies replaced all their infantry by tanks, Britain would be unable to do so because of needs of imperial policing.[55] Moreover, the political situation in India, where a degree of autonomy was granted in 1935, precluded raising additional taxes to pay the cost of mechanizing British units there, and modernisation of the Indian Army required British subsidies, which the Treasury withheld until after a review of Indian defence requirements in 1938. Indian Army units could be used elsewhere in the Empire in an emergency, but neither they nor British units deployed for imperial defence were equipped for European warfare. As with the dominions, India represented a large reserve of manpower, but the Indian Army's contribution outside the sub-continent in the early stages of the war was limited to one infantry division each in the Middle East and East Africa, and one brigade each in Burma and Malaya.[56]

The British Army's central reserve, both for imperial defence and for service in Europe, was the Field Force, formed from units based in Great

Britain. In the early 1930s it comprised four infantry divisions, one cavalry division, and one tank brigade, but in 1934 it was so unready that in the event of war only single divisions could have been sent to the Continent in each of the first two months, a third division at the end of the fourth month, and the remainder at the end of the sixth.[57] In 1935 the General Staff decided that the development of armoured fighting vehicles had reached a point where the cavalry's horses could be replaced with tanks. A new unit, the mobile division, was created, but its organisation was undecided, and even in 1938 the formation adopted was for training and administrative rather than operational purposes.[58] In 1939 it was divided into two smaller armoured divisions, neither of which was ready for action at the outbreak of war.

Prior to the introduction of conscription in April 1939, there was no question of enlarging the Regular Army. Instead the War Office looked to the twelve infantry divisions of the Territorial Army (TA) for reinforcements for the Field Force. Territorials were part-time soldiers who would require four months' intensive training before they could be sent abroad. It was not until February 1937 that the Cabinet approved a War Office proposal that the TA should receive modern equipment for training purposes, and equipment and instructors were spread very thinly when Chamberlain and the secretary of state for war, Leslie Hore-Belisha, decided in March 1939 to double the TA by duplicating every unit.[59] As the size of British infantry divisions had been reduced in 1938, the TA was now to have twenty six. However, even once they had been trained and equipped and added to the six Regular divisions, the army would be less than half its size in 1918.

Like air forces, armies had to cope with rapid technical change in the 1930s. Historians were long influenced by Liddell Hart and Major-General J. F. C. Fuller, who described the development of British armoured formations in terms of far-seeing tank enthusiasts being frustrated by reactionary top brass. For example, Brian Bond ascribed the lack of an armoured division ready to support France in 1939 to rivalry between traditional arms and the Royal Tank Regiment, and refusal by the General Staff to employ officers with experience of armoured formations to command such a division.[60] John Harris has argued that such a view is at best misleading. The tank enthusiasts wanted a mechanised force to have the minimum of supporting artillery and no conventional infantry, whereas the men they denounced as conservatives wanted an all-arms mechanised division. The problem with British tank tactics and organization, in Harris's view, was that the tank enthusiasts had too much influence, and British armoured divisions combined tanks and artillery in a less effective way than German panzer divisions.[61] In

1932 the General Staff anticipated that a future continental campaign would be characterised by mobile mechanised warfare, with the Germans particularly keen to use tanks, having been on the receiving end of these weapons in the First World War.[62] Montgomery-Massingberd, an artillery man, wanted the newest weapons, including armoured fighting vehicles, to be available to increase the mobility and firepower of the cavalry and infantry. He believed it would be better to mechanise the cavalry and infantry divisions gradually and that it had been a mistake in 1931 to introduce an entirely new formation, the Tank Brigade.[63] As a result of this policy, and the decision in December 1937 not to commit the Field Force to a European campaign at the outbreak of war, no direct replacement for the Tank Brigade's medium tanks was produced; instead orders were placed for lighter, faster machines suitable for reconnaissance and imperial defence, and for heavier machines to work with the infantry. Wartime experience showed that what an armoured division needed was a versatile medium tank.[64] Churchill, who had been a proponent of the development of the tank in the First World War, made no positive contribution to design or doctrine in the 1930s. Indeed, in April 1938 he doubted whether tanks would play as decisive a role in future as in 1918. 'Nowadays', he wrote, 'the anti-tank rifle and the anti-tank gun have made such great strides that the poor tank cannot carry a thick enough skin to stand up to them'.[65] On returning to government in 1939, he pressed for the development of huge earth-moving machines to cut trenches along which troops could advance across no man's land. The concept was applicable to a repetition of trench warfare, but not to mobile warfare.[66]

The British were not alone in being uncertain how best to employ tanks. The American army disbanded its mechanized force in 1931 and left tank development to the infantry and the cavalry until 1940.[67] Most French tanks were distributed throughout the army in an infantry support role; some were employed in light mechanized cavalry divisions, designed for reconnaissance, screening operations and forward delaying actions, but the first armoured divisions designed to break through the enemy lines were still in the course of formation in 1939 after being debated in the High Command for years.[68] The Red Army disbanded its mechanized corps in 1939, reassigning its tanks for infantry support, but reversed this decision after the success of German panzer divisions in France in 1940.[69]

The Field Force was essentially a make-weight in the scales of European land power. In November 1937 the chiefs of staff did not expect the German army to be larger than the French until 1939, and it did not seem to the Cabinet that France was in immediate danger of being overrun.[70] The assumption that the threat from the German army could for the time being be left to France was based on poor intelligence assessment of the French army's effectiveness.[71] French military policy was based on the concept of a nation in arms, with a relatively small number of regular soldiers engaged in training conscripts and reservists. Active infantry divisions were intended to be the cadre for a larger number of divisions in wartime, and thus committing active divisions to a limited war against Germany would disrupt mobilization plans. Moreover, the period served by conscripts was reduced from two years to eighteen months in 1923, and to one year in 1928, and the two-year period was not restored until 1935. French generals naturally felt their men required further training and experience of fighting on the defensive before being committed to more demanding offensive operations. Moreover, they were encouraged to think defensively by an optimistic assessment of the efficacy of anti-tank weapons.[72] The fortifications of the Maginot Line along the Franco-German frontier reflected and reinforced this strategy. However, it was one that allowed the Germans to concentrate their forces against an Eastern European ally of France in the initial stages of a war. The British Army was even less well placed to take the offensive at the outbreak of war. Anglo-French land power could act as a deterrent only insofar as it convinced the Germans that they could not win a short war, and thus faced the prospect of a long war in which the allies' sea power could be used to weaken the German economy and to mobilise their overseas resources.

3.5   Defence Industries

In the 1930s all the great powers relied almost wholly on their own industries to equip their armed forces. Britain had imported munitions on a large scale from the United States during the First World War, but American neutrality legislation in the 1930s banning the sale and shipment of arms to all belligerents made future supplies uncertain. President Roosevelt periodically raised hopes that Britain and France would have access to American munitions in war, but as late as July 1939 Congress rebuffed his attempt to repeal the arms embargo. There was little incentive, therefore, for the Chamberlain government to place orders in America. Pre-war contracts for American aircraft before the war amounted to less than 6 per cent of Britain's own output in 1939, although the comparable figure for France was 20 per cent, reflecting the relative weakness of the French aircraft industry.[73]

The condition of Britain's defence industries when rearmament began in the 1930s has been the subject of historical debate. In 1919 the

Cabinet decided that the defence departments' annual estimates of expenditure should be prepared on the basis that there would be no major war for ten years. In 1928 Churchill, as chancellor of the exchequer, persuaded the Cabinet that this assumption should be renewed annually until the Cabinet, on the advice of the chiefs of staff or the Foreign Office, decided otherwise. The Ten Year Rule, as it came to be called, strengthened the hand of the Treasury in imposing financial restraint and between the financial years 1928/29 and 1932/33 defence expenditure fell by 9.25 per cent.[74] M. M. Postan's official history of war production emphasized the extent to which Britain's defence industries had been reduced by the early 1930s to a point where the rearmament programme could not be fulfilled in a timely manner. David Edgerton, in contrast, has argued that Britain had maintained a powerful military-industrial complex, sustained by levels of defence expenditure comparable to those of other great powers and by exports to lesser powers.[75] These two positions are not incompatible. Britain's defence industries were strong relative to those of other countries in 1933, but nevertheless struggled to carry out the rearmament programme. Whereas German rearmament began in 1933, when many tradesmen were unemployed, British rearmament began in 1936, when the worst of the depression was over, and men who had not been absorbed into civil work tended to be those whose skills had atrophied or were obsolete. There were about two million unemployed in Britain in 1935, but the purpose of the Ministry of Labour's training centres was re-education and rehabilitation, not industrial mobilisation. In contrast, Germany's Bureau for Industrial Workers trained apprentices and retrained older workers, and its Labour Allocation Office directed labour into armaments industries. In both countries shortages of skilled workers could be eased by breaking work processes into simple stages that semi-skilled or unskilled workers could do, a process known as dilution, but British trade unionists were slow to accept change, fearing unemployment when the rearmament programme was over.[76] Moreover, although advised by Lord Weir that the rearmament programme could not be completed on time without diverting labour from normal industrial business, the Cabinet took the decision in February 1936 that there should be no interference with production for civil or export trade.

Britain still had the world's largest shipbuilding industry in the 1930s. However, international trade was lower in the interwar period than before 1914, and consequently there were fewer orders for merchant ships as well as for warships. Employment fell from about 300,000 at the end of the First World War to about 70,000 in 1932, rising again to 140,000 in 1939. Lack of investment resulted in output per man in the late 1930s being very little if at all greater than before 1914.[77] Warship building required highly specialist plant for armour and guns, and naval orders in the 1920s had been insufficient to sustain the capacity created by 1919. Despite the Royal Dockyards being restricted to refit and repair, and a secret cartel to prevent cutthroat competition, profits were low and private firms had to cut back on plant. Consequently naval rearmament was restricted by industrial factors. For example, capacity for making gun mountings was estimated in 1936 to be less than half of what would be required by 1939. Fire-control gear was a bottleneck that could be cleared only by drawing in new suppliers, but the most suitable engineering firms were fully engaged on commercial work. New armour-making plant was required to meet demand that was expected almost to double by 1939, and the position with guns was similar.[78] Private shipbuilding firms feared having redundant plant after the rearmament programme had been completed, and seem to have used profits to improve their financial position rather than to invest in fixed assets.[79] Government subsidies were provided and in February 1939 the chiefs of staff reported that by 1940 there would be enough industrial capacity for the navy's war needs on current plans, but more would be required for armour and guns to match Germany and Japan if Germany broke the Anglo-German Naval Agreement.[80]

The German navy planned to do so, but Germany's shipbuilding capacity had been much more drastically reduced by disarmament than Britain's after 1919, leading to inexperience on the part of firms and delays in construction. Moreover, the German navy was in competition with the Luftwaffe and the army for steel, non-ferrous metals and skilled labour. Apart from two capital ships already launched, ambitious plans for surface ships, including aircraft carriers, were abandoned shortly after the outbreak of war and resort made to the weapon of the weaker sea power: submarines.[81] Table 3.4 shows that Britain was still building more surface warships than any other nation in 1940. The figures support Edgerton's case that Britain had a powerful naval shipbuilding industry; on the other hand, construction fell short of what was required for a two-ocean navy.

Figure 3.6 shows how Germany took an early lead in air rearmament. On the other hand, British output of aircraft rose rapidly from 1938, and by 1940 exceeded that of any other power (the Soviet figures in 1939 and 1940 were 10,382 and 10,565). How can one explain this pattern? Postan believed that Air Ministry orders prior to 1935 were too small to sustain an industry capable of mass production.[82] On the other hand, the industry was not wholly dependent on Air Ministry orders; exports (not included in Figure 3.6) accounted for more than a quarter of total

Table 3.4. *Major warships launched (or conversions to aircraft carriers begun), 1936–40*

	Britain	France	Germany	Italy	Japan	USA
Capital ships	5	3	4	4	2	2
Aircraft carriers	5	0	1	1	6	4
Cruisers	28	1	5	3	5	11
Destroyers	69	10	25	16	32	73
Submarines	39	6	140	62	27	33

Source: Roger Chesneau (ed.), *Conway's All the World's Fighting Ships 1922–1946* (London: Conway Maritime Press, 1980).

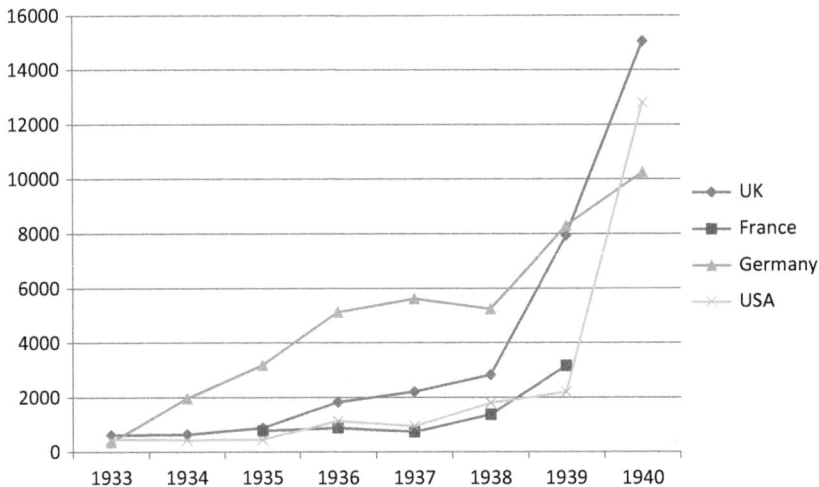

Figure 3.6 Aircraft production in the UK, France, Germany and the USA, 1933–40
Sources: Sebastian Ritchie, *Industry and Air Power: The Expansion of British Aircraft Production, 1935–1941* (London: Frank Cass, 1997), pp. 9, 90, for UK and R. J. Overy, *The Air War 1939–1945* (London: Europa Publications, 1980), pp. 21, 150, for the other powers.

production in 1934 and 1935.[83] Moreover, Edgerton has argued that aircraft were not mass produced anywhere in the interwar period, the industry being craft-based and labour intensive.[84] Germany's early start and ability to train and direct labour enabled it to increase the number of workers in its aircraft industry from 4,000 in January 1933 to 54,000 two years later, the corresponding increase in Britain being from 20,000 to 35,000.[85] Thereafter, comparisons of workers directly employed become less meaningful as both countries made increasing use of sub-contracting to firms outside the industry. In 1933 Germany started building aircraft factories financed by state subsidies but managed by private firms. In Britain a comparable scheme for what were called 'shadow factories' managed by automobile and other engineering firms to create war capacity involved 'educational' orders from 1936, but it was not until 1938 that the government decided to expand capacity by paying for the construction of new factories to be run by established aircraft firms for an agency fee.[86] Even so, neither labour nor plant seems to have been a constraint on production until 1938. The Air Ministry was aware in 1935 that the aircraft immediately available for production would soon be obsolescent, and Lord Swinton decided to order aircraft that were under development or still on the drawing board, and subject to delays as the need for modifications became evident after testing.[87] Relations between the industry and the Air Ministry became strained, as firms complained of insufficient orders to utilise their capacity and of disruption caused by frequent changes to aircraft under construction.[88] In 1937 the Bristol Aircraft Company engineer Roy Fedden reported that German practice was better in a number of ways: production was con-centrated on a smaller range of aircraft types, designs were 'frozen' so that no changes were made over a fixed period, and factories were more up to date and better organized.[89] Even so, Germany found the transition from older to newer types in 1937–38 difficult and output fell temporar-ily (see Figure 3.6). Nor was the German aircraft industry as efficient as Fedden implied: artisan methods kept labour productivity low and short-ages of steel and non-ferrous metals set an upper limit on what could be produced.[90] The decisive steps that led to British aircraft monthly pro-duction overtaking Germany's in September 1939 came in the spring of 1938: on 22 March the Cabinet agreed to reverse its decision two years earlier that rearmament orders should not interfere with production for civil or export trade, and on 27 April it authorised the Air Ministry to take delivery of as many aircraft as the aircraft industry could produce, up to a maximum of 12,000 over the next two years. To this end, Treasury control of expenditure was relaxed and industrial capacity expanded.[91] The fact that teething problems of key aircraft had been largely overcome also helped.

The War Office's suppliers fared worst under the Ten Year Rule. The army had large stocks of munitions for which it had no need to place new orders. Only 3 of the 250 national munitions factories built during the First World War were retained, in a mothballed condition, and active capacity was reduced to three royal ordnance factories and a small private sector dominated by one firm, Vickers-Armstrong. Plans for rearmament included ten new royal ordnance factories and, in accordance with the policy of non-interference with civil trade, the Treasury pressed the War Office to postpone orders until these factories had been built, rather than bring new firms into munitions production. As Churchill pointed out, there was a three-year lag between initial investment and deliveries.[92] However, much of the delay in equipping the Field Force was caused by problems in the design and development of new weapons. For example, a specification was issued in 1934 for a 25-pounder gun for the artillery, but it was not until October 1938 that trials were concluded and orders placed.[93] There were delays in the design and development of tanks, and not all teething problems had been solved when large-scale production began in 1938. Nevertheless, output overtook Germany's in 1939 and was four times that of the United States in 1940.[94] The problems of the army's suppliers down to 1938 have been cited by declinist historians as evidence of fundamental shortcomings in British industry.[95] However, the fact that Britain could produce more tanks, as well as aircraft and warships, than Germany in 1939–40 is surely evidence of formidable industrial power.

Robert Shay blamed shortcomings of British rearmament on Chamberlain's reliance on private industry's co-operation. Shay believed the invisible hand of the market could not move resources from civil to military use as quickly as the dictator's hand in Germany and that the government should have created a Ministry of Supply with quasi-wartime powers.[96] However, it is not clear that co-operation was a bad basis for government–business relations, given how output surged once the policy of non-interference with civil trade was reversed, new factories were completed and new aircraft and munitions were ready for production. In contrast, German rearmament was characterised by inefficiency and confusion, with production of weapons well below what might have been achieved for the level of expenditure.[97] Shay also believed that profiteering by the aircraft industry demonstrated the breakdown of co-operation. However, Sebastian Ritchie has shown there was no general increase in the industry's profits and that the Air Ministry was more successful than its counterparts in Germany and the United States in encouraging firms to be efficient, partly through fixed-price rather than cost-plus contracts, and partly by requiring firms to finance a greater proportion of their pre-war expansion than in these countries.[98] On balance, it would seem that the principal reason for British rearmament being slower than Germany's down to 1938 was the policy of non-interference with civil trade, and to understand why that policy was adopted, one has to look at the wider economy.

3.6   The Wider Economy

For Chamberlain the purpose of rearmament was deterrence while a settlement was reached with Germany. It followed that rearmament should not destabilise the economy. Moreover, blockade was central to grand strategy if appeasement failed, and therefore Britain had to husband enough economic strength to outlast Germany in a long war. To do so, Britain must maintain exports and overseas credit with which to pay for essential imports of food and raw materials. Inskip's interim report in December 1937 on future defence expenditure observed that if other countries detected signs of economic or financial strain in Britain, the deterrent effect of armaments would be lost.[99]

Economic constraints on rearmament were examined in Whitehall in 1936 after Churchill urged that a certain percentage of the ordinary industries of the country should be devoted to defence contracts. The illustrative figures Churchill mentioned – 25 or 30 per cent – were about four times higher than what was expected to be required for the existing rearmament programme. On the other hand, they proved to be in the order of what would be necessary to match German defence expenditure. The Board of Trade, which was the department responsible for industry as well as international trade, pointed out that Churchill's proposal would be impossible without cutting production of civil goods for the home market or for export. The shortfall for the home market could be met by imports, but these, together with a fall in exports, would result in an adverse balance-of-payments deficit on current account, to the detriment of Britain's financial strength. Treasury officials advised Chamberlain on 10 November – nine months after the Cabinet had approved the rearmament programme – that already there were signs in some industries, including steel and engineering, only indirectly connected with armaments, of firms showing less interest in export markets. Yet markets, once lost, would be hard to recover. Heavy taxation could reduce civil consumption and imports, and thereby the size of the trade deficit, but might arouse opposition to rearmament.[100] Chamberlain concluded that following Churchill's advice would 'inflict certain injury upon our trade from which it would take generations to recover'.[101] The experience of the First World War shows that Chamberlain's fears were not groundless. As British industry was diverted to munitions production, export markets were lost to rivals, notably Japan and the United States. In the mid-1920s British exports were only 75 per cent of their 1913 level and major industries such as cotton textiles and shipbuilding never fully recovered.[102] Avoiding interference with normal civil trade was, from this point of view, a means of conserving Britain's power.

On the other hand, a balance had to be struck between economic stability and security against armed attack, and that balance was altered in March 1938 when firms were asked to give priority to rearmament contracts.

Were Whitehall officials right to be concerned about the external balance? Niall Ferguson has commented that the current account deficits of the later 1930s were trivial, equivalent to about 1 per cent of GDP a year.[103] However, while this was true in 1936–38, the current account deficit increased rapidly to about 5 per cent of GDP in 1939. While many factors influence the balance of payments, it is difficult to believe this deterioration was unrelated to an increase in defence expenditure from 7.1 per cent of GDP in 1938 to 12.4 per cent in 1939.[104] In an open economy, as Britain was, there was bound to be a trade-off between armed and economic power. Britain lacked natural resources, apart from coal, and imports of raw materials had to be paid for by exporting goods and services, or by running down gold and foreign exchange reserves and overseas investments, or by borrowing abroad.[105] Even in Germany, a relatively closed economy, the ability to secure imports of iron and non-ferrous ores, rubber and oil was a limiting factor in rearmament. The Nazis pursued autarchy by exploiting low-grade ores, or developing synthetic rubber or fuel, at a greater cost than imports; they subsidised exports to earn foreign exchange; they rationed foreign exchange to secure priority for rearmament-related imports; and they economised on foreign exchange by bilateral clearing agreements even if the partners to these agreements were not the cheapest source of imports. All these measures tended to lower the standard of living. Germany gained some relief for its strained exchange position by seizing the gold reserves of Austria in 1938 and Czechoslovakia in 1939. Even so, the need to maintain exports led to restrictions being applied to production of aircraft and munitions in 1937 and 1939, and to tanks in 1939.[106] It was these restrictions that made it possible for Britain's production of aircraft and tanks to overtake Germany's in 1939–40.

Germany, with its exchange controls and clearing agreements, avoided devaluation. In contrast, speculators reacted to the prospect of war in 1938–39 by selling sterling, anticipating that it would depreciate against the dollar. The exchange rate fell from a high of $5.02 in March 1938 to a low of $4.60 six months later, at the height of the Czech crisis, and it was only by drawing on gold and foreign exchange reserves that the Bank of England was able to peg the rate at about $4.67 until August 1939, when losses became too great and the rate fell to $4.10. Christopher Price has argued that the imposition of exchange controls would have halted the depreciation of sterling and avoided the loss of half of Britain's war chest of gold and dollar reserves.[107] However, economists, including Keynes, advising the government in December 1938, took the view that Britain might be better off without gold held in London by nervous foreigners.[108] In April 1939 Keynes urged that the existing embargo on sending capital funds overseas by British nationals should be tightened, but he stopped short of suggesting that exchange controls of the kind imposed during the First World War should be restored.[109] For controls to be effective, all international financial transactions would have had to be subject to government inspection and postal censorship. The effect on London's position as an international banking centre would have been adverse, reducing financial services' contribution to the balance of payments. Alastair Parker suggested that a sharp devaluation to a level where sterling could definitely have been defended would have deterred speculation, enabling Britain to maintain its war chest, but, as he pointed out, Britain was under strong pressure from the United States' Treasury not to seek competitive advantage in international trade by devaluation.[110] In any case, sterling had to be managed responsibly because it was the reserve currency of the sterling area, which was broadly coterminous with the Commonwealth and Empire, less Canada, plus some foreign countries with close trade links with Britain. The sterling area was a source of strength as it enabled Britain to finance imports on a vast scale during the war as member countries accumulated credit balances in London. Even so, the sterling area could not supply all of Britain's needs, particularly munitions, machine tools and oil, whereas the United States could. Sterling's fall against the dollar increased the cost of such imports and thereby weakened British power.

The Treasury advised the Strategic Appreciation Sub-Committee of the CID in April 1939 that the gold reserves were for the moment greater than in 1914, but in other respects Britain was less able than it had been then to conduct a long war. Holdings of overseas investments were far less than in 1914, because many had been requisitioned and sold to finance purchases in the United States during the First World War. Nor did it seem likely that the Americans would be keen to lend as they had then, given that Britain had not repaid its war debt to the United States government (see page 95).[111] The dilemma was that rearmament on the scale reached by 1939 tended to undermine the economy's capacity to support Britain and France's long-war strategy.

Chamberlain claimed, with some justice, that the rearmament programme begun in 1936 was by far the largest ever undertaken in peacetime.[112] Figure 3.7 shows that defence expenditure took a greater share of GDP after 1936 than during the naval arms race before 1914. The experience of rearmament begun in 1950 after the Korean War broke out is also instructive: the incoming Conservative prime minister in 1951, Churchill,

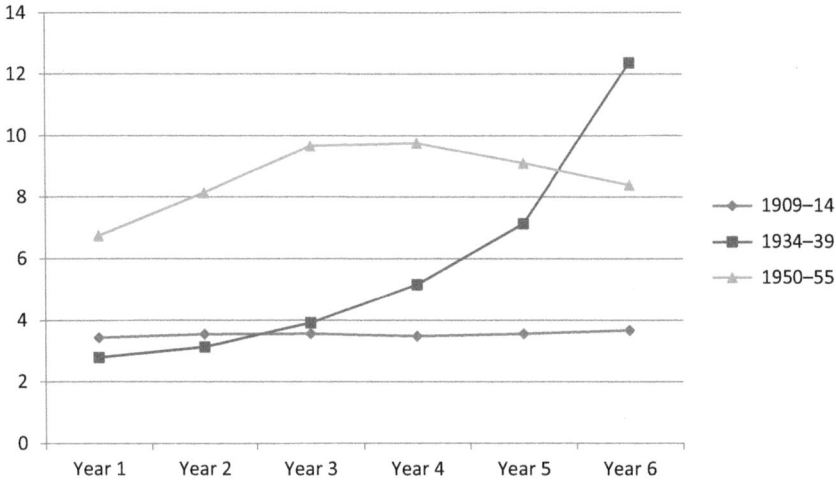

Figure 3.7 British defence expenditure as a percentage of GDP, 1909–14, 1934–9 and 1950–5 (calendar years)
Sources: B. R. Mitchell, *British Historical Statistics* (Cambridge University Press, 1988), pp. 591, 594, 829–30, and, for defence expenditure in 1937–9, Robert P. Shay, *British Rearmament in the Thirties: Politics and Profits* (Princeton, NJ: Princeton University Press, 1977), p. 297.

had to curb expenditure in response to balance-of-payments pressures and the need to maintain exports.[113] There is no reason to suppose that the percentage of GDP being spent on rearmament in 1939 did not weaken the external balance. In 1938 civil consumption and investment fell in a renewed economic recession, reducing imports. By spring 1939, however, the economy was recovering and imports were also increased by higher defence expenditure. As the economy moved towards full employment, Treasury officials had to contemplate not only higher taxation, but also controls over private investment, to transfer economic resources to government use. A totalitarian state like Germany could impose sacrifices on its people by taxation, direction of labour, controls over investment and foreign exchange, and in other ways, whereas British governments had to rely on consent. It is to the question of public willingness to make sacrifices in order to stand up to Germany that we now turn.

3.7   Public Opinion and National Morale

Public opinion is the balance of the population's attitudes towards issues such as the choice between peace and war. Morale is connected to conduct. Originally a military concept, it was extended in 1914–18 to the whole population whose active support in the face of casualties and economic hardship was necessary for victory.[114] In 1937 the chiefs of staff advised a Cabinet sub-committee of 'the necessity of maintaining our national morale' by educating the public in the limitations as well as the dangers of air attack.[115] National morale was also more likely to be maintained if the population believed in the cause for which the nation was fighting. To that extent, power depended on public opinion.

Samuel Hoare and Horace Wilson ascribed the delay in starting rearmament to the prevalence of pacifism.[116] However, the extent to which defence and foreign policy were influenced by public opinion is uncertain. Public opinion polls were not conducted on a regular basis during the years when pacifism appeared to be strongest. Charles Madge and Tom Harrison's pioneering *Britain by Mass Observation* (1939) was based on small samples.[117] Analysis of the press suggests widespread support for appeasement until Munich, and almost no support for resort to arms until Hitler's occupation of Prague showed his ambition was not restricted to German-speaking territories.[118] However, Anthony Adamthwaite has presented evidence for public opinion being deeply divided over Czechoslovakia in 1938, although Chamberlain's critics were denied opportunity to present their case on the BBC. Richard Cockett likewise argued that public opinion was less of a constraint on Chamberlain than his defenders have made out, since the prime minister himself strongly influenced it in favour of his foreign policy through speeches and management of the press, broadcasting and newsreels.[119] However, Cockett did not mention that media management was also used to support the other half of Chamberlain's dual policy: rearmament.[120]

It is not easy to interpret by-elections or their effects. The result in East Fulham in October 1933, when there was a 29.1 per cent swing from the Conservatives to Labour, was cited by Hoare as evidence of the strength of pacifism, but voters seem to have been influenced by social issues as well as by the Labour candidate's views on peace and disarmament.[121] Conservative politicians did not observe Martin Ceadel's distinction between pacifists, who were unconditionally opposed to war, and 'pacificists', who accepted that it could be justified in certain circumstances.[122] Accordingly Hoare saw the League of Nations Union's Peace Ballot in 1934–35 as the climax of the pacifist movement, although 58.8 per cent of respondents said they considered that if one nation attacked another, other nations should take military measures if necessary to stop the aggression. While this percentage was well below that for economic and non-military measures (86.9), it refutes the idea that most people were pacifist.[123]

Baldwin said in 1936 that it would have been extremely difficult to have started rearming freely in 1934, given the prevalence of pacifist opinion.[124] However, pacifism may not have been the only reason for delay. When the Defence Requirements Sub-Committee's programme was reduced by a Cabinet sub-committee in 1934, Sir Warren Fisher, the permanent secretary of the Treasury, observed that ministers believed 'our public is not as yet sufficiently apprised of the reality of our dangers to be ready to swallow at one gulp the financial results of the recommendations that we made'.[125] The relative importance of taxation and pacifism is hard to judge. From mid-1934, Chamberlain, unusually for a chancellor of the exchequer, made speeches about the nation's defences having fallen to a dangerously low level and the need to make some sacrifice for safety, particularly from air attack. On 15 October 1935, during the general election campaign, he told the public that the government had decided upon an accelerated armaments programme.[126] On the 31st, Baldwin muted this message by giving his word at a meeting of the International Peace Society that there would be 'no great armaments'.[127] However, the acceleration of defence expenditure to unprecedented levels went ahead from 1936. An American observer noted that there was almost no protest as taxes were raised to levels previously unknown in peacetime and that Britain relied much less on borrowing for rearmament than France did.[128]

It is uncertain how far public attitudes to war were influenced by fear of air attack. Brett Holman has noted greater scepticism about prophecies of civilian panic in the light of actual experience of bombing of Spanish and Chinese cities from 1936–37. However, he also reported that, when war seemed imminent in September 1938, 150,000 people fled London, whereas Susan Grayzel told how families calmly queued at civil defence centres for gas masks.[129] By the spring of 1939, civil defence measures, including air raid wardens, fire-fighting services, first aid, rescue squads and shelters, were sufficiently improved for the chiefs of staff to feel confident the civil population would not easily be demoralised. On the contrary, based on reports of reactions of civilians to air raids during the Spanish Civil War, they believed heavy casualties would stiffen national morale.[130] A similar transformation in public attitudes occurred regarding land warfare. In the early 1930s an overwhelming majority of people seemed convinced that never again should the nation's youth undergo horrors like the battles of the Somme or Passchendaele, a sentiment repeated every Armistice Day at ceremonies throughout the land. In 1934 the prime minister, MacDonald, asked the War Office to refrain from using the term 'expeditionary force' (instead of Field Force) not only in public but even in official papers.[131] A change in the public mood can be discerned in 1938 when the intake of recruits to the TA increased by 78 per cent compared with the previous year.[132]

Public attitudes to war and preparation for war responded to events. The Italian conquest of Ethiopia in 1935–36 made it harder to believe Labour and Liberal claims that collective security through the League of Nations was an alternative to rearmament. German and Italian intervention in the Spanish Civil War of 1936–39 roused the Labour movement against Fascism. The Labour Party had hitherto voted against the defence estimates in protest against what it regarded as unilateral rearmament. However, Ernest Bevin, a powerful trade union leader, and Hugh Dalton, the party's spokesman on foreign policy, argued that opposition to rearmament was inconsistent with collective security and in July 1937 Labour ceased to vote against the defence estimates. By the spring of 1938 it was no less critical than Churchill of the government's failure to match the expansion of the German air force.[133] Mass Observation surveys suggest that Hitler's bullying tactics during the Munich crisis moved public opinion decisively against appeasement.[134] As the prospect of war loomed in 1939, pessimism and defeatism were replaced by grim determination to confront Nazism, and a similar change occurred in France.[135]

3.8   Collective Security

Britain's own resources could, in theory, have been supplemented by combining with other powers. How practical was Churchill's idea of deterrence through a grand alliance of European powers? There was certainly a case for one. Victory over Germany had been achieved in the First World War in combination with France, Russia (until 1917) and the United States (from 1917), with Italy and Japan as allies. However, in the 1930s the Soviet Union was ideologically suspect, the United States was isolationist, and Italy (from 1935) and Japan were potentially hostile. The League of Nations was seen by the Labour and Liberal parties as a focus for collective security, but the United States had never been a member; Japan, Germany and Italy withdrew in the 1930s, leaving Britain, France and the Soviet Union (which joined in 1934) as the only great powers in it. Chamberlain wrote in October 1935 that 'it would be a wonderful gain for the world' if the League could halt Italian aggression against Ethiopia, but its failure to do so led him to think the League would exercise far greater influence if it were not expected to use force but only moral pressure.[136] Churchill was indifferent to the League's efforts to check aggression in Asia or Africa, but from 1936 he linked his advocacy of rearmament and a grand alliance with support for the League.[137] In contrast, the chiefs of staff advised in February 1937 that League membership increased Britain's commitments, while there was no assurance that other members of the League would act more altruistically than they had in the past.[138] In November 1937 the chiefs of staff warned they could not foresee when Britain's defence forces would be strong enough to protect its territory, trade and vital interests against Germany, Italy and Japan simultaneously, and said the importance of political or international action to gain the support of potential allies and to reduce the number of potential enemies could not be exaggerated.[139] Chamberlain was opposed to dividing Europe into two opposing blocs by forming alliances – a development he said would inevitably lead to war[140] – and his diplomacy was directed primarily at reducing the number of potential enemies.

He had been enthusiastic in 1934 about a Japanese offer of a bilateral non-aggression pact, but the Foreign Office advised that such a pact would almost inevitably mean satisfying at least some of Japan's expansionist ambitions in China and would certainly be resented in the United States. By the time Chamberlain was prime minister, Japanese aggression in China led him to hope for collaboration with the United States in the Far East. Italy was regarded by Vansittart as a potential ally against Germany, but public opinion stood in the way of the appeasement of Mussolini at the expense of Ethiopia. Italy's intervention in the Spanish Civil War and anti-British propaganda in the Middle East led Chamberlain to remark in July 1937 that there was little doubt Italy would come in on Germany's side if Britain were engaged in a war with Germany, but he felt there was no need to fear attack by Italy unless she were sure of German support.[141] Although he tried to detach Mussolini from Hitler, Chamberlain focussed his diplomatic efforts on the latter, because the threats in the Far East and the Mediterranean were most likely to materialise if Britain became involved in a war with Germany. Appeasement and deterrence were intended to secure European peace, which, besides being an end in itself, was also a means of making a worldwide empire secure.

British statesmen, including Chamberlain, recognised that the security of France was a vital British interest. However, Chamberlain was not alone in fearing that an Anglo-French alliance would encourage France to be inflexible towards Germany, making the appeasement of Europe more difficult, and would involve underwriting France's alliances with Poland, Czechoslovakia, Romania and Yugoslavia. The chiefs of staff were long reluctant to engage in staff talks with France and there were no firm military commitments until March 1939, when a common policy for the overall conduct of a war was at last discussed. Nevertheless, by

1937 British planning for war assumed France would be an ally, provide nearly all the land forces in the opening phase against Germany, and assist against Italy. In return, France expected some commitment of British land forces as a sign of tangible support. Chamberlain hoped to limit that commitment, but a policy of no liability was not a diplomatic option.[142] France, for its part, was uninterested in collective security outside Europe and the Mediterranean. As a result, the chiefs of staff expected nothing of the French in the Far East beyond the direct defence of their own colony in Indochina.

Only the United States had the means to support Britain on a global scale. However, British war planners regarded active American intervention in war as unlikely, except perhaps at a late stage, and they looked for no more than a willingness to sell arms.[143] There was little that Anglo-French diplomacy could do to reverse American neutrality legislation, since that was a matter of Congressional politics. Nevertheless, some historians believe Chamberlain was remiss in not developing a special relationship with Roosevelt. For example, Ruggiero described Chamberlain as anti-American, citing the prime minister's remark on 17 December 1937 that 'it is always best & safest to count on *nothing* from the Americans except words'. However, he failed to quote the rest of Chamberlain's sentence: 'but as this moment they are nearer to "doing something" than I have ever known them and I can't altogether repress hopes'.[144] The context of Chamberlain's remarks was the sinking by the Japanese of the American gunboat *Panay* five days earlier and the possibility of some co-ordinated Anglo-American response. In the event, none was agreed. Nevertheless, informal Anglo-American co-operation developed while he was prime minister to the extent that by 1939 the two countries were following parallel, although not joint, policies in the Pacific.[145] Rather than label Chamberlain as anti-American, it makes more sense to divide his emotions, as David Reynolds did, into doubt, fear and hope. Little that had happened since 1919, including the rejection by the Senate of the Versailles Peace Treaty and with it League membership, or the strength of isolationism in American politics, encouraged reliance on American help. There was also fear that a high price might have to be paid for such help, for example by having to make concessions in trade negotiations, or by losing control of negotiations with Germany and Italy. Nevertheless Chamberlain hoped good Anglo-American relations, and the prospect that the neutrality legislation would be repealed, would deter Germany.[146] Churchill believed that if the United States and Britain combined they would have the moral, economic and financial resources to prevent almost any aggression, but he also recognised that Americans wanted at all costs to keep out of war. In

August 1938, during the Czech crisis, he asked: 'Will the United States throw their weight into the scales of peace and law while time remains, or will they remain spectators until the disaster has occurred; and then, with infinite cost and labour, build up what need not have been cast down? This is the riddle of a sphinx'.[147]

It is far from clear that greater American support would have been forthcoming if Chamberlain had established a rapport with Roosevelt. The United States was geographically remote from Germany, Italy and Japan, and, according to Roosevelt in October 1938, less than half of the population at that date realised these powers could combine to pose a threat to American interests.[148] Although Britain and the United States shared culture and values that gave British diplomats opportunities to use soft power to influence American opinion, most Americans regarded the British Empire as their only serious foreign rival. It is hard for historians to be sure of Roosevelt's intentions: he himself said that he never let his right hand know what his left did, and that he might be entirely inconsistent.[149] In broad terms, once it was clear that appeasement had failed at Munich, he saw Britain and France as America's first line of defence and encouraged Chamberlain to stand up to Hitler. However, the president seems to have believed Britain and France were powerful enough to counterbalance Germany and that selling arms, especially aircraft, to them would enable the United States to keep out of war.[150] William Rock, taking account of the constraints on Roosevelt, concludes that a closer relationship between prime minister and president would have been unlikely to prevent war breaking out in Europe or the Pacific, although greater Anglo-American understanding would have enabled more effective preparation for war.[151]

The other great power that might have been brought into the balance against the Axis powers was the Soviet Union. Writing after the war, Churchill played up Soviet overtures indicating readiness to intervene in the Czech crisis and expressed astonishment at Chamberlain's failure to respond to them. However, Churchill also remarked that the Soviets displayed 'remarkable skill in duplicity' in negotiating simultaneously with Britain and France on the one hand and Germany on the other in 1939.[152] In a broadcast that year after Stalin had chosen a non-aggression pact with Hitler rather than an alliance with the western powers, Churchill famously described Russia as 'a riddle wrapped in a mystery inside an enigma', but added: 'perhaps there is a key. That key is Russian national interest.'[153] The Soviet Union had lost more territory than any other power as a result of the First World War, when Finland, Estonia, Latvia, Lithuania and Poland had achieved independence, and Poland and Romania had expanded at Soviet expense. For Stalin, recovery of lost territory was an alternative to collective security, as the Soviet Union's neighbours were well aware. In 1938 the Soviets refused to renounce their claim to Bessarabia, a province seized by the Romanians 20 years earlier, in order to secure Romania's assent to the passage of Soviet forces across its territory to assist Czechoslovakia.[154] Although the Soviet Union had responded to the rise of Hitler by presenting itself as a supporter of the status quo, it remained a potential disrupter. It was a member of the League of Nations, yet embodied a political ideology that other members of the League regarded as subversive. The stated aim of the Comintern was the overthrow of the international bourgeoisie by all available means, including armed force, and Churchill was not alone among Conservatives in ascribing the outbreak of the Spanish Civil War to the 'Communist pervasion of the decayed parliamentary government' there.[155] Relations between London and Moscow were marked by mutual suspicion of being inveigled into a war with Germany. The Bolshevik Revolution and subsequent Allied intervention, in which Churchill had played a prominent part, were recent memories.

Nevertheless, Churchill was much readier than Chamberlain to put ideological hostility aside and to see the Soviet Union as a potential member of a grand alliance that would deter Germany. In 1935 he met the Soviet ambassador, Ivan Maisky, and told him he did not believe the Soviet Union would pose a threat to Britain for at least ten years.[156] The Spanish Civil War revived Churchill's anti-Communism for a time, but in the Czech crisis in 1938 and the Polish crisis in 1939 he expressed faith in a solid identity of interest between the western democracies and the Soviet Union,[157] In contrast, Chamberlain, writing in March 1939, expressed distrust of Soviet motives, 'which seem[ed] to have little connection with our ideas of liberty and to be concerned only with getting everyone else by the ears'.[158] As noted on pages 31–3, there was no single Foreign Office view, officials being divided between those who believed that Soviet foreign policy was intended to further Communist objectives and was hostile to British interests, and those who thought like Churchill. British intelligence assessments did not rate the Soviet Union highly as a potential ally and doubts were greatest when Hitler threatened Czechoslovakia. By then Stalin had embarked on his great purge not only of rivals within the Communist Party but also of senior commanders in the armed forces and many officials. An assessment dated 18 April 1938 by the military attaché in Moscow pointed to the disruptive effects of the purge on Soviet industry and transport as well as the Red Army, and took the view that Stalin would not put his regime at risk by entering a war unless vital national interests were involved.[159]

Churchill was keen to include in a grand alliance lesser powers, including Czechoslovakia, Poland, Romania, Yugoslavia, Greece and Turkey. However, the weight of such states in the balance of power was limited. With the exception of Czechoslovakia, which had inherited the arms industry of a great power, Austria-Hungary, they were dependent to varying degrees on imports to equip their armed forces and would be more so in a war that required mass-production of munitions. Once rearmament began, Britain and France had little industrial capacity to spare for exports to allies.[160] The armies of the lesser powers comprised predominantly infantry and were intended primarily to defend national territories rather than to conduct offensive operations. While Serbia and Turkey had been formidable opponents of great powers in the First World War, when defensive weapons like the machine-gun had dominated the battlefield, the increasing mechanization of warfare in the 1930s placed the lesser powers at a disadvantage. Only Czechoslovakia, Poland and Sweden could design and manufacture tanks, and then not on the scale of a great power. Rather more countries had aircraft industries, but these lagged behind those of the great powers in the development of high-performance machines so that, whereas the quality of the Czech and Polish aircraft had been of international standard in the mid-1930s, they were obsolescent by 1938.[161] Despite their gallantry, the armed forces of the lesser powers fared badly against Germany in conventional warfare in 1939–41: organised Polish resistance lasted about a month; Holland surrendered after five days; Belgium after eighteen and Yugoslavia after eleven. Overall, it would seem that Churchill exaggerated the contribution the lesser powers could make to deterring aggression and Chamberlain was right to doubt their deterrent value.

3.9   Intelligence and Perceptions of Power

The importance of perceptions of power is brought out by Chamberlain's belief down to February 1939 that the Field Force need not be prepared to fight in Europe at the outbreak of war; by Roosevelt's belief that Britain and France could be enabled to act as United States' first line of defence without support from American troops; and by Stalin's apparent belief that France, supported by Britain, could contain Germany if he signed a non-aggression pact with Hitler. All three men acted on the basis of mistaken assessments of French power. By acting as they did, they changed the objective balance of power, since once France fell, Germany became much more powerful relative to other great powers.

According to John Ferris, the quality of British intelligence was not, on balance, inferior to its international rivals. Indeed the lack of co-ordination, described on pages 42–5, was worse in Germany than in Britain.[162] Christopher Andrew noted that the United States lacked a professional intelligence service and Roosevelt based his judgements on impressions drawn from a wide range of official and unofficial sources.[163] British intelligence had its successes. For example, GC&CS's ability to monitor Japanese diplomatic telegrams revealed the loose nature of relations between Japan, Germany and Italy.[164] Britain's greatest weakness was vulnerability to foreign espionage. Grossly inadequate security in the British embassy in Rome gave the Italians, and through them the Germans, access to diplomatic documents setting out British foreign policy in detail.[165] Soviet intelligence received copies of British telegrams and despatches from a number of sources in the Foreign Office as well as from the Rome embassy.[166]

However, as regards foreign and defence policy, the most serious failures in all countries seem to have arisen from how preconceptions influenced analysis and interpretation of intelligence. For example, British perceptions of Soviet war potential reflected not only difficulties in collecting intelligence in a closed society but also a belief that Russia was backward.[167] For his part, Stalin received ample intelligence from agents in Britain, but his interpretation of it was distorted by his belief in a non-existent British conspiracy to turn Hitler against the Soviet Union.[168] In Germany and Italy, perceptions of Britain's intentions depended in part on the dictators' crude social Darwinism. Hitler, from his experience of the Western Front, knew British soldiers could fight, but he believed British leaders lacked the necessary ruthlessness to maintain Britain's position in the world.[169] British interpretation of political intelligence was not helped by a mistaken belief in the Foreign Office that the Nazi regime included moderates who could influence Hitler.

Assessments of military capability were influenced by the preconceptions of the different services. Thus, for example, both British and French air intelligence officers wrongly assumed the Luftwaffe was creating an independent strategic bombing force, such as their own services aspired to, rather than a tactical air force.[170] Assessments of potential enemies' capability also depended partly on relative readiness for war. British, French, German and Italian military men all provided worst-case estimates when they felt their own preparations were inadequate. However, whereas democratic statesmen were inhibited by such advice, the dictators were much more willing to take risks. As regards the influence of intelligence on pre-war British policy, Wesley Wark has identified four phases: first, from 1933 to early 1935, when the extent and pace of German rearmament was underestimated, leading to a lack of urgency; second, from the spring of 1935 to the autumn of 1936, when intelligence was better informed, but when ministers hoped the Germans would agree to limit their armaments; third, a period, lasting until after Munich, when pessimism about Britain's ability to match German rearmament prevailed and intelligence reinforced ministers' inclination to pursue appeasement; and finally, beginning in the winter of 1938–39, a growing sense of optimism about the military balance, leading to determination to deter German aggression. A similar shift in intelligence estimates and a growing resolve to stand up to Germany occurred in France after Munich. In addition, economic intelligence that German stocks of food and raw materials might be exhausted after a year of warfare encouraged optimism in Britain about the extent to which Germany could be weakened by naval blockade, supplemented by bombing industrial targets.[171]

4   The Darkening Scene

4.1   Dealing with the Great Depression

When Chamberlain became chancellor on 5 November 1931, international relations were deteriorating under the impact of the Great
Depression, a salient feature of which was the fall in world prices – by
about 25 per cent between 1929 and 1932.[1] Farmers tried to maintain
their incomes by increasing production, thereby forcing down prices
further; industrialists, in contrast, cut production in an attempt to maintain prices. As a result, unemployment increased – in Britain's case from
10.4 per cent in 1929 to 22.1 per cent in 1932, according to contemporary statistics for workers covered by national unemployment insurance,
or from 8.0 per cent to 17.0 per cent as a proportion of the total labour
force.[2] Falling prices also increased the number of bad debts as the value
of collateral was reduced and returns from investment were lower than
expected. Banking crises occurred in Central Europe in 1931 and in the
United States in 1930–3. Governments found it harder to balance their
budgets as tax receipts fell, arousing fears about whether currencies
would remain fixed to their gold par. The international gold standard
deepened deflation as central banks raised interest rates in order to
prevent a loss of gold when currencies came under speculative pressure.[3]
Britain suspended the gold standard on 21 September 1931 when it
became clear that the Bank of England's reserves were inadequate to
defend the $4.86 exchange rate fixed by Churchill in 1925. Subsequent
fluctuations in exchange rates made it difficult for international traders to
predict prices and therefore to agree contracts. International trade had
already fallen as a result of other countries raising tariffs – with the
United States leading the way with the Smoot-Hawley Tariff Act of
June 1930, which raised already high rates by 20 per cent – but currency
instability was a further impediment.

Chamberlain's first task was to restore confidence in the financial
system. To this end he continued the policy of his Labour predecessor,
Philip Snowden, of attempting to balance the budget, even when pressed

by Keynes and others to promote recovery by lowering taxes and financing public expenditure by borrowing. However, Chamberlain's budgets were less rigidly orthodox than Snowden's: in particular, sinking funds to redeem the national debt were reduced. Advised by his senior officials, Sir Richard Hopkins and Sir Frederick Phillips, Chamberlain looked mainly to a lowering of interest rates to stimulate private investment in Britain and to reduce the cost of government debt. A façade of budgetary orthodoxy made it possible in the summer of 1932 to reduce bank rate – the Bank of England's discount rate – from 6 per cent to 2 per cent, and to convert a large tranche of the national debt incurred in the First World War from 5 per cent to 3.5 per cent. Interest paid on the national debt in 1933/34 was £62 million less than in 1931/32, a significant sum compared with total defence expenditure of £107 million in 1933/34.[4]

According to Robert Self, Chamberlain made 'a completely new and radical departure' in forward budgetary planning when he asked officials in March 1932 what scope there would be for changes in taxation and expenditure over the next three or four years. This exercise – known to Treasury officials as 'Old Moore's Almanack' after a popular compilation of astrological forecasts – was not in fact unprecedented. Churchill had asked for similar budget forecasts for 1928/29 to 1932/33 when he planned to make changes to the tax system. What Hopkins called the 'conjectures' of the Treasury and the Boards of Inland Revenue and Customs and Excise in 'Old Moore' suggested there would be little improvement in the budgetary position until 1934, but thereafter there would be scope to restore cuts in public expenditure and to reverse tax increases imposed to balance the budget during the depression.[5] As regards monetary policy, Hopkins and Philips believed there should be no return to the fixed exchange rate of the gold standard: instead, sterling was pegged early in 1932 at about $3.40, thereby making goods priced in sterling more competitive on international markets – to the benefit of exporters – and imports priced in other currencies dearer – to the benefit of domestic producers. Ralph Hawtrey, the Treasury's in-house economist, and Keynes, whom the Treasury consulted, reckoned a sterling depreciation of 30 per cent would offset the fall in world prices that had occurred since 1925. The Treasury wanted prices to rise to their pre-depression levels and Phillips thought the only way to achieve that would be to hold sterling down relative to the price of gold. Rising prices would encourage private investment and raise revenue from taxation, making it easier to balance the budget and maintain confidence.[6] Rising prices would also help the dominions and colonies, whose farmers had suffered particularly severely in the depression. Chamberlain announced this policy goal at the British Empire Economic Conference at Ottawa in

July 1932 and reiterated it frequently. By 1937 the Board of Trade's wholesale price index had risen by 20 per cent. Chamberlain's personal contribution to the policy mix was to end Britain's traditional policy of free trade – hitherto supported strongly by Treasury officials – by introducing in 1932 a general 10 per cent tariff, and protective duties of up to 33.5 per cent on some manufactured goods, to raise revenue and to improve the balance of trade.[7] Churchill, for whom free trade had been a central conviction, was converted to tariffs by the depression and supported Chamberlain.[8]

Economic historians and economists have disagreed about the effectiveness of Chamberlain's policies. Keynesians believe he would have done better to borrow on a large scale to finance public investment, whereas non-Keynesians doubt whether Keynes's proposals would have increased national income and reduced unemployment by as much as he claimed. However, Roger Middleton, himself a Keynesian, pointed out that Chamberlain's budgets provided a stable environment and made possible an expansion of low-interest credit which fuelled a housing boom as well as encouraging industrial investment. Chamberlain created conditions for an economic recovery in 1932–7 which went further than that brought about by Roosevelt's contemporary New Deal. Real GDP in Britain was 14.7 per cent higher in 1937 than in 1929, whereas in the United States it was only 5.3 per cent higher; unemployment in Britain, while still severe in 1937, at 8.5 per cent of the labour force, was lower than the corresponding American figure of 9.2 per cent.[9] Economic historians disagree about the contribution of tariffs to recovery, partly because it is difficult to distinguish between their effects from those of the reduction in sterling's exchange rate in 1931–2; partly because tariffs raised costs for some British industries, like steel, which relied on imported iron ore, and partly because, insofar as tariffs improved the trade balance, they also tended to raise the exchange rate.[10] However, taken together, Chamberlain's policies helped to bring about economic recovery while restoring financial markets' faith in British public finance. As Churchill wrote in January 1937, after Chamberlain had announced his intention to borrow for rearmament: 'The chancellor of the exchequer has happily by his prudent management of our finances restored our credit and raised it to an exceptionally high level.'[11]

Some of Chamberlain's policies had implications for international relations. The dominions followed Britain's example in departing from the gold standard (apart from Canada, which had already done so), as did India and the colonies, and foreign countries that were closely connected with Britain through trade. Treasury officials saw an opportunity to create a 'sterling area' in which Empire countries and as many foreign countries as possible would peg their currencies to the pound, making sterling an effective rival to gold for the conduct of international finance. Their plans were largely realised, although the Canadians chose to link their currency with the American dollar. The sterling area enabled a large part of the world to enjoy greater monetary stability than that experienced by countries that remained on gold. Such stability was possible only through the operations of the Exchange Equalisation Account, which was devised by Phillips for use by the Bank of England to smooth out fluctuations in exchange rates and to keep sterling low in the interests of Britain's balance of trade. The United States and France resented the Exchange Equalisation Account because they believed it gave the sterling area an unfair trading advantage.[12] Roosevelt took the dollar off the gold standard in March 1933 and stabilized it in January 1934 at 59 per cent of its former gold content in an attempt to raise prices in the United States and to help American exporters. France remained on the gold standard and the franc came under speculative pressure in the expectation that it too would be devalued, especially after Léon Blum formed a left-wing government in 1936. Roosevelt's secretary of the treasury, Henry Morgenthau, approached Chamberlain, as his opposite number, to urge co-operation on exchange-rate stabilization and the chancellor responded with a personal letter expressing the desire for the 'closest and most friendly contact' between the American and British treasuries.[13] There followed the Tripartite Agreement on 25 September 1936, whereby Britain, France and the United States undertook to consult together to prevent, as far as possible, any disturbance to the international monetary system resulting from the devaluation of the franc.

Great resentment was aroused, particularly in the United States, by Chamberlain's efforts to promote trade within the Commonwealth and Empire through the system of imperial preference in tariffs, which he negotiated with dominion prime ministers at Ottawa in 1932. Since the dominions did not want to expose their industries to British competition by lowering their tariffs, the only way to create imperial preference was to raise tariffs or impose quantitative restrictions on foreign imports, which both Britain and the dominions did. Empire products not previously subject to tariffs were exempt from the Abnormal Importations Act of November 1931 and the Import Duties Act of April 1932. American exporters objected to being discriminated against in their most valuable market, the United Kingdom, and in Empire countries, especially Canada. The American secretary of state from 1933, Cordell Hull, later described imperial preference as 'the greatest injury, in a commercial way, that has ever been inflicted on this country since I have been in public life'.[14] Hull made it his business to try to dismantle imperial preference through bilateral trade agreements with the dominions and with Britain. Trade negotiations were the responsibility of the Board of Trade but, when he became prime minister, Chamberlain saw them as an opportunity to improve relations with the United States. With that end in view, the Anglo-American Trade Agreement of November 1938 led to reductions in – but not abolition of – preferences.

4.2   The War Debts Controversy

Inter-governmental debt was another source of Anglo-American discord. The Treaty of Versailles stated that Germany was responsible for all loss and damage arising from the war, although the schedule of reparations set in 1921 had been far lower than the level that responsibility implied, and had been further modified by the Dawes Plan of 1924 and the Young Plan of 1929 to take account of Germany's capacity to pay. The other form of inter-governmental debt arose from loans to finance the conduct of the war. Britain was both a creditor and a debtor, having lent about twice as much to its allies as it had borrowed from the United States. At Churchill's instigation, the British government had declared in 1922 it would demand from its debtors no more than it was required to pay, and had thereby aroused hostile criticism in the United States, which had lent $4,604 million to Britain; $4,025 million to France; and smaller sums to Italy and other European countries. The loans had been financed by the sale of Federal government debt to the American public and the American taxpayer was liable to pay the interest on that debt. Writing off war debts would thus increase the burden of taxation in the United States. Under a settlement negotiated in 1923 by the then chancellor of the exchequer, Baldwin, Britain agreed to pay the United States annual instalments of $160 million (£33 million at the gold exchange rate of $4.86) for ten years and $184 million (£38 million) for a further 52 years. Interest of 3 per cent was payable on the capital outstanding until December 1932, and 3.5 per cent thereafter. Subsequent agreements between the United States and other countries were on more generous terms, according to their perceived ability to pay. As a result, down to mid-1931 Britain paid $1,352 million, of which $1,150 million represented interest, whereas France paid $200 million, of which only $39 million was interest.[15] Meanwhile, Churchill, as chancellor, negotiated with countries owing war debts to Britain with a view to securing payments that, together with Britain's share of German reparations, would match Britain's payments to the United States. In the event, in the financial year 1927/28 Britain received only £25 million, £8 million less than it paid to the United States, and even the maximum level of payments due to Britain from 1933, £33 million, would have been £5 million less than the payments that would then have been due to the United States.

A financial crisis in Germany in 1931 raised the prospect of default on reparations, and on 21 June the American president, Herbert Hoover, proposed a one-year moratorium from 1 July on reparations and war debts. As the depression deepened, the German government asked the Bank for International Settlements to establish an advisory committee to investigate its capacity to pay reparations, as it was entitled to do under the Young Plan, and on 23 December the committee reported that Germany would be unable to fulfil its obligations at the end of the moratorium. Chamberlain's response was to call for a comprehensive settlement of reparations as soon as possible and, ignoring the long-standing American refusal to recognise a link between war debts and reparations, he advocated a general cancellation of both. Although international diplomacy was officially a matter for the Foreign Office, he took the lead in negotiations at a conference of European powers at Lausanne in June 1932, when Britain and France agreed to reduce Germany's obligations to three billion reichsmarks (£150 million), with a three-year moratorium, and with payments thereafter dependent on economic conditions (which, in the circumstances, effectively meant the end of reparations). Chamberlain's experience at Lausanne convinced him of the efficacy of his personal touch in diplomacy, and the Lausanne settlement may be regarded as his first act of appeasement. Writing in May 1933, the permanent under-secretary of the Foreign Office, Vansittart, thought Lausanne was the only success in the previous two years regarding the liquidation of political and financial problems arising from the war. On the other hand, he feared that failure to solve the problem of war debts was 'bound to undermine, and might even destroy, the painfully erected structure of Anglo-American friendship'.[16]

Churchill had warned that it was a mistake to hold the Lausanne conference shortly before a presidential election in the United States, since any reduction of reparations was bound to lead to Republicans and Democrats vying with each other in taking a hard line against the revision of war debts.[17] The Lausanne settlement was subject to an informal understanding that Britain would not attempt to collect war debts from other countries and French willingness to forgo reparations was conditional on American willingness to forgo France's war debt. Chamberlain believed Americans could be educated to see the necessity of remission or cancellation of war debts. The case prepared in the Treasury was, briefly, as follows. Payment of reparations and war debts had been made possible in the 1920s by the flow of investment capital from the United States to continental Europe, but that flow had ceased with the depression. In the long run international debts could only be paid by exporting goods or services, but protectionist policies in the United States left debtors no option but to pay in gold. Demand for gold had consequently increased, forcing up its price, leading to a general fall in prices relative to the price of gold. As a result, all debts denominated in terms of gold were worth more in terms of goods and services. Nations were forced to increase their trade surpluses to maintain payments on international debts, but, prevented by tariffs from increasing exports, they could do so only by reducing imports. The value of international trade had decreased by 50 per cent in between 1929 and 1932, to the detriment of creditor and debtor nations alike. Revision of war debts, by Britain as well as the United States, would reverse this trend, and even partial recovery of business activity would result in additional tax receipts greater than the debt payments foregone.[18] On this occasion Keynes agreed with the Treasury's analysis. He added that the scale of Britain's debt to the United States should be reduced to the replacement cost at current prices of the wheat, cotton, copper, chemicals and munitions purchased there during the war. Moreover, he noted, protectionist congressmen would have to accept that repayment was possible only if America had a net trade deficit with the rest of the world.[19]

The Treasury's case was presented to Hoover's secretary of state, Henry Stimson, in November 1932, with a proposal that Britain's next payment due on 15 December should be suspended pending renegotiation of the 1923 settlement. Stimson's reply on the 23rd acknowledged that the fall in prices had increased the burden of debt, but pointed out that the effects of the British proposal on the American taxpayer could not be disregarded, as the ultimate decision on changes to intergovernmental debts was reserved to Congress.[20] While some Americans understood that the United States would benefit from the increased ability of Europeans to buy American goods following a cancellation of war debts, it was difficult to persuade American taxpayers, suffering as they were from the depression, to take on payment of the interest on the debts when European countries continued to spend large sums on armaments. Chamberlain deplored what he took to be a lack of moral courage on the part of American leaders in the face of opposition in Congress and was inclined not to pay the December instalment. However, he was persuaded by the governor of the Bank of England, Montagu Norman, that default on the war debt might prompt other countries, such as Australia and Argentina, to default on other debts to Britain.[21] The December payment was accordingly accompanied by a note on the

11th saying it was not to be regarded as a resumption of the instalments agreed in 1923; instead it was intended to be a capital payment pending a discussion of the whole question by the two governments.[22] The next day the French government was defeated when it asked the Chamber to sanction payment of its December instalment and France defaulted, although it had ample gold reserves. Roosevelt did not adopt Chamberlain's proposal for a moratorium, but, shortly before the next instalment was due in June 1933, suggested a part-payment of $10 million in gold with the assurance that it would be regarded as a contribution to the final settlement. After some haggling, the United States accepted a token payment of $10 million in silver at a rate of 50 cents to the ounce, equivalent to $7.5 million in gold, and Roosevelt stated publicly that he did not regard the British government to be in default.

In the autumn of 1933 Chamberlain sent a Treasury official, Sir Frederick Leith-Ross, to Washington with instructions to try to secure cancellation, but if that were impossible, to offer annual payments not exceeding $20 million (instead of $184 million), with a let-out clause whereby Britain should not be required to pay proportionately more than other debtors. Roosevelt was prepared to contemplate modification of the 1923 settlement so as to reduce Britain's liability to about $60 million a year, a sum that Leith-Ross thought was within Britain's capacity to pay, although American tariffs would make it difficult to do so. On both sides, however, there were political objections to more concessions. Leith-Ross, who had several cordial interviews with the president, had the impression that Roosevelt did not care much what was done about the debt so long as it did not cause him difficulties with Congress. The president rightly believed there was no hope of securing Congress's agreement to better terms; indeed, after another part-payment in silver was made in December, Congress passed a resolution precluding any further 'token' payment and followed this up in April 1934 with the Johnson Act, which barred nations in default of their debts from negotiating any further loans.[23] On 25 May 1934 the United States Treasury sent a bill for $262 million, being the balance of the instalments for 1933 plus the full payment due on 15 June 1934. Chamberlain would have been prepared to continue token payments had it been possible thereby to avoid default, but he was not willing to continue full payments without receiving anything from Britain's debtors, and had no wish to reopen the European debt question settled at Lausanne.[24] Notwithstanding the Johnson Act, he opted for default.

Greg Kennedy included the handling of war debts and its effects on Anglo-American relations in his indictment that Chamberlain was the worst of Britain's strategic policymakers. He blamed Chamberlain for

failing to see that an Anglo-American 'special relationship' was the key
to Britain's survival as a first-rank, global power. He believed
Chamberlain's intentions from the outset were to dodge a settlement for
as long as possible and in the end to pay the Americans nothing.[25]
However, Self's careful account of policymaking in relation to war debts
has shown that Chamberlain had to overcome strong opposition from
Cabinet colleagues, including Walter Runciman, the president of the
Board of Trade, and Philip Cunliffe-Lister, who had recently moved from
the Board of Trade to the Colonial Office, to secure agreement for such
payments as were made.[26] Chamberlain was by no means the most hawkish
minister on the subject. Kennedy saw the experience of war debt negotiations as critical in forming Chamberlain's 'mental map' of the United
States and its president as unreliable, deceitful and unhelpful.[27] However,
in that respect Chamberlain was typical of his generation of policymakers in
Whitehall; as Self pointed out, even Vansittart, who had an American wife,
complained in 1934 that the Americans 'will always let us down'.[28]

Neither Kennedy nor Self considered the merits of Chamberlain's case
on war debts. The depression had multiple causes, and the fall in prices
was also partly due to supply factors – for example increased output as a
result of mechanization of agriculture – and, arguably, mainly to restrict-
ive domestic monetary policy in the United States and Germany, and the
cessation of American overseas investment. Nevertheless, gold transfers
to the United States arising from inter-governmental debts added to the
deflationary bias of the international gold standard as the Federal
Reserve absorbed gold without permitting a proportionate increase in
the domestic monetary supply.[29] Likewise, recovery from the depression
had multiple causes, but default on war debts was one of them. Most
countries did not resume payments after the end of the Hoover moratorium and no country, except Finland, made any payments after
December 1933. William Ashworth described default as a 'piece of
healthy destruction' that removed a major element of weakness and
disturbance in international economic relations. Charles Kindleberger
observed that 'a far-seeing leadership on the part of the United States
might have been willing to waive war debts, but it would have been
difficult to persuade the American voter'.[30]

One politician who attempted that task was Churchill. In articles in
American magazines in November 1933 and March 1934 – the first
shortly before the last token payment and the second shortly before the
Johnson Act – he presented the same argument as Chamberlain's
Treasury. The question, Churchill said, was 'not the *ability* to pay, but
the method and the consequences of payment'. Debts could only be paid
from the balance of trade in goods and services, and Britain would have

to reduce purchases from the United States or, where that was not possible, as with raw cotton, to levy taxes on imports payable in dollars. Such a process, he remarked, would be injurious to both countries and could not fail to arouse increasing friction. He hailed Roosevelt's sagacity and courage in declaring that Britain was not in default after token payments; sagacity because that act recognised the realities of international trade, and courage because the president had faced the difficulty of making the ordinary public understand that debts between nations could not be treated like indebtedness in private life. Churchill continued: 'This is no time for forcing a faithful debtor into extreme courses, and I believe that, in spite of the frenzied oratory of ebullient backwoods senators, moderate opinion in America recognizes the fact.'[31] Self thought Chamberlain's attempts to educate American opinion by setting out British policy in robust speeches greatly inflamed the situation.[32] However, there was no significant difference between Churchill and Chamberlain in their analysis, and Chamberlain's language was more temperate.[33] Vansittart thought the breach over war debts came because the Americans had overplayed their hand.[34] Be that as it may, it is not clear why any historian should pillory Chamberlain alone on this subject.

The consequences of the Johnson Act were potentially severe. So long as Britain was in default, purchases of munitions and other supplies in the United States would be limited to what could be financed from its gold and dollar reserves, export earnings and the sale of assets held there by British subjects. Britain would thus not be able to draw on American resources in a future war on the same scale as in 1915–18. However, the Johnson Act was not the only barrier to be overcome. Congress also passed neutrality acts in 1935 and 1937, providing for a mandatory embargo on the sale of weapons to belligerents and prohibiting American ships from carrying munitions to them. The influence of isolationism was very strong. It is not clear how much Britain would have benefited from continuing to pay instalments on its war debt. Finland, the only nation to do so, found that the goodwill won thereby was of limited utility. When the Soviet Union invaded Finland in the winter of 1939–40, Roosevelt extended credit to the Finns to buy farm surpluses and non-military supplies in the United States, but arms had to be paid for in cash and transported in foreign ships. He refused to antagonize isolationists by asking Congress for a loan that would enable the Finns to buy arms in Sweden. His caution was well founded. A bill filed by Senator Prentiss Brown to lend the Finns $60 million to buy arms was so mutilated in Congress that the credit was limited to $20 million and restricted to non-military supplies.[35] In short, Finland was treated in exactly the same way as nations that had defaulted on war debts.

4.3   Manchuria and the End of the Ten Year Rule

Chamberlain's handling of war debts was not the only cause of tension in Anglo-American relations. The two countries were also at odds in their responses to the crisis that broke out in the Far East shortly after the National Government was formed. In September 1931 a Japanese army invaded the Chinese province of Manchuria, using a staged explosion on a Japanese-owned railway as a pretext. The Chinese government appealed to the League of Nations and to the United States as a signatory of the Nine-Power Treaty of 1922, which guaranteed the sovereignty and territorial integrity of China and the 'open door' whereby all countries could trade with China on equal terms. The League's Council called on Japan and China to stop fighting and return their forces to their own frontiers, and the American secretary of state, Stimson, published a note warmly supporting the League's action. The Japanese army continued to seize territory, and in November the Japanese government, which had little control over its forces in Manchuria, proposed a commission of inquiry. The Council agreed and on 10 December postponed any coercive measures against Japan indefinitely. Military unpreparedness meant that Britain, and therefore the League, was in no position to impose sanctions. On 7 January 1932 Stimson published notes to China and Japan setting out the doctrine of 'non-recognition', which would deny legality to any treaty or agreement that impaired the integrity of China or America's open door rights. The secretary of state evidently hoped for support from other powers, but the British foreign secretary, Sir John Simon, rebuffed him by issuing a communiqué to the effect that the British government saw no need to do more than ask Japan to confirm previous assurances that it would maintain the 'open door' in Manchuria. On 9 February, following a Japanese attack on Shanghai and a further Chinese appeal to the League, Stimson proposed that the United States and Britain should issue a very strong indictment of Japan. The British government hoped to avoid alienating either Japan or the United States. In a series of static-ridden transatlantic telephone conversations – then a novel form of diplomacy – Simon prevaricated, first by taking refuge in ambiguity, and then by referring the matter to the League. There was to be no Anglo-American démarche. Stimson felt let down. State Department officials were convinced that the British were cowardly.[36] From a British perspective, it seemed that Stimson's proposal would have alienated Japan to no good purpose, since the United States was no more prepared than Britain to take any military action. Baldwin remarked on 27 February, 'you will get nothing out of Washington but words, big words, but only words'.[37]

The crisis in the Far East challenged the Foreign Office's assumptions about the possibility of war. Vansittart, when reviewing the Ten Year Rule as recently as June 1931, had warned that Germany and the Soviet Union might become threats within that timeframe, but had made no mention of Japan.[38] The Japanese attack on Shanghai, where about three-quarters of Britain's investments in China were concentrated, brought home the extent of military weakness resulting from failure to complete the naval base at Singapore. Sir Bolton Eyres-Monsell, the first lord of the Admiralty, and Viscount Hailsham, the secretary of state for war, called for the end of the Ten Year Rule in Cabinet on 10 February 1932, but Chamberlain thought that the risk of destroying the country's financial stability was greater than the risks of military unpreparedness, a proposition with which Baldwin agreed 'with extreme reluctance'. The chancellor had yet to present to Parliament the first of a series of balanced budgets with which he hoped to restore confidence in the financial system. When, on 23 March, the Cabinet accepted the chiefs of staff's recommendation that the Ten Year Rule should be cancelled, the minutes noted that the decision was not to be taken to justify increased defence expenditure without regard to the country's serious economic situation.[39] In the event, the defence estimates for the financial year 1932/33 were the lowest of the interwar period and Britain was no more prepared to risk war by imposing sanctions on Japan in the spring of 1933 than it had been in the spring of 1932.[40]

Meanwhile, events in China had taken their course. In Shanghai the American and British consuls worked together to secure a truce on 5 May 1932. On 2 October the long-awaited report of the League commission of inquiry under Lord Lytton was published. While sympathetic towards Japanese grievances in Manchuria, it condemned the invasion of the province and refused to accept the legitimacy of the puppet state that the Japanese had set up there, recommending instead an autonomous government under Chinese sovereignty. When the League adopted the report in February 1933, Japan gave notice it would withdraw from the League and launched an attack on Jehol, part of China proper. Chamberlain, correctly anticipating that the fighting would soon be over, persuaded the Cabinet to impose an arms embargo on both China and Japan, to maintain impartiality.[41] The Chinese Nationalist government was forced to make peace in May and the Japanese army was left in occupation of the whole of the north-east of the country down to the Great Wall without any effective action having been taken by the League, Britain or the United States. Vansittart thought the obvious unwillingness of members of the League to impose sanctions had done much to discredit it, but believed Britain had avoided incurring Japanese resentment by acting impartially. Reviewing British foreign policy in May 1933, he did not think the Far Eastern situation was a threat to world peace for the time being.[42]

The Labour Party took a different view. Its leader, George Lansbury, in a speech on 27 February 1933, warned that wars tend to spread and called for 'all the sanctions, all the obligations' of the League to be carried through and for an arms embargo to be imposed on Japan alone as the aggressor.[43] Churchill, however, in a speech the same day, said he was anxious the League should not be dragged into a quarrel 'at the far end of the world', where it was powerless, although he thought it had a valuable role in Europe. He was opposed to 'throw[ing] away our old, valued friendship with Japan'. He described China as prey to anarchy and Communism – 'the same state that India would be if the guiding hand of British rule were withdrawn' – and had no doubt that the least unhappy provinces were those where the Japanese had established law and order. Like Chamberlain, he thought the correct attitude was to have an impartial arms embargo.[44] There was no hint in the speech of the judgement he made in *The Second World War* in 1948 that the Manchurian incident had undermined the moral authority of the League at a time when it was most needed.[45]

4.4   Disarmament and Defence Requirements, 1932–1934

Disarmament had been written into the Treaty of Versailles in 1919 in the preamble to the clauses restricting Germany's armed forces to an army of 100,000 men (about half the size of the British Regular Army), with no tanks or heavy artillery; a small navy with no ships more than 10,000 tons or submarines; and no military aircraft. Strict observance was said to be required 'in order to render possible the initiation of a general limitation of the armaments of all nations'.[46] The practical problems of how to achieve such a goal had occupied the attention of military, naval and air experts since 1920, without agreement being reached on which weapons were defensive and which were offensive, or how disarmament could be verified. The fundamental problem was how to reconcile German demands for equality of rights with France's fears for its security. Since becoming a member of the League of Nations in 1926, Germany had argued that either other countries should disarm down to its level, or Germany should be allowed to rearm up to their level. French reluctance to concede this point at the League's Disarmament Conference, which opened in Geneva in February 1932, led the Germans to withdraw their delegation seven months later and to return on 14 December only after Britain, France, Italy and the United States had agreed in principle to German equality of status. The prospects for successful negotiation dimmed when Hitler came to power in January 1933. Vansittart had previously thought the difficulty in the way of what he called 'world appeasement' was French determination to maintain its military and political predominance in Europe; by 1933 he recognized the legitimacy of French fears. However, he thought it was impossible for Britain to give more assurances to France than had already been given in the Treaty of Locarno, given 'the temperament of the British people and the nature of the British Commonwealth'.[47]

Chamberlain's thinking followed a similar pattern. In October 1932 he had argued in the Ministerial Committee on Disarmament that French fears might be assuaged if disarmament proceeded in stages, each stage being dependent on German good behaviour.[48] By 4 March 1933, however, he was writing to his sisters that 'the best opinion now seems convinced that the Germans are only looking for an opportunity to declare that the Disarmament Conference has failed in order to rearm and defy the world ... We are sending the P.M. out to Geneva to make a last effort to pull something out of the blaze but it is a forlorn hope and we hardly expect anything to come out of it.'[49] Ramsay MacDonald tabled a draft convention whereby Germany would remain disarmed for a further five or more years while the League established and tested a system for inspecting the state of armaments of all nations. In June Chamberlain hoped that a complete breakdown at Geneva could be avoided, but on 26 July, after seeing intelligence reports on secret German rearmament, he took the view in Cabinet that the French should not be pushed into a position of weakness.[50] Churchill had reached that position earlier. On 23 March 1933 he argued it was dangerous to press France to disarm so that Germany could have equality of status, for then Britain would be more likely to be called upon to fulfil its Locarno obligations, and he denounced the Disarmament Conference as 'a solemn and prolonged farce'.[51]

Vansittart, notwithstanding his alarm at the nature of the Nazi regime, took a different view. In February 1933 he advised that Britain had to go on negotiating, even if with diminished hopes.[52] By May he believed that Germany, on past and present form, would start another European war just as soon as it felt strong enough.[53] Nevertheless, he feared the consequence of a breakdown of the conference would be an arms race and eventually war. He thought that in such an atmosphere trade revival from the depression would be impossible.[54] Germany's future was uncertain. He thought there were three possibilities. First, economic failure could result in the collapse of Hitler's regime, leading to either a military dictatorship or a Communist takeover. Second, if Hitler were successful domestically, a European war would follow in four or five years' time. Third, there might be a preventative war before Germany was strong enough to attack anyone else, but Vansittart did not advocate such a course, simply commenting that all three alternatives were 'singularly uninviting'.[55] The conclusion he drew was that 'if we are to avoid the disaster for which Hitlerism is working … we must keep as close as possible to the United States, to France and, if possible, to Italy, and to bring the last two together'.[56] He thought that even if Anglo-American relations were to be impaired for a time by failure to find an amicable solution to the war debt problem, the United States would respond to events and, the fuller the world was of unpleasant events, the shorter American memories would be.[57] The Soviet Union did not feature in his balance-of-power calculations in 1933. He noted that Stalin's Five Year Plan had caused serious economic difficulties and interpreted Soviet avoidance of conflict with Japan in Manchuria as evidence of weakness.[58]

Churchill's initial reaction to Hitler coming to power fell some way short of a grand alliance. In March 1933 he told the House of Commons he hoped the French would 'look after their own safety, and that we should be permitted to live our life in our island without being again drawn into the perils of the Continent of Europe'. He urged greater air and naval armaments to give Britain power to decide its own destiny, but made no mention of its army.[59] In the context of the resurgence of what he called a 'war spirit' in Germany, he said: 'Thank God for the French army.'[60] In April he warned that if Germany were to gain military equality with its neighbours, while its grievances still not redressed, 'so surely should we see ourselves within measurable distance of a general European war'. He said the first rule of British foreign policy should be to emphasise respect for the peace treaties, for only then could there be peaceful mitigation of grievances.[61] In November he told the House of Commons that 'the great dominant fact is that Germany is rearming'. Isolation, he believed, was impossible, but he urged 'a certain degree of sober detachment'. He thought he saw a solution in adherence to the League of Nations, which, he argued, could be effective in Europe despite its failure in the Far East. Britain, he believed, would find its greatest safety in co-operating with other European powers, 'not taking a leading part but coming in our proper place', in 'an attempt to address Germany collectively, so that there may be some redress of her grievances before rearmament endangered the peace of the world'.[62] Collective security through the League would not then have involved the Soviet Union, which was not yet a member.

Within Whitehall, Vansittart warned ministers in August that a rearmed Germany could defeat Britain and France within the next decade, and negotiations at Geneva could at best only retard German rearmament.[63] He was not the only senior official to be alarmed. While on sick leave, the permanent secretary of the Treasury, Sir Warren Fisher, had followed events in Germany and, on returning to work in September, he urged Chamberlain that Britain's defensive position should be reviewed in the light of Hitler's rise to power.[64] By October things were going badly at Geneva: Germany withdrew again from the conference on the 14th and gave notice of its intention to withdraw from the League. The chiefs of staff's annual review highlighted how deficiencies in Britain's armed forces had accumulated under the Ten Year Rule.[65] On the 21st Chamberlain noted that common prudence suggested some strengthening of the country's defences. The Treasury was no longer expecting a budget deficit at the end of the financial year 1933/34 and more money could be found for the defence estimates without imperilling his policy of restoring confidence through sound finance.[66] Notwithstanding his resistance to increased expenditure when the Ten Year Rule was cancelled, Chamberlain had never supposed that the defence estimates could remain at the level to which they had been reduced (£103 million in the financial year 1932/33). In the 'Old Moore's Almanack' exercise in March 1932 he had pencilled in £115 million for the defence estimates in 1935/36, restoring them to the level that had prevailed before Churchill had strengthened the Ten Year Rule in 1928.[67] The question was: on what should additional funding be spent? Fisher joined the cabinet secretary, Sir Maurice Hankey, and the chiefs of staff in pressing for a review of defence requirements. On 15 November 1933 the Defence Requirements Sub-Committee (DRC) of the CID, comprising the chiefs of staff, Fisher and Vansittart, with Hankey as chairman, was formed to draw up a programme to deal with the worst deficiencies in relation to threats from Japan in the Far East, Germany in Europe, and the Soviet Union to India. The DRC quickly decided that if deficiencies were made good to meet the German threat, requirements for the defence of India could also be met, so that debate centred on the relative importance of Far Eastern and European commitments.

The first sea lord, Sir Ernle Chatfield, was principally concerned with the Japanese navy, since German naval rearmament had scarcely begun. For example, when Hankey and Fisher asked him about Germany's pocket battleships, Chatfield said new French warships could look after them. British design of new capital ships would depend on what the Japanese built.[68] Sir Archibald Montgomery-Massingberd, the chief of the imperial general staff, was principally concerned with the Field Force and its ability to defend the Low Countries against Germany. On the other hand, he refrained from asking for substantial sums to train the Territorial Army, four divisions of which would be required to support the Regular units of the Field Force four months after the outbreak of war. Major Henry Pownall, the DRC's secretary, thought it would have been dangerous to give the full figures for, if ministers knew what the total cost of the Field Force plus the Territorial Army would be, they might decide the army was too expensive and turn to the RAF instead.[69] Montgomery-Massingberd also gave a lower priority to the army's contribution to the air defence of Great Britain (anti-aircraft guns and searchlights) than Sir Edward Ellington, the chief of the Air Staff, thought wise.[70] In short, each chief of staff pursued his own service's interests.

Most historians who have studied the DRC's proceedings have concluded that discussion of grand strategy was dominated by Vansittart and Fisher, who identified Germany as the ultimate enemy against whom defence policy must be directed.[71] Given that Soviet-Japanese relations were not good, Vansittart thought Japan was unlikely to attack unless Britain were engaged in a war elsewhere. On the other hand, he reported that French intelligence reckoned Germany would be ready to attack Poland by the end of 1935 or early in 1936. Although he and Fisher wanted the Singapore base to be completed as quickly as possible, to gain Japan's respect, both were primarily concerned with the German threat.[72] Keith Neilson, however, argued that the priorities set out in the DRC's report were those of the chiefs of staff, with the Far East the first contingency to be prepared for and Germany the second. In his view, 'Hankey rightly saw that the menace from Berlin was in the future, not in the present'. Greg Kennedy likewise believed that, despite Vansittart's attempt to put Germany first, the DRC gave first priority to the Far East, particularly naval preparations.[73] Historians can come to radically different interpretations of the DRC report because Hankey, as a skilful civil servant, drafted it in a way that all the sub-committee members could sign, despite the profound disagreements revealed in their discussions. Brian McKercher has challenged Neilson and Kennedy's revisionism by pointing out that the DRC recommended more expenditure on the army than on the navy and air force combined, and that the Field Force's share (£25,680,000) exceeded that of either the navy or the air force in the five-year period 1934–8 (Table 4.1).[74]

Table 4.1 overstates McKercher's case. The navy's figure covers the cost of deficiencies such as the need to modernise capital ships, fleet fuelling reserves, stores and equipment, and the Singapore base, but not the cost of new warships. The DRC, prompted by Chatfield, regarded the replacement programme for ships and Fleet Air Arm aircraft as a continuation of normal Admiralty policy rather than as part of the deficiency programme, but forecast that expenditure under these heads would increase by a total of £25,914,000 over the five years 1934–8

Table 4.1. *DRC recommendations for additional expenditures over the five years 1934–8 to make good deficiencies for each service*

Service	Expenditure in addition to level in financial year 1933/34 (£)	Percentage share of total
Royal Navy	21,067,600	29.5
British Army	39,990,980	56.1
RAF	10,265,000	14.4
Total	71,323,580	

Source: CP 64 (34), 28 Feb. 1934, table A (1), CAB 24/247/64, reproduced in B. J. C. McKercher, Deterrence and the European Balance of Power: The Field Force and British Grand Strategy, 1934–1938', *English Historical Review*, 123, 500 (2008), 98–131, at 106.

Table 4.2. *DRC deficiency programmes plus forecast additional naval replacement programme*

Service	Expenditure (£)	Percentage share of total
Royal Navy	46,981,600	48.3
British Army	39,990,980	41.1
RAF	10,265,000	10.5
Total	97,237,580	

Source: CP 64 (34), tables A (1) and A (2), CAB 24/247/64.

compared with what it would have been had it remained at the level of the estimates for the financial year 1933/34. Including that figure with the deficiency expenditure shows that the Royal Navy was expected to continue to be the biggest spender (Table 4.2).

The recommendations regarding the RAF, as they appeared in the printed report, might support the view that the Far East was first priority, but they were based on an error. Of 441 additional aircraft said to be required to meet the worst deficiencies, 110 were to complete the 52-squadron Home Defence scheme of 1923, 88 were for the Far East and 243 were for the Fleet Air Arm, most of which would be deployed against the Japanese navy. In all, these aircraft would be the equivalent of 40 squadrons, of which 10 would be for home defence. Vansittart and Fisher urged Ellington to ask for 25 more squadrons, with the German threat in mind, but the chief of the Air Staff demurred, saying that greater expansion would require emergency measures and alterations in training standards. He was backed by Montgomery-Massingberd, who pointed out that a larger increase for the RAF would be at the expense of the other services and would be liable to upset the balance of the report.[75] Ellington stated categorically, and after the matter had been referred back to him for further investigation, that 19 squadrons could be provided from the 52 Home Defence squadrons to accompany the Field Force to the continent. On the day that the committee's report was circulated to ministers, he admitted to Hankey that his staff had told him that in a European war all, or practically all, of the 52 squadrons would be required for home defence. Ellington's letter was circulated as a DRC paper, and the recommendations of the report regarding the RAF were a dead letter before ministers read them.[76]

However modest the figures in Tables 4.1 and 4.2 may appear to historians, to Hankey the cost of the DRC's recommendations seemed 'staggering'.[77] If implemented in full (including the naval replacement programme), they would result in an increase in the defence estimates in the order of 20 per cent within two years, not an easy decision for ministers to take at a time when pacifism was perceived to be a potent political force. Moreover, as Vansittart noted in a Cabinet paper in April 1934, there was 'probably no *immediate* danger ... [and] opinions must necessarily vary and depart into the realms of prophecy in estimating the ... period [before Germany's] expansionist phase'.[78] He also recognised that it was difficult to take adequate defensive measures as long as the fate of the Disarmament Conference was uncertain.[79]

Chamberlain took the view that 'the whole lesson' of the conference was that disarmament came second and security came first.[80] He feared a breakdown of the conference, followed by an arms race, unless the French could be given the security they required. However, like Vansittart, he doubted whether a unilateral British guarantee to France would be acceptable to public opinion. He therefore put forward a plan for what he called a limited liability partnership in which the principal European powers would enter a mutual guarantee convention whereby each would commit specified units – for example two divisions of troops or five squadrons of aircraft – to support an aggrieved party in the event of aggression. However, he was unable to convince the chiefs of staff or his Cabinet colleagues that the plan was practicable. In particular, the chiefs of staff thought it would be impossible to limit liability to specified units, and that such a convention would extend Britain's commitments.[81]

The Disarmament Conference's fate did not remain uncertain for long. In April 1934 the French government rejected the latest British proposals and it was becoming increasingly clear that the Germans would not return. On 18 May, five days before the conference was due to meet, the foreign secretary, Simon, told the House of Commons that any fresh initiative at Geneva must come from other countries.[82] The conference faded from the scene in June, but arms limitation pacts, particularly regarding air and naval forces, remained British objectives.

4.5   Reshaping Grand Strategy, 1934

Although Chamberlain's limited liability plan fell on stony ground, he did succeed in bringing about radical changes to the strategic priorities set out in the DRC report. Like Sir Warren Fisher and Sir Robert Vansittart, he was more impressed by the danger from Germany than from Japan. Fisher was his closest adviser at this time, and Fisher in turn consulted Lord Trenchard, the former chief of the Air Staff. Trenchard advised Fisher that the RAF should have 100 squadrons based in Great Britain, instead of the 52 recommended in the DRC report, and that two-thirds should be bombers.[83] On 10 May 1934 the Ministerial Committee on Disarmament, to which the Cabinet had remitted consideration of the DRC report, agreed to Chamberlain's suggestion that he should prepare an alternative programme, which he did, with Fisher's help, in the light of the committee's discussions, financial limitations and probable reactions of public opinion. In putting forward his alternative proposals on 20 June, the chancellor argued that the best defence would be an air deterrent based in Great Britain of a size and efficiency calculated to inspire respect in the mind of a possible enemy. He recommended that 38 squadrons, instead of the DRC's 10, should be added to the Home Defence force, but that no new squadrons should be formed overseas, except for the three allocated by the DRC to the defence of Singapore. Naval requirements, he thought, could be met by making Fleet Air Arm and Home Defence squadrons interchangeable.[84] Hankey told Baldwin that Chamberlain's proposal was 'excessive' and 'a panic measure', in that it neglected naval and Far Eastern requirements.[85]

It was probably due to the cabinet secretary's influence that a sub-committee on the Allocation of Air Forces was set up, without any Treasury member, and with Baldwin in the chair. The sub-committee decided that, for technical reasons, Fleet Air Arm and Home Defence squadrons could not be interchangeable, and recommended instead 33 squadrons for Home Defence and four-and-a-half for the Fleet Air Arm, and 4 instead of 3 squadrons for the Far East. In the light of the sub-committee's report, the Ministerial Committee on Disarmament also rounded up Chamberlain's figure of £18.2 million for the Air Ministry over the first five years of the programme to £20 million, to pay for reserves of aircraft and bombs, which the chancellor had omitted, but accepted the Treasury's argument that provision of the bulk of these

war requirements should be deferred so as to avoid accumulating obsolescent aircraft. Hankey regarded creating squadrons without reserves as
a 'politicians' window-dressing scheme',[86] but, as noted on page 60,
Germany followed the same policy. The final air programme, as
approved by the Cabinet on 18 July, reflected Chamberlain's views rather
than those of Hankey or the Air Staff.[87]

Trenchard also gave advice about the army. He regarded deficiencies in
the army's anti-aircraft defences in Great Britain as more urgent than
deficiencies in the Field Force, but still regarded the latter's role in
securing continental air bases as important since many of the RAF's
bombers lacked the range to reach the Ruhr from bases in England.[88]
However, when the army's programme was first discussed in the
Ministerial Committee on Disarmament on 3 May 1934, Chamberlain
challenged the need for another expeditionary force along the lines of
1914, given the strength of France's frontier defences and the fact that
the German air force could fly over these. In these circumstances,
he claimed, Britain's best contribution would be air and sea power. The
secretary of state for war, Viscount Hailsham, responded that, while the
French fortifications were probably impregnable, the Belgians had not
begun theirs, and it was doubtful if the Dutch would resist the Germans.
In his view, an expeditionary force was required to deny the Germans air
and submarine bases in the Low Countries. Chamberlain probed
Hailsham's case: could British troops arrive in time to prevent the Low
Countries being overrun? Would it be better to finance the Belgians'
fortifications? Was the answer to the German air menace not an overwhelming British air force? When ministers resumed their discussion on
10 May, with a paper by the chiefs of staff on the importance of the Low
Countries before them, Chamberlain admitted he had previously misunderstood the proposal regarding an expeditionary force. He now realised
that what the DRC recommended was not the creation of an expeditionary
force out of something that did not exist, but rather preparation of the
existing Field Force to act as an expeditionary force. He remained unconvinced an expeditionary force would necessarily have to be despatched to
the continent immediately in the event of war with Germany, but he was
prepared to accept that the army had to be equipped if it was to be useful.[89]

When Chamberlain put forward his alternative proposals to the committee on 25 June, he gave first priority to an air deterrent, but, should
deterrence fail, Britain's defences would take the form partly of the
enlarged RAF, partly in the completion of anti-aircraft defences, and
'finally' in the 'conversion of the army into an effectively equipped force
capable of operating with allies in holding the Low Countries'.[90]
Hailsham complained that Chamberlain's proposed allocation for the

army, £19.1 million over five years, compared with £40 million in the DRC report, covered all the recommendations for anti-aircraft defence of Great Britain and for coastal defences at Singapore, but included only a small residuum for the Field Force. Chamberlain replied that some kind of arbitrary cut was necessary on financial grounds, and that only the timescale of the army's deficiencies programme was being altered, with most of the expenditure being delayed until after the financial year 1938/39. Hailsham received little support from other ministers, who agreed with Chamberlain that public opinion would not favour expenditure on the army, and the committee's report, which was accepted by the Cabinet on 31 July, merely rounded up Chamberlain's figure for the army's programme from £19.1 million to £20 million.[91]

Chamberlain had reason to be pleased with his impact on the DRC's recommendations for the air force and army, especially since, as he told his sisters on 1 July, he had pitched his proposals 'on purpose a little high'.[92] The Admiralty proved to be more formidable in bureaucratic politics. Unlike the army, the navy enjoyed public support, and Baldwin was apprehensive about the activities of the Navy League. When Chamberlain proposed to the Ministerial Committee on Disarmament on 25 June 1934 that the Admiralty postpone until after 1939 plans for sending to Singapore a fleet of capital ships capable of meeting the Japanese in battle, the first lord, Sir Bolton Eyres-Monsell asked how the dominions could be told that the whole basis of imperial defence was to be altered. He dismissed Chamberlain's suggestion, derived from advice by Trenchard and Fisher, that the approaches to the Indian Ocean could be defended by submarines and light craft based in Singapore, while cruisers protected the trade routes. Chamberlain argued his proposal that Britain should not lay down new capital ships on the expiry of the London Naval Treaty in 1936 would not affect the naval balance in the Far East immediately, for he accepted that the Royal Navy's existing capital ships should be modernised and it would take Japan three-and-a-half years to build new ones. If the situation in the Far East changed, he said, there would still be time to alter policy, perhaps at the expense of home defence. Meanwhile he wanted a reduction in the navy's deficiency programme from £21.1 million to £13 million and a cut of more than £11 million in the Admiralty's forecast for new construction. As before, he was pitching his proposals high. He did not really expect his colleagues to accept the idea of giving up building new capital ships. Other ministers were broadly in agreement with Eyres-Monsell that Japan posed an immediate danger, whereas (the first lord thought) Germany was unlikely to be a menace for some time and might never be a menace at all.[93]

On the other hand, as the prime minister, MacDonald, observed, the National Government was committed in Chamberlain's next budget to reverse income-tax increases and public sector pay cuts imposed in the financial crisis of 1931. These concessions would cost the Exchequer £27 million in 1934/35 and £40 million in a full year, or far more than the cost of the full DRC programme, but ministers were unwilling to take an electoral risk by withholding the concessions. No minister challenged Chamberlain on 25 June when he rejected Baldwin's suggestion of a defence loan to spread the cost of the DRC programme over a period of 10–15 years. Maintaining confidence in the financial system had priority. The fact that future construction of warships was subject to the outcome of the Naval Disarmament Conference due to be held in London the following year offered ministers a way to put off a decision. On Eyres-Monsell's suggestion, they agreed that naval construction should be considered by the first lord and the chancellor in the normal way in the autumn as part of the annual estimates, and the Admiralty's deficiency programme was made subject to the same procedure.[94]

Historians have offered very different interpretations of the effects of Chamberlain's influence on defence priorities in 1934. Peter Bell, who took a strong revisionist line on appeasement, argued the chancellor recognised that it was not practicable to prepare against simultaneous danger in Europe and the Far East, and established priorities accordingly, thereby laying the foundations for defence against Germany.[95] Keith Neilson, in line with his views about the DRC, strongly criticised Chamberlain for sacrificing naval power and the ability to defend world-wide interests for the sake of an ineffective air deterrent.[96] The gulf between Bell and Neilson's positions reflects that between Fisher and Hankey in 1934. Fisher's Treasury line was that Britain's capacity to conduct war depended not so much on what voters were willing to pay in taxes as on its purchasing power abroad, given the need to import food, raw materials and munitions. He urged that maximum strength be deployed against the principal danger. The Empire would be defenceless if Germany 'knocked out England'. Japan, by itself, could not do that, or even endanger trade routes, India, or Australia, if the Singapore base were completed, although Hong Kong and Britain's investments in China would be lost.[97] Hankey thought Fisher had never been sound about the navy or understood how Britain's interests in the Far East could be defended, and advised Baldwin in August 1934 that the Cabinet had overrated the '*imminence* of the German peril'.[98] Hankey seems, in retrospect, complacent about Germany, given that the Munich crisis was only four years away. On the other hand, Fisher (and Chamberlain) overestimated Britain's ability to deter Germany with air power. Sir Michael Howard granted that Chamberlain's ideas were 'at least coherent' compared with the chiefs of staff's willingness to dissipate British strength in the Empire's defence, but argued that failure to prepare an expeditionary force before 1939 deprived Britain of the means of maintaining the European balance of power, and asked how long Britain could be defended if Germany dominated the continent.[99] Thus it is possible to believe that Chamberlain made the right choice as between the German and Japanese threats, but the wrong choice in prioritising an air deterrent over an expeditionary force.

Chamberlain's success in reshaping grand strategy to give priority to the air force owed much to politicians' perceptions of public opinion. When defending his proposals in the Ministerial Committee on Disarmament on 25 June 1934, he argued that the defence programme could not be carried out without the support of the public, who would have to be educated in the facts of the international situation. He felt that to persuade taxpayers a war in the Far East constituted as great a menace as an air attack on Great Britain would be an extremely difficult task, the more so as 'public opinion was already alive to a considerable extent to our deficiencies in air defence'.[100] On 2 July Baldwin noted that a decision about the expansion of the RAF had to be taken before Parliament rose and 'something had to be done to satisfy the semi-panic conditions which existed now about the air'.[101]

No one had done more to rouse Parliament and the public to the air threat from Germany than Churchill. In a speech on 7 February 1934, he had warned that neglect of aerial defences would lead to the 'crash of bombs exploding in London' and 'cataracts of masonry and fire and smoke'.[102] At a time when the RAF was only about half the size of the French air force, he successfully pressed Baldwin to pledge on 8 March that Britain would have an air force as strong as France had or the one Germany was creating. Churchill's was not a lone voice. In the same debate Clement Attlee, the deputy leader of the Labour Party, remarked that air warfare was now decisive and asked whether the Air Ministry was being allocated an appropriate share of the defence budget (£17.6 million, compared with £56.6 million for the Admiralty and £40 million for the War Office).[103] Even so, when Churchill in a speech on 7 July called for an immediate vote of credit to double the size of the RAF, and another vote of credit as soon as possible to double it again, he was accused by the leader of the Liberal Opposition, Herbert Samuel, of using the 'language of blind and causeless panic'.[104] A vote of credit would have been an emergency measure to finance expenditure outside the annual budget and was therefore akin to Baldwin's suggestion of a defence loan. Another six months would pass before Chamberlain was prepared to consider borrowing for rearmament.

As a backbencher, Churchill did not attempt to set out a comprehensive view of grand strategy. In 1933 and 1934 he took a leading part in the debates on the air estimates, but apparently felt no need to do so in the debates on the navy or army estimates. In 1933 he said that the best defence against air attack was to bomb the enemy's air bases and factories, and in 1934 he called for research on how to destroy aircraft attacking Britain.[105] He accepted that German rearmament was inevitable because 'no one proposes a preventative war to prevent Germany breaking the Treaty of Versailles'. Like the government, he hoped a convention might be negotiated to limit air warfare and he argued in March 1934 that such a convention would be observed only if there was parity in air forces between the powers.[106]

Between them, Chamberlain and Churchill helped to bring about a remarkable change in the balance of defence expenditure. Had the DRC's report been accepted unchanged, the RAF would have continued to receive the smallest share (see Table 4.3a). In the event, the RAF's expenditure overtook that of the army in 1937 and of the navy in 1938 (Table 4.3b).

Table 4.3a *Forecasts of expenditure if recommendations of DRC accepted in full, and RAF share of total, 28 February 1934 (£ millions)*

Financial year	Royal Navy £ millions	British Army £ millions	RAF £ millions	RAF as % of total for three services
1934/35	56.2	44.4	17.7	14.9
1935/36	61.0	45.0	18.7	15.0
1936/37	63.3	45.2	20.3	15.8
1937/38	63.8	45.5	21.3	16.3
1938/39	65.1	45.7	21.3	16.1

Source: CP 64 (34), 28 Feb. 1934, table A (2), CAB 24/247/64

Table 4.3b *Actual expenditure and RAF's share of total, 1933/34 to 1938/39*

Financial year	Royal Navy £000s	British Army £000s	RAF £000s	RAF as a % of total for three services
1934/35	56,580	39,660	17,630	15.5
1935/36	64,806	44,647	27,496	20.1
1936/37	81,092	54,846	50,134	26.9
1937/38	101,950	77,877	82,290	31.4
1938/39	127,295	121,361	133,800	35.0

Source: *Statistical Abstract for the United Kingdom 1924 to 1938* (Cmd. 6232), p. 177, UK Parliamentary Papers 1939–40.

4.6   Anglo-Japanese Relations

Although Chamberlain reshaped defence policy, he was much less successful in his attempts to influence foreign policy. In October 1933 he
noted in Cabinet that the situation in the Far East hampered the prospects of achieving an agreement on limiting naval armaments. He said
he greatly regretted the weakening of Anglo-Japanese relations that had
resulted from the termination of the Anglo-Japanese alliance, at
American behest, at the Washington Conference in 1921–2. He asked
the foreign secretary, Simon, whether anything could be done to improve
matters. Simon claimed that Britain's attitude at Geneva during the
Manchurian crisis had ensured that relations were fairly good, but the
president of the Board of Trade, Walter Runciman, countered that
Japanese militarism, combined with attempts to flood Empire markets
with their exports, had created a bad situation. Simon undertook no
more than to consider Chamberlain's suggestion.[107] Chamberlain
returned to the subject the following month when the CID set up the
DRC, observing that, if it were possible to improve relations with Japan,
it might be possible to lower the Far East in priority compared with
Germany.[108] He regarded the danger of attack by Japan as 'by no means
negligible', but thought 'it ought to be possible to avoid it by wary and
skilful diplomacy'.[109]

The permanent secretary of the Treasury, Sir Warren Fisher thought
the United States had never been friendly to Britain since 'Colonial days'
and never would be. He believed the Americans used naval limitation
pacts to keep Britain 'on bad terms with the Japanese (and therefore
potentially weaker and less able to take an independent line vis-à-vis the
United States)'.[110] On his insistence, the DRC's report included statements that 'we cannot over-state the importance we attach to getting
back, not to an alliance (for that would not be practicable politics), but at
least to our old terms of cordiality and mutual respect with Japan', and
'there is much to be said for the view that our subservience to the United
States of America in past years has been one of the principal factors in the
deterioration of our former good relations with Japan', together with a
recommendation that, before the Naval Disarmament Conference due in
1935, 'we ought thoroughly to reconsider our general attitude'.[111]

When the DRC report was considered by the Cabinet in March 1934,
Chamberlain put forward for discussion the idea that Britain should
decline to align itself with the United States in opposing any change in
the proportions of 5:5:3 agreed at the Washington Conference for the
total tonnage of major warships in the American, British and Japanese
navies. If this were done, he said, the Japanese would no longer fear that

Britain might combine with the United States against them. He thought that, if the three countries were freed from treaty limitations, the Japanese would realise they could not compete with the Americans and, for financial reasons, would limit their building programme to something to which Britain could adjust. He therefore suggested a non-aggression pact with Japan, subject to assurances about the Japanese attitude to China. The chancellor received strong support from the first lord of the Admiralty, Sir Bolton Eyres-Monsell, who thought Japan might not press its demand for equality if it had a non-aggression pact with Britain. He remarked that such a pact might actually please the Americans since it would show Britain could exert influence on Japan. Simon also supported the idea of a non-aggression pact, but the prime minister, MacDonald, feared it would be regarded in the United States as an alliance. The dominions secretary, 'Jimmy' Thomas, said Canada would be pro-American in the matter, but Australia and New Zealand would welcome a non-aggression pact.[112]

The initial warm response from Simon and Eyres-Monsell to Chamberlain's suggestions cooled once departmental officials had a chance to advise their ministers. Vansittart had already made clear in the DRC that Anglo-American relations should not be sacrificed for an Anglo-Japanese *rapprochement*. He suspected Japanese professions in early 1934 of a desire to re-establish cordial relations with Britain were motivated by insecurity vis-à-vis the Soviet Union. Thinking in terms of the global balance of power, he saw antagonism between Japan and the Soviet Union as a restraint on either of these powers doing harm to British interests. He was also influenced by a turn in Soviet foreign policy away from co-operation with Germany, following the advent of the Nazi regime, towards seeking co-operation with France and better relations with Britain. Initially sceptical about Soviet intentions, Vansittart came by the summer of 1934 to see the advantages of a Franco-Soviet counter-weight to Germany and the disadvantages of alienating the Soviet Union by making a non-aggression pact with Japan.[113] Under Vansittart's influence, Simon became less enthusiastic about such a pact. In September he told Chamberlain that the principal effect would be to give Japan a free hand in the Far East as long as it respected British possessions, thereby encouraging Japanese designs on China and probably increasing the risk of Japanese aggression against the Dutch East Indies (now Indonesia).[114] Chamberlain persuaded Simon and a reluctant Vansittart over dinner on 24 September that the British ambassador in Tokyo, Sir Robert Clive, should sound out the Japanese government.[115] Arguing his case in Cabinet, Chamberlain said 'clearly we could not contemplate giving Japan a free hand in China or Shanghai or in the Dutch East Indies or to do what she thought fit by way of aggression against the Soviet'.[116] In the event, Clive elicited little by way of positive response from Tokyo, and Chamberlain complained bitterly to Simon that the ambassador, instructed by the Foreign Office, had not pressed the matter with sufficient enthusiasm.[117]

Meanwhile Fisher, with Chamberlain's approval, had briefed a British businessman, A. H. F. Edwardes, to lobby members of the Japanese Cabinet with what, to the Treasury, seemed promising results.[118] Fisher also tried his hand at diplomacy by lunching with the Japanese ambassador in London, Matsudaira Tsuneo, on 24 October 1934 to convey to him Chamberlain's views. Fisher reported the ambassador had said there was a 'Jingo' party in Japan but it was diminishing in power. On the question of a non-aggression pact, Matsudaira said he would be glad to include the United States in a tripartite pact as the best guarantee against war in the Far East. As for the Naval Disarmament Conference, he told Fisher that, if the Japanese claim for a common upper limit was rejected and the United States embarked on a large building programme, Japan would not follow suit if Britain did not. Chamberlain was encouraged and had no doubt that Britain could easily make an agreement with Japan were it not for the Americans.[119] He wished he could have taken part in disarmament conversations with the Japanese which took place in London in November 1934 but, as he himself said, he had no status in them.[120] Political negotiations were the province of the Foreign Office, not the Treasury.

The first sea lord, Chatfield, and the naval staff were no less opposed than Vansittart to Chamberlain's ideas. In a paper submitted in April 1934 to the Cabinet Committee on the London Naval Conference, they had made clear their preference for retaining the 5:3 ratio between the Royal Navy and the Japanese navy and for agreeing maximum tonnages for major warships, thereby contradicting Chamberlain's suggestion it would be better to be freed from treaty limitations. Fisher pointed out that Britain was in no position financially to threaten to out-build the Japanese. Chatfield allowed that, if the Japanese would not agree to the 5:3 ratio, the best thing would be to beg to differ and to avoid a quarrel rather than to combine with the Americans to insist upon it. Like Vansittart, however, he did not want to fall out with the United States, and he was certainly not willing to accept an improvement in relations with Japan as a reason for not carrying out the full naval programmes of the DRC report.[121] By July Fisher was complaining to Chatfield that, in talks with the Americans, MacDonald and Eyres-Monsell had already given an undertaking – or what the Americans would certainly interpret as an undertaking – that in the event of disagreements with Japan at the conference Britain would align itself with the United States. Such a policy, he believed, would remove any chance of getting on to permanently good terms with Japan.[122] However, the most the Treasury could achieve was the agreement of the Cabinet in October that Fisher, along with Chatfield and Robert Craigie of the Foreign Office, would advise the British delegation. The delegation itself comprised MacDonald, Eyres-Monsell and Simon, but not Chamberlain. In November Roosevelt called in *The Times* Washington correspondent and warned against an Anglo-Japanese deal. After talks between the United States and British delegations later that month, Norman Davis, the principal American negotiator, was rightly confident the chancellor's pro-Japanese line would not prevail.[123]

China's monetary problems gave Chamberlain an opportunity to take an initiative in the Far East in a sphere where the Treasury's technical expertise gave it an advantage over the Foreign Office. The American silver lobby had campaigned successfully in 1934 for a policy whereby the United States government purchased the metal at steadily increasing prices. An unintended consequence was an increase in the value of the Chinese silver dollar, causing a deepening depression in that country as prices of goods fell.[124] The Chinese government approached the British government for a £20 million loan in the autumn of 1934, and in interdepartmental discussions in December, Fisher pronounced himself in favour of an approach to Japan for a joint financial assistance for China. Chamberlain took up the idea, and the Foreign Office acquiesced in the Treasury taking the lead. In August 1935 a Treasury official, Sir Frederick Leith-Ross, was despatched to the Far East to advise the Chinese on how to rehabilitate their currency and also to seek the co-operation of Japan in a joint guarantee of a loan for China as part of a deal over Manchuria. The first objective was achieved in November when the Chinese abandoned the silver standard for a managed paper currency, but the second proved to be elusive. The powerful Japanese military had no wish for China to be strengthened through joint financial aid or otherwise. Chamberlain agreed with the Foreign Office that it would be dangerous to proceed with the loan in the face of Japanese opposition, but it was not until May 1936 that he agreed to recall Leith-Ross. Chamberlain seems to have accepted the mission was a failure as he made no attempt to take up any of the recommendations that Leith-Ross made in his report to the Cabinet.

Historians have been generally critical of Chamberlain's attempts to influence foreign policy towards Japan. Greg Kennedy cited them as further evidence that Chamberlain was the worst of Britain's strategic foreign-policy makers in the interwar period, noting how the chancellor based his ideas on unofficial sources ('anecdotal evidence, hearsay') rather than on advice from the Foreign Office and the Admiralty, whose experts made assessments from multiple intelligence sources.[125] Anthony Best, who argued the Leith-Ross mission was primarily an attempt to revive Britain's economic and political influence in East Asia rather than an exercise in appeasement, nevertheless considered Chamberlain to have been dangerously naïve regarding Japan's determination to go its own way in China.[126] Peter Bell, on the other hand, argued it was by no means certain at the time that some arrangement with Japan was unattainable and that, given the risks that Britain faced, diplomacy was an avenue worth exploring.[127] The Japanese historian Kibata Yoichi pointed out there were civilian elements in the Japanese government who wished to co-operate with Britain, although their influence was waning and that of the military was waxing.[128] Churchill began to be concerned about Japan as a predatory dictatorship only from January 1936, after further Japanese aggression in China and the collapse of the London Naval Disarmament Conference. As late as February 1937 he wrote that he had always been in favour of the Anglo-Japanese alliance, although not at the expense of Anglo-American relations.[129] There was, perhaps, more uncertainty about Japan than hindsight suggests. In the event, whatever the merits of Chamberlain's ideas, the chancellor had no influence on Anglo-Japanese relations or on naval disarmament because the Foreign Office and the Admiralty had the prestige and confidence to stand up to the Treasury.

5   The Ethiopian and Rhineland Crises

5.1   The German Threat Increases

On 15 November 1934 the Deuxième Section of the French Air Ministry supplied British Air Intelligence with secret information on German aircraft production that showed it was vastly in excess of the needs of civil aviation.[1] Six days later the Cabinet was told by the Air Ministry there was reason to believe that in a year's time Germany would have as large an air force as Britain. The matter was urgent for ministers because the subject was due to be raised by Churchill in Parliament in the following week.[2] A small Cabinet sub-committee, which did not include Chamberlain, was appointed to collate facts and to make proposals on what line to take in the debate. Assessments by the three defence departments and the Industrial Intelligence Centre (IIC) indicated that Germany's rearmament was by no means confined to the air force it was forbidden to have under the Treaty of Versailles. The German army was reported to be expanding to three times its permitted limit of 100,000 men and to be equipped with weapons such as tanks that were forbidden by the treaty.[3] However, it was the German air force that absorbed ministers' attention at a special meeting of the Cabinet on 26 November. During their discussion they decided the RAF's expansion programme, authorised only four months earlier, should be completed in two years instead of four, in anticipation of parliamentary criticism and for the deterrent effect on Germany. Chamberlain protested that nothing in the intelligence on German preparations justified this acceleration, that the Air Ministry had said the present programme was as much as could be accomplished efficiently without waste of money, and that at least an additional £500,000 would be required in the coming year and larger amounts in later years. He was overruled.[4]

Churchill's speech on 28 November was a remarkable statement of how the air threat was seen in the 1930s. He predicted that a week to ten days of intensive bombing on London would result in 30,000 or 40,000 people being killed or seriously injured. He thought 3 or 4 million citizens would flee into the open countryside, without food, shelter or sanitation, and the Regular and Territorial armies would be wholly occupied with maintaining law and order. He called for urgent research on air defence, but said that meantime the only defence was the threat of retaliatory bombing on the same scale as the aggressor. Briefed by the head of the IIC, Desmond Morton, Churchill said that Germany would achieve air parity with Britain before the end of 1935, and would be nearly twice as strong in 1937. Baldwin responded with Air Ministry estimates that Britain would have nearly 50 per cent superiority in Europe alone at the end of 1935, and, while refusing to forecast what the position would be in 1937, pledged not to accept 'any position of inferiority with regard to whatever air force may be raised in Germany'.[5]

Meanwhile the chiefs of staff had recommended that planning for a war with Germany should be completed in five years from 1934. When the CID considered the matter on 22 November 1934, Viscount Hailsham, the secretary of state for war, reminded his colleagues that the DRC had recommended in February that deficiencies should be put right in five years but the Cabinet had extended that period for financial reasons. Both the prime minister, Ramsay MacDonald, and the foreign secretary, Sir John Simon, thought war with Germany might come within five years, but MacDonald observed that the country could not 'run the risk of a financial smash' (a reference to the searing experience of 1931). The chiefs of staff's recommendation was approved on the understanding that no question of finance was involved and action was limited to drawing up plans.[6]

At the Treasury the permanent secretary, Sir Warren Fisher, felt something should be done to make the public aware of the danger posed by Germany and to prepare the way for higher taxation. In January 1935 he, the permanent under-secretary of the Foreign Office, Sir Robert Vansittart, and the cabinet secretary, Sir Maurice Hankey, suggested to MacDonald and the Conservative party leader, Stanley Baldwin, that a white paper should be published to set out reasons for an increase in defence expenditure. Hankey produced a first draft in consultation with Fisher, Vansittart and the chiefs of staff, but the version published on 1 March reflected ministers' views. Chamberlain toned down some of the Foreign Office's passages about the German threat, and Fisher complained to Baldwin that the changes from the first draft weakened the warning required to dispel the effect of 'so-called pacifist propaganda'.[7] However, Baldwin, conscious that 1935 was an election year, did not respond to Fisher's plea for stronger language. Hitler took umbrage at the white paper's reference to Germany's as-yet-undeclared rearmament and developed a diplomatic cold, so that a projected visit to

Berlin by Simon and the lord privy seal, Anthony Eden, had to be postponed. Chamberlain thought the white paper and Hitler's 'childish' reaction had given a sharp shock to public opinion.[8]

Further shocks followed. On 15 March the French Chamber of Deputies voted in favour of extending the period of compulsory military service from one year to two. Hitler responded the next day by promulgating a law establishing conscription for the German army, a clear breach of the Treaty of Versailles. Then, when Simon and Eden finally visited Berlin on 25 and 26 March, he claimed Germany had already attained parity in the air with Britain and intended soon to do so with France.[9] This revelation came a week after Churchill had claimed in Parliament that parity had been lost, despite Baldwin's pledge four months earlier.[10] The Air Ministry was still reluctant to embark on a rapid expansion programme, fearing being left at the end with a large stock of obsolescent aircraft, and arguing that training standards would be compromised.[11] Nevertheless, the Ministerial Committee on Defence Requirements set up a sub-committee on Air Parity at the end of April, and its reports led to the adoption on 21 May of a new expansion programme – Scheme C – which added 39 squadrons to the 84 to be based in Great Britain in the July 1934 programme, a total of 1,512 aircraft to be completed by 31 March 1937. Speaking as chancellor in the Ministerial Committee on Defence Requirements, Chamberlain expressed anxiety about wasteful expenditure arising from placing orders for large numbers of aircraft that had not been fully tested, but broadly supported what he regarded as a truly formidable programme that would act as a deterrent.[12]

Chamberlain's financial views were markedly less orthodox in 1935 than when he had dismissed the idea of a defence loan the previous year. In January, at a time when Lloyd George was trying to revive the Liberal Party's electoral fortunes by putting forward proposals for government borrowing for measures to cure unemployment, the chancellor asked his officials whether parts of the defence programme could be financed in that way. In particular, he had in mind the creation of industrial capacity to be used for armaments production in the event of war. Sir Richard Hopkins replied that, according to the then accepted principles of public finance, government borrowing should be restricted to projects that would produce an income that would repay the loan with interest. Idle reserves of industrial plant would not, he advised, meet this requirement. However, towards the end of the month the Treasury received intelligence that the German government was borrowing on a large scale to finance rearmament. Fisher drew the attention of MacDonald and Baldwin, as well as Chamberlain, to these reports. By the time the RAF's expansion programme was being discussed in the spring, Treasury officials were prepared to accept there might be a case for spreading the cost of rearmament over a longer period by raising a defence loan. When the DRC was reconstituted early in July to re-examine the programmes of the navy, army and air force in the light of developments since its first report 16 months earlier, it was the permanent secretary of the Treasury who suggested they should draw up a five-year programme on the assumption there would be a defence loan.[13] By August, in the light of an interim report by the DRC, Chamberlain was noting in his diary that 'Germany is said to be borrowing over £1000 million a year to get herself rearmed', and thought Britain would have to spend an extra £120 million over four or five years to hurry its own rearmament.[14] The latter sum was small both in relation to what Germany was reported to be spending and to the additional sums over the 1935 estimates that the DRC would call for in November (£417 million over five years).[15] Nevertheless, the chancellor was clearly more willing to loosen the purse strings than he had been the previous summer when he had attempted to cut the first DRC programme from £71 million to £56 million.

Chamberlain's concern about Germany influenced his views on foreign policy. Prior to Simon and Eden's visit to Berlin in March 1935, he told Eden it would be necessary to speak very plainly to Hitler and warn him there were only two ways of attaining security: a system of pacts like Locarno or, if the Germans would not participate, a system of alliances.[16] He would have liked to go with MacDonald and Simon when they met Mussolini and the French premier, Pierre Laval, at Stresa in the following month to discuss German violations of the Treaty of Versailles, but recognised that that was impossible.[17] Fascist Italy seemed to be a plausible ally against Germany, both as a signatory of the Treaty of Locarno and because Mussolini had moved troops towards the Brenner Pass when an attempted Nazi *putsch* occurred in Austria in 1934. Britain, France and Italy agreed at Stresa in April 1935 to reaffirm Locarno and to resist further German breaches of Versailles. However, Britain failed to consult France and Italy before signing, two months later, the Anglo-German Naval Agreement, which recognised Germany's right to build beyond the Versailles limit up to 35 per cent of the total tonnage of the Royal Navy's surface vessels (45 per cent for submarines, with an option to increase to 100 per cent). Chamberlain thought the terms were so good as to be suspicious, but he believed the treaty gave Britain control over the German navy and it had been right to clinch Hitler's offer.[18]

Churchill, in contrast, criticised the agreement for condoning a breach of Versailles and thereby weakening the 'Stresa Front'. It would have been far better, he said, to take the German claim to the League of

Nations to muster support there for collective security. He predicted Germany would build up to the 35 per cent limit in four or five years. Given the age of much of the Royal Navy, Britain would have to replace half of its fleet, and even then, he thought, would not have enough ships to spare from the North Sea to protect British interests in the Far East. He urged the government to raise a defence loan with the rebuilding of the fleet as the first charge on it.[19] This speech appears to have been the only occasion in the 1930s that Churchill gave the navy a higher priority than the air force. Joseph Maiolo has challenged the view, implicit in Churchill's criticism, that the Anglo-German Naval Agreement was a sign of weakness. He argued that the Admiralty saw it as a first step to reshape the international naval balance to maintain Britain's status as a great power. If Germany could be persuaded to build standard warships rather than a fleet of specialist commerce raiders, British capital ships could be designed to serve in the Far East as well as home waters. The Admiralty hoped to persuade the Cabinet to approve a two-power standard, and then the Royal Navy would build enough such ships to be able to meet its world-wide commitments.[20]

5.2   The Ethiopian Crisis

The Stresa Front's collapse proved to be inevitable owing to Mussolini's ambitions in Africa. Mussolini wanted a military triumph to match his rhetoric about the Roman Empire being reborn: hence his plans to invade Ethiopia, where Italy had suffered a humiliating defeat in a colonial war less than 40 years earlier. In January 1935 Laval met Mussolini in Rome and gave him the impression France would give Italy a free hand in Ethiopia, although the French premier later claimed he had agreed only to peaceful economic penetration of that backward country.[21] Laval was intent on securing Italian support against Germany, and Mussolini agreed to Franco-Italian staff talks that led to a military convention. Mussolini was further encouraged when MacDonald and Simon said nothing about Ethiopia at Stresa, although by then Italy was openly making military preparations for a campaign in East Africa. However, Ethiopia was a member of the League of Nations and British public opinion would expect the British government to participate in economic sanctions against an aggressor.

On 16 June Vansittart advised the newly appointed foreign secretary, Sir Samuel Hoare, that, if Mussolini were thwarted, Italy would leave the League and 'throw itself into the arms of Germany', breaking the League and the Stresa Front. The permanent under-secretary proposed that land-locked Ethiopia should be offered a port in British Somaliland

and be asked in return to cede territory to Italy.[22] Chamberlain approved this 'ingenious proposition', but Mussolini aimed at control of the whole of Ethiopia, not just its desert fringes, as he made clear to Anthony Eden (now minister for League of Nations affairs) when the latter visited Rome later that month.[23] On his way back through Paris, Eden met Laval, who suggested the best solution might be an Italian protectorate over the whole of Ethiopia, just as France had a protectorate over Morocco. It was clear the French were unlikely to take action that might deprive them of Italian support against Germany. In August, Eden and Laval agreed, as a basis for further discussion, that the League could be asked to approve a plan whereby Italy would be given a predominant role in the economic development and administrative reorganisation of Ethiopia.[24] Mussolini was too committed to military action to back down without loss of prestige and rejected the offer.

Like other ministers, Chamberlain was not much concerned with the fate of an African country in which Britain had no significant interests. On the other hand, the Peace Ballot results published in June indicated considerable public support for collective action through the League, and there was a general election pending.[25] In July he contemplated the closure of the Suez Canal to Italian forces, but only if that action were backed by France.[26] He thought that economic sanctions alone would be futile if, as he expected, Germany and the United States, did not impose them. He expressed his frustration by writing to his sisters in August: 'what I hope for is a reconstructed League to deal with European affairs and what I shall work for is a Britain strong enough to make it impossible for her wishes to be flouted again as Mussolini has flouted them now'.[27]

Hoare consulted Churchill on 21 August and found he too thought that any action against Italy should be collective, by which he meant principally Anglo-French co-operation. Churchill wished to preserve the League as a deterrent to German aggression. He therefore advised that the government should make clear that Britain was prepared to carry out its League obligations, even to the point of war, provided other members were prepared to do the same. However, he realized Laval was in an extremely difficult position in that friendship with Italy was important for the defence of France. Churchill therefore urged that a policy of sanctions should be carried no further than France was willing to go.[28] Like Vansittart, he saw that sanctions might bring Italy and Germany together, with the latter sending war materials through Austria. Nor did he think the Admiralty should despise the Italians and suppose they would never dare to fight: 'Mussolini's Italy may be quite different from that of the Great War', he wrote.[29] The Admiralty did not, in fact, underestimate the Italians: it wanted time for preparations and, although confident of success in any naval action, worried about possible loss of ships, especially given the unknown factor of Italian air power, with a consequent weakening of the fleet that could be sent to the Far East in the event of trouble with Japan.[30] Churchill 'dreamed of a Cromwellian administration which would have handled the Italian dictator in a resolute fashion', but feared that a combination of military weakness and the government's policy would lead to the crippling of the League, the humiliation of Britain, the estrangement of Italy and the subjugation of Ethiopia.[31] In a speech at the Carlton Club on 26 September he expressed surprise that 'so great man and so wise ruler' as Mussolini should be eager to 'cast an army ... upon a barren shore 2000 miles from home against the good will of the whole world and without command of the sea'. He did not, however, advocate fighting the Italians, whom he referred to as 'our comrades and old allies'.[32] He was no less keen than Vansittart to maintain Italy as a powerful and friendly factor in Europe.[33]

With Chamberlain's help, Hoare prepared a speech, to be delivered at Geneva on 12 September, to explain Britain's double policy of negotiation with Italy and loyalty to the League. In it the foreign secretary stressed that the League was weak because the United States, Germany and Japan were not members, and he repeatedly used the word 'collective' to indicate that collective security must be really comprehensive. He was amazed by the enthusiastic response of journalists, who interpreted it as a rallying call.[34] When the Italian invasion of Ethiopia began on 3 October, the League agreed to an embargo on arms exports and to limited economic sanctions but, as Chamberlain had foreseen, the United States did not participate in the latter. Laval had to agree to sanctions in order to retain the support of the Radical Party for his government, but he continued to seek a negotiated settlement with Mussolini. Italian hostility was directed at Britain and the DRC had to consider the implications for grand strategy. Vansittart now doubted the likelihood of Mussolini's co-operation in maintaining peace in Europe and warned that Italy ultimately sought dominance in the Mediterranean.[35] Hitherto DRC planning had made provision only against Germany and Japan, and Britain's defences in the Mediterranean had been neglected. Vansittart and Hankey noted that this weakness made the security of the British Empire dependent on France, since, as Chatfield warned, the Italian navy posed a threat to imperial communications through the Suez Canal.[36] Britain strengthened its forces in the Mediterranean region sufficiently to dissuade Mussolini from any 'mad dog' act.[37] However, France did not take even preliminary precautions.

When Parliament discussed the international situation before being prorogued on 25 October for the general election, Churchill insisted that Italy's war with Ethiopia was 'a very small matter' compared with the threat posed by German rearmament. He showed understanding of France's wish not to prejudice its military convention with Italy, and praised both the League for imposing economic sanctions and Mussolini for not regarding these as an act of war. Churchill professed to hope that slow pressure from sanctions, backed by British sea power, would make possible a satisfactory settlement along the lines of the Anglo-French offer to Mussolini in August. He expressed sympathy for the 'primitive, feudal' Ethiopians fighting for their independence, but said no one could pretend their country was 'a fit, worthy and equal member of a civilised league of nations'. In particular, he said that what he described as 'oppression' by the dominant race there of tribes conquered in the 1890s must not be perpetuated by the action of the League of Nations. He urged that the Ethiopians must be made to put their house in order – a statement that could be taken as code for an Italian role in supervising economic and administrative reform.[38]

Baldwin went into the 1935 general election on 14 November with a manifesto promising that the League would remain 'the keystone of British foreign policy' and that, with regard to Ethiopia, 'there will be no wavering in the policy we have hitherto pursued'.[39] Within Whitehall, Vansittart warned of a risk of war if economic sanctions were extended to oil, as had been proposed at Geneva, and that France was unreliable.[40] Oil sanctions had become a symbol of the League's determination and were regarded by the Cabinet as necessary to placate British public opinion, even though Board of Trade and Foreign Office studies had shown that an embargo by League members would be ineffective as Italy could secure adequate suppliers from non-members, particularly the United States.[41] Chamberlain noted in his diary on 29 November that the American government had gone a good deal further in support of economic sanctions than usual and, if Britain backed out because of Mussolini's threats, the United States would decline to help in any way in future, sanctions would crumble, and the League would lose its coherence. He thought Britain ought to give a lead on oil sanctions if no other country would.[42] On 2 December the Cabinet agreed Hoare should press on with peace negotiations as rapidly as possible with a view to bringing the conflict to an end before oil sanctions were tried. Chamberlain believed this was the sensible course, since the purpose of sanctions was to stop the war. Accompanied by Vansittart, the foreign secretary met Laval in Paris on 7 and 8 December to discuss a basis for a possible settlement. As with Vansittart's proposal in June, Ethiopia was to be offered access to the sea in return for territorial concessions, and Italy was to have a monopoly over the economic development of a large part of the country. Hoare went on to Switzerland to recuperate from stress, and in his absence Eden explained the new proposal, which he supported, to the Cabinet, which recorded its approval on the 9th.[43] However, the Cabinet subsequently recanted when the terms of the Hoare-Laval Pact, which had been leaked in Paris, provoked protests in the press, in Parliament and at Geneva. Even *The Times*, normally supportive of the government, did much to damn the proposals by referring on 16 December to the strip of territory that Ethiopia was to receive as a 'corridor for camels'. (It was reported that Ethiopia would not be allowed to build a railway there.)[44] Chamberlain did his best to protect Hoare, a political ally, from pressure to resign. However, the foreign secretary eventually did so on 18 December and was succeeded by Eden.

Chamberlain was thus implicated in a policy that can be characterised as appeasement in the sense of weakness and shameful failure to stand up to dictators. However, it was a policy that had its origins in, and was executed by, the Foreign Office, with Vansittart as its principal proponent. Churchill avoided making any comment on the Hoare-Laval Pact at the time by extending a holiday in Spain, but in 1948 he wrote that Vansittart 'should not be misjudged because he thought continuously of the German threat and wished to have Britain and France organised at their strongest to face this major danger, with Italy in their rear a friend and not a foe'.[45] When, in February 1936, Labour MPs called for oil sanctions, Churchill warned that these might precipitate war and apparently thought that was a decisive argument against them.[46]

It can be argued, nevertheless, that Vansittart's policy towards Italy had been misconceived. As Clement Attlee, leader of the Opposition, observed, allowing a wrong-doer to profit at the expense of the victim encouraged violence in international relations and undermined the foundations of collective security.[47] Looking back in April 1937 at the end of his period in Berlin, the British ambassador, Sir Eric Phipps, thought that no event had influenced German foreign policy more decisively than the imposition and subsequent failure of sanctions against Italy, as the reduction in British prestige and the break-up of the Stresa Front encouraged Hitler to be more adventurous and demanding.[48] However, in February 1936 Vansittart thought a League victory over Italy would not influence Hitler, who would base his judgement on his estimates of the strength and readiness of the League powers, which, given the progress of British and French rearmament, left much to be desired.[49]

Churchill, in a conversation with Hankey in April 1936, after the German remilitarization of the Rhineland, recommended giving the Italians an ultimatum that unless they agreed to come to terms with the League, Britain would close the Suez Canal (an action that would force them to supply their forces in East Africa via the Cape of Good Hope). He was, however, as Hankey noted, 'talking rather at large, and probably without having thought matters out'. That would account for Churchill's idea, put forward in the same conversation, of warning the French that if they did not support the ultimatum, Britain would come to terms with Germany.[50] Churchill later remarked that if the government was not prepared to back words at Geneva with action, 'it might have been better to keep out of it all, like the United States, and let things rip and see what happened'.[51] Duff Cooper, who would establish a reputation as an anti-appeaser when he resigned from the Chamberlain government over the Munich agreement, recalled he thought in 1935 that Italy had good grounds for complaint against Ethiopia and it would have been better to 'hold the ring for a fair fight [sic]' and to offer Britain's services as a mediator. He added that the opportunity should have been taken to dissolve the ties binding Britain to the 'decaying corpse of the League'. In retrospect he believed that retaining Italian friendship would have prevented the formation of the Axis, without which Hitler 'could hardly have launched the Second World War'.[52] Everyone agreed that collective action depended upon French support. Even the League of Nations Union made clear to Baldwin during the furore over the Hoare-Laval Pact that it had never wished Britain to take unilateral action.[53]

Shortly before the Ethiopian capital, Addis Ababa, fell to the Italians on 5 May 1936, Chamberlain noted in his diary that he had been discussing the war with Eden. Chamberlain argued that collective security in its existing form had failed and it should be replaced by a series of regional pacts to be approved by the League. Such a system, he thought, would enable Britain to participate in pacts that directly concerned its interests, such as Locarno or the Far East, but would leave Eastern Europe to other powers.[54] Chamberlain believed Eden shared his views, but was aware the foreign secretary hoped that if sanctions remained in place until the League Assembly met in September, a collective decision could be taken to end them in return for Italian commitments to maintain an open door to trade with Ethiopia and not to raise an army there.[55] Chamberlain initially agreed that sanctions should not be given up without receiving something in return.[56] However, by 10 June he had changed his mind. In what he himself called a 'blazing indiscretion', he declared in a speech at Grosvenor House that the continuation of sanctions was 'the very mid-summer of madness'. Collective security had been tried out and had failed because, he said, the task was beyond the League's powers. The conclusion he drew was that, whatever foreign policy was adopted, Britain must be adequately armed. He did not consult Eden before making these remarks because he felt the foreign secretary would, on account of his office, be obliged to ask him not to make them, even if he agreed with them. Chamberlain seems to have been expressing a widespread opinion in the Conservative Party. He described himself to his sisters as giving a lead when ministers who should have done had failed to do so.[57] Churchill was one member of the party who agreed with him. Some five weeks earlier, after the collapse of the Ethiopian field forces, he had told his constituents he found himself in agreement with Sir Austen Chamberlain that a policy of sanctions out of mere revenge and without any prospect of materially benefiting Ethiopian tribesmen could not be justified. After Eden announced the end of sanctions on 18 June, Churchill said he supported the government on the issue.[58] He was well aware that Mussolini might throw in his lot with Hitler, but had not yet abandoned hope that the Italian occupation of Ethiopia could be regularised along the lines of France's protectorate over Morocco, and Italy could resume its place in the League's system of collective security.[59]

5.3   Drawing Up the Rearmament Programme

The pace of Britain's defence preparations accelerated following reports by the DRC on 24 July and 21 November 1935.[60] The July report was a preliminary survey of defence requirements and asked for political guidance before new programmes were worked out in detail. It described how the international situation had deteriorated since the DRC's first report in February 1934. The dispute with Italy over Ethiopia threatened to weaken the unity of the powers that could hold Germany in check, while the time was rapidly approaching when Japan would be relatively at its strongest in the Far East. Germany's navy was not expected to be ready for war before 1942, but its army would approach numerical equality with the French in 1939 and have marked superiority by 1942. The DRC said there was no reason why the German air force could not match the expansion scheme approved for the RAF two months earlier for 1,512 first-line aircraft based in Britain by April 1937, or exceed that figure by a third by the end of 1938, although it was thought unlikely that German squadrons would be fully trained by then. As an autocracy, Germany could divert resources to rearmament so as to be ready for war at its own selected date. Vansittart thought Germany was unlikely to go to war deliberately before 1942, but might do so by miscalculation. Readiness for war was a relative term, he said, and Germany might take advantage of British unprepared-ness to embark on an adventure in Central or Eastern Europe. The permanent under-secretary regarded 1 January 1939 as the latest date when Germany might do so, and he could not guarantee it would remain politically quiescent until then. The report – whose signatories included the permanent secretary of the Treasury, Fisher – recommended that financial considerations should be of secondary importance when aiming at the earliest possible security, and that each service should be as ready by the end of the financial year 1938/39 as normal peacetime conditions allowed. The CID's Defence Policy and Requirements Sub-Committee (DPRC), which included Chamberlain, agreed on 29 July 1935 that the DRC should work out programmes on this basis and report on what special measures for increasing factory output would be necessary to achieve the necessary level of preparedness by the end of March 1939, and what level of preparedness could be achieved without these measures.[61]

The DRC's November report described a situation that had deteriorated further. Italy was now antagonistic to Britain. France had shown itself to be unreliable and could not be counted on as an ally unless it faced a direct threat to itself. The United States was more isolationist than ever. Japan intended to dominate the Far East, as Germany intended to dominate Europe. Diplomacy, the sub-committee advised, must aim at avoiding a situation where Britain faced hostility simultaneously from Japan in the Far East, Germany in the West and Italy on the main line of communication between the two. Italy was expected to require a period of recuperation after its efforts in Ethiopia, and the DRC advised it was neither urgently necessary nor feasible to add to the defence requirements against Germany and Japan by making provision for a permanently hostile Italy. Another new consideration was the enormous increase in Germany's capacity to produce aircraft, which raised the possibility of an attack on such a scale, the sub-committee warned, that the morale of any population might be so undermined as to make it difficult to continue the war. The DRC recommended an addition of 183 aircraft to the figure of 1,512 agreed for the RAF in May; the substitution of larger bombers for those currently in production, and the provision of substantial war reserves. However, the report set out larger increases for the other two services. Naval strength should be based on a new, two-power standard that would allow Britain to send to the Far East a fleet fully adequate to act on the defensive and be a strong deterrent to Japan, while being able at all times to meet the requirements of a war against Germany. The army's Field Force should be prepared to fight in Europe within two weeks of the outbreak of a war and – a major addition to the first DRC report in 1934 – the Territorial Army should be fully equipped so that it could provide reinforcements thereafter.[62] If the report had been accepted by ministers in full, the existing balance of expenditure between the services would have been preserved, with only a temporary increase in the RAF's share of the defence budget (see Table 5.1).

Table 5.1. *Forecasts of expenditure if recommendations of DRC accepted in full, and RAF share of total, 21 November 1935 (£ millions)*

Financial year	Royal Navy (£ millions)	British Army (£ millions)	RAF (£ millions)	RAF share RAF as % of total for three services
1935/6 (actual)	64.8	44.7	27.5	20.1
1936/37	74.9	54.0	45.0	25.9
1937/38	89.0	62.0	60.0	28.4
1938/39	90.7	72.0	64.0	28.2
1939/40	90.7	72.0	50.0	23.5
1940/41	83.3	82.0	44.0	21.0

Sources: 1935/36 – Cmd. 6232, p. 177; 1936/37 to 1940/41 – Third Report of the Defence Requirements Sub-Committee, DRC 37, 21 Nov. 1935, table IVc, CAB 16/112.

Although the report was presented to the prime minister, Baldwin, on 21 November, its contents were not discussed collectively by ministers in the DPRC until 13 January 1936. In the interim it was examined by Lord Weir, the industrialist, who was invited to join the DPRC. Weir noted that the DRC proposals would double expenditure on defence equipment over the next five years, and said he did not see how the engineering, metallurgical and shipbuilding industries could recruit the necessary additional workers without interfering with normal business activity. Runciman, the president of the Board of Trade, was as opposed as Chamberlain to interference with production for civil or export trade. Hankey, the cabinet secretary who had drafted the report, explained it set out 'a policy of perfection' over a period of three to five years, with a view to getting as much done as possible. No one challenged Weir when he said the kind of controls on industry exercised by the state in Germany and the Soviet Union could not be replicated in Britain. He saw the solution in the shadow factories scheme whereby firms outside the arms industry would be asked to create capacity for aircraft or munitions production in return for 'educational orders' and payment by the state of their outlays plus a management fee. He also advised that, while there must be no profiteering, contracts should not be delayed by financial controls.[63] From February, Treasury sanction of defence departments' expenditure was expedited by thrice-weekly meetings of a new Treasury Inter-Service Committee at which approval of new proposals was given promptly orally with formal correspondence following only as confirmation.

At the DPRC meeting on 13 January 1936 Chamberlain once more made the case for cutting down on the Field Force and increasing expenditure on the RAF. He believed that in a European war the Germans would outflank the French and Belgian fortifications by advancing through Holland, and would seize air bases in the Low Countries before an expeditionary force could be disembarked on the Continent. He therefore wanted the air force to have 'unprecedented powers of destruction' to act as 'the most terrifying deterrent we can think of'.[64] The foreign secretary, Eden, agreed with him, and added that the best chance of securing a convention with Germany to limit air armaments was to expand the RAF as quickly as possible. Weir, who had been an advocate of strategic bombing when he had been minister in charge of the RAF in 1918, thought numerical parity was scarcely enough to aim at, given London's greater vulnerability to air attack than any target in Germany. Lord Swinton, the secretary of state for air, pointed out the existing RAF programme was greater than the aircraft industry could fulfil, and ministers agreed that orders should be placed with other firms. To that extent, some diversion of industrial production from civil or export trade was accepted. However, that concession did not extend to the army, which Weir and Chamberlain argued was the most expensive way of helping allies and would make the largest demands on manufacturing resources.[65]

The changes made by the DPRC to the DRC report before it was presented to the Cabinet indicate the limits of Chamberlain's influence as chancellor on defence policy. In the case of the navy, ministers accepted his suggestion that the proposed two-power standard should not be adopted 'at present', but the Admiralty should be authorised to work out a programme to give it effect, and the committee should then consider whether it should be implemented. Industrial capacity would limit naval expansion over the next three years, and the Admiralty's 1936 and 1937 building programmes were approved in due course. Chamberlain's influence could be seen in the DPRC's recommendation that the Air Ministry should be given latitude to vary its programme to increase the RAF's offensive power by increasing the number and size of bombers ordered. In the event, Scheme F, approved by the Cabinet in February 1936, provided for 1,736 front-line aircraft to be based in Britain by 31 March 1939, with 225 per cent reserves by 1941. In the case of the army, Chamberlain was unable to reduce the size of the Field Force's Regular contingents in view of the chiefs of staff's advice on the strategical importance of the Low Countries. However, ministers agreed to reserve for three years a decision on whether or when to implement the DRC's proposals for the Territorial contingents, with consequent savings on expenditure on munitions. The forecast of expenditure set out in Table 5.1 for the financial years 1936/37 to 1938/39 was not materially changed by these decisions, but there were reductions of £8 million for 1939/40 and £17 million for 1940/41, mainly at the expense of the army.

On 25 February 1936 the Cabinet duly approved the DRC report, as modified by the DPRC, on the understanding that the rearmament programme was provisional and liable to be modified in the light of new developments. Parliament was informed by a white paper on 3 March.[66]

In the debate on the white paper on 10 March Churchill criticised the decision to postpone equipping the Territorial Army, noting the detrimental effect that would have on recruitment. However, he devoted much more of his speech to questions of air power and sea power, and to how industry could be organised to supply the armed forces' needs. He considered the rearmament programme to be inadequate in the light of the scale of German expenditure. Drawing upon estimates supplied by Sir Henry Strakosch, he warned that Germany was spending the equivalent of £600 million to £800 million a year on warlike preparations – a figure the Treasury thought was probably only slightly exaggerated. Churchill doubted whether British defence expenditure – £137 million in 1935/36 – could be increased by as much as £50 million in 1936/37, owing to the unpreparedness of British industry, and, on the basis of his own experience as minister of munitions in the First World War, he predicted that production would lag behind contracts for another two years. He also warned of the danger inherent in the way Germany was financing rearmament. He said the German government could not maintain its present level of borrowing indefinitely. At some point it must choose between bankruptcy, if it attempted to continue, and tremendous unemployment, if it stopped. Before that point was reached, 'at no distant date', it was likely that Hitler would prefer some external adventure to internal catastrophe. [67]

5.4   The Rhineland Crisis and After

On 7 March 1936, between the publication of and the debate on the defence white paper, the German army moved into the Rhineland where, under the Treaty of Versailles, it was forbidden to have any fortifications or troops. In 1948 Churchill described the failure of Britain and France to enforce the treaty on this occasion as the loss of the 'last chance of arresting Hitler's ambitions without a serious war'.[68] He blamed the French for not mobilising their army in order to compel the Germans to withdraw. However, France lacked the resources for independent action. As noted on page 68, the French army was neither equipped nor organised to take the offensive promptly. Moreover, the economy and public finances had been weakened by prolonged defence of the gold standard.[69] The prospects for international support for

France were poor. Collective security through League of Nations sanctions was proving to be ineffective over Ethiopia. Her military pact with Italy could no longer be relied on, and some troops that might have been used in the Rhineland would have had to be deployed on the Alpine frontier or retained in North Africa. The Franco-Soviet Pact of 1935 had not been ratified until February 1936 and, in the absence of staff talks, the form that any Soviet help might take was unknown. The British government took the view that the continued demilitarization of the Rhineland was not a vital British interest. Even before the Germans made their move, key French soldiers and politicians had decided it would be best to accept a *fait accompli* in the Rhineland and to use it to secure additional funding for rearmament and fresh guarantees from Britain.[70]

Eden had raised the question of the demilitarized zone in Cabinet in February 1936 in the context of Britain's rearmament programme: would not the public expect a major increase in defence expenditure to be accompanied by some attempt to come to terms with Germany? The foreign secretary proposed interdepartmental examination of possible concessions that could be offered in return for a final European settlement that included arms limitation and Germany's return to the League. As an example, he asked his Cabinet colleagues: 'Are we prepared to consider with France and Belgium the abandonment of the demilitarized zone?' The zone was the clearest remaining denial of equality to the Germans, and Vansittart thought it would be better to give it up willingly as part of a comprehensive settlement rather than under duress. The permanent under-secretary did not anticipate how quickly Hitler would move, and thought the time to begin bargaining would be after Britain had shown it meant business by making a strong start to the rearmament programme.[71] The question became more pressing on 3 March when the French foreign minister, Pierre Flandin, asked Eden at Geneva for an assurance that Britain would fulfil its Locarno commitment to provide military assistance to France and Belgium in the event of flagrant German aggression in the Rhineland in return for French compliance with oil sanctions against Italy. At a Cabinet meeting on 6 March Baldwin and Chamberlain pointed out the reality of the situation was that neither France nor Britain could take effective military action, an assessment confirmed subsequently by the chiefs of staff, who advised that it would be thoroughly dangerous to engage in hostilities with Germany when Britain's armed forces were heavily committed in the Mediterranean as a result of the Ethiopian crisis.[72] Eden was authorised to enter negotiations with Germany on an air pact, in the expectation that the demilitarized zone would be raised at an early stage, but by the next day that bargaining counter had gone.

On 11 March, after talks in Paris with Flandin and the Belgian prime minister, Paul van Zeeland, Eden warned the Cabinet the French and Belgians believed that, if the Germans were allowed to remain in military occupation of the Rhineland, war was inevitable in two or three years' time when Germany had rearmed. He himself shared their apprehension. Nevertheless, he and the other minister conducting the negotiations, Halifax (the lord privy seal), had concluded that forcing the Germans out of the Rhineland would not produce a satisfactory settlement, and recommended instead negotiations based on 'reasonable regard for the position into which Germany had got herself' and reassurance to France and Belgium of support in a new treaty to replace Locarno. The Cabinet was anxious Britain should not be charged with failing to fulfil its Locarno obligations, but was influenced by public opinion, which was believed to be strongly opposed to the use of force, and by what ministers thought would be the consequences of another great war in Europe. Baldwin remarked that the French 'might succeed in crushing Germany with the aid of Russia, but it would probably only result in Germany going Bolshevik'.[73] On 15 March Chamberlain took advantage of a visit to London by Flandin to have a frank tête-à-tête. The chancellor discouraged Flandin's idea of the Locarno powers imposing economic sanctions on Germany. Instead he suggested a truce during which an international force, largely British, would be stationed on both sides of the Franco-German frontier, and in return France would agree to negotiations for a permanent settlement on the basis of no increase in fortifications and of a new mutual assistance pact. The minutes of the Cabinet meeting the next day record that Eden joined Baldwin in congratulating the chancellor for seizing the opportunity to put forward the idea of an international force. The foreign secretary did not as yet resent Chamberlain's interference in foreign policy, and it is difficult to discern any difference between the two men on how to respond to the remilitarization of the Rhineland.[74]

In further talks with France, Italy and Belgium, Eden resisted Flandin's proposal for the permanent presence of British and Italian troops on the French side of the frontier, and Flandin rejected Chamberlain's idea of an international force on both sides of the frontier. In Cabinet, Chamberlain supported Eden's concession to Flandin that there should be Anglo-French staff talks, although several ministers objected that such talks would be unacceptable to public opinion. Eden and Chamberlain both thought the talks did not commit Britain to giving military assistance. On 19 March Eden and Flandin agreed on a text of proposals to put to Hitler, including an international force on the German side of the frontier, and no fortifications to be built on, or further troops to be sent into, the Rhineland. The last point implicitly acknowledged Germany's right to keep troops in the zone. If these proposals were accepted, Britain and France would take up Hitler's offer of 7 March to negotiate a new mutual security pact. There was, however, no ultimatum, or any other form of pressure to induce Germany to make concessions, and negotiations over the next 12 months for a new security pact or a general settlement achieved nothing. Nevertheless, on 22 March Vansittart congratulated Eden on having extricated Britain 'from a position in which it might have been either dishonoured and isolated, or forced into dangerous courses'.[75]

Churchill's initial reaction to the remilitarization of the Rhineland came at a meeting of the Foreign Affairs Committee of government-supporting MPs on 12 March 1936. He said Britain must fulfil its obligations and drew a dramatic picture of European countries hastening to assist France and Britain against Germany. However, he said nothing about these countries' military preparedness, and Sir Samuel Hoare, now a back-bencher, thought that most were totally unprepared, and that the smaller ones would be a liability rather than an asset.[76] In a Parliamentary debate on 26 March, Churchill warned that the Nazi regime had gained an enormous triumph, and the League of Nations and the rule of law had suffered an immense blow. He noted that the Germans had declined even to refrain from entrenching themselves in the Rhineland during the nego-tiations. Churchill foresaw that once the zone was fortified, which he expected it to be in a very short time, Germany would be free to deploy its main forces in Central and Eastern Europe. He did not, however, propose any action by which the German troops could be removed promptly. He said it was important to ensure the League of Nations had the authority to adjudicate in France's dispute with Germany, but regret-ted that France and Italy had been estranged from each other by the imposition of too vigorous sanctions in support of Ethiopia.[77]

Churchill advocated collective security through the League in order to win support from the British public for measures to contain Germany.[78] Chamberlain, in contrast, was openly sceptical about the effectiveness of the League in the light of its failure to prevent Italian aggression. He mocked Churchill's vision of collective security: 'My right hon. friend the Member for Epping drew a vivid picture – for he is an artist in words as well as in paint – of a state of affairs in which there should be the peaceful encirclement of a potential aggressor. You might have the peaceful encirclement of a lion if half-a-dozen people joined hands and stood all round it, and yet one could not feel quite certain that they would keep that potential aggressor from aggression.' Chamberlain went on to say that the League could only function as keeper of the world's peace if there were more definite arrangements about what part each member would play. He justified staff talks with France and Belgium on the grounds that the independence of the Low Countries was a vital British interest. However, when asked by the Labour MP Hugh Dalton what the government's attitude would be in the event of unprovoked aggression by Hitler against Czechoslovakia or Poland, Chamberlain said only that Britain would be bound to fulfil its obligations under the League of Nations 'in company with our fellow members'.[79] Churchill went no further. Even when advocating co-operation by the European powers under the aegis of the League, he said Britain should not take a leading role. Moreover, the purpose of combining with other powers would be to address Germany collectively in an attempt to agree some redress of its grievances.[80]

Churchill's ideas about how Germany could be kept in check were far from fully formed in 1936. In his conversation with Hankey in April that year, he showed he had no illusions about the weakness of the League, but thought that all its members should be induced to make an effort. He suggested permanently basing a British fleet at a Russian Baltic port to ensure naval superiority in that sea, thereby strengthening the threat to Germany of a blockade. The cabinet secretary, reporting to Inskip, dismissed this idea as fantastic. Churchill himself had doubts about how far the Soviet Union could be relied upon as an ally, although he was in frequent contact with the Soviet ambassador, Ivan Maisky, in the hope of securing Soviet support for collective security.[81] The civil war in Spain, which broke out in July 1936, and what Churchill took to be the Soviet Union's role in creating revolutionary conditions there, strengthened his doubts. Indeed in November 1936 he said it would be a crime to call on British or French soldiers to go to the aid of Russia so long as it persisted in spreading revolution. However, he hoped the Soviets would cease to do so and would become a suitable partner in maintaining peace.[82]

Churchill supported the government's policy of non-intervention in the Spanish Civil War. Germany and Italy supplied arms and men to the Nationalists, who were supported by right-wing elements, including most of the army, landowners and the church, and the Soviet Union did likewise to the left-wing Republican government. Churchill saw the war as a struggle between fascism and bolshevism, with victory for either side having disastrous consequences: in one case a government sympathetic to Italy and Germany; on the other a government that would spread Communism through France and Portugal. Of these alternatives, he initially tended to favour the former, partly because British naval power could discourage a pro-fascist Spanish government from acting against British interests, and partly because he foresaw that the Nationalist leader, General Franco, would assert independence of his Italian and German backers. Churchill refused to become the partisan of either side, and thereby distanced himself from those anti-appeasers who supported the Republican government.[83]

The policy of non-intervention had its origins in Paris, where the French premier, Léon Blum, knew that any other course of action would deepen divisions between left and right in France, and believed that open intervention by the great powers could lead to a European war. Eden thought likewise and took the initiative in negotiating a non-intervention agreement with the principal European powers. The Cabinet did not meet from the end of July until the beginning of September 1936. It was Eden who on 19 August decided to announce that Britain would apply an arms embargo to both sides in Spain irrespective of what other powers did.[84] In the event, Germany, Italy and the Soviet Union continued to send arms and men. Jill Edwards argued that British policy reflected the sympathies of a Conservative-dominated government and benefited Franco.[85] Certainly Chamberlain's prejudices are summed up in one of his letters to his sisters: 'Spain is awful. The Bolshies are ... all the time trying to make mischief.'[86] However, the policy of maintaining the territorial integrity of Spain and Spanish neutrality in any future European war, and preventing the civil war from widening into such a conflict, was Eden's. Chamberlain supported what proved to be unsuccessful attempts by the foreign secretary at mediation in late 1936 and the spring of 1937. As prime minister, Chamberlain maintained strict neutrality in the conflict, pressed for the withdrawal of foreign forces, and withheld recognition from Franco's government until February 1939, when the Republicans were on the brink of surrender.[87] Meanwhile, following a visit to Spain in the summer of 1938 by his son-in-law, Duncan Sandys, Churchill had changed his mind on Franco and decided that a victory for the Republican government would be less of a threat to the British Empire.[88] However, by February 1939 he too recognised that the Republicans could not win and he expressed the misplaced hope that Franco would favour national reconciliation, and the better-founded expectation that the generalissimo would maintain Spain's independence.[89]

One issue where one can discern a clear difference between Chamberlain and Churchill in 1936 was German claims for the restoration of colonies lost as a result of the First World War. The idea of using the ex-colonies as a bargaining counter was first put forward by Vansittart in February 1936. Starting from the premise that no lasting settlement with Hitler could be made without making provision for German territorial expansion, he had argued for Britain making colonial concessions rather than conniving at changes in Europe at the expense of other countries.[90] Following the remilitarization of the Rhineland, Baldwin set up a CID sub-committee to consider the possibility of returning colonies, and the question was also discussed in Cabinet and Parliament. Chamberlain's personal view was that the government ought to consider returning Germany's colonies 'if we were in sight of an all-round settlement', and if the interests of the populations concerned were fully safeguarded.[91] Churchill, however, said the colonies could not be handed back as long as Jews were being persecuted in Germany and the question should be regarded as closed. He counselled against raising German hopes that would have to be disappointed.[92] Hitler had no immediate plans to acquire colonies, but hoped the colonial question could be used to bring about an Anglo-German understanding that would give him a free hand in Europe. When the CID sub-committee's report was considered by the Cabinet's Foreign Policy Committee in July, Eden favoured a negative response to German claims. Chamberlain, while agreeing that the largest colony in British hands, Tanganyika (now Tanzania), was too important strategically to be returned, argued in favour of keeping the possibility of concessions open.[93] The question became more pressing when the German economic minister, Hjalmar Schacht, raised it with the French prime minister, Blum, in August 1936. Eden and Vansittart took the view that the return of colonies should be considered only after a European settlement. Chamberlain and Treasury officials thought a wholly negative response to Schacht's initiative would lead to an impasse.[94]

Eventually, in April 1937, the Cabinet's Foreign Policy Committee agreed with Chamberlain that discussion of the colonial question, and the related matters of Germany's economic difficulties and access to raw materials, could begin once the German government had demonstrated willingness to enter negotiations on a replacement for Locarno; on reassurance for the territorial integrity of Germany's eastern neighbours; on the return of Germany to the League, and on international limitation of armaments. Chamberlain recognised that Australia, New Zealand, South Africa and Japan would not surrender ex-German colonies, and with Tanganyika also excluded, there remained only two in West Africa, Togoland and Cameroon, which, apart from small strips of British territory, were in French hands.[95] When approached, the French government was understandably unwilling to make almost all of the sacrifices to secure a political settlement, and for the time being the matter lapsed.

A related matter was what Eden called 'economic appeasement'. In May 1937 he feared that if Germany became more detached from the economic system of Western Europe, it might draw closer to the Soviet Union, which could supply many raw materials.[96] The Treasury agreed it was important to restore Germany to its normal place in international trade, and Chamberlain approved the efforts of Montagu Norman, the governor of the Bank of England, to maintain links between the City and Germany.[97]

5.5 Rearmament and the Role of the Army

Churchill had radically different views from Chamberlain on the extent to which rearmament contracts should divert industry from normal trade. On 10 March 1936 he urged the creation of a 'skeleton Ministry of Munitions' or Ministry of Supply which would follow the example of Germany and other continental countries in preparing industry to switch from peace to war production. He was aware that plans for the allocation of civil industrial capacity between the services were already in hand, but he wanted practical steps to be taken to organize the manufacture of components by firms not accustomed to producing parts for aircraft or munitions, to give them experience.[98] He was less than precise on what powers over industry a minister of munitions should be given, saying on 21 May that 'only a portion' of those exercised in wartime would be needed initially, although more could be added as necessary.[99] Weir, the government's principal industrial adviser, disagreed about the need for a Ministry of Supply in peacetime, when it would lack wartime powers. He preferred to rely on the defence departments' existing supply organisations, except in the case of the War Office, where he advocated the creation of a Munitions Supply department within the ministry, which was done on 23 July 1936.[100]

On 29 July 1936, as a member of a Conservative parliamentary deputation to the prime minister, Churchill claimed the extent to which Britain was lagging behind Germany in aircraft and munitions production justified emergency measures. It was on this occasion when, as discussed on pages 74–5, he advocated devoting 25 or 30 per cent of the capacity of civil industry to rearmament contracts. He did not propose that Britain should turn itself into a war economy, but urged the government to take powers to impose priorities. For example, he said, all firms making bicycles should be told to agree among themselves a scheme whereby 25 per cent of the industry's capacity would be given over to making machine guns, and if they were unable to agree on one within a fortnight, the government would impose one. Churchill's suggestion was not wholly impractical – the Board of Trade had for more than ten years been assisting the setting up of trade associations to do this kind of work in wartime – but he was surely unrealistic about the time required for planning. He believed the public, including trade unions, would support whatever was necessary for rearmament, if the government stopped making assurances that there was no emergency and instead gave a lead.[101] Historians can only speculate if he was right.

Churchill was primarily concerned with the air force and army because he believed the navy's existing dockyards, and gun and armour plants, were capable of maintaining a fleet on a great scale.[102] Moreover, he was much less concerned with the threat from Japan than from Germany. While he was aware Japan was increasingly dominated by nationalist and militarist extremists, he thought the Japanese had little margin for additional naval construction, as their military expenditure was already so high. Given the vast distances separating the fleets of Japan, Britain and the United States, he said in March 1936 that it would take at least a decade of preparation for them to be able to attack one another.[103] This position does not seem very different from Chamberlain's view, adopted a month earlier by the Cabinet, that the DRC's proposal for a two-power standard should not be adopted for the time being, although a programme to achieve it should be worked out. Speaking to the Conservative 1922 Committee on 7 December 1936, Churchill focused mainly on Britain's weakness compared with Germany in the air, much as Chamberlain had done in discussions on the DRC report in January. Churchill emphasised that the Royal Navy was in a stronger position, relative to European powers, than in 1914. He thought it would be 'impossible and futile' to challenge Japan's supremacy in its own or Chinese waters, but it would be equally impossible for Japan to attack Australia provided the defences of Singapore were made impregnable and battleships could be based there.[104]

Churchill was opposed in 1936 to any pledge to send an expeditionary force to France. Speaking as a member of the deputation to the prime minister on 29 July, he recalled that in 1914 there had been no formal commitment, but the Anglo-French *Entente* had included a tacit understanding that, if Britain joined in the war, six British divisions would take their place on the left of the French armies. He said: 'I feel very strongly that it would be very much better if France and Belgium were taught to make their own arrangements for man-power to defend their frontiers, and we made it quite clear that they had to do that by themselves. What we do we then do in addition, extra, if we can, but there would not be any gap in the line about which, if it was not filled, we should be told we had failed.'[105] These comments were made in the context of concern, expressed by other members of the delegation, that fear of Britain being drawn into another continental campaign was adversely affecting army recruitment. In Churchill's case the threat of air attack was another factor. As in his speech in November 1934, he predicted the government would require all its 'disciplined forces', including presumably the Regular and Territorial armies, to deal with the consequences of at least three to four million panic-stricken people fleeing from air raids on London at the outbreak of war.[106] From this perspective, an expeditionary force would only be able to embark once order had been restored. However, he believed Britain should have an army capable of going to France and Belgium, and that industrial capacity should be created in peacetime so that an army 'of considerable size' – he mentioned figures ranging from 500,000 to 2 million men – could be equipped after the outbreak of war.[107]

Chamberlain reopened the question of the role of the army in October 1936 when he told the minister for co-ordination of defence, Inskip, that there must be an early decision on the future of the Territorial Army and what he thought that decision should be.[108] Chamberlain spoke in public of rearmament providing an army 'trifling in numbers beside the vast conscript armies of the Continent, but equipped with the most modern weapons and mechanical devices that science can give us'.[109] Privately he noted his belief that the five Regular divisions of the Field Force were all Britain could provide for a European war, and that Territorials should be enlisted for service only at home manning anti-aircraft defences.[110] Inskip discussed Chamberlain's ideas with Vansittart and the chief of the imperial general staff, Sir Cyril Deverell. The permanent under-secretary warned that an announcement that in the event of war the British Expeditionary Force would be limited to five divisions would start a landslide of minor states towards Germany. Deverell argued for the military necessity of the Territorial divisions as reinforcements in the light of the British Expeditionary Force's experience of attrition in 1914. Inskip told Chamberlain on 5 November that he (Inskip) was not in a position to controvert the experts' emphatic opinions and he could see no hope of limiting in advance the size of army to be sent to France.[111] Chamberlain consulted his permanent secretary, Fisher, who advised that the DRC's plan to send 17 divisions to the Continent within a limited time after the outbreak of a major war should be regarded as an *ultimate* policy, but that the expansion of the RAF and naval development should have *absolute priority* over the Territorial divisions (italics in original).[112] Taken together, the Field Force and the 12 Territorial infantry divisions would number about 600,000 men, which Fisher thought should be the maximum war strength for the army (compared with Churchill's illustrative figures of 500,000 or 2 million, or the 3,858,000 deployed in 1918).

At the beginning of December 1936 the secretary of state for war, Duff Cooper, asked the Cabinet to revise its decision made nine months earlier to withhold for three years authority to equip the Territorial Army to fight in Europe. He argued that orders placed now would encourage firms to create the industrial capacity that would be required in war.[113] Chamberlain consulted Weir, who reaffirmed the advice he had given ministers twelve months earlier that Britain's main contribution to any alliance should be its navy and a very powerful air force. Weir thought the programme for equipping the Field Force should continue but the idea of reinforcing it with Territorial divisions should be abandoned, even if that meant that advance air bases in the Low Countries could not be secured.[114] When the question of the equipment of the Territorial divisions was discussed in Cabinet on 16 December, Chamberlain rejected Duff Cooper's argument that successive chiefs of staff had advised that Britain should be prepared to send a land force to Belgium or France if these countries were attacked by Germany. The chancellor did not think the chiefs of staff had ever addressed the question of whether equipping twelve Territorial divisions in addition to the five regular ones would be the best use of resources. When Inskip said a decision was required so that orders could be placed far enough ahead for industry to plan production, Chamberlain replied that the minister of co-ordination for defence was talking from the point of view of supply rather than that of his other function to oversee strategy. Chamberlain suggested it would be madness to add to the pressure on industry by trying to equip the Territorial divisions to the same scale as the Regulars, and drew attention to the increasing cost of doing so, now estimated at £135 million compared with £45 million in the DRC report twelve months earlier. He himself doubted whether it would be right to equip the Territorials 'for the trenches'. He did not want to say that no army should go to the Continent, but he thought the idea of sending five Regular divisions at the outbreak of war and twelve Territorial divisions later required impartial examination. At Baldwin's suggestion, the Cabinet agreed to refer the role of the army to the chiefs of staff, with Inskip consulting with Chamberlain on the terms of reference.[115]

Chamberlain asked Inskip to consider whether to include in the enquiry 'someone who could put the point of view I have made. I am a little afraid lest it never have a chance'. The cabinet secretary, Hankey, advising Inskip, commented: 'If someone is to put Mr Chamberlain's point of view to the Chiefs of Staff Sub-Committee I think it will have to be Mr Chamberlain himself, for the reason that I do not know anyone else who shares it with sufficient conviction to put if forward.' Hankey added he could not conceive of any service adviser telling the government the 'modest reinforcement' of twelve Territorial divisions could be dispensed with. Chamberlain could think of someone who might – Lord

Trenchard – but Inskip did not adopt the chancellor's suggestion that the former chief of air staff should be asked to take part in the enquiry.[116] The chiefs of staff reported in January 1937 that, while (like Churchill) they were averse to any commitment in advance to support the French or Belgian armies, the British Army, including the Territorial divisions, should be equipped and trained to serve on the Continent. Like Duff Cooper and Inskip, they thought a decision in principle to modernise the Territorial divisions would make it possible to broaden the basis of munitions supply, even if industry could not provide equipment on any considerable scale in the short term.[117] Inskip suggested a compromise: whereas the chiefs of staff advised that the 'ultimate aim' be to have all twelve Territorial infantry divisions ready to take the field within four months of the outbreak of war, he recommended that enough equipment be ordered to allow one or two divisions to do so, with the equipment spread round all twelve in peacetime for training purposes.[118] After the Cabinet approved this proposal on 3 February 1937, Chamberlain claimed the decision gave him practically all he wanted. He was amused when the first lord of the Admiralty, Hoare, and the secretary of state for air, Swinton, told him independently that, notwithstanding the apparent unanimity of the chiefs of staff, the first sea lord and the chief of air staff agreed with his views.[119]

Chamberlain was working with the grain of public opinion. The arguments he put forward in the DPRC replicated doubts raised in the press and Parliament. Historians have drawn attention to the influence of Captain Basil Liddell Hart, the defence correspondent of the *Daily Telegraph* from 1925 to 1935 and of *The Times* thereafter.[120] Weir's papers include cuttings from *The Times* with Liddell Hart's assertion in 1935 that 'the offensive is as much at an advantage in the air as it is at a disadvantage on land' underlined.[121] When Liddell Hart sent a copy of his book *Europe in Arms* to Chamberlain in March 1937 the chancellor responded by writing that he had found Liddell Hart's articles in *The Times* on the role of the army 'extremely useful and suggestive', and that he was sure that never again would Britain send to the Continent an army on the scale of 1914–18.[122] Liddell Hart's was not a lone voice. Indeed Hankey thought that Trenchard was the principal exponent of the view that air forces had rendered armies obsolete.[123]

Churchill thought an army capable of fighting in Europe was essential. In November 1936 he criticised its lack of modern weapons and the way it had fallen behind the Germans in the quality of its tanks, and urged that patriotic volunteers for the Territorial Army should be properly equipped. Nevertheless, he said that the air situation was 'the greatest matter of all'. Whereas he thought the French army would continue to be superior to the German army 'for a good many months to come', Germany was increasing its lead in the air, particularly in respect of what he called 'long-distance bombing machines'.[124] Using information he received as a member of the CID's Air Defence Research Committee, Churchill badgered the Air Ministry with comparisons of relative first-line strengths, aircraft production, and recruitment and training of pilots.[125] In doing so he helped to concentrate ministers' minds on the RAF. Intelligence assessments had the same effect. In December 1936 Chamberlain still thought Britain could have a deterrent air force of equal strength to the Luftwaffe by the spring of 1939, but that month Swinton warned the CID that the Air Ministry and the IIC now believed the Germans were aiming at something much higher than their original programme and that something had to be done.[126] It is not surprising Chamberlain managed to persuade his ministerial colleagues to give a lower priority to the army than to the air force. Eden, for example, believed the best deterrent was a large force of long-range bombers backed by anti-aircraft defences, and wondered whether Germany would be impressed by an announcement that the Territorial Army units manning the latter would be strengthened by Regular units.[127]

5.6   Financing Rearmament

Financing rearmament was not an immediate problem for Treasury officials in 1936. Revenue was buoyant thanks to recovery from the depression, and expenditure was limited by contractors' ability to fulfil orders. The number of contractors was restricted by the policy of non-interference with normal trade. On the other hand, the provisional nature of the programme encouraged the defence departments to enlarge it. Whereas the DRC had estimated in November 1935 that total defence expenditure for the five financial years 1936/37 to 1940/41 would be £1016 million, by December 1936 Sir Richard Hopkins thought it prudent to think in terms of £1500 million to £1600 million over 1937/38 to 1941/42. Income tax had been raised from a standard rate of 4s.6d (23p) to 4s.9d (24p) in the pound in Chamberlain's 1936 budget, and would be raised by a further 3d (1p) in his 1937 one. Even so, it was estimated by Sir Frederick Phillips that £400 million would have to be borrowed over the next five years to pay for the additional expenditure. At the end of 1936 Phillips warned that world prices were increasing as the world recovered from the depression, and he believed interest rates would rise within two years. He advised that a 2.5 per cent defence loan of £100 million should be raised early in 1937 before they did so. Hopkins included in the Bill authorising the loan a figure of £400 million as the maximum sum to be borrowed over five years, with a sinking fund to repay the principal and interest over 30 years. He thereby hoped to avoid a repetition of the 1931 crisis, when unlimited borrowing to finance the Unemployment Insurance Fund had led financial markets to lose confidence in the Labour government.[128] However, in introducing the Bill on 17 February Chamberlain made clear that the estimate of £1500 million for defence expenditure over five years could not be considered as final or certain. He aimed at raising taxes to a level that would cover recurrent expenditure on the enlarged defence forces from 1942/43.[129]

Leading for the Labour Opposition in the debate, Frederick Pethick-Lawrence claimed that borrowing and pumping new purchasing power into the economy, at a time when rapidly increasing prices indicated a boom was coming, was 'rank inflation'. He cited *The Economist*, which had criticised Chamberlain for having refused to raise a loan to finance work for the unemployed during the depression, when borrowing would not have been inflationary, for now accentuating the boom. If expenditure on armaments was really going to be reduced in 1942, Pethick-Lawrence said, the consequence would be to deepen the slump that would follow the boom. He denounced inflation as a disguised tax that would fall on pensioners, the unemployed and others on fixed incomes, while arms manufacturers made profits. If rearmament was necessary, he said, it should be paid for out of taxation.[130] Chamberlain claimed that, 'not being a theoretical economist', he had difficulty in following Pethick-Lawrence's argument, prompting an acerbic Attlee to remark that the chancellor would not have got to his present post if he had not been able to appreciate the simple points Pethick-Lawrence had made clearly.[131] In fact the issue was not so simple: the extent to which borrowing was inflationary depended not only on the trade cycle, but also on whether the money was lent by members of the public out of savings that might otherwise have been spent, or created by banks making new deposits. Treasury officials intended to avoid the latter and did so with some success down to 1939. Hopkins remarked to Chamberlain after the debate that it was 'pure nonsense to say that we cannot borrow £80 million a year without causing inflation. It is a mere fraction of [the country's] annual savings.'[132]

Keynes, speaking to a City audience on 24 February 1937, said he felt no doubt it was safe to borrow the sum in question, provided the Treasury increased the attractiveness of its securities by offering a range of maturities to suit the market, if as much of the money as possible was spent in areas of high unemployment, and if civil capital expenditure was postponed. In an economic analysis published in *The Times* on 11 March he concluded there was a risk of inflation over the next eighteen months, while ordinary investment was still high under the impetus of economic recovery, but he anticipated that borrowing for rearmament might be helpful in countering a depression in two years' time. As a liberal economist he was opposed to war-time controls, but he warned that the defence departments must not place contracts without regard to the effects on foreign trade, the availability of labour, and competing forms of investment.[133] Treasury officials understood that running civil and defence expenditure at full blast simultaneously would create the conditions for a boom, followed by a slump, with a great excess of industrial capacity once the rearmament programme was complete. Phillips, apparently influenced by attending meetings of the Committee on Economic information (of which Keynes was a member), had advised Hopkins in January 1937 that steps should be taken to postpone civil expenditure, including roads and housing, and to prepare a programme of public works to be undertaken in the next slump.[134]

Chamberlain had a politician's understanding of the risks. Writing to his sisters on 25 April 1937, he observed: 'All the elements of danger are here, increasing cost of living, jealousy of others' profits, a genuine feeling that things are not fairly shared out & I can see that we might easily run, in no time, into a series of crippling strikes, ruining our programme, a sharp steepening of costs due to wage increases, leading to the loss of our export trade, a feverish and partly artificial boom followed by a disastrous slump and finally the defeat of the Government and the advent of an ignorant & heavily pledged Opposition to handle a crisis as severe as that of 1931'. He sought to demonstrate to workers that the government was not in league with the employers by introducing a temporary profits tax, euphemistically called National Defence Contribution (NDC). He was aware it would not be popular with business or the Conservative Party. Indeed he felt he had 'risked the premiership' just as it was about to fall into his hands with Baldwin due to retire the following month.[135] The tax was to be levied at progressive rates according to the growth of the profits compared with average profits in three pre-rearmament years, 1933, 1934 and 1935. The City and business organisations were shocked at what seemed to be a socialist measure: share prices dropped and sales of National Defence Bonds were adversely affected. The only MP to give uncritical support to Chamberlain was the House of Commons' sole representative of the Communist Party, Willie Gallacher, who praised him for his courage and urged him not to give way to pressure from business interests.[136] Even Churchill, who said Chamberlain had rehabilitated the nation's finances and provided 'with masterful ease the cash and credit necessary for rearmament', nevertheless criticised the NDC as a tax on enterprise and contrary to the capitalist system, and urged the government to find an alternative way of convincing munitions workers that it was opposed to profiteering.[137] Chamberlain's successor as chancellor, Sir John Simon, accepted that the NDC involved endless complications and agreed to a proposal from business interests for a flat 5 per cent tax on profits to raise the same revenue.[138]

The decision to borrow weakened Treasury control of the defence departments' expenditure. Hitherto they could spend in any financial year only the funds voted by Parliament for that year, and for the purposes for which they had been voted, unless a supplementary estimate was voted. Supplementary estimates were regarded as signs of lax financial control and were granted only sparingly. Normally proposals for expenditure had to wait for the annual estimates to be fixed in the spring. However, from 1935 political pressures to deal with defence deficiencies meant that supplementary estimates became the norm. Departments were not slow to propose additions to their programmes, and it was difficult for Treasury officials to refuse to authorize expenditure on things that defence experts declared to be necessary, now that funds were always available. The procedure by which the chancellor agreed estimates for expenditure in the coming financial year became almost meaningless. Rearmament contracts extended over a number of years, so that the amount spent in a given year depended upon progress made with orders. If production were behind schedule, a larger part of the cost than intended would fall on the next year. If production were ahead of schedule, a supplementary estimate would be granted, but it was difficult to refuse further orders in the following year if productive capacity would be idle as a result. Hopkins observed in January 1937 that there had been a notable increase in the pace of the Air Ministry programme, while it had become apparent that the Admiralty was ordering ships at a rate that would soon leave shipyards idle if it was restricted to the one-power standard approved by the Cabinet. He thought the only way the chancellor could resume control of expenditure was to fix an aggregate sum, which could not be exceeded, for each department.[139] This suggestion was the genesis of the financial rationing that would be applied to departments following Inskip's review of defence expenditure and policy later in 1937 (see pages 166–73).

6   Chamberlain Takes Charge

6.1   Relations with the United States and Japan

In March 1937, while still chancellor, Chamberlain had received what he called a 'curious message' from the secretary of the US Treasury, Henry Morgenthau, who asked how the United States could help to preserve world peace. Rightly suspecting the message was sent with President Roosevelt's knowledge, Chamberlain replied that the greatest single contribution the United States could make would be to amend its neutrality legislation, which, in his view, acted as an indirect but potent encouragement to aggression. He also wished to suggest a pact whereby Britain, the United States, China, Japan and the Soviet Union would guarantee the territorial status quo in the Far East. He hoped American participation might check Japanese ambitions, and thereby indirectly check any aggressive intentions on Germany's part, by allowing Britain and the Soviet Union to focus their attention on Europe. When Eden saw Chamberlain's draft reply, however, he pointed out there was no possibility of the United States committing itself to such a pact and that it would be unwise to suggest one. The most that could be hoped, in the foreign secretary's view, was to encourage the United States to show an interest in the Far East to an extent that would act as a warning and deterrent to Japan. Chamberlain accepted this advice and made no more than a tentative suggestion for 'an exchange of views on the possibility of ... try[ing] to put relations between the USA, Japan and Great Britain on a footing that would ensure harmonious co-operation'. He concluded by remarking that Anglo-American economic collaboration would also help to restore international confidence, mentioning a trade agreement which Cordell Hull, the US secretary of state, had been keen to negotiate for over a year.[1]

Chamberlain had become prime minister by the time the American response came on 1 June in the form of a memorandum from the secretary of state. Hull placed more emphasis than Chamberlain had on a trade treaty, pointed out that traditional American attitudes to alliances precluded anything more than consultation and action on parallel lines in the

Far East, and denied that American neutrality legislation had any effect other than safeguarding the United States from being drawn into war.[2] Nine days later Roosevelt, through the American diplomat Norman Davis, let Chamberlain know he would welcome a meeting in Washington. In a carefully drafted reply, Chamberlain said he shared Roosevelt's views on the potential of Anglo-American co-operation to restore world peace and stability, but suggested delaying a meeting until there was a reasonable prospect of demonstrating co-operation in a practical way: for example, a trade agreement.[3] By the time Roosevelt sent a personal letter to Chamberlain on 28 July, accepting that their meeting would require careful timing, a brutal, undeclared war had broken out in China, following a clash between Chinese and Japanese troops three weeks earlier at the Marco Polo Bridge. The letter did not reach Chamberlain, who was on holiday in Scotland, until the second half of August. The prime minister thought contact with Roosevelt, even by correspondence, would be useful, but remarked to his sisters that the Americans had a long way to go before they would be helpful partners, instancing their refusal to make a joint démarche to Japan over its actions in China. In his reply to the president, he noted that their two countries shared the same sentiments about events in the Far East and looked forward to successful trade talks, but asked the president to wait a little longer for a meeting.[4]

Roosevelt continued to explore ways in which the United States could contribute to the preservation of world peace. In a speech in Chicago on 5 October 1937 he spoke of an 'epidemic of world lawlessness' that required 'a quarantine of the patients'. He called for peace-loving nations to make a concerted effort to oppose violations of treaties, but added that he was determined to adopt every practical measure to avoid American involvement in war.[5] Chamberlain read the speech with mixed feelings. He remarked that patients subjected to quarantine did not normally go about fully armed, and that therefore there was something lacking in Roosevelt's analogy. He feared the American doctrine of parallel action might leave Britain unsupported if it protested publicly against Japanese aggression in China, and 'in the present state of European affairs ... we simply cannot afford to quarrel with Japan'. His impression was that the president was simply testing American public opinion and had not thought out the full implications of his speech. In particular, Chamberlain believed one possible effect would be that the Germans, Italians and Japanese would draw closer together. On the other hand, he hoped the totalitarian countries might draw the conclusion they could not entirely count on American isolationism, and for that reason he thought it wise to give the impression of believing Roosevelt meant much more by quarantine than he (Chamberlain) believed the president did.[6]

The League of Nations was encouraged by Roosevelt's speech to refer the Far Eastern crisis to a conference in Brussels of the nine powers (including Britain, the United States and Japan) that had signed a treaty in 1922 affirming the sovereignty and territorial integrity of China. The United States agreed to participate, but all the evidence reaching the British government suggested that Roosevelt intended to do no more than educate the American public in international affairs. Chamberlain noted in Cabinet that the expression 'quarantine' had been widely interpreted as meaning 'boycott', and the government might be accused by the Opposition parties of standing in the way of an effective restraint on Japan. He believed it was impossible to enforce effective sanctions without a risk of war, while ineffective sanctions would cause ill will (as with Italy over Ethiopia). He could not imagine anything more suicidal than to pick a quarrel with Japan; if Britain were to become involved in the Far East, the temptation for Germany and Italy to take advantage in Eastern Europe or Spain might be irresistible. The Cabinet agreed on 13 October 1937 that the line to be taken on the conference was the government would not think about compulsion until conciliation had been exhausted. Eden, however, added that Roosevelt's speech was a most important new factor in the situation and Britain should not refuse to contemplate sanctions in the extremely unlikely event of the American government being prepared to act.[7]

Three days later, in a radio broadcast to the American people, Roosevelt made clear that the purpose of the conference was mediation.[8] Chamberlain now felt there was no danger of the government being blamed for not applying sanctions, and told ministers that in speeches the object of the conference should be presented as appeasement. Eden hoped the conference would remit mediation to Britain and the United States. Chamberlain privately thought it would be better still if Britain alone were asked to mediate, for then, he believed, the Japanese would not be too intransigent.[9] In the event, the Japanese refused to attend the conference, which convened on 3 November. On the 21st the prime minister told his sisters he had had to restrain 'our bellicose F.O.' from 'fist shaking at Japan'.[10] On the 24th, the day the conference adjourned indefinitely without producing any measures to halt the war in China, Chamberlain remarked in Cabinet that the main lesson to be learned was the difficulty of securing effective co-operation from the United States.[11]

Meanwhile Hull was making a case for what he called 'economic appeasement' – a policy he attributed to Roosevelt, but which the secretary of state claimed to have worked out in detail himself. In a conversation with Lord Tweedsmuir, the governor general of Canada, which Tweedsmuir reported to Chamberlain on 25 October 1937, Hull expressed the view that

Germany had no immediate aggressive aims, and if the United States and Britain offered to help to stabilise its economy, it could be detached from its alliance with Italy and Japan. Hull was quoted as saying that there was 'a solid and rational element' in Germany with which the democracies could work. Chamberlain underlined these words and commented in the margin: 'This shows how far the USA is from understanding German mentality.'[12] Hull believed economic rivalry was a basic cause of war, and hoped liberalized trade practices by Britain and the United States would draw Germany out of autarchy and preserve peace, besides benefiting American exporters.

On 18 November, the date when it was announced that Britain and the United States had agreed a basis for trade negotiations, Chamberlain told Leo Amery, an ardent supporter of imperial preference, that Hull was so keen on an agreement that the effect on Anglo-American relations of failing to reach one would be very serious.[13] Chamberlain was prepared to go a long way to secure a treaty because he reckoned it would make the United States more willing to act with Britain and would 'frighten the totalitarians'.[14] In the event, the negotiations dragged on and in March 1938, after Hitler's seizure of Austria created a crisis atmosphere in Europe, Sir Alexander Cadogan, the permanent under-secretary at the Foreign Office, said he would normally be in favour of the prime minister visiting Washington to sign the agreement, but, in an age when transatlantic travel was by sea rather than by air, the permanent under-secretary doubted whether Chamberlain could be absent long enough from London.[15]

The prospects of Anglo-American co-operation seemed to increase when Japanese aircraft sank the American warship *Panay* in the Yangtze River on 12 December 1937, the same day as two British warships were fired on there by Japanese artillery. This was the occasion of Chamberlain's remark on 17 December, quoted on page 82, that it was always safest to count on nothing from the Americans except words, but he could not altogether repress hopes that this time they would do something. Roosevelt did initially talk with the British ambassador, Sir Ronald Lindsay on 16 December about putting Japan in 'quarantine', by which he meant a blockade on raw materials, including oil, imposed by American and British cruisers. However, the president thought action should be taken only after the next grave outrage, such as an attack on Hong Kong or French Indochina. When Lindsay, who thought Roosevelt was in his worst 'inspirational mood', pointed out that a blockade would mean war, the president denied it would.[16] On 17 December he told his cabinet that Italy and Japan had developed a technique of fighting without declaring war, and the United States should develop a technique of economic sanctions that would not lead to war. However, within a few hours he had second thoughts and told Morgenthau there was no great hurry for economic measures against Japan.[17] On 21 December Hull told Lindsay that a blockade was a remote contingency.[18]

Roosevelt decided to send a naval officer, Captain Royal E. Ingersoll, the director of the War Plans division, to Britain for technical discussions to facilitate co-operation should both countries find themselves at war with Japan. By the time Ingersoll arrived in London Roosevelt had accepted Japan's apology and payment of an indemnity for the *Panay* incident. Ingersoll made clear the United States did not contemplate any move against Japan, but his visit led on 13 January 1938 to an informal understanding about how the American and British fleets would be deployed in the event of war and to an exchange of naval codes.[19] Chamberlain was not directly involved in these talks, but, as he wrote to his sisters on 9 January, he had been trying to 'jolly [the Americans] along with a view to making some sort of joint (or at least "parallel") naval action'.[20] On the prime minister's initiative, Lindsay enquired in Washington whether any American action could be expected if Britain were to announce that 'certain naval preparations' short of mobilization were being completed. On 10 January a telegram was received from Lindsay reporting Roosevelt had decided that, in such an event, he would announce the American Pacific fleet was to be sent to dry-dock to have their hulls scraped – i.e. prepared for sea – and soon afterwards the date for manoeuvres in the Pacific would be advanced by two or three weeks.[21] These measures fell short of the parallel action the British had in mind. Chamberlain remarked on 11 January it was evident the American government felt obliged by isolationist sentiment to move with the greatest caution, and he was therefore against asking it to commit itself to any specific action in hypothetical circumstances. From a British point of view, it was not a good time to send the fleet to the Far East, and he concluded 'we had better not make any announcement yet'.[22]

That same day the US under-secretary of state, Sumner Welles, gave Lindsay a message from Roosevelt for Chamberlain, telegraphed on the 12th, outlining an initiative which the president contemplated taking in parallel with current British efforts to come to terms with German and Italy. The ambassador was told the president was communicating his scheme to the British government alone, and would proceed with it only if he received an assurance from Chamberlain of 'cordial approval and support' by 17 January, that is within five days of the message reaching London. The preamble to the scheme spoke of a world 'where physical and economic security for the individual are lacking', words that prompted Chamberlain to comment in the margin: 'Germans &

Italians will laugh at this.' There followed a call for all nations to agree upon 'the practical foundations for peace', which were set out as: (1) 'fundamental principles' to be observed in international relations, (2) limitation and reduction of armaments, (3) equal access to raw materials and (4) the laws of war which neutrals were entitled to require of combatants. When Lindsay enquired whether the fourth point might restrict the Royal Navy's right to impose a blockade, Welles said he hoped the British government would not feel unduly anxious and that the most important points were those relating to disarmament and raw materials. In particular, he was told Roosevelt thought Germany and Italy might possibly be 'bought off' by economic concessions. The president did not propose to hold a world conference, but, if his scheme received enough support from other governments, he intended to invite selected lesser powers: Belgium, Holland, Sweden, Switzerland, Hungary, Yugoslavia and Turkey, and three Latin American nations, to send representatives to Washington to formulate proposals for subsequent submission to all nations for their reactions. Roosevelt hoped this initiative would 'give an impulse' to Anglo-French negotiations with Germany and Italy.[23]

After looking at the telegrams from Lindsay of 10 and 12 January 1938 in sequence, Gill Bennett found it hard to avoid the conclusion that Roosevelt put forward his scheme at least partly to mollify the British after his negative response to their appeal for joint naval action against Japan. Moreover, the scheme provided an alternative to a draft report by the Belgian prime minister and economist, Paul van Zeeland, which contained proposals on tariff reductions and an international fund to stabilise exchange rates that might impinge on American interests.[24] Whatever the motivation, Roosevelt's scheme involved no American commitments. Lindsay, however, advised that it was a genuine effort to relax world tension, and that rejection would have an adverse effect on American public opinion. As it happened, Eden was on holiday in France and Chamberlain had taken charge of the Foreign Office. Although the foreign secretary could have been consulted by telegraph, the prime minister chose not to do so. Instead he replied to Roosevelt on 13 January that the latter's scheme might be used by Germany and Italy to hold up negotiations with Britain and to make additional demands, and asked the president to hold his hand for a while. When, on returning to London, Eden saw Chamberlain's reply he was outraged and, without consulting the prime minister, sent a message to Lindsay at 2.30 a.m. on the 16th asking him to dispel the impression of a negative attitude towards the president's scheme.[25] Later that day, a Sunday, Eden met Chamberlain at the prime minister's country residence,

Chequers, where the two men argued about how to respond to Roosevelt, and their disagreement was aired further in four meetings of the Cabinet's Foreign Policy Committee. Eden felt Chamberlain's fear that the president's initiative would adversely affect British attempts to improve relations with Germany and Italy was exaggerated. On the other hand, the foreign secretary thought it was almost impossible to overestimate the benefits an indication of American interest in Europe could produce. Eden conceded Chamberlain might be right in regarding Roosevelt's ideas as naïve and woolly, but urged nevertheless that the president should not be discouraged. Chamberlain complained that nothing practical could emerge from the initiative, which reminded him of the Kellogg-Briand pact of 1928 for the renunciation of war as an instrument of national policy, which nations had signed but not honoured.[26]

Eden threatened to resign and Chamberlain reluctantly agreed on the 21st to the despatch of a telegram asking Roosevelt to go ahead with the scheme after all, and promising to do his best to contribute to its success.[27] By then the president was less certain that he wished to proceed, perhaps partly because his secretary of state, Hull, told him the scheme was illogical in that it would be fatal to lull the democracies into a feeling of tranquillity when they ought to be making the utmost effort to rearm, whereas the Axis powers would laugh at any request to disarm.[28] Moreover, a stronger discouragement than Chamberlain's had reached the president on the 20th in the form of a message from the American ambassador in Paris, William Bullitt. Predicting that Hitler would soon seize Austria and that France would do nothing but protest feebly, Bullitt remarked that Roosevelt's idea of convening representatives of lesser powers to formulate proposals on international law 'would be as if in the palmiest days of Al Capone you had summoned a national conference of psychoanalysts to Washington to discuss the psychological causes of crime'.[29] At all events, the president's scheme was first postponed and then dropped.

Churchill wrote in 1948 that Chamberlain had 'waved aside' Roosevelt's 'effort to stabilise or bring to a head the European situation by the intervention of the United States', with the result that 'the last frail chance to save the world from tyranny otherwise than by war' was lost.[30] This judgement, which reflected Churchill's contemporary concern with securing American support in the Cold War, has been echoed by Robert Rhodes James and Andrew Roberts.[31] Robert Dallek, Greg Kennedy and William Rock, while not endorsing Churchill's counterfactual, have been critical of what they saw as Chamberlain's rebuff to Roosevelt and disregard for the importance of co-operation with the United States.[32] David

Reynolds, on the other hand, doubted whether the incident had any impact on Anglo-American relations.[33] What is the evidence that Roosevelt felt rebuffed? The main source is Welles's conversations with Lindsay.[34] As Welles was the author of the scheme, he may have been more disappointed than the president. Roosevelt's main concern in his reply to Chamberlain on 18 January related to the issue of *de jure* recognition of Italy's conquest of Ethiopia, which Chamberlain was considering as a contribution to appeasement, but which ran counter to the American principle of non-recognition of breaches of international law.[35] Roosevelt seems to have been satisfied with Chamberlain's expression of support for his scheme; at any rate, Welles told Lindsay on 9 February that the president did not share Hull's impression that the British government was not over-enthusiastic about it.[36]

It is true that Roosevelt did not take a similar diplomatic initiative again, but the atmosphere in Europe in 1938 and 1939 was hardly propitious for one. Chamberlain, for his part, doubtless preferred not to have any more such distractions while pursuing his policy of appeasement. However, the prime minister continued to support negotiations for a trade treaty, which he valued as a demonstration of Anglo-American co-operation, and Roosevelt continued to try to amend neutrality legislation, which Chamberlain thought was the greatest possible contribution the United States could make to world peace. Moreover, Anglo-American relations improved through what Gill Bennett described as 'growing intimacy' between the Foreign Office and the State Department. On 20 January 1938, Hull suggested a full, and what turned out to be continuing, exchange of diplomatic information between the two governments.[37] Likewise, the Ingersoll talks were followed by a much greater willingness to share naval intelligence and plans regarding Japan.[38] Chamberlain's cautious response to Roosevelt's scheme did not discourage Anglo-American co-operation within the constraints set by domestic politics in the United States.

Churchill's writings in the 1930s do not suggest he had higher expectations than Chamberlain of early co-operation with the United States. In November 1936, with reference to relations with Germany, Churchill wrote: 'We must not ask too much of the United States. We must try to do the work ourselves. But we may find them with us at the end of the road.'[39] He attached great importance to American goodwill, remarking in May and December 1937 that no fact in the world situation was more important than the excellent relations and understanding that had developed between the United States and Britain and France, sustained by shared values and abhorrence of Fascism. An Anglo-American trade agreement or a settlement of the war debt question would, he said, put that goodwill beyond doubt. Even so, he thought it would be a profound mistake for Britain or France to 'count for their safety upon any force save that of their own right arm', as American public opinion was more set than ever on avoiding foreign entanglements and wars and only the actions of a hostile power would change it.[40] Like Chamberlain, Churchill believed the United States could give powerful aid by modifying its neutrality legislation to allow belligerents to purchase non-military supplies on a 'cash and carry' basis, but how would such purchases be financed, given the Johnson Act's ban on debtor nations raising loans?

In response to a Treasury enquiry in February 1937, Lindsay had advised that Roosevelt would be willing to summon an international conference to cancel war debts, if the decision rested with him, for the president took 'a completely realistic view' of them. However, the ambassador added, Congress was the decisive factor and the president could not hope to overcome the opposition of pacifists and isolationists who asked why war debts should be cancelled when European countries were spending increasing amounts on armaments.[41] Churchill appreciated the importance of a debt settlement and discussed it briefly in an article in May 1937. As in 1934, he thought the transfer of £35 million a year from Britain would cause exchange-rate instability and 'distract the entire finance of international trade'. He had no answer to the war debt question, but said it should be 'perseveringly studied'.[42] The prospect of an Anglo-American trade treaty raised the possibility of resuming payments to the United States at a level that could be financed by dollar earnings from increased exports. However, Treasury officials thought there was still a danger of a collapse in the exchange rate in future periods of stress. When Tweedsmuir suggested to Chamberlain in October 1937 that successful negotiation of a trade treaty might be followed by a debt settlement, the permanent secretary of the Treasury, Sir Warren Fisher, advised a policy of silence unless Roosevelt raised the question. Fisher believed that no offer Britain could make would satisfy Congress and that the president had no wish to see the matter reopened.[43] The Treasury continued to monitor American public opinion through the Washington embassy, but the Johnson Act had been deliberately drafted to exclude the possibility of token payments or payment of capital without interest. The war debt question remained unresolved.

As for the position in the Far East, Churchill continued in 1937 to have faith in the ability of the Royal Navy to protect Australia and New Zealand when what he called the 'fortress and dockyard' at Singapore was capable of maintaining a battle fleet. Writing in May, he expected the base to be completed soon, but added that, given that it was as far from Japan as Portsmouth was from New York, it was 'in no way a threat to our old friends the Japanese'.[44] In August, after fighting between Japanese and Chinese had developed into a full-scale war, he took the view that, unless the position in Europe became sufficiently secure, and feeling in the United States sufficiently strong, for joint Anglo-American action, both the British and the Americans must expect ceaseless encroachments on their enormous commercial interests in China. The spectacle of 'the remorseless conquest' of parts of China would not, he warned, be pleasant. Nevertheless, he thought it would have to be endured. He did not expect the Japanese invasion to lead to a wider conflict; on the contrary, the fact that the Japanese army thought the time opportune to entangle its troops in China suggested its leaders did not expect a major war in 1937. The great danger to the world, he wrote, lay 'not in the quarrels of the yellow peoples', but in Europe.[45] In October 1937, shortly before the Brussels Conference, Churchill observed that nothing was more certain than that Japan could not resist indefinitely economic pressure from the United States and the British Empire, but if the Americans would not act, nothing could be done.[46] In January 1938, as Chamberlain and Eden were quarrelling over how to respond to Roosevelt's initiative, Churchill wrote it was certain that no American government was going to 'pull the chestnuts out of the fire' for the sake of British interests in China.[47]

Chamberlain's reactions to the Sino-Japanese war were no more heroic. Japanese outrages against British interests were met with diplomatic protests, but no more. Eden approved the firmness with which Chamberlain dealt with the Japanese statesman Ishii Kikujiro, who called on the prime minister on 9 December 1937 and tried to persuade him that the war in China was the fault of the Chinese. Chamberlain dismissed Ishii's arguments, pointing out that incidents in China, including an air attack on the British ambassador, the killing of British soldiers and destruction of British property, had caused resentment, and advised him the only way to restore friendly relations was for the Japanese to make peace on generous terms.[48] Chamberlain had not abandoned all hope of appeasing Japan, and said on 14 February 1938 that some effort should be made.[49] However, he made no suggestion of what might be done, the optimism with which he had approached Anglo-Japanese relations earlier having dissipated.

6.2   Seeking a General Settlement in Europe

In contrast to his pessimism about Japan, Chamberlain seems to have been optimistic about the prospects for the appeasement of Europe – markedly more so than Foreign Office officials. The latter's hopes had been dimmed by their experience of over a year of inconclusive negotiations on Hitler's offer, made at the time of the occupation of the Rhineland, of a new western mutual security pact. An attempt to pin Hitler down on the precise meaning of his offer by sending a questionnaire to Berlin in April 1936 had met with evasion, as did an invitation in July to a five-power conference to discuss the pact. Writing on 31 December 1936, the permanent under-secretary, Vansittart, had concluded that attempts at a European settlement had got nowhere.[50] Nevertheless, Chamberlain and Foreign Office were agreed that efforts to reach a comprehensive settlement of differences with Germany and Italy should continue. Likewise there was no debate as to where the main threat to peace lay. Chamberlain, in his reply to Morgenthau in March 1937 (see page 148), had written of 'the intensity and persistence of German military preparations, together with many acts of the German government in violation of treaties', and of the need for British rearmament to act as a deterrent to German ambitions.[51] Prime minister and Foreign Office were both aware that the chiefs of staff believed war should not be risked before 1939. Vansittart indeed regarded negotiations with Germany principally as a means of gaining time in which to complete rearmament. He distrusted Hitler and thought his ambitions would be limited only by the threat of force.[52] Chamberlain believed Hitler's territorial ambitions in Europe were limited to German-speaking areas, and had an idiosyncratic conception of diplomacy in which Germany, Italy and Britain would each contribute to appeasement rather than try to gain more than they gave in negotiations. Nevertheless he too connected diplomacy with rearmament. Writing to Lord Weir on 1 August 1937 he said: 'The Air Force must go on and build itself up as rapidly as possible. I hope my efforts with Germany and Italy will give us the necessary time.'[53] On the same day he told his sisters: 'I believe the double policy of rearmament and better relations with Germany and Italy will carry us through the danger period, if only the F.O. will play up.'[54]

Eden's experience of negotiations over Ethiopia and Spain left him highly distrustful of any approaches from Italy. Chamberlain complained that the Foreign Office persisted in seeing Mussolini as 'a sort of Machiavelli putting on a false mask of friendship in order to further nefarious ambitions', adding: 'if we treat him like that we shall get nowhere with him'.[55] Prime minister and foreign secretary were at odds over the need for defensive measures against Italy. Despite an Anglo-Italian agreement in January 1937 to respect each other's rights and interests in the Mediterranean area, there had been no let-up in Italian military preparations in Libya or in anti-British propaganda by Radio Bari.[56] At a CID meeting on 5 July 1937 Chamberlain argued that, if

Britain avoided a quarrel with Germany, there was no need to fear any sudden attack by Italy, and priority should be given to providing a deterrent to German aggression. Eden thought Italy might attack and rely on Germany following her, citing the example of Austria-Hungary's ultimatum to Serbia in 1914, and urged greater preparedness for such an eventuality. Eden wanted Italy to be classified by the CID as a 'possible enemy'; Chamberlain insisted on the formula that Italy could no longer be regarded as a 'reliable friend'. The CID agreed with Chamberlain that no very large expenditure should be incurred in increasing defences in the Mediterranean or Red Sea areas.[57] Two days later the Cabinet was given a letter from the ambassador in Rome, Sir Eric Drummond, warning that anti-British articles by Mussolini in the Italian press looked like an attempt to rouse public opinion for an eventual war. Even so, no minister contradicted Chamberlain's view that 'the real counter to Italy's disquieting attitude was to get on better terms with Germany'.[58] The prime minister nevertheless hoped for improved relations with Italy as a means of avoiding heavy defence expenditure in the Mediterranean area. He was not content to leave diplomacy to the Foreign Office and it was about this time that he established a secret channel of communication with the Italian embassy, using the services of his confidant Sir Joseph Ball, who established contact with Adrian Dingli, a barrister who worked as British legal counsel to the Italian embassy.[59]

In mid-July Lord Halifax suggested to Eden that the deadlock in Anglo-Italian relations could be broken if the foreign secretary established direct contact with Mussolini by sending him a personal letter. Orme Sargent, an assistant under-secretary, noted that Mussolini might expect such a letter to be from the prime minister, but seems to have assumed the letter would be drafted in the Foreign Office.[60] In the event, Eden did not take up Halifax's suggestion and instead made a conciliatory speech in the House of Commons on 19 July in which he referred to the Anglo-Italian agreement of January 1937 and Britain's wish for Anglo-Italian friendship.[61] The Italian ambassador, Count Dino Grandi, was encouraged by the speech, and perhaps also by Ball's contact with Dingli, to ask Eden on 21 July to arrange an interview with the prime minister. Vansittart's brief for Chamberlain before the interview, in contrast to Eden's speech, emphasised the threat posed by Italian troop movements to Libya, leading Sir Horace Wilson, Chamberlain's confidential adviser, to comment: 'This is not my idea of a basis for a genial conversation – it suggests an undercurrent of annoyance which, even if we feel it, should not be displayed tomorrow.' Wilson advised Chamberlain to write a personal letter to Mussolini to ensure the right message reached him.[62]

At the meeting on 27 July Grandi gave orally what he claimed was a translation from a letter to Chamberlain from Mussolini, adding comments of his own. Chamberlain remarked he had difficulty distinguishing between what was Mussolini and what was Grandi. In fact there was no letter from Mussolini. Grandi, on his own initiative, represented instructions he had received from the Italian foreign minister, Count Galeazzo Ciano, as a personal letter from the Duce, hoping thereby to achieve a diplomatic coup and restore himself to the latter's favour. Chamberlain was given to understand that Mussolini had no ambitions in Spain, other than to ensure victory for Franco over the 'Reds', and regarded the Anglo-Italian agreement of January 1937 as only a first step towards better relations. Grandi said Mussolini attached great importance to *de jure* recognition of Italy's position in Ethiopia. Chamberlain replied that, given public support in Britain for the League of Nations, such recognition could only be part of 'a great scheme of reconciliation', and such a scheme must include reassurances about Italian troop movements and propaganda. In Grandi's presence, Chamberlain then wrote a personal letter to Mussolini, expressing goodwill and the hope that mutual confidence between their two countries could be restored to what it had been before the Ethiopian crisis.[63] The prime minister's procedure was unusual, and Eden was said by his parliamentary private secretary to have been upset at not being consulted.[64] Chamberlain himself detected indications that the Foreign Office was inclined to be jealous of its functions.[65] However, the content of his letter was hardly controversial, suggesting no more than conversations with a view to removing all causes of suspicion or misunderstanding.

On 29 July, two days after the Chamberlain-Grandi conversation, Eden told the Italian ambassador that it would be helpful if Mussolini or Ciano were to reciprocate the sentiments of his speech in the House of Commons.[66] Eden's objection to Chamberlain's letter would seem to have been primarily a matter of amour propre. Grandi, this time bearing a real letter from Mussolini, dated 31 July, had a further conversation with Chamberlain on 2 August, in which a public response to Eden's speech was promised. Mussolini agreed to Chamberlain's suggestion of conversations aimed at re-establishing mutual confidence, and Grandi's artful flattery of the prime minister confirmed the latter's belief that he knew how to deal with dictators. Writing to his sisters, Chamberlain commented that, if the Foreign Office were left to itself, there would be a danger of it 'letting pass the critical moment. As it is I can look back with great satisfaction at the extraordinary relaxation of tension in Europe since I first saw Grandi. Grandi himself says it is 90 per cent due to me and it gives one a sense of the wonderful power that the premiership gives you. As chancellor of the exchequer I could hardly have moved a pebble; now I have only to raise a finger and the whole face of Europe is changed.'[67] Even allowing for the habitual style of Chamberlain family correspondence, it is not difficult to detect signs of hubris here.

Events swiftly reversed any impression of relaxation of tension. News of attacks by Italian submarines on neutral merchant shipping trading with Republican Spain led Eden to return from holiday for a ministerial meeting at the Foreign Office on 17 August 1937, when the navy was authorised to counterattack submarines that torpedoed British vessels.[68] Chamberlain's holiday in Scotland was twice interrupted by the need to return to London for meetings on Anglo-Italian relations. Eden was very reluctant to give Italy's conquest of Ethiopia *de jure* status, whereas Chamberlain thought it would be better to recognise it while something could be gained in return for the concession.[69] On the other hand, the prime minister and the foreign secretary were agreed that Mussolini's friendly message of 31 July could not justify ignoring the Mediterranean situation.[70] Eden took a leading role at an international conference at Nyon where, on 14 September, he and the French foreign minister, Yvon Delbos, secured agreement on a plan for their two countries, assisted by lesser naval powers, to patrol the Mediterranean to prevent so-called 'pirate' submarines attacking neutral shipping. The attacks ceased abruptly and, as a face-saving exercise, Mussolini agreed that the Italian navy should take part in the patrols. In a letter to Chamberlain, Eden observed that Mussolini might be very angry for a while, but he was likely to respect Britain all the more in the end.[71] Chamberlain described the conference as 'a great success', but regretted that Anglo-Italian relations had 'gone right back'.[72]

Churchill also valued Anglo-Italian friendship. Writing early in August 1937, he attached high importance to the recent exchange of letters between Chamberlain and Mussolini. Churchill saw the danger of the Spanish Civil War dividing Europe between France and the Soviet Union, on the one hand, and Germany and Italy, on the other, and considered it the 'duty of all sensible men to try to prevent such a dire confrontation'. He was opposed to an indefinite refusal to recognise the conquest of Ethiopia if that were to lead to the permanent alienation of Italy. At the same time he endorsed Eden's warnings that Italy should not encroach on the territorial integrity of Spain and its colonies. In contrast to Chamberlain's reliance on expressions of good will, Churchill emphasised the importance of sea power in ensuring that the Mediterranean route to the Far East remained open.[73] As a response to attacks on neutral shipping, he suggested to Eden shortly before the Nyon conference in September that armed decoy ships should be used to sink 'pirate' submarines (a tactic used by the Royal Navy in the First World War). Eden consulted the first lord of the Admiralty, Duff Cooper, who replied that Churchill's suggestion 'to lure Italian submarines to their destruction would be an admirable one if it were our policy to expedite the outbreak of war'.[74] That, of course, was not Churchill's intention. Indeed on 9 September, the day before the conference opened, he wrote to Eden that anti-submarine patrols in the Mediterranean must have the friendly concurrence of, and if possible participation by, Italy. 'This is the moment', Churchill added 'to rally Italy to her international duty.' Germany was not ready for a major war in 1937, he said, and matters with Italy 'should be brought to a head now', and Mussolini shown that Britain would not give way to bluff and bullying.[75] Eden wrote to Churchill at the end of the conference to say he hoped he would agree the results had been satisfactory, claiming they had 'much increased our authority among the nations'.[76] Churchill subsequently published an article in which he said that Nyon demonstrated how Britain and France could ensure peace in the Mediterranean by standing together.[77]

Chamberlain had a less robust approach and was as far as ever from leaving the task of dividing Italy from Germany to the Foreign Office. He was annoyed by Eden's response to a speech by Mussolini in which the Italian dictator championed Germany's claim to African colonies. Following a question in the House of Commons by Churchill's son-in-law, Duncan Sandys, about whether the foreign secretary would ask the Italian government which of its African possessions it would be prepared to offer to Germany, Eden declared on 1 November that he did not admit the right of any government to call on Britain to make a contribution when it was not prepared to make one itself.[78] Writing to his sisters, Chamberlain remarked that Eden should never have allowed himself to be provoked into making the retort. The prime minister took the incident as another example of what he regarded as the Foreign Office's inability to keep the major objects of foreign policy in mind. At a luncheon the next day, he whispered to Grandi that his own attitude to Anglo-Italian relations was unchanged.[79] Chamberlain also kept the secret Ball-Dingli channel to the Italian embassy open. Italian documents record a series of meetings in late 1937 held to explore how the gap between Mussolini's demands and what Chamberlain could offer could be bridged, but by the end of the year an agreement was no closer.[80]

Despite the amount of time Chamberlain spent on Anglo-Italian relations, his principal goal remained a general settlement of differences with Germany. As he wrote to his sisters on 4 July 1937, 'if only we could get on terms with the Germans I would not care a rap for Musso'.[81] As in

1936, however, the Germans proved to be elusive. Eden had hopes in June 1937 that the German foreign minister, Freiherr von Neurath, could be persuaded to come to London to discuss the policy of non-intervention in Spain, following an attack on the German warship *Deutschland* by Republican aircraft, and that advantage could be taken of the visit for a general review of the international situation. However, von Neurath, having said he was ready to discuss all aspects of Anglo-German relations, prevaricated, and Hitler, having first agreed to the visit, refused to let it go ahead on the grounds that he needed his foreign minister in Berlin at a time when another incident might occur in Spain. In a further effort to discover the objectives of German policy, Eden instructed the ambassador in Berlin, Sir Nevile Henderson, in July to broach the subject with Hermann Goering, who was second only to Hitler in the Nazi hierarchy, and who had recently alluded in conversation with Henderson to the German people regarding England as the enemy in their path. Goering was evasive when asked to define Germany's grievances, and his promise to provide a written answer to the points raised by Henderson about Austria, Czechoslovakia and Germany's ex-colonies went unfulfilled. Goering did say, however, that Hitler was bitterly disappointed by Britain's failure to enter into an Anglo-German understanding following the naval treaty of 1935.[82]

Chamberlain thus grasped eagerly in October 1937 at the opportunity for high-level contact afforded by an invitation to Lord Halifax to visit an international hunting exhibition in Berlin. When Halifax told him that Vansittart had said he should not go as he would certainly be asked awkward questions, the prime minister was 'really horrified' that the Foreign Office should allow 'another opportunity to be thrown away'.[83] Eden did not object to the visit, but was unenthusiastic and said Halifax should confine himself to listening to what the Germans had to say and to warning them off action against Austria and Czechoslovakia. Later, after it had been arranged that Halifax would meet Hitler at Berchtesgaden, Eden was annoyed by press reports on 16 November that, in his opinion, exaggerated the significance of what was intended to be an occasion for informal contact, not negotiations. Suspecting that the inspiration for the reports might have come from the prime minister's press office, Eden went to see Chamberlain. Chamberlain insisted that Halifax's visit would be valuable, and there followed what Eden called 'rather sharp' exchanges on Anglo-American relations and lack of progress on rearmament. Chamberlain ended the interview by advising Eden to go home and take an aspirin.[84]

Halifax's visit to Berchtesgaden on 19 November left him with the impression Hitler was sincere when he said the Versailles settlement must be changed by war or by reason, and that no one who had seen what war meant, as he had, could be so stupid as to want another. On the other hand, Halifax did not rate the political value of the interview very highly since he and Hitler clearly had different values and were metaphorically as well as literally not talking the same language. Chamberlain, however, judged the visit to have been a great success from the point of view of creating an atmosphere in which a European settlement could be discussed with Germany. He took as correct, 'at least for the time being', that Hitler did not intend to go to war, but would seek to dominate Eastern Europe by a close union with Austria, short of incorporation into the Reich, and by giving support to the German minority in Czechoslovakia. Chamberlain thought a basis for a settlement would be satisfactory assurances from Germany that force would not be used to deal with the Austrians or Czechoslovaks, and assurances from Britain that force would not be used to prevent changes that Germany could get by peaceful means. Halifax advised that only the colonial question offered a way in which to improve Anglo-German relations, and Chamberlain still felt a settlement was possible by redistributing African territories without having to return Tanganyika. He was optimistic Germany could be persuaded to return to the League of Nations if its coercive powers, which had failed over Ethiopia, were removed. He noted that Hitler had been non-committal about disarmament, but took some comfort from the fact he had declared himself in favour of banning bombers.[85]

Nevertheless, Chamberlain was not completely naïve. When he, Eden and Halifax met the French prime minister, Camille Chautemps, and foreign secretary, Delbos, in London on 29 and 30 November to discuss Halifax's visit, Chamberlain remarked that a colony, once given to Germany, could not be recovered, but assurances given by Germany might easily not be fulfilled. He and Chautemps agreed there could be no discussion of colonies except as part of a general settlement. Regarding Central Europe, Chamberlain said that, whatever Germany's ultimate objective – which could be assumed to include acquisition of territory – Britain and France should aim to make this more difficult, or even to postpone it until it became unrealisable. Delbos feared that what Germany really wanted was to absorb Austria and part of Czechoslovakia, thereby gaining hegemony and a new appetite for further conquest. Chamberlain, however, thought it would be impossible to win over British public opinion for armed intervention against Germany in support of Czechoslovakia. There was, he said, a feeling in Britain that the German minority had grievances that ought to be addressed – a view which Eden shared – and Delbos agreed to raise the matter with the Czechs. Regarding Austria, it was noted that Britain,

France and Italy had agreed at Stresa that the independence of Austria was a necessary element in European peace and, although Italy's interest in that country had somewhat weakened, Austria ought to feature in negotiations with Germany.[86] The Cabinet agreed with Chamberlain on 1 December that the German government should be told that matters discussed by Halifax would require a good deal of study and it should not be disappointed if some time elapsed before a further approach was made.[87] In February 1938 Chamberlain told his sisters he had been reading Stephen Roberts' book, *The House That Hitler Built*, which warned that Hitler's aims could not be achieved without war unless all German territorial demands were met. Chamberlain remarked: 'If I accepted the author's conclusions I should despair but I don't and won't.'[88]

Chamberlain was unduly optimistic about the prospects for peace, but Churchill too was far from convinced war was inevitable. On 15 October 1937 he published an article in which he said great exertions were being made to meet the dangers facing the country and 'in spite of the risks which wait on prophecy, I declare my belief that a major war is not imminent, and I still believe there is a good chance of no major war taking place again in our time'.[89] Alluding to von Neutrath's failure to come to Britain earlier in the year, Churchill remarked in speech in the Commons in December that 'the Angel of Peace is unsnubbable', and said efforts should continue in the face of rebuffs to improve relations with Germany. Churchill praised the government for following up the Halifax visit by inviting Chautemps and Delbos to London for a reaffirmation of Anglo-French solidarity, and said he was convinced the two countries were so formidable in combination they were very likely to be left undisturbed, 'at least for some time to come'. He welcomed Chamberlain's assurance that the restoration of Germany's colonies would be discussed only as part of a general settlement in Europe leading to an all-round reduction in armaments, and spoke in terms of all countries that had gained territory after the First World War contributing to appeasement.[90]

In hindsight one can see that optimism about Anglo-German relations was unfounded. Whereas Britain and France wanted a replacement for Locarno which would preserve their position under the League Covenant and, in France's case, existing treaties with Eastern European countries, Hitler wanted a bilateral pact with Britain, along the lines of the Anglo-German Naval Agreement, which would give him a free hand in Eastern Europe. By November 1937 he had concluded that the British were hostile to his territorial ambitions but were unable to oppose them effectively, and therefore he had little interest in an agreement.[91] However, both Chamberlain and Churchill saw the future as uncertain and war far from inevitable. The 1937 defence review, discussed in the next section, was thus an attempt to find a sustainable deterrent to support diplomacy.

6.3   The Inskip Defence Review

In the spring of 1937, while Chamberlain was still chancellor, Treasury officials drew his attention to the way in which defence departments were constantly adding to the rearmament programme that the Cabinet had approved in February 1936. Sir Richard Hopkins advised that financial restraint should be re-imposed by fixing a maximum limit to each department's expenditure. On 30 June 1937, a month after Chamberlain became prime minister, the Cabinet approved a recommendation by his successor as chancellor, Sir John Simon, that no further major additions should be made to departments' programmes until these programmes had been reviewed in the light of the nation's financial and industrial resources. Simon further suggested that total defence expenditure in the five financial years 1937/8 to 1941/42 should not exceed £1,500 million, of which £400 million would be borrowed. The Cabinet was given the option of increased taxation if the international situation should be judged so serious as to require higher expenditure. Ministers were warned there was no surer way to national bankruptcy than to allow borrowing to become permanent, and Treasury officials were concerned that the forces to be created by March 1942 should not be larger than what could be maintained from a tolerable level of taxation. The Cabinet agreed a defence review should decide priorities and fix maximum sums to be spent by each department for each year down to 1941/42, but, in response to concerns expressed by Sir Thomas Inskip, the minister for co-ordination of defence, ministers added that it was not intended to reverse earlier Cabinet decisions or to delay the execution of these decisions.[92]

One way in which to conduct the review would have been to reconvene the DRC official sub-committee. However, Inskip thought that would cause discord among the chiefs of staff, with each fighting for his own service. Simon therefore suggested to Chamberlain that Inskip should conduct the review himself, with the assistance of a panel of civil servants: Sir Warren Fisher, Hopkins and Edward Bridges from the Treasury; Sir Horace Wilson from the Prime Minister's Office; Sir Maurice Hankey, the cabinet secretary; and Sir Arthur Robinson, chairman of the CID's Supply Board, who was responsible for co-ordinating industrial aspects of rearmament. There was no representative of the Foreign Office. The programmes of the RAF, army and navy were discussed separately in November with the responsible ministers, Swinton, Hore-Belisha and

Duff Cooper, and then Hankey drafted a report for Inskip.[93] Inskip was no Treasury cypher. Despite Hopkins's protests, he took the view that the prospective budgetary situation in 1942 was too uncertain a guide to what could be afforded and instead focused on what could be done in the immediate future. He accepted the Treasury's argument that economic stability was a 'fourth arm of defence' that acted as a deterrent by ensuring Britain would have the financial resources with which to pay for essential imports of food and raw materials while blockading Germany in a long war. He also accepted the advice of the chiefs of staff that Germany might be tempted to try to knock out Britain, or France, rapidly, and tried to strike a balance between solvency and security. He saw the purpose of the review as identifying the right kind and size of forces to ward off defeat in the early days of a war, within the financial limit set by the chancellor for the quinquennium 1937/38 to 1941/42. That limit was revised slightly by the Treasury to £1,570 million, but fell short of forecasts totalling £1,769 million to £1,884 million for what the defence departments wanted. In allocating financial 'rations' to departments, Inskip made clear that the amount of money that could be spent in any one year was not fixed. On the contrary, he said they should press on with their programmes in 1938, which the Foreign Office advised was likely to be a critical year in international relations. Moreover, Inskip recommended there should be a further review in 1939 to consider whether the defence programmes should be enlarged in the light of developments in the international situation.[94] There was to be no slackening in the pace of defence expenditure, which, in the event, increased by 50 per cent between the financial years 1937/38 and 1938/39.

Inskip's review did, however, bring about major change in grand strategy. In an interim report he recommended, and on 22 December 1937 the Cabinet agreed, that the first two objectives should be protection of the United Kingdom and its trade routes. Britain's main resources of manpower and industrial capacity were concentrated there, and ultimate defeat would be certain unless they remained unimpaired, whatever happened elsewhere. The defence of British overseas territories and interests was given a lower priority since recovery from defeats or losses would be possible so long as the United Kingdom was undefeated. The last objective was defence of the territories of allies, which was to be provided for only after the other three objectives had been met.[95] The defence departments' programmes were recast in line with this order of priorities.

By the time the review took place it was as apparent to the Air Ministry as it was to Churchill that British aircraft production was lagging behind Germany's, and there was no immediate prospect of achieving parity in bombers. However, Whitehall was moving away from the tendency to think that the bomber would always get through. Hankey, after reading reports of the CID Sub-Committee on Air Warfare in Spain, advised Inskip in September 1937 that a combination of fighter aircraft, anti-aircraft guns and searchlights might prove very much more effective than hitherto assumed.[96] Progress with radar had been sufficiently satisfactory for the CID's Air Defence Research Committee to recommend in July that work should begin on a chain of stations to detect German aircraft approaching Britain.[97] Inskip's attention was also drawn by Hankey to a report from the chargé d'affaires at Berlin, George Ogilvie-Forbes, who said that Germany's air defences were so formidable and air raid precautions so efficient that British bombing 'would produce a far less staggering impact than might at one time have been hoped'.[98] Inskip was thus prepared to challenge the Air Ministry's doctrine that Britain must maintain parity with Germany in bombers. He told Swinton in November that 'if our air striking power were inferior to an enemy's, we should suffer more than he, but the result might not at once be critical'. In contrast, if the navy were unable to keep the trade routes open for essential food and raw materials 'we should not long survive'.[99]

Inskip was unconvinced by Air Ministry arguments that ability to bomb German air bases and factories was the best form of defence as well as deterrence, and took the view that government pledges, such as those made by Baldwin in 1934 to maintain air parity, did not imply having as many bombers as the Germans. In his interim report in December 1937 he recommended that as many fighter aircraft as were necessary for the defence of the United Kingdom should be ordered, including war reserves. On the other hand, he thought the Air Ministry should order fewer of the bombers that it wanted, and that money should be spent on building aircraft factories rather than on building up war reserves of bombers. Swinton protested in Cabinet on 22 December that without reserves the air force would have to 'go slow' during the first six months of a war while additional bombers were produced. Chamberlain, however, said the evidence showed an enemy was unlikely to succeed in inflicting a knock-out blow. He attached great importance to the maintenance of economic stability. In effect, he was prepared to abandon the bomber deterrent he had favoured since 1934 and replace it with the economic deterrent of the fourth arm of defence. He suggested that the expansion of the RAF should be considered by Inskip and Swinton along the lines of the report, with the possibility of doing something more for the RAF if there were any margin out of the global sum of £1,500 million.[100] A new programme for the RAF was not agreed until April 1938, but Inskip's interim report represented a decisive step towards a defensive air strategy at the outbreak of war. Priority for home defence also meant that no additional squadrons were to be allocated to imperial defence.

In 1937 the Admiralty was already basing its construction programme on a higher standard of naval strength than the DRC standard approved by the Cabinet in February 1936. However, the Admiralty preferred to present its proposals for new construction as an acceleration of the approved programme and not to press for a decision on the New Standard. Inskip was aware the Admiralty could keep within the approved programme after 1938 only by a drastic reduction in new orders. Nevertheless, in his interim report he recommended the Admiralty should not incur expenditure that committed it to a fleet beyond the approved standard, and that a decision whether to adopt a higher standard should be deferred.[101] He intended to ration the Admiralty's finance in a way that would allow it to aim at an intermediate goal. Duff Cooper, however, rejected the whole concept of rationing and wrote to Chamberlain on 13 March 1938 claiming that a naval deterrent was more important than air power. The question was eventually discussed in Cabinet on 20 July 1938, when Duff Cooper gained some support from Sir Samuel Hoare, now home secretary, who, as a former first lord of the Admiralty, agreed with him that it would be a shock to the dominions if they were told Britain could not attain the standard required to match Japan as well as Germany. Chamberlain remarked there was no need to reject the New Standard, but neither was there a need to make a commitment to it before it could be implemented. He said he was prepared to assist Inskip, Duff Cooper, and Simon to agree a total sum to be spent on the navy in the financial years 1938/39 to 1941/42. The figure decided, £410 million, was less than the £443 million required for the New Standard, but more than that required for the DRC Standard, £395 million, and slightly more than the £405 million that Admiralty staff thought would be enough to keep existing industrial capacity fully employed.[102] In other words, the Admiralty was able to continue to aim at the New Standard, although more slowly than it would have wished, and plans to send a fleet to the Far East were not abandoned.

Chamberlain's main focus was on the army. In seeking to change its role he had an ally in the secretary of state for war, Hore-Belisha, who looked to Liddell Hart for alternative advice to that of the chief of the imperial general staff, Sir Cyril Deverell. Hore-Belisha was persuaded by Liddell Hart that one or two mechanized (armoured) divisions would have more impact in European warfare than an expeditionary force made up of infantry divisions.[103] It would seem to have been this preconception that led Hore-Belisha, following a visit to the French manoeuvres in September 1937, to tell the Cabinet 'he gathered' that in the event of war the French wanted the British to send two mechanised divisions rather than a large number of infantry divisions. Hore-Belisha's understanding was that France's frontier defences (the Maginot Line) could be held by 100,000 men, releasing the bulk of the French army for mobile operations. Chamberlain thanked Hore-Belisha for this statement, but the latter had almost certainly misunderstood what he had heard in France, his French not being good enough for military conversations.[104] According to Inskip, no one in the Cabinet believed Hore-Belisha's report to be well founded.[105] On the other hand, faith in the Maginot Line was not limited to the secretary of state for war: Churchill had written in May 1937 of the 'brilliantly conceived fortifications upon which and through which the mobile French armies will fight and manoeuvre'.[106] The chiefs of staff's more sober assessment six months later was that the French fortifications made rapid German success on land unlikely, and that the German army would not be strong enough to take the offensive before 1939–40.[107]

On 29 October 1937 Chamberlain told Hore-Belisha he had been reading Liddell Hart's book, *Europe in Arms*, and recommended the chapter on the role of the British Army. Hore-Belisha replied two days later he had immediately read the chapter and was impressed by Liddell Hart's ideas.[108] In *Europe in Arms* Liddell Hart argued that Britain should give up the idea of sending an expeditionary force to France or Belgium and should develop an air force that could intervene from British bases at the outbreak of war. 'The promise of such help', he wrote, 'would be more comfort to a threatened neighbour, and more deterrent to a would-be aggressor, than any force of the 1914 pattern – a mere drop in the bucket of a continental struggle between mass armies'.[109] Inskip thought Chamberlain had been 'bitten' by Liddell Hart and described the prime minister as 'a bitter opponent' of a continental role for the army.[110] That may be so, but Chamberlain did not dictate what the role of the army should be; he left the task of making recommendations to the responsible minister, Inskip.

As late as 23 November 1937 Inskip had not come to a firm view about the army when he dictated a memorandum saying: 'a decision is required as to the scale of the Field Force which we must provide fully equipped and trained in up-to-date armaments for dispatch to the Continent', and also as to 'the work for which it will be ready at the outbreak of war'.[111] However, on the same day Hankey advised him, reluctantly, that the Field Force's role should be imperial defence and that it should no longer be prepared for service on the continent of Europe. A year earlier Hankey had been a defender of the continental commitment. What had changed his mind? One reason was concern about Britain's air defences: on 8 November 1937 a meeting of ministers had decided the War Office should give absolute priority to the provision of anti-aircraft defences over all other forms of war material, which implied a lower priority for the Field Force.[112] Hankey also placed a high priority on imperial defence, as his views at the time of the DRC sub-committee report in 1934 had shown. In his advice to Inskip in November 1937 he accepted the Treasury's case that financial stability and economic staying power were hardly less important than armaments as a deterrent. He noted that plans to have an expeditionary force ready to fight in a European campaign at the outbreak of war required 'vast' reserves of munitions, which would not be required in the less intensive fighting that could be expected in imperial defence. He suggested four recent developments to justify a change in policy. First, Hore-Belisha had reported that France no longer expected Britain to provide an expeditionary force on the same scale as before. Second, in October 1936 King Leopold had announced that Belgium would be neutral in the event of another war, and Germany might well respect that neutrality since the Ruhr was vulnerable to attack across Belgian territory. Third, the increasing cost of aircraft and anti-aircraft defences made it harder to provide a large army as well. Finally the defence of the Empire might absorb all of the army's manpower. [113] For example, 20,000 men were required to contain the Arab revolt in Palestine after 1936, while the garrison in Egypt, at 20,500 men, was double what it had been before the crisis over Ethiopia.

Inskip accepted Hankey's advice on the Field Force with reluctance, but asked his Cabinet colleagues to share responsibility for what was being recommended with their eyes open, observing:

If France were again to be in danger of being overrun by land armies, a situation might arise when, as in the last war, we had to improvise an army to assist her. Should this happen, the Government of the day would most certainly be criticised for having neglected to provide against so obvious a contingency.[114]

Ministers would have recalled that a shortage of shells on the Western Front in 1915 had led to the fall of the government. Nevertheless they accepted Inskip's proposal for a very substantial reduction in the scale of reserves of munitions for the Field Force. Eden was told by Vansittart that 'in a relatively short while' an expanding German army plus the Italian army would outnumber the French by three to one, and the Maginot Line did not make France impregnable. Nevertheless, although the foreign secretary expressed concern about being unable to assist allies on land when the Cabinet met on 22 December 1937, he said that, from an international point of view, the strength of the air force was more important and therefore did not ask for a change in priorities. Eden differed from Chamberlain only in believing that the air force should continue to have an offensive as well as a defensive role.[115]

Understandably, the Cabinet's decision that the Field Force should not be prepared to support European allies at the outbreak of war has sometimes been interpreted by historians to mean that the army's continental role had been abandoned.[116] However, a second report by Inskip on 8 February 1938 left open the possibility of assisting European allies on land. Previously it had been planned that a Field Force of four infantry divisions and one mobile (armoured) division would be able to disembark on the Continent within 15 days of mobilisation. Inskip now proposed to have two infantry divisions and one mobile division with full reserves of munitions, ready to go abroad within 21 days, and two infantry divisions with war equipment but only half scales of reserves of munitions, ready to begin embarkation in 40 days. In addition, there would be a pool of equipment to enable two further divisions, which might be from the Territorial Army, to take the field after four months. He assumed the Field Force would be equipped to operate in an 'Eastern' theatre, probably Egypt, where a new mobile division was being established. However, Hore-Belisha circulated a paper to the Cabinet stating that, if the situation in the rest of the world permitted, an expeditionary force could be despatched to Europe. On 16 February the Cabinet decided the French should be told about the implications of its decision on the role of the army, and adopted the wording: 'if the obligations involved in the Treaty of Locarno should arise and the government of the day, after considering our other military commitments at home and abroad, should decide to despatch a military force to France', only one mobile division and four infantry divisions would be available. Moreover, these divisions would be equipped for general purposes and not specifically for a continental campaign.[117]

The Field Force's equipment was discussed at the CID on 17 March, when Hore-Belisha challenged the absolute priority given to anti-aircraft defence. In response to a request from Chamberlain for information, the chief of the imperial general staff, now Lord Gort, explained that existing field guns and howitzers were out-ranged by foreign artillery, and added that, without replacements, 'it would be murder to send our Field Force overseas to fight a first-class power'. The CID therefore agreed that, while existing industrial capacity would be used for anti-aircraft guns, the War Office could allocate any new capacity to the requirements of the Field Force. It also agreed the Field Force's first echelon of the mobile division and two infantry divisions should be prepared for a continental campaign, but for defensive warfare only. The second echelon would have only half the war reserves of the first. Finally, the Territorial Army was not to be disbanded, and would be trained with the same kind of equipment as regular units.[118] Chamberlain thus acquiesced in decisions that left open the possibility of improvising (to use Inskip's expression) an expeditionary force to assist France.

Churchill's priorities were similar to those of the government. In December 1937 and January 1938 he praised the speed with which the navy was rearming, and claimed that the combination of the British fleet and the French army should give lesser European powers the confidence to contribute to their own safety through the League of Nations. He believed the French army was second in size only to the Soviet one, and was superior in quality to that of any country, although he accepted that 'in a few years' time' the situation would change as German manpower was organised and trained. Meanwhile he was content that the British Army should act as 'little more than an imperial police reserve', albeit one that should have the latest military equipment.[119] When on 7 March 1938 Chamberlain set out the government's defence objectives, with co-operation in defence of allies' territories lowest in priority, Churchill told the House of Commons that 'the army is not at the present time a prime factor in our safety', and apparently saw no incongruity between that statement and his advice to the government to seek allies within the ambit of the League of Nations. He saw air power as the key to deterring aggression, and criticised the government's failure to carry out Baldwin's pledge to maintain parity with Germany.[120] It is difficult to believe that if Churchill had been in Chamberlain's place the army would have fared any better in Inskip's defence review.

6.4   Eden's Resignation

Writing on 19 February 1938, three days after the Cabinet approved Inskip's second report, Chamberlain noted that France was weak politically and financially, and the United States, although friendly, was not dependable on account of isolationism. He worried that the rearmament programme was creating forces which could not be maintained without heavily increased taxation for an indefinite period. He was concerned, therefore, to reduce the number of potential enemies.[121] He had been encouraged in his belief that a rapprochement with Italy was possible by a friendly message from Mussolini conveyed through his sister-in-law, Ivy Chamberlain, who visited Rome in December 1937.[122] In correspondence in January 1938 with Eden about prospective Anglo-Italian talks, the prime minister set out his objective of restoring Anglo-Italian relations to what they had been before the Ethiopian crisis, with *de jure* recognition of the Italian conquest being a contribution to appeasement. The foreign secretary, however, worried that recognition would undermine Britain's moral position, and doubted whether the Italians would abide by any agreement. In a revealing comparison of the dictators, Eden thought a general settlement with Germany might last a reasonable time, 'especially if Hitler's own position were engaged, whereas Mussolini is, I fear, a complete gangster and his pledged word means nothing'. Eden was annoyed by further informal diplomacy in Rome by Ivy Chamberlain at the beginning of February.

Matters became more pressing after Hitler summoned the Austrian chancellor, Kurt von Schuschnigg, to Berchtesgaden on 12 February 1938 and bullied him into appointing a Nazi to the key post of minister of the interior with control of the police. Eden, speaking to the Cabinet on 16 February, said he was watching the situation carefully, but added that it was not possible to offer any resistance to German action in Austria.[123] Chamberlain was convinced Mussolini faced a choice between making friends with Britain or joining Hitler's band-wagon, and that there should be no further delay in starting talks with Italy.[124] Using Sir Joseph Ball's secret channel to the Italian embassy, he let it be known he was willing to begin discussions. However, Eden was suspicious of Grandi's 'now or never' attitude to Anglo-Italian relations. When the foreign minister and the prime minister received the ambassador at 10 Downing Street on 18 February, Grandi thought they appeared like 'two enemies confronting each other, like two cocks in fighting posture'.[125] In Grandi's absence, during an adjournment, Chamberlain remonstrated with Eden, telling him: 'Anthony, you have missed chance after chance. You simply cannot go on like this.' Eden replied that Chamberlain's methods were 'right if you have faith in the man you are dealing with'. By Eden's account, Chamberlain said he did have faith.[126] The two men agreed to take their disagreement to the Cabinet, which met, unusually, on a Saturday, 19 February. Eden said the differences between him and the prime minister were over methods, and argued that talks should not proceed until Italy had given evidence of goodwill by beginning to withdraw troops from Spain and by ending anti-British propaganda. Of the 18 other ministers present, 14 supported Chamberlain unreservedly and only four gave some support to Eden.[127] At the end of the meeting Halifax suggested a compromise whereby negotiations would be announced together with a statement that *de jure* recognition depended on evidence that Italian intervention in Spain was coming to an end. However, after Chamberlain and Eden met the next day, Sunday, the prime minister concluded that their disagreement was deeper than differences on methods and timing. Eden's explanation later in the day to the Cabinet of his decision to resign included disagreement over Roosevelt's message the previous month as well as over Italy, and said it would be better for the country to have a foreign secretary with whom the prime minister could see eye to eye.[128]

In his resignation speech on 21 February, Eden said he did not believe progress could be made in European appeasement if the impression was given that Britain yielded to constant pressure.[129] The following day Churchill praised the way Eden, by standing together with France, had halted Italian submarine attacks in the Mediterranean, and his efforts to support the rule of law in Europe and to create, through regional pacts under the League of Nations, effective deterrents to aggression. Churchill asked whether there was to be a new policy of coming to terms with the totalitarian powers in the hope that, by far-reaching acts of submission, peace could be preserved.[130] For the first time he abstained from voting with the government. Despite his opposition in August 1937 to an indefinite refusal to recognise the conquest of Ethiopia if that were to lead to the permanent alienation of Italy, Churchill told Duff Cooper on 13 February 1938 that recognition would be 'the depth of humiliation'.[131] However, it is far from certain that Chamberlain and Eden saw their differences in these terms. Their disagreement about Italy concerned how negotiations should be conducted and on what conditions recognition should be granted. Halifax could see no fundamental differences between them, and concluded that Eden resigned partly because of irritation at the prime minister's closer control of foreign policy and amateur diplomacy, partly because of excessive sensitivity to criticism from the Opposition, and partly from being overstrained.[132] Eden himself made no effort in his resignation speech to develop his differences with Chamberlain, refrained from open association with Churchill, and remained silent in Parliament until after the Munich agreement. It is difficult to see Eden's resignation as a turning point in British foreign policy. However, it diminished Chamberlain in Roosevelt's estimation. The president thought Eden had been sacrificed to appease Mussolini, and compared the prime minister to a police chief who makes a deal with leading gangsters in the hope they will keep their word.[133]

Eden had not in fact opposed negotiations to improve relations with Germany. As noted above, he was less distrustful of Hitler than of Mussolini. Even so, there had been tension between foreign minister and prime minister regarding how to deal with Berlin. Chamberlain was keen to follow up Halifax's conversations in Germany, and on 24 January

1938 he put to the Cabinet's Foreign Policy Committee an idea for handling Germany's claim for the return of its colonies. The prime minister envisaged a new colonial regime in Africa. Germany and the existing colonial powers would agree to respect native rights; allow freedom of communications and as far as possible free trade; and refrain from raising native armies or constructing submarine or air bases. Germany would be given territory to administer, but Chamberlain was vague as to what would be transferred and from whom. The minutes record Eden's insistence that a colonial settlement be conditional on a general settlement, although Chamberlain had made the condition clear from the outset of the meeting, and the impression given is that the foreign secretary was attempting to assert his authority.[134] In memoranda dated 25 January and 10 February Eden listed the contributions that Germany could make to general appeasement, focusing on undertakings to respect the sovereignty of Austria and Czechoslovakia, as only these, he thought, could balance colonial concessions.[135] In the event, Chamberlain's idea did not impress Hitler. When the ambassador in Berlin, Henderson, communicated it to him on 3 March, Hitler frankly declared he was willing to put the colonial question in cold storage for a number of years, lest as part of a settlement he would be asked to tie his hands in Central Europe. Henderson recalled that a few weeks earlier Goering had said: 'If you offered us the whole of Africa we would not accept it as the price of Austria.'[136]

7   From the *Anschluss* to Munich

7.1   First Reactions to the Threat to Czechoslovakia

On 12 March 1938 German troops entered Austria, to be greeted with enthusiasm by large sections of the population. There was no armed resistance. Hitler proclaimed the *Anschluss* (Union) of Germany and Austria. His next step was rightly expected to be exploitation of the grievances of the German-speaking minority in Czechoslovakia. That country acted as a barrier to German expansion in Central and Eastern Europe. France was committed by treaty to come to Czechoslovakia's aid if it were invaded. The Soviet Union was likewise committed, but only if the French acted first. A dispute nominally about the rights of the German-speaking inhabitants of the western borders of Czechoslovakia – the Sudetenland – could thus lead to a European war. Britain had no commitment to Czechoslovakia, other than what it owed to a fellow member of the League of Nations. On the other hand, while not obliged by the Treaty of Locarno to assist France if it attacked Germany, Britain could hardly stand aside if France were in danger of being defeated. Chamberlain had henceforth to focus on crisis management rather than, as hitherto, on negotiations aimed at a general appeasement of Europe.

Chamberlain called a Cabinet meeting on 12 March, a Saturday, as the Germans carried out their occupation of Austria. He said Hitler's action made international appeasement much more difficult and hoped the foreign secretary, Halifax, would consult with the French on how to prevent a similar event in Czechoslovakia. Discussion then focused on what could be done to expand and accelerate British rearmament and there was a consensus on the need to increase the size of the air force and accelerate anti-aircraft defences. At this point domestic politics intersected with international relations. Churchill had told Chamberlain earlier in the day of his intention to support a Labour Party motion for an enquiry into the Air Ministry, which was accused of failing to match German aircraft production either in quantity or quality. Although Churchill and Attlee had indicated they would be discreet about details of the RAF's deficiencies, ministers feared that speeches belittling the effort being made would have a very unfortunate effect on the international situation just when the only hope of saving Czechoslovakia was to create an impression of power.[1] In the event the motion was not put to the House of Commons until 25 May, but defence and foreign policy were particularly closely intertwined in the spring of 1938.

The first conclusion Chamberlain drew from the *Anschluss* was that the only argument Germany understood was force backed by overwhelming strength and the determination to use it. He recognised power could best be mobilised by forming alliances. However, he was reluctant to return to pre-1914 diplomacy. Writing to his sisters on 13 March, he remarked: 'Heaven knows I don't want to get back to alliances but if Germany continues to behave as she has done lately she may drive us to it.' He proposed to show Britain's determination not to be bullied by announcing an increase or acceleration in rearmament. He thought talks with Germany must cease for the moment, but if a violent coup in Czechoslovakia could be avoided, it might be possible to resume them. Meanwhile, he intended to continue to seek an agreement with Italy.[2]

When the Cabinet met again on 14 March, the chancellor of the exchequer, Simon, warned that approving the expansion scheme put forward by the Air Ministry would breach the previous month's decision to place a ceiling on defence expenditure. He said inflationary borrowing and other unorthodox measures could be adopted in war, but to do so in peace might weaken the country's finances prematurely. He compared the country's position to that of a runner in a race who wanted to reserve his spurt for the right time, but who did not know where the finishing tape was. Inskip, as minister for co-ordination of defence, pointed out that, if rearmament was to be accelerated, it would be necessary to ask the trade unions to accept dilution of the work of skilled labour. Such an approach was likely to be badly received. The sort of difficulty he anticipated was that the trade unions would make conditions: for example, they might demand that the government undertake to use arms in support of Czechoslovakia, or insist on action through the League of Nations. Chamberlain nevertheless said that conversations should be begun with the trade unions (and in the event Inskip's fears proved to be groundless as the Trades Union Congress leaders agreed to concern themselves only with industrial aspects of rearmament). The prime minister did not wish to rush a decision on the Air Ministry's expansion scheme and instead told Parliament in the afternoon that the government had decided to make a fresh review of the defence programmes in the light of the new international situation.[3]

The effect of the *Anschluss* on Churchill's view of the international situation can be seen in his speech in the debate on 14 March. In contrast to the optimism he had expressed about Anglo-German relations a few months earlier, he now said Europe faced a programme of aggression, unfolding stage by stage, which must be resisted if Germany were not to become more and more powerful. He pointed out how German possession of Austria had weakened the strategic position of France's allies in Central and Eastern Europe, and warned that perhaps the last chance of averting war would be for Britain and France to form a grand alliance, under the League of Nations. He spoke of 'a number of states assembled round Great Britain and France', without specifying which ones, but in an article four days later he wrote of 'powers of the second rank', a category that clearly did not include the Soviet Union.[4] Churchill found himself in close agreement with Attlee when the Labour leader said that the progressive deterioration in the world situation – Manchuria, Ethiopia, the Rhineland, Spain, China and Austria – required a collective stand under the League if all of Europe were not to be thrown into the melting pot. The cross-party nature of the opposition to Chamberlain was strengthened by Attlee's reference to what he took to be Eden's principled resignation in protest against the prime minister's policy of making separate agreements with the dictators.[5] Yet for all the rhetoric about collective action, Churchill did not advocate the use of force to reverse the *Anschluss*. Speaking to the National Labour MP Harold Nicolson on 16 March he expressed sympathy for Chamberlain's position, blaming Baldwin for the weakness of Britain's air defences. 'If we take strong action', Churchill remarked, 'London will be a shambles in half-an-hour'.[6]

Meanwhile Chamberlain had asked the chiefs of staff to report on the military implications of combining with France, Czechoslovakia, Yugoslavia, Romania, Hungary, Turkey and Greece to resist a German attempt to impose a solution to the Sudetenland problem by force; and also on the implications of guaranteeing support to France if it fulfilled its treaty obligations. In both cases, the assumptions were that Italy and Japan might be hostile, the American Neutrality Act would be in operation, and the Soviet Union would be neutral.[7] In excluding the Soviet Union as a possible ally, Chamberlain was in line with the Foreign Office's guidance for the Joint Planning Sub-Committee of the Chiefs of Staff Committee to the effect that, following Stalin's purges, the Soviet Union was in no condition to wage offensive war effectively and would go to almost any lengths to avoid hostilities. The permanent under-secretary, Sir Alexander Cadogan, advised that nevertheless the Soviets would not 'be backward in stirring up hostilities'.[8] Chamberlain shared this suspicion. He wrote to his sisters of 'the Russians stealthily and cunningly pulling all the strings behind the scenes to get us involved in war with Germany (our secret service doesn't spend all its time looking out of windows)'.[9] It is debatable whether the Soviets wanted a European war in 1938, for which they were ill prepared, but even after the opening of Soviet archives Stalin's intentions in 1938 remain a matter for conjecture.[10]

The chiefs of staff's report was not ready by the time the Cabinet's Foreign Policy Committee met on 18 March, and ministers' deliberations were informed by a Foreign Office paper on possible measures to avert German action in Czechoslovakia. The paper noted the absence of fortifications along the Czech border with Austria. Moreover, the occupation of Vienna gave Germany control of Czech access to the sea through Trieste and, as Germany already controlled Czech access through Hamburg, it could impose an economic stranglehold. Chamberlain commented: 'You have only to look at the map to see that nothing that France or we could do could possibly save Czechoslovakia from being overrun by the Germans if they wanted to do it.' A hundred miles of Polish or Romanian territory separated the Soviet Union from Czechoslovakia. Chamberlain thought Czechoslovakia 'would simply be a pretext for going to war with Germany. That we could not think of unless we had a reasonable prospect of being able to beat her to her knees in a reasonable time and of that I see no sign.' He therefore abandoned any idea of giving guarantees to Czechoslovakia or France.[11]

The Foreign Office described Churchill's proposal for a grand alliance as 'attractive', but put forward the 'decisive objection' that it would require a lengthy period of negotiations, giving the Germans the motive and opportunity to act before it could be organised. Halifax said Britain faced a choice between mobilising all its friends and resources and going full out against Germany, or telling France it could not count on British assistance and that Czechoslovakia should make the best terms it could with Germany. He thought Churchill's plan for the French army to stand on the defensive behind the Maginot Line, forcing the Germans to deploy large forces in the west, while Czechoslovakia engaged Germany's remaining forces in the east, bore no relation to reality. Chamberlain observed that the French army was no doubt good, but with regard to the air force, and financial and political stability, France was in a hopeless situation, and its influence in Central and Eastern Europe was steadily declining. Significantly, he believed the seizure of the whole of Czechoslovakia would not be in accordance with what he supposed to be Hitler's policy of bringing all Germans, but not other nationalities, into the Reich. Following the advice of the ambassador in Prague, Basil Newton, he thought it most likely Germany would absorb the Sudetenland and reduce the rest of Czechoslovakia to a condition of dependent neutrality. Halifax likewise did not believe Hitler had a 'lust for conquest on a Napoleonic scale'.[12]

By the time the Cabinet met on 22 March ministers had the chiefs of staff's advice, which confirmed Chamberlain's belief that no pressure that Britain and its possible allies could bring to bear by sea, land, or air on Germany could prevent the defeat of Czechoslovakia. The chiefs of staff commented that Czech independence could then be restored only through a prolonged conflict in which it was more than probable that Italy and Japan would intervene, turning a European war into a world war. In contrast to Churchill, the military experts thought countries like Yugoslavia, Romania, Turkey and Greece would be of limited value as allies, and might involve embarrassing commitments on account of the moral obligation to assist them against German invasion.[13] Halifax said that, in view of the report, he could not recommend a policy that would risk war. He suggested the Czech government should be persuaded to reach a settlement with the Sudeten-Germans, and that Britain and France might try to secure German acceptance of that settlement. Chamberlain said it was difficult to believe the French would not be glad to find some way out of their commitment to Czechoslovakia. Although the cabinet minutes did not attribute other comments to individuals, it is clear some ministers criticised the chiefs of staff's analysis: the Soviet Union had been excluded, and some weaknesses in Germany had possibly been underrated, as had the effects of the war in China on Japan. The chiefs of staff had not dealt with the consequences of German domination of Central and Eastern Europe, which would weaken the effects of blockade in a long war. France might then have to be supported in even more disadvantageous circumstances than at present. On the other hand, it was pointed out that two years hence the RAF would have modern aircraft, anti-aircraft defences would have up-to-date equipment and civil defence measures would be in place. Arguments relating to the security of Great Britain proved to be more persuasive than those relating to the balance of power, and the Cabinet approved the policy suggested by Halifax. The Cabinet agreed, on Inskip's initiative, to speed rearmament by dropping the policy of business as usual.[14]

Before making a speech on foreign policy in the House of Commons on 24 March, Chamberlain had a conversation with Churchill to let him know about military considerations that could not be mentioned in public. By Chamberlain's account, Churchill was pleased to be taken into confidence, and said his attitude towards the government, although critical, would be 'avuncular'. Chamberlain told his sisters that everyone in the House of Commons enjoyed Churchill's speeches, but that Churchill had no following of importance, which was true at that time.[15]

In his own speech Chamberlain said the government would not guarantee Czechoslovakia, or undertake to support France if it fulfilled its treaty obligations to that country, for to do so would remove the government's discretion over an issue where Britain's interests were not as vital as they were in the case of Belgium or France. He added, however, that if war broke out 'the inexorable pressure of facts might well prove more powerful than formal pronouncements, and ... other countries, besides those which were parties to the original dispute, would almost immediately become involved', this being especially true of countries like Britain and France with 'closely interwoven interests'. He dismissed a Soviet proposal for a conference which, he said, would tend to divide Europe into exclusive groups of nations and harm the prospects of peace. He then made the announcement that the defence programmes were to be accelerated, particularly in the cases of the RAF and anti-aircraft defences, by asking industry to give first priority to rearmament work.[16]

In response Churchill argued war could be avoided only by an 'accumulation of deterrents'. He claimed a military convention with France whereby the RAF could operate from French bases would triple the effectiveness of British bombers, while the knowledge that an attack on Britain would bring the aggressor into conflict with the French army would increase British security. He accepted that a permanent and unconditional guarantee of Czechoslovakia would take the decision for peace or war out of the British government's hands, but suggested that a guarantee could be limited to a period while an impartial commission examined the Sudeten-Germans' grievances and a settlement was negotiated. He thought there was no immediate risk of war, as he believed the German army would not be ready in 1938, and also because Germany could achieve its aims by bringing political and economic pressure to bear on Czechoslovakia. He suggested German expansion in the Danube basin could be blocked by Britain and France in combination with Yugoslavia, Romania, Bulgaria, Greece and Turkey, as well as Czechoslovakia.[17] Again he made no reference to the Soviet Union. Yet, in a conversation with the Soviet ambassador, Ivan Maisky, the previous evening, he had remarked that the only reliable means of restraining Germany was a grand alliance of Britain, France, the 'Little Entente' powers (Czechoslovakia, Yugoslavia and Romania) *and* Russia. He told Maisky he had heard from ministers the Soviet Union was experiencing a grave crisis, and took with a pinch of salt Maisky's assurances that Stalin's purges had not weakened his country.[18] Churchill was ambivalent in his attitude to Soviet assistance in the spring of 1938. In a speech on 9 May he urged the government not to go 'cap in hand to Russia, or count in any definite manner upon Russian action'; yet he also observed: 'how improvidently foolish we should be, when dangers are so great, to put needless barriers in the way of the general association of the great Russian mass with resistance to an act of Nazi aggression'.[19]

By 12 April Churchill was thinking in terms of a 'system of regional pacts – Danubian, Balkan, Scandinavian – perhaps even Anglo-Italian'.[20] He was thus not wholly opposed to Chamberlain's efforts to improve Anglo-Italian relations. Negotiations in Rome between the ambassador, Lord Perth, and the Italian foreign minister, Count Ciano, led on 16 April 1938 to what became known as the Easter Agreement, which made recognition of Italian sovereignty in Ethiopia conditional on withdrawal of Italian 'volunteers' from Spain. Chamberlain believed the agreement would have a steadying effect on the Czechoslovakian situation, since Mussolini, having expended resources in Ethiopia and Spain, would not want trouble in Central Europe. The prime minister thought Britain could 'hope for a good deal of quiet help from Italy' [21] Churchill regarded the Easter Agreement as a triumph for the Italian dictator, but even so, in an article published on 12 May, wrote of the 'hope – and growing belief – that common interests will increasingly unite Italy with France and Britain'.[22]

On the other hand, there were clear differences between Churchill and Chamberlain on how relations with France should be developed. Churchill flew on 25 March to Paris where, in a series of meetings over two days with leading French politicians and also Alexis Léger, the general-secretary of the French Foreign Office, he pressed his ideas for an Anglo-French alliance and immediate staff talks, with Central European and Balkan alliances the next step. The British ambassador, Sir Eric Phipps, who was sometimes present, thought Churchill's French was 'most strange and at times incomprehensible'. For example, on one occasion Churchill had shouted out *'nous devons faire bonne'*, as a literal translation of 'we must make good'. Phipps commented in a letter to Halifax that this remark clearly stumped the French foreign minister, Joseph Paul-Boncour, 'who may even have attributed some improper meaning to it' (*bonne* can also mean housemaid). The Cabinet enjoyed this remark when Halifax read out the letter the next day. However, Halifax also told ministers that Churchill had returned from Paris with two useful pieces of information: first, the French government had dropped any idea of intervention in the Spanish Civil War because General Gamelin, the chief of staff, had said that would require mobilisation of the army; second, Churchill had been told about French plans for action if Germany attacked Czechoslovakia.[23] Although Phipps reported that the French realised Churchill spoke only for himself and a very small section of British public opinion, they regarded him as a channel through which they could communicate with British decision-makers.

British decision-makers were far from unanimous on the subject of Anglo-French staff talks. At Cabinet on 6 April Chamberlain criticised the long-standing reluctance of the chiefs of staff to engage in serious conversations. Like Churchill in July 1936 they feared these would inevitably lead to military commitments that would limit Britain's freedom of action if war broke out. The prime minister said the *Anschluss* had shown how in modern warfare an aggressor could move so rapidly there was no time in which to make plans. He had heard it suggested the recent decision on the role of the army made staff talks particularly undesirable, but to him it seemed disloyal to leave the French in the dark as to what could be done.[24] At the CID on 11 April, however, he said he was impressed by the chiefs of staff's point that the French would expect a much larger military contribution than Britain was prepared to offer. He expected a war to begin with a German air attack on Britain, while the French stood on the defensive behind the Maginot Line. He thought it would be unsound to start talks on the pre-1914 basis and be committed to sending any military force to France except what would be required to protect the RAF's Advanced Air Striking Force, which was to be based there. Although now first lord of the Admiralty, Duff Cooper maintained his opposition to Chamberlain's ideas about the role of the army, arguing that Britain could not avoid sending an expeditionary force to the Continent in the event of war. It would be impossible, he said, for Britain to have three million young men in civilian clothes if the French had their backs to the wall. Chamberlain claimed never to have been dogmatic about the possibility of having ultimately to send a large army to the Continent, but said staff talks should not be based on that particular possibility. It was decided the army should be excluded from the talks since the assistance that could be offered on land was so limited.[25] In Cabinet on 13 April Halifax expressed concerned about the depressing effect this decision would have on French ministers, but Chamberlain resisted any change and suggested that knowing they could not count on the Field Force might encourage them to complete the Maginot Line. It was also at Chamberlain's suggestion that staff talks were to be confined to Britain's Locarno obligation to assist France and Belgium in the event of unprovoked aggression by Germany, and not extended, as the chiefs of staff wished, to take account of Italian and Japanese hostility. The Mediterranean was excluded, on the grounds that nothing should be done to jeopardise or weaken the Anglo-Italian Agreement. Likewise it was agreed there should be no naval staff talks in case the Germans made them an excuse to denounce the Anglo-German Naval Agreement, to which the Admiralty attached great importance.[26]

When the French premier, Edouard Daladier, met Chamberlain and Halifax in London on 28 April he protested that defence required the co-operation of all the armed forces and that staff talks could not be confined to the air forces. He said two British divisions at the outbreak of war would be extremely useful, particularly if they were both 'motorised'. Precisely what this term meant is obscure, since in the minutes it was used interchangeably with 'mechanised', but Daladier's reference to British industry's ability to construct tanks suggests he had something more than infantry divisions in mind. In any case, he attached more importance to the moral than the material effect of a British contribution on land. He also asked for naval talks, particularly in connection with the transport of French troops from North Africa. Chamberlain agreed staff talks should include all three services, but this concession was very limited. No date was agreed for the naval talks. The army talks were to be confined to embarkation arrangements on the 'purely hypothetical basis' that two infantry divisions might be sent if the government of the day so decided, and the divisions would not be equipped specifically for a war on the Continent.[27]

On the next day, discussion turned to what should be done about Czechoslovakia. Daladier spoke eloquently of the need to take a stand against aggression, declaring that 'the ambitions of Napoleon were far inferior to the present aims of the German Reich' and that once the Germans had secured the oil and wheat of Romania they would turn against the Western Powers. Chamberlain responded that only dire necessity would persuade him to wage a preventative war.[28] By one o'clock there appeared to be deadlock. Daladier spoke no English, but Chamberlain sat with him at lunch and, as he told his sisters, 'mustered what French I could to win his confidence'.[29] A small concession on a date for naval staff talks seemed to do the trick. The French quickly agreed to Halifax's proposal that Britain should elicit a clear statement from Berlin of what concessions by the Czechs to the Sudeten-Germans would satisfy the German government, and that Britain and France would jointly urge the government in Prague to make concessions. If the Germans nevertheless intended to resort to war, they would be doing so in the knowledge that France would be compelled to intervene, and they would be reminded of what Chamberlain had said in his speech on 24 March about how shared interests with France could lead to Britain also becoming involved.[30] Chamberlain regarded this agreement as a success for his strategy of preventing war by keeping all parties guessing, but the French were playing the same game. France's honour required the affirmation of its treaty obligation to Czechoslovakia, but the British were left uncertain whether, in the event of war, the French would do more than man the Maginot Line. French ministers rightly assumed the British government would make every effort to avoid being drawn into a war and were more than content to share responsibility for finding a solution to the Sudeten-German problem, and indeed to let the British take the lead.[31]

Meanwhile Chamberlain had taken a decision on the RAF's expansion scheme. Notwithstanding the concern of the Treasury about the effect on Britain's financial strength of exceeding the limit for defence expenditure in the Inskip Report, he told the Cabinet on 27 April that the next two years would be critical in international relations. He and Simon had accordingly authorized the maximum production of aircraft the Air Ministry thought possible by 31 March 1940; that is 12,000 compared with 7,500 under the existing programme. Chamberlain still expected criticism of the Air Ministry in Parliament, especially from Churchill. However, the junior minister who represented the ministry in the House of Commons, Earl Winterton (since the secretary of state, Lord Swinton, sat in the Lords), thought it would be possible to show that the government had a grip of the situation.[32] In the event, Winterton, badgered by Churchill, performed badly in the debate on the air estimates on 12 May 1938 and Chamberlain decided Swinton must be replaced with a secretary of state who could defend the government in the Commons.[33] When on 25 May Labour put the motion for an independent enquiry into the state of the country's air defences, Churchill's speech in support was cheered from the Labour benches, but the new secretary of state, Kingsley Wood, proved to be an able debater and the government easily won the vote against. Churchill abstained.[34]

Churchill renewed his campaign for a Ministry of Supply in a letter to *The Times* on 20 May. Colonel Hastings Ismay, the deputy secretary of the CID, was not convinced such a ministry could prepare industry for war any more effectively than the service departments' principal supply officers were already doing, especially if, as Churchill said, there should be no state interference with the functions of industry. Chamberlain used the debate on air defence on 25 May to explain what was being done to create capacity for war production through the shadow factory system and to allocate existing industrial capacity between departments, and believed he had satisfied the House, although not Churchill.[35] Churchill's immediate concern was with the production of aircraft and anti-aircraft guns, but he also urged the secretary of state for war, Hore-Belisha, on 4 June to plan on the basis of being able to equip the million volunteers who, as in 1914, would come forward in an emergency. Churchill added: 'The idea that Britain will in time of war become a great military power is one of the most important deterrents against war.'[36] Chamberlain was not yet ready to adopt this conception of deterrence.

7.2 From May 'Crisis' to September Crisis

Britain took the initiative on the future of Czechoslovakia when the British ambassador in Berlin, Nevile Henderson, asked the German foreign minister, Joachim von Ribbentrop, on 11 May 1938 to indicate the terms the German government thought would be satisfactory to the Sudeten-Germans. Ribbentrop, while claiming, falsely, that the Sudeten-German leader, Konrad Henlein, was independent of the German government, suggested the programme for autonomy set out by Henlein in a speech at Karlsbad on 24 April provided a basis for discussion.[37] Although Hitler made no secret of his support for the Sudeten-Germans' right to self-determination, it was not clear to the Foreign Office or SIS in the spring of 1938 whether Germany would insist on annexing the Sudetenland or would accept a settlement that would leave it within Czechoslovakia. In his meeting with the French ministers on 29 April, Chamberlain had observed that Henlein was not demanding an *Anschluss*, although that was what his followers were reported to want.[38] In fact, on 28 March 1938 Henlein had secretly visited Berlin, where he had been told by Hitler to demand autonomy on terms which the Czechs could not accept, thus making them seem intransigent, and thereby justifying an invasion. Henlein was further instructed to give an appearance of being moderate and reasonable, and was encouraged to visit London. There he met Churchill on 13 May, whom he deceived into believing it would be possible to reach an agreement on autonomy that would not destroy the integrity of Czechoslovakia. Churchill told Chamberlain, 'I was very much pleased with this talk', and Chamberlain replied on the 16th that 'it was encouraging rather than the reverse'.[39]

Henlein's Karlsbad demands were followed by unrest in the Sudetenland. On Saturday 21 May, after rumours of German troop movements towards the frontier and the shooting of two Sudeten-Germans by Czech police, the Czech government started calling up army reservists. Halifax sent a telegram the same day to Berlin repeating Chamberlain's warning of 24 March that, if France felt compelled to intervene in a war between Germany and Czechoslovakia, the British government 'could not guarantee that they would not be forced by circumstances to become involved also'.[40] Between themselves, however, Halifax and his permanent under-secretary, Cadogan, took the view that Britain must not go to war.[41] Chamberlain refrained from making any further warning in a statement in Parliament on 23 May about the weekend's events, simply saying the German government had been invited to co-operate in facilitating an agreement between the Czech government and Henlein's party, and that the Czech government had been urged to avoid incidents.[42] Despite the fact that the military attaché in Berlin could find no evidence of German troop movements, Chamberlain was convinced the German government had made preparations for a coup, but had been deterred from going ahead by the British warning.[43] The rumours of troop movements were, in fact, false, and Hitler was infuriated by press reports that credited Chamberlain with checking him. Chamberlain drew two conclusions from the weekend 'crisis': first, that the Germans 'who are bullies by nature are too conscious of their strength and our weakness, and until we are as strong as they are we shall always be kept in a state of anxiety'; second, the German government was 'utterly untrustworthy and dishonest'.[44]

Up to a point Churchill agreed with Chamberlain that the Czech government should come to terms with the Sudeten-Germans. In speeches on 16 and 23 May Churchill said he had good reason to believe that a friendly and lasting settlement could be negotiated, although in a speech on 31 May he added the proviso: 'only if there were no violent outside interference'.[45] On 14 July he once more said a settlement was possible within the framework of the Czechoslovak state, and he did not abandon hope of a successful outcome even after his wife's cousin, Shiela Grant Duff, a journalist then working in Prague, pointed out to him two weeks later that Henlein was not a free agent and had become more radical since he and Churchill had met.[46] However, whereas Chamberlain, in common with the chiefs of staff, believed Czechoslovakia was indefensible, Churchill thought it wrong to belittle the deterrent presented by the Czech army and its 'well-conceived system of forts', together with the prospect of intervention by France and the Soviet Union, and Britain too if public opinion were roused as it had been in 1914 by the German invasion of Belgium.[47] Churchill, unlike Chamberlain and Halifax, believed the Czech government was negotiating from a position of strength. Chamberlain feared deadlock in Prague, and on 22 June he had assured the German ambassador, Herbert von Dirksen, that Britain would intensify pressure on the Czech government to grant autonomy to the Sudeten-Germans.[48] On 26 July he announced that Lord Runciman, a former cabinet minister, would go to Czechoslovakia as an investigator and mediator. Churchill was in full agreement with this step, and on 27 August, after Runciman had been trying to bridge the gulf between the Czech government and Henlein's followers for almost four weeks, he still expressed the hope that conciliation was possible.[49]

However, by then both Chamberlain and Churchill were anxious about Hitler's intentions. Intelligence reports pointed to September being the probable danger period of the crisis. In particular, news from the Berlin embassy that the German army intended to bring an unusual number of formations up to full strength for special training that month led Chamberlain to appeal to Hitler on 11 August to reduce tension by modifying these measures. He took Hitler's lack of response to be a bad sign.[50] Then on 18 August Ewald von Kleist-Schmenzin, a German conservative politician acting on behalf of members of the German General Staff who were opposed to Hitler's war plans, flew to London looking for evidence that Britain had not been bluffing on 21 May. In conversations with Vansittart (now chief diplomatic adviser) and Churchill he said that an attack on Czechoslovakia was most likely to occur before the end of September. Von Kleist urged that a leading British statesman should make a speech warning of the catastrophe that war would lead to. Chamberlain commented on Vansittart's report: 'I take it that von Kleist is violently anti-Hitler and is extremely anxious to stir up his friends in Germany to make an attempt at [the regime's] overthrow', and added 'I think we must discount a good deal of what he says.'[51] Historians are free to speculate on the consequences of this scepticism. In 1948 Churchill suggested German generals might have overthrown the Nazi regime, although he had been advised by Orme Sargent not to overrate the possibility because the generals repeatedly planned to revolt, and then drew back.[52] Like Churchill's other counterfactuals, it cannot be proved one way or another. In 1938 SIS had no sure evidence of the existence of a cohesive opposition that could have shaken the regime, and thought the Gestapo could have ensured that the German people would have followed Hitler into war.[53] Even in retrospect the chances of success seem slight, given Nazi control of the police and the media, the lack of unity in the opposition to the regime and the fact that the principal conspirator, General Ludwig Beck, shared Hitler's objectives regarding the strategic threat posed by Czechoslovakia and the need for *Lebensraum* and colonies, and disagreed with him only on the amount of risk to be taken in 1938.[54]

Chamberlain, despite his scepticism, confessed to feeling uneasy after von Kleist's visit, and a further warning to Hitler was given in a speech by Sir John Simon at Lanark on 27 August in which reference was made to what Chamberlain had said in the House of Commons on 24 March about the likelihood of British involvement if France had to fulfil its treaty obligation to Czechoslovakia.[55] Churchill seems to have regarded Chamberlain's speech as a significant warning, as he gave von Kleist a copy, and in a speech of his own, also on 27 August, said the government was right to let foreign countries know that 'Great Britain and the British Empire must not be deemed incapable of playing their part and doing their duty'.[56]

The government was less determined than Churchill supposed. Ministers were summoned from their holidays for a meeting on

30 August when Halifax and Chamberlain reviewed the conflicting intelligence on Hitler's intentions, with Sir Nevile Henderson recalled from the Berlin embassy to answer questions. Halifax thought there were two alternative suppositions. Either Hitler was determined on war, in which case there was nothing to be done but prepare for it, or he had not yet made up his mind. In the latter case a choice had to be made between threatening him with war if he invaded Czechoslovakia or, as Halifax and Chamberlain preferred, continuing to keep him guessing. Halifax also mentioned an idea put forward by Churchill that Hitler might be deterred if Britain, France and the Soviet Union presented him with a joint note. The foreign secretary's own view was that if France and the Soviet Union were asked to sign such a note 'they would probably ask embarrassing questions' as to what Britain would do if Germany invaded Czechoslovakia. Chamberlain said no democratic state ought to make a threat of war unless it was both ready to carry it out and prepared to do so. He asked each of the 18 ministers present to express an opinion. Inskip, as minister for co-ordination of defence, noted that Britain would not reach maximum defence preparedness for another year or more. The secretary of state for air, Kingsley Wood, was very apprehensive about the prospect of war and thought a guarantee to Czechoslovakia would divide the British public. The secretary of state for war, Hore-Belisha, said a threat of war could only be made if there were overwhelming public support for such action, which he did not believe there was. Duff Cooper, first lord of the Admiralty, said nobody wanted to fight for Czechoslovakia, but that was not the issue. He expected the French to go to war as soon as the Germans crossed the Czech frontier, and he was convinced Britain could not keep out of a European conflict. He agreed with the policy of keeping Hitler guessing, but suggested making naval preparations to make sure he guessed right. Four other ministers gave some support to Duff Cooper, but the majority agreed with Chamberlain that nothing should be done to provoke Germany.[57] After the Cabinet, Chamberlain saw the American ambassador, Joseph Kennedy, who agreed it would be unwise to utter threats, but expressed his belief that if France and Britain had to fight, the United States would follow before long. Kennedy invited Chamberlain to let him know if he thought there was anything President Roosevelt could do to help.[58]

The next day Churchill called on Halifax and gave him a letter developing the idea of a joint note with France and the Soviet Union to warn Hitler that an invasion by Germany of Czechoslovakia would 'raise capital issues for all three powers'. This vague expression avoided giving a guarantee to the Czechs, and indeed Churchill thought the note should be presented only after the Czech government had made the Sudeten-Germans an offer that Runciman regarded as fair. Churchill hoped the joint note would encourage Roosevelt to press Hitler to agree to a settlement, and also give 'the best chance to the peaceful elements in German official circles to make a stand'.[59] Sir Horace Wilson advised Chamberlain that the inclusion of the Soviet Union in the joint note would infuriate Hitler and rob the démarche of any value it might have as a means of persuasion. 'All it would do', Wilson remarked, 'would be to take us nearer to the point at which we might find that we had committed ourselves to taking action, very likely finding ourselves for all practical purposes in the end tackling Germany single-handed'.[60] Wilson's comment reflected doubts whether the French army, which had begun to call up reservists, would venture beyond the Maginot Line, and whether the Soviet Union could render effective aid to Czechoslovakia. On 2 September Churchill forwarded to Halifax information from the Soviet ambassador, Ivan Maisky, that Maxim Litvinov, the Soviet foreign minister, thought the best way to overcome the reluctance of the Romanian government to allow Soviet forces to cross its territory would be if the League of Nations declared that Czechoslovakia was the victim of German aggression. Litvinov had advised the French government that the League powers should consult together and purported to believe, like Churchill, that the United States would give moral support to a joint declaration by Britain, France and the Soviet Union.[61]

Chamberlain, however, had quite a different approach in mind. Late in August he and Wilson had devised a plan, which they called Plan Z, whereby the prime minister would fly to Germany to negotiate directly with Hitler if war seemed imminent. At a time when statesmen normally travelled by boat and train, Chamberlain was justified in describing Plan Z as 'unconventional and daring'. The prime minister wanted to seize the diplomatic initiative by making a dramatic gesture and he was encouraged by Henderson to believe it might save the situation at the eleventh hour. [62] Wilson noted that the plan's success would depend on it being a complete surprise and it was vital that there be no leakage.[63] Accordingly, knowledge of it was initially confined to an Inner Cabinet of the prime minister, Halifax, Simon and Sir Samuel Hoare (the last two being former foreign secretaries), which took on the function of the Cabinet's Foreign Policy Committee during the crisis and which, like that committee, was advised by Cadogan and Vansittart. Chamberlain was aware of the risk he was taking with his reputation. As he told his sisters: 'I fully realise that if eventually things go wrong and aggression takes place there will be many, including Winston, who will say that the British government must bear the responsibility and that if only they had had the courage to tell Hitler now that if he used force we should at once declare war that would have stopped him. By that time it will be impossible to prove the contrary ... .'[64] He also believed he would not be dealing with a normal statesman in Hitler, whom he described as 'half mad' and a 'lunatic'.[65]

Chamberlain, who had been in great pain from sinus trouble in August, spent the first days of September recuperating on grouse moors in Scotland. Meanwhile Halifax had become, in Chamberlain's view, 'unsettled' under Vansittart's influence, and the Foreign Office wanted Henderson to give Hitler a private warning that Britain could not stand by if France were to become involved in hostilities and was in danger of being defeated. Wilson advised that Hitler must already be aware that was the position from earlier ministers' speeches, and Halifax himself came round to the view that a further warning would be premature at a time when he and Chamberlain still hoped negotiations in Prague would produce a settlement between the Czech government and the Sudeten-Germans.[66] On 7 September *The Times* pointed out in a leading article that the concessions now being demanded by Henlein would create a state within a state, and, controversially, asked whether the Czech government might consider whether it would not be better to cede the German-speaking areas to the Reich. The Foreign Office issued a statement that this suggestion in no way represented the British government's views, but *The Times* may have been floating a trial balloon on behalf of Chamberlain and Halifax. Certainly many foreigners found it hard to believe *The Times* was acting independently of the government, and Runciman complained the article had added to his difficulties.[67] On the same day a clash between Sudeten-Germans and Czech police in Mährisch-Ostrau provided Henlein with an excuse to suspend talks. On the next day, the 8th, Chamberlain conferred with Halifax, Simon, Wilson, Cadogan and Vansittart about Plan Z as an alternative to sending a warning to Berlin. Only Vansittart was against the plan, comparing it to the Holy Roman Emperor Henry IV's humiliation at Canossa.[68]

Vansittart still wanted a warning to be sent before Hitler committed himself irretrievably in a speech he was due to make at the Nazi Party rally at Nuremberg on 12 September. Halifax finally agreed on the 9th to send a warning to Berlin that Britain could not stand aside in a general conflict. The message was telegraphed to the embassy and taken overnight to Henderson, who was at Nuremberg, with instructions it should be given to Ribbentrop with a request that it should be transmitted to Hitler without delay. Henderson responded that the German army and air force were ready to strike and a repetition of 21 May would drive Hitler to greater menaces or violence. Henderson said he had conveyed the substance of the warning in conversations with Ribbentrop and other leading Nazis, and ministers decided he need do no more, a decision with which Cadogan agreed, although it infuriated Vansittart.[69] Halifax was far from belligerent. Shortly before the warning had been sent on the 9th he had had a conversation with the French ambassador, Charles Corbin, and told him he did not think British public opinion would be prepared to go to war if Germany attacked Czechoslovakia, and certainly not to prevent a plebiscite in the Sudetenland.[70]

On 10 September, a Saturday, Churchill saw Chamberlain, Halifax and Hoare at 10 Downing Street and demanded Germany should be told immediately that, if it set foot in Czechoslovakia, Britain would declare war. According to his information, France and the Soviet Union were ready for an offensive against Germany, but, Hoare said the government's intelligence contradicted this claim. The fact that the French and Russians had not had joint staff talks suggests Churchill's wish was father to his thought. Halifax told the Cabinet on the 12th that Hitler was 'possibly or even probably mad', and any prospect of bringing him back to a sane outlook would be destroyed by anything he would regard as a public humiliation, and for that reason he did not propose to follow Churchill's advice. Duff Cooper argued the case for making it plain Britain would fight, but ministers agreed to postpone decisions on what should be done until Hitler had made his speech that evening.[71]

In the speech Hitler demanded the right of self-determination for the Sudeten-Germans, but did not entirely close the door to a peaceful settlement.[72] However, the speech was followed by rioting in Sudeten-German areas, and Henlein finally broke off negotiations with the Czech government before fleeing to Germany. Intelligence reports in the morning of the 13th indicated that Hitler intended to invade Czechoslovakia on 25 September.[73] In deciding to go ahead with Plan Z Chamberlain was influenced not only by the deteriorating situation in Central Europe but also by telegrams on the 13th from the ambassador in Paris. According to Phipps, the French had been very frightened by a report by the American airman, Colonel Lindbergh, that German aircraft production vastly exceeded that of France, and Daladier had said that at all costs Germany must be prevented from invading Czechoslovakia because then France would be faced with fulfilling its obligations. The implication was the French were not ready for war and did not want to fight. Daladier favoured a three-power conference of France, Britain and Germany, but Chamberlain felt there was no time to organise one. He had intended to reveal Plan Z to the full Cabinet on the 14th, but late in the evening of the 13th he and the other three ministers of the Inner Cabinet decided the moment had come for him to send the telegram offering to fly to see Hitler with a view to finding a peaceful solution to the crisis.[74]

7.3   Berchtesgaden and Godesberg

Having decided to fly to Germany, Chamberlain consulted the Cabinet on 14 September about what he should say in the negotiations. He anticipated Hitler would demand a plebiscite in the Sudetenland and said it would be impossible for a democracy to go to war to prevent one. Like *The Times*, Chamberlain regarded the German-speaking areas as a source of weakness to Czechoslovakia. In order to persuade the Czechs to be prepared to sacrifice their natural frontiers, he reluctantly contemplated incurring a new liability whereby Britain, together with France, Germany and the Soviet Union, would guarantee the remainder of Czechoslovakia, which would become a neutral state. He said Britain could not save Czechoslovakia if Germany decided to overrun it, but thought the guarantee would have a deterrent effect. He did not ask the Cabinet to take a decision on the guarantee, but said ministers should be aware the idea was not altogether excluded. Ministers generally supported the idea of a plebiscite. However, they were concerned it should not be held on terms that would be seen as surrendering to force. Duff Cooper said the choice was not between war and a plebiscite, but between war now and war later. He accepted, however, that the government was constrained by the public's hatred of war and in his diary he noted the Cabinet had been unanimous and enthusiastic in approving Chamberlain's action.[75] Almost all press comment the next day was favourable to what was seen as a bold diplomatic stroke. Churchill, however, thought it was the stupidest thing that had ever been done.[76] In an article he published on 15 September, he said only blunt language would have any effect. In his view, the best hope for peace would be if Britain, France and the Soviet Union presented Hitler with a joint note setting out 'the common action' they would take following an attack on Czechoslovakia, and 'if at the same time President Roosevelt would proclaim that this note carried with it the moral sympathy of the United States and all that would follow therefrom'. If Roosevelt did, 'there would be good hopes, if not indeed almost a certainty, of warding off the catastrophe which may so easily engulf our civilisation'.[77]

Ruggiero, one of Chamberlain's most severe critics, finds fault with the prime minister for not mentioning in Cabinet on the 14th the attitude of the United States' government, and cites Inskip's diary as noting that the ambassador in Washington, Ronald Lindsay, had warned that a weak stand against Hitler would cause a serious diminution of American friendliness. However, the immediately following part of Lindsay's telegram said that 'too much must not be attached to this … . If accommodation is really wise, we should be able to recover any ground lost.'

Chamberlain, of course, did not intend to make an unwise accommodation. Ruggiero also attaches importance to Roosevelt telling a French visitor that 'you can count on us for everything except troops or loans'. However, Lindsay, reporting these words, noted that, while they reflected Roosevelt's own feelings, the president ought to have added the reservation 'subject to dictates of [American] public opinion and ... domestic politics'. Given that the Neutrality Act was in force, Inskip commented that the president ought to have added 'or lethal weapons'.[78]

The strategic context for Chamberlain's visit to Germany was set out by the chiefs of staff in a Cabinet paper on 14 September: the United States could not be relied upon to come to the assistance of Britain and France; the attitude of the Soviet Union was 'incalculable' and it was 'unsafe to assume' it would go to the assistance of Czechoslovakia. Japan and Italy might take the opportunity to threaten the Empire. Germany had an advantage over Britain and France on land and in the air, and superior Allied sea power would take time to have an effect through blockade. The chiefs of staff concluded that no pressure that Britain and France could bring to bear on Germany could prevent Germany from inflicting a decisive defeat on Czechoslovakia, and Czechoslovakia's lost integrity could be restored only by defeating Germany in a prolonged and unlimited war. Britain's air defences were described as weak and the weight of bombs that might be dropped by the Luftwaffe was greatly overestimated.[79] Chamberlain's opposition to bluff was reinforced by reading Harold Temperley's book, *The Foreign Policy of Canning, 1822–1827* (1925). He wrote to his sisters: 'Again and again Canning lays it down that you should never menace unless you are in a position to carry out your threats and although if we have to fight I should hope we should be able to give a good account of ourselves we are certainly not in a position in which our military advisers would feel happy in undertaking hostilities if we were not forced to do so.'[80]

On the 15th Chamberlain flew to Munich, where he was delighted by the enthusiastic welcome of the crowds, and then went by special train to Hitler's Alpine residence at Berchtesgaden. He was accompanied by Horace Wilson, Nevile Henderson and William Strang of the Foreign Office's Central Department, but not Halifax. By leaving his foreign secretary at home, Chamberlain was able to exclude the German foreign minister, Ribbentrop, who was regarded as a baleful influence, from meetings with Hitler, when only a German Foreign Office interpreter was present. At first sight Hitler struck Chamberlain as 'the commonest little dog' he had ever seen, but as they talked he became impressed by his power.[81] The prime minister attempted to open the discussion with general issues affecting Anglo-German relations, but Hitler insisted on focusing on what he claimed to be the threats to peace posed by the situation in the Sudetenland, where martial law had been imposed following riots, and to Germany by Czechoslovakia's treaties with France and the Soviet Union. As Hitler gave the impression he was contemplating an immediate invasion, Chamberlain asked angrily why he had allowed him to travel all the way to Berchtesgaden, since it was a waste of time. Hitler responded that, if Chamberlain could give him then and there an assurance that the British government accepted the principle of self-determination, he was quite ready to discuss how to implement it. Chamberlain replied he was not authorised to do so by the Cabinet and must consult the French government and Runciman before agreeing, but said he had no personal objection provided the practical difficulties could be overcome.[82]

The prime minister returned to London the next day, and at a meeting of the Inner Cabinet in the evening heard from Runciman that it had not been possible to find a solution to the Sudeten problem which would satisfy both the Czech government and Germany. Chamberlain told the full Cabinet on the 17th (a Saturday) that he had seen no signs of insanity in Hitler, and he believed he was telling the truth when he said his ambitions were limited to incorporating the Sudeten-Germans in the Reich. Chamberlain also supposed the situation was so urgent that hostilities would have started had he not gone to Germany. Despite his remark in May that the German government was utterly untrustworthy, he was now under the illusion he had established a relationship of mutual confidence and trust with Hitler and that Hitler was a man who could be relied upon when he had given his word.[83] Wilson had had conversations with several Germans at Berchtesgaden who spoke of the favourable impression the prime minister had made on the Fuehrer, and Chamberlain was particularly pleased with his report that Walter Hewel, the chief of Ribbentrop's staff, had said that Hitler had said he had had a conversation with a *man*.[84] As with his conversations with Grandi in 1937, Chamberlain was susceptible to flattery.

According to Inskip, the impression made on ministers by Chamberlain's account of his encounter with Hitler was 'a little painful. Hitler had made him listen to a boast that the German military machine was a terrible instrument … he had in fact blackmailed the PM'.[85] Ministers were concerned that a plebiscite should be held under fair conditions, but Chamberlain said Hitler would take violent action if acceptance of the principle of self-determination were made subject to conditions. He claimed acceptance would not allow Hitler to have self-determination on any terms he wanted, and on that basis the Cabinet gave its assent. Even Duff Cooper, who doubted whether there would be peace as long as the Nazis ruled Germany, or that Hitler would agree to fair conditions, said no government could forecast the future with certainty, and modern war was so terrible it was worthwhile postponing it in the faint hope some internal event might end the Nazi regime.[86] The most vigorous reaction in Whitehall that day came from the permanent secretary of the Treasury, Sir Warren Fisher, who, in words intended for Chamberlain, told Wilson that 'in our unwearying efforts for peace we have secured the approval of the world and surely it is vital not to jeopardise that – and to become *particeps criminis* with the Germans – by appearing to surrender to force'. In order to 'reduce the possibility of our being charged with sacrificing Czechoslovakian territorial integrity to suit our purpose', Fisher urged that the Germans should be required to demobilize and that the plebiscite should be supervised by an international police force. He added, prophetically, that 'there is of course a danger that the spectacular rise in our prestige will be followed by an unpleasant fall', and that 'for this, as for many other reasons, I should regard it as of the first importance to rope in the USA so that they may participate in the plebiscite proceedings'.[87] Chamberlain put this suggestion to the American ambassador in the evening, but Kennedy said there was no chance of it being adopted given what the State Department described as the United States' 'policy of non-action'.[88]

That same Saturday evening Chamberlain and Halifax received a deputation from the National Council of Labour: Walter Citrine of the Trades Union Congress and Hugh Dalton and Herbert Morrison of the Labour Party. Citrine said the preponderance of opinion in the National Council was that Chamberlain had done the right thing in going to Germany, although some members thought prestige had been lost thereby. All, however, believed it would be wrong to take territory from democratic Czechoslovakia and hand over the population to a dictatorship. Like Churchill (although his name was not mentioned) the National Council wanted Britain, France and the Soviet Union to issue a joint warning that they would resist any invasion of Czechoslovakia. Chamberlain asked the deputation to consider whether the British people would be prepared to fight to prevent self-determination. He himself felt that even after a victory (and terrible suffering), Czechoslovakia could not be put back together again within its present boundaries. Dalton pointed out the purpose of a joint warning was to prevent war, and asked whether Hitler was under the illusion that Britain would stand aside if there was a general conflict. Chamberlain thought Hitler realised that, if France went to war, then sooner or later Britain would come in, but Hitler did not believe France would fight. The prime minister added he did not think France would fight either, pointing to the weakness of the French air force. Citrine then asked about the government's information about the position of the Soviet Union, and he and his colleagues were astonished to be told that while the Russians might raise the matter at the League of Nations, they were unlikely to do anything effective. On being asked about Britain's own preparedness, particularly civil defence, Chamberlain said he would never say that in no circumstances would we go to war, but the present was not the moment to accept a challenge from Germany if it could be possibly be avoided. Dalton made the point that giving way to Hitler now might encourage him to try something else, and Britain might find itself in an even weaker position. Chamberlain replied that one of the choices to be made was between war today as a certainty as against a possible war in years to come. The delegation went away from the interview feeling a great deal of anxiety; unlike the prime minister, they thought there was no limit to Hitler's aggressive ambitions.[89]

The next day, Sunday the 18th, Daladier and his foreign minister, Georges Bonnet, came to London to consult with Chamberlain and the Inner Cabinet. Although Daladier spoke with what Cadogan called 'carefully modulated emotion' about French honour and obligations, the premier had already made up his mind to solve the Sudeten problem peacefully rather than by war.[90] Daladier objected to a plebiscite in the Sudetenland, on the grounds the Germans could then exploit the principle of self-determination wherever there were German minorities in Europe. He added that the government in Prague feared a plebiscite would destroy the Czechoslovak state. Chamberlain suggested the Czechs should be offered a choice between a plebiscite and a cession of areas with a majority of Sudeten-German inhabitants. Daladier thought the French government could hardly put pressure on the Czechs to agree to cede part of their territory without an international guarantee of the remainder. As noted above, Chamberlain had told the Cabinet four days earlier that the idea of a guarantee was not excluded and he agreed, albeit unwillingly, to Daladier's proposal once the latter accepted that Czechoslovakia should become a neutral state like Belgium with no obligation to come to the assistance of France or the Soviet Union.[91]

On the 19th the Cabinet endorsed the Anglo-French plan for the transfer of territory in an orderly way and, after intense pressure from the British and French governments, the Czech government accepted it on the 21st.[92] At Cabinet on that day several ministers expressed reservations about Chamberlain's suggestion that German troops should be allowed to occupy areas where the Sudeten-Germans were a very large majority before the final boundary was fixed, and it was agreed that, if possible, the entry of German troops should be delayed until after an international force had reached Czechoslovakia. There was some support for Duff Cooper's view that there was a point beyond which it would be better to fight than to make further concessions. Duff Cooper was understandably vexed the next day to read a Foreign Office telegram sent to Prague after the Cabinet meeting that seemed to reflect Chamberlain's suggestion rather than the Cabinet's decision.[93]

The reaction of the National Council of Labour to the Anglo-French plan showed a great gulf between Chamberlain and the Labour Movement. Citrine told Halifax in the evening of the 21st that the feeling of a meeting of the council earlier in the day had been one of complete and utter humiliation, and he had been asked to express their views before the prime minister left for Germany the next day. The plan, Citrine said, amounted to the dismemberment of Czechoslovakia and represented a capitulation to naked aggression. He challenged the government's assessment that France and the Soviet Union were unwilling and unready to go to the Czechs' assistance, and asked whether ministers had been misled by Bonnet, who had already acquired a reputation as a defeatist. Halifax assured him the government's appreciation of the probabilities of Soviet action came from the British ambassador in Moscow. The foreign secretary was unable to mollify the National Council, which issued a statement that denounced the 'shameful surrender' to Hitler's threats, warned that his ambitions did not stop at Czechoslovakia, and called on peace-loving nations to make an immediate and concerted effort to restore the rule of law.[94] The National Council was no doubt encouraged by a speech by Litvinov at Geneva earlier on the 21st calling for collective assistance for Czechoslovakia and saying that the Soviet Union was ready to participate immediately in staff talks with France and Czechoslovakia.[95]

Meanwhile on the 19th Churchill had had a conversation with Halifax from whom he learned about the Anglo-French plan. Churchill flew to Paris on the 20th where he consulted with two ministers, Paul Reynaud and Georges Mandel, who were on the brink of resignation over the plan.[96] On returning to London, he issued a statement which, like the National Council's, appeared in the press on the 22nd. Churchill denounced the Anglo-French plan as 'the complete surrender of the Western Democracies to the Nazi threat of force'. He argued that neutralization of Czechoslovakia would release 25 German divisions to threaten France, and also open the way for Nazi domination of Romania with its oil resources. He continued: 'The belief that security can be obtained by throwing a small state to the wolves is a fatal delusion. The war potential of Germany will increase in a short time more rapidly than it will be possible for France and Great Britain to complete the measures necessary for their defence.' Once again he said peace could be preserved permanently only by a combination of powers opposed to Nazi domination. He urged the immediate recall of Parliament to be 'informed upon these grievous matters which affect the whole life and future of our country'.[97]

Churchill's statement has to be read in the context of his subsequent activities on the 22nd. After a conversation in Downing Street – with whom is not clear – he called a meeting with political friends, including the National Labour MP and diarist Harold Nicolson, according to whom he said the Cabinet were at last taking a firm stand. Churchill expected Chamberlain to demand from Hitler (a) early demobilization, (b) gradual transfer of the Sudetenland overseen by an international commission, (c) 'no nonsense' about Polish or Hungarian claims regarding their minorities in Czechoslovakia and (d) a guarantee for 'what remains of Czechoslovakia'. When his friends said Hitler would never accept such terms, Churchill replied that 'in that case Chamberlain will return tonight and we shall have war'. The group, which included only three other MPs – Archibald Sinclair, the leader of the Liberal Opposition; Brendan Bracken, a Conservative; and Nicolson – agreed to support Chamberlain if he came back with peace with honour or in the event of war, but otherwise to join with Labour in opposing him.[98] On this evidence Churchill would seem to have been prepared to contemplate some transfer of Czech territory provided it was not done under duress. However, after the meeting he went to see Duff Cooper, who recorded that Churchill was in a state of great excitement and violent in his denunciation of Chamberlain. Duff Cooper explained the situation as he saw it and encouraged Churchill to hope for war, which, Duff Cooper believed, was what Churchill wanted.[99] The next day *The Times*, in a leading article, identified Churchill as an advocate of preventative war, but he later denied that, arguing that a preventative war was an aggressive act designed to forestall the growing strength of an opponent, whereas he was urging resistance to aggression.[100]

Churchill was encouraged to urge resistance because, in contrast to his belief six months earlier that German air attacks would turn London into a shambles, he no longer feared the effects of bombing on civilians. He still expected that several million people would have to be evacuated from London. However, as a member of the Air Defence Research Committee he had access to intelligence from Spain from which he concluded that, far from producing panic and a wish to surrender, the bombing of Madrid and Barcelona had aroused 'a spirit of furious and unyielding resistance among all classes'.[101]

Despite the statements by Churchill and the National Council of Labour, and the speech by Litvinov, Chamberlain remained focused on bilateral negotiations. Speaking to pressmen at Heston airfield before he left for Germany on 22 September, he described a peaceful solution of the Czechoslovakian problem as 'an essential preliminary' to better Anglo-German understanding, which in turn was 'an indispensable foundation' of his ultimate objective, European peace.[102] The flight was shorter this time, to Cologne instead of Munich, Hitler having made the gesture of moving the venue to Bad Godesberg, on the Rhine. A profound shock awaited the prime minister. He had expected he had only to tell Hitler that the principle of self-determination had been accepted by the Cabinet and the French government, and then discuss quietly how to implement the Anglo-French plan. Hitler, however, said the plan was no longer acceptable. After expatiating at length on the grievances of the Hungarian and Polish minorities as well as of the Sudeten-Germans, he declared the problem of Czechoslovakia had reached a critical stage and must be resolved by 1 October. He claimed the position on the frontier was untenable, with thousands of refugees crossing, and that feeling in Germany against the Czechs was rising daily. Chamberlain, although angry, responded diplomatically, saying he was disappointed and puzzled, since he had secured the agreement of the French and the Cabinet to exactly what Hitler had said he wanted, and without a drop of German blood spilt. He complained that in doing so he had taken his political life into his hands: whereas his first flight to Germany had been applauded by public opinion, today he had been accused of selling out the Czechs, with members of his own party writing in protest to him. He now found himself confronted with proposals of a kind he had not contemplated at all. Hitler said a new frontier must be drawn at once, on the basis of maps showing the proportions of the population who spoke German. He demanded the Czech army and police should withdraw to that frontier, and that German troops should occupy the evacuated territory without delay. Chamberlain thought the line Hitler had drawn on the map was more favourable to the Sudeten-Germans than public opinion in Britain would think fair, but Hitler countered that a plebiscite would ensure the final frontier would minimise the numbers of Czechs in the Reich. When Hitler said he would prefer a good understanding with Britain to a good strategic frontier with Czechoslovakia, Chamberlain warned him he would not get a good understanding if he resorted to force. Before the two men parted for the night Hitler agreed to not to take immediate military action. [103]

According to Wilson, Chamberlain was 'much disturbed' by how the meeting had gone, and the next morning the prime minister spoke for the first time of his fears about the consequences to himself and his government of a failure to break the deadlock.[104] In the morning of the 23rd

Chamberlain sent a letter to Hitler expressing willingness to put the German proposal to the Czech government so that it could examine the suggested territorial changes, but warned that any attempt to occupy the areas to be transferred by German troops forthwith would be condemned by British, French and, indeed, world opinion as an unnecessary display of force. Chamberlain thought the Czechs would be bound to resist and that there must be alternative arrangements for an orderly transfer.[105] Talks were postponed while Hitler's reply was awaited. The international tension was such that the Inner Cabinet in London felt the policy hitherto pursued of pressing the Czechs not to mobilise, for fear of provoking Hitler, could not be maintained. Chamberlain agreed at 4 p.m., but said that when this decision was communicated to Prague the Czechs should be advised to avoid unnecessary publicity.[106] At 10 p.m. Halifax telegraphed to say that public opinion was hardening against concessions beyond the Anglo-French plan, and that Hitler should be told so.[107] Chamberlain met Hitler just before 11 p.m., by which time the Germans had drafted a memorandum setting out Hitler's demands. Before the prime minister and his officials had had time to study this document properly, news came that the Czech president, Edvard Beneš, had announced general mobilization. When Hitler said it was clear the Czechs did not intend to cede territory and he must take appropriate military measures, Chamberlain remarked that in that case there was no purpose in negotiating any further and he would return to London. Hitler, however, explained that by 'military measures' he did not mean an invasion of Czechoslovakia. Attention was then focused on the memorandum, and Hitler grudgingly made minor amendments, flattering Chamberlain by saying he was the only man to whom he had ever made a concession. The date by which the Czechs were to have completed their withdrawal was changed from 28 September to 1 October, and the option of an international rather than a German-Czech boundary commission was inserted. Chamberlain made the point that, as mediator, he could not either accept or reject the memorandum, but he thought the changes would make it more acceptable to public opinion, and he undertook to submit the German proposals to the Czech government as soon as possible.[108]

When Chamberlain reported to the Inner Cabinet in the afternoon of the 24th Cadogan was horrified to find Chamberlain calmly disposed to give way to Hitler's demands and thought that the prime minister seemed hypnotised.[109] Nearly 70, Chamberlain was probably exhausted by the strain of shuttle diplomacy. He was also deluded. He told the full Cabinet he had gained Hitler's respect and had some influence over him. He believed Hitler was telling the truth when he said that once the Sudeten question was settled he had no more territorial ambitions in Europe. Chamberlain invited the Cabinet to examine the difference between the Anglo-French plan agreed on the 18th and the present proposals, and to consider whether these differences would justify going to war. He spoke with compassion of the thousands of homes he had seen stretched out below him as he flew back to London, at a time when the population was fearful of air attack, and said he felt he could not justify waging war today in order to prevent a war later.[110]

At first Halifax agreed with the prime minister, but, following a discussion with Cadogan late on the 24th he told the Cabinet in the morning of Sunday the 25th that his position was changing. He now felt the Godesberg terms involved a difference of principle from the Anglo-French plan and said that if the Czechs rejected them, and if France went to war in fulfilment of her obligations, Britain should join in too. Unlike Chamberlain, he no longer believed Hitler's aims were limited.[111] Cadogan had presumably relayed to Halifax the contents of an SIS report, dated 18 September, which gave Germany's objectives as the disintegration of Czechoslovakia, the establishment of German hegemony over the whole of Central and South-Eastern Europe, and, in the longer term, over Belgium, Holland, the Baltic States, Scandinavia and most of the Soviet Union.[112] Even so, the SIS report saw no alternative to a peaceful transfer of the Sudeten-German areas to forestall the inevitable, and to give time for rearmament, so that Halifax's change of mind must have been influenced by other factors, among which considerations of prestige seem to have been paramount. Cadogan regarded the Anglo-French plan as the limit beyond which no concessions should be made to Hitler's demands. As the permanent under-secretary wrote in his diary on the 24th: 'I *know* we and [the French] are in no condition to fight: but I would rather be beat than dishonoured. How can we look any foreigner in the face after this? How can we hold Egypt, India and the rest?'[113] These words expressed feelings late at night rather than considered advice, but they also represented recognition that prestige is a significant factor in power.

Although Halifax said on the 25th he had not reached a firm conclusion on what to do, the loss of his support was a blow to Chamberlain, the more so as other ministers agreed with Halifax it would not be right to press the Czechs to accept the Godesberg terms. Duff Cooper thought the government would be swept out of office if it accepted them and the country would go to war under worse leaders. On the other hand, the mood in Cabinet was hardly bellicose. The minister for co-ordination of defence, Inskip, thought the remedy of war was worse than the disease. The secretary of state for air, Kingsley Wood, shared the feeling of humiliation, but said that from a practical point of view Russia was weak and France was doubtful.[114] The last point had been reinforced the previous day when Phipps had telegraphed from Paris: 'All that is best in France is against war, *almost* at any price … To embark upon what will presumably be the biggest conflict in history with our ally, who will fight, if fight she must, without eyes' – a reference to German air superiority – 'and without real heart must surely give us furiously to think.'[115] Phipps was unduly influenced by Bonnet, but the British Air Ministry confirmed that France was hopelessly outclassed in everything to do with air warfare.[116]

By the time Chamberlain and the Inner Cabinet met with Daladier and Bonnet in the evening of the 25th to discuss the Godesberg terms, the Czech government had intimated it would reject them. The French ministers were evasive when pressed on what action France would take in the event of a German invasion of Czechoslovakia. The British were likewise evasive when Daladier asked whether they accepted Hitler's proposals. Chamberlain replied that the British government was only an intermediary and it was up to the Czech government to accept or reject them. Each side was trying to avoid responsibility, and no conclusion was reached other than to summon the French chief of staff, Gamelin, to explain his plans the next day.[117]

Chamberlain realised the strength of the opposition he faced in Cabinet. He had earlier that evening sent a request to Hitler via Henderson that all reports on negotiations with the French or Czechs, unless direct from the prime minister, should be ignored. Henderson told the state secretary of the German Foreign Ministry, Ernst von Weizsäcker, that Chamberlain's position was threatened by increasing difficulties and it was important not to upset British policy by false moves.[118] When the Cabinet reconvened at 11.30 p.m., Duff Cooper thought Chamberlain looked, for the first time, absolutely worn out and, despite their differences, felt sorry for him. The prime minister now shifted his position from the previous day, when he had suggested that the differences between the Anglo-French plan and the Godesberg terms were not worth fighting for. He now secured the Cabinet's agreement to send Wilson to Berlin with a personal letter for Hitler, asking for concessions to enable an orderly transfer of territory to take place. If Hitler refused, Wilson was authorised to give him a personal message from the prime minister to the effect that if France went to war, it seemed certain Britain would be drawn in. Chamberlain argued this procedure would give Hitler a way out of war without losing face, while demonstrating how hard Britain had tried to preserve peace.[119] Chamberlain had thus moved towards Halifax's position, although, as will become apparent in the next section, the prime minister and the foreign secretary were still not entirely at one.

7.4   Munich

Chamberlain conferred with Daladier and Gamelin the next day, 26 September, securing agreement for Sir Horace Wilson's mission. In the afternoon Halifax was able to forward to Wilson, who had already left for Berlin, a message from the prime minister informing him the French had definitely stated their intention of taking offensive measures if Czechoslovakia were attacked. Wilson was told to make it plain to Hitler that 'this would bring us in ... and is an inevitable alternative to a peaceful solution'.[120] Meanwhile Chamberlain had invited Churchill to Downing Street and the latter had urged immediate mobilization of the fleet. Afterwards Churchill told friends the prime minister's fundamental mistake had been a refusal to take the Soviet Union into his confidence. Churchill continued: 'Ribbentrop always said to Hitler "You need never fear England until you find her mentioning Russia as an ally. Then it means she is really going to war!"'[121] Churchill then went to see Halifax and persuaded him to agree to release a statement drafted by the Foreign Office's press officer, Rex Leeper, an opponent of appeasement, to the effect that the German claim to the transfer of the Sudeten-German areas had been conceded, but if Czechoslovakia were attacked, France was bound to come to its assistance, and Britain and the Soviet Union would certainly stand by France.[122] Neither Chamberlain's letter nor message to Hitler had mentioned the Soviet Union, and the press statement was subsequently repudiated by 10 Downing Street.

Churchill also issued a press statement on the 26th. He said there was still a good chance of peace if Britain, France and the Soviet Union jointly warned the German government that an invasion of Czechoslovakia would be taken as an act of war. He added: 'If the government and people of the United States have a word to speak for the salvation of the world, now is the time, and now is the last time when words will be of any use. Afterwards, through years of struggle and torment, deeds alone will serve ... .'[123] On the same day Roosevelt sent a message to Hitler urging a peaceful solution to the crisis through negotiation. The nearest the president came to a warning was a sentence stating that no nation could escape the consequences of a world war.[124] As his actions over the next two days would show, Roosevelt was closer to Chamberlain's position than to Churchill's. The president was not yet convinced that Nazi aims were unlimited and he was prepared to acquiesce in appeasement to preserve peace, while avoiding responsibility for the Czechs' sacrifice.[125]

When Wilson met Hitler at 5 p.m. on the 26th he found him in a state of excitement prior to making his speech later in the evening. Wilson began to read Chamberlain's letter but, after the second paragraph, which said the Czechs had rejected the Godesberg terms, had been translated, Hitler rose to leave the room. It was only with difficulty that Wilson persuaded him to hear out Chamberlain's proposal for direct negotiations between the German and Czech governments, facilitated, if both sides wished, by a British representative. Hitler made clear there could be no question of negotiations to modify the Godesberg terms, only discussions on how to implement them, and demanded acceptance by the Czechs by 2 p.m. on 28 September. Wilson judged the moment was not right to deliver the oral warning he had been told to give and asked for a further meeting the next day.[126] In a telegram to Chamberlain he said that, unless Hitler left a loophole in his speech, 'I presume we should deliver message in suitable terms and come away'.[127] In the event, although Hitler committed himself in the speech to 1 October as the date for the military occupation of the Sudetenland, he also offered to guarantee what remained of Czechoslovakia once the Polish and Hungarian claims had been met. Wilson advised Chamberlain it was 'very doubtful whether it is either necessary or wise' to deliver the oral warning. However, Chamberlain replied that it must be given, although 'more in sorrow than in anger'.[128]

Wilson was faithful to his role as his political master's voice when he met Hitler on the 27th, even trying to speak in the tone which Chamberlain would have used. He prefaced Chamberlain's message by appealing to shared anti-Communism, recalling that Hitler had once described Britain and Germany as bulwarks against the forces of destruction, particularly from the East. Wilson drew attention to the particular form of words Chamberlain had used: if in fulfilment of treaty obligations to Czechoslovakia French forces 'became actively engaged in hostilities against Germany', the British government would feel obliged to support France. When Hitler said this meant that if France attacked Germany Britain would too, Wilson said it was not known how the French intended to carry out their treaty obligation, and that a way out of war must be found. Hitler said the only possibility was for the Czechs to give way, and Wilson replied that he would try to make them sensible.[129]

On his return later that day Wilson reported first to the Inner Cabinet and then, at 9.30 in the evening, to the full Cabinet. An hour and a half before the latter, Chamberlain gave a broadcast which expressed his feelings more vividly than in the Cabinet minutes. 'How horrible, fantastic, incredible, it is', he said, 'that we should be digging trenches and trying on gas masks here because of a quarrel in a far-away country between people of whom we know nothing.' He described himself as a man of peace to the depth of his soul. However, he also said: 'if I were convinced that any nation had made up its mind to dominate the world by fear of its force, I would feel that it must be resisted', before going on: 'but war is a fearful thing, and we must be very clear, before we embark on it, that it is really the great issues that are at stake'.[130]

Chamberlain's belief that Hitler's ambitions were limited explains why he and Halifax differed in their responses to Wilson's advice. Wilson said that, assuming the Czech government would find Hitler's terms too humiliating to accept, the only plan which could prevent the country being overrun would be for it to withdraw its troops and allow German forces to occupy the Sudetenland without loss of life. A plebiscite could then be carried out by an international commission. The Czechs would have the assurance of Hitler's public declaration that the Sudetenland represented his last territorial aim in Europe, and also the Franco-British guarantee proposed in the Anglo-French plan. The alternative, he said, was the Germans would occupy a much more extensive area of Czechoslovakia. Chamberlain said he did not propose the Czech government should be advised to take this course, merely that the suggestion should be put to them. He added that the Inner Cabinet had thought Wilson's plan was perhaps the last opportunity of avoiding war, and that it should be put to the Cabinet with 'all the facts'. He then read a telegram from Henderson in Berlin saying that, unless Czechoslovakia was advised to make the best terms it could, it would be exposed to the fate of Ethiopia. The prime minister said the military attaché from Berlin advised that the Czechs' morale was poor and they would offer feeble resistance. Chamberlain added that 'more disturbing' was a telegram from the Australian prime minister, Joseph Lyons, to the effect that, the transfer of the Sudetenland having been agreed in principle, the precise means of implementing that decision did not warrant war. Finally, Chamberlain said the latest intelligence was that Poland would side with Germany.[131]

Duff Cooper complained that all the facts presented pointed to one conclusion, but there were others which pointed the other way, including Roosevelt's message and the most recent reports from Paris, which indicated a much firmer spirit in France than before. He said the proposal before the Cabinet was a policy of surrender, and Halifax concurred. The foreign secretary argued there was a much greater difference between the Anglo-French plan and the Godesberg terms than one of time, method and degree. He did not think what was being suggested would be accepted by the House of Commons. He thought there was no alternative to telling the Czech government it must take responsibility for making its own decision, and for the British government to consult with the French as to what action should be taken. Chamberlain acknowledged that Halifax had given 'powerful and perhaps convincing reasons against the adoption of his suggestion', and left the matter there. Ministers then discussed what the prime minister should say in his speech to the House of Commons the next day, and there was a consensus he should take the position that, if the French became engaged in active hostilities as a result of her obligations to Czechoslovakia, 'we should feel obliged to support them'.[132]

As Wednesday, 28 September, dawned, Britain seemed to be on the brink of war. The mobilization of the fleet was announced in the morning papers, Chamberlain having finally agreed to this measure the previous afternoon. However, late on the 27th – too late to be discussed by the Cabinet in the evening – a letter had arrived from Hitler thanking Chamberlain for his efforts and once more offering to guarantee what would be left of Czechoslovakia.[133] In the morning of the 28th Wilson contacted Fritz Hesse, press adviser to the German embassy, who, as the representative of the Ribbentrop Bureau, could communicate directly with the German foreign minister, bypassing professional diplomats. Wilson told Hesse that, while the British government was willing to agree to the substance of the Godesberg terms, it was impossible for any democratic government to advise the Czechs to accept the demand for a military occupation. If the Germans were to give way on the form of the transfer, the British government would be prepared to press acceptance on the French and Czechs, but if Hitler could not be dissuaded, Britain would declare war, as public opinion was convinced that the principles of democratic freedom were at stake.[134] At 11.30, without consulting the Cabinet or the French, Chamberlain sent Hitler a personal message offering to return to Germany to discuss arrangements for the transfer of the Sudetenland with Hitler and representatives of the Czech and, if Hitler agreed, the French and Italian governments. Chamberlain also sent a personal message to Mussolini asking him to urge Hitler to agree.[135]

When the prime minister rose to make his speech in the House of Commons shortly before 3 p.m. no reply had been received, but he had heard from Henderson that Hitler had agreed to Mussolini's request for a delay of at least 24 hours from the time set for Czech acceptance of the Godesberg terms (2 p.m. on the 28th). It was not until Chamberlain had been speaking for an hour and a quarter, and had reached the end of a detailed account of the negotiations, that he received a note telling him that Hitler had invited him, Mussolini and Daladier to a conference in Munich the next day. Chamberlain used the note as a dramatic and unexpected peroration. MPs on the government benches, and then Opposition MPs, rose in acclamation. Churchill was one of the few who remained seated. Hansard records that one MP cried, 'Thank God for the prime minister!' The leaders of the Opposition parties,

Attlee and Sinclair, welcomed the news, but not unconditionally, speaking of 'preserving peace without sacrificing principles' and the need to ensure the independence of the Czechoslovak state within its new frontiers.[136] When Chamberlain left the Chamber Churchill shook his hand and said: 'I congratulate you on your good fortune. You were very lucky.'[137]

British diplomacy was not solely responsible for Hitler's decision. Hitler had become aware of a lack of enthusiasm for war on the part of Berliners when he observed their sullen response to a three-hour military parade beginning in the late afternoon of the 27th. Given the importance he attached to will as much as material factors in war, some doubt may have entered his mind, although he was still bellicose in the evening. At 11.15 in the morning of the 28th the French ambassador, André François-Ponçet, warned him a military conflict with Czechoslovakia could not be localized, and at 11.40 the Italian ambassador, Bernardo Attolico, delivered a message from Mussolini urging delay and acceptance of Chamberlain's proposal for a four-power conference. Mussolini had been prompted not only by Chamberlain, but also by an earlier appeal, in the afternoon of the 27th, by Roosevelt to help to bring about a negotiated settlement.[138] Mussolini's intervention seems to have been decisive. Mussolini had hitherto been supportive of German aims in Czechoslovakia, but he judged the time was not ripe for a general war.[139] Roosevelt had also sent a telegram to Hitler on the 27th asking him to consider widening the current negotiations into 'a conference of all the nations directly interested in the present controversy', while making it clear the United States was not one of them.[140] When Roosevelt heard Chamberlain had accepted Hitler's invitation to go to Munich, the president sent the prime minister a two-word telegram: 'Good man.' According to Hoare, none of the expressions of support Chamberlain received encouraged him so much.[141] Donald Watt considered that, given the purpose of the conference was to arrange the transfer of the Sudetenland to Germany, Roosevelt's intervention amounted to support for appeasement.[142] Certainly Churchill must have hoped for something else from the United States when in his press statement on 26 September he had asked for its government and people to speak for the salvation of the world.

Chamberlain left Downing Street at 8 a.m. on 29 September, and even at that hour there was a small crowd of well-wishers cheering him. Almost all of the Cabinet were at the airport to see him receive an enthusiastic send off from a large crowd. Speaking to the press, he recalled that when he was a little boy he used to repeat: 'if at first you don't succeed, try, try, try again'.[143] Critics would later alter the maxim to 'if at first you don't concede, fly, fly, fly again', but no mocking was to be heard that day. In the evening the Home Office issued plans for the evacuation of 2 million Londoners.

Churchill's position was set out in a press statement the previous day: 'I have wished the Prime Minister "God-speed" in his mission, from the bottom of my heart. The indomitable exertions he has made to preserve peace make it certain that should he be forced to declare that it is our duty to take up arms in defence of right and justice, his signal will be obeyed by a united nation and accepted by a united Empire.' Churchill warned, however: 'There must be no relaxation of moral vigilance.' Noting that the purpose of the conference was to discuss 'the methods and conditions of the transference of territories and population from the Czechoslovak Republic to Nazi rule', he observed that Britain had an obligation to 'secure for the truncated Czechoslovakia a fair chance of safety and of economic life'.[144] Churchill hoped on the 29th to make Chamberlain more resolute by sending him a telegram, to be signed by Attlee, Eden, Sinclair and himself, saying that if the prime minister betrayed the Czechs he would face cross-party opposition in the House of Commons. However, Eden refused to sign on the grounds that it would be interpreted as a vendetta against Chamberlain, and Attlee would not sign without the approval of his party. There was no time to secure that, and the telegram was not sent. Churchill was recorded by the Liberal journalist Colin Coote as being in a towering rage and deepening gloom at dinner that evening.[145]

The Munich Conference was brief, the essential decision that the Czechs would be required to cede the Sudetenland having already been taken.[146] The first session began just after 12.30 p.m. on the 29th, and the agreement was signed shortly before 2 a.m. on the 30th. The proceedings would have been shorter had they not required translation into English, French and German (Mussolini claimed to understand all three languages). Neither Chamberlain nor Daladier brought his foreign secretary, and although Ribbentrop and Ciano were present, neither seems to have contributed anything substantial to the discussions between the big four. Chamberlain raised the question of Czech representation, but gave way when Hitler objected. Halifax told the Soviet ambassador in London, Maisky, that the prime minister believed the German and Italian governments would not have agreed to take part in a conference to which the Soviet Union was invited.[147]

Chamberlain agreed to accept a memorandum which Mussolini produced at the opening session as the basis of discussion at the conference. Although the memorandum was in Italian, it was a translation, via French, of a document prepared in the German Foreign Ministry the day before on the basis of a draft by Goering, and differed little from the

Godesberg terms. Chamberlain raised questions relating to compensation for property in the territory to be transferred, and whether cattle could be driven into what remained of Czechoslovakia, provoking Hitler into shouting: 'Our time is too valuable to be wasted on such trivialities.'[148] To the prime minister, however, these matters were important, since he knew he had to make the Munich agreement an improvement on the Godesberg terms if it were to be acceptable to the Cabinet and British public opinion. The main differences were that the transfer of territory inhabited predominantly by German speakers was to take place in stages between 1 and 10 October, rather than in one operation on 1 October, and an international commission made up of representatives of the four Munich powers would determine areas where plebiscites would be held. In an annex to the agreement, Britain and France gave a joint guarantee to what was left of Czechoslovakia, meaning that Britain was obliged to act only if France did so also. The annex also stated that Germany and Italy would give a guarantee once the question of the Polish and Hungarian minorities had been settled. Strang was asked by Wilson to summarise the ways in which the agreement was better than the Godesberg memorandum, and was able to produce a sizeable list, although he thought there was little substance in the differences.[149]

Chamberlain knew the Munich agreement alone was unlikely to satisfy public opinion in Britain. However, since going to Berchtesgaden he had hoped to extend his talks with Hitler to general issues of European appeasement. The two men had a private meeting in the morning of the 30th when, according to Chamberlain, they had a 'very friendly and pleasant talk' on Spain, economic relations with South-East Europe, and disarmament. Neither mentioned Germany's ex-colonies. Chamberlain had come prepared with a short paper, hastily drafted by Strang, in which the agreement was described as 'symbolic of the desire of our two peoples never to go to war with one another again'. It concluded by saying that Hitler and Chamberlain were determined to continue their effort to remove, through consultation, 'possible sources of differences and thus contribute to assure the peace of Europe'. To Strang's dismay, the prime minister inserted into the draft a reference to the Anglo-German Naval Agreement as an example of what should be done. When the paper was translated, Hitler agreed to sign it at once. [150]

It was this piece of paper that Chamberlain waved when, on his return to London later that day, he told cheering crowds, in an allusion to Disraeli's return from the Congress of Berlin in 1878: 'this is the second time in our history that there has come back from Germany to Downing Street peace with honour. I believe it is peace for our time.'[151] Alec Douglas-Home, who, as Lord Dunglass, was Chamberlain's parliamentary private secretary and had been with him to Munich, recalled that the prime minister knew at once he had made a mistake, as he could not justify the claim.[152] However, Chamberlain described the Munich agreement as a 'triumph' in Parliament on 3 October.[153] It was only on 6 October, after being challenged on how the agreement could be reconciled with continued rearmament, that he said the words 'peace for our time' had been used in a moment of some emotion, after a long and exhausting day. He continued: 'I do indeed believe that we may yet secure peace for our time, but I never meant to suggest that we should do that by disarmament, until we can induce others to disarm too. Our past experience has shown us only too clearly that weakness in armed strength means weakness in diplomacy.'[154]

Churchill apparently hoped the reaction in Britain to the Munich agreement might bring down the government, for he advised Jan Masaryk, the Czech minister in London, on 1 October that fortifications in the Sudetenland should not be handed over to the Germans for at least 48 hours. Chamberlain, who learned from MI5 about Churchill's contacts with Masaryk, dismissed this 'conspiracy' as an example of Churchill's capacity to deceive himself.[155] In the event, only one Cabinet minister, Duff Cooper, resigned. Oliver Stanley, the president of the Board of Trade, and Walter Elliot, the minister of health, talked of resignation, but were dissuaded by Chamberlain, as was Harry Crookshank, a junior minister in the Board of Trade. In Stanley's case the task was made easier by his belief that the terms of the Munich agreement were superior in many ways to the Godesberg ones that the Cabinet had rejected.[156]

In the post-Munich debate in the House of Commons Churchill dismissed Chamberlain's claim to have achieved an improvement in Hitler's terms in the course of the negotiations at Berchtesgaden, Godesberg and Munich, remarking: '£1 was demanded at the pistol's point. When it was given, £2 were demanded at the pistol's point. Finally the dictator consented to take £1 17s 6d [£1.875] and the rest in promises of good will for the future.' Churchill argued Germany could have been deterred by a combination of Britain, France and the Soviet Union, together with smaller states. He admitted there was no certainty about what would have happened, but he contended that such a combination would have strengthened the hand of proponents of peace within Germany. To be successful, such a policy would have required Britain to guarantee Czechoslovakia against unprovoked aggression (as he had suggested in March). Now, he said scathingly, the government had given a guarantee which it was in no position to fulfil. He predicted that Czechoslovakia would not survive as an independent state. For him Munich was an avoidable disaster of the first magnitude. He pointed out that now countries in Central and South-Eastern Europe would gravitate towards Germany, giving it access to resources which would diminish the deterrent effect of British naval power, while the loss of the Czech army and the break-up of France's system of alliances gave the Germans the advantage on land. Unlike Chamberlain, he did not believe cordial relations with Germany were possible, given the nature of the Nazi regime. He expected Britain and France would soon be confronted with fresh demands that would compromise their safety. However, despite what he said about the collective strength of many nations, and despite calling for greater rearmament, he went on to say that the only way to protect Britain from the Nazi menace was to achieve supremacy in the air and thus 'make ourselves an island once again'.[157] He did not explain how this would make Britain an attractive ally to continental powers. Churchill's ideas were radically different from Chamberlain's as regards diplomacy, but not as regards priority between air power and assistance to allies on land. Attlee and Sinclair likewise commented adversely on Chamberlain's failure to adopt a policy of collective security and his neglect of the Soviet Union, but did not address the question of what Britain should contribute to collective security.[158]

The debate made clear that many Conservatives shared the Opposition's sense of humiliation. However, Chamberlain's speech on the final day rallied his government and party. He cited the 20,000 letters and telegrams he had received as evidence that the British public did not regard the dispute over the Sudetenland as a reason why they should be exposed to bombing and poison gas. He then announced a review of defence preparations. Only two dozen Conservative backbenchers – including Churchill and Eden – abstained.[159]

The reactions to Munich that Chamberlain received from dominion prime ministers were supportive. On 30 September General Hertzog telegraphed from South Africa that the outcome of the conference had been received in the Union with immense relief, and expressed confidence that further such conferences would re-establish the mutual confidence among nations essential to the maintenance of peace. From Australia Joseph Lyons sent warmest congratulations at the outcome of the negotiations. Mackenzie King wrote in his own hand that Canada rejoiced at the success that had crowned Chamberlain's 'unremitting efforts for peace' and, with less than prophetic insight, predicted these would ensure him 'an abiding and illustrious place among the great conciliators'.[160] Roosevelt shared the relief that an outbreak of war had been averted, but was concerned about the future, predicting in a letter to Mackenzie King on 11 October that there would be a new crisis if Hitler did not agree to reduce armaments and lower trade barriers.[161]

Would it have been better to take a firm stand against Hitler in 1938, as Churchill advocated, or did Chamberlain make Britain secure by gaining another year to complete its air defences? Historians' answers to these questions depend upon counterfactuals with ample scope for legitimate disagreement even with hindsight (see Chapter 11). In particular, would the Soviet Union have been a trustworthy and effective partner in collective security, as Churchill believed, but SIS and the chiefs of staff doubted? Precisely what aid could Soviet, French and British forces have rendered to Czechoslovakia? Would all the dominions have supported Britain when the *casus belli* seemed to be an obscure dispute in Central Europe? How long would Japan and Italy have remained on the side-lines if war had broken out?

There is also the moral question of whether Chamberlain would have been justified in exposing citizens to air attacks when measures to protect them were incomplete and experts in the Air Ministry expected casualties to be heavier than they proved to be. Moreover, fears of the scale of suffering war would bring extended beyond air raids. In the Munich debate James Maxton, a pacifist Labour MP, pointed to the 10 million casualties in battle between 1914 and 1918 in what had been said to be a war to end war, but which had not done so. He predicted that a future war would be more destructive and asked whether a figure of 50 million lives lost would be unrealistic (it turned out to be an underestimate for 1939–45). While expressing sympathy for the Czechs, and antagonism for all that Chamberlain represented politically, Maxton nevertheless congratulated the prime minister on doing what the common people in the world wanted by securing a breathing space in which the foundations of peace might be laid.[162] Hindsight may make such a perspective unrealistic, but war was not something to be entered into lightly.

Some criticism does not depend on hindsight. David Reynolds convincingly portrayed Chamberlain as an inexperienced pioneer of summit diplomacy who preferred to deal with Hitler face to face rather than through normal diplomatic channels, but who set off for Berchtesgaden without an interpreter. While not a pushover, Chamberlain tended to give way on major issues – such as Hitler's demand for self-determination for the Sudeten-Germans – and to be content with concessions on points of detail.[163] On the other hand, as Richard Overy pointed out, Hitler abandoned his plans for a violent conquest of Czechoslovakia and came to believe he had been beguiled by Chamberlain, who used the time gained to prepare for a major war.[164] Chamberlain sincerely wished to establish good Anglo-German relations, but he was also guided by the advice of the chiefs of staff, which was firmly against war in 1938.

8   From Munich to Prague

8.1   The Aftermath of Munich

A key difference between revisionist and post-revisionist historians arises from their interpretations of Chamberlain's state of mind after Munich. David Dilks presented Chamberlain as *hoping* he had secured peace at Munich; Alastair Parker argued the prime minister *believed* he had. According to Parker, Chamberlain 'predicted for Czechoslovakia a secure national existence "comparable to that which we see in Switzerland today"'. Hansard records that what Chamberlain said on 6 October 1938 was the Munich agreement 'may perhaps enable her to enjoy in the future and develop a national existence' under a neutrality like Switzerland's.[1] In this instance Chamberlain's words support Dilks's interpretation of hope rather than Parker's interpretation of belief. However, there is evidence pointing the other way. On 2 October Chamberlain wrote to Hankey, the recently retired cabinet secretary: 'I believe with you that we have at last laid the foundations of a stable peace, though it remains to build the superstructure.'[2] Halifax's recollection in 1951 was that Chamberlain initially felt he could influence Hitler, but saw the red light almost at once when the latter made a truculent speech at Saarbrücken on 9 October.[3] An amber light would be a more appropriate metaphor, for Chamberlain proved to be persistent in hope. In the speech Hitler said Germany would strengthen its western fortifications to guard against the possibility that Chamberlain's critics – Churchill, Duff Cooper and Eden were mentioned by name – might come to power. Hitler's tone was one of resentment at British interference in German affairs.[4] Chamberlain may well then have become less optimistic than he had been. He remarked to Halifax on 11 October that their approach to dealing with the dictators was summed up in the maxim: 'while hoping for the best it is also necessary to prepare for the worst'.[5] On 15 October he wrote to his sisters: 'we are very little nearer the time when we can put all thoughts of war out of our minds and settle down to make the world a better place'.[6]

Churchill for his part was in deep despair at the likely consequences of what Chamberlain had conceded to Hitler. Writing to the French politician Paul Reynaud on 10 October, Churchill commented: 'The magnitude of the disaster leaves me groping in the dark. Not since the loss of the American colonies has England suffered so deep an injury.'[7] Unsurprisingly, relations between Churchill and Chamberlain were strained. At the end of the Munich debate on 6 October, Chamberlain moved a motion to adjourn the House until 1 November, with the proviso that the government might ask the Speaker for an earlier meeting if the public interest required one. The motion was opposed not only by the Opposition parties, but also by some Conservatives, including Churchill, who protested it was derogatory to Parliament that 'it should be sent away upon holiday in one of the most formidable periods through which we have lived'. He commented that such impatience with parliamentary government had led to dictatorship in other countries. Drawing on what he had heard from Duff Cooper about Chamberlain's consultations with the current foreign secretary, Halifax, and former foreign secretaries, Hoare and Simon, in the Inner Cabinet, he went on: 'Why we even hear that the Cabinet is undergoing rapid modification, that only a few were consulted in matters of consequence, the rest being brought in from time to time only to register decisions in respect of matters of which they had only partial cognisance and to be told that certain matters were being settled.'[8] Chamberlain was nettled by what he regarded as Churchill's hypocrisy in keeping a smiling and courteous face when he had been engaged in what the prime minister regarded as a conspiracy with the Czech minister in London, Jan Masaryk (see page 212). Chamberlain retorted that Churchill's remarks were 'unworthy' and his description of how the Cabinet worked was 'repetition of tittle-tattle'.[9] When Churchill sent a letter complaining that these comments were offensive and broke the 'relationship of courtesy which has been maintained between us for so many years', Chamberlain replied: 'I must say I think you are singularly sensitive for a man who constantly attacks others ... I had not regarded [your] remarks, wounding as they were, as requiring a breach of personal relations, but you cannot expect me to allow you to do all the hitting and never hit back.'[10]

Exhausted and close to a nervous breakdown, Chamberlain departed for Scotland to relax for ten days at The Hirsel, the country seat of the Earl of Home, Dunglass's father. After enduring criticism of his policy in the House of Commons, the prime minister could take comfort from a flood of supportive letters and gifts from the public. While this response to Munich partly reflected management of the press by Chamberlain and Sir Joseph Ball, there can be little doubt that for the time being the bulk of public opinion was influenced by relief at being spared the horrors of war rather than by shame of what had happened to Czechoslovakia. Julie Gottlieb's analysis of the records of Mass-Observation diarists and of the correspondence received by Chamberlain and his wife has shown that women in particular praised the prime minister and thereby confirmed his belief in the rightness of his policy.[11]

Why did Chamberlain not capitalise on his popularity and call a general election? Chamberlain himself gave a perfectly sensible reason in Parliament on 6 October: a general election would tend to magnify differences between parties and, as it was possible that 'great efforts' might be required from the nation in the coming months, the smaller the differences the better.[12] Churchill likewise thought an election would split the nation and reduce co-operation from the trade unions on rearmament.[13] However, presumably as a result of Hitler's remark at Saarbrücken that the government might be replaced by one opposed to appeasement, Chamberlain told his sisters on 15 October he did not believe he would succeed in establishing confidence abroad in the continuity of his policy until he had a mandate for it, and that he would watch eagerly for an opportunity to call an election.[14] He never did. The reason is not to be found in a fall in his personal popularity. Public opinion polls show that 57 per cent of respondents who expressed an opinion were satisfied with him as prime minister in October 1938, 56 per cent in December 1938 and 58 per cent in March 1939.[15] It was not certain, however, that his personal standing would translate into electoral success. The Conservative Party's constituency soundings at the beginning of October 1938 gave no definite indication as to which way electoral opinion had swung in response to Munich, and in November a Conservative Research Department analysis of by-election trends suggested a far less promising outlook than a few months previously.[16] Moreover, the value of Munich as an electoral asset was diminished by evidence that appeasement had not secured peace. Angered by the German people's lack of enthusiasm for war, Hitler abandoned the pretence of wanting peace and, beginning with the speech at Saarbrücken, adopted a rhetoric designed to rouse their martial spirit.

Although Chamberlain cited the need for national unity as a reason for not holding an election, he was unhappy when Halifax pressed him on 11 October 1938 to bring Eden back into the government and also to broaden its basis by including some members of the Labour Party. Chamberlain anticipated disagreement with Eden over the 'conciliation part' of the dual policy of appeasement and rearmament. The prime minister believed Labour ministers would form a group opposed to his foreign policy, making his position intolerable. 'I have had trouble enough with my present Cabinet', he told his sisters. While he did not mind informing the Labour leaders privately what he was going to do and why, he placed appeasement above what he considered would be sham unity.[17] He saw no need to make drastic changes in his government. The only major new figure in a Cabinet reshuffle at the end of October was Sir John Anderson, the Independent MP for the Scottish Universities and a distinguished former civil servant, who was made lord privy seal with the task of dealing with shortcomings in civil defence preparations revealed by the Munich crisis. Chamberlain continued to enjoy the support of all but a handful of MPs in his party. An attempt by Churchill to rouse a revolt during a debate on a Ministry of Supply on 17 November was a failure: only two Conservatives, Brendan Bracken and Harold Macmillan, followed him into the lobby. Indeed, Duff Cooper defended the government's record on rearmament and said the creation of a Ministry of Supply was not an issue of first-rate importance.[18] Eden continued to keep his distance from Churchill and had a larger group of supporters than him among MPs.[19]

Chamberlain set out his own position on rearmament to the Cabinet on 3 October 1938. He said he had been 'oppressed with the sense that the burden of armaments might break our backs'. He hoped the contacts he had established with Germany and Italy might lead to an agreement to stop the arms race. However, he said, it would be madness to stop rearming until it was clear that other countries would do the same, and every effort should be made to make good deficiencies in the country's defences. On the other hand, that 'was not the same thing as to say that as a thank offering for the present détente, we should at once embark on a great increase in our armaments programme'.[20] On 6 October the Committee of Imperial Defence (CID) ordered a review of measures taken during the crisis, and the minister for co-ordination of defence, Inskip, asked departments to report on how far their programmes would be completed by 1 August 1939 and what could be done to improve the position by that date.[21] Edward Bridges, writing as cabinet secretary, but drawing on his Treasury experience, feared the defence departments would use the opportunity to add to their approved programmes. Arguing that these formed a concerted plan and that the position would have been very different had there been time to complete it, he advised Chamberlain: 'what is wanted is, surely, to press on with the completion of the existing programmes, rather than to set on foot a new review of the scope of defence preparations'.[22] A Cabinet committee chaired by Inskip considered the requirements of the defence departments in the light of the crisis and had no difficulty with a modest bid by the Admiralty for additional escort vessels. Likewise the War Office's proposals for acceleration of completion of the country's anti-aircraft defences were approved. However, Inskip considered a paper by the secretary of state for war, Hore-Belisha, on the role of the Field Force following the removal of the Czech army from the continental balance of power to be beyond the competence of the committee and the paper was referred to the CID. The biggest bid came from the Air Ministry for a new expansion scheme (Scheme M) that would approximately double expenditure on the RAF by the financial year 1940/41. The secretary of state, Kingsley Wood, admitted the cost would be 'staggering', but argued that a powerful air force was necessary to back diplomacy, and would be cheaper than a major war. The chancellor of the exchequer, Simon, countered by drawing attention to the need to maintain the country's financial stability, and the committee was unable to reach a conclusion before the Cabinet met on 7 November 1938.[23]

The Cabinet's discussion was guided by the Treasury's doctrine of the fourth arm of defence. Even Kingsley Wood, who believed that bombers provided the best deterrent, agreed Britain must have sufficient financial strength to maintain a war effort. Chamberlain observed that the government was doing its best to drive two horses abreast, conciliation and rearmament, and it was difficult to keep them in step. He thought it by no means certain Britain could beat Germany in an arms race. He cordially agreed with the Air Ministry's proposal to increase the number of fighter aircraft, but said it would be difficult to represent an increase in the number of bombers as in any way defensive. He accepted that bombers were necessary, but he was very uneasy about the proposal to concentrate on new types of very heavy bombers. The prime minister recalled that before 1914 Britain had tried to gain an advantage by building a new, bigger type of battleship, the *Dreadnought*, but before long other countries began to build dreadnoughts and the level and expense of naval armaments was increased. He agreed the question was a technical one which could not be settled by laymen, but he observed that a heavy bomber cost as much as four fighters. Halifax pointed out that negotiations for qualitative disarmament would probably begin by banning very heavy bombers. The Cabinet accordingly approved the whole of the fighter programme and decided that efforts should be made to produce the maximum number possible by March 1940, but asked the secretary of state for air to give further consideration to the new bomber policy. The obverse of priority for fighters was that orders for bombers were to be limited to what would keep the aircraft industry fully employed.[24] In the event, Kingsley Wood, having consulted the Air Ministry's experts, wrote to Chamberlain on 9 December 1938 that he was satisfied the heavy bombers would give better value than medium ones, and

Chamberlain felt it was not possible for laymen to take the matter further.[25] It was left to the Treasury to ensure that fighters were given priority over bombers, and in the event technical problems in developing heavy bombers delayed their production until after the outbreak of war.

Sir Horace Wilson advised Chamberlain that it would not be possible to overtake German production unless the aircraft industry were put on a war footing, and that the Germans would then conclude Britain had decided to sabotage the Munich agreement. In that case, Wilson said, the Germans would increase the size of their aircraft industry and, 'as we know from Herr Hitler himself, there is a danger that he may feel himself forced to denounce the Naval Treaty, the existence of which is only justifiable, in his view, on the hypothesis that England and Germany do not intend to be at war'.[26] Wilson believed a Ministry of Supply would be effective only if it had compulsory powers and, following conversations with leading businessmen, he told Chamberlain on 21 October that the government could count on the co-operation of industry to expedite rearmament, and that a recession in 1938 had eased the labour-supply problem.[27] Although Hore-Belisha was keen to have a Ministry of Supply to mobilise industry for the army's needs, Chamberlain was opposed. He wrote to his sisters on the 24th: 'A lot of people seem to me to be losing their heads and talking and thinking as though Munich had made war more instead of less imminent.' He blamed the press and said he hoped to persuade editors that, while there were gaps in the rearmament pro-gramme to be filled, there was no need for huge additions to it.[28]

This hope provides the context for the approach made by George Steward, Chamberlain's press relations officer, on 11 October to Fritz Hesse, the press adviser at the German embassy who acted as Ribbentrop's personal repre-sentative. According to Hesse's account, Steward told him that German propaganda could best promote Anglo-German friendship by avoiding attacks on critics of Munich like Churchill, which gave the impression of German interference in British affairs, and instead emphasise support for Chamberlain's peace policy. In particular, Steward suggested Britain, Germany, France and Italy should make a declaration that they did not intend to exceed the level of armaments which would be achieved at com-pletion of their present rearmament programmes. Such a success would strengthen Chamberlain's position and enable him to call a general elec-tion.[29] Steward's overture had no prospect of success, since Ribbentrop himself had instigated the press campaign against British rearmament.[30] The significance of the incident lies in Hesse's report on his conversation with Steward, which contains an apparently incriminating account of Chamberlain's relations with the Cabinet and the Foreign Office. The prime minister was said no longer to ask the opinion of any minister, not even

Halifax, and the Foreign Office was reported to have tried to commit Britain to warlike action during the crisis and to be bent on revenge on Germany and particularly on Ribbentrop. The account of the Foreign Office's attitude was certainly a distortion, although whether by Steward or Hesse is not clear. Steward was also reported to have advised that in future the Foreign Office should be bypassed and all major questions directed to the prime minister, but Hesse's accuracy on this point is uncertain.[31]

On 23 November Hesse had another secret meeting with a 'representative' of Chamberlain, identified by MI5 as Steward. MI5 obtained a copy of Hesse's report to Ribbentrop from one of its informants at the embassy. According to the official history of MI5, the report showed that Hesse's interlocutor had 'secretly hinted to Hesse ... that Britain would "give Germany everything she asks for the next year"'.[32] That is a possible interpretation. Hesse's report records Steward as suggesting an Anglo-German agreement on humanising aerial warfare, which might assist in reducing the extent of rearmament, and a joint declaration recognising respective principal zones of influence. For this purpose Ribbentrop should come to London in January or February 1939 to negotiate, since Chamberlain could not travel to Germany again without further developments. Hesse continued: 'This surprising suggestion is, if I may be allowed to express an opinion, another sign of how great the wish for an understanding with us is ... and is also evidence ... that Great Britain is ready, during the next year, to accept practically everything from us ... .'[33] Hesse was inferring this conclusion from what Steward had said, but it is not certain that that was the impression Steward intended to convey. An alternative interpretation would be that Chamberlain was looking for ways to end the arms race without sacrificing Britain's interests in its zones of influence.

Be that as it may, Sir Alexander Cadogan was appalled when he read a copy of Hesse's report. He hesitated to bring it to Halifax's attention in case the secretary of state resigned, precipitating other ministerial resignations and a general election. Some kind of 'popular front' might then come to power prepared to 'stand up' to the Axis powers, the permanent under-secretary noted, and 'the Foreign Office would then definitely be associated with the war party and would be playing a large role in domestic politics'. That, Cadogan thought, was an argument against telling Halifax, because 'we might find ourselves a disunited nation at the very moment when unity would above all be desirable'.[34] Nevertheless, he decided he must speak with the secretary of state, noting in his diary: 'we must stop this sort of thing'. Cadogan felt that, if the prime minister had not inspired the approach, he should know about it. After Halifax tackled Chamberlain, Cadogan recorded that the latter was 'aghast (H. thinks genuinely)'.[35] According to Ruggiero, Chamberlain was merely feigning surprise.[36] That may be so, since it is unlikely Steward was acting without Chamberlain's knowledge. However, another interpretation of the prime minister's reaction would be that he was horrified by the conclusion drawn by Hesse from Steward's clandestine negotiations.

How different were Foreign Office views from Chamberlain's after Munich? On 9 November Halifax was presented by Cadogan with six memoranda by officials on the possible course of future British policy, together with the SIS assessment of 18 September, mentioned on page 203, of Germany's far-reaching objectives. There was a consensus on the need for greater rearmament. Cadogan observed that the dangerous military inferiority of Britain and France compared with Germany meant Hitler had not succeeded at Munich through bluff: 'It is not, in poker parlance, a bluff to bid high on four aces.'[37] William Strang, the head of the Central Department, described Munich as a debacle and thought the only hope of dealing successfully with Germany lay in becoming substantially as strong as it. The British people, he said, would have to be persuaded to make sacrifices to increase rearmament and accept compulsory military service. Cadogan argued that Germany's advantage lay not in its totalitarian system but in being more nearly self-sufficient than the United Kingdom and therefore more able to focus its industry on munitions. Britain, in contrast, had to import the greater part of its food, and consequently to maintain the sterling exchange rate. Thus the permanent under-secretary, like Chamberlain, accepted the Treasury's doctrine of economic stability as the fourth arm of defence, and doubted whether the combined efforts of Britain and France could achieve more than equality with Germany. Churchill's advocacy of a common front by Britain, France and the Soviet Union under the banner of collective security had no support in the Foreign Office. Strang thought the effects would be to polarise public opinion in Britain and France, to alienate some of the smaller Central and Eastern European powers, and to 'provoke a war in which defeat would be disastrous and victory hardly less so'.[38] Even Laurence Collier, the head of the Northern Department, who believed the Nazi menace gave Britain, France and the Soviet Union common interests, accepted that the pre-Munich balance of power in Central and Eastern Europe could not be restored and, in common with other officials, said Britain should concentrate on preserving its imperial communications through the Mediterranean. Strang thought the French should liquidate their commitments in Central Europe (including their alliance with Poland), and that Britain and France should create a barrier against Germany in the West, while maintaining relations with the Soviet Union at a level that would make it less likely that Stalin would join forces with Hitler.[39] Halifax agreed with this broad strategic analysis. In a letter to Sir Eric Phipps, the British ambassador in Paris on 1 November, the secretary of state said German predominance in Central Europe was inevitable, and that Britain and France must aim at having the armed strength to ensure their predominant position in Western Europe, the Mediterranean and the Middle East, and the closest possible ties with the United States. Halifax was ambivalent about the Soviet Union and hoped France would not allow itself to be drawn into a war with Germany on account of the Franco-Soviet alliance.[40]

As regards Germany's objectives, SIS's view was that Germany would be prepared, at least for a time, to recognise British supremacy overseas in return for a free hand in Central and South-Eastern Europe, although a demand for the return of its colonies would follow in due course.[41] SIS believed Germany aimed in the longer term at hegemony over much of Europe, but Cadogan thought a frank discussion with the Germans about their grievances with a view to a general settlement would be worthwhile. He believed the German people realised they had nearly been plunged into a war to get what they got without one at Munich, and that that experience might have shaken their belief in the Fuehrer. 'If we can show that we are willing to remedy 80 per cent of Germany's remaining grievances, will Herr Hitler get his people to fight for the other 20 per cent?' he asked. To this end he was willing to contemplate a further conference of the four Munich powers, although he was more comfortable with the idea of a direct approach to Germany by Britain.[42] Cadogan rejected Collier's critique of Germany and Italy as predatory states whose appetites would grow with each concession.[43] None of the Foreign Office officials thought German predominance in Central and South-Eastern Europe need be at the expense of British economic interests there, since the German market would not be large enough to absorb all the agricultural produce from the region. Frank Ashton-Gwatkin, the head of the Economic Relations Section, suggested that Field-Marshal Goering, who was in charge of the four-year plan for the German economy, should be invited to Britain in order to discover his views on reducing trade barriers.[44] Hopes that progress in commercial talks could lead to better political relations would persist into early 1939.

On the question of colonial restitution, there was the usual split between Cadogan and Strang on the one hand and Collier on the other. Collier thought Germany's claims should be resisted on the grounds that Germany now occupied a stronger position in Europe than in 1914 and any concession would be regarded both abroad and in Britain as a sign of complete decadence. Cadogan and Strang were prepared to consider trading colonies for an agreement on disarmament. Strang thought Britain was in a position to demand that a price be paid by Germany since the latter was in no position to undertake an offensive war in Western Europe (to which Cadogan commented: 'Perhaps not *now*').[45] Cadogan pointed out on 8 November that disarmament would not really be a quid pro quo since all parties to an agreement would be limiting their armed forces, and Germany should also be asked to give undertakings concerning frontiers in Europe 'for what that might be worth'.[46] Cadogan was clearly sceptical and said Britain was bound to make proportionate increases in its defences as long as Germany expanded its armaments, but as of 9 November he was prepared, like Chamberlain, to hope for a general settlement while preparing for the worst.

However, intelligence reports led the Foreign Office to be less hopeful than Chamberlain. The latter's belief that he had won Hitler's respect and could influence him was challenged by an MI5 report forwarded to the Foreign Office on 7 November 1938. In order to ensure the prime minister paid attention to its contents, the report included examples of Hitler's insulting references to him, and Halifax underlined in red one of Hitler's more vulgar ones: '*arschloch*' (arsehole). The negotiations during the Czech crisis were said to have convinced Hitler that Britain was decadent and lacking the will and power to defend its empire. German policy was described as 'Napoleonic', with the only doubt being what direction German expansion would take.[47] A summary of SIS reports received up to 11 November emphasised Munich had left Hitler resentful that Chamberlain had been given the credit, even by the German people, for preventing war. The regime was described as having a 'dynamic urge' towards expansion, and it was predicted that German claims in Europe or for colonies would increase.[48] The effect of intelligence reports was strengthened by the events of *Kristallnacht* when, on the night of 9–10 November, Nazi Stormtroopers and civilians attacked Jews and their property on a massive scale. At Halifax's request, the Cabinet's Foreign Policy Committee was convened at short notice on 14 November, when he said 'crazy people' were in charge of Germany. The foreign secretary added that a resolute attitude by Britain, backed by increased aircraft production, might discourage extremists, and encourage moderates, in Germany. Meanwhile he had reluctantly concluded that resumption of Anglo-German conversations would serve no useful purpose. Chamberlain commented he was inclined to discount intelligence reports.[49] He seems to have been reluctant to accept he might have been wrong about Hitler. Writing to his sisters on 13 November, the prime minister said he had had a 'very interesting report' from William

Astor, a Conservative MP and the son of Viscount and Nancy Astor who entertained Chamberlain and his wife from time to time at their home at Cliveden and whose social circle were said to be strong supporters of appeasement. William Astor had visited Berlin and formed the impression that Hitler 'definitely liked' Chamberlain and thought he could do business with him.[50]

Nevertheless, Chamberlain was horrified by the barbarity of *Kristallnacht* and accepted that any diplomatic approach to Germany was out of the question for the time being.[51] Instead he told the Foreign Policy Committee on 14 November the best way to approach the Berlin-Rome axis was at the Rome end, and that he proposed to visit Mussolini.[52] The two men had met for the first time at Munich, when, by Chamberlain's account, Mussolini had been more than friendly and had expressed the strong hope he would visit him soon in Italy. Chamberlain wrongly believed Mussolini had played an indispensable part in securing a peace settlement.[53] Implementation of the Anglo-Italian Agreement of 16 April 1938 had been delayed by the prime minister's insistence in June on evidence that the Spanish Civil War had been eliminated, or was in the process of being eliminated, as a source of international friction.[54] However, on 26 October, Halifax told the Cabinet that half the Italian 'volunteer' infantry had been withdrawn from Spain, and recommended that the Cabinet approve steps to bring the agreement into force, as the opportunity to free Mussolini from the pressure he was under from Berlin might not recur. Chamberlain concurred, saying the agreement was an essential step towards general European appeasement.[55] Chamberlain was being typically optimistic, but even the cautious Cadogan thought that, once the agreement was in force, 'we might ... find that we could get Signor Mussolini into our confidence and enlist his co-operation in Berlin'.[56] In contrast to when Eden had been foreign secretary, Chamberlain and the Foreign Office were now in step on Anglo-Italian relations. The approach to Rome was also in line with an SIS report, dated 14 November, that there was apprehension in the Fascist Grand Council about the preponderance of Germany in the Axis.[57] On 16 November, when the Anglo-Italian Agreement came into force, Mussolini sent a friendly personal telegram to Chamberlain, and agreed to a proposal by the British ambassador, Lord Perth, that the prime minister and Halifax should visit Rome.[58]

The conversations with Mussolini and his foreign minister, Ciano, from 11 to 14 January 1939 would have discouraged a less optimistic statesman than Chamberlain. He was unconvinced by Mussolini's claim that German rearmament was for defensive purposes, pointing out that no one in Britain, not even Churchill, thought in terms of an offensive war against Germany. Mussolini made it clear that no improvement in Franco-Italian relations would occur until the Spanish Civil War was over.[59] Nevertheless, Chamberlain was heartened by his own enthusiastic reception from Italian crowds demonstrating a desire for peace, and he found Mussolini much more pleasant to deal with than Hitler. The Italian dictator impressed him as 'a reasonable man ... straightforward and sincere'.[60] Away from the conference room, however, Mussolini was dismissive of Chamberlain and Halifax, remarking: 'These men are not made of the same stuff as the Francis Drakes and the other magnificent adventurers who created the empire. These, after all, are the tired sons of a long line of rich men, and they will lose their empire.'[61] Chamberlain's – and Cadogan's – hope that Mussolini could be enlisted in the cause of appeasement was unfounded. At best, as Churchill remarked, the visit to Rome did no harm.[62]

Chamberlain, Churchill and the Foreign Office were agreed on the need to keep the closest possible ties with the United States. Chamberlain took considerable interest in Anglo-American trade negotiations which had begun in February 1938. While he did not expect an agreement to lead to any great political or economic support from the United States, he recognised that failure to reach one would have a negative effect on how Anglo-American relations were perceived by Germany and Japan.[63] Cadogan observed on 14 October 1938 that 'the Americans may be backward in giving any promise of material assistance, and still more backward in implementing it, but the shadow of possible trouble with America has undoubtedly restrained Japan in recent times from doing as much damage as she would like to do to our interests in the Far East'.[64] He thought it would be worthwhile making considerable concessions to secure a trade agreement. The context of this remark was disagreement between the Foreign Office and the Board of Trade on how far negotiations should be guided by political considerations, and in particular by a list of additional American demands for free entry of goods to the British market. The president of the Board of Trade, Oliver Stanley, wanted a Cabinet ruling on how far negotiators should go in making concessions. At the Cabinet meeting on 19 October Halifax said it was desirable to go a very long way to meet the Americans, but that it was impossible to agree to all of their requests. Chamberlain thought the American secretary of state, Cordell Hull, would not be prepared to break off talks, and that it would still be possible to reach an agreement if some politically sensitive items were removed from the list.[65] At a time when Roosevelt wished to demonstrate support for the British against the Axis powers, Hull decided on 5 November to accept the British counter proposals.

Chamberlain followed up this success on 8 November by writing once more to Roosevelt to ask for the repeal of the arms embargo embodied in the American Neutrality Act. An assurance that Britain and her French allies could draw on American resources in war, the prime minister wrote, would be 'a profound moral encouragement to us in the struggle in which we are engaged', and would have 'a devastating effect on German morale'.[66] However, a report which reached Chamberlain on 14 December explained the president wished him to feel America's industrial resources were behind him in the event of war with the dictatorships, 'so far as he, the president, was able to achieve it', but the prime minister should not go further in public than stating that Britain 'could rely upon obtaining raw materials from the democracies of the world'.[67] Given isolationist influence in Congress, the extent of future American support remained uncertain. Churchill feared Munich would lead the American people to wash their hands of European affairs.[68] However, a Foreign Office appreciation for the Joint Intelligence Committee in November 1938 noted a recent marked increase in anti-totalitarian feeling in the United States. The Foreign Office thought the Neutrality Act would be altered in the Allies' favour if there were a European war, but warned 'it would be most imprudent to count on armed assistance'.[69]

On 4 January 1939 Roosevelt, in his annual message to Congress, spoke cryptically of methods short of war that would bring home to aggressor governments the sentiments of the American people, and Chamberlain responded by welcoming his words as an indication of the vital role of American democracy in world affairs, a positive response that pleased Churchill.[70] Even so, Chamberlain and Halifax were agreed on 9 January that Britain should not commit itself to taking parallel action with the Americans regarding possible economic sanctions against the Japanese.[71] On 7 February, in response to a parliamentary question, he made clear he did not intend to go to the United States to meet Roosevelt. Later, in June, he explained to Labour leaders that 'the sure way ... to lose the Americans was to run after them too hard'. To do so would reinforce American fears of European entanglements – a point, he felt, critics like Churchill did not properly appreciate.[72]

Churchill was much less hopeful than Chamberlain that an agreement with Germany was possible. It is true that, following a hostile reference to himself in a speech by Hitler on 6 November 1938, Churchill expressed regret that the German leader had not been mellowed by success, and said 'let this great man search his own heart and conscience before he accuses anyone of being a war-monger'.[73] It is hard to know whether Churchill was being irenic or ironic on that occasion. In an article published on 17 November he warned that the prime minister's hopes that Hitler sought no more territorial expansion in Europe, or that colonial restitution would bring about prolonged good relations with Germany, rested on speculation, and that appeasement might only stimulate a more ferocious appetite. Churchill was particularly concerned that negotiations on disarmament might lead to Britain giving up the right to have as powerful an air force as Germany, in the same way as the Germans had limited their navy to a third of the British under the Anglo-German Naval Agreement.[74] His fears in this respect were exaggerated, but not wholly unfounded, for even in January 1939 Chamberlain had not abandoned hope of an agreement on limitation of bombing – and hinted as much to Mussolini during the Rome visit.[75] Churchill was no more certain about Hitler's precise intentions than the Foreign Office. In late December 1938 he expected a move against Poland in February or March. By 8 January 1939, when the Polish foreign minister, Jozef Beck, appeared to have made some sort of deal with Hitler, Churchill expected the latter to press towards Hungary and Romania.[76]

8.2   Towards a Continental Commitment

Churchill was slow to see that land warfare could not be left to the French once the Czech army no longer counted in the balance of power. Although he wrote of 'the fundamental ties of self-preservation which bind us to the French Republic', he told the House of Commons on 17 November 1938 that the Field Force was 'not a vital weapon. England will not be saved or cast away by the condition of our armies'.[77] His advocacy of air power and sea power as the principal means of deterring Germany rested on his belief that, although the German army was increasing in strength, it suffered from a shortage of officers, and was inferior in quality to the French army, which had more trained reserves and longer-established units. He recognised that France had been weakened by the collapse of its system of alliances in Eastern Europe, but he did not so much as mention the Field Force in an article on Anglo-French relations published on 1 December.[78] This omission did not reflect confidence that Soviet intervention would make up for the loss of the Czech army; on the contrary, on 15 December he described Russia as 'a mystery and a riddle'.[79]

Chamberlain anticipated pressure from the French for a greater British contribution on land. On 22 November, when discussing in Cabinet forthcoming talks in Paris, he said he proposed to take 'a firm line' and stick to existing plans for the Field Force – that is two divisions at the outbreak of war – although it was 'impossible to say what might be done in the course of a long war'. If the French said they were relying on Britain for the air defence of Paris, he would make clear that the RAF was being expanded for the defence of the United Kingdom.[80] In the Anglo-French discussions on 24 November he countered Daladier's assumption that France would be the first to be attacked by arguing that, given the vulnerability of London, the first blow might be struck against Britain. Chamberlain explained that priority for air defence meant industrial capacity could be made available for the Field Force's artillery only after sufficient anti-aircraft guns had been produced. The French premier was left with no more than a hope that it might be possible for Britain to despatch two divisions eight days after the outbreak of hostilities, instead of after three weeks as under current plans, although at the outset of the talks he had emphasised the need for more divisions to support the French army.[81] Regarding Eastern Europe, Chamberlain was keen to find out more about the French attitude to the Soviet Union, because, if France were drawn into a war as a result of a dispute between Germany and the Soviets, Britain would be drawn in too. He professed himself content when Bonnet, the foreign minister, said on the 24th that French obligations under the Franco-Soviet treaty came into force only if there were a direct attack by Germany on Russian territory. Chamberlain congratulated the French on an agreement they were about to sign with Germany promising to promote peaceful relations and to consult together on any international difficulties – an agreement which, like the one he had signed with Hitler after Munich, he regarded as another step towards appeasement in Europe.[82]

Complacency gave way to concern early in December. In the first of a series of reports from the Paris embassy the military attaché, Colonel William Fraser, warned that the French might be so discouraged by the weakening of their strategic position they might not only give Germany a free hand in Eastern Europe, but Britain might be left to confront Germany alone. Phipps, the ambassador, endorsed this warning, and, when the CID met on 15 December to discuss the state of preparedness of the Field Force, Halifax said there was a 'slight danger' the French might stand aside while Germany attacked Britain if they were given the impression they would be left to bear the brunt of the slaughter on land.[83] However, at this stage all that the secretary of state for war, Hore-Belisha, proposed was a restoration of the £70 million that had been cut from the War Office's rearmament programme in April, plus additional expenditure to deal with the situation in Palestine, where the equivalent of two divisions had had to be deployed to deal with an Arab uprising.

The CID referred the question of the extent of the equipment and industrial capacity required for the army to the Chiefs of Staff Committee, where, on 21 December, the chief of the imperial general staff, Lord Gort, explained he was not asking permission to supply the Field Force with more munitions than what was required for defensive operations in Europe, but only to complete the equipment of four Regular infantry divisions and the mobile division (which was to be split into two) to enable them to be sent anywhere, with four Territorial divisions as reinforcements four months after mobilization. That said, he argued that the Dutch and Belgian armies, if left unsupported, would be unable to prevent the Germans overrunning the Low Countries and establishing air and submarine bases, whereas a British promise to send an expeditionary force would encourage the French to support the Belgians. Sir Roger Backhouse, the first sea lord, observed that British troops would be unable to reach Holland in time to stop the Germans, but nevertheless thought Gort had made an unanswerable case. In contrast, Sir Cyril Newall, the chief of air staff, was not convinced any Territorial divisions need be prepared for war; once that idea was accepted, he said, the door was opened to unlimited expansion of land warfare, to which he was opposed.[84] However, when the chiefs of staff resumed their discussion on 18 January 1939 Newall accepted that a study by the Joint Planning Sub-Committee of the relative strengths of France and Germany pointed to the probability that some assistance to France on land would be essential. Bridges, the cabinet secretary, suggested the chiefs of staff should report to the CID that, if industrial capacity were not expanded now to equip a greater army than hitherto authorised, the government's strategic choices at the outbreak of a war would be 'miserably restricted'.[85] The chiefs of staff's report on 25 January 1939 accordingly advised ministers that with only about 30 per cent of the British engineering industry currently employed on rearmament contracts, there should be ample capacity for additional army requirements. A more powerful Field Force could be justified by the priority given in the Inskip Report to the security of the United Kingdom, the chiefs of staff suggested, for they found it difficult to see how that security could be maintained if France were overrun and its ports occupied. Moreover, they added, a lack of land forces available in the first year of a war might result in a loss of opportunities for offensive action which could shorten the war.[86]

The shift in Newall's position on the army between December and January, and in Bridges' position since October, when he had been opposed to increasing the scope of the rearmament programme, reflected the effects of an accumulation of intelligence about German intentions as well as a growing awareness of the need to support France. Reports from the embassy in Berlin were markedly more pessimistic from October 1938 to February 1939, while Sir George Ogilvie-Forbes was in charge during the absence on health grounds of the ambassador, Sir Nevile

Henderson. Unlike Henderson, Ogilvie-Forbes believed there was no limit to Hitler's ambitions. Prior to December the intelligence services had not produced evidence that Hitler intended any direct attack on Britain or its Empire. On 16 December, however, Chamberlain called a meeting of the CID to hear Halifax report there was intelligence from Berlin that Hitler was unbalanced and intended to make a surprise air attack on London in March. Chamberlain said this report could not be ignored, although he did not think there was a definite plan or that Hitler would attack without giving warning by picking a quarrel. Hjalmar Schacht (the president of the Reichsbank) had told Chamberlain the previous day that Hitler was contemptuous of Britain as powerless and would be 'up to some mischief' in Eastern Europe within the next month or so. Ministers agreed that all departments should examine whether any acceleration in their programmes was possible, but no change in grand strategy was implied thereby.[87] However, on 1 January 1939 Hore-Belisha met the French chief of staff, Gamelin, in Paris and found him far less optimistic than previously about France's ability to deal with Germany and Italy if, as was thought likely, the Italian army was stiffened with German troops. Gamelin also said German forces were concentrated on the Dutch frontier and thought they might occupy Holland to establish air and submarine bases.[88] By 11 January Inskip was noting in his diary that the Paris embassy was reporting a growing feeling in France that Britain must make a continental commitment of an army large enough to make up for the loss of the Czech army, and that the French General Staff was convinced that war would break out before very long.[89]

On 19 January the Foreign Office advised the Cabinet's Foreign Policy Committee that, on the basis of intelligence reports since mid-December, it was no longer possible to assume that Germany would aim at expansion in Central and Eastern Europe rather than in the West in 1939. On the contrary, there was 'inconvertible evidence' that many people close to Hitler were considering an attack on Britain and France during the next few months or even weeks, and it was 'not at all unlikely' that he was thinking along the same lines. 'All our sources are at one in declaring that he is barely sane, consumed by an insensible hatred of this country, and capable of ordering an immediate air attack on any European country.'[90] Halifax told the committee on 23 January that the dismissal of Schacht earlier in the month indicated that Germany's financial and economic condition was becoming desperate and was 'impelling the mad dictator of that country to insane adventures'. The foreign secretary advised it should be assumed that intelligence reports of intended hostile action against Britain might be true, and the chiefs of staff were asked to report on the implications of a German invasion of

Holland.[91] Although the intelligence gave a realistic picture of the atmosphere in Berlin, the reports of an intended invasion of Holland or of Luftwaffe plans for air attacks on London were untrue, being the inventions of the German opposition to Hitler. Nevertheless, they had their intended effect of alarming the British government, which the German opposition hoped would stand up to Hitler.[92]

Chamberlain agreed with Halifax in Cabinet on 25 January that intelligence about Germany's intentions could not be ignored, especially since in Hitler 'we might be dealing with a man whose actions were not rational'. Even so, the prime minister was sceptical about the intelligence, remarking that it came from sources which had not always proved to be accurate. For example, he had been told that when he and Halifax went to Rome they would be met with demands similar to those made at Berchtesgaden, but that had not been the case. He found it hard to believe Hitler had been irritated by the result of Munich. Chamberlain thought Britain would be bound to intervene if Germany attacked Holland, but resisted the idea of a public warning to Hitler.[93] The following day he focused the Foreign Policy Committee's discussion on the chiefs of staff's report that a war in the near future would be the most serious situation the Empire had ever faced, and the outcome might well depend on the intervention of other powers, particularly the United States. The prime minister suggested the French government should be told about Britain's attitude to Holland, and the committee agreed that staff talks, for which the French had been pressing for some time, should go ahead.[94] On 1 February he explained to the Cabinet that hitherto very close contacts with staffs of potential allies, for example France and Belgium, had been avoided as they would lead to binding commitments. Nevertheless the Foreign Policy Committee now recommended diplomatic approaches to these countries for staff talks. Any attempt by Germany to gain military control over Holland, Chamberlain said, would be such evidence of an intention to dominate Europe as to require Britain to treat it as a casus belli. A German attack on Switzerland (which would threaten France by allowing the Maginot Line to be outflanked) came into the same category.[95]

The next day, 2 February, the Cabinet considered the role of the Field Force and the Territorial Army in the light of the chiefs of staff's views. Chamberlain observed that existing policy was for the Field Force to be available for general purposes – for example service in the Middle East – but now it was proposed it should be equipped with full reserves of munitions for a European campaign. He thought an unanswerable case could be made for increasing all three services if the financial aspect was ignored, but, as a former chancellor, he thought the financial position was extremely dangerous. He hoped the forthcoming staff talks would lead the French to appreciate the gigantic effort Britain was making in the air and on sea and to accept it might be best not to expand the army as well. On this occasion Chamberlain can be justly criticised for applying logic without empathy. However, the deterrent effect of the fourth arm of defence was also at stake. The chancellor, Simon, said defence expenditure was growing faster than revenue and the difficulty experienced in maintaining the sterling exchange rate was a sign the country's financial strength might be slipping away. There was, he warned, a danger of a financial crisis as severe as in 1931. However, as he told his officials after the meeting, no one in the Cabinet, except the prime minister, now placed much importance on finance. Halifax said the French were sensitive about the size of Britain's land contribution, and argued that the chancellor could take the risk of further borrowing for defence. The foreign secretary had made a statement to the Cabinet the previous week to the effect that Germany was having increasing difficulty in importing raw materials and Hitler faced a choice during 1939 between curbing armaments expenditure and securing raw materials by force. Now Halifax advised that the present international tension could not last indefinitely and must result either in war or the destruction of the Nazi regime. Chamberlain agreed with him that a decision on the army should not be delayed, but said Simon, Hore-Belisha and Lord Chatfield (who had replaced Inskip as minister for co-ordination for defence) must have an opportunity to consider the proposals for the Field Force alongside proposals the War Office was due to make shortly on the army's contribution to the air defence of Great Britain. Meanwhile the Cabinet approved Hore-Belisha's proposal for full-scale training equipment for the Territorial Army.[96]

Chamberlain chaired two ministerial meetings to discuss Hore-Belisha's proposals for the Field Force and then recommended to the Cabinet on 22 February 1939 acceptance with minor economies. He explained he had come to this conclusion with reluctance, but saw no alternative, given the strength of the German army and of feeling in France that Britain would not be playing an adequate part in war unless some contribution were made on land. He also thought British public opinion would become restive if the present position that none of the Territorial Army would be ready to go abroad until a year after the outbreak of war became known. The aim was now to have a Field Force of four infantry divisions and two mobile divisions equipped for a European campaign, with the first echelon ready to embark 21 days after the outbreak of war, and the second echelon after 60 days, with four Territorial divisions ready to embark in six months and a further eight Territorial divisions after a

year. The additional cost, £51.4 million, represented a major new financial commitment at a time when the War Office's expenditure in 1938/39
was just over £120 million, but Simon accepted that financial considerations were outweighed by other aspects.[97]

The decision to commit the Field Force to a continental campaign at
the beginning of a war has rightly been seen as a major change in British
military policy, although the extent of the military commitment was still
limited.[98] The Field Force was small compared with European conscript
armies, and time would be required to equip it for offensive operations.
Nor was there much sign of special measures to expedite production of
munitions: on 21 February Churchill once more called for a Ministry of
Supply, and Hore-Belisha was strongly in favour of one, but on 2 March
the Cabinet accepted Chatfield's recommendation that it should not be
set up in peacetime.[99]

Chamberlain's primary object in approving the continental commitment
appears to have been to sustain French morale. Norman Gibbs detected a
lingering suspicion of France when the prime minister said on 1 February
that staff talks should not commit Britain to enter a war between Italy and
France, for in such an eventuality France might benefit from Britain
keeping out in order to avoid bringing Germany in on Italy's side. The
chiefs of staff themselves warned that the French might make political
capital out of talks conducted at a higher level than those conducted since
1936.[100] An offer from Gamelin to visit London was not taken up and staff
talks did not begin until 29 March. However, that there was a commitment
to France was not in doubt. When a Labour MP asked on 6 February
whether a statement by the French foreign minister that in war all British
forces would be at the disposal of France, just as all French forces would be
at the disposal of Britain, was in accordance with the government's views,
Chamberlain said it was. Reading from what Sir Alexander Cadogan
described as a 'very strong draft' prepared in the Foreign Office, he continued: 'the solidarity of interest, by which France and this country are
united, is such that any threat to the vital interests of France from whatever
quarter it came must evoke the immediate co-operation of this country'.[101]
This declaration was described by Churchill as a 'major deterrent' to
aggression.[102] It would be a bold dictator, he said, who would take on the
combined strength of Britain and France, with their worldwide resources
and connections, including the dominions, and with the United States
extending ever greater goodwill to the democracies.[103]

The change in the army's role owed little to pressure from Churchill.
In an interview in the *New Statesman* in January 1939 he had said he did
not think Britain needed a great conscript army on the continental model
in peace. Instead he advocated enlarging the Territorial Army to create a

'skeleton' around which a great army could be built in war. He did say, however, that if not enough volunteers came forward for Territorial units he would not hesitate to make up the numbers by ballot.[104] He did not speak about the army again until 21 February, in a parliamentary debate on defence loans, too late to have influenced Chamberlain. Churchill again said there would be no point at present in trying to raise an army on a continental scale, as that would take years, but he did think Britain ought to have available in the first few months of war larger military forces than those contemplated hitherto. He advocated making industrial preparations so that hundreds of thousands of men, who would volunteer at the outbreak of war, as in 1914, could be equipped.[105] He described as 'momentous' Hore-Belisha's announcement on 8 March 1939 that planning for the Field Force was on the basis of four infantry and two mobile divisions, plus 13 Territorial divisions, and that the Territorial Army would be equipped for a European war. Churchill's congratulations were somewhat barbed, since he said the decision to equip the Territorial Army was a case of better late than never, and should have been taken in 1936. Nevertheless, he regarded the decision to prepare an expeditionary force of 19 divisions available for the common cause of peace as a 'tremendous declaration' of intent, albeit one that required to be backed by creating the industrial capacity to equip and maintain in the field a far bigger force than previously planned.[106] He no longer gave overriding priority to air defence because by the spring of 1939 British aircraft production was at last catching up with Germany's.[107]

8.3   Still Hoping for the Best

Although finally persuaded to change the role of the army as part of preparing for the worst, Chamberlain continued to hope for the best even after *Kristallnacht* had forced him to postpone any diplomatic approach to Germany. In particular, he was unwilling to exclude permanently the possibility of restoring Germany's former colonies as part of a general settlement. When in December 1938 rumours that retrocession was being considered by the government aroused opposition in the colonies, the colonial secretary, Malcolm MacDonald, asked for guidance about what he should say in Parliament. Chamberlain preferred wording that would deny the rumours but which would avoid any finality on the question.[108] Although he conceded in parliamentary debate on 19 December that he was still waiting for a sign from Germany that its leadership shared his desire for peaceful change, Chamberlain continued to look for such a sign.[109] He wondered whether Hitler's New Year speech containing the words 'general pacification of the world' was one, but was advised by Cadogan it was not.[110] Hitler was due to make another speech on 30 January 1939 and Chamberlain took the opportunity of a speech to the Birmingham Jewellers' Association two days before to say that it took two to make peace and until all international tension had been ended Britain would rearm with unrelenting vigour.[111] Sir Horace Wilson sent an advance copy to Hitler and believed it had encouraged restraint in the latter's speech. Writing to Phipps in Paris on 2 February, Wilson said his impression was that the consistency and persistence of the prime minister's policy were steadily enhancing the position at home and abroad.[112]

Chamberlain also believed his speech had led Hitler to alter his at the last moment to make it more pacific.[113] Speaking in Parliament on 31 January the prime minister said the general appeasement of Europe required a favourable atmosphere and confidence could not easily be restored after a long period of uncertainty and anxiety. He went on: 'we want to see not only words which indicate a desire for peace; before we can enter upon the final settlement we shall want to see some concrete evidence of a willingness, let us say, to enter into arrangements for, if not disarmament, at any rate, limitation of armaments'.[114] Oliver Harvey, a Foreign Office official who was normally critical of Chamberlain, thought the prime minister showed 'commendable firmness' on this occasion.[115] Chamberlain told his sisters on 5 February he had begun to feel 'we are at last getting on top of the dictators'. He gave four reasons why Hitler had 'missed the bus' at Munich. First, gaps in Britain's defences had been filled and the Germans 'could not make nearly such a mess of us as they could then, while we could make much more of a mess of them'. Second, the German people had shown they did not like the prospect of war and would protest violently if they thought they were being brought close to it again. Third, the economic position in Germany was not a good one from which to start a war. Fourth, Roosevelt had given the dictators an uneasy feeling that in case of trouble it would not take much to bring the Americans in on the democracies' side.[116] Chamberlain was further encouraged when Sir Nevile Henderson, who had returned to the embassy in Berlin, told him on 16 February that Hitler had approved a passage in a speech by the Duke of Coburg to the Anglo-German Society which referred to co-operation arising from personal contact between the two countries' leaders.[117] Writing to his sisters on the 19th, the prime minister remarked that all the information he got seemed to point in the direction of peace.[118] On the same day in a letter to Henderson he outlined steps by which that goal might be achieved. With the Spanish Civil War likely to end soon, relations between France and Italy could be improved. Then disarmament talks might be begun, starting with Mussolini, but bringing in the Germans pretty soon. If these went well, discussions about colonies could be contemplated, although that subject would have to be approached with care on account of public opinion.[119] Chamberlain showed the letter to Halifax, who did not share his optimism. The foreign secretary told Henderson it would be harder to improve Franco-Italian relations than the prime minister thought, and that there was no prospect of progress in colonial discussions 'unless and until your German friends can really show more than smooth words as evidence of friendly hearts'.[120]

Churchill was likewise unconvinced by Hitler's conciliatory words in the speech of 30 January 1939. He was more impressed by reports of German troop movements in Central Europe and by Hitler's declaration that he would support Mussolini against France.[121] Nevertheless, Churchill saw grounds for optimism. He believed French responses to Italian demands for the cession of Nice, Corsica and Tunisia revealed a new spirit of resolve to resist aggression. In an article published on 9 February, he also noted greater national unity and a stiffening of the government's attitude in Britain. There was, he said, a sense of gathering strength as orders for aircraft and munitions were at last being fulfilled, and he thought the power of the Royal Navy relative to its possible tasks was unprecedented. Like Chamberlain he attached importance to Roosevelt's action in leaking to the press his statement to a confidential meeting of the Senate Military Affairs Committee on 31 January that American munitions would be available in wartime to victims of aggression.[122] On 21 February Churchill told Parliament that the aim of foreign policy should be to bring together 'overwhelming deterrents, and then from a basis of strength and not of weakness, to attempt a general settlement followed by a general disarmament'.[123] In these respects his objectives were the same as Chamberlain's. On the other hand, Churchill was mistaken when he thought Chamberlain might be moving towards forming a deterrent through a grand alliance. In an article published on 9 March he took a visit by Chamberlain to the Soviet embassy – the first by any prime minister – to be evidence of new interest in the possibilities of co-operation, but, as we shall see, Chamberlain had not become less suspicious of Communist intentions. Churchill was on firmer ground when he said Britain was gaining ground in the arms race. Italy was suffering from the burden of maintaining large armies in Ethiopia, Libya and Spain, and was less and less able to afford imports of the materials necessary for munitions production. Drawing upon estimates by Sir Henry Strakosch, Churchill said Germany was spending more than twice the proportion of national income than Britain was on armaments, and was under a correspondingly more severe strain. However, whereas Chamberlain was inclined to think that Germany's economic difficulties would discourage Hitler from going to war, Churchill saw it would be more in keeping with Hitler's character for him to make a move before he faced a domestic crisis and before British rearmament was complete.[124]

8.4   The End of Czechoslovakia

On 9 March 1939 Chamberlain gave lobby correspondents an unofficial briefing in which he predicted that Europe would settle down to a period of tranquillity. The next day optimistic stories appeared in the press, noting the country's growing armed strength and, echoing what Chamberlain had told Henderson on 19 February, predicting that the end of the Spanish Civil War would make it easier to resolve Franco-Italian differences and improve the international atmosphere, and that a disarmament conference would be held before the end of the year. When Halifax again told Chamberlain he did not share his confidence, the prime minister replied he had been horrified that remarks, which he had intended only as a general background, had been reported verbatim. Chamberlain apologised and promised to consult Halifax before speaking to the press on foreign affairs, but, writing to his sisters, he said he felt no harm had been done and indeed that it was good to let the dictators know how things stood.[125] Chamberlain's optimism was echoed on 10 March in a speech by Samuel Hoare in which he held out the prospect of a golden age of prosperity if the leaders of the great powers worked together to dispel fear and end the arms race.[126]

On 15 March the German army occupied what was left of Czechoslovakia, and it was apparent to all that the Sudetenland had not been Hitler's last territorial claim, as he had claimed in September. The sight of German troops in Prague was all the more damaging to Chamberlain's reputation, both at the time and in history, in the light of his expressions of optimism six days earlier. Robert Self has compared the prime minister's briefing of the lobby correspondents to his promise of 'peace in our time' after Munich, and attributed both incidents to hubris.[127] Be that as it may, some explanation for Chamberlain's unfortunate timing in March 1939 is required, as he had been confident things were going his way since the beginning of February. David Gillard suggested Chamberlain might have been motivated by domestic politics. A general election had to be held within the next twenty months, and in early March the Conservative Research Department was working on a manifesto for an autumn poll in 1939. Pessimistic press comment about the international situation was believed to be reducing the government's popularity, and it was natural that Chamberlain should seek to dispel the gloom. Moreover, intelligence that the Slovaks might seek German support for independence from Prague pointed to the likelihood of trouble in Central Europe, and Chamberlain may have been seeking to offset imminent bad news by placing it in the context of hopeful prospects for peace.[128]

The prime minister had reason not to expect how bad the news would be. Foreign Office officials, in their post-Munich deliberations, had anticipated the need for Anglo-German talks to reconcile the two countries' trade interests, and in mid-February 1939 Halifax sent Ashton-Gwatkin, the head of the Economic Section, to Berlin to exchange views on the economic situation in Germany and the world generally. The foreign secretary told the Cabinet on 8 March that Ashton-Gwatkin had seen Walther Funk, the minister for economic affairs, as well as Goering and Ribbentrop and found the atmosphere very friendly. The Cabinet minutes record that Ashton-Gwatkin 'had gained the impression that no immediate adventures of a large type were contemplated. This, however, did not rule out the possibility of further pressure being brought to bear on Czechoslovakia'.[129] It was not until 11 March, two days after Chamberlain had briefed the lobby journalists, that Cadogan warned him that Sir Vernon Kell, the head of MI5, had intelligence that the Germans would invade Czechoslovakia in the next 48 hours. Forty-eight hours later Cadogan showed the prime minister a further report on German preparations, but added that neither he nor Kell could say whether the Germans would put their plan into effect.[130]

When the Cabinet met at 11.00 in the morning of 15 March, Halifax admitted there was not much more that he could tell his colleagues than what had appeared in the *Daily Telegraph* four hours earlier. The Czechoslovak president, Emil Hacha, had placed the Czech people under German protection and Hitler had guaranteed 'autonomous development of its national life', a form of words that could be interpreted to mean that a Czech state would continue to exist.[131] (It was not until the next day that Henderson used the term 'annexation' in a telegram from Berlin, and not until the 17th that it was confirmed the Czech areas in the provinces of Bohemia and Moravia would now be part of the German Reich.)[132] The independence of Slovakia had been proclaimed in Bratislava on 14 March, and Chamberlain claimed on the 15th that the Czechoslovak state which Britain had undertaken to guarantee against unprovoked aggression had broken up and therefore the guarantee had come to an end.[133] The four-power treaty of guarantee envisaged at Munich had not been signed. Foreign Office officials had never been keen on an Anglo-French guarantee: it would be ineffective and would expose Britain to the same humiliation as France had suffered through its inability to fulfil its treaty obligations to Czechoslovakia.[134] However, in a statement to Parliament on 4 October 1938 Sir Thomas Inskip had said that, although technically the treaty of guarantee was not in force, the government felt under a moral obligation to it as if it were.[135] In the event, the Germans, having at first prevaricated, had responded on 28 February 1939 to a French approach about the treaty of guarantee by making clear that Central Europe was Germany's sphere of interest and Anglo-French guarantees would not be welcome.[136] Chamberlain, in response to a question in Parliament from Attlee on 14 March, had been cautious enough to refer to the 'proposed guarantee'.[137] No minister argued on the morning of the 15th that Britain was still bound by Inskip's statement. The question arose of how the government should register its disapproval of Germany's action, and Chamberlain said it was impossible to allow a planned visit to Berlin by the president of the Board of Trade, Oliver Stanley, to go ahead. As the Opposition was demanding a debate that afternoon, it was left to Chamberlain and Halifax to settle the terms for a statement by the prime minister.

The situation in Czechoslovakia was not much clearer when Chamberlain addressed the House of Commons before 4.00 p.m. He spoke mainly from a draft prepared in the Foreign Office, but added a passage in which he said that, while he bitterly regretted what had occurred, he would not be deflected from his policy of promoting peace and substituting the method of discussion for the method of force in settling international differences. Cadogan thought the implication that appeasement would continue was 'fatal'.[138] Chamberlain himself came to realise that the detached way in which he recited the facts as he knew them had given an impression of indifference. As he told his sisters, 'as soon as I had time to think I saw that it was impossible to deal with Hitler, after he had thrown all his own assurances to the winds'.[139] Chamberlain used a speech in Birmingham on 17 March to make his feelings known. He insisted he had been justified at Munich in hoping that, once the Czechoslovakian question had been settled, it would be possible to pursue appeasement further. However, in contrast to the Austrian *Anschluss* and the Sudetenland, Hitler had gone beyond what might be justified on grounds of racial affinity. 'Is this the end of an old adventure', Chamberlain asked, 'or is it the beginning of a new? Is this the last attack upon a small state, or is it to be followed by others? Is this, in fact, a step in the direction of an attempt to dominate the world by force?' Promising a review of every aspect of national life related to national security (which, he told the Cabinet the next day would raise the issues of conscription and a Ministry of Supply), he proceeded to the peroration: 'no greater mistake could be made than to suppose that, because it believes war to be a senseless and cruel thing, this nation has so lost its fibre that it will not take part to the utmost of its power resisting such a challenge if ever it were made'.[140] Cadogan commented that the speech was 'not too bad'.[141] Chamberlain's control of the Conservative party was assured.

The German occupation of Czechoslovakia occurred during a sustained attempt within Churchill's constituency to deselect him as MP on account of his criticisms of Munich. In a speech to constituents on 10 March he refused to withdraw a single word. On the contrary, he said, he was astonished at how terribly true his warnings in October 1938 about the consequences of the abandonment of Czechoslovakia had been. On 14 March 1939, the day Slovak independence was declared, he told another meeting of constituents that 'the Czechoslovakian Republic is being broken up before our eyes'. However, he went on: 'it is no use going to [the Czechs'] aid when they are defenceless, if we would not go to their aid when they were strong'. Nevertheless, he said, it was an illusion to suppose that Britain was not involved in what was going on: 'we shall have to make all kinds of sacrifice for our own defence that would have been unnecessary if a firm resolve had been taken at an earlier stage'.[142] On 19 March he wrote to Sir Horace Rumbold, the former ambassador in Berlin: 'events have told their unanswerable tale, and Chamberlain in his speech has admitted to the altogether wrong opinion which he formed of men and things for which he is responsible'.[143]

Chamberlain had not, in fact, admitted to error on the 17th, only that his hopes had been disappointed. Even so, it was obvious enough that the German occupation of Prague completed the change in the balance of power begun by the Munich agreement. Enough Czech munitions fell into Hitler's hands to equip 20 divisions. Moreover, the output of Czech factories increased the pace of German rearmament. Slovakia's independence was illusionary: German troops were admitted to its territory, and through a series of treaties its minerals and supplies of foodstuffs were brought under German control. As Churchill had warned, the end of Czechoslovakia increased Hitler's power to establish economic hegemony in Central and South-Eastern Europe, weakening the power of naval blockade to deter him.

9   Deterrence by Guarantee

9.1   The Guarantee to Poland

The fall of Czechoslovakia was followed by a diplomatic revolution. Whereas hitherto British governments had avoided commitments in Central and South-East Europe, Chamberlain now agreed to an Anglo-French guarantee of Polish independence. Historians broadly agree on the events that led to the guarantee to Poland on 31 March, but vary in their interpretations of ministers' motives and of the guarantee's significance. Simon Newman charged policymakers with being swayed by 'an atmosphere of panic, humiliation, and moral hysteria' after the German occupation of Prague, but nevertheless presented the guarantee as the culmination of efforts since before Munich to restrict German expansion in Eastern Europe.[1] Donald Watt described the guarantee as unprecedented and even unconstitutional, in that it handed the decision for war or peace to the Polish government. He believed Chamberlain did not understand what he had done; Zara Steiner was uncertain whether Chamberlain understood the implications, but Robert Self had no doubt that Chamberlain fully comprehended the guarantee's significance.[2] Steiner argued that domestic political and moral factors were more critical than economic and military ones in determining policy, believing (in common with Churchill) that Germany was in a stronger position in 1939 than it had been in 1938.[3] In contrast, Wesley Wark emphasised growing confidence in Whitehall in February and March in Britain's ability to wage war successfully.[4]

Alastair Parker believed the guarantee was the product of Chamberlain's fear of the consequences for his government of a further foreign policy failure, arising either from a German attack on Poland or Polish submission to German demands.[5] John Ruggiero went further, dismissing the guarantee as a ploy by Chamberlain to fend off critics who were demanding Churchill's grand alliance, including with the Soviet Union.[6] However, Bruce Strang saw Halifax as the prime mover behind the guarantee, and pointed to multiple objectives: defence against parliamentary criticism certainly, but also maintenance of prestige abroad, including showing the Americans that Britain was worth supporting; securing a commitment from France to resist German expansion; as well as deterrence of Germany, and, if that failed, the dispersion of Germany's resources in a two-front war.[7] As regards appeasement, Parker conceded that Chamberlain became more willing to warn Hitler against armed aggression after the occupation of Prague, but thought that otherwise the prime minister's policy remained unchanged, except insofar as it was now more constrained by public opinion and opposition within the Cabinet.[8] Robert Self, however, considered that Chamberlain's critics have failed to appreciate how carefully balanced his policy was between appeasement and deterrence, and pointed out that, while Chamberlain did not rule out some peaceful adjustment of frontiers, he was not prepared to contemplate another Munich.[9] These varied assessments of Chamberlain and his government were all based on much the same archival evidence.[10] That evidence is re-examined here from the point of view of understanding why the guarantee took the form it did.

Although historians writing about the guarantee to Poland have naturally focussed on Europe, account has to be taken of the context of Britain's worldwide strategic situation. From 1 March to 6 April 1939 ministers responsible for defence departments and the chiefs of staff were meeting under the chairmanship of Lord Chatfield, now minister for co-ordination of defence, in an ad hoc Strategic Appreciation Committee. Issues considered included whether, in the event of war with Germany, Italy and Japan, the navy should first defeat the Italian fleet, to raise Britain's prestige with Turkey, Greece and Arab countries, before sailing to Singapore. When Chatfield had been chief of the naval staff the Admiralty view had been that it would be better to abandon the Mediterranean rather than to delay sending the fleet to the Far East, but his successor, Sir Roger Backhouse, thought that if the Americans stationed a fleet at Honolulu, the Japanese were unlikely to undertake major operations against Australia or New Zealand.[11] Churchill was evidently familiar with the debate from his contacts with the Admiralty and on 27 March he sent a memorandum to Chamberlain supporting Backhouse's case. Churchill minimised the Japanese threat, asserting it would be 'easy' to hold the 'fortress' of Singapore and that the Japanese, as 'an extremely sensible people', would not risk sending a fleet and army so far from their home waters.[12] Chamberlain made no comment on the memorandum, but a week earlier he had sent a telegram to the prime minister of Australia, Joseph Lyons, assuring him that a fleet would be despatched to Singapore in the event of war.[13] On 16 April, following prompting from Halifax, Roosevelt announced the American fleet would be moved from the Atlantic to the

Pacific, thereby fulfilling Backhouse's condition for a Mediterranean-first strategy. Even so, the Far East continued to be a cause of concern: the British ambassador in Tokyo, Sir Robert Craigie, believed Japan was unlikely to remain neutral for long in any war in which the Soviet Union was engaged.[14] While there were more important impediments to an alliance with the Soviet Union, the likely hostile reaction of Japan to one was a factor to be taken into account.

In his speech in Birmingham on 17 March, Chamberlain had said he was not prepared to engage Britain in new unspecified commitments in conditions that could not be foreseen.[15] He clearly did not then contemplate guaranteeing any East European country on terms that would leave the decision of peace or war in its government's hands. However, on the same day the Romanian minister in London, Virgil Tilea, told Halifax the Germans had more divisions in Czechoslovakia than the situation there required and that 'an almost immediate' attack on Romania could 'by no means be excluded'. Tilea said Germany had offered to guarantee Romania's frontiers in return for a monopoly of Romanian exports, a communication he claimed that seemed to the government in Bucharest to be 'something very much like an ultimatum'.[16] In the febrile post-Prague atmosphere neither the foreign secretary nor his officials paused to check the accuracy of Tilea's report. British diplomats were instructed to ask the Soviet, Polish, Yugoslav, Greek and Turkish governments what they would do about a threat to Romania. A Cabinet meeting was called for the evening of the next day, a Saturday, a sure sign of a crisis. Forty-eight hours later the permanent under-secretary, Sir Alexander Cadogan, noted in his diary: 'These are awful days. The crisis is worse, really, than last September, but the public don't know it.'[17]

The chiefs of staff, after a hurried meeting in the afternoon of the 18th, warned ministers that control of Romanian oil and agricultural resources would go a long way towards making Germany immune to blockade, thus undermining the key element in Anglo-French strategy for a long war. Moreover, political domination of Romania would enable the Germans to threaten Britain's position in the eastern Mediterranean, since the Germans could count on the friendship of their First World War ally, Bulgaria. The chiefs of staff advised that Germany must be faced with the prospect of a war on two fronts, and that an alliance with the Soviet Union and Poland as well as France might be an effective deterrent, although they added that the Soviet Union was militarily an uncertain quantity. They thought the Soviet Union could play an important part in the Far East by neutralising Japan, and advised that diplomatic action should be taken to win American support. In order to reduce the number of potential enemies, they added: 'we should endeavour to buy out' Italy.[18]

By the time the Cabinet met in the evening of the 18th the British minister in Bucharest, Sir Reginald Hoare, had reported that the Romanian foreign minister had denied Tilea's story and there was no threat to Romania's economic or political independence *for the moment*.[19] Halifax nevertheless suggested ministers should consider what should be done if such a situation should occur in future. Chamberlain said the German action in Czechoslovakia made it impossible to negotiate on the old basis with the Nazi regime, as no reliance could be placed on Hitler's word. He added that 'this did not mean that negotiations with the German people were impossible'. He did not explain how this could be done, but later in the meeting Sir John Simon, the chancellor of the exchequer, said that, if Britain's attitude to aggression were known in Germany, public opinion there might be able to prevent war starting. Chamberlain told ministers he regarded his speech at Birmingham on the previous day as a challenge to Germany on the issue of whether it intended to dominate Europe by force. He agreed with Halifax that Britain must do everything possible to rally resistance from other countries. The prime minister added he was not asking ministers to decide there and then whether to declare war on Germany if Germany invaded Romania. Rather he wanted their approval for the change of policy he had set out in his speech; that is, that Britain would resist aggression to the utmost of its power. He regarded the question of when to take a stand as a separate issue. Sir Kingsley Wood, the secretary of state for air, and Leslie Hore-Belisha, the secretary of state for war, both thought the government faced a dilemma between the dangers of putting off taking a stand and the advantages of gaining time to complete defence preparations. Chamberlain said the real issue was whether Britain could gain sufficient support from other countries to justify making a public declaration. He thought a declaration might deter Germany, at least for a time, in which case full advantage would be taken of the breathing space to continue rearmament. He identified Poland, which, unlike the Soviet Union, had a common frontier with Germany, as the key to the situation. The Cabinet approved the Foreign Office's action of approaching other countries to find out whether they would combine with Britain to resist German aggression in *South-East* Europe (implying that at this stage Poland was seen primarily as a potential ally rather than as an imminent victim of aggression).[20]

The next day, Sunday 19 March, Chamberlain, Halifax, Simon and Oliver Stanley, the president of the Board of Trade, together with Cadogan and Sir Horace Wilson, met at 11.30 a.m. to discuss the form a declaration might take. Chamberlain's idea was for countries to sign a statement that they agreed to consult together in the event of a threat to the independence of any state in South-East Europe. The public warning, he said, would be followed by private discussions about what each country could do. His proposal was similar to Churchill's idea in August 1938 for Britain, France and the Soviet Union to issue a joint note warning Germany that an invasion of Czechoslovakia would 'raise capital issues for all three powers' (see page 190). In both cases the decision of whether to go to war would be kept in the British government's hands. Chamberlain proposed that initially only France, the Soviet Union, Poland and perhaps Turkey should be invited to sign, with smaller countries being added later, as discussions with them would involve considerable delay. The declaration, he thought, should apply only to an attack on the integrity and independence of a state, not simply a violation of its frontiers.[21] To his sisters, Chamberlain described the planned declaration as 'pretty bold and startling', but added he did not anticipate an acute crisis.[22]

By the time the prime minister and his colleagues reconvened at 4.30 p.m. on the 19th, the initial responses of the countries contacted on the 17th were available. The Polish foreign minister, Jozef Beck, had been non-committal. The Greeks and Turks said their treaty obligations to Romania under the Balkan Pact would take effect only if Bulgaria attacked it. The ambassador in Belgrade reported he did not believe Yugoslavia would in any circumstances commit itself in advance to war with Germany. The Soviet foreign minister, Maxim Litvinov, on the other hand, had proposed an early meeting of British, Soviet, French, Polish and Romanian representatives in Bucharest to discuss possibilities of common action.[23] However, Halifax had seen the Soviet ambassador, Ivan Maisky, earlier in the afternoon and, while not ruling out such a conference, had told him it would be dangerous to hold one before being certain of reaching an agreed conclusion. Given the Polish and Romanian governments' suspicions of Soviet intentions, there were grounds for fearing a conference might fail.

Chamberlain explained his own thinking further when the Cabinet discussed the draft declaration on 20 March. He said it did not involve a new commitment, but public opinion would assume that, if Britain, France, Poland and the Soviet Union consulted together, some action would follow. He made clear he was talking about war: 'if Germany showed signs that she intended to proceed with her march for world domination' he said, 'we must take steps to stop her by attacking her on two fronts. We should attack Germany, not in order to save a particular victim, but in order to pull down the bully.'[24] In the case of Danzig, a free city with a German-speaking population, but which was of economic importance to Poland, Chamberlain said the test would be whether action taken by Germany constituted a threat to Polish independence. In response to Chatfield's question of whether staff talks with France should be extended to Poland and the Soviet Union, he thought it would be wise to do so in order to know what action should be taken, but that no statement need be made now.[25] The other countries had, of course, not yet seen, let alone approved, the proposed declaration.

Cadogan was working on a draft of the declaration when the French ambassador, Charles Corbin, called on him. Corbin was horrified to be told that no more than consultation was proposed and said the French government would not think that was strong enough. Cadogan met Chamberlain, Halifax and Wilson in the evening, and a slightly amended text was agreed to the effect that the four governments would undertake 'immediately to consult together as to what steps should be taken to offer joint resistance' to any action that threatened the political independence of any European state. Moreover, instructions sent to British representatives in Paris, Moscow and Warsaw made plain the declaration was intended to be only a first step towards organisation of mutual support.[26]

The only overt difference between Chamberlain and the Foreign Office at this stage concerned the prime minister's wish to send a letter to Mussolini to encourage him to rein in Hitler. Cadogan thought the draft prepared by Wilson looked too much like a request for another Munich. Chamberlain said he had no wish to convey that impression and accepted some redrafting by Cadogan. On the other hand, the prime minister said that a warning about Italian hostility to France would be out of place in the letter. Even so, Cadogan considered the final version 'not too bad'. It certainly contained a clear warning that a German attempt to dominate other states would lead to war.[27] There was nothing in it to suggest Chamberlain was inclined to follow the chiefs of staff's advice to buy out Italy. Rather he seems to have believed, or at least hoped, that Mussolini's professions of peace at their meeting in January had been sincere. However, in Rome, Chamberlain's letter was seen as a sign of weakness: Ciano, the Italian foreign minister, noted it 'was another proof of the inertia of the democracies'.[28]

The next day, 21 March, was particularly stressful for Chamberlain. In the morning, Wilson told a meeting of ministers responsible for civil defence and the defence departments that intelligence reports indicated Hitler was capable of launching a 'bolt from the blue'. He said the prime minister was concerned about the time required to activate Britain's air defences, a subject which Churchill had raised with Chamberlain the previous day. Discussion centred on anti-aircraft guns and searchlights, which were to be manned by part-time soldiers of the Territorial Army, who could only be mobilised in a state of emergency. At noon Chatfield,

Hore-Belisha and Kingsley Wood saw Chamberlain and agreed a declaration of a state of emergency would be premature. As an alternative, regular units from the Field Force were to be deployed in the London area in the guise of a training exercise.[29] In the evening, while Chamberlain and his wife were attending a state banquet at Buckingham Palace for the French president, Albert Lebrun, Hore-Belisha came up to the prime minister and whispered that intelligence had just been received that Germany had mobilised 20 divisions on its western frontier. The report later proved to be false, but was plausible because news had been received that Ribbentrop, the German foreign minister, had summoned the Lithuanian minister in Berlin and demanded the immediate return of Memel, a predominantly German-speaking port ceded to Lithuania after the First World War. That night Chamberlain, unusually, took a sleeping tablet as he felt he could not afford a broken night.[30]

Meanwhile, earlier in the evening, the French foreign minister, Georges Bonnet, who happened to be accompanying Lebrun, had discussed with Halifax the British proposal for a four-power declaration. Bonnet was primarily concerned that the French should not be left to do most of any fighting. Like the British, he believed it was essential to include Poland in the declaration, as Soviet help against Germany could only be effective with Polish collaboration. He thought Poland would be mad not to join with Britain and France, but expressed distrust of the Soviet Union. Later in the evening the British ambassador in Warsaw, Sir Howard Kennard, sent Halifax a telegram pointing out that the Polish government was bound to ask itself whether there was an actual threat that would justify provoking Germany by signing the four-power declaration, and what support the other signatories could give them. A further telegram sent at 2.00 a.m. on the 22nd reported a conversation with Beck in which the Polish foreign minister had implied that Soviet participation in any such declaration would lead Poland into difficulties with Germany, but Poland might be able to associate itself with Britain and France if the Soviet Union were omitted.[31]

When the Cabinet met in the morning of 22 March it was clear no progress had been made with Chamberlain's conception of a four-power declaration. Ministers were evidently content to acquiesce in the German annexation of Memel, which, Halifax remarked, was more justified than recent events in Czechoslovakia. Conscription was discussed, but in the context of the permanent manning of Britain's air defences, not of support for France.[32] When Chamberlain and Halifax met Bonnet in the evening, the latter confirmed the French government was prepared to sign the proposed declaration. However, Chamberlain said he now recognised that including the Soviet Union would make Polish participation very difficult. It was agreed to approach Poland with a proposal that if Romania were attacked and resisted, and Poland went to its assistance, Britain and France would join in.[33] This new conception of mutual support reduced the role of the Soviet Union to that of an arsenal from which Poland and Romania could draw supplies if deterrence failed.

Chamberlain had abandoned the idea of a four-power declaration once he realized it would expose Poland to a German threat to bomb Warsaw with only the consolation that Britain and France would subsequently make the Germans pay for their behaviour. He doubted whether it was worth including the Soviet Union in the declaration without Poland. He did not believe the Red Army could maintain an effective offensive against the Germans – a view echoing a recent assessment by the military attaché at the embassy in Moscow, Colonel Roy Firebrace – and suspected the Soviet government was bent on stirring up international strife.[34] Moreover, the Soviet Union was feared by its neighbours. In the Foreign Policy Committee on 27 March Chamberlain claimed a front against German aggression could not be formed if the Soviet Union was openly associated with it. Moreover, he said, overt Soviet participation would make it harder for Britain to establish good relations with a number of countries, including Japan, Italy and Spain. However, he believed Germany could be deterred. Apparently drawing on a recent appreciation by the military attaché in Berlin, Colonel Noel Mason-MacFarlane, he argued that Germany was not ready for war on two fronts. Germany could avoid a two-front war if Poland remained neutral, but Chamberlain's new plan was for Britain and France to undertake to support Poland and Romania, provided they resisted a threat to their independence, and provided Poland was prepared to come to the assistance of Romania if the latter were threatened. The Soviet Union would be asked to make a secret agreement to aid Poland and Romania if these countries became involved in a war with Germany, and he thought the Franco-Soviet pact (which would come into effect only if Germany attacked either France or the Soviet Union) 'might possibly' be modified for this purpose.[35]

These ideas did not go unchallenged. The Soviet government had by now accepted the proposed four-power declaration, subject to France and Poland also agreeing to sign. Samuel Hoare, the home secretary, and one of Chamberlain's closest colleagues, thought the exclusion of the Soviet Union would be widely seen as 'a considerable defeat for our policy' and feared the consequences of increasing Soviet enmity towards Britain. Halifax, however, said that if a choice had to be made between Poland and the Soviet Union, it seemed clear Poland would give greater value. In answer to a question by Chatfield, he admitted there had been no recent study of Poland's military strength comparable to Colonel Firebrace's assessment of the Soviet Union. Chatfield, while prepared to accept that Poland was 'probably' the best potential eastern ally from a military point of view, thought the Soviet Union would be a greater deterrent to Germany. When Simon asked what support Britain and France could give to Poland and Romania, Chamberlain could only reply that 'by manning the Maginot Line we would be holding up large German forces which otherwise would be available for overrunning Poland and Romania'.[36] It is striking that Chamberlain was contemplating a major change in policy without waiting for an update of the strategic assessment hurriedly prepared by the chiefs of staff on 18 March. Moreover, that assessment had been that it was unlikely the Poles would divert 'any considerable portion' of the German army and air force from the west if the Soviet Union were neutral.[37]

Although Chamberlain had presented the new policy as his own, the ideas behind it were Halifax's. Halifax felt, in his private secretary's words, that 'we should not make it too difficult for Italy to betray her ally'. Accordingly the foreign secretary thought the Soviet Union should not be in the 'forefront of the picture'.[38] Chamberlain and Halifax were probably influenced by the assessment of Sir William Seeds, the ambassador in Moscow, that Stalin might give some assistance to Romania if he feared an eventual German attack on the Ukraine, but if he believed that Germany would turn west after an attack on Romania, he would look with 'considerable satisfaction' at the damage the capitalist powers would do to each other.[39] The Foreign Policy Committee approved Chamberlain's proposals 'generally' and left it to him and Halifax to draft instructions to the embassies in Warsaw and Bucharest in the light of the discussion.[40] The Polish and Romanian governments were to be told that efforts would be made to secure the Soviet government's support and to discourage Moscow's 'tendency towards isolation'.[41] In Cabinet on 29 March Halifax sought to mollify Hoare and other doubters by agreeing that Britain and France should get as much practical assistance from the Soviet Union as possible and said he would try to keep in with the Russians.[42]

Meanwhile Chamberlain had been considering ways in which to increase Britain's own power to deter. On 18 March, on his initiative, the Cabinet had set up a sub-committee under Chatfield to review the defence programmes and consider how they could be accelerated. Chamberlain's anxiety about anti-aircraft defence has already been mentioned. The biggest question on the prime minister's mind, however, was whether to introduce conscription. Following his Birmingham speech on 17 March, when he had promised a review of every aspect of national life related to national security, there was increasing pressure in the press and from France for Britain to introduce some form of compulsory military service. Chamberlain himself thought that, if successfully introduced, conscription would have a good effect on foreign opinion. His problem was that as recently as 6 October 1938 he had repeated an earlier pledge not to do so within the lifetime of the present Parliament. Any breach of that pledge would alienate the trade unions and might well demonstrate national disunity, thereby encouraging Hitler and discouraging potential allies.[43]

There was, however, an alternative course of action. The deteriorating international situation had led to an increase in the number of men coming forward to join the Territorial Army. There had been reports of volunteers being turned away because the units in which they attempted to enlist were up to establishment. Chamberlain was due to address the 1922 Committee of Conservative backbenchers in the evening of 28 March 1939, and he wished to say something about how this surge in patriotism could be utilised. Wilson wrote to Hore-Belisha in the morning asking if men could be enrolled and given some training, even if, for the time being, equipment was not available for them. The secretary of state for war saw the prime minister in the afternoon and, when told that some action was required to show Britain meant business, suggested doubling the Territorial Army. Chamberlain was anxious to make an announcement in the next 24 hours, and Hore-Belisha called a meeting of the Army Council so that a plan could be presented to the Cabinet the next day. Treasury officials were astonished to learn from Wilson that it was proposed to increase the size of the Territorial Army from 130,000 to its war strength of 170,000, and then to double it to 340,000 by duplicating every unit. Sir Richard Hopkins remarked that the proposal was unrelated to any strategic plan. Sir Alan Barlow thought that, since the immediate military value of such a force would be nil, the effect would be likely to make Hitler think he would be better to strike at once.[44]

Hore-Belisha admitted in Cabinet on 29 March that there would be difficulties in supplying the expanded Territorial Army with instructors and training equipment, it was impossible to say how long it would take to implement the scheme, and the capital cost would be in the range £80 million to £100 million. This sum was in addition to the £51.4 million committed in February to make the Field Force ready for a European campaign, and the combined effect of the two Cabinet decisions was to make expenditure on the army greater than on the navy, marking a major change in grand strategy and a final break with the Inskip Report's doctrine of economic stability as a fourth arm of defence. The chancellor of the exchequer, Simon, had recently claimed there was no prospect of financing the air force programme in 1940/41. Even so, confronted with a huge increase in the army's programme, he agreed with Halifax that the need to impress public opinion at home and abroad with evidence of the determination of the British people was more important than the financial aspects.[45] It is evidence of the extent of the post-Prague crisis that a man normally so methodical as Chamberlain should take so momentous a decision so quickly, and with so little consideration of practical problems or economic implications, on the day before Anglo-French staff talks were due to begin. When asked on 29 March by the leader of the Liberals, Sir Archibald Sinclair, whether a Ministry of Supply would be created to ensure the men were equipped, Chamberlain replied that the government had not yet had the opportunity of considering whether that step would be necessary. Churchill pointed out that a decision to increase to 32 divisions an army whose planned strength had been increased from 5 divisions to 19 divisions only a month earlier was hardly compatible with the government's policy of non-interference with industry.[46]

The pressure on Chamberlain continued to mount. In the evening of 29 March Halifax brought a journalist, Ian Colvin, to the prime minister's room in the House of Commons. Colvin, the Berlin correspondent of the *News Chronicle*, had met Halifax and Cadogan that afternoon and told them a German attack on Poland was imminent, but that there was a good chance German generals would stop Hitler or revolt if it was made quite certain Britain would intervene.[47] Chamberlain was sceptical, as was Cadogan, and with reason. Donald Watt described the intelligence Colvin brought as a mixture of accurate information and grossly exaggerated inference. Some of the information apparently originated from someone with access to the directive that Hitler had given General Walter von Brauchitsch, the commander-in-chief of the German army, on 25 March to prepare a plan for action against Poland, but that action was hardly imminent since the first draft was dated 1 April.[48] However, Halifax seems to have been keen to use Colvin's claims to press the case for guaranteeing Polish independence. Although Beck was due to come to London on Monday, 3 April, Chamberlain was alarmed by the prospect of the Poles suddenly surrendering to a German ultimatum before then and agreed 'then and there' to some form of guarantee of assistance to Poland.[49]

Chamberlain described the rest of the week to his sisters as a 'nightmare succession' of Cabinets, Cabinet committees, meetings with the leaders of the Opposition parties, drafting telegrams and constant discussions with Halifax and Cadogan, but claimed, with doubtful validity, that he had refused to be rushed.[50] At the Cabinet meeting at 2.30 p.m. on Thursday 30 March, Halifax began by reporting that the American ambassador, Joseph Kennedy, had had a message from his counterpart in

Warsaw to the effect that Ribbentrop was anxious to repeat his success over Memel while the British and French were still discussing what action to take, and during the meeting a report was received from the War Office's deputy director of military intelligence that German military dispositions appeared to be intended to cover a coup against Danzig. Chatfield told the Cabinet the chiefs of staff had concluded it would be better to fight with Poland as an ally rather than allow it to be absorbed or dominated by Germany. It would be impossible, they thought, for Britain and France to prevent Poland from being over-run, even if the Soviet Union were a friendly neutral willing to supply war material, but the Germans would suffer heavy casualties and have to leave large occupation forces. Halifax said a declaration of Britain's intention to support Poland if it were attacked might lead Hitler to abandon his plan, thereby discrediting him with German military leaders. He wanted the Cabinet to agree on a statement the prime minister and he could issue, in consultation with the French government, at a moment's notice if necessary. Chamberlain made clear the proposal was the foreign secretary's, and wanted the draft examined from the point of view of avoiding being committed in the event of German action that did not affect the independence of Poland. In particular, he thought the declaration should end on 'a somewhat less defiant note' than in the Foreign Office draft, and should stress the desirability of settling disputes peacefully. He suggested including an indication of willingness to take part in discussions between Germany and Poland, but Halifax demurred on this last point.[51] Cadogan, who drafted a revised version for the Foreign Policy Committee later in the afternoon of the 30th, thought Britain must challenge Hitler if the Poles agreed, but noted in his diary: 'it's a *frightful gamble*'.[52] At the Foreign Policy Committee Chamberlain observed that the latest information from the military attaché in Berlin on German troop deployments did not support the theory that Germany was contemplating a coup de main against Poland. Nevertheless he undertook to make the statement in the House of Commons the next day.[53]

Chamberlain had seen the leaders of the Opposition parties earlier on the 30th and gained their general approval of what he proposed to say. However, the Labour leaders were disturbed to learn in the evening that Halifax had not seen the Soviet ambassador, Maisky, since 19 March and had cancelled a visit by him to the Foreign Office that afternoon (presumably because Halifax was at the Foreign Policy Committee). They insisted on seeing Chamberlain at short notice at 10.15 p.m. to warn him he would face hostile questions in the Commons if his statement did not mention the Soviet Union, and he agreed to postpone making it until after Halifax had seen Maisky in the morning.[54] Chamberlain was acutely aware that the fate of the generation which would fight, and of the British Empire, was in his hands, and found sleep eluded him, so that once more he had to take a pill. It is not surprising that when announcing the guarantee the next day he looked gaunt and ill.[55]

Chamberlain did not intend to hand over the decision for war or peace to the Polish government. Ministers in the Foreign Policy Committee agreed with him in the morning of 31 March that Warsaw should be warned that the forthcoming statement assumed Poland would not 'indulge in provocative behaviour or stupid obstinacy', either generally or over Danzig.[56] In the Cabinet at noon he said the condition set out in the statement that it applied only in the event of a clear threat to Polish independence gave 'some freedom for manoeuvre' since 'it would, of course, be for us to determine what action threatened Polish independence'.[57] In his statement in the House of Commons in the afternoon Chamberlain announced that, during the period in which the government was consulting with other governments about the European situation, Britain and France guaranteed to give Poland 'all support in their power' in the event of 'any action which clearly threatened Polish independence, and which the Polish government accordingly considered vital to resist with their national forces'. In response to questions from Labour MPs, he said the government would welcome the maximum co-operation from all powers, and gave an assurance there were no ideological impediments to co-operation with the Soviet Union.[58] However, writing nine days later to his sisters, he criticised the Labour Party's 'pathetic belief that Russia is the key to our salvation'.[59]

To ensure the intended limits to the guarantee were understood, Cadogan briefed *The Times*, and a leading article appeared in that newspaper on Saturday, 1 April, noting that the key word in Chamberlain's statement was 'independence' and that Britain was not bound to defend 'every inch of the present frontiers of Poland'.[60] When the Commons debated the statement on Monday, 3 April, Churchill described this passage as 'sinister', in that it sought to 'whittle away' the guarantee of Poland's integrity. He was not alone in seeing a resemblance between the article and the one in September 1938 in which *The Times* had pondered whether the best solution to the Sudeten-German problem would be for Czechoslovakia to cede the German-speaking areas.[61] The Foreign Office had already issued a prompt repudiation of *The Times*' interpretation of the Polish guarantee, but privately Chamberlain thought *The Times* had been correct to stress that the guarantee concerned 'not the boundaries of states but attacks on their independence'.[62] Churchill said there should be no negotiations about particular rights or places until respect for international law had been restored 'after the crime and treachery committed against

Czechoslovakia', and that any sign of weakness would increase the threat to peace.[63] He represented a strong strand of public opinion that would prevent any direct British participation, such as Chamberlain hankered after, in talks between Germany and Poland. Notwithstanding the criticisms of Watt and Steiner, Chamberlain understood the implications of the guarantee; he failed, however, to anticipate how far his freedom of manoeuvre would be restricted.

Chamberlain's correspondence shows the guarantee was more than a ploy to deal with domestic critics. He told his sisters the announcement on 31 March had given 'a definite check' to Hitler, whose prestige would be 'enormously' affected.[64] Writing to his friend Lord Weir on 3 April, the prime minister remarked: 'Hitler let me down shamefully, but by his own action he has created a new and less reasonable situation for himself. He has shown the world beyond question that his word is not to be trusted and has enabled me therefore to unite this country and the Empire in resistance to further aggression.' On the other hand, Chamberlain did not abandon hope of a general settlement in Europe. Showing both a lack of understanding of the nature of the Nazi regime and greater optimism about the balance of power than subsequent events would warrant, his letter continued: 'My impression is that there are those about [Hitler] who will not let him plunge the world into war in a hopeless quest.'[65] Notwithstanding his exhaustion, Chamberlain's mood was one of optimism.

Churchill chose to interpret the new policy as the adoption of his idea of a grand alliance. In the debate on 3 April he warned that the government must not stop at an arrangement limited to Britain, France and Poland. He thought the government had been right not to force the pace by ignoring the feelings of Poland, Romania and the Baltic States, but, given identity of interest between the western democracies, the Soviet Union and its neighbours, in checking German expansion towards the Ukraine, he hoped a stable, close-knit Eastern Front would be in place in a few weeks. The worst folly, he said, would be to 'chill and drive away' Soviet co-operation.[66] It is to the question of why that co-operation was not secured that we now turn.

9.2   Negotiations with the Soviets

Alastair Parker thought it 'probable' that Chamberlain was responsible for the failure of negotiations in 1939 for an Anglo-French-Soviet alliance, but admitted to uncertainty about Stalin's intentions.[67] Donald Watt placed primary responsibility on Stalin, believing he played a double game, preparing the ground for the Nazi-Soviet Pact even while

negotiations with the British and French were going on.[68] Michael
Carley and Geoffrey Roberts, however, draw on Soviet documents to
argue that Stalin approved Litvinov's offer on 17 April of a mutual
assistance pact and wanted a military alliance. In their view, Stalin did
not begin to consider the option of a pact with Hitler until about the end
of July, and did not allow the German foreign minister to come to
Moscow to negotiate one until after staff talks with Britain and France
had broken down in mid-August. Carley emphasized Chamberlain's
responsibility for the failure of the alliance negotiations, arising from
the prime minister's fear that Soviet participation in a war against
Germany would lead to the spread of Communism in Europe.[69] Zara
Steiner observed that Chamberlain's ideological antipathies clearly influenced his approach to the Soviet Union, in contrast to his policy towards
Germany.[70] Keith Neilson, although highly critical of Chamberlain's
role, argued that British policy reflected not only suspicion of
Communism's ultimate objectives but also a reluctance to engage in a
form of balance-of-power diplomacy that would place the decision for
peace or war in Stalin's hands.[71] Bruce Strang likewise emphasised both
Chamberlain's fear of dividing Europe into opposing blocs at a time
when he still hoped to reach a general settlement with Germany, and
his willingness, nevertheless, to have some loose arrangement with the
Soviet Union that did not create a Soviet sphere of influence in Eastern
Europe. Strang argued that interests rather than ideology determined the
course of negotiations. Moreover, Chamberlain did not dictate foreign
policy. Halifax, the person primarily responsible for the negotiations,
aimed to improve Anglo-Soviet relations, but, in Strang's view, was
thwarted by understandable Polish fears of Soviet intentions and by
Soviet intransigence.[72]

Churchill and Chamberlain had very different ideas in 1939 of the
value of a Soviet alliance and the urgency of agreeing one. Churchill
described the Soviet Union on 3 April as 'a ponderous counterpoise in
the scale of world peace'.[73] Chamberlain, however, was guided by the
chiefs of staff, who believed that inadequate railway links would prevent
the Red Army from providing effective military support beyond Russia's
borders, even if the Poles were willing to allow it onto their territory, and
the chiefs were doubtful about the ability of Soviet industry to supply the
types of armaments required by Poland. What mattered most, in their
view, was Soviet economic co-operation in denying Germany food and
raw materials and thus making the Anglo-French blockade effective, and
they warned ministers on 24 April of the 'very grave' implications of
any possible agreement between Germany and the Soviet Union.[74] From
this perspective, Soviet political support for Britain and France was

important, but a military alliance was not urgent. When it was put to Chamberlain in May that failure to agree to an alliance would lead to the Soviet Union coming to an understanding with Germany, he remarked that the suggestion was 'a pretty sinister commentary on Russian reliability'.[75] In the absence of trustworthy intelligence that the Germans and Soviets had started negotiations, it was suspected in Whitehall that rumours of a rapprochement were being exploited by Germany to dissuade Britain and France from committing themselves irrevocably to Poland, and by the Soviets to induce them to give in to their demands.[76] SIS reported in mid-July that the idea of an agreement between Hitler and Stalin was 'very hypothetical', and was dumbfounded when the Nazi-Soviet non-aggression pact was signed on 23 August.[77]

Meanwhile the policy of deterrence by guarantee was being extended. After agreeing terms with Beck for an Anglo-Polish mutual assistance pact on 6 April, Chamberlain left London for a much-needed holiday in Scotland.[78] On his arrival he learned the Italians had seized Albania and he had to return after only a few hours of relaxation. Chamberlain had expected some such move, but, having received personal assurances from Mussolini, had hoped it would be presented as an agreed arrangement with the Albanian authorities and thus minimise its significance.[79] In this he was disappointed as Mussolini made the most of a display of military force. Albania had been virtually an Italian protectorate since the 1920s, and Chamberlain seems to have been troubled more by the manner of the annexation than by any strategic consequences.

Churchill's reaction was quite otherwise. He demanded to know why the British fleet had been widely dispersed in the Mediterranean, including in Italian ports, at a time when Italian ships and troops were known to be concentrating against Albania. He urged Chamberlain to order a British naval occupation of the Greek island of Corfu, close to Albania, to anticipate any further action by Mussolini and to strengthen opposition in Italy to war with Britain. Failure to act, he said, would lead the Balkan states to make the best terms they could with Berlin and Rome, cutting off Britain from all hope of including these states in a grand alliance 'which once effected might spell salvation'.[80] The exhausted prime minister, who had no intention of taking this advice, complained of being badgered for a meeting of Parliament by the Opposition parties and by 'Winston, who is the worst of the lot, telephoning almost every hour of the day'. Chamberlain admitted to his sisters to suffering from 'very great' mental strain and to being 'profoundly depressed'. He resented Mussolini's failure to respond to his attempt to establish a friendly relationship, and recognised that what had happened in Albania had blocked any chance of further rapprochement with Italy, just as the occupation of Prague had blocked any rapprochement with Germany.[81]

The Foreign Policy Committee agreed on 10 April that an appropriate response would be to guarantee Greece and to approach Turkey with a view to creating a Balkan bloc in support of Romania. Two days later Chamberlain saw Churchill, who thought the government's plan was hopeful, but said that, before receiving a guarantee, Romania should first return to Bulgaria territory lost after its defeats in the Balkan and First World Wars. Chamberlain himself wished to delay a guarantee until Poland agreed to be associated with it. However, on 13 April the Cabinet decided to give way to French pressure for an immediate guarantee to Romania.[82] Chamberlain informed the leaders of the Opposition before he announced the guarantees to Greece and Romania that day, and was bitterly disappointed when Attlee accused him in Parliament of hankering after appeasement and criticizing him for failing even to mention the Soviet Union. More generally, the prime minister felt the occupation of Albania, following on that of Prague, had given his enemies the opportunity to mock him and he feared, with some reason, his authority had been weakened.[83]

Chamberlain was depressed by Churchill's speech in the debate on 13 April. While expressing support for the government's policy, 'so far as it goes', Churchill attracted cheers from the Labour benches by emphasising the need to obtain the fullest possible co-operation with the Soviet Union. He was also characteristically optimistic about the power of smaller states, describing Yugoslavia, Romania, Bulgaria, Greece and Turkey as 'an immense combination' if they were united, and thought Turkey and the Soviet Union had a common interest in denying Germany access to the Black Sea.[84] He did not explain how this particular grand alliance was to be achieved. After the debate he told David Margesson, the government chief whip, he wished to join the government, and Chamberlain did not dismiss the idea out of hand. He recognised Churchill would strengthen the government in Parliamentary debates, but feared he would wear him out with rash suggestions in Cabinet. Chamberlain considered Churchill was definitely not the man to be in charge of the Ministry of Supply that was about to be created to organise the equipment of the expanded army. Moreover, the prime minister was unwilling to close off the possibility of getting back to normal relations with the dictators, who, he thought, would regard Churchill's appointment as a challenge.[85] Relations between Churchill and Chamberlain's supporters remained strained. The former chairman of the Conservative Party, J. C. C. Davidson, wrote to Sir Horace Wilson on 9 May: 'All the tricks of publicity, and of persuasion, are being used by Winston and his friends, and should there be another Munich over Poland, to give us a breathing space, an attack will develop on the government which may well prove successful.'[86]

Meanwhile, on 14 April, Halifax had seen the Soviet ambassador, Maisky, and suggested Russia should consider following the Anglo-French example of offering a unilateral guarantee to Romania and perhaps also Poland. The Soviet foreign minister, Litvinov, responded on 17 April with a proposal for a tripartite mutual assistance pact, with a joint guarantee of the Baltic States as well as Poland and Romania, and for an agreement as soon as possible on military measures that would be taken.[87] The Foreign Office advised the Foreign Policy Committee that this proposal was 'extremely inconvenient', and that the balance of advantage of 'a paper commitment by Russia', as against the disadvantage of associating openly with the Soviets, was 'to say the least, problematical'. The gap between Britain and the Soviet Union was even greater than it appeared to be as the Foreign Office admitted that the approach to Maisky had been made in order 'to placate our left wing in England, rather than to obtain any solid military advantage'.[88] Halifax anticipated the Poles would object to a tripartite pact providing for Soviet assistance to them whether or not they wanted it, and feared they would desert the common front against Germany by coming to terms with Hitler. Accordingly the foreign secretary did not intend to ask more of the Soviets than to come in once Britain and France were already fulfilling their guarantees. Referring to the latest military advice by the chiefs of staff, he told the Cabinet on 26 April that the value of the Soviet Union as a potential ally was by no means as great as Labour party leaders believed. He would aim to secure Soviet support, or at least neutrality, if war broke out, but the effect of closer Anglo-Soviet relations on other countries, not excluding Germany, had to be borne in mind.[89] Chamberlain thought that open association with the Soviet Union would be fatal to any hope of uniting the Balkan powers to resist German aggression, and said the problem was how to keep the Russians in the background without antagonising them.[90]

The prime minister had also to consider what more could be done to deter Germany. There was great pressure not only from France but also from Roosevelt for Britain to introduce conscription. When announcing on 26 April the government's intention to do so, Chamberlain claimed release from earlier pledges by saying international conditions could no longer be described as peace. Nothing else, he said, would do more to dispel the effects of the gibe about England fighting to the last French soldier. Churchill defended the prime minister against Labour's charge that conscription would divide and weaken the country, and pointed to the need to understand French feelings on the subject. However, the immediate reason for conscription was to ensure that the country's anti-aircraft defences were permanently manned, and no extension of the 32-division army projected following the doubling of Territorial units was intended. Conscripts were to receive only six months' training, after which they would have the option of joining the Territorial Army. There was some force, therefore, in Labour's criticism that the recruitment of some 200,000 men between the ages of 20 and 21 would not deter Germany.[91]

Chamberlain had been keen to make the announcement before a speech Hitler was due to make on 28 April, so that conscription would not be seen as a response to anything said in that speech. In the event Hitler responded to the Anglo-French guarantee to Poland by denouncing the Anglo-German Naval Agreement of 1935 and the non-aggression treaty he had signed with Poland in 1934. However, Hitler's proposal in his speech that Danzig should revert to Germany, together with a road across the Polish Corridor, a territory which gave Poland access to the sea but which cut off East Prussia from the rest of Germany, was moderate by his standards. Chamberlain took Hitler's call for fresh talks to be an indication he did not think the time favourable for a new challenge.[92] In his own speeches Chamberlain sought to demonstrate that British policy was firm on Poland, but open minded on everything else. For example, on 11 May he denied Britain had any wish to obstruct German trade in Central and South-East Europe, but said Britain was not prepared to see the independence of one country after another destroyed, and warned that any use of force over Danzig would lead to war.[93] Writing to his sisters on 15 July, he said he could imagine a way could be found to satisfy German claims while safeguarding Poland's independence and economic security, if the dictators had a modicum of patience, but he rejected an agreement on the Munich model that Hitler could break when it suited him.[94] The Poles themselves, although determined to fight for their independence if necessary, harboured hopes that the Anglo-French guarantee would strengthen them in negotiations with Germany over Danzig and the Corridor.[95]

Churchill's attitude towards Germany at this time was not very different from Chamberlain's. He spoke on 28 April and again on 21 June about Germany's return to a position as a prosperous, honoured and contented member of the European family of nations, being one of the first permanent interests of the British Empire. On 28 June he appealed to Hitler to pause before casting away all he had achieved in restoring Germany after its defeat in 1918.[96] Churchill even said in an article on 4 May 1939 that, if Poland felt able to make 'adjustments' in the

Corridor and over Danzig, no one would be more pleased than its western allies, but he stressed that no pressure should be put on Poland to make concessions damaging to its interests or security.[97]

On the other hand, Churchill thought Poland should be pressed to co-operate with the Soviet Union. He was aware of the fears of the Soviets' neighbours and told Maisky on 3 April that the Poles and Romanians would need assurances that Soviet forces would eventually get out if they were let in.[98] However, in the article on 4 May he claimed the British people's acceptance of conscription gave them the right to call on Poland not to place obstacles in the way of the common cause. He also urged, in a typically Churchillian passage, that Lithuania, Latvia and Estonia should be brought into association with the Soviet Union: 'To these three countries of warlike people, possessing together armies totalling perhaps 20 divisions of virile troops, a friendly Russia supplying munitions and other aid is essential.'[99] He did not say what should be done if Poland and the Baltic States could not be persuaded to put aside their fears of the Soviet Union.

On 14 May Viacheslav Molotov, who had replaced Litvinov as foreign minister, restated the Soviet position that Halifax's idea of unilateral Soviet guarantees to Poland and Romania would give Russia no security against direct attack or an attack through Latvia, Estonia and Finland. Molotov wanted nothing less than a mutual assistance pact, backed by an agreement on military measures, between Britain, France and the Soviet Union, and guarantees of these Baltic States (Lithuania, which had no common frontier with Russia, was not included).[100] From a Soviet point of view, there was a risk that a Baltic State might not resist a German move into its territory. There was also the experience of the Franco-Soviet pact which, in the absence of a military convention, had never been effective. When the Foreign Policy Committee met two days later to discuss a response, Chamberlain found the chiefs of staff's advice on the balance of the advantages and disadvantages of a Soviet alliance had changed. In particular, they warned that failure to reach an agreement might result in the Soviet Union standing aside in a future war, hoping to take advantage later of the exhaustion of the participants. They recommended an agreement whereby, if either power were attacked in Europe, the other would come to its assistance. By confining the pact to Europe, the risk of alienating Japan would be reduced, and Spanish war weariness lessened the importance of not offending Franco. Despite press pressure across the political spectrum in support of Churchill's idea of a grand alliance, Chamberlain objected that anything in the nature of an alliance with the Soviet Union would arouse opposition in Britain and the dominions, and said he was alarmed the chiefs of staff were recommending greatly increasing Britain's liabilities and in so doing increasing the probability of war. The last point reflected his belief that dividing Europe into opposing blocs would make any negotiations with the totalitarian states difficult if not impossible.[101]

Nevertheless, opinion in the House of Commons and the Cabinet was moving against him. In a debate on 19 May Churchill joined Lloyd George and Attlee in criticising the government's dilatoriness in coming to an agreement with the Soviet Union and saw no difficulty in bringing the Baltic States into it.[102] The chiefs of staff had, in fact, warned against guarantees for the Baltic States, on the grounds that the consequence might be a war with Germany in which Poland would be neutral and there would be no effective eastern front.[103] Even so, the tenor of the debate, the absence of any opposition in the press to an alliance and the fact that among ministers only R. A. Butler, the under-secretary at the Foreign Office, shared his views, finally convinced Chamberlain talks with the Soviet Union must be conducted on the basis of Molotov's proposal. At the crucial Cabinet discussion on 24 May he accepted that a breakdown in negotiations would have a discouraging effect on the French, who were eager for an agreement.[104]

However, Chamberlain made what Watt called 'one last desperate wriggle' to limit Britain's commitment. Adopting a suggestion from Sir Horace Wilson, the prime minister persuaded Halifax to propose that Britain, France and the Soviet Union should declare their intentions to fulfil their obligations under article 16 of the covenant of the League of Nations, which included military sanctions against an aggressor. Chamberlain believed that article 16 would at some future date be amended or repealed, giving Britain a chance to revise her relations with Russia.[105] Molotov suspected, wrongly, that the reference to the League was an attempt to make co-operation dependent on the interminable delays of Geneva procedures, and reference to article 16 had to be dropped. However, the Soviet foreign minister's principal objection to the British counter-proposal of 25 May related to its implied opposition to imposing guarantees on the Baltic States against their will. He was also insistent on the simultaneous conclusion of a military as well as political agreement, although, as the British ambassador, Seeds, pointed out, staff talks must take time and thus delay the political agreement.[106] Halifax opposed sending a mission to Moscow as that would give the impression 'we were running after the Russians'.[107] It was agreed a Foreign Office official should be sent to Moscow to assist Seeds. When announcing this to the House of Commons on 7 June, Chamberlain said Britain and France were ready to give Russia full military support without delay if she were attacked by a European power. Cadogan, who had drafted the statement with Wilson, considered it went 'fairly well' with the House.[108] Chamberlain, however, resented what he regarded as encouragement for the 'Bolshies' from the Labour Party and from what he called the Winston-Eden-Lloyd George group, with whom, he said, Maisky was constantly in touch.[109]

On 14 June, the day the chosen official, William Strang, arrived in Moscow, ministers were given a forceful reminder of how far British resources were stretched when Japanese troops began a blockade of the British concession at Tientsin, a small enclave in a port in Japanese-occupied China. The incident followed a decision by Halifax not to hand over to the Japanese military authorities four Chinese citizens accused of terrorism. However, the Japanese army made ending the blockade conditional on Britain agreeing not only to surrender the men but also to other demands, including handing over silver held by the Chinese government in the concession. British diplomacy could not be backed by sending a fleet to the Far East without reducing the number of capital ships in European waters to a level that, in Chamberlain's words, would put 'temptation in Hitler's way'. Chamberlain considered economic sanctions against Japan, but, once it was clear no support for countermeasures could be expected from the United States, he agreed to negotiations in Tokyo.[110] These were conducted with great skill by the ambassador in Tokyo, Sir Robert Craigie, who secured an end to the blockade without too much loss of face. Roosevelt put mild pressure on Japan by giving notice that its trade treaty with the United States would not be renewed at the end of the year, thereby raising the possibility of sanctions.

The Moscow negotiations following Strang's arrival were conducted in two phases. The first, until the suspension of Anglo-French discussions with Molotov on 2 August, was concerned with a political agreement. Then from 12 August there were military conversations which reached deadlock on the 17th and were adjourned indefinitely on the 21st, two days before the Nazi-Soviet non-aggression pact was signed. Strang recalled that in the negotiations for the political agreement the British government was forced by Molotov's obduracy, by opinion in Parliament and the press, and by pressure from the French to move in stages towards the Soviet position.[111] Early in the negotiations, on 20 June, Chamberlain thought the Soviets had every intention of reaching an agreement and were bargaining for the best possible terms; by 19 July he doubted whether they really wanted one.[112] As Halifax observed, the guarantees to Poland and Romania gave Molotov a strong hand, since the western powers were already committed in effect to helping the Soviet Union if it was attacked by Germany through these countries. On 4 July the foreign secretary told the Foreign Policy Committee that the Soviet government would act in its own interests regardless of any undertakings it might make. For example, he thought it would not hesitate to partition Poland with Germany if it believed the moment opportune, although equally it would go to war in support of Poland if that were in the Soviet Union's interest. Halifax frankly admitted the main object of the negotiations was to prevent the Soviet Union from coming to an agreement with Germany.[113] The committee's minutes and the Cabinet's conclusions do not reveal any significant differences between prime minister and foreign secretary after 24 May. Chamberlain was still dismissive about Soviet reliability or military capacity, but knew he could not carry his colleagues with him in his opposition to negotiations.[114]

The main obstacle to a political agreement was the question of how German aggression through the Baltic States should be prevented. Molotov was concerned these countries might accept a degree of German domination that menaced Soviet security. Chamberlain observed in the Foreign Policy Committee on 26 June that Molotov's proposal to prevent 'indirect aggression' by giving the Soviet Union the right to 'assist' these countries against the wishes of their governments would drive them into the German camp.[115] Churchill, who was informed about the negotiations by Maisky, described the Soviet attitude on the Baltic States as 'just and reasonable', and commented in a speech on 28 June that he did not understand 'what we have been boggling at all these weeks'.[116] However, Chamberlain considered that Molotov's definition of indirect aggression as 'an internal coup d'état or a reversal of policy in the interests of the aggressor' would, for example, permit the Soviet Union to insist on the right to occupy a strategic position in Finland on the excuse the Finnish government was acting in the interests of Germany. Halifax warned that if the Soviet Union intervened in the internal affairs of a Baltic State, and in consequence became involved in a war with Germany, Britain and France would also become involved.[117] On 19 July Halifax reported to the Cabinet he had seen two Labour Party leaders, Arthur Greenwood and Hugh Dalton, and found they entirely agreed with the government's line on indirect aggression. Subsequently Dalton said in the House of Commons that, while the Russians were right to keep an eye on political developments in Estonia and Latvia, the British negotiators were also perfectly right to watch carefully where a wide definition of indirect aggression might lead, and to look for one that would not commit Britain beyond what was reasonable in any circumstances that might arise.[118]

By 19 July Halifax was able to tell the Cabinet that there seemed to be discussions of some kind between the German and Soviet governments, but added it was impossible to estimate their importance and surmised they probably concerned with industrial matters. Chamberlain said he could not bring himself to believe that a real alliance between Germany and the Soviet Union was possible.[119] Later the same day Halifax, with Chamberlain's support, persuaded the Foreign Policy Committee that Molotov should be pressed to concede a better definition of indirect aggression in return for immediate military conversations before a political agreement had been reached.[120] Considerable progress had been made in Moscow on a draft political agreement, including an obligation on the part of Britain, France and the Soviet Union to give each other immediate assistance if one of them became involved in hostilities with a European power; a list of states to be guaranteed by the three powers once a definition of indirect aggression had been agreed, and an undertaking to enter military talks as soon as possible to make mutual assistance effective. Molotov told Seeds and Strang on 24 July the remaining differences over the definition of indirect aggression would not raise insuperable difficulties and could be settled while military conversations went ahead.[121] Halifax thought the Soviet Union would regard willingness to start military conversations as a test of good faith, and that they would help to deter German aggression. Ministers agreed on 26 July that the British representatives should be instructed to proceed very slowly until a political agreement had been reached.[122] However, on 2 August Molotov took exception to a statement by Butler in Parliament that could be interpreted as implying the Soviet Union wished to encroach on the independence of the Baltic States, and Seeds reported he felt the negotiations had received a severe setback.[123] On the same day Ribbentrop told Georgi Astrakhov, the Soviet representative in Berlin, that Germany was anxious for better trade relations. On the following day, the 3rd, Count Schulenberg, the German ambassador in Moscow, saw Molotov, who seemed to Schulenberg to be more open than previously to an improvement in relations between the two countries, although the ambassador added that his impression was the Soviet government intended to conclude an agreement with Britain and France if they met all Soviet wishes.[124]

On 2 August Halifax told the head of the joint-staff mission for the Anglo-French-Soviet military talks in Moscow, Admiral Sir Reginald Ernle-Erle-Drax, it would be best to draw out the negotiations for as long as possible. As Seeds pointed out, however, Molotov was unlikely to make concessions on political points until considerable progress had been made with the military talks, and that delay was likely to arouse Soviet suspicions that Britain was not in earnest. In contrast, the head of the French mission, General Joseph Doumenc, had instructions to reach a military agreement as soon as possible. Soviet suspicions would not have been abated by the slow voyage by British and French staff officers to Leningrad by merchant ship, Halifax having decided that going by a fast warship might have the effect of attaching too much importance to their mission. As it happened, on 11 August, the day the Anglo-French mission finally arrived in Moscow, Molotov wrote a letter to Astrakhov in Berlin expressing interest in German approaches on a trade agreement and 'other questions'. Drax seems therefore to have been right when he thought it possible the Soviet government was already considering a rapprochement with Germany. The British delegation were consequently guarded in their replies to enquiries about British defence plans, thereby increasing Soviet suspicions.[125]

When the military negotiations opened on 12 August Drax found the Soviet representatives spoke contemptuously of Britain and France and made demands in the manner of a victorious power dictating terms to a beaten enemy. He remarked in a letter to Chatfield that the Soviets had invented a new theory of war, whereby, instead of engaging Germany with all their forces, they would, if Germany attacked France and Britain, put into the field an army equal to 70 per cent of the combined Anglo-French armies directly employed against Germany. In the event of German aggression against Poland and Russia, the Soviet figure would be 100 per cent. If Germany used the coasts of Finland, Estonia and Latvia to attack Russia, the British and French must declare war immediately and deploy forces equal to 70 per cent of Soviet strength.[126] Stalin clearly intended to avoid a disproportionate burden of land warfare falling on the Soviet Union, understandably given the Anglo-French strategy of standing on the defensive behind the Maginot Line.

The Soviets also demanded that Britain and France obtain from Poland and Romania guarantees of the right to cross their territory, and from Finland, Estonia and Latvia the use of naval bases for an Anglo-French fleet to be sent to the Baltic. The Soviet navy would also use these bases, which, in the circumstances, could only be safeguarded by Soviet troops. The key question was whether Poland would consent to the entry of Soviet forces, something that Marshall Kliment Vorshilov, the chief Soviet negotiator, described on 14 August as an essential precondition for an Anglo-French-Soviet treaty.[127] Despite strong British and French pressure from 16 August, the Polish foreign secretary, Beck, and chief of staff, General Wacław Stachiewicz, remained obdurately opposed, suspecting the Soviets of ulterior motives, although Beck did say on the 19th that the Polish attitude might change if war actually broke out.[128] On 17 August Voroshilov threatened to break off talks until such time as a clear answer was forthcoming, although he did agree to meet again on the 21st. When no answer came from Poland by then he adjourned further meetings indefinitely. Any prospect of a successful outcome from an Anglo-French point of view had already gone. A German-Soviet economic agreement on 19 August was followed on the 23rd by a non-aggression pact with a secret protocol giving Stalin a free hand in the Baltic States, eastern Poland, and the Romanian province of Bessarabia. From the Soviet Union's point of view, the military talks with the British and French had successfully put pressure on Hitler to agree to its terms.

How far was Chamberlain responsible for the failure of negotiations for an Anglo-French-Soviet alliance? He can justly be held responsible for delay down to 24 May, but thereafter Halifax was in charge. Subsequent difficulties were not simply the result of anti-Communist sentiment, since Labour leaders, who were enthusiastic about the prospect of an alliance with the Soviet Union, agreed with the Chamberlain government's stance on the Baltic States. Carley makes a fair point when he says the British and French governments failed to understand the depth of Soviet distrust after Munich.[129] However, it seems equally true the Soviets did not understand the extent of British and French distrust towards them, particularly as regards leaving in Stalin's hands the power to decide whether the domestic politics of a Baltic State should lead to a European war. Churchill, writing after the war, said Britain and France should have accepted the Soviet terms, proclaimed the triple alliance and left the means by which it could be made effective to be adjusted between allies engaged against a common enemy. However, as William Strang pointed out, Churchill was overlooking the point that it was precisely the detail of military dispositions that the Soviets insisted on settling prior to a treaty.[130] In September 1939 Churchill said the Soviets had been guilty of the grossest bad faith in the negotiations, but their demand to station troops on Polish soil had been perfectly valid militarily.[131] That may be so, but the attitude of the Poles casts doubt on the practicality of Churchill's concept of a grand coalition combining lesser powers with the Soviet Union. Moreover, he would have had to be willing to give the Soviets a free hand in the Baltic States. As Chamberlain remarked, 'it is always easy to come to an agreement quickly if you accept everything the other side puts up'.[132]

9.3   Secret Contacts with Germans

The Soviets were not alone in being in contact with the Germans during the Moscow negotiations. On 6 June a Swedish intermediary, Axel Wenner-Gren, met Chamberlain, having previously had a long talk with the Nazi leader Hermann Goering. Goering had said that, unlike

Ribbentrop, the German foreign minister, he desired peace with Britain and had put forward his views on how an understanding between the two countries could be achieved, and Wenner-Gren had sent Chamberlain an account of what Goering had said. Chamberlain pointed out that Goering appeared to be thinking in terms of concessions on Poland and colonies in return for German assurances, and asked what value could be placed on assurances when Hitler had already broken his word. In response to a suggestion that Hitler might invite him to a conference, Chamberlain said he could not imagine the agenda would not include the colonial question, but, if he were to propose even to discuss it, he would be swept out of office without a moment's delay, given the state of public opinion. Wenner-Gren subsequently produced proposals, including a restoration of Czech independence and an end to religious persecution in Germany, whereby Germany could prove its good faith to Chamberlain, but neither Goering nor the prime minister took him seriously.[133]

There were other intermediaries, British and German, who dealt with Sir Horace Wilson rather than directly with Chamberlain. Of these the most important was Helmut Wohlthat, who, as head of the German four-year economic plan, was responsible to Goering. Wohlthat met Wilson and Sir Joseph Ball at the Duke of Westminster's house in London on 6 June. The only record of what was said that survives was made by Henry Drummond Wolff, a Conservative MP who had had a three-and-a-half hour conversation with Goering in May, when the latter had undertaken to send a representative to make arrangements for official negotiations. According to Drummond Wolff, Wilson told Wohlthat the British government would be prepared to negotiate on the whole range of issues, and Ball volunteered the opinion that there would be no difficulty in handing back Germany's colonies.[134] Wohlthat returned to London on 18 July and expressed concern to Wilson about deteriorating Anglo-German relations, which he attributed to the Anglo-French-Soviet discussions leading to German fear of encirclement, and to British fear of Germany's increasing strength. Wilson responded by giving him a copy of *The Times* containing the text of a speech by Halifax which repeated the prime minister's view that there would be an opportunity for Anglo-German co-operation once Germany ceased to disturb the peace of Europe. When Wohlthat said the Fuehrer did not wish to become involved in war, Wilson replied he was not surprised, since Hitler could not have overlooked the tremendous increases Britain had made in its defensive and offensive preparations, especially in the air, and there should be no doubt as to British determination to fight if necessary. According to Wohlthat's account of the conversation, the two men discussed limitation of armaments, and Wilson thought 'it would be possible within the framework of German-British co-operation to finance the reorganisation of British and German industry' to avoid unemployment arising from the changeover from production of armaments to civilian goods.[135] This idea does not occur in Wilson's account, and Donald Watt suggested that Wohlthat misrepresented what was said in order to persuade Hitler of the case for peace.[136]

Wohlthat also had a conversation on 20 July with Robert Hudson, the junior minister in charge of the Department of Overseas Trade, who raised the question of markets for heavy industries when rearmament came to an end. According to Wohlthat, the two men discussed currency questions, an international debt settlement for Germany, and loans for the Reichsbank, although these subjects do not appear in Hudson's account.[137] The following evening, Hudson was at a dinner which was also attended by two journalists, and from their understanding of what he said in conversation they wrote stories for the *Daily Telegraph* and the *News Chronicle* to the effect that, in return for international control of German armaments, Britain had offered Germany a massive loan, possibly as much as £1,000 million, to enable German industry to convert to a peacetime basis.[138] An irate Chamberlain had to deny in Parliament that there was any proposal for a loan, and to explain that Hudson and Wohlthat had been discussing financial steps that might have to be taken to develop international trade.[139] The suggestion of credit to facilitate German trade was also raised by Ernest Tennant, a British merchant banker who acted as an intermediary with Ribbentrop, but Wilson commented on 24 July that, if Germany took action to restore international confidence, its trade could probably be improved without a large credit.[140]

Although the newspaper reports seem to have been at best highly imaginative, the Hudson affair was described by Cadogan's private secretary, Gladwyn Jebb, as 'super-appeasement'. He told the permanent under-secretary, who was on leave, that it would 'arouse all the suspicions of the Bolsheviks, dishearten the Poles ... and encourage the Germans into thinking that we are prepared to buy peace ... I must say I doubt whether folly could be pushed to a further extreme'. Cadogan seems to have been less excited, since he made no mention of the affair in his diary.[141] However, Ruggiero, unlike Watt, considered Wohlthat's ideas to have been in line with Chamberlain's agenda and believed the only reason the affair did not lead to an immediate breakdown in negotiations in Moscow was the Soviet Union's reluctance to burn its bridges.[142] The talks with Wohlthat have to be seen in the context of British efforts since 1933 to persuade Germany to abandon autarky and to co-operate in an orderly, apolitical international financial system.

Given Germany's position as a leading trading partner and the importance to the City of London of profits from financing international trade,
such efforts were guided by British self-interest.[143] Whether they
amounted to an attempt to buy peace is more contentious. Even Scott
Newton, who takes a similar position to Ruggiero on the Wilson-
Wohlthat talks, does not suggest the prime minister wavered in his
determination to honour the guarantee to Poland.[144]

On 27 July another emissary, Lord Kemsley, the proprietor of the
Sunday Times and the *Daily Sketch*, met Hitler at Bayreuth, and returned
to London on 31 July to report to Wilson that the Fuehrer had suggested
that Britain and Germany should 'put their demands on paper and this
might lead to a discussion'. That evening Chamberlain and Halifax
agreed that Kemsley should send a letter (drafted by Wilson) to Otto
Dietrich, Hitler's press secretary, putting questions to find out exactly
what was meant by the suggestion. Wilson noted it was 'recognised that
care would have to be taken to make it clear that we were not ourselves in
any way anxious to start discussions [and] that we regarded the suggestion as indicating a German initiative'.[145] Chamberlain added a sentence
to the draft to emphasise the need for Hitler to do something to restore
confidence. However, Hitler did not respond.

On 3 August Herbert von Dirksen, the German ambassador in
London, who was sympathetic to Wohlthat's ideas, told Wilson
Britain's policy of encirclement created a lack of confidence. Wilson
replied that all British commitments were entirely defensive, and once
the German government made clear there would be no further aggression, 'the policy of guarantees to potential victims *ipso facto* became
inoperative'. Wilson also pointed out it was impossible for the British
government to enter general discussions on Anglo-German relations
until public opinion felt circumstances had changed. He suggested
Hitler should reduce the military threat to Poland, exercise patience over
Danzig, set up some form of autonomy for Bohemia and Moravia, and
announce he was ready to give a lead in Europe designed to substitute
harmony and security for the present state of friction and apprehension.
Wilson added it was useless to follow up Wohlthat's ideas for economic
co-operation if German troops were marching up and down the Polish
frontier. Wilson showed his note on the conversation to Chamberlain
and Halifax, who took the view that the approach represented by
Wohlthat and Dirksen should be kept alive, if the Germans wished, by
discussing with them an agenda for talks on a general settlement.[146]
Hitler was not, however, interested in economic co-operation.
Moreover, Ribbentrop was determined to quash Goering's peace initiative. On 20 August Wilson was visited by Fritz Hesse, Ribbentrop's

representative in London, who told him that Wohlthat, as an economist, was out of his depth in political diplomacy. Hesse delivered orally a message from Ribbentrop which made three points: first, the Danzig question should be left to the Germans and Poles to settle; second, once that was done, Hitler would be prepared to offer Britain an alliance; third, refusal of this offer would mean a fight to the finish between the two countries. Hesse added that Hitler knew full well that Britain would come into a war between Germany and Poland.[147]

Close examination of the papers in the Prime Minister's Office relating to Chamberlain and Wilson's backdoor diplomacy does not support the view that the prime minister was seeking another Munich, if by that term is meant a settlement on Hitler's terms at Poland's expense. While there may be some omissions in the record, it is pure fantasy to suppose, as Ruggiero did, that Hitler was in close contact with Chamberlain and that Sir Oswald Mosley's wife, Diana, was Chamberlain's 'principal line of communication with Hitler before the war'. Ruggiero cited a secondary source, which in turn cited a Security Service file, but both sources make plain that the communication in question was between Sir Oswald, as leader of the British Union of Fascists, and Hitler. There is no evidence to support Ruggiero's conspiracy theory that Chamberlain may have leaked information about Anglo-Soviet negotiations to Hitler through secret sources.[148]

A rather different charge against Chamberlain by a number of historians is that the cumulative effect of informal contacts was to encourage Hitler in his belief that Britain would try to avoid war.[149] Certainly Chamberlain hoped for appeasement, in the non-pejorative sense, but not from weakness. On the contrary, echoing a Joint Intelligence Committee (JIC) report, he told his sisters on 23 July it was apparent Hitler realised Britain meant business and had concluded that the time was not ripe for war. However, Chamberlain was exercising his own judgement when he said that the longer war was put off the less likely it would occur, as Germany would be deterred by Britain and its allies perfecting their defences: 'that is what Winston and Co never seem to realise. You don't need offensive forces sufficient to win a smashing victory. What you want are defensive forces sufficiently strong to make it impossible for the other side to win except at such a cost as to make it not worthwhile'. Chamberlain recognised that, as rearmament progressed, Hitler might be uncertain about Britain's intentions and embark on a preventative war; hence the reassuring, if firm, tone used in informal contacts. In Chamberlain's view, the time to negotiate with the Germans would be once they realised they could not get what they wanted by force.[150] In contrast, Churchill told Sir Edmund Ironside, the chief of the imperial general staff, on 24 July that it was now too late for any appeasement and Hitler was going to make war.[151]

9.4   The Decision for War

By July 1939 Treasury officials estimated Britain would spend £750 million on defence in 1939/40, compared with £400 million in the previous financial year. On 5 July 1939 Sir Richard Hopkins was asked, most unusually, to attend a special meeting of the Cabinet. He explained that the economy would reach full employment by the late autumn, and borrowing on short-term Treasury bills thereafter would be inflationary and lead to heavy losses from the gold reserves. Inflation could be curbed by taking quasi-wartime powers, as in Germany, to divert capital from private to government use: by prohibiting new issues on the Stock Exchange and by imposing controls on bank and building society loans, and on companies' dividends and reserves. Even so, the gold reserves would continue to fall owing to the adverse balance of trade, and that adverse balance would increase insofar as additions to the rearmament programme involved imports of raw materials. Such imports represented about 25 to 30 per cent of the cost of armaments produced in Britain. Britain's ability to fight a long war was diminishing with each month that passed, he said, and the prospects were becoming 'increasingly grim' unless, when the time came, the United States repealed the Johnson Act and lent or gave the necessary dollars. Hopkins saw no reason to anticipate an early economic or financial crisis in Germany, which relied less than Britain on international trade and where a docile population acquiesced in higher taxation than in Britain.[152] The seriousness of the British position was underlined on 22 August when the chancellor of the exchequer, Simon, reported heavy losses of gold as war fears led to balances being withdrawn from London, and the Cabinet authorised him to allow sterling to depreciate to a level that could be maintained by introducing exchange controls.[153] Two days later the Bank of England's discount rate was raised from 2 per cent, at which it had remained since 1932, to 4 per cent. The international crisis was thus creating a financial crisis. However, there is no evidence that Chamberlain's hand was forced by a feeling that it would be better to fight now than later. There was no suggestion in the Cabinet's discussion on 5 July that the measures set out by Hopkins, although highly unwelcome to Conservative politicians, could only be imposed in wartime.

A more plausible case can be made for Chamberlain's options being limited by domestic political pressures. The German ambassador, Dirksen, doubted whether the prime minister's position was strong enough to allow him to revert to appeasement, noting on 24 July that the public's reaction to the talks between Wohlthat and Hudson showed that any publication of plans for negotiations with Germany 'would immediately be torpedoed by Churchill and other agitators with cries of "No second Munich"!'[154] The German press office in London described the British public as mentally and morally prepared for war.[155] After Prague, even the Conservative press turned against appeasement. As Chamberlain's acquiescence in the continuation of negotiations with the Soviet Union shows, the prime minister's power over policy depended on his ability to carry his Cabinet colleagues with him. Neither he nor they could ignore the feelings of MPs, and there was the prospect of a general election, perhaps as soon as November. However, while Chamberlain's optimism about the possibility of maintaining peace separated him from his critics, it is much less certain his sense of national honour was weaker than theirs.

The final crisis broke while Chamberlain was on holiday in Scotland. The JIC report for the week ending 17 August warned that Hitler was apparently working himself up into the same unbalanced state of mind about the Poles as he had about the Czechs. On 18 August Sir Nevile Henderson phoned from the Berlin embassy to say he was convinced Hitler had practically made up his mind that Britain and France would not intervene effectively if he attacked Poland, and urged the prime minister to send a secret and personal letter to Hitler setting out unequivocally Britain's intention to fulfil its obligations. That same day one of Sir Robert Vansittart's sources told him Hitler had decided on war, to begin between 25 and the 28 August. Sir Alexander Cadogan, who had his doubts about the chief diplomatic adviser's source, spoke by phone to Halifax, who was in Yorkshire, and the foreign secretary and the permanent under-secretary agreed not to ask the prime minister to return to London yet. Instead on Saturday the 19th Halifax, Cadogan, Vansittart and William Strang drafted a letter for Chamberlain to send to Hitler. Chamberlain returned to London early on the 21st, still hopeful he might be able to resume his holiday.[156]

By the time the Cabinet met in the afternoon of 22 August the German official news agency had announced that Ribbentrop would go to Moscow the next day to conclude negotiations for a non-aggression pact. Chamberlain remarked that the principal significance of the news was that the Germans were now convinced Britain could not save Poland and would make no attempt to fulfil the guarantee. The prime minister said it was unthinkable Britain should fail to support Poland, and an announcement should be made on the BBC that evening that whatever Germany and the Soviet Union might agree would make no difference to British obligations. He thought Parliament should be recalled on the 24th and an Emergency Powers (Defence) Bill passed in a single day to enable the government to make all necessary regulations, although these would not be introduced until they were required. He also said preliminary steps should be taken for mobilisation. Only once these things had been announced should the proposed personal letter to Hitler be sent. Otherwise, he suggested, the Germans might think it was a result of their reported agreement with the Soviets.[157] The letter itself warned Hitler it would be a dangerous illusion to suppose a war would come to a swift conclusion if Germany had early military success. It appealed for an end to the present state of tension so that Germany and Poland could discuss peacefully their differences over issues such as the treatment of national minorities. Parenthetically, it added these discussions might be conducted with the aid of a neutral intermediary, if both sides thought that would be helpful, but there was no suggestion of a conference on the Munich model. Instead Britain would be willing to join in an international guarantee of an agreement reached by direct negotiation between Germany and Poland.[158] Chamberlain felt unable to put pressure on the Poles to enter talks and Sir Horace Wilson called on the American ambassador, Joseph Kennedy, early on 23 August to see if Roosevelt would. Kennedy subsequently saw Chamberlain, whom he found depressed, and who confirmed there was nothing he could do to get the Poles to make concessions. The ambassador advised Roosevelt that the only possible action would be to work on Beck, the Polish foreign minister. However, the president did not do so; instead he sent letters on the 24th to Hitler and the president of Poland urging peaceful settlement of the two countries' differences by direct negotiation or through arbitration or conciliation by someone from one of the traditionally neutral states of Europe.[159]

Meanwhile Henderson had flown from Berlin to Berchtesgaden on the 23rd to present Chamberlain's letter to Hitler in person. Hitler responded with a tirade about British support for the Czechs in 1938 and now for the Poles, and asserted that Britain's 'blank cheque' for the latter had made them so unreasonable that negotiation was impossible. Hitler complained about his offers of friendship with Britain being 'turned down with contempt', and claimed Germany had nothing to lose from war, whereas Britain had much to lose. He was calmer, but still uncompromising, when he summoned the ambassador to a second meeting that day and handed him a written reply which warned that if Britain took further mobilisation measures, general mobilisation would immediately take place in Germany.[160] In fact the German armed forces had been ordered that day to attack Poland on 26 August.

However, Hitler apparently still hoped to avoid a general war by bullying the British, telling the state secretary of the foreign ministry, Weizsäcker, who was present at the meetings with Henderson: 'Chamberlain won't survive this discussion. His cabinet will fall this evening.'[161]

Hitler completely misunderstood the strength of Chamberlain's position. In a firm, sombre speech in Parliament on 24 August the prime minister reaffirmed Britain's commitment to Poland and to an international order based on observation of treaties and the peaceful resolution of differences between nations. The leaders of the Opposition parties closed ranks with the government to demonstrate support for these principles, and the Emergency Powers Act was passed almost unanimously.[162] The following day, with Chamberlain evidently unshaken by the signature of the Nazi-Soviet Pact, Hitler tried a different tack. He summoned Henderson at 1.30 p.m. and, in a cordial interview, offered to guarantee the existence of the British Empire, once the Polish problem had been resolved. Henderson, however, insisted Britain could not abandon Poland.[163] At 5.30 p.m. the French ambassador likewise told Hitler that France would fulfil its obligations, and shortly afterwards the Italian ambassador said Italy would remain neutral. Finally, at 6 p.m. came news that a treaty of mutual assistance between Britain and Poland had been signed late that afternoon. Hitler decided he needed more time to see whether the threat of British intervention could be removed, and at 7.30 p.m. called off the attack due to begin at 4.30 the following morning. Admiral Wilhelm Canaris, the head of the Abwehr (military intelligence) and an opponent of the Nazis, thought Hitler would never recover from this blow to his reputation, but the German army leadership was divided and took no action against the regime.[164]

Chamberlain was relieved Henderson had not been handed an ultimatum, and spent much of the next three days working on a response to Hitler's offer. On 26 August Wilson and R. A. Butler, the junior minister at the Foreign Office, produced a draft which was criticised in Cabinet for being 'too deferential', and Chamberlain, Halifax and Simon undertook to redraft it. After two further Cabinet meetings, including one on Sunday the 27th, a final text was agreed on the 28th. Chamberlain described it as 'dignified, firm, and yet quite unprovocative'.[165] Discussion of Anglo-German relations was made conditional on a bilateral settlement of the differences between Germany and Poland on terms that safeguarded essential Polish interests, and which was subject to an international guarantee.[166] Hitler should have been left in no doubt that resort to force would mean war. However, by the time Henderson gave him the letter on the evening of 28 August, Hitler had already learned the gist of the British response via an emissary from Hermann Goering, Birger

Dahlerus, a Swedish businessman, who had seen Chamberlain and Halifax on the 27th and flown back to Berlin the same day.[167] According to Richard Overy, Hitler was convinced that, if the British were so desperate as to communicate unofficially through Dahlerus, their willingness to support Poland must be in doubt.[168] It is not clear, however, that Chamberlain was responsible for Hitler's misapprehension. As Overy himself has observed, Hitler's grasp of reality was weakened by the tendency of the German foreign office and military to give him only intelligence that confirmed his hopes that Britain and France would not fight.[169] Moreover, Hitler was sceptical of Dahlerus's efforts, telling Goering that 'if the English sign a treaty [with Poland] one day, they are not going to break it in twenty-four hours'.[170] Chamberlain regarded the approach from Goering, following as it did Hitler's offer, as 'rather promising'. Even after war broke out Chamberlain thought the offer had been sincere and speculated that Hitler had subsequently had some 'brainstorm', perhaps brought about by Ribbentrop, or had been unable to stop his military machine once set in motion.[171]

In fact Hitler was plotting to isolate Poland by persuading the British to press the Poles to send a representative with full powers to negotiate to Berlin on 30 August, with a view to blaming a breakdown in the talks on Polish intransigence. When talking with Henderson on the 28th he focused on Germany's grievances.[172] On the 29th Hitler produced a note saying he accepted British mediation only out of a desire for lasting friendship and persuaded Henderson that Beck ought to go to Berlin to negotiate.[173] Chamberlain and Halifax worked late into the night of 29/30 August on a draft reply. The prime minister told the Cabinet the next day that Hitler's demand for a Polish representative to appear within 24 hours was part of the technique applied to Dr Hacha, the Czech president, in March and was unacceptable. Halifax thought Hitler's note, stripped of its bombastic language, revealed a man trying to get out of a difficult situation. The tone of the British reply was firm, with no pressure on the Poles to comply with the German demand.[174] While the final draft was being prepared in the Foreign Office, Chamberlain sent a conciliatory personal message to Hitler welcoming the exchanges of views as evidence of a mutual desire for Anglo-German understanding. However, this gesture was not preliminary to another Munich. When on 31 August Mussolini proposed to convene a conference on 5 September to revise the Treaty of Versailles, Chamberlain said it was impossible to hold one under threat of mobilised armies and that there would have to be a measure of demobilisation first.[175]

When the Germans invaded Poland on 1 September the prime minister told the Cabinet 'our consciences are clear, and there should be no possible question now where our duty lay'.[176] The main problem was seen as how to co-ordinate the British response with the French. The Cabinet decided to send a note telling Hitler that, unless he halted all aggressive action against Poland and agreed to withdraw his forces promptly, the British government would fulfil its obligations 'without hesitation' – but no time limit was given.[177] Chamberlain described this note to the House of Commons that evening as a last warning, and said the German reply was unlikely to be favourable. Greenwood, deputising for Attlee as leader of the Opposition, observed that by the Anglo-Polish Treaty Britain was bound to give Poland all the support it could at once.[178]

In the morning of Saturday, 2 September, Churchill wrote to Chamberlain pointing out that the Poles had been under heavy attack for 30 hours and said he trusted the prime minister would be able to announce an Anglo-French declaration of war at *latest* when Parliament met in the afternoon.[179] Simon was due to make a statement when Parliament assembled at 2.45 p.m. that an ultimatum would be presented to Germany soon. However, quarter of an hour earlier Ciano, the Italian foreign minister, phoned Halifax to urge acceptance of Mussolini's proposal for a conference. Halifax managed to rush from the Foreign Office to the House of Commons to stop Simon in order to gain time in which to consult with the French and to synchronise action towards Germany. MPs were promised Chamberlain would make a statement later. The Cabinet met at very short notice at 4.30 p.m., when Halifax outlined what he and the prime minister had 'provisionally' agreed about the statement's contents: the Germans should be allowed until noon the next day to reply to the British note, subject to an armistice, and until midnight on the 3rd/4th for consideration of a conference, subject to agreeing to withdraw their troops from Poland and Danzig. Ministers, however, were more concerned about British public opinion than with Anglo-French co-ordination, and would not agree to delay a declaration of war beyond midnight on the 2nd/3rd. In the event, the French wanted longer: partly to complete their defence preparations, and partly because Bonnet, the foreign minister, wanted more time to explore the conference option. By the time Chamberlain appeared in the Commons at 7.45 p.m., MPs had been in a state of tension for five hours, time many had spent drinking alcohol. The prime minister's statement that the French government was still being consulted on the time limit for a German reply provoked fury. As Chamberlain recalled, some MPs believed the government to be capable of any cowardice and treachery. Leo Amery, a former Conservative minister, called out 'speak for England' when Greenwood rose to reply for the Opposition. Greenwood recognised the need to work with the

French, but said delay imperilled national honour and pressed for a definite statement on peace or war by noon the next day. James Maxton, speaking for the pacifist wing of the Labour Party, appealed to the prime minister not to allow himself to be rushed, but this was a minority view. Churchill, who had accepted Chamberlain's offer the previous day of a place in a war cabinet, remained silent, but wrote to the prime minister afterwards urging him to take a decision independently of the French, and thus give them a lead. After the prime minister's statement, twelve discontented ministers met to discover why it had been so different from what had been decided in the afternoon. They went to see Chamberlain, who explained he had felt the disadvantage of declaring war without France outweighed the probable effect of further delay on the House of Commons and the country. The ministers met again at 10 p.m., and Simon went to see Chamberlain to demand that an ultimatum be sent before Parliament met the next day. At a hastily assembled Cabinet at 11.30 p.m. Chamberlain said he had phoned Daladier to warn him it would be impossible to delay beyond noon. Ministers agreed to an ultimatum to be delivered at 9 a.m., to expire at 11 a.m. without waiting for the French.[180]

The drama of events on 2 September led Dalton to claim that the House of Commons, and especially the Labour Party, had pushed a reluctant government into war.[181] The image of an irresolute prime minister has been taken up by some historians. Alastair Parker thought that for a few hours in the afternoon of 2 September Chamberlain was tempted by the possibility of a conference of the four Munich powers plus Poland.[182] That may be, but there is no direct evidence. Ruggiero depicted Chamberlain as fearful of going to war over Poland and being compelled by an impatient Parliament and his colleagues to abandon hope that Hitler would agree to withdraw his troops.[183] That is a possible interpretation, particularly if one has as low an opinion of Chamberlain's moral fibre as Ruggiero apparently has. However, there is nothing in the documentary record to suggest Chamberlain was sanguine about Mussolini's initiative, which nevertheless could not easily be dismissed unilaterally. Watt – no admirer of Chamberlain – acquitted the prime minister of irresolution and blamed Bonnet for the delay in presenting an ultimatum. Robert Self likewise believed Chamberlain genuinely wanted only to delay long enough to synchronize action with France and to force a German withdrawal.[184] The prime minister was in a difficult position, and was slower than Churchill to see that the way out was to take the bold course of acting independently in the expectation that France would follow. The French ultimatum on 3 September expired six hours after the British.

The most quoted sentence of Chamberlain's statement to Parliament after the declaration of war is: 'Everything that I have worked for, everything that I have hoped for, everything that I have believed in during my public life, has crashed in ruins.' Less frequently quoted are the immediately following sentences in which Chamberlain devoted 'what strength and powers I have to forwarding the victory of the cause for which we have to sacrifice so much', and looked forward to the day when Hitlerism had been destroyed.[185] Churchill refrained from saying he had been proved right and instead spoke of Chamberlain's repeated efforts for peace:

All have been ill-starred, but all have been faithful and sincere. This is of the highest moral value − and not only moral value, but practical value − at the present time, because the wholehearted concurrence of scores of millions of men and women, whose co-operation is indispensable and whose comradeship and brotherhood are indispensable, is the only foundation upon which the trial and tribulation of modern war can be endured and surmounted ... . [O]ur consciences are at rest.[186]

In other words, Chamberlain's demonstration that every means to preserve peace had been tried had united the British people and the dominions by leaving no doubt that war had been unavoidable.

10   The Test of War

10.1   The 'Phoney War'

Some of Chamberlain's critics, including Sidney Aster, Frank McDonough and John Ruggiero, see continuity between pre-war appeasement and what they regard as his strategy of remaining on the defensive for as long as he could, while looking for a way out of the war.[1] Chamberlain was certainly not by nature a war minister, as he himself was acutely aware. The loss of lives when the aircraft carrier *Courageous* and the battleship *Royal Oak* were sunk by German U-boats weighed on his mind. Even destruction of German U-boats gave him an uncomfortable feeling. On a visit to France he was sickened by the sight of barbed wire and pill boxes, which reminded him of the casualties of the First World War. Whereas he had felt indispensable before the war, he did not see he had any particular role to play until the time came to discuss peace terms.[2] Churchill, in contrast, was in his element, pressing his ideas for offensive action on the naval staff and also, on matters far removed from his brief as first lord of the Admiralty, in the War Cabinet. Even before joining the government he had had hopes of becoming wartime prime minister.[3] The active part played by the Royal Navy, while air and land warfare was largely in suspense in the west until the spring of 1940, increased his prestige, making him an indispensable member of the government. Churchill's personality and methods of working were very different from Chamberlain's, and inevitably the first lord proved to be a difficult subordinate, although at a personal level the two men got on well. Chamberlain devolved some responsibility for the conduct of the war by making Churchill chairman of the War Cabinet's Military Coordination Committee after Lord Chatfield, the minister for coordination of defence, resigned on 3 April 1940. This appointment fell short of Churchill's ambition to be minister of defence, however, and Chamberlain retained ultimate authority.[4]

Chamberlain doubted the possibility of military victory and instead hoped economic pressure from the Allied blockade would bring about a collapse on the German home front, akin to that of 1918. He wrote to his sisters on 10 September 1939 that that might be a long way off, but he had a feeling it would not be so very long. He said he opposed bombing military targets in towns, unless the Germans did, without mentioning that the Germans were already doing so in Poland.[5] His ideas have to be seen in the context of Anglo-French strategy of a long war in which the Allies would stand on the defensive in the opening phase, while they mobilised their superior resources, including those of their empires, and take the offensive only after Germany had been weakened by blockade.[6]

Churchill broadly agreed with Chamberlain as regards strategic bombing, writing on 10 September that 'we should not take the initiative ... except in the immediate zone in which the French armies are operating'. He added the Allies should follow and not precede the Germans in what he thought would be an inevitable process of increasing violence, adding that every day that passed gave time to provide more shelters for the population of London and other big cities. Moreover, he said, British rearmament was overtaking Germany's and it was not in Britain's interest that industry should be interrupted by air raids. Four days later, in the War Cabinet, he did raise the possibility of air attacks on synthetic oil plants, which were 'isolated from the civil population', even if German retaliation was provoked thereby. However, this proposal was blocked by the secretary of state for air, Sir Kingsley Wood, who said policy should be guided by the need to preserve the numerically inferior RAF for when it would be most needed, and reminded ministers the air position would be 'immeasurably improved' by March 1940.[7]

Churchill had hoped that pressure on the Poles would be relieved by French land operations against Germany's western defences, which were thinly held, but the French chief of staff, General Gamelin, initiated no more than a reconnaissance in force. The chief of the imperial general staff, Ironside, advised the War Cabinet on 4 September it was most improbable the Germans would crush Poland in a few weeks.[8] However, by the middle of the month it was clear that organised Polish resistance would soon end. Churchill was impressed by the success of the German panzer divisions, which he thought could be stopped only by steel or concrete obstacles, deep ditches and mines, defended by powerful artillery. He urged on 15 September that every effort should be made to fortify the Franco-Belgian frontier, as well as strengthen the British Expeditionary Force (BEF) in France. Chamberlain thought 'the lesson of the Polish campaign is the power of the air force when it has obtained complete mastery in the air to paralyse the operations of land forces'. Given the weakness of the French air force, he feared the Germans might wipe it out along with France's aircraft factories. He did not feel confident the RAF was strong enough yet to deny the Germans mastery in the air. Churchill, while agreeing that air power was the first priority, wanted a factory building programme sufficient to expand the army from 32 divisions to 55 divisions at an early date. Chamberlain thought a decision on the size of the army should be deferred until after resources had been allocated to the air force's expansion.[9] In the event, it was not until February 1940 that the War Cabinet authorised a modest expansion of the pre-war 32-division army to 36 divisions by September 1941, together with construction of factories required for completion of the full 55-division programme thereafter.[10]

Meanwhile the Polish campaign had come to an early end after the Red Army crossed the frontier on 17 September to occupy the zone allocated to the Soviet Union under the Molotov-Ribbentrop Pact. As the Anglo-French guarantee to Poland was limited to German aggression, the Soviet action was not regarded as a casus belli in London and Paris. Chamberlain wrote to his sisters on 23 September that the Germans could not trust the Soviets and would not move into south-eastern Europe with the Red Army on their flank. Churchill agreed, telling the War Cabinet that the Germans would have to leave 20 to 25 divisions to guard against the Russians. In the light of the new situation Chamberlain considered Hitler's alternatives in the west and dismissed them all: an attack on the Maginot Line because German losses would be too severe; an attack through Belgium because it would be a risky gamble, and an air offensive because Britain's air defences were 'incomparably better than anything the Poles could put up' and Allied retaliation 'might have unexpected results on morale in Germany'.[11] He still did not understand Hitler's character as a gambler who would always go for broke. However, the prime minister was not alone in misunderstanding the political balance in the Third Reich. On 25 September 1939 Churchill submitted a paper to the War Cabinet in which he pondered whether Hitler's generals, 'who now are presumably more powerful', would prevent him launching an air offensive 'for fear of making a mortal blood-feud with Great Britain, and perhaps drawing in the United States by the air massacres which would be inevitable'.[12] Chamberlain remained sceptical about a great German offensive in the west, but did not exclude the possibility, and Britain's best troops were concentrated in northern France.

Chamberlain correctly anticipated Hitler would make a peace offer on the grounds that war in the west could not restore the Poland of the Versailles Treaty, and wrote on 23 September 1939 that such an offer should be refused and the blockade continued. When the offer came in a speech on 6 October Chamberlain said it was 'too early for any hope of peace negotiation', since the Germans were not yet convinced they could not win the war, and commented he was glad Hitler's terms were unacceptable and therefore would not encourage 'the peace-at-any-price people'. He added that peace was possible only if the Germans replaced Hitler.[13] It is difficult to reconcile these sentiments with Sidney Aster's judgement that Chamberlain was obsessed with the chances of negotiating a settlement and was heartened by 'stop the war' advocates.[14] Moreover, there seems to have been no difference between Chamberlain and Churchill on how to respond to Hitler's peace offer. On 8 October Churchill urged a stronger tone to the Foreign Office draft reply, but said his revisions did 'not close the door on any genuine offer' that included freedom and reparations for the Poles and Czechs, and evidence that Germany's sole aim would be a peaceful Europe in which it, 'as one of its greatest nations, should play a leading and honoured part'.[15] On 9 October Chamberlain told the War Cabinet that Hitler's speech, excluding as it did discussion about Poland, was an impossible basis for negotiations, and, more generally, it was impossible to believe anything Hitler said.[16] The prime minister's statement to Parliament on 12 October was on similar lines to Churchill's revisions to the Foreign Office draft, but omitted the reference to Germany being a great nation.[17]

Stalin followed his invasion of eastern Poland by making a new pact with Germany on 28 September, promising it economic support. He induced Estonia and Latvia to agree to Soviet naval bases, and Lithuania to accept Soviet army and air units, on their territory. Finland also came under pressure to make concessions. British policy, however, focused on keeping trade links with the Soviet Union open, given the need for continuing supplies of Russian timber. Chamberlain and Churchill were agreed that the Soviet Union would always act in its own interests and that a victory for Germany followed by its domination of the Balkans would not be in accordance with these.[18] On 10 October Churchill invited the Soviet ambassador, Maisky, to the Admiralty at 10 p.m. and told him that relations between their countries had been poisoned by mutual suspicion, but their basic interests did not collide anywhere. He remarked that, if the Baltic States had to lose their independence (as they were to do in August 1940), it was better for them to be taken into the Soviet system rather than Hitler's *Lebensraum*, a sentiment that suggests Churchill would have agreed to Stalin's terms during the pre-war negotiations for an alliance. Now he asked no more of the Soviet Union than benevolent neutrality. According to Maisky, Churchill said 'with a sly smile' that Stalin was playing a big game felicitously and there was no reason for Britain to be dissatisfied.[19]

Chamberlain received intelligence reports that it had been a terrible shock to Hitler to be ousted from the eastern Baltic, and believed an

Anglo-Soviet trade agreement would discomfit the Germans further.[20] Halifax wanted trade talks to be conditional on Finland not being attacked. However, Churchill said in Cabinet on 16 November it would be a mistake to stiffen the Finns against making concessions as it was in the Allies' interest that the Soviet Union increase its strength in the Baltic, thereby limiting the risk of German domination there. The foreign secretary agreed, but only if the Finns did not regard the concessions demanded as a threat to their national independence, which, unlike Churchill, they did.[21] In the event, Churchill's approach to Maisky achieved nothing, since Molotov remained suspicious of British hostility to the Soviet Union, not least over Finland.[22]

In line with his pre-war ideas about a grand alliance, Churchill challenged the Foreign Office's policy of creating a neutral Balkan bloc, telling the War Cabinet on 21 September he would like to see all the Balkan countries, plus Turkey, brought into the war, as otherwise Britain and France would be left to bear the full brunt of the German attack in the west. Halifax replied that such a policy would probably present Germany with a series of easy victories, and he was backed by Ironside, who reminded ministers of how Romania had been quickly defeated when it had entered the war prematurely in 1916. The chiefs of staff advised that, if countries were to be encouraged to enter the war, it was essential to make sure they were ready to do so.[23] Britain and Turkey were close to concluding negotiations for a mutual assistance treaty, including provision for Turkey to aid Britain and France in fulfilling their guarantees to Greece and Romania. Ironside said Turkey would be unable to transport a large force to Romania by sea in time to prevent that country being overrun. Churchill believed the arrival of even three or four Turkish divisions in Romania 'would be of the greatest assistance', and that transport by land would be possible if, as he suggested, Bulgaria were persuaded to join a Balkan bloc by Romania ceding disputed territory to her. However, Halifax saw no prospect of Romania agreeing to do so.[24]

Chamberlain agreed with Churchill that the Allies would be net gainers if Turkey and Yugoslavia intervened if Germany attacked Romania, but doubted the Turks' willingness to do so as their attitude during the treaty negotiations had made him extremely suspicious.[25] The treaty, which was eventually signed on 19 October 1939, was linked to a military convention whereby Turkey would not be obliged to act until Britain had delivered war material to be purchased with a £25 million credit.[26] It was not clear how soon that could be done when British industry was fully occupied with the needs of the expanding army and RAF. Churchill himself described the treaty as a sham, but thought an offer of support from French troops in Syria and British troops in Egypt might persuade the Turks to fulfil their obligations to Romania.[27] He continued to be much more optimistic than his colleagues about the Balkans, telling the War Cabinet on 30 November he believed Greece, Romania and Yugoslavia were 'gradually veering towards the Allies', and that if these countries were to come into the war on the Allied side, Italy might do so too.[28] In the event, despite Churchill's hopes, the Balkan states remained neutral and disunited.

Chamberlain had noted on 1 October that the Germans' success in Poland might make Mussolini feel he ought to enter the war on the winning side while there was still time, but the prime minister was confident the Italian king, church and people would be opposed to fighting Britain on Germany's behalf.[29] Chatfield, the minister for co-ordination of defence, told the War Cabinet on 6 October that uncertainty about Italy's intentions dominated strategy by compelling the Allies to retain large forces in the Mediterranean. He suggested approaching the Italians with a view to establishing détente and an agreement on mutual withdrawal of troops from North Africa. Churchill hoped the Italians might be persuaded to co-operate in keeping the Mediterranean free from submarine warfare.[30] In a War Cabinet paper on 18 October he wrote: 'everyone can see how necessary it is to have Italy friendly and how desirable to have her as an ally'. He expressed hope that good relations could be developed from common interests: 'Once engaged on this path, one thing leads to another, and confidence ripens into comradeship'.[31] The idea of comradeship with Fascist Italy was a remarkable illusion. Mussolini had opted for non-belligerency because Italy was not ready for war from an economic or military point of view; could not count on sufficient supplies from Germany to be able to withstand an Allied blockade, and German victory was uncertain, but he remained an opportunist.[32] He was unlikely to see any advantage in allying with Britain and France: whereas in 1915 Italy had been persuaded to enter the war by promises of Austrian and Turkish territory, in 1939 Italy's territorial claims were against France. By the spring of 1940 Italian newspapers and broadcasts had taken on a decidedly anti-Allied stance. Chamberlain remarked at the War Cabinet on 14 April that Italy was doubtless waiting on events in order to take sides with the victor, and meanwhile he thought Mussolini would go as far as he dared to help Hitler without actually getting involved in the war.[33]

The neutral country with the greatest potential to influence the outcome of the war was, of course, the United States. When the chancellor of the exchequer, Simon, explained to the War Cabinet on 22 September that plans to expand the air force and army implied dollar expenditure on American machine tools on a scale inconsistent with a three-year war, Chamberlain said the Treasury's figures could not be challenged, but uncertain factors should not be forgotten. He hoped the United States would help with financial difficulties if the war lasted three years. He added that the only thing that mattered was victory, even if Britain were bankrupted. A credit balance in dollars would be no comfort, he said, if the war was lost.[34] The immediate problem was the American Neutrality Act. Chamberlain wrote to Roosevelt on 4 October that success would come by convincing the Germans they could not win, and that repeal of the arms embargo would have a devastating effect on German morale.[35] Roosevelt secured Congressional approval at the beginning of November for Britain and France to purchase munitions for cash (the Johnson Act's prohibition on loans remained in force). Chamberlain sent him a note on the 8th to say it was a 'profound moral encouragement' for the Allies to know they could draw on American resources.[36] However, there was no sudden increase in orders for munitions. Instead scarce dollars were spent on raw materials and machine tools for use in British factories.[37] The long-war strategy was still intact. Churchill was among those who thought time was on the Allied side. In a broadcast on 12 November he said 'if we come through the winter without any large or important event occurring we shall in fact have gained the first campaign of the war'.[38]

Chamberlain did not expect the United States to enter the war. Indeed he wrote to his sisters on 27 January 1940: 'Heaven knows I don't want the Americans to fight for us – we should have to pay too dearly for that if they had a right to be in on the peace terms.'[39] At a time when Chamberlain was confident that blockade and weakness on the German home front could bring victory, neither he nor the Foreign Office welcomed Roosevelt's action in sending the American under-secretary of state, Sumner Welles, on a tour of Rome, Berlin, Paris and London in February and March 1940 to investigate the possibility of a negotiated peace. Welles concluded from his visit to Germany that peace was possible only on the basis of Hitler remaining in power and the Allies being given security through far-reaching disarmament. Chamberlain thought Welles was mistaken in supposing there was any chance of Hitler agreeing to give up his aims and told Welles it was fantastic to expect countries to disarm until Germany had a government which had the same attitude to peace as the Allies.[40] It is hard to square this episode with a belief that Chamberlain's reason for remaining on the defensive was that he was looking for a way out of the war.

10.2   Norway and the Fall of Chamberlain's Government

Churchill agreed with the strategy of weakening Germany through blockade, but was much less inclined than Chamberlain to be content with an otherwise passive stance. In particular, Churchill was the principal advocate of taking initiatives in the Baltic and Scandinavia. One of his most important contacts in Whitehall before the war had been Major Desmond Morton, head of the Industrial Intelligence Centre, which became the Intelligence Division of the Ministry of Economic Warfare at the outbreak of war. Morton believed, over-optimistically, that German steel mills were sufficiently dependent on Swedish iron ore for interception of its supply to have a decisive effect on production within months.[41] Shortly after becoming first lord of the Admiralty, Churchill ordered a study to be made of a naval offensive to establish a blockade in the Baltic. He suggested that two or three older battleships should be strengthened against bombs and mines to head an 'expeditionary fleet', which would take three months' supply of fuel in specially protected tankers. He thought command of the Baltic would also make it possible to bring Sweden and Norway into the war on the Allied side and might have 'far-reaching' influence upon the Soviet Union.[42] The naval staff identified major practical problems with the scheme, particularly as regards making the ships secure against air attack, and by January 1940 he accepted it could not go ahead that year, although he still had hopes for 1941. The idea that the Scandinavian countries could be persuaded to abandon their neutrality by the appearance of the Royal Navy in the Baltic was typical of Churchill's optimism.

Meanwhile he had taken up another scheme to interrupt German ore supplies. During winter, when the northern part of the Baltic was frozen, Swedish iron ore was shipped from the Norwegian port of Narvik. Churchill explained to the War Cabinet on 19 September 1939 that merchant ships were able to evade the British blockade by keeping within the three-mile limit of Norwegian territorial waters. He said that, if pressure on the Norwegian government did not halt the trade with Germany, he would propose laying mines in Norwegian waters to force the ore-carrying vessels into the open sea, where they could be inspected by the Royal Navy for contraband, as had been done in the First World War (after the United States had become a belligerent).[43] He returned to the question on 30 November, but Halifax urged caution about breaching Norwegian neutrality, and Churchill agreed the Americans' attitude might be a determining factor.[44] On the same day the Soviet Union invaded Finland, and the possible extension of the conflict to Scandinavia provided a new context for Churchill's ideas.

The Finns' heroic defence of their country aroused considerable sympathy abroad. The only practical route whereby men and supplies could be sent to support them was through Scandinavia. Aid to Finland, using Narvik as a base, would provide the Allies with an opportunity to take control of the Swedish ore-field at Gällivare. On 22 December the War

Cabinet considered a French proposal for a joint démarche to Sweden and Norway stating the British and French governments were studying how to help Finland; they hoped for Swedish and Norwegian collaboration, and were ready to consider measures to guard against any consequences to Sweden and Norway. Churchill wanted to go further by urging Sweden and Norway to give all possible help to Finland now, and to say explicitly that Britain and France would guarantee to send adequate forces to assist them if they were attacked by the Soviet Union or Germany. He hoped conflict with Soviet forces would be avoided, since they were far from Gällivare, but agreed that Germany could be expected to invade Sweden if ore supplies were interrupted. Churchill thought a Scandinavian campaign would enable Britain to exploit its advantage in amphibious warfare, and mentioned April as the likely time for a campaign. He urged that meantime steps should be taken to halt the Narvik ore trade. However, Halifax pointed out that a military operation to control the Gällivare ore-field would depend on Norwegian and Swedish good will, which would be lost if Churchill's proposed naval operation went ahead, and Chamberlain agreed with the foreign minister that it would be a mistake to prejudice the greater objective.[45]

At the War Cabinet on 10 January 1940, Halifax and Chamberlain favoured bringing diplomatic pressure to bear on Stockholm and Oslo to curb ore exports to Germany, but Churchill protested against further waste of time and urged immediate naval action to stop the trade through Narvik. He doubted if the Germans would respond by invading Norway, but argued it was to the Allies' advantage that 'the Scandinavian countries should be embroiled with Germany and that the war should extend to Scandinavia'. On a recent visit to France he had found the French high command fully agreed with this view and was ready to assist with alpine troops. He thought the neutrals should not be allowed to tie the hands of the Allies when the Allies were fighting to maintain the neutrals' liberties. The War Cabinet deferred a decision pending further negotiations with Sweden, but did agree to planning and initial preparations for a Scandinavian campaign.[46] Ten days later Churchill made a world broadcast in which he criticised neutral states for not taking a stand against German aggression: 'Each one hopes that if he feeds the crocodile enough, the crocodile will eat him last'. Chamberlain thought the broadcast did 'incalculable harm' by offending small neutral countries, especially in Scandinavia.[47]

The chiefs of staff were in favour of the Gällivare operation, although their advice on how to go about it was less than clear. They were prepared to risk conflict with Soviet forces, of which they had a poor opinion, if, as the Ministry of Economic Warfare believed, it would be a decisive blow against Germany.[48] The French high command was keen for offensive action in Scandinavia as the prospect of continuing German-Soviet collaboration had undermined its belief that the Allies could win a long war. Instead French planners looked for ways in which to achieve a rapid victory.[49] Agreement was reached on 5 February 1940 at the Supreme War Council – which brought together the leading members of the British and French governments – on a plan for an Allied expedition to Narvik. However, at the War Cabinet on 18 February the secretary of state for war, now Oliver Stanley, warned that most of the divisions earmarked for operations in Scandinavia had not reached a 'very advanced state of training', and Chamberlain remarked that doubts about the quality of the troops were a new and disturbing feature in the discussion.[50] Churchill was undeterred. On the next day he persuaded the War Cabinet to allow him to make preparations for minelaying off Narvik, pending a final decision. He predicted the Germans might be provoked into 'an imprudent action which would open the door for us'.[51] However, Chamberlain consulted the leaders of the Opposition parties about whether Britain would be justified in breaking international law by taking action in Norwegian waters and was told by Attlee it would be wrong to expose Norway to attacks by Germany. The prime minister was also concerned about the effects on American public opinion. He told Churchill the project should be put aside for the moment – a decision Churchill described as 'disastrous', but which he accepted in the War Cabinet on 29 February.[52]

All hopes for using aid for Finland as cover for a take-over of the Swedish ore-field vanished when news came on 13 March that the Finns had signed an armistice with the Soviets. Most of the British troops that had been earmarked to go to Finland were sent to France. Nevertheless, the French still pressed for the Narvik mining operation to go ahead, in the hope the German reaction might provide the Allies with an opportunity to occupy Gällivare. Indeed the French government was so anxious for offensive action that it also proposed bombing the Soviet oil field at Baku to stop exports to Germany. The Baku project was supported by Churchill's friend, Morton, at the Ministry of Economic Warfare although there was little evidence that the Soviets were supplying Germany with significant quantities of oil.[53] Halifax sensibly wondered whether Allied bombers would be able to do serious damage.[54] Churchill, without offering any evidence, said Baku oil was comparable to Swedish iron ore in importance to the German economy, and wanted the foreign secretary to sound out the Turks about co-operation in a bombing operation, adding, somewhat optimistically, that 'it was just possible that such action might not involve us in war with

Russia'.[55] At the Supreme War Council meeting on 28 March, however, Chamberlain pointed out that German oil supplies also came from Romania and Galicia (in Soviet-occupied Poland). He offered the new French premier, Paul Reynaud, no more than a study of the possibilities of an attack on Baku, a move clearly designed to sidetrack the proposal. Chamberlain said it would be most unwise to think the Allies could win the war by short cuts. The main weapon, he said, must be blockade, which required patience as its effects were slow. He did not intend to stop short of victory, and described a 'patched-up' peace as the worst possible outcome.[56] Whatever Chamberlain's shortcomings as a war leader, here is further evidence he was not anxious to negotiate a settlement with Germany.

The Supreme War Council agreed that the Narvik minefield should be laid on 5 April and also – subject to approval by the French *Conseil de Guerre* – that floating mines should be dropped into German rivers. The latter was a scheme devised by Professor Lindemann and had been advocated by Churchill since November. However, Edouard Daladier, now minister of war, feared it would provoke German retaliation in the form of air raids against France and the *Conseil* withheld its assent. Churchill flew to Paris but failed to persuade Daladier to change his mind or Reynaud to overrule his minister of war. The upshot was a delay to the Narvik operation until 8 April.[57] Even as Royal Navy units steamed towards the Norwegian coast, the Germans were also on the move. The prolonged negotiations with Scandinavian governments had given the Germans ample notice of Allied intentions and to prepare to occupy Denmark and Norway, while respecting Swedish neutrality.

There is a temptation, from which Churchill was not free, to believe the Norwegian campaign would have had a more favourable outcome if Chamberlain had not held up the Narvik operation for so long.[58] Churchill had doubted whether the Germans would react strongly to naval measures to block the ore trade, although the chiefs of staff had warned that they would, and, with its best divisions in France, the army was not ready for a new theatre of war. Ironside had noted in his diary in January that Churchill's scheme was 'half-cock' and 'the Dardanelles over again' (a reference to Churchill's action in 1915 in launching a naval attack without army support).[59] The chiefs of staff's own planning against German intervention was inadequate. Eight battalions were assigned to protect Narvik, Trondheim and Bergen, and deny the Germans the use of the airfield at Stavanger. No artillery was considered necessary, and there was no mention of air support. The defence of Oslo was left to the Norwegians, who, although they had initial success against German warships, proved to be unable to prevent German airborne troops from seizing the airport there on 9 April and establishing command of the air. Whereas the chiefs of staff had assumed British command of the sea would prevent the Germans from occupying central or northern Norway, German troops also seized Narvik, Trondheim, Bergen and Stavanger by surprise attacks from ships sent before the British arrived. RAF reconnaissance aircraft had spotted unusual activity in north German harbours, and there were numerous SIS reports that gave indications of German intentions. Failure to anticipate the invasion reflected badly on British intelligence which, despite the establishment of the JIC, was still ill-coordinated. Indeed, despite months of planning for a Scandinavian campaign, the British remained remarkably uninformed about Norway's armed forces and topography. There was not even a military attaché at the embassy in Oslo.[60]

Given Churchill's interest in military detail, he cannot be absolved from shortcomings in British planning. He had, for example, confidently declared that the mountainous nature of the Norwegian countryside excluded the use of tanks, but the Germans were able to employ tanks to good effect against British troops in central Norway.[61] Moreover, he interfered with the conduct of operations. When late in the evening of 7 April the German fleet was reported to be at sea, Churchill and Admiral Pound, the first sea lord, ordered troops aboard four cruisers to be disembarked so that the ships could hunt for the Germans. The other chiefs of staff were not informed, let alone consulted. In John Kiszely's estimation, the land campaign never recovered from the delay and confusion caused by this blunder.[62] On 14 April, as chairman of the Cabinet's Military Coordination Committee, Churchill insisted on half of the convoy carrying the force going to Narvik being diverted to Namsos, in an attempt to take Trondheim, although Ironside rightly warned the result would be confusion. Chamberlain complained that Churchill changed his mind four times about whether to carry out the Trondheim operation, with the final decision of the Military Coordination Committee on 26 April being not to do so.[63] By the beginning of May it was clear the Allies had been defeated in central Norway, and Narvik remained in German hands.

No one was more responsible than Churchill for the fiasco in Norway, but it was Chamberlain who paid the political price. The Opposition parties made the adjournment debate on 7 and 8 May a vote of confidence. Attlee declared that Norway came 'as the culmination of many other discontents' since 1931. He mocked Chamberlain's claim in a recent speech that Hitler had 'missed the bus' by not attacking Britain and France after the Polish campaign and denounced the government for failing to organise the country effectively.[64] As for the Norwegian campaign, Admiral Sir Roger Keyes, a First World War hero now a

Conservative MP, appeared in his uniform, to denounce the government's ineptitude, while expressing admiration for Churchill. Leo Amery, another Conservative supporter of Churchill, called for a real National Government that would include the Labour Party, and, addressing himself to the present National Government, quoted Cromwell's words when dismissing the Long Parliament: 'You have sat too long here for any good you have been doing. Depart, I say, and let us have done with you. In the name of God go!'[65] Churchill loyally defended the government, but some 40 Conservatives voted against it and 80 or more abstained, reducing its majority to 81.

It was clear the government would have to be reconstructed to bring in Labour and Liberal ministers, but Labour would not serve under Chamberlain. Halifax, as a peer, could not lead effectively from outside the House of Commons. It fell to Churchill, therefore, to be prime minister. Chamberlain continued to be leader of the Conservative Party and was a member of Churchill's War Cabinet along with Attlee and Arthur Greenwood from the Labour Party, and Halifax. The new government was formed in the evening of 10 May 1940, the day the Germans launched their offensive in the west. Chamberlain regarded it as providential that he should be relieved of the primary responsibility for decisions which would bring 'death & mutilation & misery to so many'.[66] Churchill, in contrast, experienced 'a profound sense of relief' now he had the authority to direct the conduct of the war. As he recalled, 'I felt I was walking with destiny and that all my past life had been but preparation for this hour and this trial'.[67]

10.3   Finest Hour

The German offensive that began on 10 May breached the neutrality of Holland, Belgium and Luxembourg. The rival armies were evenly matched: 144 Allied divisions faced 141 German divisions, and the Allies had more artillery and tanks. The British and French air forces combined had more aircraft than the Germans, but both were strategically dispersed, on account of fears of German strategic bombing. The Germans gained a decisive advantage by concentrating both the Luftwaffe and panzer divisions at a weak point in the Allied line.[68] On 14 May news came of a breakthrough at Sedan. On the same day the Dutch army capitulated. The French premier, Reynaud, phoned Churchill early in the morning of the 15th to tell him the battle was lost and to beg for more assistance. Churchill replied that Britain could not send troops more quickly than it was doing.[69]

At the War Cabinet later that morning it was decided to start bombing synthetic oil refineries and rail marshalling yards in the Ruhr. Churchill enthused that the operations would 'cut Germany at its tap root' and might have an immediate effect on the land battle.[70] In the event, the RAF's attacks, conducted at night, were wholly ineffective, but intelligence reports fed unrealistic, albeit diminishing, hopes that the Ruhr raids would have a decisive effect on German morale.[71] In the morning of the next day, the 16th, when the War Cabinet considered an appeal from the French chief of staff, Gamelin, for ten additional fighter squadrons to be sent at once to France, Churchill said a balance had to be struck between what he called the 'very grave risk' of weakening Britain's air defences and the need to bolster French morale, and he favoured sending only six.[72] He decided to make what Chamberlain described as a 'courageous visit' to Paris that afternoon to discuss the situation and found the French so depressed that he asked for approval by the War Cabinet by midnight for all 10 squadrons to be sent, and a hastily convened meeting chaired by Chamberlain at 11 p.m. gave it.[73]

Chamberlain seems to have been shaken by the news from France. He told the American ambassador, Joseph Kennedy, on 16 May that, if the French collapsed, Britain's only chance of escaping destruction would be if Roosevelt made an appeal for an armistice, but Chamberlain thought it unlikely the Germans would respond.[74] In the evening of the 17th Churchill asked him to examine the consequences of Paris falling to the Germans and the problems that would arise if the BEF had to be withdrawn from France. Chamberlain produced a report within 24 hours. He told the War Cabinet that, if Britain had to fight on single-handed until the United States 'could be induced to come to our help', it would be imperative to change 'our present rather easy-going methods and resort to a form of government which would approach the totalitarian'. In particular, he said, the government should take powers to exercise complete control over property, businesses and labour, and the War Cabinet asked him to work out legislation. Chamberlain recommended that the prime minister should prepare the way by speaking to the nation to explain the seriousness of the situation and the need for sacrifices.[75] Churchill's broadcast, his first as prime minister, on Sunday 19 May confidently predicted the front in France would be stabilised, but warned the German air force would then turn on Britain and in that supreme emergency the 'interests of property and the hours of labour' would be as nothing compared with the struggle for freedom.[76] Under the Emergency Powers (Defence) Act of 22 May 1940, the minister of labour and national service, the trade unionist Ernest Bevin, was empowered to direct any person in the United Kingdom to do any work in any place.

Meanwhile the military position deteriorated further. On 19 May the chief of the imperial general staff, Ironside, warned the War Cabinet that the British and Belgian armies were in danger of being cut off from the main French armies as the Germans advanced towards the coast. Churchill decided no more fighters should be sent to France; instead Fighter Command should be conserved to cover the evacuation of the British Expeditionary Force (BEF) from the continent, should that be necessary.[77] Chamberlain noted in his diary the same day that the Germans could be expected to present an ultimatum soon, and 'though the terms will probably be such as to force us to fight on, we should be fighting only for better terms, not for victory'.[78] Churchill was hardly more positive in a telegram to Roosevelt on the 20th when he said 'our intention is, whatever happens, to fight on to the end in this Island' and, if the Americans supplied modern aircraft, 'we hope to run [the Germans] very close in the air battles'. Churchill did not suggest Britain could win single-handed. Indeed he put pressure on the president by offering the apocalyptic vision of a successor government of a defeated Britain using its fleet as a bargaining counter to negotiate the best terms it could with Germany, and thereby raising the prospect of Hitler controlling a larger navy than the United States.[79]

The Germans reached the Channel coast on 20 May, but Churchill was heartened the next day when General Maxime Weygand, who had replaced Gamelin as chief of staff, put forward a plan for simultaneous counter-attacks by the BEF and the French to close the gap created by the German advance. Churchill flew to Paris on the 22nd to meet Reynaud and Weygand, and, according to Ironside, returned in the evening 'almost in buoyant spirits' to tell the War Cabinet he had agreed the attacks should begin the next day. Ironside said more time would be required for preparation and doubted whether French morale was good. Moreover, the German advance had cut the BEF off from its supply depots and it was consequently short of food and munitions.[80] Over the next three days it was unclear what was happening in France, but in the evening of the 25th Churchill accepted the Weygand plan could not succeed and that the BEF would have to be evacuated by sea.

Unsurprisingly, Chamberlain was pessimistic when he heard of this decision at the War Cabinet early on Sunday, 26 May, as ministers had already been told there was little chance of the navy being able to take off more than a fraction of the troops. Reynaud came to London that day and, after learning via Churchill that the French no longer believed the war could be won on land, Chamberlain commented it was 'plain from his [Reynaud's] attitude that he had given up all idea of serious fighting and if we are to go on we shall be alone'. On 27 May news came that the Belgian army was on the brink of surrender, exposing the BEF's left flank, leading Chamberlain to believe it was 'unlikely that any substantial number of the BEF will get away'.[81] It was against this background of military catastrophe that the War Cabinet debated from 26 to 28 May whether Britain and France should approach Mussolini to explore the possibility of his mediation leading to a negotiated peace with Germany.

German military success had made Italian entry into the war increasingly likely and Allied diplomacy sought at least to delay that eventuality. On 16 May Churchill had sent a personal message to Mussolini that combined expressions of goodwill and defiance, but had received an answer which even Ciano, the Italian foreign minister, described as 'needlessly harsh in tone'.[82] On 24 May the War Cabinet agreed to a French proposal for making an approach to Mussolini through Roosevelt, offering to enter negotiations on Italian claims in the Mediterranean in return for Italy keeping out of the war. On the following day Churchill authorised secret direct contact between Sir Robert Vansittart, the chief diplomatic adviser, and the Italian embassy.[83] However, at a 9 a.m. War Cabinet on 26 May the prime minister baulked at an enquiry from the Italian ambassador, Giuseppe Bastianini, about whether Britain would agree to a peace conference. Halifax, still foreign secretary, was prepared to consider proposals that might lead to peace and security as he believed Germany could no longer be defeated and the question was how to safeguard Britain's independence and Empire. Churchill opposed any negotiations that would lead to acceptance of German domination of Europe.[84]

At a second meeting in the afternoon Halifax argued that the last thing Mussolini wanted was German domination of Europe and he would therefore be anxious to moderate Hitler's demands.[85] Ministers then held an informal meeting at which the cabinet secretary, Sir Edward Bridges, was not present for the first 15 minutes. It was during this time when, according to Chamberlain's diary, Churchill said 'it was incredible that Hitler would consent to any terms that we could accept – though if we could get out of this jam, by giving up Malta and Gibraltar and some African colonies, he [Churchill] would jump at it'.[86] These words, which do not appear in Martin Gilbert's official biography, have been interpreted by David Reynolds as evidence of Churchill wrestling with doubt, and they are certainly at odds with the myth, propagated by Churchill, that the question of whether to fight on was never considered by ministers.[87] In the part of the discussion recorded by Bridges, Churchill said there was no limit to the terms Germany would impose if she could, and no approach should be made to Mussolini before Britain had been involved in serious fighting. Attlee and Chamberlain, overrating the effects of the blockade, believed Germany had only a limited time in which to achieve victory. Halifax thought that Hitler, on account of this supposed internal weakness of the Nazi regime, might not insist on outrageous terms and had hopes that Mussolini might act as a mediator, but Chamberlain doubted Mussolini's ability to act independently of Hitler.[88]

Most of the discussion at the morning meeting of the War Cabinet on 27 May centred on a report by the chiefs of staff on how Britain could continue the war single-handed if French resistance collapsed and a substantial proportion of the BEF was lost. The chiefs of staff thought Britain would be unable to do so with any chance of success unless the United States provided full economic and financial support. Germany would, however, have to achieve air superiority before attempting an invasion. Britain's weak spot was identified as its aircraft factories, which the chiefs feared might be put out of action by air raids at night, when the air defences would be less effective.[89] Having read the report, Chamberlain suggested he should see the dominion high commissioners to tell them that, even if France fell, the government had good reason to believe Britain could withstand an attack by Germany and was resolved to fight on. However, he said this statement would apply to the immediate situation following a French collapse, and would not preclude considering terms offered on their merits.[90] Chamberlain thus took an intermediate position between Churchill and Halifax.

At the afternoon meeting Halifax explained Reynaud wanted a direct Anglo-French approach to Mussolini, asking for his co-operation in seeking a peace settlement that would secure the independence of the Allies, and promising to do their best to meet his claims in the Mediterranean. Chamberlain thought such an approach would serve no useful purpose since Mussolini would hold off from bargaining until Paris had fallen. On the other hand, Chamberlain was concerned about the effect a completely negative attitude would have on the French. Sir Archibald Sinclair, the secretary of state for air, who was not a member of the War Cabinet, but who had been invited by Churchill to take part in the discussion as leader of the Liberal Party, and who, as an old Western Front comrade, could be relied upon to support the prime minister, said any suggestion of bartering away British territory would encourage the Germans and Italians, and weaken morale, making it difficult to continue what was a desperate struggle. The Labour members, Attlee and Greenwood, agreed. Churchill said the only way Britain could restore its prestige in Europe was to hold out against the Germans for two or three months, and 'even if we were beaten we would be no worse off than we would be if we were now to abandon the struggle'. He believed negotiations would prove to be a slippery slope from which it would be difficult to turn back. The War Cabinet then agreed to a proposal by Chamberlain that the French should be asked to await the outcome of the approach through Roosevelt that had been agreed on the 24th.[91]

There the matter might have rested, but Halifax protested he did not recognise any resemblance between the action he had proposed and Churchill's suggestion that Britain would be suing for terms and the result would be disaster. He recalled that Churchill himself had said the previous day he (the prime minister) would be thankful to get out of the present difficulties on terms which would not affect matters vital to British independence, and would be prepared to discuss cession of British territory. Now, however, Churchill seemed to be suggesting that under no conditions would any course other than fighting to a finish be contemplated. Halifax considered the matter was probably academic, since it was unlikely that acceptable terms would be offered, but, if they were, he doubted he could agree to continue the war to see if Britain could stand up to air attacks. He was prepared to take that risk if Britain's independence was at stake, but, if it was not, he would accept an offer which would save the country from avoidable disaster. (In the privacy of his diary Halifax wrote that Churchill had been talking 'the most frightful rot'.) Challenged by Halifax, Churchill said he would not join with France in asking for terms, but conceded that if he were told what the terms were he would consider them. Halifax was so exasperated he contemplated resignation, but was dissuaded by a combination of Churchill's charm and sober advice from Sir Alexander Cadogan and Chamberlain.[92]

The next two War Cabinet meetings – at 10 p.m. on the 27th and 11.30 a.m. on the 28th – were principally concerned with the grave implications for the BEF of the Belgian surrender, which took effect at dawn on the 28th. The War Cabinet, plus Sinclair, met that day at 4 p.m. to discuss a further request from Reynaud for a direct Anglo-French approach to Italy now that it had become clear Mussolini would not respond favourably to one by Roosevelt. Churchill said Reynaud wanted Italian mediation that would lead to a conference with Hitler. The prime minister warned that when Hitler's terms were rejected, as they would be, 'we should find that all the forces of resolution which were now at our disposal would have vanished'. The position would be entirely different, he said, after Germany had made an unsuccessful attempt to invade Britain. Halifax still thought Britain could get better terms before the French left the war and while British aircraft factories were intact. Chamberlain, however, together with Attlee and Greenwood, agreed with Churchill's diagnosis. Mediation at this stage, when the Allies had suffered military disaster, and when it seemed their resources were exhausted, would have the most unfortunate results, Chamberlain said, and he thought France as well as Britain would fare better by continuing the struggle. On the other hand, Chamberlain agreed with Halifax that, if peace terms were offered that did not threaten Britain's independence, they should be considered (as Churchill had grudgingly conceded the previous day). Chamberlain was concerned the response to Reynaud's request should not give France the pretext to give up the struggle at once. At this point the meeting adjourned as Churchill was due to meet with ministers who were not members of the War Cabinet, some 25 in all, at 6 p.m. Dalton, the minister of economic warfare, recorded in his diary that Churchill was magnificent when he gave them a frank and calm account of the situation: the difficulty of evacuating the BEF from Dunkirk, the need to prepare public opinion for bad news, and the danger of invasion. Churchill's dismissal of the idea of peace negotiations with Hitler was met with enthusiasm, which the prime minister reported to the War Cabinet when it resumed at 7 p.m. Chamberlain meanwhile had drafted a reply to Reynaud, designed to persuade him it was worthwhile to go on fighting, and Churchill expressed himself as 'exceedingly satisfied' with its terms.[93] The question of whether to negotiate peace terms never returned to the War Cabinet agenda.

Martin Gilbert and John Lukacs' extensive accounts of the War Cabinet's debate from 26 to 28 May both focus on how Churchill's passionate arguments, based on the need to maintain national morale, overcame Halifax's cool, rational analysis.[94] Robert Self, however, considered Chamberlain's intervention on 28 May was decisive, in that if he had come down in favour of Halifax, the prime minister's case for continuing to fight would have been 'dangerously compromised, even undermined'.[95] Churchill might still have prevailed, since he had the support of the Labour members of the War Cabinet, but his position would have been awkward if both of the other Conservative members, including the leader of the party, had opposed him. In the event Chamberlain was firmly in favour of fighting on. It is impossible to reconcile Chamberlain's role in the War Cabinet's debate with depictions of him as a man anxious to make peace.

The evacuation of the BEF from Dunkirk between 26 May and 3 June 1940 was much more successful than anticipated, some 222,500 British troops and more than 100,000 French troops being taken off. Even so, the BEF had lost 68,000 men killed, wounded or taken prisoner, and the artillery, tanks and vehicles of nine divisions had been lost. The War Cabinet decided on 3 June that no further fighter squadrons were to be sent to France in view of the heavy casualties suffered since 10 May and the need to maintain Fighter Command at a level adequate to defend the United Kingdom.[96] In an attempt to maintain French morale, Churchill departed from this decision by promising Reynaud on 5 June to send two fighter squadrons, but on 8 June the prime minister told the War

Cabinet's Defence Committee that no more should be sent since Britain could carry on the struggle only if its air defences were unimpaired.[97] On 10 June Mussolini declared war in order to share the spoils of Germany's imminent victory. Churchill's efforts to raise French morale by flying two more times to France for meetings of the Supreme War Council on 11 and 12 June at Briare, near Orleans, and on 13 June at Tours, were unavailing, and on 14 June, the day the Germans entered Paris, he agreed to the withdrawal of the remaining 150,000 British troops in France. After Reynaud resigned on 16 June, Marshal Philippe Pétain formed a new government and immediately asked for an armistice, which took effect on 25 June.

Even before the fall of France Chamberlain was attacked in Labour and Liberal newspapers for the unpreparedness of the BEF, and the government's Home Intelligence reports on public opinion indicated widespread hostility to him and his government on this account. The authors of the polemic *Guilty Men* published in July, opened with an account of Dunkirk, attributing the defeat to a lack of tanks and dive bombers, and blaming Chamberlain, although to a lesser extent than Baldwin, for failing to rearm sufficiently to deter aggression.[98] However, plenty of tanks were being produced in Britain in 1939–40, and responsibility for design faults or the organisation of armoured divisions lay with the War Office. Likewise the RAF's lack of dive bombers reflected Air Ministry doctrines on the tactical and strategical employment of aircraft. The BEF had shortcomings in equipment and, as regards Territorial units, training, and Chamberlain could fairly be criticized for these insofar as they arose from restrictions on rearmament down to February 1939 and the hasty expansion of the army thereafter. However, not all of the BEF's deficiencies could be blamed on him: for example, it had a less flexible command and control doctrine than the Germans; a communications system that was inappropriate for mobile warfare; lack of training in combined arms tactics; and neglect of intelligence and signal security.[99] Even so, the army's performance in Belgium and France was better than *Guilty Men* implied. A War Office committee reviewing lessons learned from the campaign noted that the BEF had never been forced to retreat by frontal attack. All withdrawals had been undertaken to conform to the movements of Allied forces on its flanks.[100]

The priority given by Chamberlain and Churchill to the air force was reflected in aircraft production, where British output exceeded German by 40 per cent in 1940. Contrary to what Churchill implied in his memoirs, increased output in 1940 owed nothing to the appointment of Lord Beaverbrook to head a new Ministry of Aircraft Production in May, but was instead the consequence of new industrial capacity created when

Chamberlain was prime minister coming on stream.[101] Chamberlain was encouraged by the success of the RAF in skirmishes with the Luftwaffe early in July. In response to accusations that the 'Men of Munich' had failed to prepare for war, he remarked 'if I am personally responsible for the deficiencies of tanks ... I must be equally personally responsible for the efficiency of the air force and the navy'.[102] He shared Churchill's confidence that Britain could repel a German invasion. On 14 July he wrote to his sisters: 'We must just go on fighting as hard as we can in the belief that some time – perhaps sooner than we think – the other side will crack.'[103] A peace offer by Hitler on 19 July 1940 in the Reichstag led Chamberlain to comment that there was nothing in it to encourage a peace party in Britain, and to remark yet again on Hitler's untrustworthiness.[104] The Luftwaffe's major assault was launched on 10 August, but Fighter Command withstood the test, and on 17 September Hitler postponed his planned invasion indefinitely.

Churchill's advent as prime minister did, of course, make a difference. His speeches, in which he offered nothing but 'blood, toil, tears and sweat' and said the British would fight on the beaches, on landing grounds, in the fields, in the streets, and in the hills, and would never surrender, perfectly matched the nation's mood. No one did more to convince servicemen and civilians that what he called the Battle of Britain would prove to be 'their finest hour'.[105] However, Britain's strategic position was such that even Churchill had to resort to appeasement of Japan. On 24 June, the day before the ceasefire in France, Japan demanded that Britain stop the transit of war materials to China via the Burma Road (in what is now Myanmar). The American government made clear Britain must not count on any material help from the United States, and Chamberlain was relieved when Churchill, 'with the responsibilities of a PM on his shoulders', was firmly against taking a bold line with the Japanese. On 18 July Churchill announced a three-month closure of the Burma Road, to gain time, he claimed, for a 'just' solution to be found to the Sino-Japanese dispute by 'a process of peace and conciliation', to which Britain would contribute.[106] It was a sign of growing confidence after the Battle of Britain that he felt able to reopen the road at the end of the three-month period.

10.4   The Limits of British Power

War highlighted Britain's need for American assistance. In the crisis after 10 May 1940 Churchill pressed Roosevelt to sell aircraft, anti-aircraft equipment and steel without regard to the financial position. 'We shall go on paying dollars for as long as we can', he told the president on 15 May, 'but I should like to feel reasonably sure that when we can pay no more, you will give us the stuff all the same'. Roosevelt gave no such reassurance at that time.[107] Chamberlain was at one with Churchill on the need for purchases in the United States: on 16 June he suggested that American manufacturers be assured that, if the French abandoned the struggle, Britain would take over all their contracts.[108] On 22 August the Treasury warned that, at the current rate of expenditure, Britain would run out of gold at the end of December, and would have to rely thereafter on expedients like requisitioning wedding rings and gold ornaments. Churchill responded by saying there could be no question of curbing orders in North America: 'If the military position should unexpectedly deteriorate we should have to pledge everything that we had for the sake of victory, giving the United States, if necessary, a lien on any and every part of British industry'.[109]

The only thing certain about American aid was that it would not be unconditional. In his letter to Roosevelt on 15 May Churchill had been particularly concerned to borrow older American destroyers for the Royal Navy, such vessels being urgently required as anti-submarine escorts. However, Roosevelt had first to be persuaded that the British would not be defeated and the destroyers would not fall into German hands. It was not until early August, when his special emissary, Colonel William Donovan, returned from London after meetings with Churchill and senior officials, visits to factories and a tour of Britain's defences, that the president was reassured on these points. Even then Roosevelt felt he could not release the destroyers without some quid pro quo to satisfy domestic critics in an election year when he hoped to secure an unprecedented third term as president. It was not until 2 September that agreement was reached whereby Britain would receive 50 destroyers dating from the First World War in return for leases of land in Newfoundland (then administered by Britain) and British colonies in the Caribbean on which the United States could build air and naval bases, plus a public declaration that, if Britain were defeated, the Royal Navy would not be surrendered or scuttled. Roosevelt's request for the declaration reflected a continuing element of doubt in America about the outcome of the war.[110]

The British had by no means abandoned hope of victory. On 4 September the chiefs of staff produced a paper on 'Future Strategy' which identified oil as Germany's key weakness. Existing stocks and sources of supply were thought to be adequate only until mid-1941, and Germany was expected before then to attempt to seize control of the Eastern Mediterranean to enable her to import oil from Romania and the Soviet Union by sea. The elimination of Italy from the war would thus be a major strategic success. The chiefs of staff advised that, before taking major offensive operations against Germany in 1942, Britain should seek to weaken her through blockade, air attacks, minor amphibious operations and sabotage of economic targets and communications by the Special Operations Executive (SOE) recently created by Churchill. They regarded the entry of the United States into the war as highly desirable, but not essential, provided the Americans gave all the economic and financial support Britain required.[111]

On 17 December 1940, after the presidential election, Roosevelt came up with the idea of lend-lease, whereby supplies would be handed over to Britain, if the president thought that was the best way of employing them for the defence of the United States. Congress was persuaded to pass the Lend-Lease Act in March 1941 by the president's promise that the United States would receive, not money, but some 'consideration' to be negotiated in return. Members of the Roosevelt administration wished to prevent Britain's defeat by Germany, but they also wished to promote the interests of the United States. Henry Morgenthau, the secretary of the treasury, was suspicious of how the sterling area operated to Britain's advantage in trade, and intended to reconstruct international monetary relations in a way that would secure American dominance, as happened at the Bretton Woods conference in 1944. Cordell Hull, the secretary of state, hoped to press Britain into abandoning imperial preference and any other form of discrimination against American goods. Article VII of the Mutual Aid Agreement signed in February 1942 committed Britain to embrace multilateralism. Lend-lease was administered in a way that deliberately kept Britain in a state of financial weakness and reliant on American goodwill. When Britain's dollar reserves tended to rise as a result of American expenditure in the sterling area after the United States entered the war in December 1941, the range of non-military supplies covered by lend-lease was reduced, thereby forcing Britain to spend its dollars.[112] Churchill's policy of victory at any cost also led to Britain incurring huge debts in sterling area countries for goods and services. Overseas investments were sold and the gold reserves reduced to the bare minimum required for the management of the sterling area. The financial strength that had underpinned Britain's position as a great power was exhausted and in 1945 Britain faced what Keynes called 'a financial Dunkirk', unable to sustain a world role without continuing dependence on the United States.[113]

Even after Churchill abandoned financial prudence in 1940, Britain's armed forces struggled to protect all of its empire. They enjoyed success against the Italians. An attack by a single aircraft carrier on the naval base at Taranto on the night of 9/10 November 1940 put half the Italian battle fleet out of action and three of Italy's seven heavy cruisers were sunk in a battle off Cape Matapan on the night of 28/29 March 1941. Between 9 December 1940 and 8 February 1941 an Italian army was destroyed by a British and imperial force about a third of its size in a desert campaign. However, Hitler sent aid to Mussolini and in April 1941 the German *Afrika Korps*, led by General Erwin Rommel, advanced to the Egyptian frontier. On 28 April Churchill issued a directive in which he stated that the loss of Egypt and the Middle East would be a disaster second in magnitude only to a successful invasion of Britain. On the other hand, he believed the danger of Japan entering the war was remote, and that, if she did, the United States would almost certainly come in on Britain's side. The chief of the imperial general staff, Sir John Dill, pointed out on 6 May that 'it was an accepted principle of our strategy that in the last resort the security of Singapore comes before that of Egypt'; yet Singapore's defences were well below what was needed. Churchill responded that Singapore required only a fraction of the forces required for the defence of Egypt, and that therefore Singapore and Egypt were not comparable alternatives.[114] Churchill persisted in referring to Singapore as a 'fortress', although the chiefs of staff had advised in August 1940 that it would be necessary to defend the whole of Malaya, and not just the naval base. Primary responsibility for the defence of Malaya had been given to the RAF, but Churchill repeatedly questioned the need to station aircraft there far from active operations. Of the 22 planned squadrons, only 12 were in place when the Japanese attacked on 7 December 1941. Moreover, most were equipped with obsolescent aircraft.[115]

The disagreement between Dill and Churchill was symptomatic of the strategic overstretch that had been apparent since the Defence Requirements Sub-Committee's report in 1934. Like Chamberlain, Churchill gave priority to the threat from Germany. By late 1941 wartime losses had reduced the size of the fleet that could be sent to the Far East. Churchill hoped to deter Japan by stationing the new capital ship, the *Prince of Wales*, and the battle-cruiser *Repulse* at Singapore. Their purpose was primarily political, to impress both the Japanese and the Americans regarding Britain's determination to defend its interests. When war broke out, Churchill thought the ships should cross the Pacific to join what was left of the American fleet after the Japanese attack on Pearl Harbor. The decision to use them in an attempt to disrupt Japanese landings on the coast of Malaya was taken by their commander, Admiral Sir Tom Phillips, who, as director of plans at the Admiralty from 1935 to 1938, had over-estimated the effectiveness of anti-aircraft guns. Churchill was not, there-fore, directly responsible for the loss of the ships when they were sunk by Japanese aircraft.[116] However, the inability of the RAF to provide the navy or ground forces with adequate air cover can be traced to his opposition to stationing aircraft in the Far East. Churchill admitted he had not taken the same interest in the Far East as in Europe and the Middle East. He was surprised to learn that Singapore was not a fortress, lacking as it did defences on its landward side.[117] The surrender of Singapore on 15 February 1942, and the loss of 9,000 men killed and wounded, and 130,000 taken prisoner, to a numerically inferior Japanese force was, as Churchill himself said, 'the worst disaster and largest capitulation in British history'.[118] Few people bore more responsibility than he did. British prestige in the Far East never recovered.

Churchill achieved victory in partnership with Stalin (following Hitler's attack on the Soviet Union in June 1941) and Roosevelt. However, even in victory he was no more able to influence events in Central and Eastern Europe than Chamberlain had been in 1938. David Carlton and John Charmley judged concessions made by Churchill to Stalin, particularly as regards Poland, whose borders were redrawn and whose government in exile in London was replaced by one acceptable to the Soviets, to be morally equivalent to Chamberlain's appeasement.[119] Churchill was outraged by Stalin's decision to hold back the Red Army in August and September 1944 in order to let the Germans defeat the anti-Communist Polish Underground Army rising in Warsaw, but acquiesced in Stalin's refusal to enable the British and American air forces to drop supplies to the Poles. As he subsequently admitted: 'terrible and even humbling submissions must at times be made to the general aim'.[120] After the Yalta conference in February 1945, when agreement was reached on a provisional government and elections in Poland, Hugh Dalton recorded Churchill as saying: 'Poor Neville believed he could trust Hitler. He was wrong. But I don't think I'm wrong about Stalin.'[121] In the event, although Stalin did not insist initially on a wholly Communist regime, Poland became a Soviet satellite and non-Communist elements were eliminated from the government when his suspicions of American intentions led him to erect the Iron Curtain. Similar fates befell Czechoslovakia, Romania, Hungary and Bulgaria. The Baltic States were re-absorbed into the Soviet Union. Churchill's experience of dealing with Stalin suggests that an alliance with the Soviet Union in 1938 or 1939 would have entailed ruthless realpolitik at the expense of states on its borders.

11 Counterfactuals and Conclusions

11.1 What Would Churchill Have Done?

The reader is invited to imagine, on the basis of evidence presented in earlier chapters, what might have happened if Churchill rather than Chamberlain had become chancellor of the exchequer in 1931 and had succeeded Baldwin as prime minister in 1937. Churchill's presence in the National Government would have made no difference to British policy towards Japan. On the contrary, Churchill sympathised with Japanese actions in China arising from the Manchurian 'incident' in 1931 and did not think the League of Nations could be effective in the Far East. By 1936 he was aware Japan was increasingly dominated by nationalist and militarist extremists, but when full-scale warfare broke out in China in 1937 he thought that, unless American public opinion were sufficiently aroused to make joint Anglo-American action possible, Japanese depredations on British interests there must be endured, since the major threat to Britain's security lay in Europe.

Would Churchill have been more successful than Chamberlain in developing a co-operative relationship with the United States? Churchill had warmer feelings towards Americans, but his views on war debt payments and the Johnson Act were the same as Chamberlain's. It is difficult to see how Churchill could have been much more accommodating than Chamberlain over the Tripartite Pact on exchange rate stability in 1936 or in the negotiations leading to the Anglo-American Trade Agreement of 1938. Churchill would no doubt have been more willing than Chamberlain was to meet Roosevelt in Washington, but would a visit by a British prime minister have reduced isolationist feeling, or would Americans have felt he was trying to involve them in Europe's quarrels? Churchill accused Chamberlain of discouraging Roosevelt from taking an interest in European affairs, but nevertheless sub-rosa co-operation developed between the Foreign Office and the State Department, and the US Navy and the Admiralty, in 1938–9. The fundamental obstacle to greater Anglo-American co-operation was American isolationism which prevented the repeal of neutrality legislation or the Johnson Act, and thereby lessened the deterrent value of Roosevelt's intention to support Britain and France through sales of aircraft and munitions.

Churchill's conception of collective security evolved through time. In November 1933 he believed co-operation with other European powers through the League of Nations could lead to peaceful mitigation of German grievances. His views on how to respond to Italian aggression in 1935 were shaped, like the government's, by a wish to preserve the League as a deterrent to German aggression, a recognition of the need not to take economic sanctions further than France was willing to go, and a hope of maintaining friendly relations with Italy. There is little reason, therefore, to suppose Britain would have backed collective security through the League any more vigorously in 1935–6 if Churchill had been in government. Consequently Hitler would still have been encouraged by what he took to be British weakness in handling Mussolini to occupy the Rhineland in March 1936. Churchill fully understood the far-reaching strategic consequences of Hitler's action, but equally recognised that British public opinion would not support the government in taking a leading role in any measures, even under the League, to secure the withdrawal of German troops. Although he was in frequent contact with the Soviet ambassador, Ivan Maisky, in the hope of securing Soviet support for collective security, the outbreak of the Spanish Civil War in July 1936 revived his anti-Communist instincts, and the Soviet Union did not feature prominently in his proposals for a grand alliance to contain Germany until 1938.

As prime minister from 1937, Churchill would no doubt have had a more robust attitude than Chamberlain towards Germany and Italy. Even so, Churchill approved the Foreign Office's efforts to enter dialogue with their German counterparts in 1937, being still uncertain about the likelihood of war. It was not until the Nazi takeover of Austria in March 1938 that he once more took up the theme of collective security through the League of Nations. He realised that France's system of alliances in Central Europe had been weakened. Nevertheless he did not propose any measures to restore Austrian independence, being deterred by the vulnerability of London to air attack (see page 179). As for Anglo-Italian relations, Churchill hoped, even after the outbreak of the Second World War, that common interests could draw Italy closer to Britain and France, and in this respect he was hardly less naïve than Chamberlain about Mussolini.

The difference between Churchill and Chamberlain in foreign policy became apparent during the crisis leading to the Munich conference. Whereas Chamberlain's fear of dividing Europe into opposing blocs led him to adopt bilateral negotiations with Hitler, Churchill thought in terms of deterrence through a grand alliance of Britain, France, the Soviet Union and lesser European powers, with moral support from the United States. His ideas were at variance with official advice in 1938. As regards the lesser powers, the chiefs of staff did not share his belief in their military value, and Foreign Office officials thought negotiations would take too long for alliances with them to be of any use in the immediate crisis. As for the Soviet Union, the Foreign Office advised that Stalin's purges had left the Red Army unable to conduct offensive operations effectively and that he would keep out of a war if he could. A prime minister could, of course, have disregarded this advice, but it is not clear it was wrong. The problems of the lesser powers and the Soviet Union were linked by the Poles' and Romanians' distrust of any Soviet presence on their territory, making it difficult for the Red Army to get to grips with the Germans. The Soviet Union might have agreed to Churchill's idea at the end of August 1938 for a joint note with Britain and France stating that a German invasion of Czechoslovakia would raise 'capital issues' (whatever that might mean) for all three signatories (see page 190). However, there is no certainty that Hitler would have been deterred by a declaration that was not backed by a military alliance. Churchill would not have travelled to Germany to negotiate, but he was apparently prepared to agree to a gradual transfer of the Sudetenland supervised by an international commission, provided the Germans demobilized first, Polish and Hungarian territorial claims were disregarded, and the remainder of Czechoslovakia was given a guarantee (see page 200). However, unlike Chamberlain, he was prepared to fight rather than accept what he considered to be a dishonourable settlement and, with the support of Halifax and Duff Cooper, would surely have carried the Cabinet with him in rejecting Hitler's terms. Hitler's likely reaction is hard to gauge: the prospect of Anglo-French intervention in September 1938 led him to abandon his plan to invade Czechoslovakia, but only after he was assured that the Sudetenland would be transferred to Germany. If he had been denied that success he might have gambled on war, especially as he might reasonably have suspected that neither France nor the Soviet Union was eager to fulfil its obligations. It is possible that German generals who feared Hitler was taking too great a risk might have attempted to overturn the Nazi regime, but their ability to do so is far from certain.

Would the prospects of deterring Hitler have been greater if Churchill's views on rearmament had prevailed? Given his orthodox economic ideas, and his attitude to Japan's incursions into China, it seems unlikely he would have taken the financial brake off defence expenditure before Hitler came to power. Churchill would have agreed to a defence loan in 1934, a year before Chamberlain did. From July 1936 Churchill, unlike Chamberlain, was willing to risk the loss of export markets, and he favoured the creation of a Ministry of Supply that could have diverted industrial capacity to munitions production more quickly than Chamberlain's policy of non-interference with normal trade. Defence expenditure could have reached the 1939 level in 1938. On the other hand, the RAF could have expanded faster than it did only by ordering obsolescent aircraft. Likewise new artillery and tanks for the army only became available for production in 1938. Britain could have had stronger armed forces in 1938, but not necessarily in proportion to the additional expenditure.

No one, with the possible exception of Baldwin, did more than Churchill to create fear of the bomber. Like Chamberlain, Churchill consistently gave top priority to air power, but, given the limitations of the aircraft available and the problems of training aircrew in a period of rapid expansion, any bomber force before the war would have had limited effectiveness. Naval power was Churchill's second priority, but he was generally content with the size of the Admiralty's programmes in the 1930s because, like Chamberlain, he prioritised the threat from Germany rather than from Japan. The army ranked lowest in Churchill's priorities. As late as the winter of 1937–8, while the Inskip Report was being discussed in Cabinet, he believed the French army would be superior to the German for some time to come, and agreed that meantime the British Army's role could be confined to imperial defence (see page 173). Such an army would have lacked the reserves of munitions for offensive operations in Europe and could have contributed little to a grand alliance in the early stages of a conflict. Historians who are critical of Chamberlain's influence on defence policy should not assume there was a Churchillian alternative that would have made a decisive difference.

11.2   Would It Have Been Better to Fight in 1938?

Chamberlain never doubted he had been right not to go to war in September 1938. Writing to his sisters at the end of December 1939, he said Hitler 'could have dealt France and ourselves a terrible, perhaps a mortal, blow then', but had missed his opportunity. On 25 May 1940, the day before the evacuation from Dunkirk started, Chamberlain told them 'it is as clear as daylight that if we had had to fight in 1938 the results would have been much worse'. He claimed the record would show he had realised how militarily weak Britain was and had done his best to postpone, if he could not avert, war to gain time for preparation.[1]

Churchill presented a very different picture of Munich and its consequences in his history of the second world war: the Soviet Union's
'undoubted willingness to join the Western Powers and go [to] all lengths
to save Czechoslovakia' had been ignored; the Czech army had been lost,
and the output of the mighty Skoda munitions works had increased the
pace of German rearmament.[2] Historians of appeasement are broadly
divided into those who agree and those who disagree with the counterfactual that it would have been better to take a stand and if necessary fight
in 1938 rather than in 1939.[3] Given that the fortunes of war are inher-
ently unpredictable, the debate is exceptionally difficult to resolve.

Churchill's version of Munich was challenged by Samuel Hoare, who
had been a member of Chamberlain's Inner Cabinet. He questioned
Churchill's belief that the Soviet Union was eager to join Britain and
France in support of Czechoslovakia. The Soviets, Hoare suspected,
were playing for time, and would not have been dissatisfied had war
broken out between Britain and Germany. He thought Churchill overlooked the political, economic and military weakness of France. Hoare
recalled the chiefs of staff had advised that the Czech army could hold
out only for a few weeks. He admitted the relative position with Germany
regarding land forces became worse in the year after Munich, but considered that Churchill did not attach sufficient importance to the advantages delay conferred in giving time to improve air defence with modern
fighters, an extensive system of radar and up-to-date anti-aircraft guns,
and also civil defence through the provision of shelters.[4]

Hoare's criticism can be countered by pointing out that the Luftwaffe's
medium bombers lacked the capability to carry out a strategic offensive,
and, operating from German bases, would have lacked protection by
shorter-ranged fighter escorts.[5] Moreover, the chiefs of staff advised
ministers in September 1938 that initially practically the whole of the
German air force would be concentrated against Czechoslovakia.
However, they added that at some point the main German effort would
be directed against Britain or France, as the Germans had a strong
motive to eliminate one of their principal opponents as quickly as possible so as to avoid a long war.[6] The Air Staff admitted to being in
considerable doubt as to the range and capability of German bombers
and lacked intelligence on the Luftwaffe's poor serviceability rate. Worst
case assumptions led to a greatly exaggerated estimate of the weight of
bombs that might be dropped on Britain.[7]

Chamberlain's belief that Hitler could have struck a terrible, perhaps
mortal, blow in 1938 reflected this error. However, although exaggerated, the threat posed by the Luftwaffe was not negligible. There was
nothing the British Army could have done to prevent the Germans from

occupying Holland, where they could have established air bases close enough to London to allow fighter-escorted raids on the capital. Even medium bombers could then have had an impact comparable to German biplanes in 1917–18, when Londoners took refuge in Underground stations or trekked to open fields beyond the city, and the output of munitions was interrupted.[8] A knockout blow was beyond the capability of the Luftwaffe, but the government would have been expected to protect the population.

Ministers were well aware of the deficiencies in Britain's air defences. In September 1938 nineteen out of Fighter Command's 29 squadrons were equipped with obsolete or obsolescent aircraft, many of them slower than the German bombers they were intended to intercept. Since the obsolete fighters were no longer in production, squadrons equipped with them would have been dependent on reserves, which were calculated to last only one and a half weeks of wartime wastage. Only five squadrons had been equipped with the latest Hurricane fighters, but, as is common with new aircraft, there were 'teething' problems: in particular, lack of heating for the wing-mounted guns meant these could not be fired above about 15,000 feet. Radar coverage was limited to the south-east of England, and other aspects of the air defence system were far from complete. Only about a third of planned fixed defences (anti-aircraft guns, balloon barrages and searchlights) were in place. Civil defence organisation was embryonic, particularly as regards fighting fires, and there was public concern about the lack of gas masks for babies or small children.[9] How much time would have been available to remedy these deficiencies would have depended on how long the Czechs would have resisted, which in turn would have depended, in part, on what action Britain, France and the Soviet Union took.

Writing in mid-September 1938, Churchill predicted the Germans would suffer 300,000 or 400,000 casualties in three or four weeks if they invaded Czechoslovakia – an extraordinary figure given that German casualties in a similar period during the invasion of Poland in 1939 were just under 45,000.[10] Historians generally agree the Czechs could not have held out indefinitely without outside support.[11] Nevertheless there is scope for disagreement about how long resistance would have lasted, whether the French and the Soviets would have intervened effectively, and whether the Germans would have been able subsequently to campaign as successfully in the west as they did in 1940.

Figures for the strength of the Czech army vary. Churchill credited it with 36 or 37 divisions. Pierre Caquet, Milan Hauner and David Vital included fortress troops and estimated the army's strength to be equivalent to 40 to 42 divisions. Katriel Ben-Arie reached a figure of 57 divisions by adding independent battalions made up of border guards, customs officials, etc. Williamson Murray, however, considered a figure of approximately 30 as appropriate for comparative purposes. Moreover he pointed out that the near equality with the 37 German divisions deployed against Czechoslovakia in September 1938 is deceptive, since all the German divisions were regular units whereas about a third of the Czechs' were reserve ones.[12] The disparity in regular formations would have been only partially offset by the Czechs' fortifications. These were strong on the northern frontier with Silesia, but weak in many places in the west, facing Bavaria, and weaker still in the south, facing Austria, where fortification had begun only after the *Anschluss*. The Czechs' air force was similar in size and obsolescence to Poland's. In Murray's judgement, Czech resistance would probably have lasted as long as Poland's, about a month, even without support from allies.[13]

Murray did not take account of Czechoslovakia's nationalities problem. According to French intelligence, only 51 per cent of the army were Czechs and 23 per cent were German-speaking. The latter, along with the five per cent of the population who identified as Hungarian, were of doubtful loyalty. To mitigate the risk of mass desertions, such as had occurred in the Austro-Hungarian army in the First World War, when Czech units had gone over to the Russians, the proportion of non-Slav troops in any regiment was capped at 15 per cent. Even so, such a unit might be decimated by desertion. Moreover, Slovak troops were said by a German military attaché to be unenthusiastic, on account of the way in which Czechs monopolised promotions, and the subsequent history of Czech-Slovak relations tends to confirm his impression.[14] The nationalities problem makes it unusually difficult to form a view of how effective Czech resistance would have been.

What support would the Czechs have received from the western powers? The chiefs of staff advised that the British and French should not initiate a bombing war by attacking targets in Germany, at least until Britain was ready to defend itself and to strike effectively.[15] The French air force was in no condition to conduct an air offensive. Like the Poles in 1939, the Czechs would have had no support from the western powers in the air war. As for land forces, the British had only two divisions available to send to France in the autumn of 1938. Churchill wrote in his memoirs that the French army, with an advantage of over ten to one in regular divisions on the western front, could 'most certainly have rolled forward across the Rhine or into the Ruhr'.[16] Caquet has argued that General Gamelin, the French chief of staff, had a plan whereby upwards of 40 French divisions could have broken through the Germans' incomplete fortifications in 18 days and reached the Rhine in the second month of the war.[17] However, it is not certain how quickly the plan would have been initiated. The commander of the French air force, General Joseph Vuillemin, predicted the Germans would achieve air superiority, enabling them to interfere at will with French troop movements and launch massive attacks against French cities. At a meeting in London on 26 September 1938 Gamelin suggested he would have to wait until the major cities had been evacuated before beginning military operations, and even then he seemed to the British to envisage no more than a reconnaissance in force followed by a withdrawal to the Maginot Line once the Germans transferred their main effort from east to west. As one of his interlocutors, Major-General Henry Pownall, the War Office's director of military operations and intelligence, noted in his diary, 'that wouldn't have helped the Czechs much'.[18] Caquet disputed the British account of the meeting, but even if a French offensive had been begun promptly it might have been too slow to save Czechoslovakia.

Soviet capabilities and intentions are an even greater source of uncertainty in view of Stalin's purges of senior officers in the armed forces. The French high command suspected their partners in the Franco-Soviet alliance were trying to bring about a European war which would exhaust the other powers and leave the Soviet Union dominant. Soviet evasiveness during preliminary staff conversations in 1937 had strengthened this suspicion.[19] However, Hugh Ragsdale, using Russian sources, argued that Stalin wished to postpone war until the Soviet armed forces had recovered from the purges and had updated their equipment, probably about 1942. In the meantime, deterrence of Germany through collective security suited Soviet interests.[20]

What would Stalin have done in the event of a German attack on Czechoslovakia? The Czechs apparently negotiated an agreement in September 1938 for the Soviets to send 700 aircraft once suitable airfield facilities and appropriate anti-aircraft defences had been prepared.[21] However, there was no common border between the two countries, and the information reaching the Foreign Office was that Romania would not allow Soviet aircraft to fly over its territory.[22] Even if permission had been given, or Romanian objections had been ignored, the logistics of such an operation would have been formidable. Most Czech airfields were too short for modern Soviet bombers, and Czech and Soviet aircraft used different kinds of fuel. Soviet intervention would have required preparation of airfields and accumulation of fuel stocks, both of which could readily have been disrupted by the Luftwaffe.[23] Vansittart thought Soviet air assistance to Czechoslovakia would not be 'on a very grand scale'.[24]

The Red Army was able to deploy the equivalent of 90 divisions on the western border of the Soviet Union, a force equal to the whole of the

German army, including reserve units.[25] As with the air force, however, the problem was how to render assistance to the Czechs. Churchill believed Romania could have been persuaded to allow a Soviet army on to its soil and that that country's railways 'might well have supported' 30 divisions.[26] In fact Romania's railways and roads were inadequate to supply a substantial Soviet force in Czechoslovakia. Moreover, there is no evidence the Red Army's logistic units would have been equal to the task; on the contrary, they failed miserably even on Soviet territory during the Winter War with Finland in 1939–40.[27] It is far from certain, therefore, that Soviet intervention would have prolonged Czech resistance. As Churchill himself said in January 1940, the Winter War dispelled illusions about the capabilities of the Red Army and Air Force.[28] Caquet has claimed the Soviet Baltic fleet would have been able to block German iron ore imports from Sweden, but the fleet's inefficiency, exposed in 1941, suggests otherwise.[29] The main advantage of Soviet participation in a grand alliance in 1938, as the British chiefs of staff pointed out in 1939, would have been to strengthen the Allied blockade by preventing German trade with Russia.

Even if Czechoslovakia could not have been saved from being overrun, it might still have been better to fight in 1938 rather than 1939. Murray believed the German army and economy would have been weaker in 1938–9 than they were in 1939–40, since most of the Czech munitions that were taken over intact in March 1939 would have been destroyed during the fighting, along with some industrial plant.[30] Adam Tooze, on the basis of his study of the German economy, considered that Hitler 'almost certainly saved his regime from disaster' by agreeing to the Munich settlement. Steel shortages imposed limits on munitions and aircraft production. With Britain and France able to draw on the resources of the United States, Tooze reckoned that 'any conventional strategic analysis suggested Germany was outmatched'.[31] However, a conventional analysis would not have predicted the outcome of the campaign in the west in 1940.

Murray argued that the panzer divisions, equipped in 1939 predominantly with light rather than medium tanks, 'certainly could not have undertaken the offensive' as successfully as in 1940, but a note of caution appeared in his conclusion that 'it is most unlikely' (and therefore not impossible) that France would have been knocked out of the war.[32] Tooze also considered that the panzer divisions which were victorious in Poland would have been 'clearly inadequate' against French tanks.[33] However, victory in 1940 was not simply a result of tank-versus-tank battles, but also of German superiority in command and control technique, and in particular in the combined use of artillery, infantry and aircraft in support of tanks. Victory was a result of superior tactics and strategy. The Germans' strategy might well have been different in a 1939 campaign, as their initial plan had the limited aim of capturing the coast facing Britain and the more ambitious plan to cut off the British and French forces in Belgium was adopted only in February 1940. Even so, the Germans would still have had their tactical advantage. In the 1940 campaign, French casualties alone numbered 292,000 killed or wounded and almost two million taken prisoner against 153,000 Germans killed or wounded and about 17,500 missing.[34] A narrower margin in a 1939 campaign might still have been a decisive victory.

In any event, Britain's air defences would probably not have been seriously tested before some point in the summer of 1939. There would have been time after September 1938 to replace the obsolete and some of the obsolescent fighters; radar coverage would have been extended; more anti-aircraft guns would have been added to the ground defences, and adequate civil defence would have ensured the maintenance of morale under air attack. With hindsight, it can be argued that it was not necessary to gain time by sacrificing Czechoslovakia at Munich. On the other hand, it would have required a certain ruthlessness, which Churchill had, but Chamberlain did not, to expose the British people to air attack in 1938 when the country's defences were incomplete.

A decision to fight in 1938 would have required the people of Britain and the Commonwealth to be willing to undergo the hardships of a prolonged and unlimited war to restore Czechoslovakia after it had been overrun. Lord Halifax confessed Munich had been a 'horrible and wretched business', but claimed the experience had convinced the country and Commonwealth there was no alternative to war.[35] Lord Ismay, a soldier who had served in the CID secretariat in the 1930s and had been Churchill's chief staff officer during the war, reckoned it would have been far better to fight in 1938, from a purely military point of view. However, he doubted whether the British nation or the Commonwealth would have been united in doing so, and observed: 'lack of unity on the home front in time of war may well be more disastrous in its consequences than inferiority of armaments'.[36] Chamberlain may not have been far wrong in his belief that public opinion would not allow the government to risk war over Czechoslovakia.[37] In a poll in August 1938 only 47 per cent of men aged 30 years or less said that in the event of war they would co-operate fully with the authorities by joining the services or a civil defence organisation; a further 13 per cent said they would give qualified support.[38] The hysterical expression of relief that followed the Munich agreement also casts doubt on the readiness of the British people for war. As for Commonwealth unity, the dominions secretary, Malcolm

MacDonald, warned the Cabinet's Foreign Policy Committee in March 1938 that South Africa and Canada would see no reason whatever why they should go to war to prevent Germans from rejoining their father-land.[39] The answer to the question whether it would have been better to fight in 1938 than 1939 depends on the relative importance one attaches to morale and to material factors.

11.3   Concluding Reflections

Had Churchill been in Chamberlain's place, rearmament would have been faster and a firm stand would have been taken over Czechoslovakia. However, it does not follow that war could have been prevented as easily as Churchill claimed. Indeed, even with hindsight, there is a good deal of uncertainty as to what might have happened. Chamberlain hoped, and for a time believed, that appeasement would preserve peace by removing potential causes of war. The dispute over the Sudetenland seemed to him to be a case in point. He also hoped his diplomacy would gain time to make Britain's air defences secure. On the other hand, the sacrifice of Czechoslovakia altered the European balance of power, perhaps decisively, in Germany's favour. For Chamberlain's critics, Munich was worse than a crime; it was a mistake.

Chamberlain's critics have tended to assume that British rearmament was inadequate although he authorised what from 1936 was the fastest increase in defence expenditure in peacetime. Certainly British rearma-ment initially lagged behind Germany's, but, as Churchill recognised, German levels of military expenditure were unsustainable. British grand strategy was based on deterrence, with armed forces that could be maintained indefinitely, or, failing that, on a long war in which blockade and superior economic staying power would be decisive. Britain spent less than Germany because a balance had to be struck between rearma-ment and economic stability. By 1939, however, intelligence reports suggested Hitler would, for economic reasons, have to choose between peace and war soon. The period of deterrence came to be measured in months rather than years, and Chamberlain accepted the need to accept economic risks that Churchill would have taken earlier. It is worth reflecting on the scope of the rearmament programme in the spring of 1939. Britain was re-equipping as large a navy as the United States, was on the cusp of producing more aircraft than Germany, was exercising primary responsibility for the defence of a Commonwealth and Empire that covered a quarter of the world's land surface and yet found resources with which to create an army that would deny Germany a numerical advantage on land in Western Europe. It is not clear that more could have been attempted. The war showed Britain's resources were not inexhaustible. Strategic choices had to be made. Chamberlain bore some of the responsibility for defeat in France in 1940, but Churchill was primarily responsible for the Singapore disaster.

Chamberlain's critics are on firmer ground when they blame him for failures in foreign policy. His inexperience of diplomacy, over-confidence, and susceptibility to flattery were serious defects. His success as chancellor had in no small part been due to his willingness to accept advice from Treasury officials. In his attempts to influence defence policy, both as chancellor and prime minister, he recognised his limitations as a layman. He challenged the chiefs of staff when they failed to present the Cabinet with alternatives from which ministers could choose, and he looked to men like Warren Fisher, Weir, Trenchard and Liddell Hart for ideas, but he stuck to broad issues of grand strategy and priorities. He did not attempt to take on the work of the defence departments himself. In contrast, he did not hesitate to act as his own foreign secretary and side-lined the Foreign Office through informal contacts first with Italy and then with Germany. He relied far too much on advice from Horace Wilson, whose approach to dealing with dictators appears to have been influenced by his experience in industrial relations. Chamberlain's failure to take an interpreter for his first meeting with Hitler typified a lack of professionalism. As a negotiator, Chamberlain was at a disadvantage against someone as ruthless and shameless as Hitler, the extent of whose ambitions he failed to grasp.

Churchill proved to be correct when he said appeasement (in the pejorative sense) merely enlarged the dictators' appetites. Historians are bound to respond to the moral issues raised by the coercion of the government of a small country into surrendering part of its territory. However, it is arguable that Munich was not morally different from the Hoare-Laval Pact, which Churchill implicitly endorsed. In 1935, as in 1938, a small country was called upon to make territorial sacrifices. The fact that Ethiopia was an African country that Churchill considered to be unfit to be a member of a civilised league of nations does not make a difference in twenty-first-century eyes. Churchill thought it was expedient to make concessions to Mussolini for the sake of the European balance of power, but that is a strategic argument, not a moral one.

There are other difficult moral issues on which reasonable people may disagree. The right of European people to self-determination was an important element in the peace settlement of 1919; indeed Czechoslovakia owed its existence to that principle. However, the ethnographic map of Central Europe was complex. The British Labour Party had protested against the incorporation of predominantly German-speaking areas into

Czechoslovakia after the war and was not unanimously against territorial revision even in 1938, although it regarded surrender to the threat of force as shameful.[40] Chamberlain was sincere when he told Labour leaders he did not believe Czechoslovakia could be restored to its existing form after a victory over Germany. He could not conceive that the problem of German minorities would be removed by ethnic cleansing, as happened in Czechoslovakia and Poland after the war, when, with Churchill's acquiescence, millions of German-speaking people were expelled in circumstances that led to hundreds of thousands of deaths.[41] German-speaking people had lived in Bohemia and Moravia since medieval times and, as part of the Austrian Empire, these provinces had been within the German Confederation until 1866, when Bismarck expelled Austria from the Confederation. Even so, J. W. Bruegel argued that disloyalty to Czechoslovakia developed among Sudeten-Germans only after Hitler rose to power, and annexation by the Reich was opposed by substantial numbers of German-speaking Social Democrats.[42] Directly after Munich Churchill said he believed the Sudeten-Germans would have voted against being placed under Nazi rule if they had been allowed to vote.[43] Like so many of his counterfactuals it is hard to prove one way or another. The pro-Nazi Sudeten German Party had won 60 per cent of German speakers' votes in the 1935 election, a margin sufficient to ensure success in areas where ninety per cent or more of the population was German-speaking. However, in some mixed areas a combination of democratic German speakers plus Czechs probably would have rejected Nazi rule. The Munich agreement provided for plebiscites in mixed areas, but none were held and the new frontier was settled by direct negotiation between the German and Czech governments. The extent of opposition to Hitler's Reich among Sudeten-Germans thus remains unknown. However, even allowing for passions arising from a brutal occupation, the post-war expulsion by the Czechs of all German speakers, including Social Democrats and other anti-Nazis, makes one wonder whether Czechoslovakia had been viable as a multi-ethnic state.

Another moral question is: how readily should war be used as an instrument of foreign policy? In the autumn of 1938 – although not in the spring – Churchill was willing to risk exposing the people of Britain to air attacks, having seen reports of how the citizens of Madrid and Barcelona had reacted to bombing. Chamberlain was much less willing. The reactions of the two men to the situation reflected not only different assessments of Hitler's ultimate aims, but also contrasting personalities: the warrior and the man of peace.

Nevertheless, a year later Chamberlain became the first statesman to declare war on Hitler's Germany, followed within a few hours by the

French premier, Daladier, but with Roosevelt on the sidelines and Stalin preparing to participate in the partition of Poland. Chamberlain's critics have given him little or no credit for declaring war, or, for that matter, for introducing conscription for the first time in Britain in peacetime. He has been portrayed as responding to domestic political pressures, which is undoubtedly true, but not the whole truth. Chamberlain still hoped to preserve peace after the German occupation of Prague, but no longer trusted Hitler. A policy of keeping Germany guessing was replaced in the spring of 1939 by one of giving guarantees to threatened countries. Chamberlain would have welcomed 'adjustments' in the Polish Corridor and over Danzig, provided they were not made under duress, but so would Churchill (see pages 260–1). Chamberlain acted reluctantly at each step on the road to war, as he was bound to do when millions of lives depended on his decision, but in the end he accepted responsibility for stopping Hitler.

There are basically three charges made against Chamberlain's actions in 1939. First, that he sabotaged an alliance with the Soviet Union. Second, that his diplomacy, particularly the back-door variety, encouraged Hitler to believe Britain would not stand by Poland. Third, that the outbreak of war did not mark the end of appeasement and he hoped for a peace settlement short of victory. Chamberlain was suspicious of Soviet intentions, and was with difficulty persuaded to agree to negotiations for an Anglo-Franco-Soviet alliance. However, although he had excluded the Soviet Union from the negotiations leading to the Munich settlement, he was not wholly opposed to including the Soviets in a deterrent to future German aggression. In March 1939 he proposed that the Soviet Union, together with Britain, France and Poland, sign a declaration stating they would consult together in the event of a threat to the independence of a European state – an arrangement similar to what Churchill had proposed in August 1938. What Chamberlain baulked at was any arrangement that would leave the decision for peace or war in Soviet hands. Whether this attitude was reasonable depends on the view one takes of Stalin: was the Soviet dictator concerned only to defend the status quo, or was he opportunistic in the pursuit of Soviet aims, both territorial and in expanding Communist influence? Soviet actions during and after the war strongly suggest, but do not prove, the latter.

As for the consequences of the way Chamberlain handled Anglo-German relations in the summer of 1939, particularly informal contacts, the evidence is capable of different interpretations. How can one account for divergences between British and German accounts of what was said? Was economic appeasement an attempt to buy peace, or simply encouragement to Germany to rejoin the multilateral international economy (to Britain's, and particularly the City of London's, advantage)? Chamberlain's irenic mode of diplomacy may have encouraged Hitler to risk Anglo-French intervention, but Germans who were familiar with the position in London knew Chamberlain would fulfil the guarantee to Poland. If any one man enabled Hitler to go to war that man was Stalin, by agreeing to the Nazi-Soviet Pact.

The evidence for Chamberlain regarding Britain as honour bound to fulfil its guarantee to Poland is very strong. The delay in declaring war can be explained entirely in terms of the need to keep in step with France. As for the notion that appeasement continued after the outbreak of war, Chamberlain was as certain as Churchill that peace with Hitler was impossible. When Britain faced defeat shortly before Dunkirk, Chamberlain supported Churchill's decision to fight on.

Churchill disagreed profoundly with Chamberlain over Munich. Nevertheless, unlike some anti-revisionist historians, he was willing to credit Chamberlain with honourable motives. Moreover, Churchill had no doubt that a real change in foreign policy took place in the spring of 1939 and he would have been willing to serve in Chamberlain's government thereafter. It is possible to consider that Chamberlain was guilty as charged by Churchill over Munich without agreeing with historians who go further than Churchill when criticising other aspects of Chamberlain's foreign and defence policies. As for Munich itself, Churchill's claim that Hitler could easily have been stopped by a combination of Britain, France and the Soviet Union cannot be proved either way. On the one hand, Hitler did backtrack from his intention to invade Czechoslovakia when confronted with the threat of Anglo-French intervention. On the other hand, given his gambler's instinct, he might well have gone ahead if denied the prize of the Sudetenland. As in September 1939, the British people would then have faced the uncertain prospect of a long and bloody war.

Notes

Chapter 1

1 Cato [Michael Foot, Peter Howard and Frank Owen], *Guilty Men* (London, 1940).
2 John F. Naylor, *Labour's International Policy: The Labour Party in the 1930s* (London, 1969).
3 Keith Feiling, *The Life of Neville Chamberlain* (London, 1946), pp. v, 314, 319–20, 353.
4 Winston S. Churchill, *The Second World War*, vol. I: *The Gathering Storm* (London, 1948), pp. 251, 271–2. Pagination is different in later editions.
5 A. J. P. Taylor, *The Origins of the Second World War* ([1961] Harmondsworth, 1964), pp. 7–8, 198, 234–5, 300–1. References are to the edition which contains Taylor's foreword 'Second Thoughts' expounding his thesis in the light of reactions to it.
6 D. C. Watt, 'Appeasement: The Rise of a Revisionist School?' *Political Quarterly*, 36, 2 (1965), pp. 191–213.
7 Keith Robbins, *Munich 1938* (London, 1968).
8 W. N. Medlicott, *Britain and Germany: The Search for Agreement 1930–1937* (London, 1969).
9 N. H. Gibbs, *Grand Strategy*, vol. I: *Rearmament Policy* (London, 1976); Robert P. Shay, *British Rearmament in the Thirties: Politics and Profits* (Princeton, 1977); G. C. Peden, *British Rearmament and the Treasury, 1932–1939* (Edinburgh, 1979). For impact of these books, see J. L. Richardson, 'New Perspectives on Appeasement: Some Implications for International Relations', *World Politics*, 40 (1988), no. 3, 289–316.
10 David Dilks, '"We Must Hope for the Best and Prepare for the Worst": The Prime Minister, the Cabinet and Hitler's Germany, 1937–1939', *Proceedings of the British Academy*, 73 (1987), 309–352, and John Charmley, *Chamberlain and the Lost Peace* (London, 1989).
11 Keith Middlemas, *Diplomacy of Illusion: The British Government and Germany, 1937–1939* (London, 1972); Sidney Aster, *1939: The Making of the Second World War* (London, 1973); Larry W. Fuchser, *Neville Chamberlain and Appeasement: A Study in the Politics of History* (New York, 1982); Williamson

Murray, *The Change in the European Balance of Power, 1938–1939: The Path to Ruin* (Princeton, 1984).

12 R. A. C. Parker, *Chamberlain and Appeasement: British Policy and the Coming of the Second World War* (London, 1993), pp. 10, 292–3, 343, 345–7.

13 R. A. C. Parker, *Churchill and Appeasement: Could Churchill Have Prevented the Second World War?* (London, 2000), p. 259.

14 Michael Jabara Carley, *1939: The Alliance That Never Was and the Coming of World War II* (Chicago, IL, 1999); Louise Grace Shaw, *The British Political Elite and the Soviet Union 1937–1939* (London, 2003).

15 Keith Neilson, *Britain, Soviet Russia and the Collapse of the Versailles Order, 1919–1939* (Cambridge, 2005), pp. 322, 326.

16 Zara Steiner, *The Triumph of the Dark: European International History 1933–1939* (Oxford, 2011), pp. 647–656.

17 Niall Ferguson, *The War of the World: History's Age of Hatred* (London, 2006), pp. 325–330; G. C. Peden, 'Keynes, the Economics of Rearmament and Appeasement', in Wolfgang J. Mommsen and Lothar Kettenacker (eds.), *The Fascist Challenge and the Policy of Appeasement* (London, 1983), pp. 142–156.

18 Tim Bouverie, *Appeasing Hitler: Chamberlain, Churchill and the Road to War* (London, 2019); David Faber, *Munich: The 1938 Appeasement Crisis* (London, 2008); Graham Macklin, *Chamberlain* (London, 2006); Frank McDonough, *Neville Chamberlain, Appeasement and the British Road to War* (Manchester, 1998); Adrian Phillips, *Fighting Churchill, Appeasing Hitler: How a British Civil Servant Helped Cause the Second World War* (London, 2019); Nick Smart, *Neville Chamberlain* (London, 2010). John Ruggiero, *Neville Chamberlain and British Rearmament: Pride, Prejudice, and Politics* (Westport, CT, 1999) was a partial exception in that he took some account of economic factors, but his focus was on Chamberlain's relations with the Labour movement.

19 James P. Levy, *Appeasement and Rearmament: Britain 1936–1939* (Lanham, MD, 2006), pp. 159–161; Christopher Layne, 'Security Studies and the Use of History: Neville Chamberlain's Grand Strategy Revisited', *Security Studies*, 17 (2008), no. 3, 397–437.

20 Greg Kennedy, '"Rat in Power": Neville Chamberlain and the Creation of British Foreign Policy, 1931–39', in T. G. Otte (ed.), *The Makers of British Foreign Policy: From Pitt to Thatcher* (Basingstoke, 2002), pp. 173–95.

21 John Ruggiero, *Hitler's Enabler: Neville Chamberlain and the Origins of the Second World War* (Santa Barbara, CA, 2015), pp. 186–7.

22 Peter Neville, *Hitler and Appeasement: The British Attempt to Prevent the Second World War* (London, 2006), pp. 181–4, 188–90.

23 Robert Self, *Neville Chamberlain, a Biography* (Aldershot, 2006), pp. 296, 450.

24 Andrew David Stedman, *Alternatives to Appeasement: Neville Chamberlain and Hitler's Germany* (London, 2011).

25 Richard H. Powers, 'Winston Churchill's Parliamentary Commentary on British Foreign Policy', *Journal of Modern History*, 26 (1954), no. 2, 179–82.

26 Robert Rhodes James, *Churchill: A Study in Failure, 1900–1939* (London, 1970).

27 Randolph Churchill and Martin Gilbert, *Winston S. Churchill*, 8 vols. (London, 1966–88). Gilbert was solely responsible for volumes 3 to 8.

28 John Charmley, *Churchill: The End of Glory* (London, 1993).
29 B. J. C. McKercher, 'The Limitations of the Politician-Strategist: Winston Churchill and the German Threat, 1933–39', in John H. Maurer (ed.), *Churchill and Strategic Dilemmas before the World Wars* (London, 2003), pp. 88–120.
30 Donald Cameron Watt, 'Churchill and Appeasement', in Robert Blake and Wm. Roger Louis (eds.), *Churchill* (Oxford, 1993), pp. 199–214.
31 David Reynolds, *In Command of History: Churchill Fighting and Writing the Second World War* (London, 2004), pp. 94–7.
32 David Carlton, *Churchill and the Soviet Union* (Manchester, 2000), pp. 209–10.
33 Paul Addison, *Churchill: The Unexpected Hero* (Oxford, 2005); Stuart Ball, *Winston Churchill* (London, 2003); Andrew Roberts, *Churchill: Walking with Destiny* (London, 2018).
34 Paul Kennedy, 'The Tradition of Appeasement in British Foreign Policy, 1865–1939', *British Journal of International Studies*, 2 (1976), no. 3, 195–215.
35 *Documents on British Foreign Policy 1919–1939*, series 1A, vol. 3 (*DBFP* 1A/3), appendix, p. 789.
36 House of Commons Debates (HC Deb), 26 March 1936, vol. 310, cc. 1446, 1523, api.parliament.uk/historic-hansard/index.html.
37 Martin Gilbert, *Churchill's Political Philosophy* (Oxford, 1981), pp. 67, 71–3.
38 HC Deb, 6 October 1938, vol. 339, cc. 544–7.
39 W. N. Medlicott, review of Arthur H. Furnia, *Diplomacy of Appeasement: Anglo-French Relations and the Prelude to World War II* in *International Affairs*, 38 (1962), no. 1, 84–5.
40 *The Times*, 3 October 1936, p. 7.
41 Richard Titmuss, *Problems of Social Policy* (London, 1950), p. 13; Terence O'Brien, *Civil Defence* (London, 1955), p. 677.
42 Harold Macmillan, *Winds of Change, 1914–1939* (London, 1966), p. 575.
43 Gaines Post, *Dilemmas of Appeasement: British Deterrence and Defense, 1934–1937* (Ithaca, NY, 1993), pp. 14–17; Richard Overy, 'Air Power and the Origins of Deterrence Theory before 1939', *Journal of Strategic Studies*, 15 (1992), no. 1, 73–101.
44 Malcolm Smith, 'Rearmament and Deterrence in Britain in the Thirties', *Journal of Strategic Studies*, 1 (1978), no. 3, 313–37, at 327.
45 B. J. C. McKercher, 'Deterrence and the European Balance of Power: The Field Force and British Grand Strategy, 1934–1938', *English Historical Review*, 123 (2008), no. 500. 98–131.
46 G. C. Peden, 'A Matter of Timing: The Economic Background to British Foreign Policy, 1937–1939', *History*, 69 (1984), no. 225, 15–28.
47 David Dilks, *Churchill and Company: Allies and Rivals in War and Peace* (London, 2012), p. 239.
48 John Maynard Keynes, *Collected Writings* (*JMK*), vol. XIV ed. Donald Moggridge (London, 1973), p. 113; Keynes, *Treatise on Probability* [1921], *JMK*, vol. VIII (1973).
49 Abraham Ascher, 'Was Hitler a Riddle?' *Journal of the Historical Society*, 9 (2009), no. 1, 1–21.

50 Winston S. Churchill, 'Hitler and his Choice', *Great Contemporaries* (London, 1937), pp. 225–32 at 225.

51 Esmonde Robertson (ed.), *The Origins of the Second World War* (London, 1971), pp. 83–104; Kathleen Burk, *Troublemaker: The Life and History of A. J. P. Taylor* (New Haven, CT, 2000), p. 288.

52 Ian Kershaw, *Hitler: 1936–1945: Nemesis* (London, 2000), pp. xli, 47–49, 222–3.

53 Christopher Andrew, *The Defence of the Realm: The Authorized History of MI5* (London, 2009), pp. 201–9; John Ferris, *Behind the Enigma: The Authorized History of GCHQ, Britain's Secret Cyber-Intelligence Agency* (London, 2020), p. 151.

54 Gill Bennett, 'Declassification and Release Policies of the UK's Intelligence Agencies', *Intelligence and National Security*, 17 (2002), no. 1, 21–32; Kevin Quinlan and Calder Walton, 'Missed Opportunities? Intelligence and the British Road to War', in Frank McDonough (ed.), *The Origins of the Second World War: An International Perspective* (London, 2011), pp. 205–222.

55 Carl von Clausewiz, *On War*, ed. Michael Howard and Peter Paret (Princeton, 1976), pp. 85–6, 119–21.

56 William Ashworth, *Contracts and Finance* (London, 1953).

Chapter 2

1 Wilson, 'Munich, 1938', October 1941, CAB 127/158, fol. 1.

2 Andrew Roberts, *Churchill: Walking with Destiny* (London, 2018), p. 44.

3 *The Neville Chamberlain Diary Letters (NCDL)*, 4 vols., ed. Robert Self (Aldershot, 2000–5), vol. IV, pp. 394, 441–2.

4 See, for example, Alan Allport, *Britain at Bay: The Epic Story of the Second World War: 1938–1941* (London, 2020), pp. 77–8; John Ruggiero, *Hitler's Enabler: Neville Chamberlain and the Origins of the Second World War* (Santa Barbara, CA, 2015), pp. 3, 49–50; Nick Smart, *Neville Chamberlain* (London, 2010), pp. xii–xiv.

5 *The Austen Chamberlain Diary Letters 1916–1937*, ed. Robert Self (Cambridge, 1995), pp. 282–4.

6 Paul Addison, *Churchill: The Unexpected Hero* (Oxford, 2005), p. 3.

7 *Winston S. Churchill Companion (WSCC)*, 5 vols., ed. Martin Gilbert (London, 1967–82), vol. II, part 2, p. 863.

8 Peter Clarke, 'Churchill's Economic Ideas, 1900–1930', in Robert Blake and Wm. Roger Louis (eds.), *Churchill* (Oxford, 1993), pp. 79–95.

9 Sir Alan Barlow to Sir Richard Hopkins, 22 June 1938, Treasury records: T 177/42, The National Archives of the United Kingdom (TNA).

10 Martin Gilbert, *Winston S. Churchill*, vol. III (London, 1971), pp. 111–13.

11 Addison, *Churchill*, p. 90.

12 Maurice Cowling, *The Impact of Hitler: British Politics and British Policy 1933–1940* (Cambridge, 1975), p. 241.

13 Robert Self, *Neville Chamberlain: A Biography* (Aldershot, 2006), pp. 15, 115.

14 'Chamberlain: A Candid Portrait', n.d. but 1939, David Margesson papers, MRGN 1/5, Churchill Archives, Cambridge.

15 *Clem Attlee: The Granada Historical Records Interview* (London, 1967), p. 20.
16 Character study by Butler, n.d. but 1939, RAB F80, fol. 101, R. A. Butler papers, Trinity College Library, Cambridge.
17 MRGN 1/5.
18 Chamberlain to Liddell Hart, 8 March 1937, LH 1/159, and Churchill to Liddell Hart, 16 February 1936, LH 1/171, Liddell Hart papers, Liddell Hart Centre for Military Archives, King's College, London.
19 Churchill to Chamberlain, 12 March 1938, Prime Minister's Office correspondence and papers: PREM 1/237, TNA.
20 *NCDL*, vol. IV, pp. 179, 311.
21 Winston S. Churchill, *The Second World War*, vol. I: *The Gathering Storm* (London, 1948), p. 173.
22 *WSCC*, vol. V, part 3, p. 687.
23 Churchill, *Second World War*, vol. I, p. 389.
24 Ibid., pp. 255, 280.
25 *NCDL*, vol. IV, p. 81.
26 Alvin Finkel and Clement Leibovitz, *The Chamberlain-Hitler Collusion* (Halifax, NS, 1997).
27 Winston S. Churchill, 'After President Roosevelt's Message', *Step by Step 1936–1939* (London, 1939), pp. 352–6 at 356.
28 David Marquand, *Ramsay MacDonald* (London, 1977), pp. 749–59, 772.
29 Churchill, *Second World War*, vol. I, pp. 169–70, 615; G. M. Young, *Stanley Baldwin* (London, 1952), pp. 11–12.
30 Philip Williamson, 'Baldwin's Reputation: Politics and History, 1937–1967', *Historical Journal*, 47 (2004), no. 1, 127–68.
31 *Baldwin Papers: A Conservative Statesman, 1908–1947*, ed. Philip Williamson and Edward Baldwin (Cambridge, 2004), p. 379.
32 Neville Chamberlain, *The Struggle for Peace* (London, 1939), p. 347 and passim.
33 Michael L. Roi and B. J. C. McKercher, '"Ideal" and "Punch-Bag": Conflicting Views of the Balance of Power and Their Influence on Interwar Foreign Policy', *Diplomacy and Statecraft*, 12 (2001), no. 2, 47–78.
34 Chamberlain's diary, 28 January 1935, Neville Chamberlain papers NC2/23, Cadbury Research Library, University of Birmingham.
35 Eunan O'Halpin, *Head of the Civil Service: A Study of Sir Warren Fisher* (London, 1989); G. C. Peden, 'Sir Warren Fisher and British Rearmament against Germany', *English Historical Review*, 94 (1979), no. 370, 29–47.
36 Self, *Neville Chamberlain*, p. 292.
37 'Talk with Horace Wilson', Thomas Jones papers, CH, Class P, vol. 3, fol. 68, National Library of Wales; Note of conversation with Sir Alexander Cadogan, 14 November 1951, Templewood papers, part XIX, file 5, Cambridge University Library; *The Diaries of Sir Alexander Cadogan, 1938–1945 (CD)*, ed. David Dilks (London, 1971), pp. 53, 127, 178; G. C. Peden, 'Sir Horace Wilson and Appeasement', *Historical Journal*, 53 (2010), no. 4, 983–1014.
38 For Ball's activities see Arnold Beichman, 'Hugger-mugger in Old Queen Street: The Origins of the Conservative Research Department', *Journal of Contemporary History* 13 (1978), no. 4, 671–88; Richard Cockett, 'Ball,

Chamberlain and *Truth*', *Historical Journal*, 33 (1990), no. 1, 131–42; *Memoirs of a Conservative: J. C. C. Davidson's Memoirs and Papers*, ed. Robert Rhodes James (London, 1969), pp. 271–2; William C. Mills, 'Sir Joseph Ball, Adrian Dingli, and Neville Chamberlain's "Secret Channel" to Italy, 1937–40', *International History Review*, 24 (2002), no. 2, 278–317; Adrian Phillips, *Fighting Churchill, Appeasing Hitler: How a British Civil Servant Helped Cause the Second World War* (London, 2019), pp. 51–5, 287–9. Unfortunately the only book-length account of Ball's activities to draw on his surviving papers, Jonathan Pile, *Churchill's Secret Enemy* (2012) is a privately-published series of notes rather than a continuous text, and lacks page numbers or proper references to sources.

39 Donald Boadle, 'The Formation of the Foreign Office Economic Relations Section, 1930–1937', *Historical Journal*, 20 (1977), no. 4, 919–36.

40 Chamberlain's diary, January 1934 (no day), NC2/23.

41 David Dutton, *Simon: A Political Biography of Sir John Simon* (London, 1992), pp. 124–5, 170, 177.

42 MacDonald diary, 3 March 1935, PRO 30/69/1753, TNA.

43 *NCDL*, vol. IV, pp. 141, 150 and 153.

44 Viscount Templewood, *Nine Troubled Years* (London, 1954), pp. 135–8.

45 Viscount Simon, *Retrospect* (London, 1952), p. 238; Templewood, *Nine Troubled Years*, pp. 372–82.

46 Most notably in his memoirs, Earl of Avon, *The Eden Memoirs: Facing the Dictators* (London, 1962). For Eden's defence of this image against academic criticism, see Peter Beck, 'Politicians Versus Historians: Lord Avon's "Appeasement Battle" Against "Lamentably, Appeasement-minded" Historians', *Twentieth Century British History*, 9 (1998), no. 3, 396–419.

47 Eden to Baldwin, 21 February 1934, Stanley Baldwin papers, Cambridge University Library, quoted in David, Carlton, *Anthony Eden* (London, 1981), p. 45.

48 HC Deb, 3 October 1938, vol. 339, cc. 86.

49 Michael L. Roi, *Alternative to Appeasement: Sir Robert Vansittart and Alliance Diplomacy, 1934–1937* (Westport, CT, 1997), p. 125.

50 *NCDL*, vol. IV, p. 418.

51 Templewood, *Nine Troubled Years*, p. 138.

52 Robert Vansittart, *The Mist Procession* (London, 1958), p. 542; Avon, *Facing the Dictators*, pp. 241–2.

53 Roi, *Alternative to Appeasement*, pp. 125–31.

54 *The Diplomatic Diaries of Oliver Harvey 1937–1940*, ed. John Harvey (London, 1970), p. 22.

55 Roi, *Alternative to Appeasement*, pp. 35–36, 69–80, 105–7, 123–5, 153–4 ; Keith Neilson and T. G. Otte, *The Permanent Under-Secretary for Foreign Affairs, 1854–1946* (Abingdon, 2009), pp. 210–33.

56 Gladwyn Jebb, *The Memoirs of Lord Gladwyn* (London, 1972), p. 59.

57 *CD*, pp. 103–5.

58 Jebb, *Memoirs*, p. 70.

59 *CD*, pp. 47–48, 67.

60 Cadogan to the Earl of Birkenhead, 20 January 1965, Cadogan papers, ACAD 4/4, Churchill Archives Centre, Cambridge.

61 Jebb, *Memoirs*, p. 73.
62 Valentine Lawford, *Bound for Diplomacy* (London, 1963), pp. 268–9.
63 Keith Neilson, 'Orme Sargent, Appeasement and British Policy in Europe, 1933–39', *Twentieth Century British History*, 21 (2010), no. 1, 1–28.
64 Keith Neilson, *Britain, Soviet Russia and the Collapse of the Versailles Order, 1919–1939* (Cambridge, 2005), pp. 32–5, 129–30, 157–62; William (Baron) Strang, *Home and Abroad* (London, 1956), pp. 146, 149–52.
65 Sir Nevile Henderson, *Failure of a Mission: Berlin 1937–1939* (London, 1940), pp. vi–vii, 17; Sir Nevile Henderson, *Water under the Bridges* (London, 1945), p. 216; Peter Neville, 'The Foreign Office and Britain's Ambassadors to Berlin, 1933–39', *Contemporary British History*, 18 (2004), no. 3, 110–29.
66 Donald Cameron Watt, *How War Came: The Immediate Origins of the Second World War, 1938–1939* (London, 1989), p. 614. See also Aaron L. Goldman, 'Two views of Germany: Nevile Henderson versus Vansittart and the Foreign Office, 1937–1939', *British Journal of International Studies*, 6 (1980), no. 3, 247–77; Peter Neville, 'Rival Foreign Office Perceptions of Germany, 1936–39', *Diplomacy and Statecraft*, 13 (2002), no. 3, 137–52; G. Bruce Strang, 'Two Unequal Tempers: Sir George Ogilvie-Forbes, Sir Nevile Henderson and British Foreign Policy, 1938–39', *Diplomacy and Statecraft*, 5 (1994), no. 1, 107–37.
67 *CD*, p. 151.
68 Treasury Organisation Committee minutes, 2 November 1936, T 199/50c.
69 Avon, *Facing the Dictators*, pp. 319–20, 521.
70 For the work of this committee, see Susan Howson and Donald Winch, *The Economic Advisory Council, 1930–1939: A Study in Economic Advice during Depression and Recovery* (Cambridge, 1977), chs. 5–6.
71 *JMK*, vol. 10, pp. 330–31.
72 G. C. Peden, *British Rearmament and the Treasury, 1932–1939* (Edinburgh, 1979), pp. 24–5; John Winnifrith, 'Edward Ettingdean Bridges- Baron Bridges 1892–1969', *Biographical Memoirs of Fellows of the Royal Society*, 16 (1970), 37–56.
73 Bridges to J. A. N. Barlow (Treasury under-secretary), 19 April 1937, T161/780/9 (S.41999).
74 Gaines Post, *Dilemmas of Appeasement: British Deterrence and Defense, 1934–1937* (Ithaca, NY, 1993), pp. 3–4, 21, 331–6.
75 Ruggiero, *Hitler's Enabler*, p. 4.
76 'Defence Co-ordination: Note by the chancellor of the exchequer', n.d., PREM 1/196, fos. 57–61, written in response to Hankey's CP 30 (36), 7 February 1936, CAB 24/259/30.
77 Lord Chatfield, *It Might Happen Again*, vol. II: *The Navy and Defence* (London, 1947), pp. 169, 172, 179.
78 Viscount Swinton, *I Remember* (London, 1948), pp. 109–11, 146–7; W. J. Reader, *Architect of Air Power: The Life of the First Viscount Weir of Eastwood 1877–1959* (London, 1968), p. 293.
79 *NCDL*, vol. IV, p. 251.
80 R. J. Minney, *The Private Papers of Hore-Belisha* (London, 1960), pp. 66–67. For Liddell Hart's role, see Alex Danchev, *Alchemist of War: The Life of Basil Liddell Hart* (London, 1998), pp. 187–94.

81 Brian Bond, 'Leslie Hore-Belisha at the War Office', in Ian Beckett and John Gooch (eds.), *Politicians and Defence: Studies in the Formulation of British Defence Policy 1845–1970* (Manchester, 1981), pp. 110–31 at 130.

82 Chatfield, *It Might Happen Again*, vol. II, p. 98.

83 Self, *Neville Chamberlain*, p. 337.

84 Sir John Simon (chancellor of the exchequer) to Chamberlain, 25 October 1937, PREM 1/250.

85 Chatfield, *It Might Happen Again*, vol. 2, p. 62.

86 *The Ironside Diaries 1937–1940*, ed. Roderick Macleod and Denis Kelly (London, 1962), p. 101.

87 Sir Basil Liddell Hart, *Memoirs*, 2 vols. (London, 1965).

88 Sir John Kennedy, *The Business of War: The War Narrative of Major-General Sir John Kennedy*, ed. Bernard Fergusson (London, 1957), p. 5.

89 John Kiszely, *Anatomy of a Campaign: The British Fiasco in Norway* (Cambridge, 2017), pp. 13, 295–7.

90 Donald Ferguson to chancellor of the exchequer, 27 April 1935, T 172/1830; *Chief of Staff: The Diaries of Lieutenant-General Sir Henry Pownall*, vol. I: *1933–1940*, ed. Brian Bond (London, 1972), p. 34.

91 Fisher to Sir Horace Wilson, 15 May 1939, Sir Warren Fisher papers, Coll Misc 0461/2/13, LSE Library, London.

92 Interview with Bridges, 17 December 1952, Templewood papers, part XIX, file 5.

93 Keith Jeffery, *MI6: The History of the Secret intelligence Service, 1909–1949* (London, 2010), pp. 303–6.

94 Christopher Andrew, *The Defence of the Realm: The Authorized History of MI5* (London, 2009), pp. 195–213.

95 JIC 8th & 9th meetings, 26 April and 26 May 1937, CAB 56/1.

96 Jebb, *Memoirs*, p. 71.

97 F. H. Hinsley et al, *British Intelligence in the Second World War: Its Influence on Strategy and Operations*, vol. I (London, 1979), p. 11.

98 Minute by Sargent, 5 July 1934, Foreign Office records: FO 371/17695 (C4297/20/18), TNA.

99 Wing-Commander C. E. H. Medhurst to Desmond Morton, 2 August 1935, Air Ministry records: AIR 5/1154, TNA.

100 Gill, Bennett, *Churchill's Man of Mystery: Desmond Morton and the World of Intelligence* (Abingdon, 2007), pp. 150–90.

101 Hinsley, *British Intelligence*, vol. I, p. 59.

102 'The Financial and Economic Position in Germany, Autumn 1938', 6 December 1938, FO 371/2104 (C15551/541/18). For discussion in the Treasury of Pinsent's estimates of German financing of armaments see T 172/2085.

103 F. H. Hinsley, 'Churchill and the Use of Special Intelligence', in Blake and Louis (eds.), *Churchill*, pp. 407–26.

104 Vansittart, *Mist Procession*, p. 499; Churchill, *Second World War*, vol. I, p. 63.

105 *WSCC*, vol. V, part 3, pp. 1015–16, 1046.

106 Bennett, *Churchill's Man of Mystery*, pp. 173–4.

107 *WSCC*, vol. V, part 3, p. 557.

108 Christopher M. Bell, *Churchill and Sea Power* (Oxford, 2013), pp. 147–9.

109 *WSCC*, vol. V, part 2, pp. 1314–15. The Churchill-Strakosch correspondence is in the Winston Churchill papers, Churchill Archives, Cambridge, CHAR 2/277.

110 HC Deb, 7 June 1935, vol. 302, cc. 2247–52; Churchill to Baldwin, 6 July, and Baldwin to Churchill, 8 July, 1935, *WSCC*, vol. V, part 2, pp. 1207–8; Churchill to Kingsley Wood, 2 June 1938, WSCC, vol. V, part 3, pp. 1057–8.

111 Churchill to Hankey, 18 April 1938, with Hankey's comment for the secretary of state for air, CAB 21/630. The sub-committee's minutes are in CAB 16/132.

112 Gilbert, *Winston S. Churchill*, vol. V, pp. 877–81, 944, 951–3

Chapter 3

1 Paul Kennedy, *The Rise and Fall of the Great Powers: Economic Change and Military Conflict from 1500 to 2000* (London, 1988).

2 Gordon Martel, 'The Meaning of Power: Rethinking the Decline and Fall of Great Britain', *International History Review*, 13 (1991), no. 4, 662–694; Keith Neilson, '"Greatly Exaggerated": The Myth of the Decline of Great Britain before 1914', ibid., 695–725; John Ferris, '"The Greatest Power on Earth": Great Britain in the 1920s', ibid., 726–50; B. J. C. McKercher, '"Our Most Dangerous Enemy": Great Britain Pre-eminent in the 1930s', ibid., 751–83.

3 Paul K. MacDonald and Joseph M. Parent, 'Graceful Decline: The Surprising Success of Great Power Retrenchment', *International Security*, 35 (2011), no. 4, 7–44.

4 The purpose of the Maddison project was to measure economic change over time. Angus Maddison adjusted his estimates of German GDP to take account of frontier changes by omitting production in territories lost after 1945 – see Angus Maddison, *Monitoring the World Economy 1820–1992* (Paris, 1995), pp. 131, 229. To estimate German GDP within the pre-1938 borders this adjustment must be reversed by increasing his figures by 10.75 per cent.

5 Randall L. Schweller, *Deadly Imbalances: Tripolarity and Hitler's Strategy of World Conquest* (New York, 1998), pp. 26–31.

6 Zara Steiner, *Triumph of the Dark: European International History 1933–1939* (Oxford, 2011), pp. 798–800.

7 Mark Harrison, 'The Economics of World War II: An Overview', in Mark Harrison, (ed.), *The Economics of World War II: Six Great Powers in International Comparison* (Cambridge, 1998), pp. 1–42, at 3.

8 'Imperial Defence, 1937', review by chiefs of staff, 22 February 1937, *DBFP* 2/18, Appendix I, pp. 965–89.

9 Andrew Stewart, 'The British Government and the South African Neutrality Crisis, 1938–39', *English Historical Review*, 123 (2008), no. 503, 947–972; Paul Canning, 'Yet Another Failure for Appeasement? The Case of the Irish Ports', *International History Review*, 4 (1982), no. 3, 371–392.

10 G. C. Peden, 'The Burden of Imperial Defence and the Continental Commitment Reconsidered', *Historical Journal*, 27 (1984), no. 2, 405–423.

11 Iain E. Johnston-White, *The British Commonwealth and Victory in the Second World War* (London, 2017), pp. 114–18, 175–80, 227–8.

12 COS 843, 20 February 1939, para. 6, Cabinet Office records: CAB 53/45/2, TNA.

13 N. H. Gibbs, *Grand Strategy*, vol. I: *Rearmament Policy* (London, 1976), pp. 23, 332–58.

14 Joseph Maiolo, *The Royal Navy and Nazi Germany: A Study in Appeasement and the Origins of the Second World War* (London, 1998), pp. 15–17, 91–101, 147–52.

15 Christopher M. Bell, *Churchill and Sea Power* (Oxford, 2013), pp. 103–114, 121–5, 131–4.

16 James Neidpath, *The Singapore Naval Base and the Defence of Britain's Eastern Empire 1919–1941* (Oxford, 1981); Andrew Field, *Royal Navy Strategy in the Far East 1919–1939: Planning for War against Japan* (London, 2004).

17 Maiolo, *Royal Navy*, p. 34.

18 Wesley Wark, 'In Search of a Suitable Japan: British Naval Intelligence in the Pacific before the Second World War', *Intelligence and National Security*, 1 (1986), no. 2, 189–211, at 194–5. British intelligence on the capabilities of the Japanese armed forces was heavily influenced by ethnocentric assumptions of European superiority – see Antony Best, *British Intelligence and the Japanese Challenge in Asia, 1914–1941* (London, 2002), pp. 119–20, 140, 168–70.

19 'Naval Policy in the Event of a Far Eastern War', minute by Director of Plans, Captain V. H. Danckwerts, 5 May 1939, enclosing revised memorandum, Admiralty records: ADM 116/3863, TNA; COS 931, 24 June 1939, CAB 53/50/1.

20 COS 639, 12 November 1937, paras. 23 and 41, CAB 53/34/3.

21 COS 843, 20 February 1939, paras 4(v), 146–53 and 339–50, CAB 53/45/2.

22 David Reynolds, *The Creation of the Anglo-American Alliance 1937–41: A Study in Competitive Co-operation* (London, 1981), pp. 58–62.

23 Bell, *Churchill*, pp. 31, 233.

24 'Naval Construction: 1933/34 Programme', T 161/624/5 (original reference S.36130/34); 'Capital Ships: Vulnerability to Air Attack' (report and papers of CID Sub-Committee), CAB 16/147.

25 HC Deb, 11 March 1937, vol. 321, cc. 1399–1400; Winston S. Churchill, 'Rebuilding the Battle Fleet' and 'Defending the Empire', *Step by Step 1936–1939* (London,1939), pp. 114–17, 130–3.

26 HC Deb, 17 March 1938, vol. 333, cc. 658–9; Winston S. Churchill, 'Let Tyrant Criminals Bomb', in *The Collected Essays of Sir Winston Churchill*, ed. Michael Wolff, vol. I (London, 1976), pp. 421–7 at 424.

27 Winston Churchill, *The Second World War*, vol. I: *The Gathering Storm* (London, 1948), p. 322.

28 COS 697, 16 March 1938, paras. 59–63, 88, 90, CAB 53/37/4.

29 Churchill, *Second World War*, vol. I, p. 101.

30 HC Deb, 26 June 1923, vol. 165, c. 2142.

31 Churchill, *Second World War*, vol. I, p. 101.

32 Gibbs, *Grand Strategy*, p. 599.

33 F. H. Hinsley et al, *British Intelligence in the Second World War*, vol. I (London, 1979), pp. 299–300.

34 M. M. Postan, *British War Production* (London, 1952), p. 471. Both Gibbs' and Postan's figures exclude transport aircraft.

35 R. J. Overy, *The Air War 1939–1945* (London, 1980), p. 23; R. J. Overy, 'German Air Strength 1933 to 1939: A Note', *Historical Journal*, 27 (1984), no. 2, 465–71.

36 R. J. Overy, 'Hitler and Air Strategy', *Journal of Contemporary History*, 15 (1980), no. 3, 405–21.

37 CID 271st meeting, 14 October 1935, CAB 2/6; 'French Air Force', T 161/842/3 (S.41152).

38 Tami Davis Biddle, *Rhetoric and Reality in Air Warfare: The Evolution of British and American Ideas about Strategic Bombing, 1914–1945* (Princeton, 2002), chs. 2 and 3; Richard Overy, *The Bombing War: Europe 1939–1945* (London, 2013), pp. 41–54; Matthew Powell, 'Debate, Discussion, and Disagreement: A Reassessment of the Development of British Tactical Air Doctrine, 1919–1940', *War in History*, 28 (2021), no. 1, 93–117.

39 James S. Corum, 'From Biplanes to Blitzkrieg: The Development of German Air Doctrine between the Wars', *War in History*, 3 (1996), no. 1, 85–101; R. J. Overy, 'From "Uralbomber" to "Amerikabomber": The Luftwaffe and Strategic Bombing', *Journal of Strategic Studies*, 1 (1978), no. 2, 154–78.

40 Alexander Boyd, *The Soviet Air Force since 1918* (London, 1977), pp. 55–8, 67–9.

41 Lucio Ceva and Andrea Curami, 'Air Army and Aircraft Industry in Italy 1936–1943', in Horst Boog (ed.), *The Conduct of the Air War in the Second World War: An International Comparison* (Oxford, 1992), pp. 85–107.

42 Anthony Cain, *Forgotten Air Force: French Air Doctrine in the 1930s* (Washington, DC, 2002).

43 HC Deb, 10 November 1932, vol. 270, c. 632.

44 John Ferris, 'Fighter Defence before Fighter Command: The Rise of Strategic Air Defence in Great Britain, 1917–1934', *Journal of Military History*, 63 (1999), no. 4, 845–84.

45 'Air Ministry Memorandum in Reply to Parliamentary Deputation to the Prime Minister on July 28 and 29 1936', para. 204, PREM 1/193; G. C. Peden, *Arms, Economics and British Strategy: From Dreadnoughts to Hydrogen Bombs* (Cambridge, 2007), pp. 117, 159.

46 Sir Thomas Inskip to Chamberlain, 26 October 1937, CAB 64/9.

47 Neville Jones, *The Beginnings of Strategic Air Power: A History of the British Bomber Force 1923–1939* (London, 1987), pp. 112–21, 133–6, 146–9.

48 Air Ministry note, 22 October 1937, CAB 64/9; Alexander Rose, 'Radar and Air Defence in the 1930s', *Twentieth Century British History*, 9 (1998), no. 2, 219–45.

49 Uri Bialer, *The Shadow of the Bomber: The Fear of Air Attack and British Politics 1932–1939* (London, 1980), pp. 133–46.

50 'Defence Expenditure', note by T. S. V. Phillips, 29 June 1937, ADM 205/80.

51 COS 639, 12 November 1937, CAB 53/34/3.

52 COS 697, para. 63, CAB 53/37/4.
53 Williamson Murray, *The Change in the European Balance of Power, 1938–1939: The Path to Ruin* (Princeton, 1984), p. 251.
54 Hinsley, *British Intelligence*, p. 78.
55 Defence Requirements Sub-Committee minutes, 23 January 1934, CAB 16/109.
56 Brian Bond, *British Military Policy between the Two World Wars* (Oxford, 1980), pp. 98–126.
57 Defence Requirements Sub-Committee Report, DRC 14, 28 February 1934, CAB 24/247/64.
58 'The Mobile Division/Cavalry Mechanization', October 1935–December 1937, War Office records: WO 32/2826, TNA; David French, 'The Mechanization of the British Cavalry between the World Wars', *War in History*, 10 (2003), no. 3, 296–320.
59 Hew Strachan, 'The Territorial Army and National Defence', in Keith Neilson and Greg Kennedy (eds.), *The British Way in Warfare: Power and the International system, 1856–1956* (Farnham, 2010), pp. 159–78.
60 Bond, *British Military Policy*, chs. 5 and 6.
61 J. P. Harris, *Men, Ideas and Tanks: British Military Thought and Armoured Forces, 1903–1939* (Manchester, 1995), pp. 211–15, 221–8, 289–90, 305–7.
62 J. P. Harris, 'British Military Intelligence and the Rise of the German Mechanized Forces 1927–1939', *Intelligence and National Security*, 6 (1991), no. 2, 395–417.
63 'The Autobiography of a Gunner', Montgomery-Massingberd papers, MSS 10/11, Liddell Hart Centre for Military Archives, King's College, London.
64 Leslie Hore-Belisha to Chamberlain, 31 January 1938, PREM 1/241; M. M. Postan, D. Hay and J. D. Scott, *Design and Development of Weapons* (London, 1964), pp. 310–13, 327–9.
65 Winston S. Churchill, 'How the Wars of the Future Will be Waged', in *Collected Essays*, ed. Wolff, vol. I, pp. 391–7 at 394.
66 David Edgerton, *Britain's War Machine: Weapons, Resources and Experts in the Second World War* (London, 2011), pp. 89–92.
67 David E. Johnson, *Fast Tanks and Heavy Bombers: Innovation in the US Army, 1917–1945* (Ithaca, NY, 1998), ch. 10.
68 Robert A. Doughty, 'The French Armed Forces', in Allan R. Millett and Williamson Murray (eds.), *Military Effectiveness*, vol. II: *The Interwar Period* (Boston, MA, 1988), pp. 39–69, at 55–6.
69 Roger R. Leese, *The Soviet Military Experience: A History of the Soviet Army, 1917–1991* (London, 2000), p. 94.
70 COS 639, para. 36, CAB 53/34/3.
71 Martin Alexander and W. J. Philpott, 'The Entente Cordiale and the Next War: Anglo-French Views on Future Military Co-operation, 1928–39', in Martin Alexander (ed.), *Knowing Your Friends: Intelligence Inside Alliances and Coalitions from 1914 to the Cold War* (London, 1998), pp. 53–84.
72 Martin Alexander, *The Republic in Danger: General Maurice Gamelin and the Politics of French Defence, 1933–40* (Cambridge, 1992), pp. 258–9; Eugenia

C. Kiesling, "'If It Ain't Broke, Don't Fix It: French Military Doctrine between the Wars', *War in History*, 3 (1996), no. 2, 208–23.

73 Gavin Bailey, *The Arsenal of Democracy: Aircraft Supply and the Anglo-American Alliance* (Edinburgh, 2013), pp. 40–8.

74 *Statistical Abstract for the United Kingdom 1924 to 1938* (Cmd. 6232), pp. 176–7, UK Parliamentary Papers 1939–40.

75 Postan, *British War Production*, pp. 1–52; David Edgerton, *Warfare State: Britain, 1920–1970* (Cambridge, 2006), pp. 15–48.

76 R. A. C. Parker, 'British Rearmament 1936–9: Treasury, Trade Unions and Skilled Labour', *English Historical Review*, 96 (1981), no. 379, 306–43 (from 327).

77 J. R. Parkinson, 'Shipbuilding', in Neil Buxton and Derek Aldcroft (eds.), *British Industry between the Wars* (London, 1979), pp. 79–102.

78 G. A. H. Gordon, *British Seapower and Procurement between the Wars: A Reappraisal of Rearmament* (London, 1988); Christopher W. Miller, *Planning and Profits: British Naval Armaments Manufacture and the Military-Industrial Complex, 1918–1941* (Liverpool, 2018), pp. 10–15, 28–43, 48–76; Postan, *British War Production*, pp. 2–4, 47–51.

79 Hugh Peebles, *Warshipbuilding on the Clyde* (Edinburgh, 1987), pp. 142–153.

80 COS 843, 20 February 1939, paras. 11 and 383, CAB 53/45/2.

81 Wilhelm Deist, 'The Rearmament of the Wehrmacht', in Militärgeschichtliches Forschungsamt (ed.), *Germany and the Second World War*, vol. I: *The Build-up of German Aggression* (Oxford, 1990), pp. 373–540 at 456–80.

82 Postan, *British War Production*, p. 5.

83 Peter Fearon, 'Aircraft Manufacturing', in Buxton and Aldcroft, *British Industry*, pp. 216–40 at 217–19.

84 Edgerton, *Warfare State*, pp. 43–4.

85 Edward L. Homze, *Arming the Luftwaffe: The Reich Air Ministry and the German Aircraft Industry, 1919–39* (Lincoln, NE, 1976), pp. 93, 108; Fearon, 'Aircraft', p. 216.

86 Neil Forbes, 'Democracy at a Disadvantage? British Rearmament, the Shadow Factory Scheme and the Coming of War, 1936–40', *Jahrbuch für Wirtschaftsgeschichte/ Economic History Yearbook*, 55 (2014), no. 2, 49–69; Homze, *Arming the Luftwaffe*, pp. 76–9; William Hornby, *Factories and Plant* (London, 1958), pp. 218–26; Sebastian Ritchie, *Industry and Air Power: The Expansion of British Aircraft Production, 1935–1941* (London, 1997), pp. 57–61, 91–105.

87 Viscount Swinton, *I Remember* (London, 1948), p. 110.

88 Sir Horace Wilson to Chamberlain, 15 March, and Sir Charles Bruce-Gardner (chairman of the Society of British Aircraft Constructors) to Swinton, 20 April, 1938, PREM 1/236.

89 'Précis of Reports on Visits to Germany by A.H. R. Fedden', October 1937, CAB 104/32.

90 Richard Overy, 'The German Pre-War Aircraft Production Plans: November 1936–April 1939', *English Historical Review*, 90 (1975), no. 357, 778–797; Homze, *Arming the Luftwaffe*, pp. 149–55, 190, 227–8.

91 CC 15 (38), 22 March 1938, CAB 23/93/2; G. C. Peden, *British Rearmament and the Treasury, 1932–1939* (Edinburgh, 1979), pp. 156–8.
92 HC Deb. 21 May 1936, vol. 312, cc. 1442–3.
93 Postan, Hay and Scott, *Design and Development of Weapons*, pp. 258–9, 261.
94 Benjamin Coombs, *British Tank Production and the War Economy 1934–1945* (London, 2013), pp. 18–19, 47–9; Postan, *British War Production*, pp. 109–10.
95 For example, Correlli Barnett, *The Collapse of British Power* (London, 1972), pp. 476–85.
96 Robert P. Shay, *British Rearmament in the Thirties: Politics and Profits* (Princeton, 1977), pp. 128–33, 289–94.
97 R. J. Overy, 'Hitler's War and the German Economy: A Reinterpretation', *Economic History Review*, 35 (1982), no. 2, 272–91.
98 Shay, *British Rearmament*, pp. 249–63, 290; Sebastian Ritchie, 'The Price of Air Power: Technological Change, Industrial Policy, and Military Aircraft Contracts in the Era of British Rearmament, 1935–39', *Business History Review*, 71 (1997), no. 1, 82–111.
99 CP 316 (37), para. 11, CAB 24/273/41.
100 *WSCC*, vol. V, part 3, p. 285; Sir Horace Hamilton to Sir Richard Hopkins, 17 October 1936, enclosing note by Board of Trade Statistics Department, and memorandum by Edward Bridges, 10 November 1936, T 161/720/6 (S49175).
101 *NCDL*, vol. IV, pp. 219–20.
102 Nicholas Crafts, 'Walking Wounded: The British Economy in the Aftermath of World War I', in Stephen Broadberry and Mark Harrison (eds.), *The Economics of the Great War: A Centennial Perspective* (London, 2018), pp. 119–25, at 120, https://voxeu.org/content/economics-great-war-centennial-perspective.
103 Niall Ferguson, *The War of the World: History's Age of Hatred* (London, 2006), pp. 329–30.
104 R. G. Ware, 'The Balance of Payments in the Interwar Period', *Bank of England Quarterly Bulletin*, 14 (1974), no. 1, 47–52, at 49, and London and Cambridge Economic Service, *The British Economy: Key Statistics 1900–1970* (London, 1971), p. 17. Defence expenditure from Shay, *British Rearmament*, 297, adjusted to calendar years. GDP from B. R. Mitchell, *British Historical Statistics* (Cambridge, 1988), p. 829.
105 CP 149 (39), para. 3, CAB 24/287/32.
106 R. J. Overy, *War and Economy in the Third Reich* (Oxford, 1994), pp. 177–204; Adam Tooze, *The Wages of Destruction: The Making and Breaking of the Nazi Economy* (London, 2006), pp. 90–5, 208–10, 224–42, 246, 250–3, 302–5.
107 Christopher Price, *Britain, America and Rearmament in the 1930s: The Cost of Failure* (Basingstoke, 2001), pp. xiii–xiv, 85–6, 134–5, 150–2. For discussion on Price's economic ideas, see Peden, *Arms, Economics*, pp. 133–6.
108 26th Report of the Committee on Economic Information, EAC (SC) 33, 16 December 1938, para. 23, CAB 58/30.
109 *JMK*, vol. XXI, p. 512.

110 R. A. C. Parker, 'The Pound Sterling, the American Treasury and British Preparations for War, 1938–1939', *English Historical Review*, 98 (1983), no. 387, 261–279.

111 SAC 4th meeting, 6 April 1939, CAB 16/209.

112 *The Times*, 30 January 1937, p. 14.

113 Peden, *Arms, Economics*, pp. 249–260.

114 Daniel Ussishkin, *Morale: A Modern British History* (New York, 2017), pp. 73–86.

115 'Planning for War with Germany', Defence Plans (Policy) Sub-Committee, DP(P) 2, 15 February 1937, CAB 16/182.

116 Viscount Templewood, *Nine Troubled Years* (London,1954), pp. 126–9, 133–4; Hoare's notes of conversation with Wilson, 5 March 1947 and 27 May 1948, Templewood papers, part XIX, file 5.

117 Tom Harrison and Charles Madge, *Britain by Mass-Observation* (London, [1939] 1986), ch. 2.

118 Franklin Gannon, *The British Press and Germany, 1936–1939* (Oxford, 1971); Benny Morris, *The Roots of Appeasement: The British Weekly Press and Nazi Germany during the 1930s* (London, 1991).

119 Anthony Adamthwaite, 'The British Government and the Media, 1937–1938', *Journal of Contemporary History*, 18 (1983), no. 2, 281–97; Richard Cockett, *Twilight of Truth: Chamberlain, Appeasement, and the Manipulation of the Press* (London, 1989).

120 Nicholas Pronay, 'Rearmament and the British Public: Policy and Propaganda', in James Curran, Anthony Smith and Pauline Wingate (eds.), *Impacts and Influences: Essays on Media Power in the Twentieth Century* (London, 1987), pp. 53–96.

121 Martin Ceadel, 'Interpreting East Fulham', in Chris Cook and John Ramsden (eds.), *By-Elections in British Politics* (London, 1973), pp. 118–39; C. T. Stannage, 'The East Fulham By-Election, 25 October 1933', *Historical Journal*, 14 (1971), no. 1, 165–200.

122 Martin Ceadel, 'The Peace Movement between the Wars: Problems of Definition', in Richard Taylor and Nigel Young (eds.), *Campaigns for Peace: British Peace Movements in the Twentieth Century* (Manchester, 1987), pp. 73–99.

123 Templewood, *Nine Troubled Years*, pp. 127–8; Martin Ceadel, 'The First British Referendum: The Peace Ballot, 1934–5', *English Historical Review*, 95 (1980), no. 377, 810–39.

124 *Baldwin Papers: A Conservative Statesman, 1908–1947*, ed. Philip Williamson and Edward Baldwin (Cambridge, 2004), pp. 375–6.

125 Fisher to Sir Ernle Chatfield, 11 July 1934, Stanley Baldwin papers, vol. 131, fol. 194, Cambridge University Library.

126 Chancellor's speeches, T 172/1526 and T172/1527.

127 *The Times*, 1 November 1935, p. 21.

128 William T. Stone, 'Economic Consequences of Rearmament', *Foreign Policy Reports* (New York), 1 October 1938, 166–7, 169–70, in FO 371/21632 (C534635).

129 Brett Holman, *The Next War in the Air: Britain's Fear of the Bomber, 1908–1941* (London, 2014), pp. 74, 170; Susan R. Grayzel, *At Home and*

Under Fire: Air Raids and Culture in Britain from the Great War to the Blitz (Cambridge, 2012), pp. 256–66.

130 'Anglo-French Staff Conversations: British Strategical Memorandum', AFC 1, para. 29, 20 March 1939, CAB 29/159.

131 CID minutes, 266th meeting, 22 November 1934, CAB 2/6.

132 Cmd. 5948, UK Parliamentary Papers 1938–39.

133 John F. Naylor, *Labour's International Policy: The Labour Party in the 1930s* (London, 1969), pp. 70–2, 191–6, 229–31; John Swift, *Labour in Crisis: Clement Attlee and the Labour Party in Opposition, 1931–40* (Basingstoke, 2001), p. 107; Ben Pimlott, *Hugh Dalton* (London, 1985), pp. 241–2.

134 Frank McDonough, 'When Instinct Clouds Judgement: Neville Chamberlain and the Pursuit of Appeasement with Nazi Germany, 1937–9', in Frank McDonough (ed.), *The Origins of the Second World War: An International Perspective* (London, 2011), pp. 186–204, at 198–9.

135 Paul Horsler, 'Cometh the Hour, Cometh the Nation: Local-Level Opinion and Defence Preparations Prior to the Second World War, November 1937–September 1939' (PhD thesis, London School of Economics and Political Science, 2016); Daniel Hucker, *Public Opinion and the End of Appeasement in Britain and France* (Farnham, 2011).

136 *NCDL*, vol. IV, pp. 157, 287.

137 Winston Churchill, *Arms and the Covenant* (London, 1938), pp. 247, 308.

138 *DBFP* 2/18, appendix I, pp. 968–9.

139 COS 639, 12 November 1937, para. 42, CAB 53/34/3.

140 HC Deb, 4 April 1938, vol. 334, c. 61.

141 CID minutes, 296th meeting, 5 July 1937, CAB 2/6.

142 William Philpott and Martin Alexander, 'The French and the British Field Force: Moral Support or Material Contribution?' *Journal of Military History*, 71 (2007), no. 3, 743–72.

143 'Anglo-French Staff Conversations: British Strategical Memorandum', 20 March 1939, AFC 1, paras. 2, 5, CAB 29/159.

144 John Ruggiero, *Hitler's Enabler: Neville Chamberlain and the Origins of the Second World War* (Santa Barbara, CA, 2015), p. 62. For the complete sentence see *NCDL*, vol. IV, p. 294.

145 Greg Kennedy, *Anglo-American Strategic Relations and the Far East 1933–1939* (London, 2002), p. 262. Kennedy did not credit Chamberlain with this development but it could hardly have taken place without at least the prime minister's tacit approval.

146 Reynolds, *Creation of the Anglo-American Alliance*, pp. 10, 16–20, 51–3, 57.

147 Churchill, 'The United States and Europe', *Step by Step*, pp. 267–71 at 267.

148 'Note of Conversation between President Roosevelt and Colonel Arthur Murray', 21 October 1938, PREM 1/367.

149 B. J. C. McKercher, *Transition of Power: Britain's Loss of Pre-eminence to the United States, 1930–1945* (Cambridge, 1999), p. 158.

150 Callum MacDonald, 'Deterrent Diplomacy: Roosevelt and the Containment of Germany, 1938–40', in Robert Boyce and Esmonde M. Robertson (eds.), *Paths to War: New Essays on the Origins of the Second World War* (London: Macmillan, 1989), pp. 297–329.

151 William R. Rock, *Chamberlain and Roosevelt: British Foreign Policy and the United States, 1937–1940* (Columbus, OH, 1988), p. 293.

152 Churchill, *Second World War*, vol. I, pp. 229–32, 238–40, 305.

153 *The Listener*, 1 October 1939, p. 647.

154 Michael J. Carley, '"Only the USSR Has ... Clean Hands": The Soviet Perspective on the Failure of Collective Security and the Collapse of Czechoslovakia, 1934–1938 (Part 2)' *Diplomacy and Statecraft*, 21 (2010), no. 3, 368–96, at 371.

155 Churchill, *Second World War*, vol. I, p. 167.

156 *The Complete Maisky Diaries*, 3 vols., ed. Gabriel Gorodetsky (New Haven, 2017), vol. I, p. 50.

157 For the evolution of Churchill's position from 1934, see David Carlton, *Churchill and the Soviet Union* (Manchester, 2000), pp. 46–64.

158 *NCDL*, vol. IV, p. 396.

159 *DBFP* 3/1, no. 148; Keith Neilson, '"Pursued by a Bear": British Estimates of Soviet Military Strength and Anglo-Soviet Relations, 1922–1939', *Canadian Journal of History*, 28 (1993), no. 2, 189–221.

160 Glyn Stone, 'The British Government and the Sale of Arms to the Lesser European Powers, 1936–39', *Diplomacy and Statecraft*, 14 (2003), no. 2, 237–70.

161 COS 697, 16 March 1938, paras 18–31, CAB 53/37/4; COS 872, 3 April 1939, paras 12–14, 19–21, CAB 53/47/3; JIC 99, 18 May 1939, CAB 56/4; *WSCC*, vol. V, part 3, p. 1345; Jerzy Cynk, *History of the Polish Air Force 1918–1968* (Reading, 1972), pp. 93–114.

162 John Ferris, *Intelligence and Strategy: Selected Essays* (Abingdon, 2005), pp. 99–137.

163 Christopher Andrew, *For the President's Eyes Only: Secret Intelligence and the American Presidency from Washington to Bush* (London, 1995), pp. 81–99.

164 John Ferris, *Behind the Enigma: The Authorized History of GCHQ, Britain's Secret Cyber-Intelligence Agency* (London, 2020), pp. 153–8.

165 David Dilks, 'Flashes of Intelligence: The Foreign Office, the SIS and Security before the Second World War', in Christopher Andrew and David Dilks, (eds.), *The Missing Dimension: Government and Intelligence Communities in the Twentieth Century* (London, 1984), pp. 101–25.

166 Christopher Andrew and Vasili Mitrokhin, *The Mitrokhin Archive: The KGB in Europe and the West* (London, 1999), pp. 65–9, 75–86, 107–8.

167 Martin Kahn, 'British Intelligence on Soviet War Potential in 1939: A Revised Picture and some Implications (a Contribution to the "Unending Debate")', *Intelligence and National Security*, 28 (2013), no. 5, 717–47.

168 Andrew and Mitrokhin, *Mitrokhin Archive*, pp. 85–6, 120, 122.

169 Adolf Hitler, *Mein Kampf* (London, [1925] 1969), p. 133; Manfred Messerschmidt, 'Foreign Policy and Preparation for War', in Militärgeschichtliches Forschungsamt (ed.), *Germany and the Second World War*, vol. I, pp. 541–717 at 628.

170 Wesley Wark, *The Ultimate Enemy: British Intelligence and Nazi Germany, 1933–1939* (Ithaca, NY, 1985), pp. 35–6, 65–9; Peter Jackson, *France and*

the Nazi Menace: Intelligence and Policy Making 1933–1939 (Oxford, 2000),
pp. 271–4.
171 Wark, *Ultimate Enemy*, pp. 226–33; Jackson, *France and the Nazi Menace*,
pp. 337–42, 350–64; W. N. Medlicott, *The Economic Blockade*, 2 vols.
(London, 1952 and 1959), vol. I, pp. 1–3, 26–7.

Chapter 4

1 According to the Board of Trade's index of wholesale prices – see B. R.
Mitchell and Phyllis Deane, *Abstract of British Historical Statistics* (Cambridge,
1962), p. 477. The index included a large element of import prices, and at a
time when Britain was the world's largest importer of food and raw materials
reflected the price of internationally traded goods.
2 Department of Employment and Productivity, *British Labour Statistics:
Historical Abstract 1886–1968* (London, 1971), Table 160; Charles
Feinstein, *National Income, Expenditure and Output of the United Kingdom
1855–1965* (Cambridge, 1972), Table 58.
3 For the workings of the gold standard, see Barry Eichengreen, *Golden Fetters:
The Gold Standard and the Great Depression 1919–1939* (New York, 1992).
4 Forrest H. Capie, Terence C. Mills and Geoffrey E. Wood, 'Debt
Management and Interest Rates: The British Stock Conversion of 1932',
Applied Economics, 18 (1986), no. 10, 1111–26; Roger Middleton, *Towards
the Managed Economy: Keynes, the Treasury and the Fiscal Policy Debate of the
1930s* (London, 1985), pp. 78–115.
5 Sir Richard Hopkins, 'Speculative Forecast of 1935 on the Basis of "Old
Moore's Almanac"', 21 March 1932, T 171/296; Robert Self, *Neville
Chamberlain, a Biography* (Aldershot, 2006), p. 209; G. C. Peden, *The Treasury
and British Public Policy, 1906–1959* (Oxford, 2000), pp. 209–10, 265–6.
6 Susan Howson, *Domestic Monetary Management in Britain 1919–38*
(Cambridge, 1975), pp. 82–6.
7 Peden, *Treasury and British Public Policy*, pp. 240–1, 260–3; Tim Rooth,
*British Protectionism and the International Economy: Overseas Commercial
Policy in the 1930s* (Cambridge, 1993), pp. 63–70.
8 Andrew Roberts, *Churchill: Walking with Destiny* (London, 2018), p. 356.
9 Roger Middleton, 'British Monetary and Fiscal Policy in the 1930s', *Oxford
Review of Economic Policy*, 26 (2010), no. 3, 414–41. For comparison of extent
of economic recovery in Britain and the United States, see Nick Crafts and
Peter Fearon, 'Lessons from the 1930s Great Depression', ibid., 285–317, at
287. For argument that effects of Keynes's proposals would have been less
than he claimed, see Nicholas Crafts and Terence Mills, 'Self-defeating
Austerity? Evidence from 1930s Britain', *European Review of Economic
History*, 19 (2015), no. 2, 109–27.
10 Forrest Capie, *Depression and Protection: Britain between the Wars* (London,
1983), pp. 96–143; Michael Kitson and Solomos Solomou, *Protectionism and
Economic Revival: The British Interwar Economy* (Cambridge, 1990), esp.
pp. 89–99.

11 Winston S. Churchill, 'How to Meet the Bill', *Step by Step 1936–1939* (London, 1939), pp. 98–101 at 99.

12 Ian M. Drummond, *The Floating Pound and the Sterling Area 1931–1939* (Cambridge, 1981); Susan Howson, *Sterling's Managed Float: The Operations of the Exchange Equalisation Account, 1932–39* (Princeton, 1980).

13 *From the Morgenthau Diaries*, 3 vols., ed. John Morton Blum, vol. 1 (Boston, MA, 1959), p. 143.

14 Rooth, *British Protectionism*, p. 286.

15 'United Kingdom War Debt to the United States', no date, but position in file indicates December 1936, T 160/934/5 (F.13300/12).

16 Vansittart, 'The Foreign Policy of His Majesty's Government in the United Kingdom with a List of Commitments Arising out of that Policy and the Foreign Policy of Other Nations', 19 May 1933, paras. 4 and 213, Lord Vansittart papers, VNST I/1/7, Churchill Archives Centre, Cambridge.

17 HC Deb, 10 May 1932, vol. 265, c. 1750.

18 CP 416 (32), 1 December 1932, CAB 24/235/16.

19 *JMK*, vol. XVIII, pp. 382–6.

20 *Note Addressed by the United States Government to His Majesty's Government in a Reply to a Note Dated 10 November 1932 Relating to the British War Debt*, 23 November 1932 (Cmd. 4203), UK Parliamentary Papers 1932–33.

21 *NCDL*, vol. III., pp. 359–60 (26 November 1932); Meeting of members of Cabinet held in Prime Minister's room, 28 November 1932, T 172/1507.

22 *Further Note Addressed by His Majesty's Government to the United States Government Relating to the British War Debt*, 11 December 1932, (Cmd. 4215), UK Parliamentary Papers 1932–33.

23 Sir Frederick Leith-Ross, *Money Talks: Fifty Years of International Finance* (London, 1968), pp. 172–9.

24 CC 22 (34), 30 May 1934, CAB 23/79/7.

25 Greg Kennedy, '"Rat in Power": Neville Chamberlain and the Creation of British Foreign Policy, 1931–39', in T. G. Otte (ed.), *The Makers of British Foreign Policy: From Pitt to Thatcher* (Basingstoke, 2002), pp. 173–95, at 175–6.

26 Robert Self, *Britain, America and the War Debt Controversy: The Economic Diplomacy of an Unspecial Relationship, 1917–1941* (London, 2006), pp. 117–18, 172–3, 186–7.

27 Greg Kennedy, 'Neville Chamberlain and Strategic Relations with the United States during his Chancellorship', *Diplomacy and Statecraft*, 13 (2002), no. 1, 95–120, at 113–14.

28 Robert Self, 'Perception and Posture in Anglo-American Relations: The War Debt Controversy and the "Official Mind", 1919–1940', *International History Review*, 29 (2007), no. 2, 282–312.

29 Eichengreen, *Golden Fetters*, pp. 205–7, 247–9.

30 William Ashworth, *A Short History of the International Economy since 1850*, 2nd edition (London, 1962), p. 243; Charles P. Kindleberger, *The World in Depression 1929–1939* (London, 1973), p. 295.

31 Winston S. Churchill, 'The Truth About War Debts', *Answers*, 17 March 1934, reproduced in *Finest Hour, The Journal of Winston Churchill*, no. 153 (winter 2011/12), 26–28.

32 Self, *Neville Chamberlain*, p. 182.
33 See HC Deb, 14 December 1932, vol. 273, cc. 353–68; 14 June 1933, vol. 279, cc. 284–8.
34 Lord Vansittart, *The Mist Procession* (London, 1958), p. 466.
35 William E. Leuchtenburg, *Franklin Roosevelt and the New Deal* (New York, 1963), pp. 296–7; Max Jacobson, *The Diplomacy of the Winter War* (Cambridge, MA, 1961), pp. 191–7.
36 Keith Neilson, 'Perception and Posture in Anglo-American Relations: The Legacy of the Simon-Stimson Affair, 1932–1941', *International History Review*, 29 (2007), no. 2, 313–37
37 Thomas Jones, *A Diary with Letters 1931–1950* (London, 1954), p. 30.
38 'Ten Year Rule', 12 June 1931, VNST I 1/5.
39 CC 12 (32), 10 February 1932, CAB 23/70/12 and CC 19 (32), 23 March 1932, CAB 23/70/19.
40 Sir Maurice Hankey diary, 4 March 1933, HNKY 1/7, Churchill Archives Centre, Cambridge.
41 *NCDL*, vol. III, pp. 378–9.
42 'Foreign Policy', 19 May 1933, VNST I 1/7, paras. 6 and 208.
43 HC Deb, vol. 274, cc. 42–8.
44 *Winston Churchill: His Complete Speeches 1897–1963*, 8 vols., ed. Robert Rhodes James, vol. V (New York, 1974), pp. 5227–8.
45 Winston S. Churchill, *The Second World War*, vol. I: *The Gathering Storm*, (London, 1948), p. 69.
46 Treaty of Versailles, part V.
47 'Foreign Policy', 19 May 1933, VNST I 1/7, paras. 7 and 9.
48 *NCDL*, vol. III, pp. 353, 355–8.
49 Ibid., p. 379.
50 Ibid. p. 392; CC 48 (33), 26 July 1933, CAB 23/76/20.
51 HC Deb, 23 March 1933, vol. 276, cc. 542, 545–8, 551.
52 Untitled minute, 26 February 1933, VNST I 2/2.
53 Minute, 6 May 1933, on Sir Horace Rumbold's despatch No 425 from Berlin, VNST I 2/3.
54 'Foreign Policy', 19 May 1933, VNST I 1/7, para. 8.
55 Minute to Secretary of State, 10 May 1933, VNST, I 2/4.
56 Minute, 6 May 1933, VNST I 2/3.
57 Marginal note on untitled minute, 26 February 1933, VNST I 2/2.
58 'Foreign Policy', 19 May 1933, VNST I 1/7, paras. 111–16.
59 HC Deb, 14 March 1933, vol. 275, c. 1820.
60 HC Deb, 23 March 1933, vol. 276, c. 542.
61 HC Deb, 13 April 1933, vol. 276, cc. 2788–91.
62 HC Deb, 7 November 1933, vol. 281, cc. 137–42.
63 CP 212 (33), 30 August 1933, CAB 24/243/12.
64 Fisher to Chamberlain, 1 October 1938, PREM 1/252.
65 CID paper 1113-B, 12 October 1933, CAB 4/22.
66 *NCDL*, vol. III, p. 408.
67 Fisher and Hopkins, 'Speculative Forecast of 1935 on the Basis of "Old Moore's Almanack"', 21 March 1932, T 171/296.

68 DRC 6th meeting, 23 January 1934, CAB 16/109.
69 *Chief of Staff: The Diaries of Lieutenant-General Sir Henry Pownall*, ed. Brian Bond, vol. I (London, 1972), p. 29.
70 DRC 1st and 7th meetings, 14 November 1933 and 25 January 1934, CAB 16/109.
71 See, for example, Peter Bell, *Chamberlain, Germany and Japan, 1933–4* (London, 1996), pp. 34–8, 43–5; Brian Bond, *British Military Policy between the Wars* (Oxford, 1980), pp. 195–7; Michael Howard, *The Continental Commitment: The Dilemma of British Defence Policy in the Era of the Two World Wars* (London, 1972), p. 105; Charles Morrisey and M. A. Ramsay, '"Giving a Lead in the Right Direction": Sir Robert Vansittart and the Defence Requirements Sub-Committee', *Diplomacy & Statecraft*, 6 (1995), no. 1, 39–60; Michael L. Roi, *Alternative to Appeasement: Sir Robert Vansittart and Alliance Diplomacy, 1934–1937* (Westport, CT, 1997), pp. 28–35; Wesley Wark, *The Ultimate Enemy: British Intelligence and Nazi Germany, 1933–1939* (Ithaca, NY, 1985), pp. 28–32.
72 DRC 3rd and 4th meetings, 4 December 1933 and 18 January 1934, CAB 16/109.
73 Keith Neilson, 'The Defence Requirements Sub-Committee, British Strategic Foreign Policy, Neville Chamberlain and the Path to Appeasement' *English Historical Review*, 118 (2003), no. 477, 651–84, at 672 and 679; Greg Kennedy, *Anglo-American Strategic Relations and the Far East 1933–1939* (London, 2002), pp. 55–7.
74 Brian McKercher, 'Deterrence and the European Balance of Power: The Field Force and British Grand Strategy, 1934–1938', *English Historical Review*, 123 (2008), no. 500, 98–131, at 112.
75 DRC 10th and 12th meetings, 16 and 26 February 1934, CAB 16/109; DRC Report, 28 February 1934, para. 28, ibid. (also CAB 24/247/64).
76 N. H. Gibbs, *Grand Strategy*, vol. I: *Rearmament Policy* (London, 1976), pp. 97–8.
77 Hankey diary, 4 March 1934, HNKY 1/7.
78 CP 104 (34), 7 April 1934, CAB 24/248/40.
79 Record of meeting at Foreign Office, 30 April 1934, Sir Eric Phipps papers, PHPP I 1/12, Churchill Archives Centre, Cambridge.
80 CC 10 (34), 19 March 1934, CAB 23/78/10.
81 Ibid.; *NCDL*, vol. IV, pp. 65, 67, 69; Neville Chamberlain diary, 20 April 1934, NC2/23, Cadbury Research Library, University of Birmingham; DC (M) (32) 95, 28 March 1934, CAB 27/510.
82 HC Deb, 18 May 1934, vol. 289, c. 2115.
83 Andrew Boyle, *Trenchard, Man of Vision* (London, 1962), pp. 681–2.
84 DC(M) (32) 120, 20 June 1934, CAB 27/511.
85 Hankey to Baldwin, 29 June 1934, CAB 21/434.
86 Hankey diary, 9 August 1934, HNKY 1/7.
87 CP 193 (34), 16 July 1934, CAB 24/250/18; CC 14 (34), 18 July 1934, CAB 23/79/14.
88 Boyle, *Trenchard*, p. 681.

89 DC(M) (32) 109, 9 May 1934, CAB 27/510; DC(M) (32) 44th and 45th meeting, CAB 27/507.

90 DC(M) (32) 120, CAB 27/511; DC(M) (32) 50th meeting, 25 June 1934, CAB 27/507.

91 DC(M) (32) 51st meeting, 26 June 1934, CAB 27/507; CP 205 (34), 1 August 1934, CAB 24/250/30.

92 *NCDL*, vol. IV, p. 77.

93 DC(M) (32) 120, 20 June 1934, CAB 27/511; DC(M) (32) 50th, 51st, 52nd and 55th meetings, 25 June, 26 June, and 2 July 1934, CAB 27/507; Boyle, *Trenchard*, p. 681; Chamberlain diary, 6 June 1934, NC2/23.

94 DC(M) (32) 120, 20 June 1934, CAB 27/511; DC(M) (32) 50th and 55th meetings, 25 June and 24 July 1934, CAB 27/507; CP 205 (34), 1 August 1934, CAB 24/250/30.

95 Bell, *Chamberlain, Germany and Japan*, pp. 146, 159–60, 176–8.

96 Neilson, 'Defence Requirements Sub-Committee', 680–3.

97 NCM (35) 3, 23 April 1934, CAB 29/148.

98 Hankey to Baldwin, 23 August 1934, Baldwin papers 1/40–48.

99 Howard, *Continental Commitment*, pp. 100, 109–11, 120.

100 DC(M) (32) 50th meeting, 25 June 1934, CAB 27/507.

101 DC(M) (32), 52nd meeting, 2 July 1934, CAB 27/507.

102 HC Deb, 7 February 1934, vol. 285, c. 1197.

103 HC Deb, 8 March 1934, vol. 286, cc. 2042–3, 2046, 2069–74, 2078.

104 *Churchill Complete Speeches*, vol. V, p. 5376; HC Deb, 13 July 1934, vol. 292, c. 675.

105 HC Deb 4 March 1933, vol. 275, cc. 1820; HC Deb, 8 March 1934, vol. 286, c. 2070.

106 HC Deb 8 March 1934, vol. 286, cc. 2069, 2071.

107 CC 57 (33), 26 October 1933, CAB 23/77/8.

108 261st CID meeting, 9 November 1933, CAB 2/6.

109 Comment on minute by Fisher, 15 January 1934, T 161/624/5 (S.36130/34).

110 Note by Sir Warren Fisher, 29 January 1934, DRC 12, CAB 16/109.

111 DRC 14, 28 Februay 1934, paras. 8 and 9, CAB 24/247/64. See also Fisher to Hankey, DRC 16, 12 February, and note by Fisher, DRC 19, 17 February, 1934, CAB 16/109.

112 CC 9 (34), 14 March 1934, CAB 23/78/9.

113 Simon Bourette-Knowles, 'The Global Micawber: Sir Robert Vansittart, the Treasury and the Global Balance of Power, 1933–35', *Diplomacy and Statecraft*, 6 (1995), no. 1, 91–121.

114 Simon to Chamberlain, 7 September 1934, MSS Simon 79, Bodleian Libraries, Oxford.

115 *NCDL*, vol. IV, p. 90.

116 CC 32 (34), 25 September 1934, CAB 23/79/17.

117 Chamberlain diary, 17 October 1934, NC2/23.

118 Gill Bennett, 'British Policy in the Far East 1933–1936: Treasury and Foreign Office', *Modern Asian Studies*, 26 (1992), no. 3, 545–68, at 557–8.

119 Chamberlain diary, 25 October 1934, NC2/23; *NCDL*, vol. IV, pp. 94–5.

120 *NCDL*, vol. iv, p. 101.

121 Naval staff memorandum, NCM (35) 1, 14 April, and Fisher's comments thereon, NCM (35) 3, 23 April, 1934, CAB 29/148; Chatfield to Fisher, 4 June 1934, Chatfield papers (CHT) 3/1, National Maritime Museum, Greenwich, London.

122 Fisher to Chatfield, 11 July 1934, Baldwin papers 131/189, referring to Anglo-American naval discussions on 2 July - see NCM (35) 14, CAB 29/148.

123 Stephen E. Pelz, *Race to Pearl Harbor* (Cambridge, MA, 1974), p. 143; Kennedy, *Anglo-American Strategic Relations*, pp. 195–6, 199.

124 Milton Friedman, 'Franklin D. Roosevelt, Silver, and China', *Journal of Political Economy*, 100 (1992), no. 1, 62–83.

125 Kennedy, 'Rat in Power', pp. 179–81, 189.

126 Anthony Best, 'The Leith-Ross Mission and British Policy towards East Asia, 1934–7', *International History Review*, 35 (2013), no. 4, 681–701, at 688, 697.

127 Bell, *Chamberlain, Germany and Japan*, pp. 162–3.

128 Kibata Yoichi, 'Anglo-Japanese Relations from the Manchurian Incident to Pearl Harbor: Missed Opportunities?' in Ian Nish and Kibata Yoichi (eds.), *The History of Anglo-Japanese Relations, 1600–2000*, vol. II: *The Political-Diplomatic Dimension, 1931–2000* (Basingstoke, 2000), pp. 1–25, at 7–11.

129 Winston S. Churchill, 'The Mission of Japan', in *The Collected Essays of Sir Winston Churchill*, ed. Michael Wolff (London, 1976), pp. 365–72.

Chapter 5

1 Despatch from Group Captain R. M. Field, air attaché, Paris, 15 November 1934, CAB 21/417.

2 CC 41 (34), 21 November 1934, CAB 23/80/9.

3 CP 865 (34), 23 November 1934, CAB 24/251/40.

4 CC 42 (34), 26 November 1934, CAB 23/80/10.

5 HC Deb, 28 November 1934, vol. 295, cc. 858–62, 866–7, 882–3.

6 CID paper no. 1149-B, 23 October 1934, CAB 4/23; CID minutes, 266th meeting, 22 November 1934, CAB 2/6.

7 *NCDL*, vol. IV, p. 122; Fisher to Baldwin, 26 February 1935, Baldwin papers, 1/80. Earlier drafts of the white paper are in CAB 21/407.

8 *NCDL*, vol. IV, p. 119.

9 CP 69 (35), 26 March 1935, CAB 24/254/25.

10 HC Deb, 19 March 1935, vol. 299, cc. 1049–63.

11 Ministerial Committee on Defence Requirements, 61st meeting, 30 April 1935, CAB 27/508.

12 Ministerial Sub-Committee on Air Parity reports, DCM (32) 141 and 143; Ministerial Committee on Defence Requirements, 20 May 1935, CAB 27/508; *NCDL*, vol. IV, p. 137; CC 29 (35), 21 May 1935, CAB 23/81/28.

13 G. C. Peden, *British Rearmament and the Treasury, 1932–1939* (Edinburgh, 1979), pp. 72–4.

14 Chamberlain diary, 2 August 1935, NC2/23.
15 Third DRC Report, DRC 37, 21 November 1935, table IVc, CAB 16/112.
16 *NCDL*, vol. IV, p. 122.
17 Ibid., p. 128.
18 Ibid., p. 141.
19 HC Deb, 22 July 1935, vol. 304, cc. 1550–7.
20 Joseph A. Maiolo, *The Royal Navy and Nazi Germany, 1933–39* (Basingstoke, 1998), pp. 20–2, 26–8, 32–7.
21 G. Bruce Strang, 'Imperial Dreams: The Mussolini-Laval Accords of January 1935', *Historical Journal*, 44 (2001), no. 3, 799–809.
22 *DBFP* 2/14, doc. 308.
23 *NCDL*, vol. IV, p. 141; *DBFP* 2/14, docs. 320, 323, 325.
24 *DBFP* 2/14, docs. 327, 458, 465.
25 Daniel Waley, *British Public Opinion and the Abyssinian War* (London, 1975), pp. 19–32.
26 Chamberlain diary, 5 July 1935, NC2/23.
27 *NCDL*, vol. IV, p. 149.
28 *DBFP* 2/14, doc. 483.
29 *WSCC*, vol. V, part 2, p. 1251.
30 Richard Hammond, 'An Enduring Influence on Imperial Defence and Grand Strategy: British Perceptions of the Italian Navy, 1935–1943', *International History Review*, 39 (2017), no. 5, 810–35.
31 Churchill to James Garvin (editor of the *Observer* newspaper), 1 September 1935, cited in Gaines Post, *Dilemmas of Appeasement: British Deterrence and Defense, 1934–1937* (Ithaca, NY, 1993), p. 125.
32 *Winston Churchill: His Complete Speeches 1897–1963*, ed. Robert Rhodes James, vol. V (New York, 1974), p. 5673.
33 *WSCC*, vol. V, part 2, pp. 1270–2.
34 Viscount Templewood, *Nine Troubled Years* (London, 1954), pp. 166, 169–71.
35 Michael L. Roi, *Alternative to Appeasement: Sir Robert Vansittart and Alliance Diplomacy, 1934–37* (Westport, CT, 1997), p. 99.
36 DRC 17th meeting, 10 October 1935, CAB 16/112.
37 For Britain's defensive precautions see Steven Morewood, '"This Silly African Business": The Military Dimension of Britain's Response to the Abyssinian Crisis', in G. Bruce Strang (ed.), *Collision of Empires: Italy's Invasion of Ethiopia and Its International Impact* (Farnham, 2013), pp. 73–107.
38 HC Deb, 24 October 1935, vol. 305, cc. 357–67.
39 www.conservativemanifesto.com/1935/1935-conservative-manifesto.shtml
40 *DBFP* 2/15, no. 251.
41 G. Bruce Strang, '"The Worst of All Worlds": Oil Sanctions and Italy's Invasion of Abyssinia', 1935–36', *Diplomacy and Statecraft*, 19 (2008), no. 2, 210–35.
42 Keith Feiling, *The Life of Neville Chamberlain* (London, 1946), p. 272.
43 CC 50 (35), 2 December 1935, CAB 23/82/18; Chamberlain diary, 8 December 1935, NC2/23; CP 235 (35), 8 December 1935, CAB 24/257/55; CC 52 (35), 9 December 1935, CAB 23/82/20.

44 *The Times*, 16 December 1935, p. 15.
45 Winston S. Churchill, *The Second World War*, vol. I: *The Gathering Storm* (London, 1948), p. 143.
46 HC Deb, 24 February1936, vol. 309, c. 189–90.
47 HC Deb, 19 December 1935, vol. 307, c. 2018.
48 *DBFP* 2/18, no. 399.
49 CP 42 (36), 11 February 1936, p. 5, CAB 24/260/7.
50 Hankey's note of conversation with Churchill, 19 April 1936, CAB 21/435.
51 Churchill, *Second World War*, vol. I, p. 143.
52 Viscount Norwich, *Old Men Forget* (London, 1953), pp. 190–1.
53 Record of meeting with League of Nations Union Deputation, 13 December 1935, PREM 1/195.
54 Chamberlain diary 27 April 1936, NC2/23.
55 Earl of Avon, *The Eden Memoirs: Facing the Dictators* (London, 1962), p. 384.
56 CC 39 (36), 27 May 1936, CAB 23/84/10.
57 *The Times*, 11 June 1936, p. 10; *NCDL*, vol. IV, pp. 194–5.
58 *Churchill Complete Speeches*, vol. VI, p. 5772.
59 *WSCC*, vol. V, part 3, pp. 171–3.
60 DRC 25 and DRC 37, CAB 16/112. A copy of the latter is enclosed with CP 26 (36), CAB 24/259/26.
61 DPR 4th meeting, CAB 16/136.
62 DRC 37, CAB 16/112.
63 Minutes of DPR(DR) meeting, 13 January 1936, CAB 16/123; W. J. Reader, W. J. *Architect of Air Power: The Life of the First Viscount Weir of Eastwood* (London, 1968), pp. 235–8.
64 Minutes of DPR(DR) meetings, 13 and 14 January 1936, CAB 16/123; 'Defence Co-ordination: Note by the chancellor of the exchequer', n.d., PREM 1/196, fol. 60.
65 Memorandum by Lord Weir, DPR(DR) 4, 9 January 1936; DPR(DR) minutes, 14, 16, and 31 January 1936, CAB 16/123; Chamberlain diary 19 January 1936, NC2/23.
66 DPR(DR) minutes 14, 16, 20 and 27 January 1936, CAB 16/123, and DPR (DR) 9, 6 February 1936, CAB 24/159/26; CC 10 (36), 25 February 1936, CAB 23/83/10; *Statement Relating to Defence* (Cmd. 5107), UK Parliamentary Papers 1935–6.
67 HC Deb, 10 March 1936, vol. 309, cc. 2006–9; S. D. Waley, 'Germany's Expenditure on Armaments', 30 June 1936, T 172/2085.
68 Churchill, *Second World War*, vol. I, p. 152.
69 Barry Eichengreen, *Golden Fetters: The Gold Standard and the Great Depression 1919–1939* (New York, 1992), pp. 348–57, 365–73.
70 Martin Alexander, *The Republic in Danger: General Maurice Gamelin and the Politics of French Defence, 1933–1940* (Cambridge, 1992), pp. 73–9; Peter Jackson, *France and the Nazi Menace: Intelligence and Policy Making, 1933–1939* (Oxford, 2000), pp. 171–7; Stephen A. Schuker, 'France and the Remilitarization of the Rhineland', *French Historical Studies*, 14 (1986), no. 3, 299–338.
71 CP 42 (36), 11 February 1936, enclosing memorandum by Vansittart on 'Britain, France and Germany', 3 February 1936, CAB 24/260/7.

72 CC 15 (36), 5 March 1936, CAB 23/83/15; *DBFP* 2/16, doc. 134.

73 CC 18 (36), 11 March 1936, CAB 23/83/18.

74 *DBFP*, 2/16, doc. 115; CC 20 (36), 16 March 1936, CAB 23/83/20.

75 James Emmerson, *The Rhineland Crisis: A Study in Multilateral Diplomacy* (London, 1977), pp. 188–90, 193–8 (quotation on 198).

76 'Foreign Affairs Committee', notes by T. L. Rowan, PREM 1/194, fol. 59.

77 HC Deb, 26 March 1936, vol. 310, cc. 1446, 1524–8, 1530. See also 6 April 1936, vol. 310, cc. 2484–5.

78 HC Deb, 26 March 1936, vol. 310, cc. 1527–31.

79 Ibid., cc. 1529, 1538–49 (quotation at 1548).

80 HC Deb, 6 April 1936, vol. 310, cc. 2488–9. See also 5 November 1936, vol. 317, cc. 313–14.

81 Hankey's note of conversation, 19 April 1936, CAB 21/435.

82 HC Deb, 5 November 1936, vol. 317, cc. 318–19.

83 R. A. C. Parker, *Churchill and Appeasement: Could Churchill Have Prevented the Second World War?* (Basingstoke, 2000), pp. 106–7, 117–19, 124–5, 146–7.

84 Avon, *Facing the Dictators*, pp. 401–17.

85 Jill Edwards, *The British Government and the Spanish Civil War, 1936–1939* (Basingstoke, 1979).

86 *NCDL*, vol. IV, p. 214 (24 October 1936).

87 Glyn Stone, 'Neville Chamberlain and the Spanish Civil War, 1936–9', *International History Review*, 35 (2013), no. 2, 377–95; Scott Ramsay, 'Ensuring Benevolent Neutrality: The British Government's Appeasement of General Franco during the Spanish Civil War 1936–1939', *International History Review*, 41 (2019), no. 3, 604–23.

88 Winston Churchill, 'The Spanish Ulcer', *Step by Step 1936–1939* (London, 1939), pp. 312–16.

89 Churchill, 'Hope in Spain', ibid., pp. 331–4.

90 CP 42 (36), CAB 24/260/7.

91 CC 20 (36), 16 March 1936, CAB 23/83/20.

92 HC Deb, 6 April 1936, vol. 310, cc. 2483–4; 21 April 1936, vol. 311, cc. 101–2.

93 FP (36) 3rd and 4th meetings, 21 and 27 July 1936, CAB 27/622.

94 For these developments see Andrew J. Crozier, *Appeasement and Germany's Last Bid for Colonies* (Basingstoke, 1988), pp. 175–203.

95 *DBFP* 2/18, doc. 366.

96 Bernd-Jürgen Wendt, '"Economic Appeasement" – A Crisis Strategy', in Wolfgang J. Mommsen and Lothar Kettenacker (eds.), *The Fascist Challenge and the Policy of Appeasement* (London, 1983), pp. 157–72, at 164.

97 Neil Forbes, 'London Banks, the German Standstill Agreements, and "Economic Appeasement" in the 1930s', *Economic History Review*, 40 (1987), no. 4, 571–87.

98 HC Deb, 10 March 1936, vol. 309, cc. 2010–14.

99 HC Deb, 21 May 1936, vol. 312, cc. 1443–4.

100 Reader, *Architect of Air Power*, pp. 244–50.

101 *WSCC* , vol. V, part 3, pp. 285, 294.

102 HC Deb, 10 March 1936, vol. 309, cc. 2015–16.

103 HC Deb, 16 March 1936, vol. 310, cc. 97–8.
104 *WSCC*, vol. V, part 3, pp. 466–70.
105 Ibid., p. 278.
106 Ibid., p. 275; HC Deb, 28 November 1934, vol. 295, c. 859.
107 *WSCC*, vol. V, part 3, p. 282.
108 *NCDL*, vol. IV, p. 211 (10 October 1936)
109 *The Times*, 3 October 1936, p. 7.
110 Chamberlain's diary, 25 October 1936, NC2/23.
111 Secret note, 27 October, and Inskip to Chamberlain 5 November, 1936, CAB 64/35.
112 Chamberlain to Fisher, 30 November 1936, with Fisher's comments, T 161/1071/1 (S.42580/1).
113 CP 326 (36), 3 December 1936, CAB 24/265/46.
114 'Some Notes for the chancellor of the exchequer', December 1936, Weir 17/10, Lord Weir papers, Churchill Archives Centre, Cambridge.
115 CC 75 (36), 16 December 1936, CAB 23/86//19.
116 Chamberlain to Inskip, 16 December, Hankey to Inskip, 17 December, 1936, and Chamberlain to Inskip, 24 December, 1936, CAB 64/35.
117 CP 41 (37), 28 January 1937, CAB 24/267/42.
118 CP 46 (37), 2 February 1937, CAB 24/267/47.
119 *NCDL*, vol. IV, p. 233; CC 5 (37), 3 February 1937, CAB 23/87/7.
120 Brian Bond, *Liddell Hart: A Study of His Military Thought* (London, 1977), pp. 88–118; Michael Howard, *The Continental Commitment: The Dilemma of British Defence Policy in the Era of the Two World Wars* (London, 1972), p. 107; Alex Danchev, *Alchemist of War: The Life of Basil Liddell Hart* (London, 1998), pp. 187–95.
121 Weir 17/10, Churchill Archives Centre, Cambridge.
122 Chamberlain to Liddell Hart, 8 March 1937, Liddell Hart papers, I/159, Liddell Hart Centre for Military Archives, King's College, London.
123 Hankey, 'Role of the British Army', 18 January 1937, CAB 63/52.
124 HC Deb, 12 November 1936, vol. 317, cc. 1106, 1110–13 (quotations at 1100 and 1113).
125 See, for example, Churchill's notes circulated to the CID on 17 December 1935 and Foreign Office officials' comments thereon, in *WSCC*, vol. V, part 2, pp. 1345–8, 1356–7; comments by Lord Swinton and the Air Staff on a paper by Churchill, 26 June 1936, and Hankey to Inskip, 29 June 1936, *WSCC*, vol. V, part 3, pp. 216–21; HC Deb, 27 January 1937, vol. 319, cc. 998–1003, 1012–17.
126 Chamberlain to Swinton, 8 December 1936, T 172/2111; 286th CID meeting, 17 December 1936, CAB 2/6.
127 Eden to Inskip, 25 February 1937, FO 954/4A, vol. 4, fos. 98–100.
128 Peden, *British Rearmament*, pp. 76–8.
129 HC Deb, vol. 320, cc. 1206–17; *Defence Loans* (Cmd. 5368), UK Parliamentary Papers 1936–37.
130 HC Deb, 17 February 1937, vol. 320, cc. 1223–30; *The Economist*, 23 January 1937, pp. 157–8. Pethick-Lawrence was familiar with Keynes's ideas – see Richard Toye, 'The Labour Party and the Economics of

Rearmament, 1935–39', *Twentieth Century British History*, 12 (2001), no. 3, 303–26, at 310.

131 HC Deb, 17 February 1937, vol. 320, cc. 1313–14.
132 Hopkins's notes on the Second Reading of the Borrowing Bill, 23 February 1937, T 175/96.
133 *JMK*, vol. XXI, pp. 401–9.
134 Phillips to Hopkins, 19 January 1937, T 161/783/6 (S.48431/02/1).
135 *NCDL*, vol. IV, pp. 246–8.
136 HC Deb, 31 May 1937, vol. 324, cc. 819–20.
137 HC Deb, 1 June 1937, vol. 324, cc. 882–97.
138 Simon diary, 15 January 1938, MSS Simon, vol. 7.
139 Note by Hopkins, 19 January 1937, T 161/783/6 (S48431/02/1).

Chapter 6

1 *NCDL*, vol. IV, p. 241; *DBFP* 2/18, nos. 202, 268 and 285. There is a copy of Chamberlain's reply to Morgenthau in PREM 1/261, fos. 60–5.
2 Sir Ronald Lindsay, British ambassador in Washington, to Eden, 1 June 1937, enclosing memorandum to be communicated to Chamberlain, PREM 1/261.
3 Chamberlain to Norman Davis, n.d., but position in file indicates 8 July 1937, PREM 1/261, fos. 70–3.
4 Roosevelt to Chamberlain, 28 July 1937, in Elliott Roosevelt (ed.), *The Roosevelt Letters: Being the Personal Correspondence of Franklin Delano Roosevelt*, 8 vols. (1949–52), vol. III, p. 215; *NCDL*, vol. IV, p. 267; Chamberlain to Roosevelt, n.d. PREM 1/261, fos. 16–19.
5 millercenter.org/the-presidency/presidential-speeches/october-5-1937-quar-antine-speech.
6 *NCDL*, vol. IV, pp. 273–4.
7 CC 36 (37), 6 October 1937, CAB 23/89/7, and CC 37 (37), 13 October 1937, CAB 23/89/8.
8 millercenter.org/the-presidency/presidential-speeches/october-12-1937-fire-side-chat-10-new-legislation.
9 CC 38 (37), 20 October 1937, CAB 23/89/9; *NCDL*, vol. IV, p. 275.
10 *NCDL*, vol. IV, p. 285.
11 CC 43 (37), 24 November 1937, CAB 23/90A/5.
12 Tweedsmuir to Chamberlain, 25 October 1937, 25 October 1937, PREM 1/229, fol. 16.
13 *The Empire at Bay: The Leo Amery Diaries 1929–1945*, ed. John Barnes and David Nicholson (1988), p. 452.
14 *NCDL*, vol. IV, p. 284.
15 Frank Ashton-Gwatkin to Horace Wilson, 16 March 1938, PREM 1/261.
16 *DBFP* 2/21, no. 433.
17 Robert Dallek, *Franklin D. Roosevelt and American Foreign Policy, 1932–1945* (New York, 1979), pp. 154–5.
18 *DBFP* 2/21, no. 442.

19 Ibid., no. 486; Lawrence Pratt, 'The Anglo-American Naval Conversations on the Far East of January 1938', *International Affairs*, 47 (1971), no. 4, 745–63.

20 *NCDL*, vol. IV, p. 296.

21 *DBFP* 2/21, nos. 471, 478.

22 Ibid., no. 480.

23 *DBFP* 2/19, nos. 422–4.

24 Gill Bennett, 'The Roosevelt Peace Plan of January 1938', *FCO Historical Branch Occasional Papers*, no. 1 (November 1987), 27–37, at 31–2, Foreign Office records: FO 973/522, TNA.

25 *DBFP* 2/19, no. 425, 430, 443.

26 Ibid., no. 445; Earl of Avon, *The Eden Memoirs: Facing the Dictators* (London, 1962), pp. 552–67; 'Full record of conversation between Chamberlain and Eden re Roosevelt initiative', FP (36) 17th meeting, 19 January 1938, Avon papers AP 20/6/29B.

27 *DBFP* 2/19, no. 455.

28 Cordell Hull, *Memoirs*, 2 vols. (London, 1948), vol. I, p. 547.

29 Quoted in William R. Rock, *Chamberlain and Roosevelt: British Foreign Policy and the United States, 1937–1940* (Columbus, OH, 1988), p. 68.

30 Winston S. Churchill, *The Second World War*, vol. I: *The Gathering Storm* (London, 1948), pp. 199, 271.

31 Robert Rhodes James, *Anthony Eden* (London, 1986), p. 188; Andrew Roberts, *Churchill: Walking with Destiny* (London, 2018), p. 422.

32 Dallek, *Roosevelt and American Foreign Policy*, pp. 156–7; Greg Kennedy, *Anglo-American Strategic Relations and the Far East 1933–1939* (London, 2002), pp. 239–40; Rock, *Chamberlain and Roosevelt*, pp. 71–2.

33 David Reynolds, *The Creation of the Anglo-American Alliance 1937–41: A Study in Competitive Co-operation* (London, 1981), 32, 303.

34 *DBFP* 2/19, nos. 441 and 447; *Foreign Relations of the United States* (*FRUS*), 1938, vol. I, no. 79.

35 *DBFP* 2/19, no. 446.

36 Lindsay's telegram no. 114, PREM 1/259, fol. 16.

37 Bennett, 'Roosevelt peace plan', 33.

38 Kennedy, *Anglo-American Strategic Relations*, pp. 36–40.

39 'Mr Churchill's Plea to Germany', *Daily Telegraph*, 19 November 1936, Churchill Press Cuttings, CHPC 15, Churchill Archives Centre, Cambridge.

40 Winston Churchill, 'America Looks at Europe' and 'What We Ask of the United States', *Step by Step 1936–1939* (London, 1939), pp. 134–7, 193–6 (quotation at 194).

41 Lindsay to Sir Frederick Leith-Ross, 1 March 1937, T 160/934/6 (F.1330013).

42 Churchill, 'America Looks at Europe', *Step by Step*, pp. 134–7 at 137.

43 Memorandum by Fisher, 12 November 1937, PREM 1/229.

44 Churchill, 'Defending the Empire', *Step by Step*, pp. 130–3 at 132.

45 *WSCC*, vol. V, part 3, pp. 755–6 (30 August 1937).

46 Winston S. Churchill, 'War is Not Imminent', *Step by Step*, pp. 176–9 at 177.
47 Churchill, 'What Japan Thinks of Us', Ibid., pp. 205–8 at 207.
48 'Viscount Ishii', note by Chamberlain for foreign secretary, 9 December 1937, with comment by Eden, PREM 1/314, fos. 67–70.
49 Conference of ministers, 14 February 1938, PREM 1/308, fol. 56.
50 For the questionnaire in April 1936, see *DBFP* 2/16, no. 277 and Appendix I. For the conference proposal, see *DBFP* 2/17, nos. 15 and 186. For Vansittart, see ibid., Appendix II, para 18.
51 *DBFP* 2/18, no. 268 enclosure.
52 *DBFP* 2/17, Appendix II, para. 22–26.
53 Chamberlain to Weir, 1 August 1937, Weir MSS GB 248 DC 096/22/2, Glasgow University Archives.
54 *NCDL*, vol. IV, p. 264.
55 Ibid., vol. IV, p. 270.
56 *DBFP* 2/17, no. 530; 2/18, no. 615.
57 CID minutes, 296th meeting, 5 July 1937, CAB 2/6.
58 CC 29 (37), 7 July 1937, CAB 23/88/17. Drummond's letter is summarised in *DBFP* 2/19, at p. 44n.
59 William C. Mills, 'Sir Joseph Ball, Adrian Dingli, and Neville Chamberlain's "Secret Channel" to Italy, 1937–1940', *International History Review*, 24 (2002), no. 2, 278–317.
60 *DBFP* 2/19, no. 45.
61 HC Deb, 19 July 1937, vol. 326, c. 1804–5.
62 Wilson to Chamberlain, 26 July 1937, PREM 1/276, fol. 346.
63 *DBFP* 2/19, nos. 64 and 65.
64 J. P. L. Thomas, 'Material for *Facing the Dictators*', undated, Avon papers AP 7/24/81.
65 *NCDL*, vol. IV, p. 264.
66 *DBFP* 2/19, no. 77.
67 *NCDL*, vol. IV, p. 265.
68 *DBFP* 2/19, nos. 94 and 96.
69 Eden to Halifax, 11 August 1937, Avon papers AP 13/1/58E; *NCDL*, vol. IV, p. 267.
70 *DBFP* 2/19, no. 111.
71 Avon, *Facing the Dictators*, p. 469.
72 *NCDL*, vol. IV, p. 271.
73 Churchill, 'Anglo-Italian Friendship – How?' *Step by Step*, pp. 155–8.
74 Churchill to Eden, 3 September, and Duff Cooper to Eden, 5 September, 1937, FO 954/7B.
75 Churchill to Eden, 9 September 1937, Ibid.
76 Avon, *Facing the Dictators*, p. 468.
77 Churchill, 'War Is Not Imminent', *Step by Step*, pp. 176–9.
78 HC Deb, 1 November 1937, vol. 328, cc. 519, 579.
79 *NCDL*, vol. IV, p. 281.

80 William C. Mills, 'The Chamberlain-Grandi Conversations of July-August 1937 and the Appeasement of Italy', *International History Review*, 19 (1997), no. 3, 594–619, at 615.
81 *NCDL*, vol. IV, p. 259.
82 *DBFP* 2/18, no. 574; 2/19, nos. 41, 52, and annex IV to no. 160.
83 *NCDL*, vol. IV, p. 278.
84 Eden to Chamberlain, 16 November 1937, Avon papers AP 20/5/13; Avon, *Facing the Dictators*, pp. 509–12.
85 *NCDL*, vol. IV, pp. 286–7; *DBFP* 2/19, no. 336.
86 *DBFP* 2/19, no. 354.
87 CC 45 (37), 1 December 1937, CAB 23/90A/7.
88 *NCDL*, vol. IV, p. 300; Stephen Roberts, *The House That Hitler Built* (London, 1937), pp. 313–17, 362–3.
89 Churchill, 'War Is Not Imminent', *Step by Step*, pp. 176–9 at 177.
90 HC Deb, 21 December 1937, vol. 299, cc. 1831–6.
91 G. T. Waddington, '*Hassgegner*: German Views of Great Britain in the Later 1930s', *History*, 81 (1996), no. 261, 22–39.
92 CC 27 (37), 30 June 1937, CAB 23/88/15; CP 165(37), 25 June 1937, CAB 24/270/10.
93 Simon to Chamberlain, 25 October 1937, PREM 1/250. The records of the review's meetings are in CAB 64/30.
94 Memorandum by Inskip, 23 November 1937, T161/855/3 (S.48431/01/1); Defence Expenditure in Future Years: Interim Report', CP 316 (37), 15 December 1937, CAB 24/273/41, para. 6–14, and 'Further Report' CP 24 (38), 8 February 1938, CAB 24/274/24, paras. 35–62.
95 CP 316 (37), paras. 41–4.
96 Hankey to Inskip, 27 September 1937, CAB 64/3.
97 Swinton to Simon, 12 July 1937, T 161/855/4 (S.48431/01/2).
98 Hankey to Inskip, 27 September 1937, enclosing DPR 219, 6 September 1937, CAB 64/3.
99 Inskip to Swinton, 4 November 1937, CAB 64/30.
100 CP 316 (37), CAB 24/273/41, paras. 80–100; CC 49 (37), 22 December 1937, CAB 23/90A/11.
101 CP 316 (37), paras. 51–60; G. C. Peden, *British Rearmament* and *the Treasury, 1932–1939* (Edinburgh, 1979), pp. 116, 162–4.
102 Duff Cooper correspondence with Chamberlain, 23 December 1937, 13 March, 28 April and 27 May 1938, PREM 1/346; CC 34 (38), 20 July 1938, CAB 23/94/7; T. L. Rowan, note on new naval construction, 3 January 1939, T 161/909/2 (S.36130/39); *The Duff Cooper Diaries*, ed. John Julius Norwich (London, 2005), p. 252.
103 Brian Bond, *Liddell Hart: A Study of his Military Thought* (London, 1977), pp. 91–4.
104 CC 35 (37), 29 September 1937, CAB 23/89/6; John Kennedy, *The Business of War: The War Narrative of Major-General Sir John Kennedy*, ed. Bernard Fergusson (London, 1957), p. 43.
105 Inskip diary, 11 January 1939, INKIP 2, Churchill Archives Centre, Cambridge.
106 Churchill, 'Germany and the Low Countries', *Step by Step*, pp. 126–9 at 128.

107 COS 639, 12 November 1937, para. 4, CAB 53/34/3.

108 R. J. Minney, *The Private Papers of Hore-Belisha* (London, 1960), p. 54.

109 Basil Liddell Hart, *Europe in Arms* (London, 1937), pp. 78–9.

110 Inskip diary, 16 December 1939, INKP 2.

111 Inskip memorandum, 23 November 1937, T 161/855/ 3 (S.48431/01/1).

112 N. H. Gibbs, *Grand Strategy*, vol. I: *Rearmament Policy* (London, 1976), p. 467.

113 Hankey, 'Cost of Defence', 23 November 1937, T 161/855/3 (S.48431/01/1).

114 CP 316 (37), 15 December 1937, para.75, CAB 24/273/41.

115 Vansittart to Eden, 13 and 17 December 1937, FO 954/7B, fos. 496–7; CC 49 (37), 22 December 1937, CAB 23/90A/11.

116 Brian Bond, *British Military Policy between the Two World Wars* (Oxford, 1980), p. 263; Michael Howard, *The Continental Commitment: The Dilemma of British Defence Policy in the Era of the Two World Wars* (London, 1972), p. 117; B. J. C. McKercher, 'Deterrence and the European Balance of Power: The Field Force and British Grand Strategy, 1934–1938', *English Historical Review*, 123 (2008), no. 500, 98–131, at 128.

117 CP 24(38), 8 February 1938, CAB 24/274/24; CP 26(38), 10 February 1938, CAB 24/274/26; CC 5 (38), 16 February 1938, CAB 23/92/5.

118 CID minutes, 17 March 1938, CAB 2/7.

119 Churchill, 'Panorama of 1937' and 'Britain Rearms', *Step by Step*, pp. 197–200, 201–4 (quotations at 203); *WSCC*, vol. V, part 3, p. 869.

120 HC Deb, 7 March 1938, vol. 332, cc. 1561–2, 1600–13.

121 Chamberlain diary, 19 February 1938, NC2/24, printed in *DBFP* 2/19, appendix I, at p. 1138.

122 *DBFP* 2/19, no. 392.

123 CC 5 (38), 16 February 1938, CAB 23/92/5.

124 Chamberlain diary, 19 February 1938, NC2/24, printed in *DBFP* 2/19, Appendix I, at p. 1141.

125 *Ciano's Diplomatic Papers*, ed. Malcolm Muggeridge (London, 1948), p. 183.

126 Eden diary, 21 February 1938, AP 20/1/18.

127 CC 6 (38), 19 February 1938, CAB 23/92/6.

128 CC 7 (38), 20 February 1938, CAB 23/92/7; *CD*, pp. 51–3; *The Diplomatic Diaries of Oliver Harvey 1937–1940*, ed. John Harvey (London, 1970), pp. 94–7.

129 HC Deb, 21 February 1938, vol. 332, c. 49.

130 HC Deb, 22 February 1938, vol. 332, cc. 237, 245.

131 *Duff Cooper Diaries*, p. 241.

132 'Record of Events connected with Anthony Eden's resignation, February 19th–20th, 1938', Hickleton papers (microfilm), Churchill Archives Centre, Cambridge, HLFX2: A4.410.11.

133 Roosevelt to John Cudahy, 9 March 1938, *Roosevelt letters*, vol. III, p. 232.

134 FP (36) 21st meeting, CAB 27/623, printed in *DBFP* 2/19, no. 465.

135 *DBFP* 2/19, nos. 469, 504.

136 Ibid., no. 615 (quotation on p. 994).

Chapter 7

1 CC 12 (38), 12 March 1938, CAB 23/92/12; Attlee to Chamberlain, 11 January 1938, PREM 1/238; Churchill to Chamberlain, 12 March 1938, PREM 1/237.
2 *NCDL*, vol. IV, p. 305.
3 CC 13 (38), 14 March 1938, CAB 23/92/13; Horace Wilson to prime minister, 25 March 1938, PREM 1/251, fol. 85; H.C. Deb., 14 March 1938, vol. 333, c. 52.
4 HC Deb, 14 March 1938, vol. 333, c. 93–100 (quotation at c. 99); Winston S. Churchill, 'The Austrian Eye-Opener', *Step by Step 1936–1939* (London, 1939), pp. 223–6 at 224.
5 HC Deb, 14 March 1938, vol. 333, cc. 53–6.
6 *Harold Nicolson: Diaries and Letters 1930–39*, ed. Nigel Nicolson (London, 1966), p. 332.
7 COS 697, note by secretary, 16 March 1938, CAB 53/37/4.
8 Cadogan to Hankey, 19 March 1938, FO 371/21656 (C1651/G).
9 *NCDL*, vol. IV, p. 307.
10 Igor Lukes, 'Stalin and Czechoslovakia in 1938–9: An Autopsy of a Myth', *Diplomacy and Statecraft*, 10 (1999), nos. 2–3, 13–47; Silvio Pons, *Stalin and the Inevitable War 1936–1941* (London, 2002), pp. 131–5; Hugh Ragsdale, *The Soviets, the Munich Crisis, and the Coming of World War II* (Cambridge, 2004), pp. 182–4; Zara Steiner, 'The Soviet Commissariat of Foreign Affairs and the Czechoslovakian Crisis in 1938: New Material from the Soviet Archive', *Historical Journal*, 42 (1999), no. 3, 751–79.
11 FP (36) 26th meeting, 18 March 1938, with Appendix I, memorandum signed by Halifax, same date, CAB 27/623; *NCDL*, vol. IV, p. 307.
12 FP (36) 26th meeting, 18 March 1938, CAB 27/623; *DBFP* 3/1, no. 86.
13 COS 698 (Revise), 28 March 1938, CAB 53/37/5 is the final version of the report.
14 CC 15 (38), 22 March 1938, CAB 23/93/2.
15 *NCDL*, vol. IV, p. 311.
16 HC Deb., 24 March 1938, vol. 333, cc. 1401–6, 1410–11.
17 Ibid., cc.1444–55.
18 *The Complete Maisky Diaries*, 3 vols., ed. Gabriel Gorodetsky (New Haven, CT, 2017), vol. I, p. 275.
19 *Winston Churchill: His Complete Speeches*, ed. Robert Rhodes James, vol. VI (New York, 1974), pp. 5955–63.
20 *WSCC*, vol. V, part 3, p. 990.
21 *NCDL*, vol. IV, pp. 322, 325.
22 Churchill, 'Britain and Italy', *Step by Step*, pp. 240–4 at 244.
23 *WSCC*, vol. V, part 3, pp. 960, 964; CC 17 (38), 30 March 1938, CAB 23/93/4.
24 CC 18 (38), 6 April 1938, CAB 23/93/5.
25 CID minutes, 319th meeting, 11 April 1938, CAB 2/7.
26 CC 19 (38), 13 April 1938, CAB 23/93/6.
27 N. H. Gibbs, *Grand Strategy*, vol. I: *Rearmament Policy* (London, 1976), p. 638; *DBFP* 3/1, no. 164.

28 *DBFP* 3/1, no. 164.
29 *NCDL*, vol. IV, p. 318.
30 *DBFP* 3/1, no. 164.
31 Anthony Adamthwaite, *France and the Coming of the Second World War, 1936–1939* (London, 1977), pp. 178–81.
32 CC 18 (38), 6 April 1938, CAB 23/93/5 and CC 21 (38), 27 April 1938, CAB 23/93/8.
33 *NCDL*, vol. IV, pp. 322–3.
34 HC Deb, 25 May 1938, vol. 336, cc. 1233–53, 1280–94, 1342–53.
35 *WSCC*, vol. V, part 3, pp. 1034–5, 1040–2; H.C. Deb., 25 May 1938, vol. 336, cc. 1260–6, 1286–8; *NCDL*, vol. IV, p. 326.
36 *WSCC*, vol. V, part 3, p. 1053. See also Churchill, 'National Service', *Step by Step*, pp. 250–4.
37 *DBFP* 3/1, no. 206.
38 Ibid., no. 164.
39 *WSCC*, vol. V, part 3, pp. 1021–4; R. A. C. Parker, *Churchill and Appeasement: Could Churchill Have Prevented the Second World War?* (London, 2000), p. 164.
40 *DBFP* 3/1, no. 250.
41 *CD*, p. 79.
42 H.C. Deb., 23 May 1938, vol. 336, cc. 824–6.
43 *NCDL*, vol. IV, p. 325.
44 Ibid., pp. 324, 325.
45 *Churchill Complete Speeches*, vol. VI, pp. 5963–6, 5976.
46 *WSCC*, vol. V, part 3, pp. 1100–1, 1112–13, 1138.
47 Churchill, 'Shadows Over Czechoslovakia', *Step by Step*, pp. 255–8 at 257.
48 *NCDL*, vol. IV, p. 338; *Documents on German Foreign Policy*, series D, vol. 2 (*DGFP*, D/2), no. 266.
49 Winston S. Churchill, *The Second World War*, vol. I: *The Gathering Storm* (London, 1948), pp. 227–8.
50 *DBFP*, 3/2, no. 608 and p. 687.
51 Chamberlain to Halifax, 19 August 1938, *DBFP* 3/2, Appendix IV, 686.
52 Churchill, *Second World War*, vol. I, pp. 243–5; David Reynolds, *In Command of History: Churchill Fighting and Writing the Second World War* (London, 2004), p. 96. The Churchillian case is put most strongly in Patricia Meehan, *The Unnecessary War: Whitehall and the German Resistance to Hitler* (London, 1992).
53 'The Crisis and Aftermath', 14 November 1938, CAB 104/43.
54 Joachim Fest, *Plotting Hitler's Death: The German Resistance 1933–1945* (London, 1996), pp. 77–84; Klemens von Klemperer, *German Resistance against Hitler: The Search for Allies Abroad, 1938–1945* (Oxford, 1992), pp. 105–10; Manfred Messerschmidt, 'Foreign Policy and Preparation for War', in Militärgeschichtliches Forschungsamt (ed.), *Germany and the Second World War*, vol. I (Oxford, 1990), pp. 541–717, at 658–60.
55 *DBFP* 3/2, Appendix IV, p. 686, and no. 704.
56 Ibid., Appendix IV, pp. 688–9; Churchill, *Second World War*, vol. I, p. 228.
57 Meeting of ministers, 30 August 1938, CAB 23/94/10; *The Duff Cooper Diaries 1915–1951*, ed. John Julius Norwich (London, 2005), p. 255.

58 Note by Wilson, 30 August 1938, PREM 1/265, fos. 183–5.
59 *WSCC*, vol. V, part 3, pp. 1130–1.
60 Wilson to prime minister, 31 August 1938, PREM 1/265, fos. 117–19
61 *WSCC*, vol. V, part 3, pp. 1137–8.
62 *NCDL*, vol. IV, p. 342.
63 Note by Wilson, 30 August 1938, PREM 1/266A, fol. 363.
64 *NCDL*, vol. IV, p. 344.
65 Ibid. 342, 344.
66 Notes by Wilson for prime minister, 5 September, and Halifax to Chamberlain, 5 September, and Chamberlain to Halifax, 6 September, 1938, PREM 1/265, fos. 41–5, 57, 61–6; Inskip diary, 8 September 1938, INKP 1, Churchill Archives Centre, Cambridge.
67 *The Times*, 7 September 1938, p. 13; *DBFP* 3/2, p. 271n; Richard Cockett, *Twilight of Truth: Chamberlain, Appeasement and the Manipulation of the Press* (London, 1989), pp. 71–4.
68 *CD*, p. 95.
69 *DBFP* 3/2, nos. 815, 819, 823, 825, and Appendix I, pp. 649–50; *CD*, pp. 95–6.
70 *DBFP* 3/2, no. 814.
71 CC 37 (38), 12 September 1938, CAB 23/95/1; Inskip diary, 12 September 1938, INKP 1; Viscount Templewood, *Nine Troubled Years* (London, 1954), pp. 301–2; *Duff Cooper Diaries*, p. 258.
72 *The Times*, 13 September 1938, p. 7.
73 *Duff Cooper Diaries*, p. 259.
74 *NCDL*, vol. IV, pp. 345–6; CC 38 (38), 14 September 1938, CAB 23/95/2; *DBFP* 3/2, nos. 855, 857–8, 861; Inskip diary, 13 September 1938, INKP 1.
75 CC 38 (38), 14 September 1938, CAB 23/95/2; *Duff Cooper Diaries*, p. 259.
76 *The Diplomatic Diaries of Oliver Harvey 1937–1940*, ed. John Harvey (London, 1970), p. 180.
77 Churchill, 'The European Crisis', *Step by Step*, pp. 281–4 at 284.
78 John Ruggiero, *Neville Chamberlain and British Rearmament: Pride, Prejudice and Politics* (Westport, CT, 1999), p. 141; *DBFP*, 3/2, no. 841; Inskip diary, 12 September, 1938, INKP 1.
79 CP 199 (38), CAB 24/278/34.
80 *NCDL*, vol. IV, p. 344.
81 Inskip diary 17 September 1938, INKP 1.
82 *DBFP* 3/2, nos. 895–6; *NCDL*, vol. IV, pp. 346–8.
83 CS 5 (38), 16 September 1938, CAB 27/646; CC 39 (38), 17 September 1938, CAB 23/95/3.
84 'The Prime Minister's Visit to Germany: Notes by Sir Horace Wilson', 16 September 1938, NC 8/26/2; *NCDL*, vol. IV, p. 348.
85 Inskip diary, 17 September 1938, INKP 1.
86 CC 39 (38), 17 September 1938, CAB 23/95/3; *Duff Cooper Diaries*, p. 261.
87 Fisher to Wilson 'for N.C.', 17 September 1938, T 273/405.
88 Note on Wilson to Prime Minister, 17 September 1938, T 273/405; David Reynolds, *The Creation of the Anglo-American Alliance 1937–41* (London, 1981), p. 34.

89　PREM 1/264, fos. 14–19; Walter Citrine, *Men and Work: The Autobiography of Lord Citrine* (London, 1964), pp. 361–6; Hugh Dalton, *The Fateful Years: Memoirs 1931–1945* (London, 1957), pp. 176–83.

90　Adamthwaite, *France and the Coming of the Second World War*, pp. 213–14; *CD*, p. 100.

91　*DBFP* 3/2, no. 928.

92　CC 40 (38), 19 September 1938, CAB 23/95/4; *DBFP* 3/2, nos. 937, 961, 964, 981, 988, 991, 1000–2.

93　CC 41 (38), 21 September 1938, CAB 23/95/5; *Duff Cooper Diaries*, pp. 262–3; *DBFP* 3/2, no. 1003.

94　PREM 1/264, fos. 3–11; *The Times*, 22 September 1938, p. 12.

95　*The Times*, 22 September 1938, p. 9.

96　Churchill, *Second World War*, vol. I, p. 237.

97　*The Times*, 22 September 1938, p. 15.

98　*Nicolson Diaries 1930–9*, pp. 363–4.

99　*Duff Cooper Diaries*, p. 263.

100　*The Times*, 23 September 1938, p. 13; *WSCC*, vol. V, part 3, p. 1247.

101　Churchill, 'Is Air Power Decisive?' *Step by Step*, pp. 276–80 at 279; Winston S. Churchill, 'Let the Tyrant Criminals Bomb', *The Collected Essays of Sir Winston Churchill*, ed. Michael Wolff (London, 1976), pp. 421–7 at 426.

102　*The Times*, 23 September 1938, p. 12.

103　*DBFP* 3/2, no. 1033; *DGFP*, D/2, no. 562; Paul Schmidt, *Hitler's Interpreter*, ed. R. H. C. Steed (London, 1951), pp. 96–7.

104　Wilson, 'Munich, 1938', October 1941, pp. 27, 40, CAB 127/158.

105　*DBFP* 3/2, no. 1048.

106　*Harvey Diplomatic Diaries*, pp. 193–4; *DBFP* 3/2, no. 1049.

107　*DBFP* 3/2, no. 1058.

108　Ibid., no. 1073; *DGFP*, D/2, nos. 583–4; Nevile Henderson, *Failure of a Mission* (London, 1940), p. 157; Schmidt, *Hitler's Interpreter*, pp. 100–2.

109　*CD*, p. 103.

110　CC 42 (38), 24 September 1938, CAB 23/95/6.

111　CC 43 (38), 25 September 1938, CAB 23/95/7.

112　'What Should We Do?' 18 September 1938, FO 371/21659 (C14471/42/18).

113　Note by Cadogan, 20 September 1938, on minute by Orme Sargent, PREM 1/266A, fos. 267–8; *CD*, p. 104.

114　CC 43 (38), CAB 23/95/7; *Duff Cooper Diaries*, pp. 265–6.

115　*DBFP* 3/2, no. 1076.

116　John Herman, *The Paris Embassy of Sir Eric Phipps: Anglo-French Relations and the Foreign Office, 1937–1939* (Brighton, 1998), pp. 116–19.

117　*DBFP* 3/2, no. 1093.

118　*DGFP*, D/2, no. 610.

119　*Duff Cooper Diaries*, p. 267; CC 44 (38), CAB 23/95/8.

120　*DBFP* 3/2, no. 1111.

121　*Nicolson Diaries 1930–9*, p. 367.

122　Ibid; *DBFP* 3/2, p. 550n.

123　*WCCC*, v, part 3, p. 1177.

124 *FRUS*, 1938, vol. I, no. 631.
125 C. A. MacDonald, *The United States, Britain and Appeasement* (London, 1981), pp. 99–100, 102–5.
126 *DBFP* 3/2, nos. 1097, 1118.
127 Ibid., no. 1116.
128 Message from Wilson, 26 September 1938, PREM 1/266A, fos. 76–7; *DBFP* 3/2, no. 1121.
129 *DGFP*, D/2, no. 634.
130 *The Times*, 28 September 1938, p. 10.
131 CC 46 (38), 27 September 1938, CAB 23/95/10; Henderson's telegram is in *DBFP* 3/2, no. 1126. The advice of the military attaché, Colonel F. N. Mason MacFarlane, is in CS (38) 15, 27 September 1938, CAB 27/646.
132 CC 46 (38), 27 September 1938, CAB 23/95/10; *Duff Cooper Diaries*, pp. 267–9.
133 *DBFP* 3/2, no. 1144.
134 *DGFP*, D/2, no. 657.
135 *DBFP* 3/2, nos. 1158–9.
136 HC Deb., 28 September 1938, vol. 339, cc. 26–7.
137 *Nicolson Diaries 1930–9*, p. 371.
138 *FRUS*, 1938, vol. I, no. 652.
139 Ian Kershaw, *Hitler: 1936–1945 Nemesis* (London, 2000), pp. 118–21; G. Bruce Strang, 'War and Peace: Mussolini's Road to Munich', *Diplomacy and Statecraft*, 10 (1999), no. 2–3, 160–90.
140 *FRUS*, 1938, vol. I, no. 662.
141 Templewood, *Nine Troubled Years*, pp. 325–6. Templewood mistakenly gave the date of the telegram to Chamberlain as 23 September instead of the 28th: see Robert Dallek, *Franklin D. Roosevelt and American Foreign Policy, 1932–1945* (New York, 1979), pp. 165–6.
142 Donald Watt, 'Roosevelt and Neville Chamberlain: Two Appeasers', *International Journal*, 28 (1973), no. 2, 185–204.
143 *The Times*, 30 September 1939, p. 12.
144 *WSCC*, vol. V, part 3, pp. 1184–5.
145 Ibid., pp. 1188 and 1189n.
146 What follows draws upon *DBFP* 3/2, no. 1227; *DGFP*, D/2, no. 674; David Reynolds, *Summits: Six meetings that Shaped the Twentieth Century* (London, 2007), pp. 85–90; Keith Robbins, *Munich 1938* (London, 1968), pp. 316–19.
147 *DBFP* 3/2, no. 1221.
148 Schmidt, *Hitler's Interpreter*, p. 110.
149 Lord Strang, *Home and Abroad* (London, 1956), p. 148. The Godesberg terms and the Munich agreement are in *DBFP* 3/2, nos. 1068 and 1224. For Chamberlain's account of the differences see HC Deb., 3 October 1938, vol. 339, cc. 42–5.
150 *NCDL*, vol. IV, p. 350; *DBFP* 3/2, no. 1228; Strang, *Home and Abroad*, p. 147.
151 *The Times*, 1 October 1938, pp. 12, 14.
152 Alec Douglas-Home, *The Way the Wind Blows* (London, 1976), p. 67.

153 HC Deb, 3 October 1938, vol. 339, c. 45.

154 HC Deb, 6 October 1938, vol.339, c.551.

155 Parker, *Churchill and Appeasement*, p. 185.

156 Stanley to Chamberlain, 3 October 1938, PREM 1/266A.

157 HC Deb., 5 October 1938, vol. 339, cc. 359–73 (quotation at 372).

158 HC Deb., 3 October 1938, vol. 339, cc. 56–9, 71, 74.

159 HC Deb, 6 October 1938, vol. 339, cc. 544–53. The speech led Crookshank to withdraw his resignation – see Diary of Viscount Crookshank, 4 & 6 October 1938, Ms Eng Hist d.359, Bodleian Libraries, Oxford.

160 Copies of the telegrams and letter, all dated 30 September 1938, are in MSS Dawson, vol. 93, fos. 156–8, Bodleian Libraries, Oxford.

161 *The Roosevelt Letters*, ed. Elliott Roosevelt, vol. III (London, 1952), p. 243.

162 HC Deb, 4 October 1938, vol. 339, cc. 193–7.

163 Reynolds, *Summits*, pp. 37–95.

164 Richard Overy, 'Germany and the Munich Crisis: A Mutilated Victory?' *Diplomacy and Statecraft*, 10 (1999), no. 2, 191–215.

Chapter 8

1 David Dilks, '"We Must Hope for the Best and Prepare for the Worst": The Prime Minister, the Cabinet and Hitler's Germany, 1937–1939', *Proceedings of the British Academy*, 73 (1987), 309–52; R. A. C. Parker, *Churchill and Appeasement: Could Churchill Have Prevented the Second World War?* (London, 2000), pp. 184, 189; HC Deb, 6 October 1938, vol. 339, c. 547.

2 Chamberlain to Hankey, 2 October 1938, HNKY 4/30, cited in R. A. C. Parker, *Chamberlain and Appeasement: British Policy and the Coming of the Second World War* (London, 1993), p. 182.

3 Samuel Hoare's notes of conversation with Halifax, 5 December 1951, Templewood papers, XIX:5, Cambridge University Library.

4 *The Times*, 10 October 1938, p. 14, and 12 October 1938, p. 14.

5 Halifax to Chamberlain, 11 October 1938, NC7/11/31/124A.

6 *NCDL*, vol. IV, p. 355.

7 *WSCC*, vol. V, part 3, p. 1208.

8 HC Deb, 6 October 1938, vol. 339, cc. 493–4.

9 HC Deb, 6 October 1938, vol. 339, cc. 494–5; *NCDL*, vol. IV, pp. 351–3.

10 Churchill to Chamberlain, 6 October 1938, Chamberlain papers NC7/9/38; *WSCC*, vol. V, part 3, pp. 1204–5.

11 *NCDL*, vol. IV, pp. 351, 354–5; Richard Cockett, *Twilight of Truth: Chamberlain, Appeasement and the Manipulation of the Press* (London, 1989), pp. 78–83; Julie Gottlieb, *'Guilty Women', Foreign Policy, and Appeasement in Inter-War Britain* (Basingstoke, 2015), pp. 204–11.

12 HC Deb, 6 October 1938, vol. 339, c.548.

13 Winston S. Churchill, 'The Morrow of Munich', *Step by Step 1936–1939* (London, 1939), pp. 300–3.

14 *NCDL*, vol. IV, p. 356.

15 British Institute of Public Opinion, *Public Opinion Quarterly*, 4 (1940), no. 1, 2.

16 Robert Self, *Neville Chamberlain, a Biography* (Aldershot, 2006), pp. 335, 341.
17 Halifax to Chamberlain, 11 October 1938, Chamberlain papers, NC7/11/31/124A; *NCDL*, vol. IV, p. 356.
18 HC Deb, 17 November 1938, vol. 341, cc. 1128–9, 1176–85.
19 Martin Gilbert, *Winston Churchill*, vol. V: *1922–1939* (London, 1976), p. 1019.
20 CC 48 (38), 3 October 1938, p. 304, CAB 23/95/12.
21 CP 219 (38), 13 October 1938, CAB 24/279/19.
22 Memorandum by Bridges, 18 October 1938, PREM 1/252.
23 Minutes and papers of Cabinet Committee on Defence Programmes and Acceleration, 27 October–1 November 1938, CAB 27/648; CP 247 (38), 3 November 1938, CAB 24/280/2.
24 CC 53 (38), 7 November 1938, CAB 23/96/5.
25 Kingsley Wood to prime minister, 9 December, and Chamberlain's note on minute by Wilson, 13 December, 1938, PREM 1/236.
26 Wilson to J. H. Woods (the chancellor of the exchequer's principal private secretary), 1 November 1938, PREM 1/236.
27 Wilson to prime minister, 21 October 1938, PREM 1/336.
28 *NCDL*, vol. IV, p. 358.
29 *DGFP*, D4, no. 251.
30 Ibid, no. 253.
31 Ibid, no. 251.
32 Christopher Andrew, *The Defence of the Realm: The Authorised History of MI5* (London, 2009), p. 206.
33 Copy of Hesse's report to Ribbentrop', 26 November 1938, FO 1093/107.
34 Cadogan, 'Self-typed notes, no copy', 29 November 1938, ibid. For fuller discussion of Cadogan's reaction, see G. Bruce Strang, 'Sir Alexander Cadogan and the Steward-Hesse Affair: Assessments of British Cabinet Politics and Future British Policy, 1938', *International History Review*, 43 (2021), no. 3, 657–76.
35 Cadogan diary, 28 and 29 November 1938, ACAD 1/7, Churchill Archives Centre, Cambridge.
36 John Ruggiero, *Hitler's Enabler: Neville Chamberlain and the Origins of the Second World War* (Santa Barbara, CA, 2015), p. 104.
37 Cadogan memorandum, 8 November 1938, in 'Possible Future Course of British Policy', FO 371/21659 (C14471).
38 Memoranda by Strang, 10 October and Cadogan, 14 October, 1938, ibid.
39 Memoranda by Strang, 10 October, and Collier, 29 October, 1938, ibid.
40 *DBFP* 3/3, no. 285.
41 'What Should We Do?' 18 September 1938, FO 371/21659 (C14471).
42 Cadogan memorandum, 8 November 1938, ibid.
43 Marginal note on Collier memorandum, 29 October 1938, ibid.
44 Ashton-Gwatkin memorandum, 27 October 1938, ibid.
45 Strang memorandum, 10 October 1938, with Cadogan marginal comment, ibid.
46 Cadogan memorandum, 8 November 1938, ibid.

47 Andrew, *Defence of the Realm*, pp. 203–6.
48 'The Crisis and Aftermath: Tendencies and Reactions', 14 November 1938, CAB 104/43.
49 FP (36) 32nd meeting, 14 November 1938, CAB 27/624.
50 *NCDL*, vol. IV, p. 362. For the Astors see Norman Rose, *The Cliveden Set: Portrait of an Exclusive Fraternity* (London, 2000).
51 *NCDL*, vol. IV, p. 363.
52 FP (36) 32nd meeting, 14 November 1938, CAB 27/624.
53 *NCDL*, vol. IV, p. 350.
54 *DBFP* 3/3, no. 326.
55 CC 50 (38), 26 October 1938, CAB 23/96/2.
56 Memorandum by Cadogan, 8 November 1938, FO 371/21659 (C14471).
57 'The Crisis and Aftermath', 14 November 1938, CAB 104/43.
58 *DBFP* 3/3, no. 456.
59 Ibid., no. 500 (third conversation).
60 Chamberlain to the king, 17 January 1939, PREM 1/327. See also *NCDL*, vol. IV, pp. 373–4.
61 *Ciano's Diary, 1939–1943*, ed. Malcolm Muggeridge (London, 1947), pp. 9–10.
62 *WSCC*, vol. V, part 3, p. 1347.
63 CC 49 (38), 19 October 1938, CAB 23/96/1.
64 Cadogan memorandum, 14 October 1938, FO 371/21659 (C14471).
65 CC 49 (38), 19 October 1938, CAB23/96/1; CP 225 (38), 14 October 1938, CAB 24/279/25.
66 Chamberlain to Roosevelt, 8 November 1938, PREM 1/366.
67 'Note of certain conversations between President Franklin D. Roosevelt and Colonel Hon. Arthur Murray during Colonel and Mrs Murray's stay with the President at Hyde Park, October 16th to 24th, 1938, PREM 1/367. Chamberlain annotated the report: 'to be carefully preserved. Note formula [about American support] which may be used'.
68 *WSCC*, vol. V, part 3, p. 1224.
69 JIC 78, 16 November 1938, CAB 56/4.
70 William R. Rock, *Chamberlain and Roosevelt: British Foreign Policy and the United States, 1937–1940* (Columbus, OH, 1988), pp. 146–7; *WSCC*, vol. V, part 3, p. 1343. Rock does not mention Chamberlain's response.
71 Halifax to Chamberlain, 9 January 1939, and Chamberlain's marginal comment, PREM 1/314.
72 David Reynolds, *The Creation of the Anglo-American Alliance 1937–41* (London, 1981), p. 51.
73 *WSCC*, vol. V, part 3, p. 1260.
74 Churchill, 'Morrow of Munich', *Step by Step 1936–1939* (London, 1939), pp. 300–3.
75 Chamberlain comment on note by Wilson, 16 January 1939, PREM 1/318, fol. 3.
76 *WSCC*, vol. V, part 3, pp. 1323, 1343.
77 Churchill, 'Morrow of Munich', *Step by Step*, pp. 300–3 at 301; HC Deb, 17 November 1938, vol. 341, c.1138.

78 Churchill, 'France and England', *Step by Step*, pp. 304–7.
79 Churchill, 'New Lights in Eastern Europe', *Step by Step*, pp. 308–11 at 309.
80 CC 56 (38), 22 November 1938, CAB 23/96/8.
81 *DBFP* 3/3, no. 325.
82 CC 56 (38), 22 November 1938, CAB 23/96/8; *DBFP* 3/3, no. 325.
83 Fraser to Phipps, 5 December, and Phipps to Halifax, 7 December, 1938, FO 371/21597 (C15175/36/17), cited in Talbot C. Imlay, *Facing the Second World War: Strategy, Politics, and Economics in Britain and France 1938–1940* (Oxford, 2003), p. 84; CID minutes, 341st meeting, 15 December 1938, CAB 2/8.
84 265th Chiefs of Staff Committee meeting, 21 December 1938, CAB 53/10/3.
85 268th Chiefs of Staff Committee meeting, 18 January 1939, CAB 53/10/ 4.
86 COS 827, 25 January 1939, CAB 53/44/3 (also CAB 24/283/1).
87 Full note of CID minutes, 342nd meeting, 16 December 1938, in envelope marked 'Confidential Library', CAB 2/8.
88 R. J. Minney, *The Private Papers of Hore-Belisha* (London, 1960), pp. 168–9.
89 INKP 2.
90 Gladwyn Jebb, 'Summary of Information from Secret Sources', 19 January 1939, Figure 3.2 CAB 27/627.
91 FP (36) 35th meeting, 23 January 1939, CAB 27/624.
92 Donald Cameron Watt, *How War Came: The Immediate Origins of the Second World War, 1938–1939* (London, 1989), pp. 100–6.
93 CC 2 (39), 25 January 1939, CAB 23/97/2
94 FP (36) 36th meeting, 26 January 1939, CAB 27/624.
95 CC 3 (39), 1 February 1939, CAB 23/97/3.
96 CC 5 (39), 2 February 1939, CAB 23/97/5; copy of note by Simon on Cabinet of 2 February, T 175/104 (part 2). For Halifax's statement see CC 2 (39), 25 January 1939, CAB 23/97/2.
97 CC 8 (39), 22 February 1939, CAB 23/97/8.
98 Michael Howard, *The Continental Commitment: The Dilemma of British Defence Policy in the Era of the Two World Wars* (London, 1972), pp. 127–8; Brian Bond, *British Military Policy between the Two World Wars* (Oxford, 1980), pp. 299–301.
99 HC Deb, 21 February 1939, vol. 344, c. 251–3; CC 9 (39), 2 March 1939, CAB 23/97/9.
100 N. H. Gibbs, *Grand Strategy*, vol. I: *Rearmament Policy* (London, 1976), pp. 655–6.
101 HC Deb, 6 February 1939, vol. 343, c. 623; *CD*, p. 147.
102 HC Deb, 21 February 1939, vol. 344, c. 254.
103 *Winston S. Churchill: His Complete Speeches*, ed. Robert Rhodes James, vol. VI (New York, 1974), p. 6071.
104 *New Statesman and Nation*, 17 (7 January 1939), pp. 5–7, at 6.
105 HC Deb, 21 February 1939, vol. 344, cc. 256–7.
106 HC Deb, 8 March 1939, vol. 344, c. 2173; 14 March 1939, vol. 345, cc. 251–7.
107 See Churchill's comment that in 1939 British aircraft factories would be earning sums of money on a scale hitherto only seen in Germany – HC Deb, 21 February 1939, vol. 344, c. 250.

108 Chamberlain's note on memorandum by Wilson, 6 December 1938, PREM 1/247, fol. 3; HC Deb, 7 December 1938, vol. 342, cc. 1239–40, 1247.

109 HC Deb, 19 December 1938, vol. 342, c. 2524.

110 Note by Strang, 5 January 1939, FO 371/22988 (C204), fol. 39.

111 Neville Chamberlain, *The Struggle for Peace* (London, 1939), p. 385.

112 Sir Eric Phipps papers, PHPP 3/5, fol. 47, Churchill Archives Centre, Cambridge.

113 *NCDL*, vol. IV, p. 382.

114 HC Deb, 31 January 1939, vol. 343, cc. 81–2.

115 *The Diplomatic Diaries of Oliver Harvey 1937–1940*, ed. John Harvey (London, 1970), p. 250.

116 *NCDL*, vol. IV, pp. 377–8.

117 *NCDL*, vol. IV, pp. 382, 385; *DBFP* 3/4, Appendix I (iii).

118 *NCDL*, vol. IV, p. 382.

119 *DBFP* 3/4, Appendix I (iii).

120 Ibid., Appendix I (iv).

121 Churchill, 'The Lull in Europe', *Step by Step*, pp. 327–30.

122 Churchill, 'Mussolini's Cares' and 'The Lull in Europe', *Step by Step*, pp. 322–5 and 327–30; B. J. C. McKercher, *Transition of Power: Britain's Loss of Global Pre-eminence to the United States 1930–1945* (Cambridge, 1999), p. 274.

123 HC Deb, 21 February 1939, vol. 344, c. 253.

124 Churchill, 'Is It Peace?' *Step by Step*, pp. 335–9. For Strakosch's estimates of German expenditure on armaments, see *WSCC*, vol. V, part 3, pp. 1377–8.

125 Earl of Halifax, *Fulness of Days* (London, 1957), p. 232; *NCDL*, vol. IV, p. 393.

126 *The Times*, 11 March 1939, p. 7.

127 Self, *Neville Chamberlain*, p. 49.

128 David Gillard, *Appeasement in Crisis: From Munich to Prague, October 1938–March 1939* (Basingstoke, 2007), pp. 110–13.

129 CC 10 (39), 8 March 1939, CAB 23/97/10.

130 *CD*, pp. 155–6.

131 CC 11 (39), 15 March 1939, CAB 23/98/1; *DBFP* 3/4, no. 256.

132 *DBFP* 3/4, nos. 288, 301.

133 CC 11 (39), CAB 23/98/1.

134 Minute by O. E. Sargent, 4 October 1938, FO 371/21788 (file C13965).

135 HC Deb, 4 October 1938, vol. 339, c. 303.

136 *DGFP*, D/2, no. 175.

137 HC Deb, 14 March 1939, vol. 345, c. 223.

138 HC Deb, 15 March 1939, vol. 345, cc. 435–40; *CD*, p. 157.

139 *NCDL*, vol. IV, p. 393.

140 Chamberlain, *Struggle for Peace*, pp. 413–20; CC 12 (39), 18 March 1939, CAB 23/98/2.

141 *CD*, p. 160.

142 *Churchill Complete Speeches*, pp. 6072, 6081.

143 *WSCC*, vol. V, part 3, p. 1398.

Chapter 9

1 Simon Newman, *March 1939: The British Guarantee to Poland* (Oxford, 1976), pp. 3–6, 136.

2 Donald Cameron Watt, *How War Came: The Immediate Origins of the Second World War* (London, 1989), p. 186; Zara Steiner, *The Triumph of the Dark: European International History* (Oxford, 2011), p. 740; Robert Self, *Neville Chamberlain, a Biography* (Aldershot, 2006), p. 357.

3 Zara Steiner, 'British Decisions for Peace and War 1938–1939: The Rise and Fall of Realism', in Ernest R. May, Richard Rosecrance and Zara Steiner (eds.), *History and Neorealism* (Cambridge, 2010), pp. 129–154.

4 Wesley K. Wark, *The Ultimate Enemy: British Intelligence and Nazi Germany, 1933–1939* (Ithaca, NY, 1985), pp. 213–21.

5 R. A. C. Parker, *Chamberlain and Appeasement: British Policy and the Coming of the Second World War* (London,1993), pp. 213–15.

6 John Ruggiero, *Hitler's Enabler: Neville Chamberlain and the Origins of the Second World War* (Santa Barbara, CA, 2015), pp. 121–2.

7 G. Bruce Strang, 'Once More unto the Breach: Britain's Guarantee to Poland, March 1939', *Journal of Contemporary History*, 31 (1996), no. 4, 721–52.

8 Parker, *Chamberlain and Appeasement*, pp. 203–5.

9 Self, *Neville Chamberlain*, pp. 354, 361–2, 376–7.

10 The exception being Simon Newman, who did not have access to Chamberlain's private papers.

11 SAC 1st meeting, 1 March 1939, CAB 16/209.

12 'Memorandum on Sea-Power', PREM 1/345 (reproduced in *WSCC*, vol. V, part 3, pp. 1414–17).

13 Chamberlain to Lyons, 21 March, PREM 1/309.

14 Craigie's Telegram 269, 23 March 1939, CAB 104/69.

15 Neville Chamberlain, *The Struggle for Peace* (London,1939), pp. 419–20.

16 *DBFP* 3/4, no. 395.

17 *CD*, p. 161.

18 COS 283rd meeting, 18 March 1939, CAB 53/10/7.

19 *DBFP* 3/4, no. 399. Emphasis in the original.

20 CC 12 (39), 18 March 1939, CAB 23/98/2.

21 FO 371/22967 (C3858/15/18), cited in David Gillard, *Appeasement in Crisis: From Munich to Prague, October 1938–March 1939* (Basingstoke, 2007), p. 133.

22 *NCDL*, vol. IV, p. 394.

23 *CD*, p. 161; *DBFP* 3/4, nos. 400, 406, 421, 424, 426.

24 CC 13 (39), 20 March 1939, CAB 23/98/3.

25 Ibid.

26 *CD*, p. 161; *The Diplomatic Diaries of Oliver Harvey 1937–1940*, ed. John Harvey (London, 1970), p. 265; *DBFP* 3/4, no. 446.

27 Cadogan to Wilson, and Chamberlain's note on memorandum by Wilson, both 19 March 1939, PREM 1/327; *CD*, p. 162; *DBFP* 3/4, no. 448.

28 *Ciano's Diary, 1939–1943*, ed. Malcolm Muggeridge (London, 1947), p. 54.

29 Notes of ministerial meetings, 21 March 1939, CAB 21/592; *WSCC*, vol. V, part 3, p. 1400.
30 *NCDL*, vol. IV, p. 395.
31 *DBFP* 3/4, nos. 458, 465, 479.
32 CC 14 (39), 22 March 1939, CAB 23/98/4.
33 *DBFP* 3/ 4, no. 484.
34 *NCDL*, vol. IV, p. 396. Firebrace's assessment of the Red Army is in *DBFP* 3 /4, no. 183, enclosure 2.
35 FP (36) 38th meeting, 27 March 1939, CAB 27/624 (also CP 74 (39), CAB 24/284/21); *DBFP* 3/4, no. 522.
36 FP (36) 38th meeting, CAB 27/624.
37 COS 283rd meeting, 18 March 1939, CAB 53/10/7.
38 *Harvey Diplomatic Diaries* (25 March 1939), p. 268.
39 *DBFP* 3/4, no. 476.
40 FP (36) 38th meeting, 27 March 1939, CAB 27/624.
41 *DBFP* 3/4, no. 538.
42 CC 15 (39), 29 March 1939, CAB 23/98/5.
43 Peter Dennis, *Decision by Default: Peacetime Conscription and British Defence 1919–39* (London, 1972), pp. 190–5.
44 R. J. Minney, *The Private Papers of Hore-Belisha* (London, 1960), pp. 186–7; Wilson to Hore-Belisha, 28 March, and memorandum by Wilson 29 March, 1939, PREM 1/296; minute by J. A. N. Barlow, with comment by Hopkins, 28 March 1939, T 175/104 (part 2).
45 Undated memorandum by Sir Edward Bridges, enclosing Chatfield letter to Hore-Belisha, 31 March 1939, PREM 1/296; CC 15 (39), 29 March 1939, CAB 23/98/5.
46 HC Deb, 29 March and 3 April 1939, vol. 345, cc. 2049–50, 2504–5.
47 Ian Colvin, *Vansittart in Office* (London, 1965), pp. 303–11; *Harvey Diplomatic Diaries*, p. 271.
48 *NCDL*, vol. IV, p. 400; *CD*, pp. 164–5; Watt, *How War Came*, pp. 183–4.
49 *NCDL*, vol. IV, p. 400.
50 Ibid.
51 CC 16 (39), 30 March 1939, CAB 23/98/6.
52 *CD*, p. 165. Emphasis in original.
53 FP (36) 39th meeting, 30 March 1939, CAB 27/624.
54 Hugh Dalton, *The Fateful Years: Memoirs 1931–1945* (London, 1957), pp. 237–8.
55 *NCDL*, vol. IV, p. 399; *Harold Nicolson: Diaries and Letters 1930–1939*, ed. Nigel Nicolson (London, 1966), p. 393.
56 FP (36) 40th meeting, 31 March 1939, CAB 27/624; *DBFP* 3/4, no. 584.
57 CC 17 (39), 31 March 1939, CAB 23/98/7.
58 HC Deb, 31 March 1939, vol. 345, cc. 2415–17.
59 *NCDL*, vol. IV, p. 404.
60 Gordon Martel (ed.), *The Times and Appeasement: The Journals of A. L. Kennedy, 1932–1939* (Cambridge, 2000), pp. 286–7.
61 HC Deb, 3 April 1939, vol. 345, c.2501. Hugh Dalton also drew a parallel between the two *Times* articles (cc. 2577–8).

62 *NCDL*, vol. IV, p. 401.
63 HC Deb. 3 April 1939, vol. 345, c. 2501.
64 *NCDL*, vol. IV, p. 402.
65 Chamberlain to Weir, 3 April 1939, Weir MSS, GB 248 DC 096/22/2, Glasgow University Archives.
66 HC Deb, 3 April 1939, vol. 345, cc. 2500–3.
67 Parker, *Chamberlain and Appeasement*, p. 245.
68 Watt, *How War Came*, pp. 361–84, 447–61.
69 Michael J. Carley, *1939: The Alliance That Never Was and the Coming of World War II* (Chicago, 1999); Michel J, Carley, 'Fiasco: The Anglo-Franco-Soviet Alliance That Never Was and the Unpublished British White Paper, 1939–1940', *International History Review*, 41 (2019), no. 4, 701–28; Geoffrey Roberts, 'Stalin and the Outbreak of the Second World War', in Frank McDonough (ed.), *The Origins of the Second World War* (London, 2011), pp. 409–28.
70 Steiner, *Triumph of the Dark*, p. 737.
71 Keith Neilson, *Britain, Soviet Russia and the Collapse of the Versailles Order, 1919–1939* (Cambridge, 2006), pp. 271–332.
72 G. Bruce Strang, 'John Bull in Search of a Suitable Russia: British Foreign Policy and the Failure of the Anglo-French-Soviet Alliance Negotiations, 1939', *Canadian Journal of History*, 41 (2006), no. 1, 47–84; G. Bruce Strang, 'The Spirit of Ulysses? Ideology and British Appeasement in the 1930s', *Diplomacy and Statecraft*, 19 (2008), no. 3, 481–526.
73 HC Deb, vol. 345, c.2501.
74 COS 872, 3 April 1939, CAB 53/47/3, paras. 1, 31–4; CP 95 (39), 24 April 1939, CAB 24/285/17, paras. 18–19, 25, 40–1. See also Martin Kahn, 'British Intelligence on Soviet War Potential in 1939: A Revised Picture and Some Implications (a Contribution to the "Unending Debate")', *Intelligence and National Security*, 28 (2013), no. 5, 717–47.
75 *NCDL*, vol. IV, p. 417 (21 May 1939).
76 David Dilks, 'Appeasement and "Intelligence"', in David Dilks (ed.), *Retreat from Power: Studies in Britain's Foreign Policy of the Twentieth Century*, vol. I (London, 1981), pp. 139–69, at 162–4.
77 Keith Jeffery, *MI6: The History of the Secret Intelligence Service 1909–1949* (London, 2010), pp. 311–12.
78 For the terms see *DBFP* 3/5, no. 16.
79 *NCDL*, vol. IV, p. 403.
80 *WSCC*, vol. V, part 3, pp. 1434–6, 1438–9.
81 *NCDL*, vol. IV, pp. 403, 405.
82 FP (36) 41st meeting, 10 April 1939, CAB 27/624; CC 20 (39), 13 April 1939, CAB 23/98/10.
83 HC Deb, 13 April 1939, vol. 346, cc. 13, 19; *NCDL*, vol. IV, pp. 405–6.
84 HC Deb, 13 April 1939, vol. 346, cc. 29, 35–7; Winston S. Churchill, 'The Anglo-Turkish Alliance', *Step by Step 1936–1939* (London, 1939), pp. 361–5.
85 *NCDL*, vol. IV, pp. 407, 409–10.
86 *Memoirs of a Conservative: J. C. C. Davidson's Memoirs and Papers 1910–1937*, ed. Robert Rhodes James (London, 1969), p. 424.

87 *DBFP* 3/5, nos. 170, 176, 201.
88 FP (36) 43rd meeting, 19 April 1939, CAB 27/624, Appendix II.
89 CC 24 (39), 26 April 1939, CAB 23/99/3; CP 95 (39), 24 April 1939, CAB 24/285/17.
90 *NCDL*, vol. IV, p. 412.
91 CC 22 (39), 22 April 1939, CAB 23/99/1; HC Deb, 26 April 1939, vol. 346, cc. 1150–3, 27 April 1939, cc. 1347, 1353, 1375–7; Dennis, *Decision by Default*, pp. 219–22.
92 *DGFP*, D/6, no. 277; Adolf Hitler, *Speech Delivered in the Reichstag, April 28th 1939* (Berlin, 1939), pp. 36–8; *NCDL*, vol. IV, pp. 410–11.
93 Horace Wilson to Nevile Henderson, 12 May 1939, PREM 1/331A; *The Times*, 12 May, p. 10.
94 *NCDL*, vol. IV, p. 428.
95 Anita Prażmowska, *Britain, Poland and the Eastern Front, 1939* (Cambridge, 1987), pp. 67–71.
96 *Winston Churchill: The Complete Speeches*, ed. Robert Rhodes James, vol. VI (New York, 1974), pp. 6117, 6139, 6141.
97 Churchill, 'The Russian Counterpoise', *Step by Step*, pp. 357–60 at 358.
98 HC Deb, 3 April 1939, cc. 2500–3; *Nicolson Diaries 1930–9*, p. 394.
99 *Nicolson Diaries 1930–9*, p. 345.
100 *DBFP* 3/5, no. 520.
101 FP (36) 47th meeting , 16 May 1939, and chiefs of staff's aide-memoire , 'Negotiations with the Soviet', both enclosed in CP 116 (39), 17 May 1939, CAB 24/286/13; *NCDL*, vol. IV, p. 418. For press pressure, even from Conservative newspapers, see Daniel Hucker, 'Public Opinion, the Press and the Failed Anglo-Franco-Soviet Negotiations of 1939', *International History Review*, 40 (2018), no. 1, 65–85.
102 H.C Deb, 19 May 1939, vol. 347, cc. 1840–4.
103 'Negotiations with the Soviet', CP 116 (39), CAB 24/286/13.
104 CC 30 (39), 24 May 1939, CAB 23/99/9; *NCDL*, vol. IV, p. 418.
105 Watt, *How War Came*, p. 247.
106 *DBFP* 3/5, nos. 624, 648, 657, 662, 670, 697.
107 FP (36), 49th meeting, 5 June 1939, CAB 27/625.
108 HC Deb, 7 June 1939, vol. 348, cc. 400–1; *CD*, p. 186.
109 *NCDL*, vol. IV, p. 420.
110 Ibid., p. 424; FP (36) 52nd meeting, 19 June; 53rd meeting, 20 June, and 54th meeting, 26 June, 1939, CAB 27/625; CC 33 (39), 21 June 1939, CAB 23/100/1, and CC 34 (39), 28 June 1939, CAB 23/100/2.
111 Lord Strang, *Home and Abroad* (London, 1956), pp. 156–9, 173–98; Lord Strang, 'The Moscow Negotiations, 1939', in Dilks (ed.), *Retreat from Power*, vol. I, pp. 170–86.
112 FP (36) 53rd meeting, 20 June, and 58th meeting, 19 July, 1939, CAB 27/625.
113 FP (36) 54th meeting, 26 June, and 56th meeting, 4 July, 1939, CAB 27/625.
114 *NCDL*, vol. IV, p. 428.
115 FP (36), 54th meeting, 26 June 1939, CAB 27/625.

116 *Churchill Complete Speeches*, vol. VI, p. 6144.

117 *DBFP* 3/6, no. 227; FP (36) 56th meeting, 4 July, and 58th meeting, 19 July, 1939, CAB 27/625.

118 CC 38 (39), 19 July 1939, CAB 23/100/6; HC Deb, 31 July 1939, vol. 350, cc. 2011–12.

119 CC 38 (39), 19 July 1939, CAB 23/100/6.

120 FP (36), 58th meeting, 19 July 1939, CAB 27/625.

121 *DBFP* 3/6, nos. 414–16, 493.

122 CC 39 (39), 26 July 1939, CAB 23/100/7.

123 *DBFP* 3/6, no. 525. For Butler's statement see HC Deb., 31 July 1939, vol. 350, c. 2099.

124 Carley, *1939*, pp. 190–2.

125 Admiral Sir R. Plunkett Ernle-Erle-Drax, 'Mission to Moscow, August 1939, part 1', *Naval Review*, vol. XI (1952), no. 3, 250–65; part 2, vol. XI (1952), no. 4, 399–413; part 3, vol. XII (1953), no. 1, 57–63 (copy in Drax papers, Churchill Archives, Cambridge: DRAX 6/14); *DBFP* 3/6, no. 647; Carley, *1939*, p. 194.

126 Drax, 'Mission to Moscow, part 1', vol. XI (1952), no. 3, 261–2, and part 2, vol. XI, no. 4, 400–2.

127 *DBFP* 3/7, no. 34; *Soviet Peace Efforts on the Eve of World War II*, ed. Andrei Gromyko et al (Moscow, 1976), no. 317.

128 *DBFP* 3/7, nos. 30, 38, 39, 52, 60, 70, 90, 119.

129 Carley, *1939*, p. 77.

130 Winston S. Churchill, *The Second World War*, vol. I: *The Gathering Storm* (London, 1948), p. 284; Strang, 'Moscow Negotiations', p. 185.

131 War Cabinet paper WP (39) 52, 25 September 1939, CAB 66/2/2.

132 HC Deb. 19 May 1939, vol. 347, c. 1838.

133 *DBFP* 3/6, Appendix III.

134 Adrian Phillips, *Fighting Churchill, Appeasing Hitler: How a British Civil Servant Helped Cause the Second World War* (London, 2019), pp. 286–8.

135 *DBFP* 3/6, no. 354; *The Times*, 30 June 1939, p. 9; *DGFP*, D/6, no. 716, at p. 982.

136 Watt, *How War Came*, pp. 395–400, 402–3.

137 *DBFP* 3/6, no. 370; *DGFP*, D/6, no. 716.

138 Watt, *How War Came*, pp. 400–1.

139 HC Deb, 24 July 1939, vol. 350, cc. 1025–8; *NCDL*, vol. IV, pp. 430–1, 435.

140 Minute by Wilson, 24 July, PREM 1/335.

141 *The Memoirs of Lord Gladwyn* (London, 1972), p. 93; *CD*, p. 192.

142 Ruggiero, *Hitler's Enabler*, pp. 154–7.

143 David Blaazer, 'Finance and the End of Appeasement: The Bank of England, the National Government and the Czech Gold', *Journal of Contemporary History*, 40 (2005), no. 1, 25–39; Neil Forbes, *Doing Business with the Nazis: Britain's Economic and Financial Relations with Germany, 1931–1939* (London, 2000); Scott Newton, *Profits of Peace: The Political Economy of Anglo-German Appeasement* (Oxford, 1996); Bernd-Jürgen Wendt, '"Economic Appeasement" – A Crisis Strategy', in Wolfgang

J. Mommsen and Lothar Kettenacker (eds.), *The Fascist Challenge and the Policy of Appeasement* (London, 1983), pp. 157–72.

144 Newton, *Profits of Peace*, p. 122.

145 Minute by Wilson, 1 August 1939, PREM 1/332.

146 *DBFP* 3/6, no. 533; minute by Wilson, 4 August 1939, PREM 1/330.

147 Minute by Wilson, 20 August 1939, PREM 1/331A.

148 Ruggiero *Hitler's Enabler*, pp. 137–8 citing Christopher Andrew, *The Defence of the Realm: The Authorized History of MI5* (London, 2009), p. 192, whose source is B7, 'Lady Diana Mosley', 26 June 1940, Security Service records: KV 2/884, TNA.

149 For example, Newton, *Profits of Peace*, p. 128; Parker, *Chamberlain and Appeasement*, pp. 268–9; Zara Steiner, *Triumph of the Dark*, p. 858; Watt, *How War Came*, p. 407.

150 *NCDL*, vol. IV, pp. 428, 431. The JIC report is SWR 9, 19 July 1939, FO 1093/125.

151 *The Ironside Diaries 1937–1940*, ed. Roderick Macleod and Denis Kelly (London, 1962), p. 83.

152 Hopkins to T. Padmore (private secretary to Horace Wilson), 3 July 1939, T 175/115; CP 148 (39), 3 July 1939, CAB 24/287/31; CP 149 (39), 3 July 1939, CAB 24/287/32; CC 36 (39), 5 July 1939, CAB 23/100/4.

153 CC 41 (39), 22 August 1939, CAB 23/1009, Annex C.

154 *DGFP*, D/6, no. 710, at p. 970.

155 Ibid., no. 630.

156 SWR 13, 17 August 1939, FO 1093/125; *DBFP* 3/7, no. 56; *CD*, pp. 196–7; *NCDL*, vol. IV, p. 440.

157 CC 41 (39), 22 August 1939, CAB 23/100/9.

158 *DBFP* 3/7, no. 145.

159 *FRUS* , 1939, vol. I, nos. 350, 355; *Heritage to Fortune: The Letters of Joseph P. Kennedy*, ed. Amanda Smith (New York, 2001), pp. 356–8, 361.

160 *DBFP* 3/7, nos. 200, 211, 248.

161 Ian Kershaw, *Hitler 1936–1945: Nemesis* (London, 2000), p. 213.

162 HC Deb, 24 August 1939, vol. 351, cc. 2–16.

163 *DBFP* 3/7, nos. 283–4.

164 Kershaw, *Hitler 1936–1945*, pp. 214–15, 225; Richard Overy, *1939: Countdown to War* (London, 2009), pp. 33–40.

165 *NCDL*, vol. IV, p. 441; CC 43–5 (39), 26–8 August 1939, CAB 23/100/ 11–13; David Euan Wallace Diary, Ms Eng Hist c. 495, Bodleian Libraries, Oxford.

166 *DBFP* 3/7, no. 426.

167 Johan Birger Dahlerus, *The Last Attempt* (London, 1948), pp. 72–8.

168 Overy, *1939*, p. 53.

169 Richard Overy, 'Strategic Intelligence and the Outbreak of the Second World War', *War in History*, 5 (1998), no. 4, 456–64, at 455, 462–4.

170 Watt, *How War Came*, p. 522.

171 *NCDL*, vol. IV, pp. 443–4.

172 *DBFP* 3/7, nos. 450, 455, 472.

173 *DBFP* 3/7, nos. 490, 493, 501–2.

174 CC 46 (39), 30 August 1939, CAB 23/100/14; *DBFP* 3/7, no. 543.
175 *DBFP* 3/7, nos. 525, 590.
176 CC 47 (39), 1 September 1939, CAB 23/100/15.
177 *DBFP* 3/7, no. 669.
178 HC Deb, 1 September 1939, vol. 351, cc. 130–1, 133–4.
179 *WSCC*, vol. V, part 3, p. 1605. Emphasis in the original.
180 *NCDL*, vol. IV, p. 443; HC Deb, 2 September 1939, vol. 351, cc. 280–6;
     CD, p. 212; Minney, *Private Papers of Hore-Belisha*, pp. 225–8; *WSCC*, vol.
     V, part 3, p. 1606 (for Churchill), and pp. 1607–9 (for Sir Reginald
     Dorman-Smith's recollections); Halifax's 'Record of Events before the
     War', RAB G10/100, R. A. Butler papers, Trinity College Library,
     Cambridge; Hoare's 'Notes on Crisis', Templewood papers, X: 5,
     Cambridge University Library; Inskip diary, INKP 2; Sir John Simon diary,
     MSS. Simon, vol. 11, Bodleian Libraries, Oxford; David Euan Wallace
     diary, Ms. Eng. Hist. c.495, Bodleian Libraries, Oxford; CC 48 and 49
     (39), 2 September 1939, CAB 23/100/16 and 17.
181 Dalton, *Fateful Years*, p. 270.
182 Parker, *Chamberlain and Appeasement*, pp. 338–9.
183 Ruggiero, *Hitler's Enabler*, pp. 168–9.
184 Watt, *How War Came*, pp. 543–6, 569–89; Self, *Neville Chamberlain*, p. 379.
185 HC Deb, 3 September 1939, vol. 351, c. 292.
186 Ibid., c. 295.

Chapter 10

1 Sidney Aster, '"Guilty Men": The Case of Neville Chamberlain', in Robert
   Boyce and Esmonde Robertson (eds.), *Paths to War: New Essays on the Origins
   of the Second World War* (London, 1989), pp. 233–68, at 256; Frank
   McDonough, 'When Instinct Clouds Judgement: Neville Chamberlain and
   the Pursuit of Appeasement with Nazi Germany, 1937–9', in Frank
   McDonough (ed.), *The Origins of the Second World War* (London, 2011),
   pp. 186–204, at 202; John Ruggiero, *Neville Chamberlain and British
   Rearmament: Pride, Prejudice and Politics* (Westport, CT, 1999), p. 7.
2 *NCDL*, vol. IV, pp. 445, 451, 458, 481.
3 *The Ironside Diaries 1937–1940*, ed. Roderick Macleod and Denis Kelly
   (London, 1962), p. 83.
4 David Dilks, 'The Twilight War and the Fall of France: Chamberlain and
   Churchill in 1940', *Transactions of the Royal Historical Society*, 28 (1978), 61–86.
5 *NCDL*, vol. IV, p. 445.
6 N. H. Gibbs, *Grand Strategy*, vol. I: *Rearmament Policy* (London, 1976),
   pp. 657–63, 668–78.
7 *The Churchill War Papers* (*CWP*), ed. Martin Gilbert, vol. I (New York,
   1993), p. 60; War Cabinet (WM series) (39) 15th conclusions, confidential
   annex, 14 September 1939, CAB 65/3/6.
8 WM (39) 2nd conclusions, 4 September 1939, CAB 65/1/2.
9 *CWP*, vol. I, pp. 98, 101.
10 M. M. Postan, *British War Production* (London, 1952), pp. 74–5.
11 *NCDL*, vol. IV, pp. 450–1; WP (39) 52, 25 September 1939, CAB 66/2/2.

12 WP (39) 52, 25 September 1939, CAB 66/2/2.
13 *NCDL*, vol. IV, pp. 451, 454–6.
14 Aster, '"Guilty Men"', in Boyce and Robertson (eds.), *Paths to War*, p. 256.
15 David Reynolds, *In Command of History: Churchill Fighting and Writing the Second World War* (London, 2004), p. 121.
16 WM (39) 42nd conclusions, 9 October 1939, CAB 65/1/42.
17 HC Deb, 12 October 1939, vol. 353, cc. 563–8; *NCDL*, vol. IV, p. 459.
18 *The Listener*, 1 October 1939, pp. 647–8; *NCDL*, vol. IV, p. 453.
19 *The Complete Maisky Diaries*, ed. Gabriel Gorodetsky, vol. II (New Haven, CT, 2017), pp. 636–9.
20 *NCDL*, vol. IV, p. 464.
21 WM (39) 85th conclusions, 16 November 1939, CAB 65/2/19; Martin Gilbert, *Winston S. Churchill*, vol. VI: *Finest Hour 1939–1941* (London, 1983), p. 99.
22 Michael J. Carley, '"A Situation of Delicacy and Danger": Anglo-Soviet Relations, August 1939–March 1940', *Contemporary European History*, 8 (1999), no. 2, 175–208, at 190–3.
23 WM (39) 22nd conclusions, confidential annex, 21 September 1939, CAB 65/3/11.
24 WM (39) 15th conclusions, 14 September 1939, CAB 65/1/15.
25 *CWP*, vol. I, p. 101; *NCDL*, vol. IV, p. 446.
26 Llewellyn Woodward, *British Foreign Policy in the Second World War*, vol. I (London, 1970), pp. 26–7.
27 WP (39) 52, 25 September 1939, CAB 66/2/2.
28 WM (39) 99th conclusions, 30 November 1939, CAB 65/2/33.
29 *NCDL*, vol. IV, pp. 446–7, 453.
30 WM (39) 39th conclusions, 6 October 1939, CAB 65/1/39; Gilbert, *Churchill*, vol. VI, p. 57.
31 WP (39) 92, 18 October 1939, CAB 66/2/42.
32 R. J. B. Bosworth, *Mussolini* (London, 2002), pp. 352–6; Ivonne Kirkpatrick, *Mussolini: A Study in Power* (New York, 1964), pp. 424–32.
33 WM (40) 92nd conclusions, 14 April 1940, CAB 65/6/37; *NCDL*, vol. IV, p. 521.
34 WP (39) 48, 21 September 1939, CAB 66/1/42; Sir John Simon Diary, 23 September 1939, MSS Simon, vol. 11.
35 David Reynolds, *The Creation of the Anglo-American Alliance 1937–41* (London, 1981), p. 76.
36 William R. Rock, *Chamberlain and Roosevelt: British Foreign Policy and the United States, 1937–1940* (Columbus, OH, 1988), p. 229.
37 W. K Hancock and M. M. Gowing, *British War Economy* (London, 1949), p. 106.
38 *The War Speeches of the Rt. Hon. Winston Churchill*, ed. Charles Eade, vol. I (London, 1951), pp. 120–1.
39 *NCDL*, vol. IV, p. 492.
40 WM (40) 67th conclusions, 13 March 1940, CAB 65/6/12; *NCDL*, vol. IV, p. 510. For a fuller account of this episode see Rock, *Chamberlain and Roosevelt*, pp. 262–76.
41 Patrick Salmon, 'British Plans for Economic Warfare against Germany 1937–1939: The Problem of Swedish Iron Ore', *Journal of Contemporary History*, 16 (1981), no. 1, 53–71.

42 Winston S. Churchill, *The Second World War*, vol. I: *The Gathering Storm* (London, 1948), pp. 550–2.

43 WM (39) 20th conclusions, 19 September 1939, CAB 65/1/20.

44 WM (39) 99th conclusions, 30 November 1939, CAB 65/2/33.

45 WM (39) 122nd conclusions, confidential annex, 22 December 1939, CAB 65/4/29; WP (39) 170, 21 December 1939, CAB 66/4/20.

46 WM (40) 8th conclusions, confidential annex, 10 January 1940, CAB 65/11/8.

47 *CWP*, vol. I, p. 673; *NCDL*, vol. IV, p. 492.

48 Bernard Kelly, 'Drifting Towards War: The British Chiefs of Staff, the USSR and the Winter War, November 1939–March 1940', *Contemporary British History*, 23 (2009), no. 3, 267–91.

49 Talbot Imlay, 'A Reassessment of Anglo-French Strategy during the Phoney War, 1939–1940', *English Historical Review*, 119 (2004), no. 481, 333–72 at 343–8.

50 WM (40) 45th conclusions, confidential annex, 18 February 1940, CAB 65/11/32.

51 WM (40) 46th conclusions, confidential annex, 19 February 1940, CAB 65/11/33.

52 *NCDL*, vol. IV, pp. 504–5; WM (40) 55th conclusions, 29 February 1940, CAB 65/5/55.

53 Imlay, 'Reassessment of Anglo-French Strategy', 366–7.

54 WM (40) 72nd conclusion, 19 March 1940, CAB 65/6/17.

55 WM (40) 76th conclusions, 27 March 1940, CAB 65/6/21.

56 Woodward, *British Foreign Policy*, vol. I, p. 111.

57 *CWP*, vol. I, p. 389; Gilbert, *Churchill*, vol. VI, pp. 89, 194, 202, 207–10.

58 Reynolds, *In Command*, p. 125.

59 *Ironside Diaries*, pp. 191–2.

60 J. L. Moulton, *The Norwegian Campaign of 1940* (London, 1966), pp. 69–71; John Kiszely, *Anatomy of a Campaign: The British Fiasco in Norway* (Cambridge, 2017), pp. 73–7, 95–6, 100–5; Tony Insall, *Secret Alliances: Special Operations and Intelligence in Norway 1940–1945 – The British Perspective* (London, 2019), pp. 27–34.

61 WM (39) 118th conclusions, 18 December 1939, CAB 65/2/52; Moulton, *Norwegian Campaign*, pp. 184–6, 191.

62 Kiszely, *Anatomy*, pp. 115, 127.

63 *Ironside Diaries*, pp. 256–62; *NCDL*, vol. IV, p. 527; *CWP*, vol. I, pp. 1139–42.

64 HC Deb, 7 May 1940, vol. 360, c. 1093; *The Times*, 5 April 1940, p. 8.

65 HC Deb, 7 May 1939, vol. 360, cc. 1125–30, 1149–50.

66 *NCDL*, vol. IV, p. 531.

67 Churchill, *Second World War*, vol. I, pp. 526–7.

68 Richard Overy, *Air Power, Armies, and the War in the West, 1940*, Harmon Memorial Lecture, US Air Force Academy, Colorado (1989); Hans Umbreit, 'The Battle for Hegemony in Western Europe' in Militärgeschichtliches Forschungsamt (ed.), *Germany and the Second World War*, vol. II: *Germany's Initial Conquests in Europe* (Oxford, 1991), pp. 227–326 at 248–50, 279.

69 *CWP*, vol. II, pp. 35–6.

70 WM (40), 123rd conclusions, 15 May 1940, confidential annex, CAB 65/13/9.

71 Alan Allport, *Britain at Bay: The Epic Story of the Second World War: 1938–1941* (London, 2020), pp. 235–8.

72 WM (40) 124th conclusions, 16 May 1940, confidential annex, CAB 65/13/10.

73 WM (40) 124th and 125th conclusions, 16 May 1940, CAB 65/7/19 and 20; *NCDL*, vol. IV, p. 531; *CWP*, vol. II, p. 60.

74 Neville Chamberlain diary, 16 May 1940, NC2/24.

75 WM (40) 128th conclusions, 18 May 1940, confidential annex, CAB 65/13/11.

76 *The Listener*, 23 May 1940, pp. 997–8 at 998.

77 WM (40) 129th conclusions, 19 May 1940, CAB 65/7/24; T. C. G. James, *The Growth of Fighter Command 1936–1940*, ed. Sebastian Cox (London, 2002), p. 91.

78 NC2/24.

79 *CWP*, vol. II, p. 93.

80 *Ironside Diaries*, p. 328; WM (40) 134th conclusions, 22 May 1940, confidential annex, CAB 65/13/15.

81 Chamberlain diary 26 and 27 May 1940, NC2/24; *NCDL*, vol. IV, p. 534.

82 *CWP*, vol. II, p. 50; Malcolm Muggeridge (ed.), *Ciano's Diary 1939–1943* (London, 1947), p. 252.

83 WM (40) 137th and 138th conclusions, 24 and 25 May 1940, CAB 65/7/32 and 33.

84 WM (40) 139th conclusions, 26 May 1939, confidential annex, CAB 65/13/20.

85 WM (40) 140th conclusions, 26 May 1939, confidential annex, CAB 65/13/21.

86 NC2/24.

87 David Reynolds, 'Churchill and the British "Decision" to Fight On in 1940', in Richard Langhorne (ed.), *Diplomacy and Intelligence during the Second World War* (Cambridge, 1985), pp. 147–67, at 166; Churchill, *Second World War*, vol. II, p. 157.

88 WM (40) 140th conclusions, 26 May 1940, confidential annex, CAB 65/13/21.

89 WM (40) 141st conclusions, 27 May 1940, confidential annex, minute 9, CAB 65/13/22; WP (40) 168, 'British Strategy in a Certain Eventuality', 25 May 1940, CAB 66/7/48; WP (40) 169, 'British Strategy in the Near Future', 26 May 1940, CAB 66/7/49.

90 WM (40) 141st conclusions, 27 May 1940, confidential annex, minute 1, CAB 65/13/22.

91 WM (40) 142nd conclusions, 27 May 1940, confidential annex, CAB 65/13/23; WM (40) 142nd conclusions, 27 May 1940, CAB 65/7/37.

92 WM (40) 142nd conclusions, 27 May 1940, confidential annex, CAB 65/13/23; Halifax diary, 27 May 1940, quoted in Earl of Birkenhead, *Halifax: The Life of Lord Halifax* (London, 1965), p. 458; *CD*, p. 291.

93 WM (40) 145th conclusions, 28 May 1940, confidential annex, CAB 65/13/24; *The Second World War Diary of Hugh Dalton 1940–45*, ed. Ben Pimlott (London, 1986), pp. 26–9.

94 Gilbert, *Churchill*, vol. VI, pp. 402–21; John Lukacs, *Five Days in London: May 1940* (New Haven, CT, 1999).

95 Robert Self, *Neville Chamberlain, a Biography* (Aldershot, 2006), p. 438.

96 WM (40) 153rd conclusions, 3 June 1940, confidential annex, CAB 65/13/31.

97 War Cabinet Defence Committee, 14th meeting, 8 June 1940, CAB 69/1.

98 Cato [Michael Foot, Peter Howard and Frank Owen], *Guilty Men* (London, 1940), pp. 1–16, 43–6.

99 David French, *Raising Churchill's Army: The British Army and the War against Germany 1919–1945* (Oxford, 2000), pp. 43, 159–74; Edward Smalley, 'Signal Failure: Communications in the British Expeditionary force, September 1939–June 1940', *War in History*, 28 (2021), no. 1, 143–65.

100 Final Report of the [Bartholomew] Committee to Review the Lessons Learned from the Recent Fighting in Flanders', 1940, WO 32/9581.

101 Postan, *British War Production*, pp. 471, 484; Churchill, *Second World War*, vol. II, pp. 286–7; A. J. Robertson, 'Lord Beaverbrook and the Supply of Aircraft, 1940–1941', in Anthony Slaven and Derek Aldcroft (eds.), *Business, Banking and Urban History: Essays in Honour of S. G. Checkland* (Edinburgh, 1982), pp. 80–100.

102 *NCDL*, vol. IV, pp. 547, 553.

103 Ibid., p. 551. See also pp. 547, 550 and 554 for invasion threat.

104 Ibid., p. 552.

105 HC Deb, 13 May 1940, vol. 360, c. 1502; 4 June 1940, vol. 361, c. 796; 18 June 1940, vol. 362, c. 61.

106 *NCDL*, vol. IV, pp. 551, 553; HC Deb, 18 July 1940, vol. 363, cc. 399–400.

107 Churchill to Roosevelt, 15 May, and Roosevelt to Churchill, 16 May, 1940, *CWP*, vol. II, pp. 45–6, 69–70.

108 WM (40) 168th conclusions, confidential annex, 16 June 1940, CAB 65/13/45.

109 WM (40) 232nd conclusions, 22 August 1940, confidential annex, CAB 65/14/23.

110 Reynolds, *Creation of the Anglo-American Alliance*, pp. 114, 121–32.

111 COS (40) 683, 4 September 1939, CAB 80/17.

112 Kathleen Burk, 'American Foreign Economic Policy and Lend-Lease', in Ann Lane and Howard Temperley (eds.), *The Rise and Fall of the Grand Alliance* (London, 1995), pp. 43–68.

113 *JMK*, vol. XXIV, pp. 398–411, at 410.

114 'Directive by the Prime Minister and Minister of Defence', 28 April 1941; Dill, 'The Relation of the Middle East to the Security of the United Kingdom', 6 May 1941, and Prime Minister to CIGS, 13 May 1941, all WO 216/5.

115 *CWP*, vol. III, pp. 81, 476, 774, 1412, 1413; Brian Farrell, *The Defence and Fall of Singapore 1940–1942* (Stroud, 2005), pp. 63–4, 86–7, 123.

116 Christopher M. Bell, 'The "Singapore Strategy" and the Deterrence of Japan: Winston Churchill, the Admiralty and the Despatch of Force Z', *English Historical Review*, 116 (2001), no. 467, 604–34.

117 Reynolds, *In Command*, pp. 295–6.

118 Winston S. Churchill, *The Second World War*, vol. IV: *The Hinge of Fate* (London, 1951), p. 81.

119 David Carlton, *Churchill and the Soviet Union* (Manchester, 2000), pp. 104–12, 117–18, 128–31; John Charmley, *Churchill: The End of Glory* (London, 1993), pp. 559–61.

120 Winston S. Churchill, *The Second World War*, vol. VI: *Triumph and Tragedy* (London, 1954), p. 124.

121 Dalton, *Second World War Diary*, p. 836

Chapter 11

1 *NCDL*, vol. IV, pp. 483, 533.
2 Winston S. Churchill, *The Second World War*, vol. I: *The Gathering Storm* (London, 1948), p. 271.
3 The case for fighting in 1938 is set out in Williamson Murray, *The Change in the European Balance of Power, 1938–1939* (Princeton, 1984), pp. 217–63, and P. E. Caquet, 'The Balance of Forces on the Eve of Munich', *International History Review*, 40 (2018), no. 1, 20–40. For the contrary view, see Keith Robbins, *Munich 1938* (London, 1968), pp. 327–58.
4 Lord Templewood, *The Listener*, vol. 40, 7 October 1948, p. 533, and *Nine Troubled Years* (London, 1954), pp. 331–5.
5 Murray, *Change in the European Balance*, pp. 245–53.
6 CP 199 (38), 14 September, 1938, CAB 24/278/34.
7 Wesley K. Wark, *The Ultimate Enemy: British Intelligence and Nazi Germany, 1933–1939* (Ithaca, NY, 1985), pp. 66–9.
8 Terence O'Brien, *Civil Defence* (London, 1955), pp. 10–11.
9 T. C. G. James, *The Growth of Fighter Command 1936–1940*, ed. Sebastian Cox (London, 2002), pp. 42–51; O'Brien, *Civil Defence*, pp. 153–65.
10 Winston S. Churchill, 'The European Crisis', *Step by Step* (London, 1939), pp. 281–4 at 283; Horst Rohde, 'Hitler's First Blitzkrieg and its Consequences for North-eastern Europe', in Militärgeschichtliches Forschungsamt (ed.), *Germany and the Second World War*, vol. II: *Germany's Initial Conquests in Europe* (Oxford, 1991), pp. 67–150 at 124.
11 Caquet, 'Balance of Forces', 31; Peter Jackson, 'French Military Intelligence and Czechoslovakia, 1938', *Diplomacy and Statecraft*, 5 (1994), no. 1, 81–106, at 99; Murray, *Change in the European Balance*, p. 234; David Vital, 'Czechoslovakia and the Powers, September 1938', *Journal of Contemporary History*, 1 (1966), no. 4, 37–67, at 48–9. Katriel Ben-Arie, 'Czechoslovakia at the Time of Munich: The Military Situation', *Journal of Contemporary History*, 25 (1990), no. 4, 431–46, is a partial exception, since he thought there was a fair chance the Czech army could have held out indefinitely, but even he assumed substantial assistance in the form of Soviet aircraft.
12 Churchill, *Second World War*, vol. I, p. 263; Caquet, 'Balance of Forces', 28–9; Milan Hauner, 'Czechoslovakia as a Military Factor in British Considerations of 1938', *Journal of Strategic Studies*, 1 (1978), no. 2, 194–222; Vital, 'Czechoslovakia', 44–5; Ben-Arie, 'Czechoslovakia at the Time of Munich', 438–9; Murray, *Change in European Balance*, p. 231.
13 Murray, *Change in the European Balance*, pp. 222–9, 231, 233–4.
14 Jackson, 'French Military Intelligence', 93–4; *The Times*, 28 September 1938, p. 11; *DGFP*, C/3, no. 69.
15 COS 770, 23 September 1938, CAB 53/41/5, and COS 773, 24 September 1938, CAB 53/41/6.
16 Churchill, *Second World War*, vol. I, p. 271.
17 Caquet, 'Balance of Forces', 34–5.
18 *Chief of Staff: The Diaries of Lieutenant-General Sir Henry Pownall*, ed. Brian Bond, vol. I: *1933–1940* (London, 1972), p. 163. See also Peter Jackson,

France and the Nazi Menace: Intelligence and Policy Making, 1933–1939 (Oxford, 2000), pp. 275–80, 284–5.

19 Jackson, 'French Military Intelligence', 88–9.

20 Hugh Ragsdale, *The Soviets, the Munich Crisis and the Coming of World War II* (Cambridge, 2004), pp. 182–92.

21 Ibid., p. 120.

22 *DBFP* 3/2, no. 791.

23 Igor Lukes, 'Stalin and Czechoslovakia in 1938–39: An Autopsy of a Myth', *Diplomacy and Statecraft*, 10 (1999), no. 2–3, 13–47, at 34–5.

24 *The Political Diary of Hugh Dalton, 1918–40, 1945–60*, ed. Ben Pimlott (London, 1986), p. 240.

25 Geoffrey Jukes, 'The Red Army and the Munich Crisis', *Journal of Contemporary History*, 26 (1991), no. 2, 195–214 at 202–3.

26 Churchill, *Second World War*, vol. I, p. 239.

27 Ragsdale, *Soviets, the Munich Crisis*, pp. 157–60, 166.

28 *CWP*, vol. I, pp. 671–2.

29 Caquet, 'Balance of Forces', 30. For Soviet naval inefficiency see Evan Mawdsley, *The War for the Seas: A Maritime History of World War II* (New Haven, CT, 2019), pp. 135–44.

30 Murray, *Change in the European Balance*, pp. 234, 256–63.

31 Adam Tooze, *The Wages of Destruction: The Making and Breaking of the Nazi Economy* (London, 2006), pp. 274, 302–3, 309.

32 Murray, *Change in the European Balance*, p. 262.

33 Tooze, *Wages of Destruction*, p. 329.

34 Hans Umbreit, 'The Battle for Hegemony in Western Europe', in Militärgeschichtliches Forschungsamt (ed.), *Germany and the Second World War*, vol. II, pp. 227–339 at 240, 244–7, 304, 316.

35 Earl of Halifax, *Fulness of Days* (London, 1957), p. 198.

36 *The Memoirs of General the Lord Ismay* (London, 1960), p. 92.

37 *DBFP* 3/1, no. 164, at 221.

38 Tom Harrison and Charles Madge, *Britain by Mass-Observation* (London, [1939] 1986), pp. 47–9.

39 Ritchie Ovendale, 'Britain, the Dominions and the Coming of the Second World War, 1933–9', in Wolfgang J. Mommsen and Lothar Kettenacker (eds.), *The Fascist Challenge and the Policy of Appeasement* (London, 1983), pp. 323–38 at 329.

40 John F. Naylor, *Labour's International Policy* (London, 1969), pp. 237–8, 243–4.

41 R. M. Douglas, *Orderly and Humane: The Expulsion of the Germans after the Second World War* (New Haven, CT, 2012), pp. 27, 75, 84–92.

42 J. W. Bruegel, *Czechoslovakia before Munich: The German Minority Problem and British Appeasement Policy* (Cambridge, 1973).

43 HC Deb, 5 October 1938, vol. 339, c. 365.

Bibliography

Archival Sources

The National Archives of the United Kingdom, London

Records of the Following:
Admiralty
Air Ministry
Cabinet Office
Foreign Office
MacDonald, Ramsay, diary
Prime Minister's Office
Security Service
Treasury
War Office

Other Archives

Bodleian Libraries, Oxford:
Crookshank, Viscount
Dawson, Geoffrey
Rumbold, Sir Horace
Simon, Viscount
Wallace, (David) Euan
British Library of Political and Economic Science, London School of Economics:
Fisher, Sir Warren
Cadbury Research Library, University of Birmingham:
Avon, Earl of (Sir Anthony Eden)
Chamberlain, Neville
Cambridge University Library:
Baldwin, Stanley
Templewood, Viscount (Sir Samuel Hoare)
Churchill Archives Centre, Churchill College, Cambridge:
Cadogan, Sir Alexander
Churchill, Winston S.
Drax, Admiral Sir Reginald Plunkett-Ernle-Erle
Grigg, Sir James

Hailsham, Viscount
Halifax, Earl of, microfilm from Hickleton papers
Hankey, Sir Maurice
Hore-Belisha, Leslie
Inskip, Sir Thomas (Viscount Caldecote)
Margesson, David
Phipps, Sir Eric
Swinton, Earl of
Vansittart, Sir Robert
Weir, Viscount
Glasgow University Archives:
Weir, Viscount
Liddell Hart Centre for Military Archives, King's College, London:
Ismay, Lord
Liddell Hart, Sir Basil
Montgomery-Massingberd, Sir Archibald
National Maritime Museum, Greenwich:
Chatfield, Lord
Trinity College Library, Cambridge:
Butler, R. A.

Published Primary and Contemporary Material

Amery, Leo, *The Empire at Bay: The Leo Amery Diaries 1929–1945*, ed. John Barnes and David Nicholson, London: Hutchison, 1988.
Attlee, Clement, *Clem Attlee: The Granada Historical Records Interview*, London: Panther Record, 1967.
Baldwin, Stanley, *Baldwin Papers: A Conservative Statesman, 1908–1947*, ed. Philip Williamson and Edward Baldwin, Cambridge: Cambridge University Press, 2004.
British Institute of Public Opinion, *Public Opinion Quarterly* (1940), no. 1, 2.
Cadogan, Sir Alexander, *The Diaries of Sir Alexander Cadogan 1938–1945*, ed. David Dilks, London: Cassell, 1971.
Cato pseud [Michael Foot, Peter Howard and Frank Owen], *Guilty Men*, London: Victor Gollancz, 1940.
Chamberlain, Sir Austen, *The Austen Chamberlain Diary Letters 1916–1937*, ed. Robert Self, Cambridge: Cambridge University Press, 1995.
Chamberlain, Neville, *The Struggle for Peace*, London: Hutchinson, 1939.
  The Neville Chamberlain Diary Letters, 4 vols., ed. Robert Self, Aldershot: Ashgate, 2000–5.
Churchill, Winston S., *Great Contemporaries*, London: Thornton Butterworth, 1937.
  Arms and the Covenant, London: George G. Harrap, 1938.
  Step by Step 1936–1939, London: Thornton Butterworth, 1939.
  The War Speeches of the Rt. Hon. Winston Churchill, 3 vols., ed. Charles Eade, London: Cassell, 1951–52.

Winston S. Churchill, Companion, 5 vols., ed. Martin Gilbert, London: Heinemann, 1967–82.

Winston Churchill: His Complete Speeches 1897–1963, 8 vols., ed. Robert Rhodes James, New York: Chelsea House Publishers, 1974.

The Collected Essays of Sir Winston Churchill, 4 vols., ed. Michael Wolff, London: Library of Imperial History, 1976.

The Churchill War Papers, 3 vols., ed. Martin Gilbert, New York: W. W. Norton, 1993–99.

'"The Truth About War Debts", 17 March 1934, Reproduced in Finest Hour', *The Journal of Winston Churchill,* no. 153 (Winter 2011/12), 26–28.

Ciano, Galeazzo, *Ciano's Diary, 1939–1943,* ed. Malcolm Muggeridge, London: William Heinemann, 1947.

Ciano's Diplomatic Papers, ed. Malcolm Muggeridge, London: Odhams, 1948.

Colville, John, *The Fringes of Power: Downing Street Diaries, 1939–55,* London: Hodder and Stoughton, 1985.

Cooper, (Alfred) Duff, *The Duff Cooper Diaries 1915-1951,* ed. John Julius Norwich, London: Weidenfeld and Nicolson, 2005.

Dalton, Hugh, *The Political Diary of Hugh Dalton, 1918–40, 1945–60,* ed. Ben Pimlott, London: Jonathan Cape, 1986.

The Second World War Diary of Hugh Dalton, 1940–45, ed. Ben Pimlott, London: Jonathan Cape, 1986.

Documents on British Foreign Policy, series 1A and 2nd and 3rd series, 1946-86.

Documents on German Foreign Policy, series D, vols. I–VI, 1949–56.

The Economist.

Foreign Relations of the United States.

Harrison, Tom and Charles Madge, *Britain by Mass-Observation,* [1939] London: Cresset, 1986.

Harvey, Oliver, *The Diplomatic Diaries of Oliver Harvey 1937–1940,* ed. J. Harvey, London: Collins, 1970.

Hitler, Adolf, *Mein Kampf,* London: Hutchinson, [1925] 1969.

Speech Delivered in the Reichstag, April 28th 1939, Berlin: Müller & Sohn, 1939.

House of Commons Debates, api.parliament.uk/historic-hansard/index.html.

Ironside, Sir Edmund, *The Ironside Diaries 1937–1940,* eds. Roderick Macleod and Denis Kelly, London: Constable, 1962.

Jones, Thomas, *A Diary with Letters 1931–1950,* London: Oxford University Press, 1954.

Kennedy, A. L, *The Times and Appeasement: The Journals of A. L. Kennedy, 1932–1939,* ed. Gordon Martel, Cambridge: Cambridge University Press, 2000.

Kennedy, Joseph P, *Hostage to Fortune: The Letters of Joseph P. Kennedy,* ed. Amanda Smith, New York: Viking Penguin, 2001.

Keynes, John Maynard, *Collected Writings,* 30 vols., eds. Elizabeth Johnson and Donald Moggridge, London: Macmillan; Cambridge University Press, 1971-89.

Liddell Hart, Basil, *Europe in Arms,* London: Faber and Faber, 1937.

The Listener

Maisky, Ivan, *The Complete Maisky Diaries,* 3 vols., ed. Gabriel Gorodetsky, New Haven: Yale University Press, 2017.

Morgenthau, Henry, *From the Morgenthau Diaries*, 3 vols., ed. John Morton Blum, Boston, MA: Houghton Mifflin, 1959–67.

New Statesman and Nation

Nicolson, Harold, *Harold Nicolson: Diaries and Letters 1930–1939*, ed. Nigel Nicolson, London: Collins, 1966.

Phipps, Sir Eric, *Our Man in Berlin: The Diary of Sir Eric Phipps, 1933–1937*, ed. Gaynor Johnson, Basingstoke: Palgrave/Macmillan, 2008.

Pownall, Sir Henry, *Chief of Staff: The Diaries of Lieutenant-General Sir Henry Pownall*, 2 vols., ed. Brian Bond, London: Leo Cooper, 1972–4.

Roberts, Stephen, *The House That Hitler Built* (London: Methuen, 1937).

Roosevelt, Franklin D, *The Roosevelt Letters: Being the Personal Correspondence of Franklin Delano Roosevelt*, 8 vols., ed. Elliott Roosevelt, London: George G. Harrap and Co., 1949–52.

Soviet Peace Efforts on the Eve of World War II, ed. Gromyko, Andrei, et al, Moscow: Progress Publishers, 1976.

The Times

UK Parliamentary Papers

Memoirs

Avon, Earl of, *The Eden Memoirs: Facing the Dictators*, London: Cassell, 1962.

Butler, Lord, *The Art of the Possible*, London: Hamish Hamilton, 1971.

Chatfield, Lord, *It Might Happen Again*, vol. II: *The Navy and Defence*, London: William Heinemann, 1947.

Churchill, Winston S, *The Second World War*, 6 vols., London: Cassell, 1948–54.

Citrine, Walter, *Men and Work: The Autobiography of Lord Citrine*, London: Hutchinson, 1964.

Dahlerus, Johan Birger, *The Last Attempt*, London: Hutchinson, 1948.

Dalton, Hugh, *The Fateful Years: Memoirs, 1931–1945*, London: Frederick Muller, 1957.

Davidson, J. C. C., *Memoirs of a Conservative: J. C. C. Davidson's Memoirs and Papers, 1910-1937*, ed. Robert Rhodes James, London: Weidenfeld and Nicolson, 1969.

Douglas-Home, Alec, *The Way the Wind Blows*, London: Collins, 1976.

Drax, R. Plunkett-Ernle-Erle, 'Mission to Moscow, part 1', *Naval Review*, vol. XI (1952), no. 3, 250-65; part 2, vol. XI, (1952), no. 4, 399-414; part 3, vol. XII (1953), no. 1, 57-63.

Gladwyn (see Jebb).

Halifax, Earl of, *Fulness of Days*, London: Collins, 1957.

Henderson, Nevile, *Failure of a Mission: Berlin 1937–1939*, London: Hodder and Stoughton, 1940.

Water under the Bridges, London: Hodder and Stoughton, 1945.

Home (see Douglas-Home).

Hull, Cordell, *Memoirs*, 2 vols., London: Hodder and Stoughton, 1948.

Ismay, Baron, *Memoirs of General the Lord Ismay*, London: Heinemann, 1960.

Jebb, Gladwyn, *The Memoirs of Lord Gladwyn*, London: Weidenfeld and Nicolson, 1972.

Kennedy, John, *The Business of War: The War Narrative of Major-General Sir John Kennedy*, ed. Bernard Fergusson, London: Hutchinson, 1957.

Kirkpatrick, Ivone, *The Inner Circle*, London: Macmillan, 1959.

Lawford, Valentine, *Bound for Diplomacy*, London: John Murray, 1963.

Leith-Ross, Sir Frederick, *Money Talks: Fifty Years of International Finance*, London: Hutchinson, 1968.

Liddell, Hart, Sir Basil, *Memoirs*, 2 vols., London: Cassell, 1965.

Macmillan, Harold, *Winds of Change 1914–1939*, London: Macmillan, 1966.

Norwich, Viscount [Duff Cooper], *Old Men Forget*, London: Hart-Davis, 1953.

Schmidt, Paul, *Hitler's Interpreter*, ed. R. H. C. Steed, London: William Heinemann, 1951.

Simon, Viscount, *Retrospect*, London: Hutchinson, 1952.

Strang, William (Baron), *Home and Abroad*, London: André Deutsch, 1956.

Swinton, Viscount, *I Remember*, London: Hutchinson, 1948.

Templewood, Viscount [Samuel Hoare], *Nine Troubled Years*, London: Collins, 1954.

Vansittart, Robert (Baron), *The Mist Procession*, London: Hutchinson, 1958.

Winterton, Earl, *Orders of the Day*, London: Cassell, 1953.

Secondary Material

Adamthwaite, Anthony, *France and the Coming of the Second World War, 1936–1939*, London: Frank Cass, 1977.

'The British Government and the Media, 1937–1938', *Journal of Contemporary History*, 18 (1983), no. 2, 281–97.

Addison, Paul, *Churchill: The Unexpected Hero*, Oxford: Oxford University Press, 2005.

Alexander, Martin, *The Republic in Danger: General Maurice Gamelin and the Politics of French Defence, 1933-40*, Cambridge: Cambridge University Press, 1992.

Alexander, Martin, and W. J. Philpott, 'The Entente Cordiale and the Next War: Anglo-French Views on Future Military Co-operation, 1928–39', in Martin Alexander (ed.), *Knowing Your Friends: Intelligence Inside Alliances and Coalitions from 1914 to the Cold War*, London: Frank Cass, 1998, pp. 53–84.

Allport, Alan, *Britain at Bay: The Epic Story of the Second World War: 1938–1941*, London: Profile Books, 2020.

Andrew, Christopher, *For the President's Eyes Only: Secret Intelligence and the American Presidency from Washington to Bush*, London: HarperCollins, 1995.

The Defence of the Realm: The Authorized History of MI5, London: Allen Lane, 2009.

Andrew, Christopher, and Vasili Mitrokhin, *The Mitrokhin Archive: The KGB in Europe and the West*, London: Allen Lane, 1999.

Ascher, Abraham, 'Was Hitler a Riddle?' *Journal of the Historical Society*, 9 (2009), no. 1, 1–21.

Ashworth, William, *Contracts and Finance*, London: HMSO, 1953.

A Short History of the International Economy since 1850, 2nd edition, London: Longmans, Green and Co, 1962.

Aster, Sidney, *1939: The Making of the Second World War*, London: André Deutsch, 1973.

'"Guilty Men": The Case of Neville Chamberlain', in Robert Boyce and Esmonde Robertson (eds.), *Paths to War: New Essays on the Origins of the Second World War*, London: Macmillan, 1989, pp. 233–68.

Bailey, Gavin, *The Arsenal of Democracy: Aircraft Supply and the Anglo-American Alliance*, Edinburgh: Edinburgh University Press, 2013.

Ball, Stuart, *Winston Churchill*, London: British Library, 2003.

Barnett, Correlli, *The Collapse of British Power*, London: Eyre Methuen, 1972.

Beck, Peter, 'Politicians Versus Historians: Lord Avon's "Appeasement Battle" Against "Lamentably, Appeasement-minded" Historians', *Twentieth Century British History*, 9 (1998), no. 3, 396–419.

Beichman, Arnold, 'Hugger-mugger in Old Queen Street: The Origins of the Conservative Research Department', *Journal of Contemporary History* 13 (1978), no. 4, 671–88.

Bell, Christopher M., *The Royal Navy, Seapower and Strategy between the Wars*, London: Macmillan, 2000.

'The "Singapore Strategy" and the Deterrence of Japan: Winston Churchill, the Admiralty and the Despatch of Force Z', *English Historical Review*, 116 (2001), no. 467, 604–34.

Churchill and Sea Power, Oxford: Oxford University Press, 2013.

Bell, Peter, *Chamberlain, Germany and Japan, 1933–4*, London: Macmillan, 1996.

Ben-Arie, Katriel, 'Czechoslovakia at the Time of Munich: The Military Situation', *Journal of Contemporary History*, 25 (1990), no. 4, 431–46.

Bennett, Gill, 'The Roosevelt Peace Plan of January 1938', *FCO Historical Branch Occasional Papers*, no. 1 (Nov. 1987), 27–37, Foreign Office records: FO 973/522, TNA.

'British Policy in the Far East 1933-1936: Treasury and Foreign Office', *Modern Asian Studies*, 26 (1992), no. 3, 545–68.

'Declassification and Release Policies of the UK's Intelligence Agencies', *Intelligence and National Security*, 17 (2002), no. 1, 21–32.

Churchill's Man of Mystery: Desmond Morton and the World of Intelligence, Abingdon: Routledge, 2007.

Best, Antony, *Britain, Japan and Pearl Harbor: Avoiding War in East Asia, 1936–1941*, Oxford: Oxford University Press, 1995.

British Intelligence and the Japanese Challenge in Asia, 1914–1941, London: Palgrave Macmillan, 2002.

'The Leith-Ross Mission and British Policy towards East Asia, 1934-7', *International History Review*, 35 (2013), no. 4, 681–701.

Bialer, Uri, *The Shadow of the Bomber: The Fear of Air Attack and British Politics 1932–1939*, London: Royal Historical Society, 1980.

Biddle, Tami Davis, *Rhetoric and Reality in Air Warfare: The Evolution of British and American Ideas about Strategic Bombing, 1914–1945*, Princeton, NJ: Princeton University Press, 2002.

Birkenhead, Earl of, *Halifax: The Life of Lord Halifax*, London: Hamish Hamilton, 1965.

Blaazer, David, 'Finance and the End of Appeasement: The Bank of England, the National Government and the Czech Gold', *Journal of Contemporary History*, 40 (2005), no. 1, 25–39.

Blake, Robert, and Wm. Roger Louis (eds.), *Churchill*, Oxford: Oxford University Press, 1993.

Boadle, Donald, 'The Formation of the Foreign Office Economic Relations Section, 1930–1937', *Historical Journal*, 20 (1977), no. 4, 919–36.

Bond, Brian, *Liddell Hart: A Study of His Military Thought*, London: Cassell, 1977.

  British Military Policy between the Two World Wars, Oxford: Clarendon Press, 1980.

  'Leslie Hore-Belisha at the War Office', in Ian Beckett and John Gooch (eds.), *Politicians and Defence: Studies in the Formulation of British Defence Policy 1845–1970*, Manchester: Manchester University Press, 1981, pp. 110–31.

Bosworth, R. J. B., *Mussolini*, London: Arnold, 2002.

Bourette-Knowles, Simon, 'The Global Micawber: Sir Robert Vansittart, the Treasury and the Global Balance of Power, 1933–35', *Diplomacy and Statecraft*, 6 (1995), no. 1, 91–121.

Bouverie, Tim, *Appeasing Hitler: Chamberlain, Churchill and the Road to War*, London: The Bodley Head, 2019.

Boyd, Alexander, *The Soviet Air Force since 1918*, London: Macdonald and Jane's, 1977.

Boyle, Andrew, *Trenchard, Man of Vision*, London: Collins, 1962.

Bruegel, J. W., *Czechoslovakia before Munich: The German Minority Problem and British Appeasement Policy*, Cambridge: Cambridge University Press, 1973.

Burk, Kathleen, 'American Foreign Economic Policy and Lend-Lease', in Ann Lane and Howard Temperley (eds.), *The Rise and Fall of the Grand Alliance*, London: Macmillan, 1995, pp. 43–68.

  Troublemaker: The Life and History of A. J. P. Taylor, New Haven, CT: Yale University Press, 2000.

Buxton, Neil, and Derek Aldcroft (eds.), *British Industry between the Wars*, London: Scolar Press, 1979.

Cain, Anthony, *Forgotten Air Force: French Air Doctrine in the 1930s*, Washington, DC: Smithsonian Institution Press, 2002.

Canning, Paul, 'Yet Another Failure for Appeasement? The Case of the Irish Ports', *International History Review*, 4 (1982), no. 3, 371–92.

Capie, Forrest, *Depression and Protection: Britain between the Wars*, London: George Allen and Unwin, 1983.

Capie, Forrest H., Terence C. Mills and Geoffrey E. Wood, 'Debt Management and Interest Rates: The British Stock Conversion of 1932', *Applied Economics*, 18 (1986), no. 10, 111–26.

Caputi, Robert J., *Neville Chamberlain and Appeasement*, Selinsgrove, PA: Susquehanna University Press, 2000.

Caquet, P. E., 'The Balance of Forces on the Eve of Munich', *International History Review*, 40 (2018), no. 1, 20–40.

Carley, Michael Jabara, *1939: The Alliance That Never Was and the Coming of World War II*, Chicago, IL: I. R. Dee, 1999.

'"A Situation of Delicacy and Danger": Anglo-Soviet Relations, August 1939–March 1940', *Contemporary European History*, 8 (1999), no. 2, 175–208.

'"Only the USSR Has ... Clean Hands": The Soviet Perspective on the Failure of Collective Security and the Collapse of Czechoslovakia, 1934–1938 (Part 2)' *Diplomacy and Statecraft*, 21 (2010), no. 3, 368–96.

'Fiasco: The Anglo-Franco-Soviet Alliance That Never Was and the Unpublished British White Paper, 1939–1940', *International History Review*, 41 (2019), no. 4, 701–28.

Carlton, David, *Anthony Eden*, London: Allen Lane, 1981.

Churchill and the Soviet Union, Manchester: Manchester University Press, 2000.

Ceadel, Martin, 'Interpreting East Fulham', in Chris Cook and John Ramsden (eds.), *By-Elections in British Politics*, London: Macmillan, 1973, pp. 118–39.

'The First British Referendum: The Peace Ballot, 1934–5', *English Historical Review*, 95 (1980), no. 377, 810–39.

'The Peace Movement between the Wars: Problems of Definition', in Richard Taylor and Nigel Young (eds.), *Campaigns for Peace: British Peace Movements in the Twentieth Century*, Manchester: Manchester University Press, 1987, pp. 73–99.

Ceva, Lucio, and Andrea Curami, 'Air Army and Aircraft Industry in Italy 1936–1943', in Horst Boog (ed.), *The Conduct of the Air War in the Second World War: An International Comparison*, Oxford: Berg, 1992, pp. 85–107.

Charmley, John, *Chamberlain and the Lost Peace*, London: Weidenfeld and Nicolson, 1989.

Churchill: The End of Glory, London: Hodder and Stoughton, 1993.

Churchill's Grand Alliance: The Anglo-American Special Relationship 1940–57, London: Hodder and Stoughton, 1995.

Churchill, Randolph, and Martin Gilbert, *Winston S. Churchill*, 8 vols., London: Heinemann, 1966–88. Gilbert was solely responsible for volumes 3 to 8.

Clarke, Peter, 'Churchill's Economic Ideas, 1900–1930', in Robert Blake and Wm. Roger Louis (eds.), *Churchill*, Oxford: Oxford University Press, 1993, pp. 79–95.

Clausewitz, Carl von, *On War*, eds. Michael Howard and Peter Paret, Princeton, NJ: Princeton University Press, 1976.

Cockett, Richard, *Twilight of Truth: Chamberlain, Appeasement, and the Manipulation of the Press*, London: Weidenfeld and Nicolson, 1989.

'Ball, Chamberlain and *Truth*', *Historical Journal*, 33 (1990), no. 1, 131–42.

Colvin, Ian, *Vansittart in Office*, London: Victor Gollancz, 1965.

Coombs, Benjamin, *British Tank Production and the War Economy, 1934–1945*, London: Bloomsbury, 2013.

Cooper, Chris, '"We Have to Cut Our Coat According to Our Cloth": Hailsham, Chamberlain, and the Struggle for Rearmament, 1933-4', *International History Review*, 36 (2014), no. 4, 653–72.

Corum, James S., 'From Biplanes to Blitzkrieg: The Development of German Air Doctrine between the Wars', *War in History*, 3 (1996), no. 1, 85–101.

Cowling, Maurice, *The Impact of Hitler: British Politics and British Policy 1933-1940*, Cambridge: Cambridge University Press.

Crafts, Nicholas, 'Walking Wounded: The British Economy in the Aftermath of World War I', in Stephen Broadberry and Mark Harrison (eds.), The Economics of the Great War: A Centennial Perspective, https://voxeu.org/content/economics-great-war-centennial-perspective (2018), pp. 119–25

Crafts, Nicholas, and Peter Fearon, 'Lessons from the 1930s Great Depression', Oxford Review of Economic Policy, 26 (2010), no. 3, 285–317.

Crafts, Nicholas, and Terence C. Mills, 'Self-defeating Austerity? Evidence from 1930s Britain', European Review of Economic History, 19 (2015), no. 2, 109–27.

Crozier, Andrew J., Appeasement and Germany's Last Bid for Colonies, Basingstoke: Macmillan, 1988.

Cynk, Jerzy, History of the Polish Air Force 1918-1968, Reading: Osprey, 1972.

Dallek, Robert, Franklin D. Roosevelt and American Foreign Policy, 1932-1945, New York: Oxford University Press, 1979.

Danchev, Alex, Alchemist of War: The Life of Basil Liddell Hart, London: Weidenfeld and Nicolson, 1999.

Davis, Richard, Anglo-French Relations before the Second World War: Appeasement and Crisis, Basingstoke: Palgrave, 2001.

Deist, Wilhelm, 'The Rearmament of the Wehrmacht', in Militärgeschichtliches Forschungsamt (ed.), Germany and the Second World War, vol. I: The Build-up of German Aggression, Oxford: Clarendon Press, 1990, pp. 373–540.

Dennis, Peter, Decision by Default: Peacetime Conscription and British Defence 1919-39, London: Routledge and Kegan Paul, 1972.

Department of Employment and Productivity, British Labour Statistics: Historical Abstract 1886-1968, London: HMSO, 1971.

D'Este, Carlo, Warlord: The Fighting Life of Winston Churchill from Soldier to Statesman, London: Allen Lane, 2009.

Dilks, David, 'The Twilight War and the Fall of France: Chamberlain and Churchill in 1940', Transactions of the Royal Historical Society, 28 (1978), 61–86.

'Appeasement and "Intelligence"', in David Dilks (ed.), Retreat from Power: Studies in Britain's Foreign Policy of the Twentieth Century, vol. I, London: Macmillan, 1981, pp. 139–69.

'Flashes of Intelligence: The Foreign Office, the SIS and Security before the Second World War', in Christopher Andrew and David Dilks, (eds.), The Missing Dimension: Government and Intelligence Communities in the Twentieth Century, London: Macmillan, 1984, pp. 101–25.

Neville Chamberlain, vol. I: 1869-1929, Cambridge: Cambridge University Press, 1984.

'"We Must Hope for the Best and Prepare for the Worst": The Prime Minister, the Cabinet and Hitler's Germany, 1937-1939', Proceedings of the British Academy, 73 (1987), 309–52.

Churchill and Company: Allies and Rivals in War and Peace, London: I. B. Tauris, 2012.

Doerr, Paul W., British Foreign Policy 1919-1939, Manchester: Manchester University Press, 1998.

Doughty, Robert A., 'The French Armed Forces', in Allan R. Millett and Williamson Murray (eds.), *Military Effectiveness*, vol. II: *The Interwar Period*, Boston, MA: Unwin Hyman, 1988, pp. 39–69.

Douglas, R. M., *Orderly and Humane: The Expulsion of the Germans after the Second World War*, New Haven, CT: Yale University Press, 2012.

Drummond, Ian M., *The Floating Pound and the Sterling Area 1931–1939*, Cambridge: Cambridge University Press, 1981.

Dutton, David, *Simon: A Political Biography of Sir John Simon*, London: Aurum Press, 1992.

Neville Chamberlain, London: Arnold, 2001.

'Guilty Men? Three British Foreign Secretaries of the 1930s', in Frank McDonough (ed.), *The Origins of the Second World War: An International Perspective*, London: Continuum, 2011, pp. 144–67.

Edgerton, David, *Warfare State: Britain, 1920–1970*, Cambridge: Cambridge University Press, 2006.

Britain's War Machine: Weapons, Resources and Experts in the Second World War, London: Allen Lane, 2011.

Edwards, Jill, *The British Government and the Spanish Civil War, 1936–1939*, Basingstoke: Macmillan, 1979.

Eichengreen, Barry, *Golden Fetters: The Gold Standard and the Great Depression 1919–1939*, New York: Oxford University Press, 1992.

Emmerson, James, *The Rhineland Crisis: A Study in Multilateral Diplomacy*, London: Temple Smith, 1977.

Evans, Richard J., *The Third Reich in Power*, London: Allen Lane, 2005.

Faber, David, *Munich: The 1938 Appeasement Crisis*, London: Simon and Schuster, 2008.

Farrell, Brian, *The Defence and Fall of Singapore 1940–1942*, Stroud: Tempus, 2005.

Fearon, Peter, 'Aircraft Manufacturing', in Neil Buxton and Derek Aldcroft (eds.), *British Industry between the Wars*, London: Scolar Press, 1979, pp. 216–40.

Feiling, Keith, *The Life of Neville Chamberlain*, London: Macmillan, 1946.

Feinstein, Charles, *National Income, Expenditure and Output of the United Kingdom 1855–1965*, Cambridge: Cambridge University Press, 1972.

Ferguson, Niall, *The War of the World: History's Age of Hatred*, London: Allen Lane, 2006.

Ferris, John, '"The Greatest Power on Earth": Great Britain in the 1920s', *International History Review*, 13 (1991), no. 4, 726–50.

'Fighter Defence Before Fighter Command: The Rise of Strategic Air Defence in Great Britain, 1917–1934', *Journal of Military History*, 63 (1999), no. 4, 845–84.

Intelligence and Strategy: Selected Essays, Abingdon: Routledge, 2005.

"Now That the Milk Is Spilt": Appeasement and the Archive on Intelligence', *Diplomacy and Statecraft*, 19 (2008), no. 3, 527–65.

Behind the Enigma: The Authorised History of GCHQ, Britain's Secret Cyber-Intelligence Agency, London: Bloomsbury, 2020.

Fest, Joachim, *Plotting Hitler's Death: The German Resistance 1933–1945*, London: Weidenfeld and Nicolson, 1996.

Field, Andrew, *Royal Navy Strategy in the Far East 1919-1939: Planning for War against Japan*, London: Frank Cass, 2004.

Finkel, Alvin, and Clement Leibovitz, *The Chamberlain-Hitler Collusion*, Halifax, NS: James Lorimer, 1997.

Finney, Patrick (ed.), *The Origins of the Second World War*, London: Arnold, 1997.

Forbes, Neil, 'London Banks, the German Standstill Agreements, and "Economic Appeasement" in the 1930s', *Economic History Review*, 40 (1987), no. 4, 571–87.

Doing Business with the Nazis: Britain's Economic and Financial Relations with Germany, 1931–1939, London: Frank Cass, 2000.

'Democracy at a Disadvantage? British Rearmament, the Shadow Factory Scheme and the Coming of War', *Jahrbuch für Wirtschaftsgeschichte/ Economic History Yearbook*, 55 (2014), no. 2, 49–69.

French, David, *Raising Churchill's Army: The British Army and the War against Germany 1919–1945*, Oxford: Oxford University Press, 2000.

'The Mechanization of the British Cavalry between the World Wars', *War in History*, 10 (2003), no. 3, 296–320.

Friedman, Milton, 'Franklin D. Roosevelt, Silver, and China', *Journal of Political Economy*, 100 (1992), no. 1, 62–83.

Fuchser, Larry W., *Neville Chamberlain and Appeasement: A Study in the Politics of History*, New York: Norton, 1982.

Gannon, Franklin, *The British Press and Germany, 1936–1939*, Oxford: Clarendon Press, 1971.

Gibbs, N. H., *Grand Strategy*, vol. I: *Rearmament Policy*, London: HMSO, 1976.

Gilbert, Martin, *The Roots of Appeasement*, London: Weidenfeld and Nicolson, 1966.

Winston S. Churchill, 8 vols. *(first two with Randolph Churchill)*, London: Heinemann, 1966–88.

Churchill's Political Philosophy, Oxford: Oxford University Press, 1981.

Winston Churchill: The Wilderness Years, London: Macmillan, 1981.

'Horace Wilson: Man of Munich? *History Today*, 32 (1982), no. 10, 3–9.

Churchill and America, London: Free Press, 2005.

Gillard, David, *Appeasement in Crisis: From Munich to Prague, October 1938–March 1939*, Basingstoke: Palgrave, 2007.

Goldman, Aaron L., 'Two views of Germany: Nevile Henderson Versus Vansittart and the Foreign Office, 1937–1939', *British Journal of International Studies*, 6 (1980), no. 3, 247–77.

Gooch, John, *Mussolini and His Generals: The Armed Forces and Fascist Foreign Policy, 1922–1940*, Cambridge: Cambridge University Press, 2007.

Goodman, Michael S., *The Official History of the Joint Intelligence Committee*, vol. I: *From the Approach of the Second World War to the Suez Crisis*, Abingdon: Routledge, 2016.

Gordon, G. A. H., *British Seapower and Procurement between the Wars: A Reappraisal of Rearmament*, London: Macmillan, 1988.

Gottlieb, Julie, *'Guilty Women', Foreign Policy, and Appeasement in Inter-War Britain*, Basingstoke: Palgrave Macmillan, 2015.

Grayzel, Susan R., *At Home and Under Fire: Air Raids and Culture in Britain from the Great War to the Blitz*, Cambridge: Cambridge University Press, 2012.

Greenwood, Sean, 'Sir Thomas Inskip as Minister for the Co-ordination of Defence, 1936–1939' in Paul Smith (ed.), *Government and Armed Forces in Britain 1856–1990*, London: Hambledon Press, 1996.

Hammond, Richard, 'An Enduring Influence on Imperial Defence and Grand Strategy: British Perceptions of the Italian Navy, 1935–1943', *International History Review*, 39 (2017), no. 5, 810–35.

Hancock, W. K., and M. M. Gowing, *British War Economy*, London: HMSO, 1949.

Harris, J. P., 'British Military Intelligence and the Rise of the German Mechanized Forces 1927–1939', *Intelligence and National Security*, 6 (1991), no. 2, 395–417.

Men, Ideas and Tanks: British Military Thought and Armoured Forces, 1903–1939, Manchester: Manchester University Press, 1995.

Harrison, Mark, 'The Economics of World War II: An Overview', in Mark Harrison (ed.), *The Economics of World War II: Six Great Powers in International Comparison*, Cambridge: Cambridge University Press, 1998, pp. 1–42.

Haslam, Jonathan, *The Soviet Union and the Struggle for Collective Security in Europe, 1933–39*, London: Macmillan, 1984.

Hauner, Milan, 'Czechoslovakia as a Military Factor in British Considerations of 1938', *Journal of Strategic Studies*, 1 (1978), no. 2, 194–222.

Herman, John, *The Paris Embassy of Sir Eric Phipps: Anglo-French Relations and the Foreign Office, 1937–1939*, Brighton: Sussex Academic Press, 1998.

Hinsley, F. H., et al, *British Intelligence in the Second World War: Its Influence on Strategy and Operations*, 4 vols., London: HMSO, 1979–90.

'Churchill and the Use of Special Intelligence', in Robert Blake and Wm. Roger Louis (eds.), *Churchill*, Oxford: Oxford University Press, 1993, pp. 407–26.

Holman, Brett, *The Next War in the Air: Britain's Fear of the Bomber, 1908–1941*, Abingdon: Ashgate, 2014.

Homze, Edward L., *Arming the Luftwaffe: The Reich Air Ministry and the German Aircraft Industry, 1919–39*, Lincoln, NE: University of Nebraska Press, 1976.

Hornby, William, *Factories and Plant*, London: HMSO, 1958.

Horsler, Paul, 'Cometh the Hour, Cometh the Nation: Local-Level Opinion and Defence Preparations Prior to the Second World War, November 1937-September 1939', PhD thesis, London School of Economics and Political Science, 2016.

Howard, Michael, *The Continental Commitment: The Dilemma of British Defence Policy in the Era of the Two World Wars*, London: Temple Smith, 1972.

Howson, Susan, *Domestic Monetary Management in Britain 1919–38*, Cambridge: Cambridge University Press, 1975.

Sterling's Managed Float: The Operations of the Exchange Equalisation Account, 1932–39, Princeton Studies in International Finance, no. 46, Nov. 1980.

Howson, Susan, and Donald Winch, *The Economic Advisory Council, 1930–1939: A Study in Economic Advice during Depression and Recovery*, Cambridge: Cambridge University Press, 1977.

Hucker, Daniel, *Public Opinion and the End of Appeasement in Britain and France*, Farnham: Ashgate, 2011.

'Public Opinion, the Press and the Failed Anglo-Franco-Soviet Negotiations of 1939', International *History Review*, 40 (2018), no. 1, 65–85.

Imlay, Talbot C., *Facing the Second World War: Strategy, Politics, and Economics in Britain and France 1938–1940*, Oxford: Oxford University Press, 2003.

'A Reassessment of Anglo-French Strategy during the Phoney War, 1939–1940', *English Historical Review*, 119 (2004), no. 481, 333–72.

Insall, Tony, *Secret Alliances: Special Operations and Intelligence in Norway 1940–1945 – The British Perspective*, London: Biteback Publishing, 2019.

Jackson, Peter, 'French Military Intelligence and Czechoslovakia, 1938', *Diplomacy and Statecraft*, 5 (1994), no. 1, 81–106.

France and the Nazi Menace: Intelligence and Policy Making 1933–1939, Oxford: Oxford University Press, 2000.

Jacobson, Max, *The Diplomacy of the Winter War*, Cambridge, MA: Harvard University Press, 1961.

James, T. C. G., *The Growth of Fighter Command 1936-1940*, ed. Sebastian Cox, London: Frank Cass, 2002.

Jeffery, Keith, *MI6: The History of the Secret Intelligence Service, 1909-1949*, London: Bloomsbury, 2010.

Johnson, David E., *Fast Tanks and Heavy Bombers: Innovation in the US Army, 1917-1945*, Ithaca, NY: Cornell University Press, 1998.

Johnston-White, Iain E., *The British Commonwealth and Victory in the Second World War*, London: Palgrave Macmillan, 2017.

Jones, Neville, *The Beginnings of Strategic Air Power: A History of the British Bomber Force 1923-1939*, London: Frank Cass, 1987.

Jukes, Geoffrey, 'The Red Army and the Munich Crisis', *Journal of Contemporary History*, 26 (1991), no. 2, 195–214.

Kahn, Martin, 'British Intelligence on Soviet War Potential in 1939: A Revised Picture and Some Implications (a Contribution to the "Unending Debate")', *Intelligence and National Security*, 28 (2013), no. 5, 717–47.

Kelly, Bernard, 'Drifting Towards War: The British Chiefs of Staff, the USSR and the Winter War, November 1939-March 1940', *Contemporary British History*, 23 (2009), no. 3, 267–91.

Kennedy, Greg, *Anglo-American Strategic Relations and the Far East 1933-1939*, London: Frank Cass, 2002.

'Neville Chamberlain and Strategic Relations with the United States during his Chancellorship', *Diplomacy and Statecraft*, 13 (2002), no. 1, 95–120.

'"Rat in Power": Neville Chamberlain and the Creation of British Foreign Policy, 1931-39', in T. G. Otte (ed.), *The Makers of British Foreign Policy: From Pitt to Thatcher*, Basingstoke: Palgrave, 2002, pp. 173–95.

Kennedy, Paul, 'The Tradition of Appeasement in British Foreign Policy, 1865–1939', *British Journal of International Studies*, 2 (1976), no. 2, 195–215.

The Rise and Fall of the Great Powers: Economic Change and Military Conflict from 1500 to 2000, London: Unwin Hyman, 1988.

Kershaw, Ian, *Hitler: 1889–1936 Hubris* and *1936–1945 Nemesis*, London: Allen Lane, 1998 and 2000.

Kibata, Yoichi, 'Anglo-Japanese Relations from the Manchurian Incident to Pearl Harbor: Missed Opportunities?' in Ian Nish and Yoichi Kibata (eds.), *The History of Anglo-Japanese Relations, 1600–2000*, vol. II: *The Political-Diplomatic Dimension, 1931-2000*, Basingstoke: Macmillan, 2000, pp. 1–25.

Kiesling, Eugenia C., '"If It Ain't Broke, Don't Fix It: French Military Doctrine between the Wars', *War in History*, 3 (1996), no. 2, 208–23.

Kindleberger, Charles P., *The World in Depression 1929-1939*, London: Allen Lane, 1973.

Kirkpatrick, Ivone, *Mussolini: A Study in Power*, New York: Hawthorne, 1964.

Kiszely, John, *Anatomy of a Campaign: The British Fiasco in Norway*, Cambridge: Cambridge University Press, 2017.

Kitson, Michael, and Solomos Solomou, *Protectionism and Economic Revival: The British Interwar Economy*, Cambridge: Cambridge University Press, 1990.

Klemperer, Klemens von, *German Resistance against Hitler: The Search for Allies Abroad, 1938-1945*, Oxford: Clarendon Press, 1992.

Lammers, Donald, 'From Whitehall after Munich: The Foreign Office and the Future Course of British Policy', *Historical Journal*, 16 (1973), no. 4, 831–56.

Layne, Christopher, 'Security Studies and the Use of History: Neville Chamberlain's Grand Strategy Revisited', *Security Studies*, 17 (2008), no. 3, 397–437.

Leese, Roger R., *The Soviet Military Experience: A History of the Soviet Army, 1917–1991*, London: Routledge, 2000.

Leuchtenburg, William E., *Franklin Roosevelt and the New Deal*, New York: Harper and Row, 1963.

Levy, James P., *Appeasement and Rearmament: Britain 1936–1939*, Lanham, MD: Rowman and Littlefield, 2006.

London and Cambridge Economic Service, *The British Economy: Key Statistics 1900-1970*, London: Times Newspapers, 1971.

Lukacs, John, *Five Days in London: May 1940*, New Haven, CT: Yale University Press, 1999.

Lukes, Igor, 'Stalin and Czechoslovakia in 1938–39: An Autopsy of a Myth', *Diplomacy and Statecraft*, 10 (1999), nos. 2–3, 13–47.

Lukes, Igor, and Erik Goldstein (eds.), *The Munich Crisis, 1938: Prelude to World War II*, London: Frank Cass, 1999.

MacDonald, C. A., *The United States, Britain and Appeasement*, London: Macmillan, 1981.

'Deterrent Diplomacy: Roosevelt and the Containment of Germany, 1938–40', in Robert Boyce and Esmonde M. Robertson (eds.), *Paths to War: New Essays on the Origins of the Second World War*, London: Macmillan, 1989, pp. 297–329.

MacDonald, Paul K., and Joseph M. Parent, 'Graceful Decline: The Surprising Success of Great Power Retrenchment', *International Security*, 35 (2011), no. 4, 7–44.

Macklin, Graham, *Chamberlain*, London: Haus, 2006.

Maddison, Angus, *Monitoring the World Economy 1820-1992*, Paris, Development Centre of the OECD, 1995.

Maiolo, Joseph, *The Royal Navy and Nazi Germany: A Study in Appeasement and the Origins of the Second World War*, London: Macmillan, 1998.

Cry Havoc: How the Arms Race Drove the World to War, 1931-1941, London: John Murray, 2010.

'"To Gamble All on a Single Throw": Neville Chamberlain's Strategy in the Phoney War', in C. Baxter, M. Dockrill, and K. Hamilton (eds.), *Britain in Global Politics*, vol. I: *From Gladstone to Churchill*, Basingstoke: Palgrave Macmillan, 2013, pp. 220-41.

Manne, Robert, 'The British Decision for Alliance with Russia, May 1939', *Journal of Contemporary History*, 9 (1974), no. 3, 3–26.

Marquand, David, *Ramsay MacDonald*, London: Jonathan Cape, 1977.

Martel, Gordon, 'The Meaning of Power: Rethinking the Decline and Fall of Great Britain', *International History Review*, 13 (1991), no. 4, 662–94.

Mawdsley, Evan, *The War for the Seas: A Maritime History of World War II*, New Haven, CT: Yale University Press, 2019.

McDonough, Frank, *Neville Chamberlain, Appeasement and the British Road to War*, Manchester: Manchester University Press, 1998.

'When Instinct Clouds Judgement: Neville Chamberlain and the Pursuit of Appeasement with Nazi Germany, 1937-9', in Frank McDonough (ed.), *Origins of the Second World War: An International Perspective*, London: Continuum, 2011, pp. 186–204.

McKercher, B. J. C., '"Our Most Dangerous Enemy": Great Britain Pre-eminent in the 1930s', *International History Review*, 13 (1991), no. 4, 751–83.

Transition of Power: Britain's Loss of Pre-eminence to the United States, 1930-1945, Cambridge: Cambridge University Press, 1999.

'The Limitations of the Politician-Strategist: Winston Churchill and the German Threat, 1933–39', in J. H. Maurer (ed.), *Churchill and Strategic Dilemmas before the World Wars*, London: Allen Lane, 2003, pp. 88–120.

'The Foreign Office, 1930-39: Strategy, Permanent Interests and National Security', *Contemporary British History*, 18 (2004), no. 3, 87–109.

'Deterrence and the European Balance of Power: The Field Force and British Grand Strategy, 1934-1938', *English Historical Review*, 123 (2008), no. 500, 98–131.

'National Security and Imperial Defence: British Grand Strategy and Appeasement, 1930-1939', *Diplomacy and Statecraft*, 19 (2008), no. 3, 391–442.

'*Anschluss*: The Chamberlain Government and the First Test of Appeasement, February-March 1938', *International History Review*, 39 (2017), no. 2, 274–94.

Medlicott, W. N., *The Economic Blockade*, 2 vols., London: HMSO, 1952-9.

Review of Arthur H. Furnia, *Diplomacy of Appeasement: Anglo-French Relations and the Prelude to World War II* in *International Affairs*, 38 (1962), no. 1, 84–5

British Foreign Policy since Versailles, 1919-1963, London: Methuen, 1968.

Britain and Germany: The Search for Agreement 1930–1937, London: Athlone Press, 1969.

'The Hoare Laval Pact Reconsidered' in David Dilks (ed.), *Retreat from Power: Studies in Britain's Foreign Policy of the Twentieth Century*, vol. I, London: Macmillan, 1981, pp. 118–38.

Meehan, Patricia, *The Unnecessary War: Whitehall and the German Resistance to Hitler*, London: Sinclair Stevenson, 1992.

Messerschmidt, Manfred, 'Foreign Policy and Preparation for War', in Militärgeschichtliches Forschungsamt (ed.), *Germany and the Second World War*, vol. I, Oxford: Clarendon Press, pp. 541–717.

Middlemas, Keith, *Diplomacy of Illusion: The British Government and Germany, 1937–1939*, London: Weidenfeld and Nicolson, 1972.

Middleton, Roger, *Towards the Managed Economy: Keynes, the Treasury and the Fiscal Policy Debate of the 1930s*, London: Methuen, 1985.

'British Monetary and Fiscal Policy in the 1930s', *Oxford Review of Economic Policy*, 26 (2010), no. 3, 414–41.

Miller, Christopher W., *Planning and Profits: British Naval Armaments Manufacture and the Military-Industrial Complex, 1918-1941*, Liverpool: Liverpool University Press, 2018.

Millett, Alan R., and Williamson Murray (eds.), *Military Effectiveness*, vol. II: *The Interwar Period*, Boston, MA: Unwin Hyman, 1988.

Mills, William C., 'The Chamberlain-Grandi Conversations of July-August 1937 and the Appeasement of Italy', *International History Review*, 19 (1997), no. 3, 594–619.

'Sir Joseph Ball, Adrian Dingli, and Neville Chamberlain's "Secret Channel" to Italy, 1937-40', *International History Review*, 24 (2002), no. 2, 278–317.

Minney, R. J., *The Private Papers of Hore-Belisha*, London: Collins, 1960.

Militärgeschichtliches Forschungsamt (ed.), *Germany and the Second World War*, vols. I and II, Oxford: Clarendon Press, 1990-1.

Mitchell, B. R., *British Historical Statistics*, Cambridge: Cambridge University Press, 1988.

Mitchell, B. R., and Phyllis Deane, *Abstract of British Historical Statistics*, Cambridge: Cambridge University Press, 1962.

Mommsen, Wolfgang J., and Lothar Kettenacker (eds.), *The Fascist Challenge and the Policy of Appeasement*, London: George Allen and Unwin, 1983.

Morewood, Steven, '"This Silly African Business": The Military Dimension of Britain's Response to the Abyssinian Crisis', in G. Bruce Strang (ed.), *Collision of Empires: Italy's Invasion of Ethiopia and Its International Impact* (Farnham: Ashgate, 2013), pp. 73–107.

Morris, Benny, *The Roots of Appeasement: The British Weekly Press and Nazi Germany during the 1930s*, London: Frank Cass, 1991.

Morrisey, Charles, and M. A. Ramsay, '"Giving a Lead in the Right Direction": Sir Robert Vansittart and the Defence Requirements Sub-Committee', *Diplomacy & Statecraft*, 6 (1995), no. 1, 39–60.

Moulton, J. L., *The Norwegian Campaign of 1940*, London: Eyre and Spottiswoode, 1966.

Murray, Williamson, *The Change in the European Balance of Power, 1938-1939: The Path to Ruin*, Princeton, NJ: Princeton University Press, 1984.

Naylor, John F., *Labour's International Policy: The Labour Party in the 1930s*, London: Weidenfeld and Nicolson, 1969.

A Man and an Institution: Sir Maurice Hankey, the Cabinet Secretariat and the Custody of Cabinet Secrecy, Cambridge: Cambridge University Press, 1984.

Neidpath, James, *The Singapore Naval Base and the Defence of Britain's Eastern Empire 1919-1941*, Oxford: Oxford University Press, 1981.

Neilson, Keith, '"Greatly Exaggerated": The Myth of the Decline of Great Britain before 1914', *International History Review*, 13 (1991), no. 4, 695–725.

'"Pursued by a Bear": British Estimates of Soviet Military Strength and Anglo-Soviet Relations, 1922-1939', *Canadian Journal of History*, 27 (1993), no. 2, 189–221.

'The Defence Requirements Sub-Committee, British Strategic Foreign Policy, Neville Chamberlain and the Path to Appeasement' *English Historical Review*, 118 (2003), no. 477, 651–84.

Britain, Soviet Russia and the Collapse of the Versailles Order, 1919-1939, Cambridge: Cambridge University Press, 2006.

'Perception and Posture in Anglo-American Relations: The Legacy of the Simon-Stimson Affair, 1932-1941', *International History Review*, 29 (2007), no. 2, 313–37.

'Orme Sargent, Appeasement and British Policy in Europe, 1933-39', *Twentieth Century British History*, 21 (2010), no. 1, 1–28.

Neilson, Keith, and Greg Kennedy (eds.), *The British Way in Warfare: Power and the International System, 1856-1956*, Farnham: Ashgate, 2010.

Neilson, Keith, and T. G. Otte, *The Permanent Under-Secretary for Foreign Affairs, 1854-1946*, Abingdon: Routledge, 2009.

Neville, Peter, *Appeasing Hitler: The Diplomacy of Sir Neville Henderson, 1937-39*, Basingstoke: Macmillan, 2000.

'Sir Alexander Cadogan and Lord Halifax's "Damascus Road" Conversion over the Godesberg Terms 1938', *Diplomacy and Statecraft*, 11 (2000), no. 3, 81–90.

'Rival Foreign Office Perceptions of Germany, 1936-39', *Diplomacy and Statecraft*, 13 (2002), no. 3, 137–52.

'The Foreign Office and Britain's Ambassadors to Berlin, 1933-39', *Contemporary British History*, 18 (2004), no. 3, 110–29.

Hitler and Appeasement: The British Attempt to Prevent the Second World War, London: Hambledon Continuum, 2006.

Newman, Simon, *March 1939: The British Guarantee to Poland*, Oxford: Clarendon Press, 1976.

Newton, Scott, *Profits of Peace: The Political Economy of Anglo-German Appeasement*, Oxford: Clarendon Press, 1996.

O'Brien, Terence, *Civil Defence*, London: HMSO, 1955.

O'Halpin, Eunan, *Head of the Civil Service: A Study of Sir Warren Fisher*, London: Routledge, 1989.

Ovendale, Ritchie, *'Appeasement' and the English Speaking World: Britain, the United States, the Dominions, and the Policy of Appeasement 1937-1939*, Cardiff: University of Wales Press, 1975.

'Britain, the Dominions and the Coming of the Second World War, 1933-9', in Wolfgang J. Mommsen and Lothar Kettenacker (eds.), *The Fascist Challenge and the Policy of Appeasement*, London: George Allen & Unwin, 1983, pp. 323-38.

Overy, Richard J., 'The German Pre-War Aircraft Production Plans: November 1936-April 1939', *English Historical Review*, 90 (1975), no. 357, 778–97.

'From "Uralbomber" to "Amerikabomber": The Luftwaffe and Strategic Bombing', *Journal of Strategic Studies*, 1 (1978), no. 2, 154–78.

The Air War 1939-1945, London: Europa, 1980.

'Hitler and Air Strategy', *Journal of Contemporary History*, 15 (1980), no. 3, 405–21.

'Hitler's War and the German Economy: A Reinterpretation', *Economic History Review*, 35 (1982), no. 2, 272–9.

'German Air Strength 1933 to 1939: A Note', *Historical Journal*, 27 (1984), no. 2, 465–71.

Air Power, Armies, and the War in the West, 1940, Harmon Memorial Lecture, US Air Force Academy, Colorado (1989).

'Air Power and the Origins of Deterrence Theory before 1939', *Journal of Strategic Studies*, 15 (1992), no. 1, 73–101.

War and Economy in the Third Reich, Oxford: Clarendon Press, 1994.

'Strategic Intelligence and the Outbreak of the Second World War', *War in History*, 5 (1998), no. 4, 456–64.

'Germany and the Munich Crisis: A Mutilated Victory?' *Diplomacy and Statecraft*, 10 (1999), no. 2, 191–215.

1939: Countdown to War, London: Allen Lane, 2009.

The Bombing War: Europe 1939-1945, London: Allen Lane, 2013.

Parker, R. A. C., 'British Rearmament 1936-9: Treasury, Trade Unions and Skilled Labour', *English Historical Review*, 96 (1981), no. 379, 306–43.

'The Pound Sterling, the American Treasury and British Preparations for War, 1938–1939', *English Historical Review*, 98 (1983), no. 387, 261–79.

Chamberlain and Appeasement: British Policy and the Coming of the Second World War, London: Macmillan, 1993.

Churchill and Appeasement: Could Churchill Have Prevented the Second World War? London: Macmillan, 2000.

Parkinson, J. R., 'Shipbuilding', in Neil Buxton and Derek Aldcroft (eds.), *British Industry between the Wars*, London: Scolar Press, 1979, pp. 79–102.

Peden, G. C., *British Rearmament and the Treasury, 1932-1939*, Edinburgh: Scottish Academic Press, 1979.

'Sir Warren Fisher and British Rearmament against Germany', *English Historical Review*, 94 (1979), no. 370, 29–47.

'Keynes, the Economics of Rearmament and Appeasement', in Wolfgang J. Mommsen and Lothar Kettenacker (eds.), *The Fascist Challenge and the Policy of Appeasement*, London: George Allen and Unwin, 1983, pp. 142–56.

'The Burden of Imperial Defence and the Continental Commitment Reconsidered', *Historical Journal*, 27 (1984), no. 2, 405–23.

'A Matter of Timing: The Economic Background to British Foreign Policy, 1937-1939', *History*, 69 (1984), no. 225, 15–28.

The Treasury and British Public Policy, 1906-1959, Oxford: Oxford University Press, 2000.

Arms, Economics and British Strategy: From Dreadnoughts to Hydrogen Bombs, Cambridge: Cambridge University Press, 2007.

'Sir Horace Wilson and Appeasement', *Historical Journal*, 53 (2010), no. 4, 983–1014.

Peebles, Hugh, *Warshipbuilding on the Clyde*, Edinburgh: John Donald, 1987.

Pelz, Stephen E., *Race to Pearl Harbor*, Cambridge, MA: Harvard University Press, 1974.

Phillips, Adrian, *Fighting Churchill, Appeasing Hitler: How a British Civil Servant Helped Cause the Second World War*, London: Biteback Publishing, 2019.

Philpott, William, and Martin Alexander, 'The French and the British Field Force: Moral Support or Material Contribution?' *Journal of Military History*, 71 (2007), no. 3, 743–72.

Pile, Jonathan, *Churchill's Secret Enemy*, Amazon, 2012.

Pimlott, Ben, *Hugh Dalton*, London: Jonathan Cape, 1985.

Pons, Silvio, *Stalin and the Inevitable War 1936-1941*, London: Frank Cass, 2002.

Post, Gaines, *Dilemmas of Appeasement: British Deterrence and Defense, 1934-1937*, Ithaca, NY: Cornell University Press, 1993.

Postan, M. M., *British War Production*, London: HMSO, 1952.

Postan, M. M., D. Hay and J. D. Scott, *Design and Development of Weapons*, London: HMSO, 1964.

Powell, Matthew, 'Debate, Discussion, and Disagreement: A Reassessment of the Development of British Tactical Air Doctrine, 1919-1940', *War in History*, 28 (2021), no. 1, 93–117.

Powers, R. H., 'Winston Churchill's Parliamentary Commentary on British Foreign Policy', *Journal of Modern History*, 26 (1954), no. 2, 179–82.

Pratt, Lawrence, 'The Anglo-American Naval Conversations on the Far East of January 1938', *International Affairs*, 47 (1971), no. 4, 745–63.

East of Malta, West of Suez, Cambridge: Cambridge University Press, 1975.

Prażmowska, Anita, *Britain, Poland and the Eastern Front, 1939*, Cambridge: Cambridge University Press, 1987.

Price, Christopher, *Britain, America and Rearmament in the 1930s: The Cost of Failure*, Basingstoke: Palgrave, 2001.

Pronay, Nicholas, 'Rearmament and the British Public: Policy and Propaganda', in James Curran, Anthony Smith and Pauline Wingate (eds.), *Impacts and Influences: Essays on Media Power in the Twentieth Century*, London: Methuen, 1987, pp. 53–96.

Quinlan, Kevin, and Calder Walton, 'Missed Opportunities? Intelligence and the British Road to War', in Frank McDonough (ed.), *Origins of the Second World War: An International Perspective*, London: Continuum, 2011, pp. 205–22.

Ragsdale, Hugh, *The Soviets, the Munich Crisis, and the Coming of World War II*, Cambridge: Cambridge University Press, 2004.

Ramsay, Scott, 'Ensuring Benevolent Neutrality: The British Government's Appeasement of General Franco during the Spanish Civil War 1936–1939', *International History Review*, 41 (2019), no. 3, 604–23.

Ramsden, John, *Man of the Century: Winston Churchill and His Legend since 1945*, London: HarperCollins, 2002.

Reader, W. J. *Architect of Air Power: The Life of the First Viscount Weir of Eastwood*, London: Collins, 1968.

Reynolds, David, *The Creation of the Anglo-American Alliance 1937-41: A Study in Competitive Co-operation*, London: Europa, 1981.

'Churchill and the British "Decision" to Fight On in 1940', in Richard Langhorne (ed.), *Diplomacy and Intelligence during the Second World War*, Cambridge: Cambridge University Press, 1985, pp. 147–67.

In Command of History: Churchill Fighting and Writing the Second World War, London: Allen Lane, 2004.

Summits: Six meetings that Shaped the Twentieth Century, London: Allen Lane, 2007.

Rhodes James, Robert, *Churchill: A Study in Failure, 1900–1939*, London: Weidenfeld and Nicolson, 1970.

Anthony Eden, London: Weidenfeld and Nicolson, 1986.

Richardson, J. L., 'New Perspectives on Appeasement: Some Implications for International Relations', *World Politics*, 40 (1988), no. 3, 289–316.

Ritchie, Sebastian, *Industry and Air Power: The Expansion of British Aircraft Production, 1935–1941*, London: Frank Cass, 1997.

'The Price of Air Power: Technological Change, Industrial Policy, and Military Aircraft Contracts in the Era of British Rearmament, 1935-39', *Business History Review*, 71 (1997), no. 1, 82–111.

Robbins, Keith, *Munich 1938*, London: Cassell, 1968.

Roberts, Andrew, *'The Holy Fox': A Biography of Lord Halifax*, London: Weidenfeld and Nicolson, 1991.

Churchill: Walking with Destiny, London: Allen Lane, 2018.

Roberts, Geoffrey, 'Stalin and the Outbreak of the Second World War', in Frank McDonough (ed.), *The Origins of the Second World War*, London: Continuum, 2011, pp. 409–28.

Robertson, A. J., 'Lord Beaverbrook and the Supply of Aircraft, 1940-1941', in Anthony Slaven and Derek Aldcroft (eds.), *Business, Banking and Urban History: Essays in Honour of S. G. Checkland*, Edinburgh: John Donald, 1982, pp. 80–100.

Robertson, Esmonde, ed., *The Origins of the Second World War*, London: Macmillan, 1971.

Rock, William R., *Chamberlain and Roosevelt: British Foreign Policy and the United States, 1937–1940*, Columbus, OH: Ohio State University Press, 1988.

Rohde, Horst, 'Hitler's First Blitzkrieg and its Consequences for North-eastern Europe', in Militärgeschichtliches Forschungsamt (ed.), *Germany and the Second World War*, vol. II: *Germany's Initial Conquests in Europe*, Oxford: Clarendon Press, 1991, pp. 67–150.

Roi, Michael L., *Alternative to Appeasement: Sir Robert Vansittart and Alliance Diplomacy, 1934-1937*, Westport, CT: Praeger, 1997.

Roi, Michael L., and B. J. C. McKercher, '"Ideal" and "Punch-Bag": Conflicting Views of the Balance of Power and Their Influence on Interwar Foreign Policy', *Diplomacy and Statecraft*, 12 (2001), no. 2, 47–78.

Rooth, Tim, *British Protectionism and the International Economy: Overseas Commercial Policy in the 1930s*, Cambridge: Cambridge University Press, 1993.

Rose, Alexander, 'Radar and Air Defence in the 1930s', *Twentieth Century British History*, 9 (1998), no. 2, 219–45.

Rose, Norman, *Vansittart: Study of a Diplomat*, London: Heinemann, 1978.

The Cliveden Set: Portrait of an Exclusive Fraternity, London: Jonathan Cape, 2000.

Roskill, S., *Hankey, Man of Secrets*, 3 vols., London: Collins, 1970–4.

Naval Policy between the Wars, vol. II: *The Period of Reluctant Rearmament 1930–1939*, London: Collins, 1976.

Ruggiero, John, *Neville Chamberlain and British Rearmament: Pride, Prejudice, and Politics*, Westport, CT: Greenwood Press, 1999.

Hitler's Enabler: Neville Chamberlain and the Origins of the Second World War, Santa Barbara, CA: Praeger, 2015.

Salmon, Patrick, 'British Plans for Economic Warfare against Germany 1937-1939: The Problem of Swedish Iron Ore', *Journal of Contemporary History*, 16 (1981), no. 1, 53–71.

Schuker, Stephen A., 'France and the Remilitarization of the Rhineland', *French Historical Studies*, 14 (1986), no. 3, 299–338.

Schweller, Randall L., *Deadly Imbalances: Tripolarity and Hitler's Strategy of World Conquest*, New York: Columbia University Press, 1998.

Self, Robert, *Britain, America and the War Debt Controversy: The Economic Diplomacy of an Unspecial Relationship, 1917-1941*, London: Routledge, 2006.

Neville Chamberlain, a Biography, Aldershot: Ashgate, 2006.

'Perception and Posture in Anglo-American Relations: The War Debt Controversy and the "Official Mind", 1919-1940', *International History Review*, 29 (2007), no. 2, 282–312.

Shaw, Louise Grace, *The British Political Elite and the Soviet Union 1937-1939*, London: Frank Cass, 2003.

Shay, Robert P., *British Rearmament in the Thirties: Politics and Profits*, Princeton, NJ: Princeton University Press, 1977.

Smalley, Edward, 'Signal Failure: Communications in the British Expeditionary Force, September 1939-June 1940', *War in History*, 28 (2021), no. 1, 143–65.

Smart, Nick, *Neville Chamberlain*, London: Routledge, 2010.

Smith, Malcolm, 'The Royal Air Force, Air Power and British Foreign Policy, 1932–37', *Journal of Contemporary History*, 12 (1977), no. 1, 153–74.

'Rearmament and Deterrence in Britain in the Thirties', *Journal of Strategic Studies*, 1 (1979), no. 3, 313-37.

British Air Strategy between the Wars, Oxford: Oxford University Press, 1984.

Stafford, David, *Churchill and the Secret Service*, London: John Murray, 1997.

Stannage, C. T, 'The East Fulham By-Election, 25 October 1933', *Historical Journal*, 14 (1971), no. 1, 165–200.

Baldwin Thwarts the Opposition: The British General Election of 1935, London: Croom Helm, 1980.

Stedman, Andrew David, *Alternatives to Appeasement: Neville Chamberlain and Hitler's Germany*, London: I. B. Tauris, 2011.

Steiner, Zara, 'The Soviet Commissariat of Foreign Affairs and the Czechoslovakian Crisis in 1938: New Material from the Soviet Archive', *Historical Journal*, 42 (1999), no. 3, 751–79.

The Lights That Failed: European International History 1919-1933, Oxford: Oxford University Press, 2005.

'British Decisions for Peace and War 1938-1939: The Rise and Fall of Realism', in Ernest R. May, Richard Rosecrance and Zara Steiner (eds.), *History and Neorealism*, Cambridge: Cambridge University Press, 2010, pp. 129–54.

The Triumph of the Dark: European International History 1933-1939, Oxford: Oxford University Press, 2011.

Stewart, Andrew, 'The British Government and the South African Neutrality Crisis, 1938-39', *English Historical Review*, 123 (2008), no. 503, 947–72.

Stewart, Graham, *Burying Caesar: Churchill, Chamberlain and the Battle for the Tory Party*, London: Weidenfeld and Nicolson, 1999.

Stone, Glyn, 'The British Government and the Sale of Arms to the Lesser European Powers, 1936-39', *Diplomacy and Statecraft*, 14 (2003), no. 2, 237–70.

'Neville Chamberlain and the Spanish Civil War, 1936-9', *International History Review*, 35 (2013), no. 2, 377–95.

Strachan, Hew, 'The Territorial Army and National Defence', in Keith Neilson and Greg Kennedy (eds.), *The British Way in Warfare: Power and the International System, 1856–1956*, Farnham: Ashgate, 2010, pp. 159–78.

Strang, G. Bruce, 'Two Unequal Tempers: Sir George Ogilvie-Forbes, Sir Nevile Henderson and British Foreign Policy, 1938-39', *Diplomacy and Statecraft*, 5 (1994), no. 1, 107–37.

'Once More unto the Breach: Britain's Guarantee to Poland, March 1939', *Journal of Contemporary History*, 31 (1996), no. 4, 721–52.

'War and Peace: Mussolini's Road to Munich', *Diplomacy and Statecraft*, 10 (1999), nos. 2–3, 160–90.

'Imperial Dreams: The Mussolini-Laval Accords of January 1935', *Historical Journal*, 44 (2001), no. 3, 799–809.

'John Bull in Search of a Suitable Russia: British Foreign Policy and the Failure of the Anglo-French-Soviet Alliance Negotiations, 1939', *Canadian Journal of History*, 41 (2006), no. 1, 47–84.

'The Spirit of Ulysses? Ideology and British Appeasement in the 1930s', *Diplomacy and Statecraft*, 19 (2008), no. 3, 481–526.

'"The Worst of All Worlds": Oil Sanctions and Italy's Invasion of Abyssinia', 1935–36', *Diplomacy and Statecraft*, 19 (2008), no. 2, 210–35.

'Mésentente Cordiale: Italian Policy and the Failure of the Easter Accords, 1937-1938', *Diplomacy and Statecraft*, 32 (2021), no. 1, 31–59.

'Sir Alexander Cadogan and the Steward-Hesse Affair: Assessments of British Cabinet Politics and Future British Policy, 1938', *International History Review*, 43 (2021), no. 3, 657–76.

Strang, William, The Moscow Negotiations, 1939', in David Dilks (ed.), *Retreat from Power: Studies in Britain's Foreign Policy of the Twentieth Century*, vol. I, London: Macmillan, 1981, pp. 170–86.

Swift, John, *Labour in Crisis: Clement Attlee and the Labour Party in Opposition*, Basingstoke: Palgrave, 2001.

Taylor, A. J. P., *The Origins of the Second World War*, Harmondsworth: Penguin, [1961] 1964.

Thomas, Martin., *Britain, France and Appeasement: Anglo-French Relations in the Popular Front Era*, Oxford: Berg, 1996.

Thorne, Christopher, *The Limits of Foreign Policy: The West, the League and the Far Eastern Crisis of 1931-1933*, London: Hamish Hamilton, 1972.

Thorpe, D. R., *Eden: The Life and Times of Anthony Eden, First Earl of Avon*, London: Chatto and Windus, 2003.

Titmuss, Richard, *Problems of Social Policy*, London: HMSO, 1950.

Todman, Daniel, *Britain's War: Into Battle 1937-1941*, London: Allen Lane, 2016.

Tooze, Adam, *The Wages of Destruction: The Making and Breaking of the Nazi Economy*, London: Allen Lane, 2006.

Toye, Richard, 'The Labour Party and the Economics of Rearmament, 1935-39', *Twentieth Century British History*, 12 (2001), no. 3, 303–26.

Umbreit, Hans, 'The Battle for Hegemony in Western Europe' in Militärgeschichtliches Forschungsamt (ed.), *Germany and the Second World War*, vol. II: *Germany's Initial Conquests in Europe*, Oxford: Clarendon Press, 1991, pp. 227–326.

Ussishkin, Daniel, *Morale: A Modern British History*, New York: Oxford University Press, 2017.

Vital, David, 'Czechoslovakia and the Powers, September 1938', *Journal of Contemporary History*, 1 (1966), no. 4, 37–67.

Waddington, G. T., '*Hassgegner*: German Views of Great Britain in the Later 1930s', *History*, 81 (1996), no. 261, 22–39.

Waley, Daniel, *British Public Opinion and the Abyssinian War*, London: Temple Smith, 1975.

Ware, R. G., 'The Balance of Payments in the Interwar Period', *Bank of England Quarterly Bulletin*, 14 (1974), no. 1, 47–52.

Wark, Wesley K., *The Ultimate Enemy: British Intelligence and Nazi Germany, 1933-1939*, Ithaca, NY: Cornell University Press, 1985.

'In Search of a Suitable Japan: British Naval Intelligence in the Pacific before the Second World War', *Intelligence and National Security*, 1 (1986), no. 2, 189–211.

Watt, Donald Cameron, 'Appeasement: The Rise of a Revisionist School?' *Political Quarterly*, 36 (1965), no. 2, 191–213.

'Roosevelt and Neville Chamberlain: Two Appeasers', *International Journal*, 28 (1973), no. 2, 185–204.

'Churchill and Appeasement', in Robert Blake and Wm. Roger Louis (eds.), *Churchill*, Oxford: Oxford University Press, 1993, pp. 199–214.

How War Came: The Immediate Origins of the Second World War, 1938-1939, London: William Heinemann, 1989.

Wendt, Bernd-Jürgen, '"Economic Appeasement" – A Crisis Strategy', in Wolfgang J. Mommsen and Lothar Kettenacker (eds.), *The Fascist Challenge and the Policy of Appeasement*, London: George Allen & Unwin, 1983, pp. 157–72.

Wheeler-Bennett, John, *John Anderson, Viscount Waverley*, London: Macmillan, 1962.

Williamson, Philip, *Stanley Baldwin: Conservative Leadership and National Values*, Cambridge: Cambridge University Press, 1999.

  'Baldwin's Reputation: Politics and History, 1937-1967', *Historical Journal*, 47 (2004), no. 1, 127–68.

Wilson, Thomas, *Churchill and the Prof*, London: Cassell, 1995.

Winnifrith, John, 'Edward Ettingdean Bridges – Baron Bridges 1892-1969', *Biographical Memoirs of Fellows of the Royal Society*, 16 (1970), 37–56.

Witham, Charles, 'Seeing the Wood for the Trees: The British Foreign Office and the Anglo-American Trade Agreement of 1938', *Twentieth Century British History*, 16 (2005), no. 1, 29–51.

Woodward, Llewellyn, *British Foreign Policy in the Second World War*, 5 vols., London: HMSO, 1970–6.

Young, G. M., *Stanley Baldwin*, London: Rupert Hart-Davis, 1952.

Index